# Creative Accounting, Fraud and International Accounting Scandals

For other titles in the Wiley Finance series
please see www.wiley.com/finance

# Creative Accounting, Fraud and International Accounting Scandals

Edited by

## Michael John Jones

A John Wiley and Sons, Ltd., Publication

Copyright © 2011     Michael Jones
Published in 2011 by    John Wiley & Sons Ltd, The Atrium, Southern Gate, Chichester,
West Sussex PO19 8SQ, England
Telephone (+44) 1243 779777

Email (for orders and customer service enquiries): cs-books@wiley.co.uk
Visit our Home Page on www.wiley.com

*Library of Congress Cataloging-in-Publication Data*

Jones, Michael, 1953–
  Creative accounting, fraud and international accounting scandals / edited by Michael Jones.
    p. cm.
  Includes index.
  ISBN 978-0-470-05765-0
  HF5636.J65 2010
  364.16′3–dc22

                        2010024558

*British Library Cataloguing in Publication Data*

A catalogue record for this book is available from the British Library

ISBN  978-0-470-05765-0

Typeset in 11/13pt Times by Aptara Inc., New Delhi, India
Printed and bound in Great Britain by CPI Antony Rowe, Chippenham, Wiltshire

To my family for all their love and support.

# Contents

# List of Contributors

**Michael Jones (editor)**

Michael Jones, MA Oxon, is Professor of Financial Reporting at Bristol University. Formerly, he taught accounting for 33 years, first at Hereford Technical College, then at Portsmouth Polytechnic (now University) then at Cardiff Business School (1989–2009). He has taught financial accounting at all levels from GCSE level to final-year degree and MSc courses. He has published over 140 articles in both professional and academic journals. These articles cover a wide range of topics, such as financial accounting, the history of accounting and international accounting. He is joint editor of the British Accounting Review and serves on two more editorial boards. As well as being Director of the Financial Reporting and Business Communication Unit, he chairs the British Accounting Association Financial and Reporting Special Interest Group. He has served on the British Accounting Association Committee and on the Committee for Professors of Accounting and Finance. He has written three textbooks: *Accounting*, *Financial Accounting* and *Management Accounting*. (Author, Chapters 1–7, 21–23)

**Bhabatosh Banerjee**

Dr Bhabatosh Banerjee, MCom, PhD, AICWA, is Professor of Commerce and Co-ordinator, MBA in Finance, University of Calcutta; Editor, *Indian Accounting Review*; and President, Indian Accounting Association Research Foundation. A former Dean of Commerce and Management (1987–89 and 2003–5), Dr Banerjee has 39 years' postgraduate teaching experience including two years in the USA (1995–97). The first recipient of the International Educator Award (2006) from the Indian Accounting Association, his numerous research publications include *Contemporary Issues in Accounting Research* (ed.) (1991), *Accounting Education in India* (1994) and *Regulation of Corporate Accounting and Reporting in India* (2002). (Author, Chapter 12 on India)

**Garry Carnegie**

Garry Carnegie is Professor of Accounting in the School of Accounting, RMIT University, Melbourne. Prior to joining academe, Professor Carnegie gained experience in IT, public accounting and in the financial services industry. He has held full-time professorial posts at Deakin University, Melbourne University/Private University of Melbourne and the

University of Ballarat. Professor Carnegie's expertise embraces financial reporting and accountability as well as accounting history. His published research appears in books and monographs and also in articles in respected journals in the fields of accounting, accounting history, archaeology, economic history, law, museum management and public administration. He is joint editor of *Accounting History*, the journal of the Accounting History Special Interest Group of the Accounting and Finance Association of Australia and New Zealand. (Co-author, Chapter 8 on Australia)

**Nieves Carrera**
Nieves Carrera has a PhD in Business Administration and Quantitative Methods from University Carlos III Madrid (Spain) and a degree in Economics (University of Vigo, Spain). Before joining the Instituto de Empresa Business School, she was a lecturer in accounting at the School of Accounting and Finance (Manchester University). Her research interests cover different aspects of auditing and financial reporting, such as the role of women in the auditing profession, the structure of the audit market and the impact of regulation on the audit market and on financial reporting. (Author, Chapter 16 on Spain)

**Catherine Huirong Chen**
Catherine Chen, PhD, MBA, BSc, is a Senior Lecturer, Business School, Middlesex University. Catherine's main research interests are in corporate governance and executive remuneration. She obtained her PhD in Accounting and Finance at Cardiff Business School. Her PhD thesis examined the determinants of executive remuneration in China, focusing on the role of the board of directors, ownership structure and market comparison factors. (Co-author, Chapter 9 on China)

**Eugene Comiskey**
Eugene E. Comiskey is the Fuller E. Callaway Chair, Professor of Accounting and Associate Dean for Faculty and Research at the Georgia Institute of Technology. He received his doctorate in accounting from Michigan State University and is a Certified Public Accountant (CPA). Dr Comiskey has co-authored four books with Dr Charles Mulford, as well as about 70 journal articles in a wide range of both professional and academic journals. He has served on a number of committees for the American Accounting Association and has also served as its director of research, president of its financial reporting and accounting section, as an editorial consultant and as a member of its editorial board. (Co-author, Chapter 19 on the USA)

**David Gwilliam**
David Gwilliam is Professor of Accounting at the University of Exeter, UK, having previously held academic posts at the University of Cambridge, London School of Economics and Political Science and University of Wales, Aberystwyth in the UK, and Monash University in Australia. He is a Fellow of the Institute of Chartered Accountants in England and Wales, having qualified with Price Waterhouse, and was the P.D. Leake lecturer at ICAEW in 2003. David's research interests include accounting and audit regulation, accounting and the law, and corporate governance. (Co-author, Chapter 18 on the UK)

## Yuanyuan Hu

Yuanyuan Hu, PhD, MAcc, MA, BSc, is a lecturer in accountancy at the School of Accountancy, Massey University, New Zealand. Yuanyuan has research interests in the areas of corporate social and environmental reporting, corporate social accountability and responsibility, Chinese accounting and corporate governance. The prime focus of her PhD, awarded by Cardiff University, was on the willingness of Chinese listed companies to participate in corporate environmental reporting. (Co-author, Chapter 9 on China)

## Richard Jackson

Richard Jackson is Associate Professor of Accounting and Finance and former Head of Department of Accounting at the University of Exeter, UK, having moved from the University of Wales, Aberystwyth, UK. He is a Fellow of the Institute of Chartered Accountants in England and Wales, having qualified with Ernst & Young. Richard was the Henry Ford II Scholar at Cranfield University, and later worked with NatWest Group and Accenture prior to his academic career. His research interests include earnings management and dynamics, market asset valuation and econometric methodology. (Co-author, Chapter 18 on the UK)

## Kristina Jonäll

Kristina Jonäll, Ekon Lic (Licentiate of Philosophy), is a doctoral student in the Financial Reporting & Analysis Group at the Department of Business Administration at the Göteborg School of Business, Economics and Law. Her research is in the accountability aspects of business communication. Her licentiate thesis explored how textual analysis can be a useful tool to analyse business communication. She is also a participant in the research programme 'The Role of Trust in Communication of Accounting Information Research'. (Co-Author, Chapter 17 on Sweden)

## George Kontos

George Kontos graduated from the Athens University of Economics and Business. He has over 30 years' experience in the banking industry, of which the last 12 years have been as the Group Financial Reporting Officer for Alpha Bank SA. He is a member of the board of directors for Alpha Bank Romania, Alpha Bank Srbija and Alpha Bank Skopje AD. Since 2001, he has also been a lecturer in bank accounting at the University of Piraeus. (Co-author, Chapter 11 on Greece)

## Maria Krambia-Kapardis

Maria Krambia-Kapardis, PhD, MBus, BEc, ACA, has until recently been Professor of Accounting and holder of the PricewaterhouseCooper Chair in Applied Accounting Research, Intercollege, Nicosia, Cyprus. She is now Associate Professor of Accounting at the Cyprus University of Technology. She has published books, many articles in academic journals internationally and presented her work at local and international conferences. Her research interests include forensic accounting, fraud investigation and prevention, Corporate Social Responsibility and Corporate Governance. (Co-author, Chapter 11 on Greece)

## Henk Langendijk

Henk Langendijk has a Masters degree in Business Economics from the University of Amsterdam. He has practical business experience in accountancy and consulting in the Netherlands with the audit firms Arthur Andersen and BDO. He is currently Professor in Financial Accounting and Reporting at Nyenrode Business University and the University of Amsterdam. His PhD was entitled: 'The market for statutory audits in the Netherlands' (University Leiden). His recent research is in the field of IFRS-conversions, quality of financial reporting (creative accounting and fraudulent reporting) and corporate governance. He has published numerous books in the field of accounting and many articles in international journals, such as the *Accounting Auditing Accountability Journal*, *Corporate Governance: An International Review*, the *European Accounting Review*, the *European Journal of Finance* and national Dutch accounting journals. He is editor of the Dutch accountancy journal *Maandblad Accountancy en Bedrijfseconomie*. (Author, Chapter 15 on the Netherlands)

## Hansrudi Lenz

Hansrudi Lenz has been a Professor of Accounting and Auditing at the University Wuerzburg since 1996. He received his doctoral and post-doctoral degrees in Business Administration from the Free University of Berlin in 1986 and 1994, respectively. His main areas of research are related to accounting and auditing. He has published several articles in refereed German and international journals. Professor Lenz acquired professional experience as an employee in the controlling department of the Treuhandanstalt (former state-owned holding company for all former East German firms) and in a management holding in Berlin. He is currently chairman of the Accounting Commission of the German Academic Association of Business Research. (Author, Chapter 10 on Germany)

## Andrea Melis

Andrea Melis is Associate Professor of Accounting and Business Economics at the Department of *Ricerche aziendali*, University of Cagliari, Italy. His Masters degree was taken at the Nottingham Business School (UK) and he received a PhD from the University of Rome TRE, Italy. His main research interests are financial reporting and corporate governance. He has published two monographs on corporate governance, several chapters in edited books and articles in international journals such as *Accounting*, *Business and Financial History*, *Corporate Governance: An International Review*, *Corporate Ownership and Control*, *The ICFAI Journal of Accounting Research* and other premier accounting and business journals in Italy. (Author, Chapter 13 on Italy)

## Nikolaos Milonas

Nikolaos T. Milonas, PhD, MPhil, MBA, BA, is a Professor of Finance at the Department of Economics at the University of Athens. He has held academic positions at Baruch College (CUNY), the University of Massachusetts at Amherst, the Athens Laboratory of Business Administration (ALBA) and the University of Wales, Cardiff Business School. He has teaching and research interests in the stock market, institutional investing, derivative markets and energy risk management. He is the author of two recent books on mutual funds and derivative markets and of numerous articles appearing in leading academic journals, including the *Journal of Finance*, *Journal of Futures Markets*, *European*

*Financial Management*, *Financial Review*, *Housing Finance Review* and *Applied Financial Economics*. (Co-author, Chapter 11 on Greece)

## Charles Mulford

Charles W. Mulford is Invesco Chair and Professor of Accounting in the College of Management at the Georgia Institute of Technology. He has a doctorate in accounting from the Florida State University and is a Certified Public Accountant (CPA). Dr Mulford has co-authored four books with Dr Eugene Comiskey: *Financial Warnings*, published in 1996; *Guide to Financial Reporting and Analysis*, published in 2000; *The Financial Numbers Game: Identifying Creative Accounting Practices*, published in 2002; and *Creative Cash Flow Reporting: Uncovering Sustainable Financial Performance*, published in 2005. In 2002, he founded the Georgia Tech Financial Analysis Lab, which is dedicated to conducting independent stock market research. Dr Mulford has appeared on numerous broadcast networks, including CNBC, ABC News and Bloomberg TV. In addition, he has been quoted in several business publications, including *The Wall Street Journal*, *The Financial Times*, *Business Week*, *Forbes* and *Fortune*. (Co-author, Chapter 19 on the USA)

## Brendan O'Connell

Brendan has extensive teaching and research experience in leading Australian and US universities including Monash University, Deakin University and the University of Richmond in Virginia. He has published numerous papers in leading academic journals, such as the *Journal of Accounting Auditing and Finance*, *Critical Perspectives on Accounting*, *Issues in Accounting Education*, the *Australian Accounting Review* and the *Journal of Applied Finance* on topics such as earnings management, financial statement fraud, business ethics, accounting education and securitization. Brendan was guest editor of a special issue of *Critical Perspectives on Accounting* entitled 'Enron.con' and a special issue of *Accounting History* that provided an historical perspective on accounting and audit failure within corporate collapse. He is also a member of the editorial board of the *Australian Accounting Review*. His case studies on the collapses of Enron and HIH Insurance are now part of the CPA programme in Australia. In 2004, Brendan was a recipient of $95 000 from the Australian Research Council Discovery Grant Scheme to study 'Audit Failure in Corporate Collapse: An Historical Perspective'. Prior to working in academia, he worked in both accounting and the investment banking industry. (Co-author, Chapter 8 on Australia)

## Simon Norton

Dr Simon D. Norton is a lecturer in the law relating to banking, the capital markets, and financial services at Cardiff Business School, Cardiff University. His areas of research, and in which he has published, include: corporate governance in the context of financial institutions; the impact of banking activities upon the natural environment, including the Equator Principles and the United Nations Environmental Programme; and Islamic finance and financial innovation in the context of Sharia principles. Dr Norton gained his doctorate in shipping finance, and is actively involved in the promotion of professional standards and training in the ship broking industry. (Author, Chapter 20 Creative Accounting and the Financial Crisis of 2008–2009)

## Gunnar Rimmel

Gunnar Rimmel, Ekon Dr (PhD), is Associate Professor and Head of the Financial Reporting & Analysis Group at the Department of Business Administration at the Göteborg School of Business, Economics and Law. After the public defence of his thesis 'Human Resources Disclosures' in 2003, he received a post-doctoral position from the Adlerbertska Research Foundation. In recent years, he has been involved in a number of international research projects and has been a visiting research fellow at Kobe University. He was Secretary General of the 25th Annual Congress of the European Accounting Association (EAA) and currently is a member of the EAA Conference Committee. (Co-author, Chapter 17 on Sweden)

## Kazuyuki Suda

Kazuyuki Suda, PhD, BEcon, MCom, is Professor of Accounting at the Graduate School of Finance, Accounting and Law, Waseda University. He has been a Visiting Professor of Accounting at the University of Alberta (1996–97) and Visiting Research Associate at the University of Rochester (1987–88). He was a Chair of the Specified Issues Study Committee of the Japanese Accounting Association (2004–6) and a Vice President of the Japanese Association for Research on Disclosure from 2005 to date. He has served as a member of the Technical Committee of Accounting Standards Board of Japan, the Examinations Committee of Security Analysts Association of Japan, and a Commission of CPA Examinations of Certified Public Accountants and Auditing Oversight Board in Japan. He has published many books in Japanese as well as articles in English. (Author, Chapter 14 on Japan)

## Jason Zezhong Xiao

Jason Xiao, PhD, MSc, MEcon, ITML, is Director of the Chinese Accounting, Finance and Business Research Unit and Professor of Accounting at Cardiff Business School, Cardiff University. Jason has researched into accounting and corporate governance in China and accounting information systems. He has published over 30 articles in international journals and over 50 articles in Chinese journals and is a member of five journal editorial boards. He is a member of ACCA's Research Committee and a board director of the Chinese Auditing Association. (Co-author, Chapter 9 on China)

# Preface

Enron, WorldCom and Parmalat are well-known accounting scandals. However, what is not so well known is that every country has its own accounting scandals. The basic motivation for this book is to explore the role of accounting, particularly creative accounting and fraud, in accounting scandals across different countries. I therefore approached people from different countries to see if they would be prepared to help me. In almost every case they did not say 'what accounting scandals?' but 'which accounting scandals would you like me to write about?'

Accounting scandals, by their nature, are extreme cases. They generally involve creative accounting and fraud. The title of the book reflects this: *Creative Accounting, Fraud and International Accounting Scandals*. This book covers 58 high-profile accounting scandals across 12 countries. However, it also deals with many other cases of creative accounting and fraud.

Accounting scandals are inherently interesting because they indicate extreme abuse of financial reporting. They show how, in extremis, the accounting numbers can be manipulated so as to deceive and defraud. This book provides an insight into the methods of creative accounting and fraud, the motivations that underpin the scandals and the consequences of the scandals, both in the short term and the long term.

The book aims to inform. The information is presented in as accessible a way as possible. There is a focus on presenting the big picture. The book should prove very interesting to readers. It provides a global approach to the topic. It covers 12 countries with representatives from Australasia (Australia), Asia (China, India and Japan), Europe (Germany, Greece, Italy, the Netherlands, Sweden, Spain and the UK) and North America (USA). It therefore represents leading global economies, developed and developing countries as well as the majority of the world's population. In addition, there is a chapter dealing with bank failures in the recent credit crunch.

The book is presented in three broad sections. In the first section I explore the basic themes which underpin the book. I examine the creative accounting environment, motives, methods and impression management. I site this within the academic and largely descriptive professional literature.

In the next section, individual authors, all native to their respective countries, provide an in-depth look at the major accounting scandals and instances of creative accounting that have occurred since the 1980s. Each author contextualizes the accounting issues and looks at the motives, methods and consequences of the creative accounting and the accounting scandals. These chapters give a unique insight into the global nature of the problem. There is also a final chapter in this section looking at the consequences of the recent global banking crisis.

To write this book I depended upon the expertise of the individual authors. This book would not have been possible without my reliance on their research and local knowledge. To the best of my knowledge the facts which they have described and on which this book is based are correct.

The authors were given general parameters within which to write their chapter. I rely upon the expertise and factual accuracy of the individual country author chapters to synthesise and distil the material. The material in Chapters 21–23 and Appendices 1 and 2 thus relies principally on these individual chapter contributions. Generally, I have not changed the accounting terminology that they have used. Therefore, within the book certain accounting terms are used somewhat interchangeably such as inventory or stock; accounts receivable or trade receivables or debtors; accounts payable or trade payables or creditors; property, plant and equipment or fixed assets. This is because different countries have their own terminology or use International Accounting Standards Board terminology.

In the last three chapters, I draw out some general themes from the chapters. I look at the methods used, the motivations for the creative accounting, fraud and accounting scandals, the role of powerful individuals, and I highlight failures of internal control and external auditing. Finally, I investigate the long-term impact of accounting scandals on the regulatory environment.

This book has several novel and original features:

- An accessible overview of the methods, motives and nature of creative accounting and fraud drawing on prior literature and past accounting scandals.
- For the first time, an in-depth study of international accounting scandals in both developed and developing countries.
- Individual chapters are written by experienced authors native to each country.
- A global synthesis of the motivations, methods, control failings and consequences of major accounting scandals is provided.
- An historical overview of accounting scandals and creative accounting is provided from the ancient period into the 1980s.
- A chapter looking at the banking crisis of 2008/9 from an accounting perspective.

As such, this book provides a rare glimpse into the murky world of accounting scandals. It will be ideal for the general reader, professional accountant and businessman worldwide. It is also well suited for undergraduate students taking courses in forensic accounting and fraud. It may also prove a useful supporting book on more general accounting and finance courses. The book is uniquely positioned to support specialised MSc courses in accounting and finance or MBA courses.

Michael Jones
August 2010

# Acknowledgements

I am extremely grateful to the 21 authors who have helped me to write this book. Without them, a book of this type would have been impossible. They have provided the detailed factual knowledge of their particular scandals and the national accounting environments in which those scandals occurred. I have relied upon the factual accuracy of their work when preparing the rest of the book.

I am very appreciative of the help and unfailing support of my partner, Jill Solomon, whose insightful comments have helped me immensely. I should also like to thank Steve Hardman, Jenny McCall and the team at John Wiley for their help and support. Finally, last but certainly not least, I should like to thank Jan Richards for her unstinting patience and hard work in turning my generally illegible scribbling into the final manuscript.

# Part A

Part 3

# 1

# Introduction – Setting the Scene

Michael Jones

## 1.1 INTRODUCTION

Accounting scandals, creative accounting and fraud are perennial. They range from ancient Mesopotamia to the South Sea Bubble in 1720 to Enron and Parmalat today. They occur in all eras and in all countries. As accounting forms a central element of any business success or failure, the role of accounting is crucial in understanding such business scandals. Accounting enables businesses to keep a set of records to give investors and other users a picture of how well or badly the firm is doing. However, sometimes when businesses are doing badly managers are tempted to use accounting to enhance the apparent performance of the firm in an unjustified way. In addition, managers may wish to use the flexibility within accounting to serve a range of managerial interests such as to boost profits or increase assets. This can be done legally by using creative accounting to exploit the flexibility within accounting. Alternatively, in other cases management will indulge in false accounting or fraud. In this case, management will step outside the rules and regulations that govern accounting. Often this will be because management has got into serious financial difficulties and is looking for any way to postpone corporate collapse. Managers may use prohibited accounting techniques, falsify records or even record fictitious transactions. In some cases, companies start with creative accounting, but end up committing fraud.

This book aims to explore the role of accounting, particularly creative accounting and fraud, in accounting scandals. The terminology of creative accounting is explored first, and I then provide an overview of the three parts of the book. In Part A the background and context of creative accounting and fraud are explored. This part draws upon the established academic and professional literature and thinking about creative accounting and fraud. It provides an overview of the main terminology, looks at the creative accounting environment, the motivations for indulging in creative accounting and fraud, the methods of creative accounting and fraud, the evidence for creative accounting, impression management and, finally, looks at 18 major accounting scams and scandals across time. This is from ancient times until about 1980.

Part B looks at a series of international accounting scandals. Accounting scandals in 12 countries are investigated, covering Asia, Australasia, Europe and North America. Country specialists contribute chapters on Australia, China, Germany, Greece, India, Italy, Japan, the Netherlands, Spain, Sweden, the UK and the USA. In addition, there is a separate chapter dealing with the global banking crisis of 2008–9 from an accounting perspective. As can be

*Creative Accounting, Fraud and International Accounting Scandals*   Edited by Michael Jones
© 2011 Michael Jones. Published by John Wiley & Sons, Ltd

seen from their biographies, these experienced academics, using their knowledge and experience, provide an informed view of creative accounting, fraud and international accounting scandals in their respective countries. Finally, in Part C, I draw out some themes and implications from the country studies. In particular, I look at the impact of accounting scandals and synthesise the country studies using the data available from the individual chapters.

## 1.2 EXPLORING THE TERMS

The term 'creative accounting' came to prominence in a book published by Ian Griffiths in 1986. This book, called *Creative Accounting* (Griffiths, 1986), written in the UK context, began with the assertion that:

> Every company in the country is fiddling its profits. Every set of accounts is based on books which have been gently cooked or completely roasted. The figures which are fed twice a year to the investing public have been changed in order to protect the guilty. It is the biggest con trick since the Trojan horse.
>
> Any accountant worth his salt will confirm that this is no wild assertion. There is no argument over the extent and existence of this corporate contortionism, the only dispute might be over the way in which it is described. Such phrases as 'cooking the books', 'fiddling the accounts', and 'corporate con trick' may raise eyebrows where they cause people to infer that there is something illegal about this pastime. In fact, this deception is all in perfectly good taste. It is totally legitimate – it is creative accounting.

Since Griffiths' book there have been many other explorations of creative accounting. In the UK, for example, there have been at least three books. *Accounting for Growth* by Terry Smith, a city analyst, looked at the reporting practices of 185 UK companies and found numerous examples of creative accounting. Hardly any companies were immune (Smith, 1991). Trevor Pijper, in *Creative Accounting: The Effectiveness of Financial Reporting in the UK*, investigated the situation in the UK at the start of the 1990s, finding many companies that had indulged in creative accounting. In particular, Pijper looked in depth at Polly Peck, a UK company that controversially collapsed in 1990 (Pijper, 1993). Finally, McBarnet and Whelan, in *Creative Accounting and the Cross-eyed Javelin Thrower*, explored UK financial reporting in 1999. They looked at many instances of creative accounting, especially those detected by the Financial Reporting and Review Panel, which 'policed' UK financial reporting (McBarnet and Whelan, 1999). Meanwhile, in the USA, a very influential book by Charles Mulford and Eugene Comiskey, entitled *The Financial Numbers Game*, investigated the pre-Enron financial reporting in the USA and documented numerous examples of both creative accounting and fraud. Enron is shown to be only one high-profile example of frequently occurring financial manipulations in the USA (Mulford and Comiskey, 2002). This leads us to the question, what exactly are creative accounting and fraud and how can they be distinguished from other commonly used terms such as earnings management, income smoothing and aggressive accounting?

### 1.2.1 Creative Accounting

Although creative accounting is a popularly used term, there is much less agreement on its exact definition than might be supposed. In essence, there is the wide definition, as adopted by Mulford and Comiskey (2002, p. 15) in the USA and the narrower definition as practised in the UK. I give two representative definitions in Figure 1.1, and also the preferred definition that I will use in the book.

Generally, therefore, the wider US definition sees creative accounting as including fraud whereas the UK definition sees creative accounting as using the flexibility within the regulatory system, but excludes fraud. The preferred definition in this book sees creative accounting as excluding fraud. It is defined as 'Using the flexibility in accounting within the regulatory framework to manage the measurement and presentation of the accounts so that they give primacy to the interests of the preparers not the users'. Creative accounting is thus seen as working within the regulatory system. It is thus not illegal. Companies using creative accounting are not breaking the law, just using the flexibility in accounting to serve their own interests.

Creative accounting is thus designed, by exploiting loopholes in the existing regulatory system, to serve preparers' not users' interests. In Europe, the financial statements of published companies, for example, are required to present a 'true and fair' view of the accounts. In the USA, a similar phrase 'present fairly' is used. In these Anglo-Saxon countries (and in many other countries) there is the overriding notion that accounts should faithfully represent economic reality.[1] Users are supposed to be given a set of financial accounts which reflect economic reality. Creative accounting, by contrast, privileges the interests of the preparers (i.e. the managers). It is able to do this because of the fundamental need for financial reports to be flexible so as to give a true and fair view of accounts. All companies are different and operate in different environments.

The flexibility in financial reporting is meant to reflect this. However, this flexibility can be used, and often is, for creative accounting. As Figure 1.2 shows, there is a continuum from no flexibility to flexibility to give a true and fair view, to flexibility to give a creative view, to flexibility to give a fraudulent view.

Thus, if there is no flexibility, there will be no creative accounting. However, there will also not be a true and fair view. This is unacceptable as a fundamental purpose of accounting is to provide users, generally shareholders, with information so that they can make economic decisions such as whether to buy, sell or hold shares. A regulatory framework, which varies from country to country but may include national standards (most countries, e.g. the UK and the USA), international standards (widely used), company law (some countries, such as the UK and Germany) or independent accounting commissions (such as the Securities and Exchange Commission in the USA) has, therefore, grown up to set up accounting rules and regulations which companies and other organizations should follow so as to deliver 'a true and fair view' to account users. This is the ideal scenario, where the preparers of accounts use the flexibility in the accounts to deliver 'a true and fair view'. However, the flexibility within the accounting rules and regulations opens the door for the managers to use creative accounting. In a sense, there is nothing wrong in this as they are not breaking any rules. However, they are departing from the basic purpose of accounting, which is to provide users with a true and fair view. When the managers actually go outside the regulatory framework, they are not then complying with existing regulations. Technically, they may then be indulging in false accounting or in fraud. However, this is a difficult

---

[1] For ease of understanding the phrase 'true and fair' commonly used in Europe is used in this book to convey the notion of economic reality.

**Narrow definitions of creative accounting**

"The exploitation of loopholes in financial regulation in order to gain advantage or present figures in a misleadingly favourable light."

*Oxford Dictionary of English*

"A form of accounting which, while complying with all regulations, nevertheless gives a biased impression (generally favourable) of the company's performance."

Chartered Institute of Management Accounting (2000), *Official Terminology*

**Wide definition of creative accounting**

"Any and all steps used to play the financial numbers game, including the aggressive choice and application of accounting principles, both within and beyond the boundaries of generally accepted accounting principles, and fraudulent financial reporting. Also included are steps taken toward earnings management and income smoothing."

Mulford and Comiskey (2002, p. 15)

**Preferred definition of creative accounting**

"Using the flexibility in accounting within the regulatory framework to manage the measurement and presentation of the accounts so that they give primacy to the interests of the preparers not the users."

**Fraud**

"A knowing misrepresentation of the truth or concealment of a material fact to induce another to act to his or her detriment."

*Black's Law Dictionary*, 7th edn (1999)

"… 'fraud' comprises both the use of deception to obtain an unjust or illegal financial advantage and intentional misrepresentations affecting the financial statements by one or more individuals among management, employees, or third parties. Fraud may involve:

- Falsification or alteration of accounting records or other documents.

- Misappropriation of assets or theft.

- Suppression or omission of the effects of transactions from records or documents.

- Recording of transactions without substance.

- Intentional misapplication of accounting policies.

- Wilful misrepresentation of transactions or of an entity's state of affairs."

Auditing Standards Board, *Statement of Auditing Standard*, SAS 110

**Figure 1.1**   Definitions of creative accounting and fraud

**Fraudulent financial reporting**

"International misstatements or omissions of amounts or disclosures in financial statements, done to deceive financial statement users, that are determined to be fraudulent by an administrative, civil or criminal proceeding."

Mulford and Comiskey (2002, p. 3)

"International material misstatement of financial statements or financial disclosures or the perpetration of an illegal act that has a material direct effect on the financial statements or financial disclosures."

Beasley, Carcello and Hermanson (1999)

**Preferred definition of fraud**

The use of fictitious accounting transactions or those prohibited by generally accepted accounting principles gives the presumption for fraud which becomes proved after an administrative or court proceeding.

**Figure 1.1**  Definitions of creative accounting and fraud (*Continued*)

area. False accounting or fraud, in effect, must be proved in a court of law or by a regulatory body.

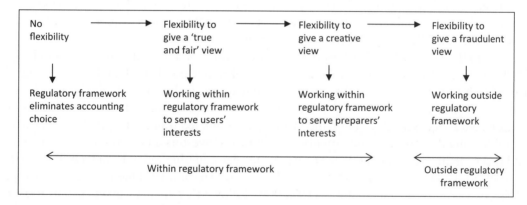

**Figure 1.2**  Flexibility within accounting
*Source*: Adapted from Jones (2006).

### 1.2.2  Fraud

The difference between creative accounting and fraud is, therefore, essentially that creative accounting is working within the regulatory framework. An exact definition of fraud is elusive; for instance, in the UK there is no legal definition of fraud (Levi, Information Gathering Working Party and Doig, 1999). However, fraud involves working outside the regulatory framework. In each country, the definition of fraud will be slightly different; however, in essence, it involves breaking the law and/or violating the regulatory framework. Fraud can be committed by individuals or management. For individuals, accounting fraud would generally involve theft of, for example, inventory or cash. For management, there is also the crime of preparing false financial statements intended to deceive users. When there are suspicions that fraud is taking place, then we can say there is alleged fraud. However, it is only when there is a proven court case that we have a demonstrable case of fraud. Thus, in Polly Peck, a UK company that collapsed in 1991, Asil Nadir has been accused of fraud and false accounting by the Serious Fraud Office in the UK but has not yet been brought to court. The charges remain alleged, with Asil Nadir protesting his innocence. However, in the USA Kenneth Lay and Jeffrey Skilling were both brought to trial and found guilty of accounting fraud at Enron (White, 2006). Also in the USA, the Rigas family who owned Adelphi Communications, a cable operator, were accused of a whole range of accounting malpractices in June 2002. 'The Justice Department and the U.S. Postal Inspection Service charged the five executives with securities, wire and bank fraud, saying they "looted Adelphia on a massive scale" and used it as a "personal piggy bank". Rigas private funds sloshed with Adelphia's in the same cash-management system' (Lieberman and Farrell, 2002, p. 3). For their role in the fraud, key members of the founding family were convicted of financial statement fraud.

Financial statement fraud is a subset of fraud in general. There have been some attempts to estimate both the extent of fraud and of financial statement fraud, which is the main focus of this particular book. The most comprehensive study, particularly of financial statement fraud, is provided by Beasley, Carcello and Hermanson (1999) in a research report commissioned by the Treadway Commission in the USA. This is dealt with, in depth, in Chapter 5. I therefore focus here on other indications of the extent of fraud in four studies from the UK, USA, Australia and globally.

First, in the UK the Fraud Advisory Panel (Levi, Information Gathering Party and Doig, 1999) outlined various ranges of the annual cost of major frauds in the UK. These ranged from £16 billion from the Association of British Insurers; £5 billion from the Serious Fraud Office as well as Ernst & Young; £1–2 billion from benefit fraud and £400–700 million from KPMG. The Serious Fraud Office workload of alleged frauds in April 1997 was over £2 billion and the most common frauds were those on investors and creditors, and on banks and other institutions. The number of cases of false accounting ranged from a high of 2106 in 1989 to a low of 1395 in 1995 (from 1986–96). The most frequently occurring type of fraud was false documentations (£977 000) followed by theft of assets (£640 100) in 1997/98.

In the USA, the Association of Certified Fraud Examiners in 1996 published a Fraud Report (Association of Certified Fraud Examiners, 1996). It collected the experience of 2608 Certified Fraud Examiners. They studied $15 billion of cases, and established that fraud and abuse cost US organisations more than $400 billion annually. Men commit 75 % of frauds, with small businesses being the most vulnerable. The most common account affected by fraud was cash, with fraudulent financial statements accounting for about 5 % of cases.

Third, in Australia and New Zealand, KPMG carried out a Fraud Survey in 2004 (KPMG, 2004). Its main findings were that 45 % of its respondents experienced at least one fraud, with a loss of $456.7 million and 27 657 instances of fraud. The typical fraudster was male, about 31 years old, with no prior record of dishonesty, in a non-management position who misappropriated funds of \$337 734 and acting alone was motivated by greed. The most common fraud by managers was the theft of inventory/plant, followed by the misappropriation of funds, cheque forgery and false invoicing.

Fourth, Ernst & Young carry out an annual survey of fraud. Their 2002 survey found that 85 % of frauds were by insiders on the payroll (Ernst & Young, 2002). Generally, more frauds happened in less developed regions, such as Africa, than in more developed regions, like Europe. The size of more than half the losses was less than \$100 000.

In general, financial statement fraud can be categorised in two major ways. First, it is when a company uses accounting practices which are outside those permitted by the regulatory framework. In other words, they are not allowed by accounting standards or accounting laws. Generally, to be designated as fraud these practices will have been shown to be fraudulent in a court of law. Often, it is difficult to distinguish between creative accounting and fraud as it will all be a matter of interpreting the basic assumptions that underpin accounting.

The second major type of fraud is where transactions have been invented. In other words, non-existent transactions have been recorded in the books, such as fictitious sales or fictitious inventory. For example, in the USA there have been two high-profile fraud cases in the twentieth century that have involved substantial fraud. In McKesson and Robbins a fictitious subsidiary had been invented, while in the case of the Equity Funding Corporation of America a whole edifice of false insurance policies had been constructed.

### 1.2.3  Other Terms

There are many other terms which are used in connection with creative accounting. Some of these are discussed below. They are also set out more formally in Figure 1.3.

---

**Aggressive accounting**

This is a very similar term to creative accounting. It involves the use of accounting rules and regulations to deliver a particular result, but working within the regulatory system.

**Earnings management**

This involves using the flexibility within accounting to deliver a predetermined profit. This may be, for example, to meet a consensus earnings figure expected by city analysts.

**Impression management**

This represents an attempt by the management of the firm to give to users the impression of the firm which managers want. This will include creative accounting. However, impression management is more usually associated with presentational issues such as accounting narratives and graphs.

**Profit smoothing**

This involves the use of accounting techniques to ensure a steady profit. In other words, the natural peaks and troughs of accounting profit are eliminated.

---

**Figure 1.3**   Other terms used in creative accounting

### 1.2.3.1  Aggressive Accounting

This term is broadly the same as creative accounting. It is the use of accounting rules and regulations to deliver a particular set of financial results. It involves the deliberate choice of accounting figures which will have more to do with achieving a specific managerial objective, such as increased earnings, rather than presenting a true and fair view. In this book, aggressive accounting is seen to be broadly synonymous with creative accounting.

### 1.2.3.2  Earnings Management

Earnings management is a term commonly used by academics. There have been numerous academic papers written on all aspects of the subject. Earnings management is where managers manage the accounts in order to achieve a specific objective. So, for example, it is common practice for analysts to issue profit forecasts for firms trading on the world's stock exchanges. Firms like to meet these forecasts because if they do not, share prices of the errant companies often fall. Firms which are falling short of their targets will, therefore, sometimes seek to manage their profits. There are many other examples of earnings management. For example, to ensure that debt covenants are not breached, for profit smoothing, or to sustain earnings and share price in takeovers. A fuller discussion of the earnings management literature is given in Chapter 5.

### 1.2.3.3  Impression Management

Impression management involves managers influencing the financial reports in their favour. It is not fraudulent. It is a very wide term and although it includes creative accounting, it is normally more associated with the presentational aspects of reporting such as accounting narratives, graphs and photographs. Accounting narratives, such as the Chairman's State-ment in the UK and the Management Discussion and Analysis in the USA, may be subject to narrative enhancement. In other words, management may present news selectively, bias the news or use attribution (attribute good news to themselves but attribute bad news to uncontrollable external influences such as world events).

There are many possible ways in which graphs might be used creatively. For example, they may only be used when there is a favourable trend to display. Or alternatively they might be drawn so as to enhance favourable results and downplay unfavourable results. Finally, photographs may be used to present an overall image of the company. For ex-ample, many of the high-profile oil companies use nature photographs to try to present a green image. A fuller discussion of the impression management literature is provided in Chapter 6.

### 1.2.3.4  Profit Smoothing

The stock market generally rewards companies that produce steady profits, but penalises those with erratic profits. Companies therefore will prefer to report steady year-on-year growth rather than confront the market with volatile profits. Company managers will, therefore, use various techniques to smooth profits. Essentially this means massaging down high profits and enhancing poor profits. Fortunately for the creative accountant, lots of opportunities arise for massaging profits. The company can, for example, use provision or 'cookie jar' accounting. This is where a firm may set up a provision for an expense one year. This will reduce profits. The next year it may reverse the provision saying that the expenses it expected to incur were overestimated. Consequently, in year two profits will be more because of the reversed provision. Companies can then save up their profits for a rainy day.

## 1.3 STRUCTURE OF THE BOOK

I will now briefly outline the contents of the rest of the book. In the rest of Part A, the context of creative accounting is examined. This draws upon existing academic and professional literature. In Chapter 2, I look at the main actors involved in creative accounting: managers, investment analysts, auditors, regulators, shareholders, merchant bankers and other users. The different interests which these groups have are highlighted. Managers may benefit from creative accounting as it gives them the flexibility to deliver the results they want. Existing shareholders may also gain, unless the company collapses, due to its enhanced share prices caused by creative accounting. For merchant bankers, there may be potentially lucrative fees to be earned by creating complex creative accounting schemes. By contrast, other groups are harmed by creative accounting. Regulators dislike creative accounting because it can be used to bypass accounting rules and undermines the currency of accounting. Shareholders, and other users, may suffer if the company collapses. For auditors, creative accounting creates a potential conflict with management, and also a potential problem if the company collapses as the auditor may be blamed.

The motivations to indulge in creative accounting and fraud are varied and are examined in Chapter 3. There are two sets of general incentives: personal and city. The personal incentives relate to the managers. They may wish, for example, to try to increase their salaries, bonuses, enhance their shares and share options. In other words, there are incentives for them to manipulate accounting policies in order to maximise their own personal benefit. They also may wish to meet city expectations. If the business does not deliver the expected profits then its share price may be punished. As a result, managers will try to meet analysts' expectations and may indulge in profit smoothing or in other creative accounting techniques.

There are also a range of special circumstances. For example, managers may wish to increase net assets so as to stop breaching debt covenants or creative accounting may be used to increase the share price of a company when it is purchasing another through a share issue. In certain circumstances, there may also be incentives to reduce profits. For example, in regulated industries when governments may penalise excessive profits or in situations where a new incoming management team may wish to make the current year's profits worse so that future profits will look better.

There are numerous ways of exploiting the inherent flexibility of accounting so as to indulge in creative accounting. In Chapter 4, I look at four main strategies: increasing income, decreasing expenses, increasing assets and decreasing liabilities.

### 1.3.1 Increase Income

The aim here is to maximise revenues which will feed directly into profit. There are several main ways. Generally, these will involve the premature recognition of sales or the maximisation of other income such as interest receivable or non-operating profit. In most cases, these techniques will exploit the flexibility in accounting regulation. However, in some cases completely fictitious sales will be created. At its most extreme, as in McKesson and Robbins in the USA in 1931, a wholly fictitious trading subsidiary was set up. More recently in Germany, as we will see in Chapter 10, at Flowtex, fictitious drilling machines were 'manufactured' and 'leased'.

### 1.3.2 Decrease Expenses

By decreasing expenses, profit is naturally increased. Expenses can be decreased in a number of ways. For example, in provision accounting, in good years expenses will be set up for provisions such as restructuring. Then, in bad years these provisions can be fed back into the profit and loss account reducing expenses and increasing profits. Such provisions are particularly popular on acquisition or when a new management takes over a company. Other ways of decreasing expenses can be (i) to capitalise expenses such as interest payable so that they are recorded as assets not expenses, or (ii) to lengthen asset lives so as to reduce depreciation, or (iii) to reduce bad debts. Finally, a good way of decreasing expenses is to increase closing inventory. Closing inventory is taken off cost of sales and thus by increasing closing inventory, cost of sales is reduced and profits increased.

### 1.3.3 Increase Assets

Many of the strategies that decreased expenses will also boost assets. Thus, lengthening depreciation levels and capitalising interest will boost fixed assets, while reducing bad debts will increase accounts receivable. However, some other techniques can be used to increase assets. For example, goodwill, brands and other intangible assets can be enhanced in value and included in the accounts. In addition, tangible fixed accounts can be revalued.

### 1.3.4 Decrease Liabilities

Another way of increasing net assets is by decreasing liabilities. Two common ways are off-balance sheet financing and reclassifying debt as equity. Off-balance sheet financing attempts to quarantine debt in subsidiary companies which are not then consolidated. Enron, for example, set up numerous off-balance sheet subsidiaries. Reclassifying debt as equity seeks to classify outside, third-party debt as insider capital. This serves to reduce the apparent levels of debt.

There have been many studies into creative accounting, and both descriptive and statistical studies are discussed in Chapter 5. The descriptive studies, reports and books discuss and provide illustrative examples of creative accounting. In the statistical studies, large numbers of company accounts are typically analysed by accounting academics to see if they can discern any aggregate evidence of creative accounting.

The eight books and two reports present an impressive array of evidence about creative accounting and fraud both in the UK and the USA. Innovative methods and illustrations of creative accounting are documented. For example, UBS Phillips & Drew in *Accounting for Growth* in 1991 looked at 185 well-known UK companies' annual reports. They identified 11 creative accounting techniques and then showed which UK companies used them as well as using vignettes to illustrate individual practices (UBS Phillips & Drew, 1991).

The statistical studies have looked at a range of issues and generally have found evidence supportive of the existence of creative accounting.

- Companies were found to income smooth. In other words, companies increased profits in poor years, but decreased them in good years.
- Companies used creative accounting to meet their own annual earnings forecasts and also those of market analysts.
- Managers manipulated earnings so that they could receive higher bonuses.
- Companies manipulated earnings and net asset values so as not to breach their debt covenants.
- Certain companies, particularly those in regulated industries, manipulated their earnings so as to ward off government interference.
- When there was a change of management, especially when the changes were forced, then incoming managers, in particular, were found to decrease income in the year of changeover so that future profits could be enhanced.
- In takeover situations, it was found that acquiring companies' earnings increased before the acquisition. This increased share prices and thus meant acquiring companies had to pay fewer shares for their acquisitions. Similarly, company earnings increased before a share issue.
- Those firms which failed to meet analysts' expectations were more likely to make disclosures to attempt to manage stock market reactions.

The use of accounting narratives, graphs and photographs to manage impressions is outlined in Chapter 6. Impression management is where managers present the numbers and narratives in an annual report in such a way as to give users a particular impression of the firm's results. Managers may, for example, use accounting narratives to:

(i) stress the positive and downplay the negative;
(ii) convey bad news by using technical language which is difficult to read;
(iii) use differential reporting, with companies reporting bad news focusing less on the actual results and preferring to focus on the future;
(iv) use attribution to take the credit themselves for good news, while blaming the environment for bad news.

Managers can use graphs for impression management in three ways. First, by being selective in their use and presenting only those graphs which convey good news (selectivity). Second, by drawing graphs which present an enhanced picture of the company's underlying performance (measurement distortion). Third, by enhancing the presentation of graphs using a variety of presentational techniques (presentational enhancement). Finally, photographs can be used to create an overall impression of a firm. Thus, companies selling alcohol may try to convey a fun-loving, exciting environment.

Accounting scandals have always been with us. The role of creative accounting and fraud in them has always been fairly fluid. One period's creative accounting can, after a change in accounting rules and regulations, become a subsequent period's fraud. Chapter 7 looks at accounting scandals over time and shows the role played by creative accounting and fraud.

Eighteen different examples of accounting scams and scandals are outlined across five time periods: the ancient and medieval period; the seventeenth and eighteenth centuries; the nineteenth century; the twentieth century up to 1945; and the twentieth century from 1945 up to the 1980s. The cases range from the doctoring of a cruciform monument in the second millennium BC in Mesopotamia in an attempt to convince the King that the revenues of the temple were greater than they actually were to the Renouf and Judge corporations in New Zealand in the 1980s, where creative accounting was apparently used to enhance earnings and share price (see Chapter 7). Geographically, the countries where scandals occur are diverse: Australia, Italy, Mesopotamia, New Zealand, the UK and the USA.

These illustrative examples include clear examples of creative accounting, such as P&O's manipulation of the results of its New Zealand subsidiary at the start of the twentieth century so as to transfer funds secretly to the UK to frauds such as Equity Funding of America. In this latter case, more than $3 billion life insurance policies were found to be fraudulent.

In Part B, we look at accounting scandals in 12 different countries. The main countries (with the authors and the most important cases presented) are shown in Table 1.1.

The author(s) of each chapter were asked to analyse cases of creative accounting, fraud and accounting scandals in their respective countries since the 1980s. In particular, they were asked to discuss, explain and evaluate the major accounting scandals. In addition, as a final chapter (Chapter 20) in this Part, we look at the global banking crisis. This chapter written by Simon Norton deals with the major recent US cases of Bear Stearns, Lehman Brothers and Madoff Securities International Ltd.

In Table 1.1, I list the countries, the authors and the major cases in each country. Usually, this is one case, such as HIH in Australia, but in Germany, the Netherlands, Spain, Sweden and the USA, two cases are covered. In Japan, three major cases are identified across the period. As we see below, the authors discuss not only these major cases, but also instances of creative accounting and other important scandals that have occurred, usually post-1980. I now look, briefly, at these major chapters.

Gary Carnegie and Brendan O'Connell look at accounting scandals in Australia in Chapter 8. They demonstrate that Australia has a long history of accounting scandals. Five case studies are examined, in depth: Adelaide Steamship, Bond Corporation, Harris Scarfe, One.Tel and HIH. In particular, they focus on HIH, which in 2001 was the largest ever corporate collapse in Australia's history. They show that HIH collapsed through underprovisioning and from mismanagement.

Accounting scandals in China are investigated in Chapter 9 by Catherine Chen, Yuanyuan Hu and Jason Xiao. They focus on six accounting scandals (Yuanye, Great Wall Fund Raising, Hongguang, Daqing Lianyi, Kangsai Group and Lantian Gufen) before carrying out an in-depth study into Zhenzhou Baiwen. Zhenzhou Baiwen, a company involved in household appliances and department stores, appeared to be very successful. However, at

**Table 1.1**   Main countries discussed in this book

| Chapter | Country | Authors | Major cases |
|---|---|---|---|
| 8 | Australia | Garry Carnegie<br>Brendan O'Connell | HIH Insurance |
| 9 | China | Catherine Chen<br>Yuanyuan Hu<br>Jason Xiao | Zhenzhou Baiwen |
| 10 | Germany | Hansrudi Lenz | ComRoad<br>Flowtex |
| 11 | Greece | George Kontos<br>Maria Krambia-Kapardis<br>Nikolaos Milonas | Bank of Crete |
| 12 | India | Bhabatosh Banerjee | Satyam |
| 13 | Italy | Andrea Melis | Parmalat |
| 14 | Japan | Kazuyuki Suda | Kanebo<br>Livedoor<br>Nikko Cordial |
| 15 | Netherlands | Henk Langendijk | Royal Ahold |
| 16 | Spain | Nieves Carrera | Afinsa and Fórum<br>Filatélico |
| 17 | Sweden | Gunnar Rimmel<br>Kristina Jonäll | ABB<br>Skandia |
| 18 | United Kingdom | David Gwilliam<br>Richard Jackson | Polly Peck |
| 19 | United States | Charles Mulford<br>Eugene Comiskey | Enron<br>WorldCom |

the turn of the new millennium it ran into trouble and the authors show that its apparent success was based on creative accounting and fictitious sales.

Chapter 10, on accounting scandals in Germany, was written by Hansrudi Lenz. He looks at six important cases: Co-op, Balsam, Bremer Vulkan Verbund, Philipp Holzmann, Flowtex and ComRoad. Flowtex and ComRoad are particularly interesting. They both involve extensive frauds. Flowtex manufactured and leased fictitious drilling equipment, while ComRoad's CEO and his wife had virtually constructed a fictitious customer/supplier.

Accounting scandals in another European country, Greece, are analysed in Chapter 11. Three cases are singled out for special attention by George Kontos, Maria Krambia-Kapardis and Nikolaos Milonas: ETBA Finance, Dynamic Life and the Bank of Crete. The Bank of Crete was a major scandal in which one man, George Koskotas, systematically used weaknesses in the internal accounting system of the bank to embezzle huge sums of money. The wider implications of the case for the Greek economic and political structure are examined.

In Chapter 12 we move to India. Bhabatosh Banerjee demonstrates first that creative accounting is very common in India. He outlines eight different instances of creative accounting, ranging from the creation and write-back of provisions by Bombay Dyeing and Manufacturing Company to the capitalisation of interest by companies such as the Oil and Natural Gas Commission. Only one major Indian case is dealt with, Satyam – not because there are no more, but because the Indian judicial process is very long and they are still sub judice.

Andrea Melis investigates creative accounting and accounting scandals in Italy in Chapter 13. He looks at Pirelli's legal but creative use of consolidation accounting, before looking at the topics of stock options and creative accounting within football clubs. Then, Professor Melis investigates the most spectacular accounting fraud in Italy: Parmalat. He demonstrates that at Parmalat there was falsification of earnings, assets and liabilities with poor internal controls and serious failings by the external auditors.

Next, in Chapter 14, Kazuyuki Suda investigates a series of high-profile accounting scandals in Japan. Ten scandals are analysed: Sanyo Special Steel, Fuji Sash, Sawako, Sanyo Electric, Livedoor, Morimoto-gumi, Nikko Cordial, Riccar, Yamaichi and Kanebo. These scandals were apparently motivated by the avoidance of bankruptcy and by the need to fulfil public construction contracts and managerial compensation. The Kanebo case is particularly interesting, and represents the largest ever amount of earnings manipulation in Japan. It resulted in the break-up of the auditing firm ChuoAoyama PricewaterhouseCoopers.

In Chapter 15, Henk Langendijk looks at the Dutch experience of accounting scandals. First of all, he looks at two relatively minor accounting scandals at Rijn Schelde-Verolme (RSV) and Fokker. He then focuses on one major company accounting scandal, Royal Ahold. At Royal Ahold, consolidation and vendor allowances were both abused.

In Chapter 16, Nieves Carrera examines major financial scandals in Spain. First of all, accounting scandals in the banking sector, such as Caja Rural de Jaen and Banesto, are discussed. An important scandal in the investment services sector, Gescartera, is then studied. The third sector that Professor Carrera examines is the real estate sector, with the case of Promotora Social de Viviendas and Iniciativas de Gestión de Servicios. Finally, two major scandals involving investment in stamps, Afinsa and Fórum Filatélico, are examined. Both companies are found to have indulged in many accounting irregularities.

The Swedish chapter, Chapter 17, was written by Gunnar Rimmel and Kristina Jonäll, who look at four major accounting scandals: Fermenta, Prosolvia, ABB and Skandia. The latter two cases are covered in depth. ABB's accounting was found to be hard to decipher, with continual reorganisations and the redemption of its own shares. Skandia, an insurance company, used embedded value accounting which led the company to appear to be prosperous despite significant negative cash flows.

In Chapter 18, David Gwilliam and Richard Jackson investigate creative accounting and fraud in the UK. They analyse three main cases: BCCI, Mirror Group and Polly Peck. They focus on Polly Peck. They show that this fast-growing company, involved in food purchase, production and packaging, seemingly adopted very dubious accounting practices. In particular, weak internal controls apparently allowed huge sums of cash to be transferred out of the UK to Turkey. In addition, many of the financial statements for Polly Peck's Turkish subsidiaries appear to have been vastly inflated. Asil Nadir, who ran the company, has, however, always protested his innocence and in August 2010 returned to face trial.

The penultimate chapter in Part B, Chapter 19, is on accounting scandals in the USA. Charles Mulford and Eugene Comiskey demonstrate that in the USA since the 1990s there have been numerous cases of premature or fictitious revenue recognition, capitalisation of costs and/or extended amortisation periods, overstated assets and/or understated liabilities, and other creative accounting practices such as the abuse of restructuring charges and creative financial statement classification. They focus, in particular, upon Enron and WorldCom. They show that Enron's fraud involved off-balance sheet liabilities, fictitious income and misreported cash flow. Meanwhile, at WorldCom, the fraud – although on a massive scale – was quite simple, involving, in particular, the capitalisation of operating expenses.

The final chapter in this section, Chapter 20, is based on the recent worldwide banking crisis. Simon Norton shows the causes of the crisis and how accounting has been implicated in corporate collapses. He demonstrates the role played by fair value and also by creative accounting techniques such as off-balance sheet financing. He focuses on three important cases: Lehman Brothers, Madoff Investment Securities and Bear Stearns. Lehman Brothers is shown to involve creative accounting rather than fraud. Madoff's fraud involved a 'Ponzi' scheme where new investors essentially funded returns to existing investors. Bear Stearns is an example of creative accounting being used to repackage higher risk products to lower risk ones.

In Part C of the book, I attempt to synthesise and discuss the overall findings. In Chapter 21, I look at some themes which emerged from the various chapters. I look at the major methods used, as far as they can be identified, from the various chapters. There were examples of increasing income, decreasing expenses, increasing assets and decreasing liabilities. Particularly popular were attempts to boost earnings through related parties, capitalising expenses and off-balance sheet financing. There were also frequent cases of fraud, such as embezzlement and fictitious transactions. I also look at the incentives for creative accounting and fraud. Generally, from the evidence in the individual chapters, this was most often used to cover up bad performance, for personal benefit and to meet listing requirements.

In Chapter 21, I also look at three themes which emerged from prior chapters: the role of overstrong personalities, the failure of internal controls and of internal auditing. First, there were many examples of how overstrong individuals used the power of their personalities to carry all before them. They managed to convince investors and the wider business world to trust them. Second, many instances of a failure of internal controls were identified. These included ineffective boards of directors, lack of independent scrutiny via non-executive directors or supervisory boards, and failure of internal audit. Finally, in many cases across the accounting scandals, there was evidence of a severe failure of external auditing.

In Chapter 22, the penultimate chapter, I investigate, using the evidence from prior country chapters and the longitudinal chapter, the immediate and long-term impact of creative accounting and the international accounting scandals. In the short term, there are effects upon both insiders and outsiders. Directors are most often fined or jailed. Auditors are often sanctioned, while investors and creditors often lose money. The longer-term effects may involve new regulatory measures to stop abuses. Over time, the regulatory framework becomes more sophisticated.

Finally, in Chapter 23, I summarise the main findings from the book in terms of prior literature and the individual country studies. I look at certain key themes examined, such as the motivation for individuals to indulge in creative accounting and fraud, the main methods of creative accounting, the role of overstrong personalities, the failures of internal controls and external auditing. I then consider some lessons for the future. I examine how the potential for creative accounting and fraud is enhanced by motives and environmental opportunities. I then evaluate some potential solutions, such as more appropriate rewards and incentives, better regulations, enhanced supervision, harsher penalties and improved ethics. Finally, I suggest that whatever the attempts to prevent creative accounting and fraud, history suggests that international accounting scandals are likely to continue in one form or another.

# 1.4 CONCLUSION

The term 'creative accounting' can be defined in many ways. In particular, a broad definition of the term includes fraud. The narrower definition, as preferred by this book, sees creative accounting as using the flexibility in accounting within the regulatory framework to manage the measurement and presentation of the accounts so that they give primacy to the interests of the preparers not the users. Creative accounting is not therefore illegal, and works within the current regulatory framework. Fraud, by contrast, is illegal. Fraud involves working outside the regulatory framework. The term 'fraud', however, in this book is reserved for cases which have been tried in court or by regulatory commissions. Otherwise, the term 'alleged fraud' is used. Other terms associated with creative accounting are aggressive accounting, earnings management, impression management and profit smoothing. Aggressive accounting in this book is broadly considered to be synonymous with creative accounting. Earnings management involves using the flexibility within accounting to deliver a predetermined profit. This may be, for example, to meet a consensus earnings figure expected by city analysts or to profit smooth. Impression management can include earnings management. More particularly, it is concerned with the presentation of the accounts, in particular accounting narratives, graphs and photographs. Finally, profit smoothing involves the use of accounting techniques to ensure a steady profit. In other words, the natural peaks and troughs of accounting profit are eliminated.

This book looks at the use of creative accounting and fraud in a global context across 12 countries from Asia, Australasia, Europe and North America. Representatives of both developed and developing countries are thus included. The motives, methods and consequences of the major accounting scandals are examined. There is also consideration of the role played by accounting in recent bank failures. Then, some overall conclusions are drawn which identify the major motivations for the scandals, the major methods of creative accounting and fraud used, the role of overstrong individuals, internal and external control failures, and regulatory and other consequences.

# REFERENCES

Association of Certified Fraud Examiners (1996), *Report to the Nation on Occupational Fraud and Abuse*, USA.

Beasley, M.S., Carcello, J.V. and Hermanson, D.R. (1999), *Fraudulent Financial Reporting 1987–1997: An Analysis of U.S. Public Companies*. Research commissioned by the Committee of Sponsoring Organizations of the Treadway Commission.

Ernst & Young (2002), *Fraud: The Unmanaged Risk. 8th Global Survey*, Ernst & Young, South Africa.

Griffiths, I. (1986), *Creative Accounting*, Sidgwick and Jackson, London.

Jones, M.J. (2006), *Accounting*, John Wiley & Sons Ltd, Chichester.

KPMG (2004), *Forensic Fraud Survey 2004*, KPMG, Australia.

Levi, M., Information Gathering Working Party and Doig, A. (1999), *Study of Published Literature on the Nature and Extent of Fraud in the Public and Private Sector*, The Fraud Advisory Panel, Working Party Paper.

Lieberman, D. and Farrell, G. (2002), 'Adelphia founder, 2 sons, 2 others arrested in accounting fraud', *US Today*, 24 June.

McBarnet, D. and Whelan, C. (1999), *Creative Accounting and the Cross-eyed Javelin Thrower*, John Wiley & Sons Ltd, Chichester.

Mulford, C. and Comiskey, E. (2002), *The Financial Numbers Game. Detecting Creative Accounting Practices*, John Wiley & Sons Inc., New York.

Pijper, T. (1993), *Creative Accounting. The Effectiveness of Financial Reporting in the UK*, Macmillan, London.

Smith, T. (1991), *Accounting for Growth. Stripping the Camouflage from Company Accounts*, Century Books, London.

UBS Phillips & Drew (1991), *Accounting for Growth*, UBS Phillips & Drew, London.

White, B. (2006), 'Government scores its biggest victory', *Financial Times*, p. 26.

# 2

# The Creative Accounting and Fraud Environment

Michael Jones

## 2.1 INTRODUCTION

Creative accounting and fraud do not occur in a vacuum. There are a number of interested parties. These range from managers, investment analysts, auditors, regulators, shareholders, merchant bankers to other users. As can be seen from Figure 2.1, all of these parties play a key role in creative accounting. In the case of fraud, the legal authorities will also take an interest. The corporate environment of the firm and economic climate are also important. There needs to be, in particular, effective corporate governance. For instance, Crutchley, Jensen and Marshall (2007, p. 53) comment: '[W]e find that the corporate environment most likely to lead to an accounting scandal is characterised by rapid growth, with high earnings smoothing, fewer outsiders on the audit committee, and outsider directors that seemed overcommitted.' Finally, the economic environment of the company, or the personal circumstances of an individual, are important. Creative accounting and fraud are more likely when a company is facing financial difficulties.

The managers set the creative accounting agenda. They wish to portray the accounts in a light favourable to themselves. This may be to increase profits or increase net assets. The flexibility in accounting allows them to select accounting techniques which can deliver the profit figure that serves their interests. As we will see in Chapter 3, there are a variety of motivations why managers may wish specifically to adopt creative accounting. Managers may take professional advice from, for example, merchant banks to devise creative accounting schemes which, while complying with the letter of the law, transgress its spirit. Regulators seek to control and limit creative accounting by setting rules and regulations. Over time, the regulatory framework will be shaped by creative accounting and will, in turn, shape creative accounting. Meanwhile, the auditors will seek to ensure that the accounts are 'true and fair' and will use the regulatory framework as a legitimation tool and reference point. Whereas the managers set the agenda, the users attempt to detect creative accounting and cope with its consequences. Investment analysts are seeking to price stocks and shares efficiently; they will, therefore, seek to adjust the accounts for creative accounting. For ordinary shareholders, creative accounting can affect the share price and they will also wish to try to detect it. If a company gets into difficulties or, even worse, goes bankrupt, they will be major losers. Finally, bankers and creditors would worry that creative accounting

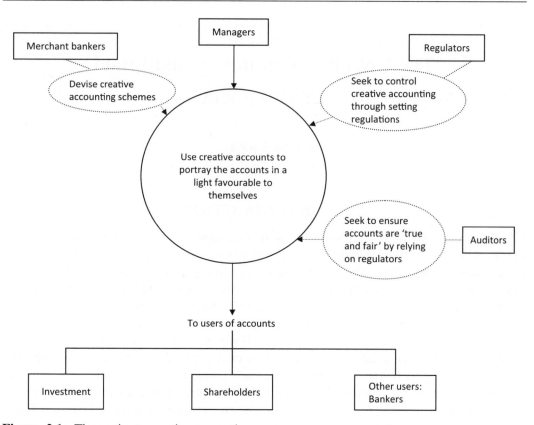

**Figure 2.1**   The parties to creative accounting

could be used to cover up poor results and leave them exposed if the company collapses. All of these are affected by creative accounting in different ways.

In terms of the corporate environment of the firm, good corporate governance will minimize the opportunities for creative accounting, and particularly fraud. There need to be, for example, effective internal controls, the presence of independent non-executive directors, the segregation of chairman and chief executive officer, and an independent audit committee. Finally, the economic environment of the company and individual is important.

## 2.2 THE MAIN ACTORS

### 2.2.1 Managers

For managers, creative accounting is a way to influence the accounts. Managers have their own agenda. In theory, managers manage the companies which are owned by the shareholders. They are, therefore, in effect, stewards and should run the companies for the good of the shareholders. However, in practice, self-interest may dictate that managers may wish to use the flexibility within the accounting system, provided by creative accounting, to manage the results in certain ways. There may be managerial incentives to increase or decrease profits, or to increase assets or decrease liabilities. These incentives may vary. For example, there may be personal incentives for managers to use creative accounting, such as to increase profit as their salary may be profit-related or they may have shares whose value is dependent on the company's underlying earnings. Or the managers may wish to meet city expectations of profit forecasts and need to manipulate profits to achieve them. Or there may be special circumstances, such as a need to boost net assets so as to avoid violating debt covenants. These motivations for creative accounting are discussed in more detail in the next chapter. If the yearly profit figures do not 'deliver' the right results when prepared under normal, generally accepted accounting principles, the managers may turn to creative accounting. If they do not, then managers may be afraid that the share price might fall or that they personally might lose out, perhaps through a reduced bonus.

The personal circumstances of managers may contribute to the pressures on them. For example, an excessive lifestyle, gambling or debts will make fraud, in particular, more likely. Also, there is a need for three preconditions to exist: the opportunity to indulge in creative accounting or fraud, the knowledge of how to do it, and the pressure of acceptable self-verbalizations to convince themselves that their behaviour is morally acceptable (Cressey, 1983).

From the perspective of the creative accountant, creative accounting is relatively easy to achieve. There are potentially hundreds of different items in the accounts – all of which have the potential to be used creatively. As we see in Chapter 4, sales can be increased, expenses decreased, assets increased or liabilities decreased so as to increase profit or net assets. Alternatively, sales can be decreased, expenses increased, assets decreased and liabilities increased if the company wants to decrease profits or net assets. Similarly, in the presentation of the accounts managers can use accounting narratives, graphs or photographs to manage the impression of the company's performance which is conveyed.

The creative accountant is aided in his creativity by the fact that it is often extremely difficult for an outsider to detect creative accounting. To take a simple example: a company is operating a fleet of lorries and each lorry will do 100 000 miles in its working life. Currently, each lorry's estimated annual mileage is 20 000 miles. Each lorry costs £50 000 and, therefore, £10 000 is written off each lorry each year in depreciation. If the managers think that next year the lorry will only do 10 000 miles, then depreciation will fall to £5000 per year. Profit will increase by £5000. This is true and fair and reflects economic reality. It is not creative accounting. However, there may be pressures on managers to interpret the amount of miles the lorries will do generously, so as to reduce profit. This is then creative accounting. This managerial interpretation is helped by the fact that we are looking to the future and relying on estimates and assumptions. It is often not possible for an outsider to know whether the manager is being creative or not. Managers themselves will argue that they are either taking generous or prudent views of the underlying assumptions and estimates which underpin accounting transactions. The situation is complicated by the fact that different managers would take different views and that there are potentially many true and fair views. It is this subjectivity that makes creative accounting so easy to carry out and so difficult to detect. Ultimately, it is only the managers themselves that know whether or not they are being creative.

Sometimes, managers start with creative accounting: stretching the accounting assumptions to their limit by, for example, manipulating depreciation charges or inventory valuation. If this fails to achieve the desired accounting figures, the creative accountant may move on to become a potential fraudster working outside the regulatory system or even inventing fictitious transactions.

### 2.2.2 Investment Analysts

Investment analysts operate in the city and investigate the accounts of companies so that stocks and shares can be priced efficiently. In order to do this effectively they need to be able to spot and detect creative accounting and, indeed, fraud. However, there is a lot of evidence to show that they often spot neither. For example, Gwilliam and Russell (1991) showed that in 1989 analysts failed to spot that Polly Peck's earnings were overstated or that the company was losing huge amounts on its overseas borrowings. Indeed, only days before one of the most spectacular collapses in British corporate history, analysts were predicting a substantial increase in profits. In another example, Breton and Taffler (2001) presented analysts with a set of doctored accounts. They used nine creative accounting techniques across different accounting areas, for example, deferred taxation, pensions, off-balance sheet financing and hidden interest charges. Very few analysts actually adjusted, or even detected, any of the creative accounting practices that had been used.

Although analysts are supposed to be independent observers of the companies they follow, in practice, they may not be. This is because the merchant banks, which they work for, may be employed in other consultancy capacities by these companies. As a result, the analysts may hedge their reports on the companies and, for example, give 'hold' recommendations rather than sell recommendations on shares.

### 2.2.3 Regulators

Regulators are keen to control creative accounting. Accounting rules and regulations are designed to be flexible enough to deliver a true and fair view. That is enough flexibility for the regulators. The regulators fear that creative accounting will debase the currency of accounting. In other words, as with Gresham's Law in economics, in which bad money drives out good, they are concerned that bad accounting will drive out good accounting. Over time, both national and international regulatory frameworks have grown up. Accounting scandals occur regularly, and a common consequence is the introduction of new rules and regulations aimed at preventing a new scandal. Similarly, creative accounting tends to erode the currency of accounting in a more insidious way, but also indirectly leads to more regulations.

Let us take three examples. First, in the UK in 1969 there was a takeover by General Electric Company (GEC) of Associated Electrical Industries (AEI). As part of their defence, AEI published a forecast of £10 million profit. However, in the end AEI made a £4.5 million loss. Much of this £14.5 million shortfall was attributable to the flexibility of accounting and, although the term was not yet in common usage, arguably to creative accounting. The ensuing controversy was an important contributory factor in the setting up, for the first time in the UK, of a standard-setting body, the Accounting Standards Committee. Second, in the UK one of the main reasons for the creation of the Accounting Standards Board in 1990 was that, after several high-profile accounting scandals, such as BCCI, Mirror Group and Polly Peck, there was a need to tighten up and improve existing accounting standards. The existing Accounting Standards Committee was not thought to be effective enough. Similarly, the Sarbanes-Oxley Act was an attempt by US regulators to crack down on accounting abuses in the USA after a series of high-profile accounting scandals such as Enron and WorldCom.

Essentially, therefore, the regulators are involved in a never-ending battle with the creative accountant. In most countries today, there is a complex set of accounting regulations – often comprising a mixture of companies' acts, accounting standards, government regulations and Securities and Exchange Commission regulations. The exact mix will vary from country to country. Also at the international level, the International Accounting Standards Board sets international accounting standards. In combination, this regulatory framework strives to deliver to users a view of the company that is in compliance with generally accepted accounting principles. In many countries there is also the belief that the financial statements should comply with 'economic reality', generally expressed as 'a true and fair view' (as in the European Union), or to present fairly (as in the USA). The regulators' job is hindered by the fact that the very flexibility in the accounts that is essential to deliver a true and fair view is the same that can be used by the creative accountant to deliver a 'creative view'.

### 2.2.4 Auditors

For auditors, creative accounting and, more particularly, fraud create a real headache. The auditors' job is to check the accounts to see that they provide a fair presentation of the results. Creative accounting arguably prevents the creation of a true and fair view. In particular, auditors will be scared that if a company has used questionable accounting practices and then subsequently collapses, they will be blamed. Technically, auditors should issue a qualified report if they notice anything amiss. However, in many high-profile corporate collapses such as Polly Peck or Enron, there was no warning from the audited companies' pre-collapse accounts of impending problems. Nor is this unusual in cases of corporate collapse. County Natwest Woodmac, for example, investigated the accounts of 45 UK companies which collapsed in 1990. They found that in only three companies had auditors qualified the accounts. In the USA, Beasley, Carcello and Hermanson (1999) found that 78 out of 141 auditors' reports, on the last financial statements before a fraud was detected, were clean. In Chapter 10 of this book, in Germany it was reported that in only three out of 24 cases, where misstatements were detected by the German Financial Reporting Enforcement Panel, had the auditors spotted the financial reporting irregularity. However, strictly speaking, even if the auditors do suspect creative accounting, as it is within the law there is very little that they can realistically do. If the auditors qualify the accounts, they will be worried that it will accelerate a company's collapse, as it will erode the confidence of investors. On a more mercenary level, they will probably lose the audit fee and be asked to step down as auditors. However, if the auditors do not spot creative accounting, and more particularly fraud, then there are grave risks to their reputation. They may well be sued by investors in negligence cases. Often auditors will lean heavily on the regulatory framework to help them justify their actions in relation to creative accounting. It is thus essential for a country to have effective rules and regulations to which the auditors can turn.

A particular problem for auditors is maintaining sufficient independence from their clients. This is complicated. Although it is, in theory, the shareholders who appoint auditors, in practice, this appointment is made generally on the recommendation of management. There is the perennial problem that it is the management that pay the auditors who report on them. Auditors need to be careful that this does not compromise their position. The situation is further complicated by the fact that it has been argued that the auditors in the 1990s became compromised by their consultancy revenues. As Duska (2005, p. 21) commented on the US accounting environment: Accounting firms also got caught. It was no accident that since the majority of revenues and hence profits for accounting firms in the 1990s began to come from consulting rather than auditing, accounting firms lost their focus on the importance of responsible auditing. This was highlighted, in particular, by the collapse of Arthur Andersen whose consultancy income from Enron was more than that from auditing.

With fraud the issues are more clear-cut, but again fraud can be difficult to detect. This is particularly so when it is a matter of interpreting accounting rules and regulations. It becomes an argument about the underlying estimates and assumptions to draw up the accounts. The situation can be very serious, especially when there is systematic fraud. If the auditors do not spot creative accounting, and more particularly fraud, then there are grave risks to their reputation. They may well be sued by investors in negligence cases. At the very least, the auditors may be taken to court and sued if an accounting scandal leads to a company's collapse. For example, Stoy Hayward, a British auditor, faced a fine of £75 000 and was ordered to pay £250 000 in costs after the collapse of Polly Peck (Perry, 2002). In more severe cases, the auditing company may collapse entirely. This was the case with Arthur Andersen, in the USA. Andersen's were the auditors of Enron, and one of the auditors was found shredding incriminating documents. In Japan, in 2006, a Japanese auditing firm, ChuoAoyama PricewaterhouseCoopers, was found guilty of negligence in auditing Kanebo. As a result, its audits of 2000 Japanese firms were suspended.

### 2.2.5 Shareholders

For external shareholders, creative accounting can be a blessing or a curse. It really depends on what happens to the company. If the company continues to trade, shareholders may actually gain in the short term because creative accounting, if used to give a more flattering view of a firm than is warranted, may actually artificially inflate a share's price. However, the danger to the shareholder is that if the company collapses then the shareholders stand to lose their money. The shareholders of Enron, and many other failed companies, thus have every reason to resent creative accounting for, by aiding the collapse of Enron, creative accounting caused them to lose money. In an even more extreme nineteenth-century case, the shareholders of the City of Glasgow Bank, which collapsed in 1878, had unlimited liability. As a result of a fraud which was not their fault, the majority of the bank's investors were made bankrupt. A particular problem for external shareholders is that they are not privy to information about the true state of a company. Insider shareholders, such as managers, may be able to sell their shares using inside knowledge to avoid financial loss.

### 2.2.6 Merchant Banks

Creative accounting schemes can be very complex. Accountants will often turn to merchant banks for advice on creative accounting schemes. In the Enron scandal, for example, questions were raised about the role of banks in setting up complex deals to set up off-balance sheet financing schemes. The criticism was particularly strong in the US Senate. Iwata (2002) states that at the US Senate Permanent Subcommittee during a ten-hour hearing there was 'document after document appearing to show the banks and their overseas law firms set up and ran secretive, off-shore "shell" companies that funnelled billions of dollars in financing to Enron over the past decade'. Robert Roach, chief investigator for the Senate Permanent Subcommittee on Investigations stated that '[t]he financial institutions were aware that Enron was using questionable accounting. They actively aided Enron in return for fees and favourable consideration in other business dealings.' In their defence, however, representatives from the banks stated that Enron had deceived them, they had followed generally accepted accounting principles and that the accounting transactions were perfectly appropriate. In effect, there was widespread press criticism as to whether corporate advisors were compromising their ethical standards in return for fees. Whatever the particular merits of the Enron case, merchant bankers are, in theory, arguably one of the big gainers from creative accounting, for it is merchant bankers who potentially can devise and peddle creative accounting schemes. As regulations get more complex, so do the schemes of avoidance. There evolves what can be called a creative accounting arms race. A simple creative accounting technique arises, regulators issue a regulation or standard that curbs this technique. The merchant banker devises another scheme to get round the new regulation. The regulator refines the accounting rules, the merchant bank then responds and so on. This is well documented by Atul Shah (1998). He found that in the late 1980s in the UK, merchant banks were often used by companies when issuing complex convertible securities. Indeed, they actively marketed the schemes to companies.

### 2.2.7 Other Users

Finally, other users generally are potentially harmed by creative accounting. These other users may be, for example, bankers, suppliers or employees. These groups generally depend on the accounts to give a fair presentation of the firm's performance. Creative accounting produces a misleading impression which serves managerial rather than stakeholder interests. Bankers might, for example, think that they are making loans on the basis of a healthy balance sheet only to find later that creative accounting has been used to enhance assets or remove liabilities. Suppliers may be lending money thinking the company has a healthy cash flow only to find later that the cash flow has been massaged. Employees may also be misled into thinking that the company is in a healthy position with regards to profits or cash when, in fact, it is not.

### 2.2.8 Legal Authorities

In the case of an alleged fraud, the prosecutors and legal authorities will take an interest. The exact mechanisms and penalties will vary from country to country. However, in all countries there are generally institutional mechanisms in place to deal with alleged fraudulent financial statements. For instance, in the USA from 2002, the Corporate Fraud Task Force, the SEC and the Department of Justice are all active in fraud enforcement. Criminal penalties for securities fraud have sentences of up to 25 years and fines of up to $ 2 million (Green, 2004, p. 4). The former CEO of Enron, Jeffrey Skilling, for example, received a 24-year sentence.

# 2.3 EFFECTIVE CORPORATE GOVERNANCE

A company needs effective corporate governance to reduce the likelihood of creative accounting and, in particular, fraud. This involves effective internal controls and effective independent scrutiny of the executive directors by non-executives. In particular, there are perhaps four main areas which a company ought to pay attention to in order to mitigate the risk of fraud: effective internal controls, the division of responsibility between chief executive and chairman, an audit committee and representation on the board of directors.

## 2.3.1  Effective Internal Controls

Internal controls include a control environment, risk assessment and management, monitoring and control activities. The presence of strong controls inhibits the possibility of financial malpractice. The collection of controls provides a key mechanism, combined with internal audit, whereby financial malpractice can be minimised.

## 2.3.2  Division of the Responsibility between Chief Executive and Chairman

One person being both chairman and chief executive is particularly dangerous. This is an essential division of authority in the board room. It prevents the unmitigated exercise of power by one person. Asil Nadir, for example, was CEO and chairman of Polly Peck.

## 2.3.3  Audit Committee

The audit committee is a relatively new development. It is responsible for supervising the auditors. It is important that the audit committee, to be effective, is independent; in particular, not staffed by friends, acquaintances or family members of existing executive directors. It also needs to meet frequently and to be staffed by experienced individuals.

## 2.3.4  Independent Board of Directors

There is a need for the board of directors itself to be strong. To be effective, there need to be independent non-executive directors. As with the audit committee, the board of directors should not be friends, acquaintances or family members of existing executive directors.

# 2.4 ECONOMIC ENVIRONMENT

The economic environment constitutes the overall framework within which the company works. In times of economic downturn, companies may well face financial difficulties. These can either be unique to the company or to the national economic cycle. In times of a downturn there is increased pressure on the company because of potential pressure on profits. At such times, the management will have increased motivation to increase profits. Increased profits, in turn, will bolster the share price. As a result, there will be increased pressure on managers to adopt creative accounting techniques. These will be used to bolster profits. Often this is because management is waiting for the good times to return. In rare cases, where creative or aggressive accounting fails, there may be pressure for management to move over the line from creative accounting to fraud.

## 2.5 CONCLUSION

All in all, the various parties to creative accounting have mixed interests. Some would appear actually to benefit from creative accounting. Managers because it gives them the flexibility to deliver the results they want to present; existing shareholders, unless the company collapses, because it may increase the share price. And, finally, merchant bankers, because they can earn potentially huge fees peddling and devising complex creative accounting schemes.

By contrast, certain other groups are harmed. Regulators dislike creative accounting because it can be used to bypass accounting rules and regulations and this undermines the credibility of the accounts. Auditors are scared that if creative accounting contributes to a company's collapse, they will be blamed and held negligent. Shareholders and other users may also suffer if the company collapses. Suppliers and bankers may get a false sense of security when accounts have been subject to creative accounting. Suppliers might have been less willing to sell goods to the company and bankers less willing to lend money to the company if they had known the company's true situation. Finally, employees might be misled by a company's results. In most cases, these groups suffer no direct harm. However, when a company collapses and creative accounting is implicated then these groups are likely to lose money. More generally, creative accounting undermines the reliance which investors and other users can place on the accounts. As such it serves to undermine the general confidence in financial reporting. As a result, investors may be less likely to invest and the economy may suffer as a result.

In fraud cases, by contrast, generally the only real gainers are the fraudsters themselves. They will be robbing the company and defrauding the shareholders, creditors and other users, benefiting themselves at the expense of other users. Where there is an alleged fraud, the legal authorities will become involved.

To avoid creative accounting, and in particular fraud, it is necessary to have good corporate governance. Four elements of corporate governance are particularly important: strong internal controls, the separation of the posts of chief executive and chairman, the existence of an audit committee and the presence of independent directors.

Creative accounting and fraud are linked to the economic environment. In particular, when the economy is suffering a downturn, there is increased pressure on company management to use financial engineering to boost profits. At first, they may use creative accounting. However, if this fails, they may resort to fraud.

## REFERENCES

Beasley, M.S., Carcello, J.V. and Hermanson, D.R. (1999), *Fraudulent Financial Reporting: 1987–1997: An Analysis of U.S. Public Companies*. Research commissioned by the Committee of Sponsoring Organizations of the Treadway Commission.

Breton, G. and Taffler, R.J. (2001), 'Accounting information and analyst stock recommendations: a content analysis approach', *Accounting and Business Research* **31**(2), 92–101.

Cressey, R. (1983), *Other People's Money: A Study in the Social Psychology of Embezzlement*, Free Press, Illinois.

Crutchley, C.E., Jensen, M.R.H. and Marshall, B.B. (2007), 'Climate for scandal: corporate environments that contribute to accounting fraud', *The Financial Review* **42**, 53–73.

Duska, R. (2005), 'The good auditor – skeptic or wealth accumulator? Ethical lessons learned from the Arthur Andersen debacle', *Journal of Business Ethics*, **57**, 17–29.

Green, S. (2004), *Manager's Guide to the Sarbanes-Oxley Act*, John Wiley & Sons Inc., New York.

Gwilliam, D. and Russell, T. (1991), 'Polly Peck: where were the analysts?', *Accountancy*, January, 25–26.

Iwata, E. (2002), 'Banks face accusations in Enron case', *USA Today*, 24 July.

Perry, M. (2002), 'Stoys faces fine and lessons over Polly Peck', *Accountancy Age*, 15 January.

Shah, A.K. (1998), 'Exploring the influences and constraints on creative accounting in the United Kingdom', *The European Accounting Review*, **7**(1), 83–104.

# Motivations to Indulge in Creative Accounting and Fraud

Michael Jones

## 3.1 INTRODUCTION

In a perfect world there would be no incentives for managers to indulge in creative accounting or fraud. This is because the business operations of the company would be in line with managerial and city expectations. Results would be excellent and bonuses and share prices would be high. Unfortunately, however, in the real world the company does not always live up to expectations. This is where the problems start and the temptations for creative accounting arise. It may be very tempting to book more sales than would actually be recorded by following the spirit of the accounting rules and regulations. Alternatively, it might be that profits are disappointing so it might seem like a good idea to use the flexibility in the accounting regulatory system to boost them. Finally, debt might seem a bit high and therefore massaging it downwards might seem a good idea.

Generally the incentives will be to maximise reported sales, maximise reported profits, increase net assets and decrease liabilities. However, this is not universally true. For example, income smoothing will involve reducing profits in bumper years. Similarly, in some cases, such as regulated industries subject to governmental price controls, it might be prudent to reduce profits in years in which the firms could be accused of making excessive profits. If this is not done then, there is a risk that the government may intervene to fix prices or profits.

The incentives for fraud are similar to those for creative accounting, but they are more extreme. In general terms, KPMG determined that the most common motivating factors for fraud were greed, gambling and lifestyle (KPMG, 2004a). Whereas creative accounting involves working within the regulatory framework, fraud involves working outside it. In extreme cases, it will involve actually fabricating accounting figures such as sales. In the case of Parmalat, for example, there was a fake Bank of America note worth €3.950 billion. Surprisingly, given the fact that the Bank of America did not receive a letter and there was no account, Grant Thornton received a letter in reply with the Bank of America's letterhead. Questions were raised as to whether the auditors had themselves directly contacted the Bank or whether they had relied on Parmalat's internal mail system. In addition, at Parmalat there were fictitious sales (e.g. 300 000 tons of powdered milk worth $620 million; Langendijk, 2004). In the City of Glasgow Bank, for example, in 1878

*Creative Accounting, Fraud and International Accounting Scandals*  Edited by Michael Jones
© 2011 Michael Jones. Published by John Wiley & Sons, Ltd

the bank directors systematically used fictitious accounting entries to try to maintain the bank's market valuation. In McKesson and Robbins in the USA in the 1930s a wholly fictitious subsidiary company was constructed.

Fraud commonly begins with management using creative accounting. A typical scenario might be that a company has a poorer year than expected. As a temporary measure the firm adopts some creative accounting techniques in order to cover up the shortfall. In the next year, however, the company expects to be able to dispense with creative accounting. Unfortunately, results in the next year are even worse. The company then uses more extensive creative accounting techniques. Eventually the company cannot deliver the expected results within the regulatory system. Therefore, it starts on the slippery road to false accounting and fraud. Jensen and Murphy's (2004, p. 44) analysis of the stock market in the late 1990s is persuasive. They argue that overvalued shares led to managers making 'increasingly aggressive accounting and operating decisions ... When these fail to resolve the issues, managers, under incredible pressure, turn to further manipulation and even fraud.'[1]

There is an obvious analogy with compulsive gambling. The gambler starts with small bets and loses money. Bigger bets are then made until the gambler is out of his/her depth. In essence, this is what happened to cause the collapse of Barings, a UK bank. Nick Leeson, a trader, gradually made bigger and bigger losing trades until, finally, his position was untenable; he could no longer cover up his losses and was then detected. The bank could not bear the losses of this one man's trading and collapsed. There was almost a total failure of the internal controls of Barings. Beasley, Carcello and Hermanson (1999) looked at all Accounting, Auditing and Enforcement Releases which captured violations of the US Securities Exchange Act from January 1987 to December 1997. They found that the most common reasons for committing fraud were to: (i) avoid a loss and bolster other financial results; (ii) increase the share price, benefit from insider trading and obtain higher share prices when making new issues; (iii) obtain a national stock exchange listing or avoid delisting; and (iv) cover up assets misappropriated for personal gain. The first three of these are also common to creative accounting.

Brennan and McGrath (2007) looked at 14 US and European fraud cases. They found that generally the main motive was to influence share prices, particularly to meet external forecasts and for personal gain. Meanwhile, a consultation paper by the UK's Auditing Practices Board (1998) reviewed recent fraud cases in the UK and concluded that 65 % of the cases of fraud proved to be the misstatement of financial information by management principally to maintain share prices or disguise losses. Finally, KPMG (2004b, p. 9) state that 'the motivations for financial statement fraud are varied, but often reflect the desire to meet earnings forecasts, clear executive compensation hurdles linked to profitability or market capitalisation, avoid breaching debt covenants tied to financial performance, or cover-up poor management decisions'.

In Figure 3.1, I outline some major potential incentives for creative accounting. These incentives may also apply for fraud, which is fortunately much rarer. There are 17 incentives given in Figure 3.1. They can perhaps be grouped into four main categories of incentives. The first three I term 'personal incentives', 'market incentives' and 'special cases'. There is also a case of it's not illegal so why not do it? The fourth category I call 'to cover up fraud'. These are not necessarily discrete categories, but provide a useful framework for a

---

[1] As cited in Grant and Visconti (2006, p. 365).

**A. Personal incentives**
Increased salaries
Bonus-related pay
Shares and share options
Job security
Personal satisfaction
**B. Market expectations**
Meeting analysts' expectations
Profit smoothing
The norm
**C. Special circumstances**
Manage gearing and borrowing
New issues
Mergers and acquisitions
Decrease regulatory visibility
New management team
Waiting for the good times
Believe current regulations incorrect
Not illegal, so why shouldn't we use creative accounting?
**D. Cover-up fraud**
Misappropriation of assets

**Figure 3.1**    Incentives for creative accounting and sometimes fraud

broad overview. In practice, in the real world, it is often difficult to disentangle the actual incentives which have driven managerial actions.

### 3.1.1 Personal Incentives

There are five personal incentives: increased salaries; bonus-related pay; shares and share options; job security and personal satisfaction. Essentially, these incentives lead the managers to adopt creative accounting or fraud as they will benefit directly. In certain circumstances, individual managers may be in severe financial difficulties and desperately need money. More often the motivation would seem just to be greed. Many of these incentives have been empirically tested and found to exist (see Chapter 5).

#### 3.1.1.1 Increased Salaries

In many cases, directors will be subject to quite extensive performance-related pay. In the case of salaries, they may be rewarded if certain targets are reached. These may be sales targets or profit targets. Just as a salesman may have incentives to maximise sales because his salary is linked to profit, so directors may have similar incentives.

#### 3.1.1.2 Bonus-related Pay

This is similar to increased salaries. However, in this case a bonus is paid if certain results are met. Once more, managers have great incentives to use the underlying flexibility within accounting quite legally to increase profits. Mulford and Comiskey (2002, p. 6) cite the case of Lawrence Coss, chairman of Green Tree Financial Corp., a US company. His bonus was calculated as 2.5 % of Green Tree's pre-tax profit. Mr Coss was paid in shares, but the share price was set at a historic price much lower than market price. In 1994, 1995 and 1996, Green Tree's profit before tax was $302 million, $410 million and $498 million, respectively. Mr Coss's bonus based on these amounts would, therefore, have been $7.5 million, $10.2 million and $12.4 million, respectively. However, as he was paid in shares he received an annual share bonus of $28.5 million in 1994, $65.1 million in 1995 and $102.0 million in 1996.

### 3.1.1.3  Shares and Share Options

As with Mr Coss, a common form of directors' remuneration is the provision of shares and share options in a company. Gary Strauss (2002) commented on the US position: 'Stock options have been a core part of CEO compensation plans for much of the past decade, enriching scores of executives. But the windfalls that options can bring have created an emphasis on short-term corporate performance and put more pressure on companies to goose revenue and profit.' Share performance is affected by many factors within and external to a firm. However, a principal driver of share price is profit. Put simply, if a company is making good profits, especially those expected by the city, its share price will rise. By contrast, disappointing profits will cause share prices to drop. A share option simply gives the directors the option to buy shares at a set price. Once again, as the directors benefit directly they have every incentive to make sure that by hook or by crook the company achieves a good profit. Share price and share option remuneration is particularly popular in countries with strong equity markets, such as the UK and USA.

### 3.1.1.4  Job Security

Directors and managers may also be concerned generally about their jobs. They may receive large remuneration packages and have a good standard of living. If they report disappointing results they may feel themselves vulnerable. Managers may fear redundancy and directors may fear board room reshuffles. Better to avoid both scenarios by creatively managing the results.

### 3.1.1.5  Personal Satisfaction

All managers are human. Therefore, like all human beings, managers crave personal recognition and esteem. If the results for a particular period are poor, then managers may lose some self-esteem. This is heightened by the fact that companies are regularly ranked by sales or profit before taxation. They can avoid this by massaging the profits upwards.

### 3.1.2  Market Expectations

The city is an important driver for creative accounting. Essentially, managers deliver the profits, while analysts help to determine the share prices. This can cause problems for managers if the profits do not live up to the expectations of the analysts. Analysts' forecasts are regularly published. If companies do not meet these forecasts then it is likely that their share prices will suffer. This is something which most companies seek to avoid as it sends the wrong signals to the city. There are three main incentives here: meeting analysts' expectations, profit smoothing and the norm.

### 3.1.2.1  Meeting Analysts' Expectations

There is an annual city reporting cycle. The companies report annually in a formal way through the annual report. There is also an interim report and in some countries, such as the USA, there are also quarterly reports. Companies may additionally make other earnings announcements. On the basis of past results, current information and other factors, analysts predict the expected profits of the firm. The share price then reflects these analysts' expectations. If the firm makes the expected results then the share price will generally not fall. If, however, for any reason the firm fails to make its anticipated profits then its share price is likely to suffer. This is bad news for the directors, especially if their remuneration is dependent on the company's share price. Consequently, there are great pressures to make analysts' earning expectations. If there is a shortfall then directors may indulge in creative accounting so as to close the earnings gap.

These pressures are expressed clearly in remarks by the chairman of the US SEC in 1988 (Levitt, 1988):

> Increasingly, I have become concerned that the motivation to meet Wall Street earnings expectations may be overriding common sense business practices. Too many corporate managers, auditors, and analysts are participants in a game of nods and winks. In the zeal to satisfy consensus estimates and project a smooth earnings path, wishful thinking may be winning the day over faithful representation. As a result, I fear that we are witnessing an erosion in the quality of earnings, and therefore, the quality of financial reporting. Managing may be giving way to manipulation; integrity may be losing out to illusion. . . . While the problem of earnings manipulation is not new, it has swelled in a market that is unforgiving of companies that miss their estimates. I recently read of one major U.S. company, that failed to meet its so-called 'numbers' by one penny, and lost more than six percent of its stock value in one day.[2]

### 3.1.2.2  Profit Smoothing

Whereas companies may indulge in last-minute accounting adjustments to meet analysts' expectations, profit smoothing is much more systematic and considered. It involves a long-term strategy to keep a smooth and steady set of profits. Essentially, erratic profits may make a company vulnerable to share price swings or in certain more extreme instances even a hostile takeover. The market will perceive a company with erratic profits to be riskier and less well managed than one with steady profits. The example in Figure 3.2 is illustrative of profit smoothing.

In both cases, the two companies make the same profits over the same time period. However, company X makes a steady set of profits. They rise on a linear trend. The market can predict future profits and is comfortable about the future. By contrast, company Y is much more erratic. As a result its share price may swing erratically. Ironically, at the end of period 4, it may find itself with a weak share price and vulnerable to a possible takeover by

---

[2] As cited in Payne and Robb (1999, p. 372).

Two firms (X and Y) in the same industry have the following profit trends. Which is likely to be favoured by the stock market?

| Years | 1 | 2 | 3 | 4 |
|---|---|---|---|---|
| | (£m) | (£m) | (£m) | (£m) |
| X | 1 | 2 | 4 | 8 |
| Y | 4 | (1) | 15 | (3) |

At first glance, X looks the better bet. Its profits steadily rise, doubling each year. However, company Y, with irregular, fluctuating profits actually makes the same cumulative profits as X (i.e. £15m). Overall, the stock market will probably favour X with its steady growth. Indeed, in year 4, company X might even be able to make a successful bid for Y! Company X's share price at that date may well be much higher than company Y's. It will be perceived as less risky. There is thus every incentive for X to use creative accounting to smooth out its profits.

**Figure 3.2**    Profit smoothing

*Source*: Adapted from Jones (2006, p. 33).

company X. As a result, the management of company Y may feel it necessary to indulge in creative accounting to protect itself against such an eventuality.

### 3.1.2.3   *The Norm*

In a sense, managers may find it acceptable to indulge in creative accounting because it is an accepted norm within the city. In other words, if everybody else is using creative accounting then managers may feel that it is perfectly in order for them to do so. This argument was expressed by Watts and Zimmerman (1986, p. 204): 'The market expects managers to manipulate the numbers to their own advantage reporting arbitrarily high earnings rather than taking actions that increase earnings because they increase firm value.' Using this argument the city automatically builds in a discount for creative accounting: if you do not indulge in it you suffer because your results will be discounted anyway. Therefore, it makes sense for your company to indulge in creative accounting too. Tied in to this motivation is the belief that there is nothing wrong with presenting your results in their best light. For instance, if you go on a date or to an interview, then you try to do your best. Looked at in this light, creative accounting is a similar understandable human reaction. Managers are just putting the most favourable interpretation on their results.

### 3.1.3  Special Circumstances

There are also a range of special circumstances in which managers may wish to use creative accounting or sometimes fraud. Eight of these are discussed below, but they are by no means exhaustive: manage gearing and borrowing; new issues; mergers and acquisitions; decrease visibility; new management team; waiting for the good times; believe current regulations incorrect; and 'it's not illegal'.

### 3.1.3.1  Manage Gearing and Borrowing

Firms often borrow money. Lenders are often anxious about recovering that loan. They usually have loan agreements with the borrowing firms. These may, for example, set penalties or even automatic debt repayment if the loan covenants are breached. One such loan covenant might be that gearing levels (i.e. the relationship of debt to shareholders' funds) should not exceed a certain preset level. If its external debt rises, this may give a firm a problem. If, for example, a firm's loan agreement says that a certain loan must be repaid automatically if gearing rises to 30 % and the accounts show 35 %, there is every incentive for the borrowing firm to use off-balance sheet financing techniques to remove some debt from the balance sheet so that it does not breach its loan covenants.

### 3.1.3.2  New Issues

New issues arise in two principal circumstances. In the first, a company is coming to the stock market for the first time. In the second, an existing firm wishes to raise more money from a share issue. In both cases, there is every incentive for the company to make its results look as good as possible. In short, if the firm looks an attractive proposition then more shareholders will subscribe for shares. The share price will then rise and, therefore, the amount raised by the new issue will rise. Creative accounting, or indeed fraud, may make the difference between a successful and an unsuccessful share issue/launch.

### 3.1.3.3  Mergers and Acquisitions

Companies often find themselves involved in merger and acquisition activity. Whether the firm is the bidder or the target, there are incentives to indulge in creative accounting. From the bidder's perspective a good set of results will allow the bid to be made from a position of strength. In particular if, as is very common, the bidder is offering its own shares as part of the purchase price then the higher its share price, the fewer shares it has to offer. Research showed that in the late 1980s in the UK one very acquisitive company, Hanson, launched 16 takeover bids. Only one was launched when the share price of Hanson was comparatively weak (Mansell, 1987). As discussed earlier, a company's share price will depend on its profitability and a company's profitability can be enhanced through creative accounting. However, in this case, there is no evidence of creative accounting although there were certainly incentives present.

From the target's perspective, the better the results that the company has the more the acquirer will have to pay for it. In addition, if the target is fighting the takeover, if it has higher profits and appears to be doing better than it actually is, this may also help its defence efforts. This was the situation in 1969 in the UK when the General Electric Company (GEC) took over Associated Electrical Industries (AEI). There was speculation that management maximised profits by using the flexibility permitted by the accounting system. This is discussed in more detail in Chapter 7.

### 3.1.3.4   Decrease Regulatory Visibility

Certain companies operate in a regulatory environment or in an environment where they may fear government interference. It may therefore be in the interests of oil companies, water companies or banks in certain circumstances not to make excessive profits. Essentially, they may fear government intervention to reduce profits, either through fixing selling prices or through a windfall tax. For example, in the UK in the 1970s two industries, electricity and gas, used income decreasing policies so as apparently to justify price rises (McInnes, 1990).

### 3.1.3.5   New Management Team

When a new management team comes in there may be every incentive to blame the previous managers for any poor results. They may adopt what is called a 'big bath' policy. This involves management making already poor results even poorer. This is done for two reasons: it enables the incoming management to start from a low base and it also enables future profits to be boosted. Future profits can, for example, be boosted by making immediate provisions for expenses that will be incurred in the future. This will reduce future expenses and thus increase future profits. Alternatively, if management reduces the current inventory valuation then when this inventory is sold in future periods this will increase future profits. Similarly, it is possible to manipulate the value of other assets such as accounts receivable or fixed assets.

### 3.1.3.6   Waiting for the Good Times

A powerful incentive for an ailing firm to use creative accounting is when it is suffering financially, but believes that good times are around the corner. The firm, therefore, uses creative accounting to help it ride out the bad times. More specifically, a company may use creative accounting, or even fraud, to maintain a stock exchange listing or even avoid delisting. How many companies successfully do this is unknown. Hindsight only tends to reveal those companies that adopted this strategy and which subsequently ran into even more difficulties when the expected good times failed to arise.

Essentially, this is what happened in two well-known UK accounting scandals: City of Glasgow Bank (1878) and the Royal Mail Steam Packet Company (1931). In the case of the City of Glasgow Bank the directors knew they were in trouble. However, they had a recovery strategy which was to invest in Australian property. Unfortunately, this investment failed. As a result, the company ultimately collapsed.

With the Royal Mail Steam Packet Company there had been a severe decline in the profitability of the shipping industry since the First World War. The chairman, Lord Kylsant, appeared to believe that better times were around the corner and used creative accounting in an attempt to keep the company afloat until then. The company was gradually using up the profits that it had accumulated in the good times. Creative accounting was a useful tool for this. Unfortunately, the good times failed to arrive and the company ran into difficulties.

### 3.1.3.7  Believe Current Regulations Incorrect

A particular and rare potential incentive is where managers may wish to give a true and fair view, but honestly believe that a strict interpretation of the current accounting rules and regulations will prevent this. In this case, they may feel that adopting a more liberal 'creative accounting' approach will enable them to do so. In other words, they are using creative accounting to portray the 'true' position of the firm. However, the number of companies which use this reasoning, and honestly believe it, is probably less than those who use it as a convenient excuse to adopt creative accounting!

### 3.1.3.8  It is not Illegal so Why Shouldn't We Use Creative Accounting?

A final reason, if perhaps not an incentive, is that creative accounting is not illegal. Therefore, as managers are not doing anything wrong, why shouldn't they use creative accounting? This is a perfectly legitimate argument, even though it is not necessarily following the spirit of the regulations. The fact that they may believe others are also adopting creative accounting reinforces this argument.

## 3.1.4  Cover-up Fraud

### 3.1.4.1  Misappropriation of Assets

This category was specifically identified by Beasley, Carcello and Hermanson (1999). It involves cases where a manager has already misappropriated assets. In order to cover this up, the manager then manipulates the financial statements.

## 3.2  CONCLUSION

In a perfect world there would be no need for creative accounting or fraud. However, when the results do not fulfil expectations then there may be several reasons why a company may wish to adopt creative accounting. First, there are a range of personal incentives. Managers may wish to use creative accounting to increase reported earnings so that they will receive increased salaries, greater bonuses or more lucrative grants of shares or share options. In other words, they may wish to maximise their own personal remuneration. In addition, managers may feel their jobs are more secure or wish to increase their personal esteem.

Second, there are pressures from the city to use creative accounting. These pressures may sometimes also cause managers to indulge in fraud. Managers may wish to meet analysts' expectations, both in the short term by last-minute earnings adjustments and also in the long term through profit smoothing. Managers may also consider that as the market will expect and discount earnings for creative accounting, they also ought to use creative accounting. If they do not, the argument runs, they will be placing themselves and their shareholders at a disadvantage.

Third, there are a range of special circumstances:

- Managers may wish to manage earnings and net assets so as not to breach loan covenants.
- Companies seeking to raise new capital by way of a share issue will wish to raise as much money as possible. If earnings are higher it is likely that the share price will be too, thus they can raise more money with the same number of shares or the same amount of money by issuing fewer shares. They may, therefore, have incentives to manipulate earnings.
- Companies in takeover situations may have incentives to indulge in creative accounting. Bidding companies may wish to increase earnings so as to make a share-based offer look more attractive. For targets, the managers may wish to increase earnings so as to make the company worth more in order to make it more difficult to take over.
- Companies in high-profile, regulated industries may wish to depress earnings so as to make it less likely that governments will intervene to fix prices.
- On a change of management incoming managers, in particular, will have incentives to make the current results look poor so that the future earnings of the company will look better.
- In some circumstances, managers may feel that creative accounting should be used because it better reflects a true and fair representation of the company's position than current regulations.
- There is nothing illegal about creative accounting. Therefore, some managers will be happy to use creative accounting as they will be keeping to the letter, if not the spirit, of the law.
- Finally, in a special case, managers may manipulate the financial statements so that their misappropriation of assets will remain undetected.

# REFERENCES

Auditing Practices Board (1998), *Fraud and Audit: Choices for Society*, Auditing Practices Board Consultation Paper.

Beasley, M.S., Carcello, J.V. and Hermanson, D.R. (1999), *Fraudulent Financial Reporting 1987–1997: An Analysis of U.S. Public Companies*. Research commissioned by the Committee of Sponsoring Organizations of the Treadway Commission.

Brennan, N.M. and McGrath, M. (2007), 'Financial statement fraud: some lessons from US and European case studies', *Australian Accounting Review*, **17**(2), 49–61.

Grant, R.M. and Visconti, M. (2006), The strategic background to corporate accounting scandals, *Long Range Planning*, **39**, 361–383.

Jensen, M.C. and Murphy, K.J. (2004), 'Remuneration: where we've been, how we got to here, what are the problems, and how to fix them', *European Corporate Governance Institute*, Finance Working Paper.

Jones, M.J. (2006), *Accounting*, John Wiley & Sons Ltd, Chichester.

KPMG (2004a), *Forensic Fraud Survey 2004*, KPMG, Australia.

KPMG (2004b), *Across the Board. A Newsletter for Australian Directors*, 7.

Langendijk, H. (2004), *Parmalat Finaziaria S.p.A.: A Case of Manipulating Financial Statements through Fraud*, NIVRA – Nyenrode Press, Breukelen, Netherlands.

Levitt, A.L. (1988), 'Remarks by Chairman Arthur Levitt Securities and Exchange Commission. The "numbers game".' NYU Centre for Law and Business, New York, 28 September, http://www.sec.gov/news/speeches/spch220.txt.

Mansell, S. (1987), *Accountancy Age*, 20 February.

McInnes, W.M. (1990), 'Further evidence on accounting choices: the South of Scotland Electricity Board, 1978–1988', *Accounting and Business Research*, **21**(81), 57–66.

Mulford, C. and Comiskey, E. (2002), *The Financial Numbers Game. Detecting Creative Accounting Practices*, John Wiley & Sons Inc., New York.

Payne, J.L. and Robb, S.W.G. (1999), 'Earnings management: the effect of ex ante earnings expectations', *Journal of Accounting, Auditing and Finance*, 371–392.

Strauss, G. (2002), 'Bush's call for reform draws mixed reviews', *USA Today*, 10 July.

Watts, P.L. and Zimmerman, J.L. (1986), *Positive Accounting Theory*, Prentice-Hall, Englewood Cliffs, New Jersey.

# Methods of Creative Accounting and Fraud

Michael Jones

## 4.1 INTRODUCTION

There are innumerable different methods of creative accounting. These arise because of the inherent flexibility within accounting. Each set of accounts consists of a myriad of different items of income, expenses, assets, liabilities and equities. For each different item there will be an accounting policy. As there are many accounting policies the opportunity arises to adapt and alter accounting policies so as to change the reported accounting figures. Indeed, one easy way to confuse investors is to continually change your results. As Robert Townsend (1970, p. 89) states: 'The easiest way to do a snow job on investors (or on yourself) is to change one factor in accounting each month. Then you can say, "It's not comparable with last month or last year and we can't really draw any conclusion from the figures".' The consistency concept limits but does not curtail companies' ability to do this. In the USA, WorldCom, which collapsed in 2002, was accused of repeatedly revising and restating its accounts. It was a pioneer of what was called proforma accounting.

The three main financial statements in a company's accounts are the income statement (also known as the profit and loss account), the balance sheet (also known as the statement of financial position) and the cash flow statement. In each of the three statements there will be different objectives for the creative accountant. In the income statement the main aim is usually to alter the profit figure. If the aim is (as is most common) to inflate profit, then incomes will be increased and expenses decreased. If profit is to be reduced then income needs to be decreased and expenses increased. In the balance sheet, the usual aim will be to increase the company's net worth. This can be done by increasing assets and decreasing liabilities. Finally, in the cash flow statement the aim will generally be to increase operating cash flow at the expense of other cash flows. In a sense, creative cash flow accounting is more difficult to achieve than creative profit creation. Cash is harder to manufacture than profit. As UBS Phillips & Drew (1991, p. 1) state: 'CASH IS KING. In the end, investment and accounting all come back to cash. Whereas "manufacturing" profits is relatively easy, cash flow is the most difficult parameter to adjust in a company's accounts. Indeed, tracing cash movements in a company can often lead to the identification of unusual accounting practices.'

I explore below some of the main methods by which these statements can be massaged. However, it should be stressed that the aim of the creative accountant is to adjust the accounts without the investors noticing. For if the stock market detects creative accounting practices then it will adjust the share price accordingly and the creative accountant's efforts will have been in vain. To indulge in creative accounting successfully, the creative accountant will also have to either hoodwink the auditors or persuade them that the accounting practices are acceptable. Inevitably, therefore, the creative accounting policies used by companies are often subtle, sometimes very complex and hard to detect. The methods given in this chapter are thus generally simplified. In practice, the actual methods used, although following the same general principles, will be more complex. They are often by their very nature difficult to detect and decipher. Many examples of creative accounting are given in the individual country chapters. After looking at the various methods of creative accounting, I will present a simple example which illustrates some of the creative accounting techniques. I will then look at some types of fraud. In many cases, fraud can be a continuation of creative accounting. However, it is interesting to consider separately two special aspects: the creation of fictitious entries and the misappropriation of assets. As with creative accounting, there are numerous different potential frauds, as will be seen in the individual country chapters.

Before looking at the actual methods the basic principles of what the creative accountant is trying to achieve will be examined. Then I will discuss how the basic technical nature of accounting helps the creative accounting process.

## 4.2 BASIC PRINCIPLES

Overall, the basic principles of creative accounting involve the three main financial statements. There are, as we can see from Figure 4.1, five main strategies.

The first two strategies aim to increase the profit in the income statement. This can be done either by increasing income or by decreasing expenses. For most companies, sales are the biggest source of income. So focusing on increasing sales is a common creative accounting strategy. However, there are other sorts of income, such as investment income,

---

**1. Increase income**

One way of increasing profit. Under this strategy, sales or other income is increased.

**2. Decrease expenses**

This is the second way of increasing profit. There are two main sub-strategies:

    2A. Just decrease expenses.

    2B. Decrease expenses and increase assets at the same time.

**3. Increase assets**

One way of increasing the net worth of the company.

**4. Decrease liabilities**

A second way of increasing the net worth of the company.

**5. Increase cash flow**

Either by increasing cash operating income or decreasing cash operating expenses.

---

**Figure 4.1**   Creative accounting strategies

which also may be manipulated. The two main methods of reducing expenses are either by utilising provisions or by capitalising expenses (making them assets). Strategies three and four focus on the balance sheet. The third strategy is to boost assets, thus strengthening and increasing the company's net worth. The fourth strategy has the same effect; however, here we focus on reducing the liabilities. Finally, the fifth strategy is to increase cash flow. As it is almost impossible to increase cash per se (you either have it or you don't), this strategy is more about timing or presentation. There may be efforts made to accelerate the collection of the cash, which may mean collecting less cash now rather than more cash later. Alternatively, it will focus on increasing operating cash flow, which is the key cash flow for analysts. This is generally by trying to classify non-operating cash inflows as operating cash inflows and operating expenses as non-operating expenses.

## 4.3 NATURE OF ACCOUNTING

Most people, apart from accountants, are unaware that at the heart of accounting is an accounting equation. This stems from the basic symmetry in accounting in which the debits equal the credits. In effect, in accounting terminology debits equal credits. Debits are expenses and assets and credits are incomes, liabilities and capital. This can be expressed in two ways. The first is set out below.

| DEBITS | = CREDITS |
|---|---|
| Assets and Expenses | = Income and Liabilities and Capital |

Every accounting transaction has a debit and a credit. So if a business sells £100 worth of goods this results in a debit and a credit. In this case, the cash which is an asset (a debit) will increase and be matched by sales of £100 which are an income (a corresponding credit).

So how does this basic symmetry help the creative accountant? The key is that it is easy to change the basic elements of the accounting equation. Thus, if we classify expenses as assets the books will still balance. Alternatively, if we record liabilities as income the books will still balance. The basic nature of accounting thus facilitates creative accounting. Furthermore, in cases of fraud, fictitious transactions will still have their debits and credits (albeit non-existent in this case).

## 4.4 METHODS OF CREATIVE ACCOUNTING

We will now discuss some of the main methods of creative accounting. The five main strategies will be discussed in turn. The aim is to present a flavour of creative accounting. The techniques used in practice will often be impossible to detect, even by experienced analysts. Most of these techniques are illustrated in actual cases in the individual country chapters later in the book.

Generally, the techniques presented here will be methods of creative accounting rather than fraud. However, the two often overlap. In essence, any method of creative accounting, if stretched to its absolute limit, would step outside the boundaries of the regulatory system. Clear cases of fraudulent methods will be highlighted. In addition, if any of a company's income or assets are misappropriated by a private individual, this can constitute fraud or fictitious accounting transactions can occur. These two special cases are dealt with at the end of the chapter.

### 4.4.1 Strategy 1: Increase Income

The text box below outlines five of the most common methods of increasing income.

---

**Strategy 1: Increase income**

  (i) Premature sales recognition
 (ii) Increase interest receivable
(iii) Include non-operating profits
 (iv) Treat loans as sales
  (v) Swaps.

---

#### 4.4.1.1   Premature Sales Recognition

This is perhaps one of the most common and pervasive forms of creative accounting. It stems from the basic question: when is a sale a sale? At first sight this may seem a silly question. However, the more complex business becomes, the more difficult the exact definition of a sale becomes. There is often, for example, a lot of latitude in determining the exact timing of a sale. Ian Griffiths (1995, p. 16) sums this up: 'Once it is accepted that actual cash flows do not present a true and fair view of the company's performance, then the door marked creativity is pushed wide open. As long as a company can justify with a degree of reasonableness that its income recognition policy is soundly based then it has *carte blanche* to do pretty much what it likes.'

Years ago I was involved in auditing a UK company which sold combine harvesters which are used to bring in the harvest in the UK in August. The company had a year end of 30 June. The farmers wanted to be invoiced in March so that they could get tax relief on the purchase (their tax year ended 5 April). The company was quite happy to hold the stock until August and wait for payment until August. It could, however, take the sale in March and it would form part of that year's sales. In this particular case, this accounting policy benefited all parties.

In the USA, Mulford and Comiskey (2002) document many incidences of companies taking sales early. For example, Midisoft Corp., in 1994, claimed to recognise revenue when the products were shipped. However, it recognised sales which were not shipped until the end of its financial year and for products which the company had no reasonable expectation would be paid (Mulford and Comiskey, 2002, p. 10). In addition, they cite many companies which were subject to the US Securities and Exchange Commission's accounting and auditing enforcement releases. Thus, Advanced Medical Products, Inc. improperly recognised revenues upon shipments to field representatives (improperly as they were still controlled by the company), improperly held open its accounting periods and continued booking sales, recognised sales without shipping the goods and recognised full sale on partial shipments (Mulford and Comiskey, 2002, p. 67).

In a recent UK case involving Interserve, a building services maintenance company, a £25 million hole in the accounts was found by the company's new head of the industrial division, Bruce Melizan. Sources close to the company said that employees apparently were over-invoicing. Invoices were entered into the accounts, inflating sales; they were then cancelled by raising credit notes. New invoices were then reissued, rolling the situation forward (Sukhraj, 2006, p. 6). Four executives lost their jobs (Richardson, 2007).

In the UK, the Financial Reporting Review Panel (FRRP), charged with policing UK company accounts, took issue with the 2004 accounts of Inveresk, a paper manufacturer (Release FRRP PN 93, 1 June 2006). Inveresk entered into a contract to sell Borelands reservoir in Inverkeitling. However, the contract was conditional on detailed planning consent. Only outline planning consent was granted by the time the land was sold in March 2005 to a third party. Inveresk, contrary to the advice of auditors KPMG, booked the sale in its 2004 accounts. The FRRP argued that the sale should not be taken in 2004. The directors accepted the panel's findings. As a result, a reported profit of £184 000, when corrected, became a loss of £417 000 (Grant, 2006, p. 7).

When I audited a manufacturing company in the 1970s in the UK, I found that the company was despatching goods in the first week in January, but was recording them as December sales. As a consequence, this affected both the profit and sales booked. The company agreed to change its policy when challenged.

### 4.4.1.2  Increase Interest Receivable

One of a company's sources of revenue is interest from investments such as stocks and shares or bank and building society accounts. This is usually fairly immutable. However, sometimes it can be massaged. In Polly Peck, for example, a high-flying UK company that collapsed in 1989, there is an example of currency mismatching which led to very high figures for income receivable (see UBS Phillips & Drew, 1991, p. 18). Essentially, Polly Peck borrowed in Swiss francs. Swiss francs are a very strong currency. Strong currencies have typically low rates of interest. Polly Peck then invested this money in a bank in Turkey. The Turkish dinar is a weak currency. However, the compensation was that it paid a high rate of interest. As a result, Polly Peck's income statement looked good. It received £68.1 million from its investment in a Turkish bank and paid out only £55.6 million to the Swiss bank. Profit was, therefore, boosted by £12.5 million. However, all was not what it seemed for the Turkish dinar depreciated against the Swiss franc. As a result, hidden away in the balance sheet was a capital loss of £44.7 million. This loss was not spotted by the investment analysts. In addition, to add insult to injury, the money was locked into Turkey and could not be transferred to the UK.

### 4.4.1.3  Include Non-operating Profits

Generally, analysts are more interested in trading profits rather than one-off non-trading items. However, companies often try to include in their normal profits one-off sales or profits. In Chapter 19, we will see that IBM's accounting was challenged by the US

Securities Exchange Commission for netting off a one-off disposal of assets in 1999 against operating costs. Other companies may try to include in operating income items such as one-off profits from selling assets. Indeed, it used to be common practice for companies to write down fixed assets to below their book value so that when they were sold a profit could be booked.

### 4.4.1.4  *Treat Loans as Sales*

Loans and sales are obviously very different things. One is income, the other essentially a liability. However, as they are both credits in the accounts there is room for the creative accountant to treat loans as income in some cases. For example, a UK manufacturing company was accused of treating loans from the government as sales. In addition, it was alleged that the company had loaned money to customers so that they could purchase its products. At Enron, the collapsed US energy company, this technique was taken to a new level and alleged to be fraudulent. Loans from merchant bankers were treated as up-front payments for energy contracts.

### 4.4.1.5  *Swaps*

In essence, a swap is where one company swaps a product with another. Swaps are in danger of stepping outside the regulatory framework. In essence, a swap is where two companies exchange products and then claim them as sales. It would be the same as two school children collecting cards. One might swap some cards with the other. However, both end up with the same number of cards. In business, however, some creative managers try to claim that a swap is actually a sale. In the communications industry such swaps of capacity are common. Enron and Qwest made a $500 million broadband swap in 2001. Enron treated these swaps as sales (Fusaro and Miller, 2002).

### 4.4.2  Strategy 2: Decrease Expenses

The other major strategy to increase profit is to decrease expenses. There are probably even more ways to do this than to increase sales. These are outlined in the text box and then discussed below.

---

**Strategy 2: Decrease expenses**

   (i) Use provision accounting
  (ii) Reduce tax
 (iii) Big bath or excessive one-year write-offs
 (iv) Decrease expenses and increase assets
  (v) Increase closing inventory
 (vi) Capitalise expenses
 (vii) Lengthen depreciation lives
(viii) Be generous with bad debts.

---

### 4.4.2.1   Use Provision Accounting

In accounting, it is necessary to make numerous estimates. Provision accounting involves setting up provisions for estimated expenses. For example, one company may take over another. It may have restructuring and reorganization costs. It will make a provision for these in the year of acquisition; this will increase expenses in this year. However, the company will argue that this is a one-off cost which should be excluded from the all-important ongoing profit from normal operations. It will then find that it has over-estimated these expenses and feed them back into the income statement. The same basic principle of establishing over-generous provisions, which are then excluded from operating profit and later released back into profits, can be used in a variety of situations.

UBS Phillips & Drew (1991) report the case of the takeover of Crowther by Coloroll in 1988 in the UK. Originally, the purchase price was £215 million and net assets acquired were £70 million. Goodwill was thus £145 million. However, Coloroll then wrote off a further £75 million through incidental costs, stock and debtor write-offs, redundancy and relocation costs and other items. 'Clearly if any of the written down stock is subsequently sold then the reported profit is enhanced. Similarly, if any written down debtors are realised in full then this also feeds through to the P&L' (UBS Phillips & Drew, 1991, p. 4). By adopting this strategy, Coloroll used the permissible flexibility in the contemporary rules for provision accounting at the time as a way of boosting future profit.

### 4.4.2.2   Reduce Taxation

Corporate taxation is a major corporate expense. Companies will try to reduce taxation. They will often employ teams of corporate tax accountants to reduce their tax bills. These tax avoidance schemes are generally beyond the scope of this book. In fact, they are worthy of a book by themselves. However, by adopting such schemes many profitable UK and US companies pay hardly any tax. In a survey, for example, UBS Phillips & Drew (1991) identified 24 out of 185 major UK companies which had a tax rate of less than 25%. It is also important to point out that such tax avoidance, which equates to creative accounting, is quite legal. By contrast, tax evasion, which equates to fraud, is illegal. As with creative accounting schemes, there is a vast industry which advises companies on potential tax avoidance schemes.

### 4.4.2.3   Big Bath

The big bath is a managerial strategy to get rid of all the bad news in one go. The reason that it falls into the strategy of reducing expenses is that it serves to write off in one year expenses that would be incurred in future years. Two common areas where the big bath method is used are in acquisition accounting and also when a new management takes over a company. In acquisition accounting it is linked with provision accounting. The basic idea is that you write off as many costs as possible now so that future performance looks better. Thus, you write down trade receivables so that you can collect more next year.

The example of Sears is given by Mulford and Comiskey (2002, p. 33). In 1992, Sears restructured its balance sheet by $2.65 billion in order to discontinue its domestic catalogue operations and other unprofitable operations. In 1992 the company reported a pre-tax loss of $4.3 billion. By writing off these restructuring costs as permitted by US GAAP, Sears had increased an already existing loss. However, as a result its earnings would be higher in future years as there would be fewer expenses in these years.

In the case of a new management team coming in, the incentives are similar. If the new management team has been brought in to turn around a failing company they may well take advantage of the flexibility of the accounting rules and regulations to write off as many expenses as possible. This has a triple benefit to the new management team. First, it makes the performance of their predecessors look worse. There is thus added justification for their replacement. Second, the new management team start off from a low base. Therefore, any improvements which they make are exaggerated. And, third, by accelerating the writing off of future costs they are likely to make the future performance of the company look better.

### 4.4.2.4  *Increase Closing Inventory*

Inventory is a particular favourite for the creative accountant. Closing inventory appears both on the balance sheet and also in the income statement, where it reduces the cost of sales. If, therefore, inventory increases so will profit. The attractive thing about inventory is that generally there is an annual stock-take in which the inventory is counted and valued. This makes it a particularly easy asset to manipulate, as Figure 4.2 shows.

There are two main ways in which inventory can be massaged. The first is by manipulating the quantity of the inventory. The second is by valuing it. The quantity can be manipulated by doing a particularly rigorous stock-take in years when profit needs to be increased and then a slack stock-take if the inventory is too high.

---

If there is only one asset, inventory, worth say £ 20 million, then if equity is £ 10 million and this year's profit is £ 10 million, we have balance sheet A:

**Balance sheet A**

|            | £ m  |            | £ m |
|------------|------|------------|-----|
| Equity     | 10   | Inventory  | 20  |
| Profit     | 10   |            | —   |
|            | 20   |            | 20  |

The company could:

(1) Adopt a more generous inventory valuation policy, perhaps by lowering the provisions for obsolete inventory (increases inventory by £ 1.0 million).

(2) Do a particularly rigorous stock-take (increases inventory by £ 0.5 million undiscovered inventory). The balance sheet now looks like balance sheet B:

**Balance sheet B**

|            | £ m  |            | £ m  |
|------------|------|------------|------|
| Equity     | 10.0 | Inventory  | 21.5 |
| Profit     | 11.5 |            |      |
|            | 21.5 |            | 21.5 |

Hey presto! We have increased our profits by £ 1.5 million.

---

**Figure 4.2**  Manipulating inventory

*Source:* Adapted from Jones (2006, p. 336).

With valuation there are several possibilities. There are provisions for obsolete and slow-moving inventory. However, these are subject to managerial subjectivity and so can be altered. The actual method of inventory valuation can also be changed. There are three main methods: AVCO (average cost method), FIFO (first-in-first-out) and LIFO (last-in-first-out). In some countries, such as the USA, all three methods are permitted. However, all three will give different levels of inventory and different profit levels, as Figure 4.3 on the next page shows.

Finally, production overheads are allowed to be included in inventory. They will thus boost inventory and thus profits. However, there is a great deal of subjectivity for what actually is a production overhead. As a result, the inventory figure can be massaged.

In practice, therefore, inventory is often inflated to serve managerial ends. I once had a neighbour who worked as a management accountant. The neighbour was looking particularly glum one Friday night. I asked what was wrong. The neighbour said that his head office financial controller had been on the phone. The current profit of the subsidiary was too low, he said. The management had been instructed to deliver a £0.5 million profit by head office and they were short of about £50 000. The neighbour was glum because he would have to spend all weekend diligently going through the inventory records in great detail to find the extra £50 000.

### 4.4.2.5  Capitalise Expenses

The capitalisation of costs utilises the basic principle that a debit balance in the accounts can either be an expense or an asset. By reclassifying expenses the creative accountant not only increases profit, but also increases assets. It is a win/win situation. The fixed assets (i.e. property, plant and equipment) will generally be depreciated. However, this means that the cost is spread over many years. There are many examples of capitalised costs, for example interest payable, software development costs, and research and development. Take interest payable as an example. When companies borrow money to construct fixed assets then they often argue that the cost of this interest is really part of the fixed assets and should, therefore, be capitalised. A study by UBS Phillips & Drew in 1991 in the UK showed that some UK companies would have actually made a loss not a profit if they had expensed rather than capitalised their interest. Moreover, they state that virtually every UK listed property company used capitalised interest to defer the effect on the income statement. When property prices are rising this is not a problem; however, when they fall this can cause problems.

The most high-profile case of companies improperly capitalising their expenses was in the USA. WorldCom is a US telecommunications firm. In 2001, it capitalised enormous amounts of costs. Analysts suspect these included wages and salaries of workers who maintained the telecom systems. As Matt Krantz (2002) saw it, 'WorldCom used the gimmick to a level never before seen. The company showed a $1.4 billion profit in 2001, rather than a loss, by using what's essentially the oldest trick in the book. Put simply what WorldCom did was treat revenue expenses such as painting a door as capital expenses such as replacing the door.'

The way in which WorldCom might have improperly capitalised $3.9 billion expenses is that it first paid costs such as wages and salaries to workers for performing maintenance on

Inventoryco purchases its inventory on the first day of the month. Its purchases and sales are as follows:

|  |  | Kilos | Cost per kilo | Total cost |
|---|---|---|---|---|
| January 1 | Purchases | 10 000 | £ 1.00 | £ 10 000 |
| February 1 | Purchases | 15 000 | £ 1.50 | £ 22 500 |
| March 1 | Purchases | 20 000 | £ 2.00 | £ 40 000 |
|  |  | 45 000 |  | £ 72 500 |
| March 30 | Sales | (35 000) |  |  |
| March 30 | Closing inventory | 10 000 |  |  |

What is the closing inventory valuation using FIFO, LIFO and AVCO?

(i) FIFO

The first inventory purchased is the first sold.

10 000 kilos January

15 000 kilos February

10 000 kilos March

35 000

The 10 000 kilos from March are left at £ 2.00 per kilo = £ 20 000.

(ii) LIFO

The last inventory purchased is assumed to be the first sold.

20 000 kilos from March

15 000 kilos from February

35 000

The 10 000 kilos from January are left at £ 1 per kilo = £ 10 000.

**Figure 4.3**  Different stock valuations methods give different profits

*Source:* Adapted from Jones (2006, pp. 413–414).

(iii) AVCO

The inventory is pooled and the average cost of purchase is taken. We purchased 45 000 kilos for £ 72 500 (i.e. £ 1.61 per kilo).

Therefore, 10 000 kilos × average cost of £ 1.61 = £ 16 110.

Our inventory valuations vary.

£

FIFO   20 000

LIFO   10 000

AVCO 16 110

Whichever valuation method is used, both cost of sales and profit are affected. Essentially, the cost of purchases will be split between inventory and cost of sales.

|  | Total cost | Cost of sales | Inventory |
|---|---|---|---|
|  | £ | £ | £ |
| FIFO | 72 500 | 52 500 (N1) | 20 000 |
| LIFO | 72 500 | 62 500 (N2) | 10 000 |
| AVCO | 72 500 | 56 390 (N3) | 16 110 |

|  |  |  | £ |
|---|---|---|---|
| (N1) FIFO represents: | January | 10 000 kilos at £ 1.00 | 10 000 |
|  | February | 15 000 kilos at £ 1.50 | 22 500 |
|  | March | 10 000 kilos at £ 2.00 | 20 000 |
|  |  |  | 52 500 |
|  |  |  | £ |
| (N2) LIFO represents: | February | 15 000 kilos at £ 1.50 | 22 500 |
|  | March | 20 000 kilos at £ 2.00 | 40 000 |
|  |  |  | 62 500 |
|  |  |  | £ |
| (N3) AVCO represents: |  | 35 000 kilos at £ 1.611 | 56 390 |

Profit is affected because if cost of sales is less, inventory, and thus profit, is higher and vice versa. In this case, using FIFO will show the greatest profit as its cost of sales is lowest and inventory highest. LIFO will show the lowest profit. AVCO is in the middle!

**Figure 4.3**   *(Continued)*

telecom systems. These were excluded from income and capitalized. Then over time they were depreciated.

Jim Hopkins (2002) suggests that WorldCom's actions in capitalising the costs of its leading network capacity, which it helped to resell to its customers, can be seen to be the same as the following:

1. Lease a house.
2. Plan to rent out the house because your rent will be more than the lease.
3. Pay the lease payments to the owner, worsening your financial position.
4. Fail to find anybody to rent.
5. Treat the lease payments as an asset because it will help you one day find somebody to rent.
6. Go to the bank to get a loan for a car and present the lease payments as assets.

However, WorldCom is only one of many companies to capitalise expenses. In the USA, America Online paid a $3.5 million fine to the Securities and Exchange Commission (SEC) to settle charges that it had capitalised the costs of mailing out thousands of diskettes (Hopkins, 2002). America Online had not acted illegally, but the SEC disagreed with its accounting treatment.

Meanwhile, in the UK in 2001, the FRRP forced Finelot plc to write off costs it had previously capitalised. The company had capitalised £966 000 of costs paid to a third party to carry out pre-production work for a new lifestyle magazine. The FRRP ruled that these costs did not include a substantial element of scientific or technical knowledge and should therefore be written off as expenses not capitalised. The directors accepted the FRRP's findings and adjusted their accounts (Financial Reporting Review Panel, July 2003, PN75).

### 4.4.2.6  Lengthen Depreciation Lives

Depreciation is a non cash expense; it involves allocating the cost of assets over a period of time. It is an expense and is recorded in the income statement. Depreciation is subject to many assumptions, such as the life of the asset and the end value of the asset. Assets can also be revalued. Finally, there are many depreciation methods, such as straight-line depreciation or reducing balance depreciation. As a result, by valuing assets differently, changing the life of the assets or the depreciation method, the actual depreciation charge can change.

Perhaps the simplest way of changing the depreciation level is by changing the life of the assets. In essence, lengthening an asset's life will reduce the level of depreciation. If management believes that the asset will last longer, then lengthening the asset life is perfectly legitimate. However, if it is done because management wants to reduce profit, then that is creative accounting. A simple example of the effect that changing an asset's life can have is given in Figure 4.4.

Generally, one might expect that with the pace of modern technology the length of asset lives would, in general, decrease. However, this is not reflected in company accounts. UBS Phillips & Drew comment: 'most changes in depreciation policy tend to be a lengthening of the expected lives rather than a shortening. Indeed it is difficult to identify any UK company which has recently reduced the depreciation life of any of its assets which has been of

A business makes a profit of £ 20 000. It has £ 200 000 worth of fixed assets (i.e. property, plant and

equipment).

Currently it depreciates them straight line over 10 years. However, the company is thinking of

changing its depreciation policy to 20 years straight line. Will this affect profit?

|  | Original policy £ | New policy £ |
|---|---|---|
| Profit before depreciation | 20 000 | 20 000 |
| Depreciation | (20 000) | (10 000) |
| Profit after depreciation | – | 10 000 |

The answer is yes. By changing the depreciation policy, profit has increased by £10 000. In

fact, the company looks much healthier.

**Figure 4.4**   Depreciation

*Source:* Adapted from Jones (2006, p. 337).

significance in terms of depressing reported profits. This is despite a general perception
that many mechanical assets' true life expectations are shortening' (UBS Phillips & Drew,
1991, p. 11).

Another way of reducing depreciation is by writing down the value of fixed assets. If the
fixed asset's value is less then depreciation will be too. UBS Philips & Drew (1991, p. 5)
cited the example of Tiphook which used the flexibility in UK accounting to its maximum
effect in the late 1980s. Tiphook, a UK company, acquired a sea container fleet of dry
containers. It paid £350m for them. However, it treated them as if it had always owned
them and thus wrote them down to £211m. As a result it saved annual depreciation of
£15m. It also set up a refurbishment provision of £12m, which saved annual charges for
repairs to the income statement. Finally, the written-down asset costs meant that any profits
on disposal would be more.

### 4.4.2.7   *Be Generous with Bad Debts*

Most businesses are based on credit. Sales result in trade receivables (debtors). Some of
those trade receivables may not pay. Companies, therefore, make provision for those bad
and doubtful debts. However, these provisions are based upon judgement. Therefore, in
times when the aim is to increase profit, one can assume that there will be a very low level
of non-payment forecast by management.

An extraordinary instance of being over-generous with bad debts was H.G. Palmer Ltd.
This Australian company failed to write off its trade receivables systematically year after
year until by 1965 its outstanding trade receivables balance at £22 million outstripped its
sales of £15 million. As a result it was forced to write off trade receivables finally in 1965,
causing a loss of £4 million.[1]

---

[1] For more on this see Chapter 9. Also Clarke, Dean and Oliver (2003, chapter 5).

### 4.4.3 Strategy 3: Increase Assets

The first method of strengthening a balance sheet is to increase the assets. Many of the techniques in strategy 2 also indirectly had this effect. However, under this strategy, as the text box below shows, we cover those techniques which are focused mainly on improving the asset base rather than on increasing profit.

---

**Strategy 3: Increase assets**

 (i) Enhance goodwill
 (ii) Enhance brands and other intangibles
(iii) Revalue fixed assets
(iv) Mark-to-market.

---

#### 4.4.3.1   Enhance Goodwill

Goodwill is an intangible asset. In other words, you cannot see it or touch it like a tangible fixed asset such as a building or a motor car. Goodwill arises when one company takes over another. It represents the purchase price paid less the fair value of the net assets acquired. The exact rules for recording goodwill vary from country to country. Under the IASB rules and in the USA, goodwill is capitalised and then left on the balance sheet unless its value is impaired. If the value of goodwill can be maximised that will increase the value of the assets on the balance sheet. It also has the advantage that fair value on acquisition will be reduced. If the assets such as inventory are written down on acquisition then this will increase profits later on when they are sold. Companies, therefore, have incentives to maximize goodwill on acquisition and then subsequently argue against its impairment.

Under some other regulatory regimes, such as non-listed companies in the UK, goodwill can be amortised (i.e. written off over time). As a result, profit can be manipulated by increasing or decreasing the write-off period in the same sort of way that you can with depreciation.

#### 4.4.3.2   Enhance Brands and Other Intangibles

Brand valuation is an extremely contentious issue within accounting. Brands such as 'Coca Cola' and 'Guinness' are extremely valuable. However, they are not typically recorded in the accounts under conventional GAAP. Some accountants, however, believe that by including the value of brands in the accounts this better reflects the true worth of a company. But other accountants believe that brand valuation is very subjective and that the true reason for their inclusion in the accounts is just to boost asset values in the balance sheet. As accounting goes, brand accounting is a relatively new idea. From the mid-1980s, UK companies such as Grand Metropolitan and Cadburys began to include acquired brands in their balance sheet. These brands, once established in the balance sheet, were not amortised. In 1990, for example, Grand Metropolitan had brands in the balance sheet of £2317 million. This compared with shareholders' funds of £3427 million and net borrowings of £2888 million (UBS Philips & Drew, 1991, p. 14). In the UK, only acquired brands can be included in the balance sheet. In other countries, the regulatory regimes differ and in many countries you are not allowed to include brands at all.

The problem with including brands is that there is no clear and self-evident way of valuing them. They are, therefore, very subjective in nature. As a result, they can be massaged and manipulated very easily if necessary. As companies become more complex, the proportion of their assets which are intangible grows. Traditionally, intangibles have not been included in balance sheets because they are very difficult to value. However, increasing numbers of different intangibles are now listed in company balance sheets (such as corporate names, patents and trademarks, personnel skills, computer software, know-how and mastheads). Given the difficulty in valuing them, there is once more scope for creativity.

As we shall see in Chapter 13, an example of the subjectivity of intangible assets comes from Parmalat. In Italy, football clubs were allowed to capitalise their players' transfer costs. Parmalat owned Parma AC, a football club. Its policy was to value its intangible assets, such as footballers. The value of Parma AC's footballers in 2002 was €279.2 million. This was more than for two much more famous European football clubs: Manchester United (€79.1 million) and Juventus, another rich Italian club (€116 million) at about the same time (Langendijk, 2004).

### 4.4.3.3   Revalue Tangible Fixed Assets

In some countries such as the UK, it is permitted to depart from the strict historical convention (in which tangible fixed assets are carried at cost). In the UK, for example, non-listed companies were traditionally permitted, if they wished, to periodically revalue their land and property. These revaluations will generally increase the value of corporate property portfolios and thus of balance sheet assets. There is, of course, an element of subjectivity in such revaluations which opens the door for creative accounting. As Rutherford (1999) demonstrated, companies very much prefer the ability to revalue their properties. In addition, there was much lobbying in the UK in 1978 against the mandatory depreciation of property. Rutherford cites the chairman of a motor and engineering group: 'We intend to revalue our properties every five years ... I am more attracted to a professional valuer's opinion than that of a committee of accountants. What do accountants know about valuations? ... Over recent years any properties sold have been sold at a handsome profit, even against the valuation' (*Accountancy Age*, 1979, p. 2). This policy, which was in accord with UK regulations, had certain advantages to companies. It increased asset prices and thus the balance sheet through revaluation and increased profits by not depreciating the assets.

Thomas (2002, p. 43) commented on Enron: 'For a company such as Enron, under continuous pressure to beat earnings estimates, it is possible that valuation estimates might have considerably overstated earnings. Furthermore, unrealized trading gains (from the revaluation of fixed assets) accounted for slightly more than half of the company's $1.41 billion reported pre-tax profit for 2000 and about one-third of its reported pre-tax profit for 1999.'

#### 4.4.3.4  Mark-to-market

The problem of how to value assets is a difficult one. This is particularly tricky with complex and active markets. Enron used mark-to-market accounting to price many complex contracts. Under US rules, then prevailing, companies with outstanding energy-related or derivative contracts had to adjust them to market value in that accounting period, taking immediately unrealized gains and losses.

### 4.4.4  Strategy 4: Decrease Liabilities

The second method of increasing balance sheet values is to reduce liabilities. The two main methods of doing this, as the text box shows, involve off-balance sheet financing and reclassifying debt as equity.

---

**Strategy 4: Decrease liabilities**

 (i) Off-balance sheet financing
(ii) Reclassifying debt as equity.

---

#### 4.4.4.1  Off-balance Sheet Financing

Off-balance sheet financing is one of the most complex and complicated forms of creative accounting. It is difficult to do justice to this topic in a few pages. Often companies are following schemes which have been devised by merchant banks. Regulators are also constantly bringing in new regulations aimed at stopping the worst abuses. So in this section I will just look at some of the major principles that underpin off-balance sheet financing schemes.

   The basic objective of off-balance sheet financing is the wish to remove liabilities from the balance sheet. The motives behind this will vary. In some cases, it may be because the company is in danger of breaching its loan covenants by having too much debt on its balance sheet. In other cases, it may just be to make the balance sheet look stronger. If we look at this a little differently, many companies borrow money to purchase assets and to finance their general operations. They want to record their assets but not the liabilities. Merchant banks will often devise very complicated schemes. The essence of these schemes is that the company gets access to the use of assets but the associated loan with which the asset was purchased is not recognised on the balance sheet.

   Enron had many unconsolidated subsidiaries often with racy names from the *Star Wars* films, like Raptor and Chewco. Under the prevailing regulations in the USA at the time, these subsidiaries did not have to be consolidated if 3 % of the equity was owned by outsiders and if they were independently controlled. In some of Enron's subsidiaries this was the case. However, in others Enron loaned the money to purchase the equity and Enron employees controlled these subsidiaries. The role of these subsidiaries was secretly to fund Enron. They would thus raise money from merchant banks and pass the money on to fund Enron's operations. The subsidiary would thus be a shell which contained unconsolidated liabilities that should properly have been recorded on Enron's group balance sheet. In many cases, it seems that Enron was acting outside the US GAAP. In other subsidiaries, assets were transferred that were losing value, such as overseas energy facilities or broadband. These losses were kept out of Enron's books. To compensate the investors in the Special Purpose Entities (SPEs), Enron issued shares. As the value of the assets fell, Enron was forced to issue more and more shares (Thomas, 2002). Andrew Fastow, Chief Financial Officer, boasted to *CFO* magazine: 'we accessed £1.5 billion in capital but expanded the Enron balance sheet by only $65 million. Enron effectively "hid virtually all the debt"' (Fusaro and Miller, 2002).

In the UK, in 1988 LEP, a UK listed company, provides another example of an off-balance sheet vehicle. LEP sold a development property, St Paul's Vista, to an associated company. LEP had an effective interest of 90 % in this company, but quite legitimately, under UK companies' legislation at the time, the company was treated as a net investment and was not consolidated. St Paul's Vista had a net book value of £111.3 million and LEP received £120 million, thus realising an £8.7 million profit. UBS Phillips & Drew (1991, p. 9) point out that by treating what was really an inter-group transfer as a sale to a third party, LEP's profit more than doubled.

As well as unconsolidated borrowings a problem arises when one company guarantees another's debts. This is known as associate debt guarantees. Often this can be picked up by studying a company's contingent liabilities. Essentially, a contingent liability is a liability which may or may not occur; in other words, it is contingent upon a set of circumstances occurring. The case of British and Commonwealth in 1989 is informative. In 1988, British and Commonwealth paid £416 million for Atlantic Computers. British and Commonwealth guaranteed the debts of Atlantic Computers. Atlantic Computers leased equipment. Unfortunately, Atlantic Computers had adopted a flawed business strategy. As UBS Phillips & Drew (1991, p. 13) point out, it allowed customers two leasing options: the flex and the walk. The flex allowed the customer to upgrade the computer equipment after two or three years and the walk to terminate the lease at once. The flex resulted in Atlantic Computers having to find a home for the old equipment and supplying new equipment. To keep the customers happy it had to keep the initial lease payments low. Customers, therefore, had the incentive to keep flexing and deferring liabilities. For the walk, Atlantic Computers had to keep paying the lease payments or find another customer. Both these options led to increasing contingent liabilities. When Atlantic Computers collapsed, British and Commonwealth ended up as guarantor and could not meet its commitments. However, all this was not obvious from the notes to the accounts.

Contingent liabilities exist for many items. Some of the most common are health-related and environmental. So, for example, some of the tobacco companies carry large contingent liabilities against the cost of smoking-related law suits. Or there are environmental liabilities on the 'polluter pays' principle. However, these contingent liabilities are generally buried in the accounts and are often obtusely worded.

### 4.4.4.2  *Reclassifying Debt as Equity*

This is another very complicated accounting topic. It is also another area where regulators have been extremely active. Essentially, equity represents owners' capital. It is the equivalent of net assets on a company's balance sheet. Debt capital, by contrast, is outside capital. It is generally the result of corporate borrowing. The relationship between the two is known as gearing. Thus, a highly geared company will have a high proportion of debt to equity. High gearing also generally means that a company will have to make substantial annual interest payments. Companies with high gearing ratios are inherently more risky than companies with low gearing ratios. Companies with high gearing may also be worried about breaching their loan covenants.

There are thus incentives for companies to reclassify debt as equity. This is where complicated financing schemes may come in, often peddled by merchant banks. An area which the merchant banks may exploit is that of convertible loan stock bonds. Convertible loan stock bonds are loans that can be converted into equity at a future time. The trick will be to try to dress up what are really loans as equity. An example of this is the convertible with the put option. A put option obliges a company to redeem the loan stock at a premium to the issue price after a period of, say, five years. However, if the share price rises above this, then the investor would be likely to convert. Because of this the interest level on the loan could be set at a low rate. The technical charge to the income statement is, therefore, low. The necessity for companies to encourage their investors to exercise the conversion option can be intense. For example, as we will see in Chapter 14, two Japanese companies, Sawako and Yaohan Japan, indulged in many dubious practices to inflate their profits with the probable intention of encouraging their shareholders to convert their bonds into ordinary shares.

In the UK, Shah (1996) cites the example of the premium put convertible bond used first in 1987. This had low interest rates, but a high conversion premium. At the time the bond was issued it was not necessary under current accounting regulations to account for the supplemental interest this caused. Companies were permitted, and preferred, to use accounting practices which led them to reduce interest payments. Burton's, for example, issued £110m of premium put convertibles with 4.75 % p.a. interest rate. There was an effective interest rate of 9.98 %. Burton's saved £5.75m per year. This financial instrument became increasingly popular. However, Shah found that the supplemental interest was not expensed by any of the companies using this bond. 'This evidence suggests that the accounting advantages (in terms of higher reported earnings) were an important motive underlying the design and popularity of the instrument' (Shah, 1996, p. 6).

Parmalat, the Italian company, provides an interesting example of turning debt into equity (Langendijk, 2004). Parmalat Participacoes do Brazil Ltd issued a convertible bond amounting to €500 million. The buyer made an irrevocable agreement to convert the debt to shares in 2008. It was, therefore, correctly treated as equity. However, the investor was not identified. It was suspected to be another subsidiary of Parmalat, Parmalat Finance Corp.

### 4.4.5 Strategy 5: Increase Operating Cash Flow

The cash flow of a business is much harder to massage than its profit. This is because generally, cash is subject to much less estimation than profit. However, sometimes, in unusual circumstances, companies will be able to accelerate cash flow from a later period to an earlier period. There are two ways of presenting the cash flow statement: the direct method and the indirect method. The direct method records actual cash inflows and outflows. The indirect method is harder to follow for the uninitiated but tends not to focus so much on the cash flows. It divides the flows by function, such as operating cash flows, investing cash flows or financing cash flows. In particular, it focuses on operating cash flows which are the main concern of the analysts. Most companies present the cash flow statement using the indirect method. This may be because it gives them more flexibility. It is prepared from the existing income statement and the last two years' balance sheets.

The focus is generally on operating cash flow. As the text box shows, there are two main methods which both focus on massaging operating cash flows. International accounting standards use three headings in the cash flow statement: cash flow from operating activities, cash flow from investing activities and cash flow from financing activities. Cash flow from operating activities represents cash from trading. This is the cash flow which most concerns analysts and which companies wish to maximise. Cash flow from investing activities includes purchases of fixed assets and interest received. Finally, cash flow from financing activities includes loans and dividends paid.

---

**Strategy 5: Increase operating cash flows**

(i)  Maximise operating cash inflows
(ii) Minimise operating cash outflows.

---

### 4.4.5.1  Maximise Operating Cash Inflows

Strictly, operating cash inflow should include only inflows from trading and items of a continuing nature. However, companies may try to include under this heading one-off items such as from the sale of assets. In Enron's case, bank loans, as we will see in Chapter 19, were treated as operating cash flow. These are items which should really be recorded elsewhere. In addition, companies will try to make the definition of what is an operating cash inflow as wide as possible and, at the same time, narrow the definition of investing and financing cash flows. Essentially, companies are trying to classify as many as possible of their positive cash flows as operating cash flows.

### 4.4.5.2  Minimise Operating Cash Outflows

Here the same principles operate as in the last section, but in reverse. Companies may try to include any one-off operating losses or expenses under the financing or investing cash flows not operating cash flows. They will attempt to narrow the definition of operating cash outflows but to widen the definition of financing and investing cash outflows. Basically, companies are trying to classify as few as possible of their cash outflows as operating cash flows.

## 4.5 SIMPLE NUMERICAL EXAMPLE

A simple example is given below in Table 4.1 to illustrate some of the points made in this chapter. It should, however, be stressed that, in practice, there would be many more subtle adjustments which together would massage the profit in the desired direction. In effect,

**Table 4.1a**   Example of creative accounting

<table>
<tr><td colspan="4" align="center">Creato plc<br>Income statement for year ended 31 December 2009</td></tr>
<tr><td></td><td>Notes</td><td>£m</td><td>£m</td></tr>
<tr><td>Sales</td><td>1</td><td></td><td>100</td></tr>
<tr><td>Less cost of sales</td><td></td><td></td><td></td></tr>
<tr><td>Opening inventory</td><td></td><td>10</td><td></td></tr>
<tr><td>Add purchases</td><td></td><td><u>40</u></td><td></td></tr>
<tr><td></td><td></td><td>50</td><td></td></tr>
<tr><td>Less closing inventory</td><td>2</td><td>(15)</td><td><u>35</u></td></tr>
<tr><td>Gross profit</td><td></td><td></td><td>65</td></tr>
<tr><td>Less expenses</td><td></td><td></td><td></td></tr>
<tr><td>Depreciation</td><td>3</td><td>12</td><td></td></tr>
<tr><td>Interest payable</td><td>4</td><td>15</td><td></td></tr>
<tr><td>Other expenses</td><td></td><td><u>43</u></td><td><u>70</u></td></tr>
<tr><td>Loss for year</td><td></td><td></td><td><u>(5)</u></td></tr>
</table>

*Notes*

1. Creato has a prudent income recognition policy, a less conservative one would create an additional £10m sales by premature sales recognition.
2. Closing inventory could be valued, less prudently, at £18m by taking a generous inventory valuation policy and by carrying out a particularly comprehensive stock-check.
3. Depreciation is charged over five years. This takes a pessimistic view of the expected lives of the assets; a more optimistic view would be of a 10-year life.
4. £10m of the interest payable is interest on borrowings used to finance a new factory.

*Source:* Jones (2006, p. 340).

where there is a range of assumptions and estimates management is adopting those which will increase profit.

If we indulge in a spot of creative accounting (Table 4.1b) we can transform Creato plc's income statement.

Hey presto! We have transformed a loss of £5m into a profit of £23m.

## 4.6 FRAUD

In many cases, the boundary between creative accounting and fraud is less than clear. For instance, at Enron the first SPEs that were created were perfectly legitimate. However, gradually more and more questionable SPEs were used. The Association of Certified Fraud Examiners (1996) divided fraud into asset misappropriation, fraudulent statements, and bribery and corruption. The most pertinent for this book are the first two categories. In particular, many accounting scandals have at their heart fraudulent statements caused by fictitious transactions. For the major scandals these fictitious transactions are systematic in nature. In many cases, the same techniques were used for financial statement fraud as for creative accounting. Thus, Beasley, Carcello and Hermanson (1999) in the USA found that, out of a sample of 204 companies using a fraud method, 50 % used improper revenue recognition, while 50 % had overstated assets. Of the other categories, 18 % had understated expenses/liabilities, 12 % had misappropriated assets, 8 % had inappropriate disclosure and 20 % used other miscellaneous techniques. The two biggest categories

**Table 4.1b**

**Creato plc**
**Income statement for year ended 31 December 2009**

|  |  | £m | £m |
|---|---|---|---|
| Sales | 1 |  | 110 |
| Less *cost of sales* |  |  |  |
| Opening inventory |  | 10 |  |
| Add purchases |  | <u>40</u> |  |
|  |  | 50 |  |
| Less closing inventory | 2 | <u>18</u> | <u>32</u> |
|  |  |  | 78 |
| *Gross profit* |  |  |  |
| Less *expenses* |  |  |  |
| Depreciation | 3 | 6 |  |
| Interest payable | 4 | 5 |  |
| Depreciation on capitalised interest payable | 4 | 1 |  |
| Other expenses |  | <u>43</u> | <u>55</u> |
| *Profit for year* |  |  | <u>23</u> |

*Notes*
1. We can simply boost sales by £10m and be less conservative.
2. If we value closing inventory at £18m, this will reduce cost of sales, thus boosting gross profit.
3. By doubling the life of our property, plant and equipment, we can halve the depreciation charge.
4. If we have borrowed the money to finance property, plant and equipment, then we can capitalise some of the interest payable. Interest payable thus reduces from £15m to £5m. We assume here that we will then depreciate this capitalised interest over 10 years (this company's new policy for property, plant and equipment). Thus, we are charging £1m depreciation on the capitalised interest payable. We thus boost profit by £9m (i.e. £10m saved less £1m extra depreciation).
*Source:* Adapted from Jones (2006).

were subdivided further. Under improper revenue recognition, 26 % recorded fictitious revenues, 24 % recorded revenues prematurely and 16 % were overstated. For overstatement of assets, 37 % had overstated existing assets, 12 % had recorded fictitious assets and 6 % had capitalised items which should have been expensed. As the text box shows it is, therefore, perhaps possible for the purpose of this book to divide fraud into two broad groups: the misappropriation of assets and fictitious transactions.

---

**Methods of fraud**

 (i) Misappropriation of assets
    (a) Inventory
    (b) Cash
    (c) Other.
 (ii) Fictitious transactions (fraudulent financial statements)
    (a) One-off: sales, cash and inventory
    (b) Systematic.

---

The misappropriation of assets is basically stealing from the company. This can be done either by the employees or by the directors. Many assets can be misappropriated, but probably those that are either cash or can be turned into cash, such as inventory, are the most common. In Chapter 11, we will see a particularly striking example of the misappropriation of the Bank of Crete's funds by Koskotas. The creation of fictitious transactions can be one-off or more systematic. In some cases, totally fictitious subsidiaries have been created. In Chapter 10, there are two interesting examples from Germany, ComRoad and Flowtex, of the extensive fabrication of company transactions.

### 4.6.1 Misappropriation of Assets

There are many forms of misappropriation. In essence, this is the easiest and most straight-forward of fraud cases: almost synonymous with 'dipping one's hand in the till'.

#### 4.6.1.1  Inventory

Given that inventory can be sold, it makes an attractive target for fraud by management or employees. The examples are legend. However, I list some of my favourite ones below. First, the town of Kidderminster in the UK is famous for making carpets. They were losing carpets every day, but could not understand how they were being stolen. The thefts went on all year. Then, in the middle of winter, an employee fell over at the front gates of the factory. The security guard went over to help and found that a carpet wrapped around the man's waist, hidden under a long coat, had slipped and straitjacketed his legs. No longer able to walk, he fell over in front of the security official at the security office and was caught.

Second, in one famous case, the company's inventory was stored in liquid form. I believe it was in the brewing industry. When the auditors came to inspect the inventory they were taken around all the vats in turn in a set order. All the vats the auditors saw were full. However, unbeknown to them the liquid was being pumped from vat to vat while they walked around. Inventory was thus inflated.

In my third favourite case it was the time of the annual stock-check. Normally, and for years, the stock-check had been carried out by the local inventory manager of the subsidiary and his team. However, this year staff from head office were called in. They were particularly enthusiastic on their day out and, therefore, looked at all the inventory available. They even went to the furthest corners of the warehouse and found lots of cardboard boxes with no inventory in. These they threw away. It later transpired that the stock manager had for years been misappropriating the inventory, but leaving the empty boxes behind at the back of the warehouse. In years past, they had been counted as full. This was the end of a long and successful fraud.

#### 4.6.1.2  Cash

Cash is the lifeblood of any business. Without cash a business will soon go bankrupt. Indeed, a company can be making profits, sometimes quite healthy ones, but then run out of cash and thus go bankrupt. Management and employees may be tempted to steal cash. It is a common fraud. In the UK, in June 2006 for example, a Scottish bank employee, Donald MacKensie, was found to have stolen £21 million. He was jailed for 10 years. Ironically, he had been named the Royal Bank of Scotland's business manager of the year for three successive years (2002, 2003 and 2004) (Lister, 2006). He set up false accounts, but had to pay the interest on them. This meant he had to borrow more money. He was only caught by accident when a new computer system for loans crashed.

### 4.6.1.3 *Other*

There are a variety of other ways in which assets can be misappropriated. Generally, there is much more scope for directors to do this than employees. In the case of Polly Peck in the UK, which went bankrupt in 1989, it was stated at a disciplinary hearing that not only did Mr Nadir steal large amounts of money from the company, but that there were '£47.7 million of net assets which were not legally held in the name of PPI (Polly Peck International) or its subsidiaries. It was not established [by auditors Stoy Hayward] why it was that such assets were not properly registered in the name of the company . . .' (Joint Disciplinary Tribunal Complaints against Stoy Hayward, March 2002).

In the case of Adelphia Communications in the USA, the Justice Department and US Postal Inspection Service charged five executives of Adelphia with 'fraud, looting the company and using it as a "personal piggy bank" where "Rigas private funds sloshed with Adelphia's in the same cash-management system"' (Lieberman & Farrell, 2002, p. 3). For example, Timothy Rigas was accused of using a company jet for an African safari holiday and company planes also were alleged to have brought guests to a family wedding. Finally, Adelphia was charged with spending $13 million to build a golf club on land mostly owned by chief executive John Rigas. John and Timothy Rigas were subsequently jailed.

### 4.6.2 Fictitious Transactions

Fictitious transactions can be one-off to conceal or create a particular activity or systematic. Generally, fictitious one-off transactions concern sales or cash. Systematic fictitious transactions are obviously much more complicated. They represent fraudulent financial statements, which are at the heart of most of the accounting scandals in this book.

### 4.6.2.1 *Fictitious Sales*

A final way of increasing sales is clearly fraudulent. It is simply to make them up. There are many instances of this. Parmalat, the disgraced Italian milk company, is alleged to have made up powdered milk sales to Cuba. There were, in fact, alleged to be 300 000 tons of powdered milk at a value of $620 million. Indeed, if the figures were true then Cubans would have been 'swimming' in milk. In addition, Parmalat used fraudulent double invoicing where there was one real and one false invoice. Both invoices were entered into the books, but only one sent to the customer (Langendijk, 2004). Sales were thus inflated.

Many other companies are alleged to also have inflated sales or just made them up. For example, in the USA the directors of Adelphia Communications were alleged to have secretly inflated cable TV subscription numbers and, in 2000, to have counted subscribers from Brazil and Venezuela where Adelphia Communications had just a minority stake. In addition, in 2001, the company was alleged to have sold 525 000 digital decoder boxes for $101 million to an unaudited company owned by the Rigas family that controlled Adelphia

Communications. However, this company had no cable systems (Lieberman and Farrell, 2002). Key members of the Rigas family were found guilty of financial fraud and jailed.

### 4.6.2.2   Fictitious Cash and Inventory

The creation of fictitious cash transactions has a long history. In the nineteenth century, for example, there were two notorious fraud cases involving false cash transactions: Walter Watts and Joseph Cole (Evans, 1859). In the first case, Walter Watts lived a life of luxury and, in particular, was patron of the Marylebone Theatre. However, it was subsequently discovered that his lavish lifestyle was the result of gigantic frauds at the Globe Assurance Office where he worked. He invested false annuities and then diverted the money into his own account. In addition, he tampered with the dividend account and once again misappropriated funds. The fraud was perpetuated for between five and six years. Watts was convicted and sentenced to 10 years' transportation. Rather than face this, he committed suicide.

In the second case, Joseph Cole was a general merchant. His early business ventures proved unsuccessful. He realised that the large banking discount houses made advances on warrants, but seldom examined the documents. He therefore created duplicate warrants for inventory. Essentially, he issued two warrants for one cargo. He thus simulated at least £500 000 false warrants for which he received loan advances. Eventually, suspicions were aroused and enquiries made. Joseph Cole fled. He was arrested, found guilty, and jailed for four years.

More recently, Parmalat, an Italian company, got into serious financial difficulty in 2003. It was unable to make a €150 million bank payment. It was found that €3.9 billion of the company's funds supposedly held in the Cayman Islands did not exist.

### 4.6.2.3   Systematic

There are several well-known examples of cases where directors systematically constructed a whole edifice of false accounts: City of Glasgow Bank, McKesson and Robbins, Equity Funding Corporation of America and more recently ComRoad and Flowtex in Germany. Although taking place in different time periods, these accounting frauds all have similarities: they were enacted by directors, they were sustained and they involved multiple and systematic transactions. They are discussed here briefly, but covered in more detail in Chapters 7 and 10.

In the case of the City of Glasgow Bank, which collapsed in 1878, the directors issued false balance sheets for a number of years. The directors were trying to recover from some bad business decisions. In the McKesson and Robbins case in the 1930s in the USA, George Coster set up and maintained for many years a totally fictitious Canadian subsidiary alongside a perfectly real and successful US company. Then, in the Equity Funding Corporation of America in the 1960s, Goldblum and Levin created a massive edifice of false insurance accounts. At ComRoad, the directors fabricated extensive transactions with VT Electronics, a non-existent overseas supplier supposedly based in Hong Kong. Finally, at Flowtex the company built up a whole edifice of false transactions involving fictitious leases of drilling equipment.

## 4.7 CONCLUSION

This flexibility in accounting opens the door for many different methods of creative accounting. This is helped by the nature of accounting. The boundary between creative accounting and fraud is often unclear. The basic accounting equation is assets plus expenses equals income plus liabilities plus capital. Therefore, it is possible to maintain the symmetry within accounting but classify expenses as assets and loans as income. There are five main strategies for the creative accountant. Strategy 1 involves increasing profit by increasing income, for example, by treating loans as sales, by the premature recognition of sales, by maximising other income or by treating loans as sales. Strategy 2 also involves increasing profit, this time by decreasing expenses by methods such as provision accounting, increasing inventory, capitalising expenses, lengthening asset lives, minimizing bad debts, minimising tax or using the big bath technique. Strategy 3 focuses on increasing the net worth of the balance sheet by increasing the assets, for example, by including brands and intangibles, goodwill and revaluing fixed assets. Strategy 4 also involves boosting the net worth of the balance sheet, however, this time by reducing liabilities through, for example, off-balance sheet financing or reclassifying debt as equity. Finally, Strategy 5 involves maximising operating cash flow. This can be done in two ways. The first involves maximising operating cash flows. The second, minimising operating cash outflows. Finally, the special cases of fraud are examined; in particular, the misappropriation of inventory, cash and assets as well as the invention of fictitious transactions or even fictitious businesses.

## REFERENCES

*Accountancy Age* (1979), 'Lunacy chairman depreciation rule', 27 April, p. 2.

Association of Certified Fraud Examiners (1996), *Report to the Nation on Occupational Fraud and Abuse*, USA.

Beasley, M.S., Carcello, J.V. and Hermanson, D.R. (1999), *Fraudulent Financial Reporting 1987–1997: An Analysis of U.S. Public Companies*. Research commissioned by the Committee of Sponsoring Organizations of the Treadway Committee.

Clarke, F., Dean, G. and Oliver, K. (2003), *Corporate Collapse. Accounting, Regulatory and Ethical Failure* (revised edition), Cambridge University Press, Cambridge.

Evans, D.M. (1859), *Facts, Failures and Frauds: Revelations, Finances, Mercantile and Criminal*, Groombridge and Sons, London.

Financial Reporting Review Panel (FRRP) (2003), *Rulings on various cases* (http://www.frrp.org.uk).

Fusaro, P.C. and Miller, R.M. (2002), *What Went Wrong at Enron*, John Wiley & Sons Inc., New York.

Grant, P. (2006), 'Paper maker bows to FRRP's ruling', *Accountancy Age*, 8 June, p. 7.

Griffiths, I. (1995), *New Creative Accounting*, Macmillan, London.

Hopkins, J. (2002), 'CFOs join their bosses on the hot seat', *USA Today*, 16 July.

Jones, M.J. (2006), *Accounting*, John Wiley & Sons Ltd, Chichester.

Joint Disciplinary Tribunal Complaints against Stoy Hayward (2002), *Polly Peck Investigation of the Facts*, The Accountants' Joint Disciplinary Scheme, March.

Krantz, M. (2002), 'Capitalizing on the oldest trick in the book', *USA Today*, 27 June.

Langendijk, H. (2004), *Parmalat Finanziaria S.p.A.: A Case of Manipulating Financial Statements through Fraud*, NIVRA – Nyenrode Press, Breukelen, Netherlands.

Lieberman, D. and Farrell, G. (2002), 'Adelphia founder, 2 sons, 2 others arrested in accounting fraud', *US Today*, 24 June.

Lister, D. (2006), 'Bank manager jailed for 10 years over £ 21m fraud', *The Times*, 28 June, p. 13.

Mulford, C. and Comiskey, E. (2002), *The Financial Numbers Game. Detecting Creative Accounting Practices*, John Wiley & Sons Inc., New York.

Richardson, S. (2007), 'Interserve takes GBP43m hit after financial scandal', *Financial Times*, 16 March.

Rutherford, B. (1999), 'Creative compliance and behaviour in response to mandatory changes in accounting policy', *Accounting History*, **4**(1), 32–58.

Shah, A.K. (1996), 'Creative compliance in financial reporting', *Accounting Organizations and Society*, **21**(1), 23–29.

Sukhraj, P. (2006), 'Interserve faces probe over £25m invoice hole', *Accountancy Age*, 31 August, p. 6.

Thomas, C.W. (2002), 'The rise and fall of Enron', *Journal of Accountancy*, April, 41–47.

Townsend, R. (1970), *Up The Organisation,* Knopf, in *Wiley Book of Business Quotations*, 1998, p. 89.

UBS Phillips & Drew (1991), *Accounting for Growth*, UBS Phillips & Drew, London.

# 5

# Evidence for Creative Accounting and Fraud

Michael Jones

## 5.1 INTRODUCTION

There have been many studies that have investigated the evidence for creative accounting and, to a lesser extent, fraud. These studies can roughly be divided into descriptive and statistical studies. This chapter will investigate these studies. The descriptive studies look at the topic of creative accounting and fraud and then cite examples of individual companies and case studies.[1] Some of the statistical studies use very complicated and complex statistical methodologies. Generally, the statistical studies more often focus on creative accounting in aggregate rather than on fraud. However, there is also a body of literature which seeks to relate corporate governance characteristics (such as presence of an audit committee) to the incidence of fraud. The aim of this chapter will be just to give a simplified overview of these studies.[2] Generally, here the intent is to focus on one or two of the most illustrative and informative studies in each category.

## 5.2 THE DESCRIPTIVE STUDIES

These studies are usually reports or books that address the topic of what they normally call creative accounting.[3] Figure 5.1 lists 10 of these studies. The earliest of these was the seminal book by Ian Griffiths in 1986 that first brought the topic of creative accounting out into the open (Griffiths, 1986). Two influential reports followed by County Natwest WoodMac (1991) and UBS Phillips & Drew (1991). The report by UBS Phillips & Drew was particularly influential as it was written by a pair of well-respected UK analysts who actually named companies that they believed were using creative accounting techniques. Two books by Trevor Pijper (1993) and McBarnet and Whelan (1999) then surveyed the UK scene over a 10-year period. Clarke, Dean and Oliver (2003) reviewed corporate collapses from the 1960s up to 2002 in Australia. This was followed up by Clarke and Dean (2007), which looked at financial reporting against the backdrop of Enron. Then there are three books from the USA. Charles Mulford and Eugene Comiskey (2002) wrote an influential

---

[1] This is not meant to be exhaustive and cover all reports and books, but to give a flavour of prior research.

[2] Readers who wish to study the topic in more detail are referred to the original articles. This chapter does not deal with books and articles which cover only one company. There is, in particular, a wealth of articles and books on Enron and WorldCom.

[3] Beasley, Carcello and Hermanson (1999) and Wells (2005) deal more specifically with fraud.

*Creative Accounting, Fraud and International Accounting Scandals*   Edited by Michael Jones
© 2011 Michael Jones. Published by John Wiley & Sons, Ltd

**(1) Ian Griffiths, *Creative Accounting* (1986)**

This was the seminal book on creative accounting. It brought to the public notice that the flexibility in the accounts could be used for creative accounting. This book was updated in 1995 and called *New Creative Accounting*.

**(2) County Natwest WoodMac, *Company Pathology* (1991)**

This report was an interesting step in creative accounting because it named companies who had indulged in creative accounting. It studied 45 UK companies that failed in 1989 and 1990.

**(3) UBS Phillips & Drew, *Accounting for Growth* (1991)**

This was another UK report that named names. It looked at 185 UK companies' annual reports and then highlighted some of the most common accounting techniques used by companies to enhance their results. I analysed this book in an article entitled 'Accounting for growth: surviving the accounting jungle'. The report was followed by a book, also called *Accounting for Growth*.

**(4) Trevor Pijper, *Creative Accounting* (1993)**

This book built on *Accounting for Growth*. It looked at the effectiveness of financial reporting in the UK against the background of the introduction of a new and more effective regulatory regime, the Accounting Standards Board, that was born in the aftermath of several high-profile UK accounting scandals.

**(5) Frank Clarke, Graeme Dean and Kyle Oliver, *Corporate Collapse, Accounting, Regulatory and Ethical Failure* (2003, first issued 1997)**

This book provides a comprehensive look at Australian corporate collapses in the 1960s, 1970s and 1980s. The book is set within the general context of creative accounting. It advocates a rethink of group accounting.

**(6) Frank Clarke and Graeme Dean, *Indecent Disclosure: Gilding the Corporate Lily* (2007)**

This book builds on the previous book by Clarke, Dean and Oliver (2003). It was written after, and influenced by, events at Enron. The authors look again at several Australian scandals and argue that the current corporate governance schemes and regulations may be doing more harm than good. They develop an alternative financial reporting framework for groups.

**(7) McBarnet and Whelan, *Creative Accounting and the Cross-eyed Javelin Thrower* (1999)**

This book surveyed UK financial reporting in 1999. This was after almost 10 years of the new regulatory framework established in 1990. Many instances of creative accounting were found.

**Figure 5.1**    Descriptive studies of creative accounting and fraud

---

**(8) Charles Mulford and Eugene Comiskey, *The Financial Numbers Game* (2002)**

This book was published just before the Enron and WorldCom financial scandals in the USA. However, this book documented numerous cases of creative accounting and fraud and showed that all was not well in the USA. The same authors also produced a follow-up book, *Creative Cash Flow Reporting* in the USA in 2005.

**(9) Beasley, Carcello and Hermanson, *Fraudulent Financial Reporting 1987–1997: An Analysis of U.S. Public Companies* (1999)**

This report was a follow-up to an earlier report published in 1987. It reviewed fraudulent financial reporting in the USA. It found the companies involved were relatively small and that top management was frequently involved. The study looked at the nature of the frauds, the role of the external auditor and the consequences and implications of the frauds.

**(10) Joseph Wells, *Principles of Fraud Examination* (2005)**

This book provides a comprehensive examination of occupational fraud and abuse. It covers corruption, asset misappropriation and fraudulent statements. The latter section is particularly relevant and looks at, *inter alia*, methods of financial statement fraud.

---

**Figure 5.1**    (*Continued*)

book on creative accounting in the USA just before the Enron and WorldCom scandals. There are also two US publications on fraud. First, Beasley, Carcello and Hermanson (1999) looked at the nature and extent of fraud in the USA. Then, Joseph Wells (2005) produced a book on both individual and financial statement fraud drawing on examples from the USA.

### 5.2.1 Ian Griffiths, *Creative Accounting* (1986)

This book began with the immortal lines that I quoted in the Introduction: 'Every company in the country is fiddling its profits. Every set of accounts is based on books which have been gently cooked or completely roasted. The figures which are fed twice a year to the investing public have been changed in order to protect the guilty. It is the biggest con trick since the Trojan horse.' It set out to demonstrate that most UK companies were indulging in creative accounting. By this it meant that companies, although working within the regulatory framework, were using accounts to serve managerial purposes rather than giving shareholders a true picture of what was going on. This book was revised and updated in 1995. However, the basic story was still the same. Despite a new regulatory regime, – the UK's Accounting Standards Board (ASB), set up in 1990 – creative accounting was still alive and well. In fact, one of the major reasons for the creation of the ASB was the perceived prevalence of creative accounting.

Griffiths' book covered a range of issues such as the presentation of the accounts, income and expenses, foreign currency, pensions, stock, current assets, share capital, cash and borrowing, off-balance sheet financing, acquisitions and mergers, brands and goodwill, and deferred taxation. For each topic he showed the ways in which the figures could be presented creatively. Usually, he used made-up examples to illustrate the points he made. However, sometimes he mentioned real-life examples. For example, he cites Lucas, a UK company that in the mid-1980s quite legally took a pension holiday (i.e. did not contribute to its employees' pension scheme because they were in surplus). As a result, Lucas's profits increased by £40 million over a two-year period (Griffiths, 1995, p. 43).

### 5.2.2  County Natwest WoodMac, *Company Pathology* (1991)

The Griffiths book brought the phenomenon of creative accounting to prominence. However, it was the two reports by County Natwest WoodMac and UBS Phillips & Drew which really started to name names and give practical, concrete examples of creative accounting. County Natwest WoodMac produced *Company Pathology* in 1991. County Natwest WoodMac was the investment arm of a leading high street bank, National Westminster. The report was, therefore, written by a city insider and drew its inspiration from the study of pathology. The authors felt that there might be something to be learnt from the analysis of deceased companies.

They studied 45 listed, USM or Third Market companies with administrators or administrative receivers appointed in 1989 or 1990. The purpose of their report was to highlight shortcomings in the UK financial reporting. They showed that only three of the 45 auditors' reports were qualified. All the other auditors' reports gave the companies a clean bill of health. They looked at the last published accounts of the companies before they failed. Of the 44 reports published, 29 showed a rise, nine a fall and six a loss. There was thus no obvious signal that most of the companies were about to fail. The report also criticised accounting standards: 'Accounting Standards give companies too much scope for creative accounting. One set of accounts were described by an experienced and well-qualified fund manager as "*a complete joke*"' (County Natwest WoodMac, 1991, p. 4). In particular, the report highlighted the weakness of the prevailing foreign currency provisions. They cited Polly Peck, which was a high-profile UK corporate collapse in 1998.

As pointed out in Chapter 4, Polly Peck had borrowed money in Swiss francs and deposited it in Turkey/northern Cyprus.[4] Under the prevailing rules, the company was able to take high levels of interest earned in an inflationary regime to the income statement. However, the capital loss was taken straight to reserves. As the authors state you would, however, have to be very astute and attentive to spot and understand what was going on. In fact, nobody did until after the event. It is this lack of astuteness and attentiveness upon which the creative accountant thrives.

The report then went on to list six areas that it identified as questionable accounting practices. Despite the passage of time, since the 1980s most are still questionable today. First, many companies had capitalised interest and other costs; this was particularly true of property developers. In the case of Reliant this capitalised interest was over 100 % of pre-tax profit. This capitalised interest not only made profits higher, but in Reliant's case it turned a loss into a profit. Second, one company, Leading Leisure, had added £10 million to profits by selling properties to joint venture companies (companies jointly owned with other companies). There was also evidence that loans made to joint

---

[4] The north of Cyprus was invaded by Turkey in 1974. It is not recognised by the UN as an independent nation.

venture companies may have enabled those companies to purchase the properties. In other words, Leading Leisure was selling properties to itself and booking them as profits. Third, many companies were classifying and excluding from profits extraordinary items (supposed to be one-off unusual costs) when really they were normal operating costs. They were thus artificially boosting their normal trading profits. Fourth, many companies were classifying their leases as operating rather than as finance leases so they did not have to be capitalised and counted as part of the company's borrowing. However, these leases were to all intents and purposes really finance leases which should have been capitalized. These companies were thus creatively reducing the debt which appeared on their balance sheets. Fifth, many companies were revaluing investment properties to open market value. This policy, as the authors state, gives directors considerable latitude. It also generally, given the rise of property prices, increased the value of the company's assets. Sixth, in echoes of Enron: 'There was widespread use of joint ventures to keep the finance for property developments off-balance sheet, with borrowings being secured on the developments' (County Natwest WoodMac, 1991, p. 21). The report gave the example of Rush and Tomkins. This company had group loans and overdrafts of £25 million. However, it also had £89 million of loans through joint venture companies. However, this was not clear from a study of its accounts. When the company collapsed a year later it owed about £300 million.

### 5.2.3 UBS Phillips & Drew, *Accounting for Growth* (1991)

This UK report also named names. It thus shone a spotlight onto practices which had hitherto been clouded in mystery. It created quite a storm in the City of London at the time. It was compiled by two analysts, Terry Smith and Richard Hannah. Subsequently, Terry Smith left Phillips & Drew. This was the result of the furore which the book caused. Smith then published a book, entitled *Accounting for Growth* on his own (Smith, 1991). This book went into more details of individual companies than the original report.

The original report looked at the reporting practices of 185 large, listed UK companies circa 1990. As well as copious specific examples of companies which adopted accounting practices that enhanced reported earnings per share, the report produced the so-called blob index. This listed 185 UK companies and indicated which of 11 'creative accounting' practices the firms adopted. I subsequently analysed this blob index, as discussed below. As can be seen in Table 5.1, the 11 techniques were found to be used with differing degrees of frequency.

Provisions were by far the most popular technique. Many companies used acquisitions as an opportunity to tidy up their balance sheets. They wrote down assets such as inventory and trade receivables so that they could sell these assets later and book more profit. With fixed assets, by writing them down they could charge less depreciation in future which also boosted profits. Also, when they were sold later on, profits on disposal would be greater.

Ten other techniques were found to be prevalent in the early 1990s. These techniques were all permitted by contemporary accounting rules and regulations. Indeed, some such as the capitalisation of expenses are still permitted now. First, 34 % of companies boosted pre-tax profits by non-trading exceptional items. They were thus including in operating profit non-operating items. Second, companies were creatively using extraordinary items. This gave the appearance of better ongoing profits than was actually the case. With

**Table 5.1**  Ranking of accounting practices used by 185 major UK companies in *Accounting for Growth*

| Type | No. | % | Ranking |
|---|---|---|---|
| Provisions | 105 | 57 | 1 |
| Nontrading profits | 63 | 34 | 2 |
| Extraordinary costs | 54 | 29 | 3 |
| Pension funds | 52 | 28 | 4 |
| Capitalization | 50 | 27 | 5 |
| Low-tax charge | 24 | 13 | 6 |
| Off-balance sheet debt | 23 | 12 | 7 |
| Depreciation | 17 | 9 | 8 |
| Currency mismatch | 16 | 9 | 9 |
| Brand names | 14 | 8 | 10 |
| Earnouts | 9 | 5 | 11 |

*Source:* Jones (1992, p. 22)

non-acquisition costs many companies were writing down, for example, fixed assets, inventory and trade receivables of a continuing business as a one-off extraordinary item. This had the same effect as acquisition-related provisions. Potential expenses were excluded from current trading profits and future years would benefit when, for example, the fixed assets and inventory were sold or trade receivables collected. Subsequently, rule changes have stopped the widespread abuse of extraordinary items. However, companies still try to increase their ongoing profits from trading. Third, the strong performance of pension funds encouraged many companies to stop paying into their employee pension schemes. These pension holidays thus boosted company profits at the expense of the employee pension schemes; 28 % of UK companies were found to do this. The full significance of this came much later. In the UK in the 1990s, the stock market foundered and since then pension schemes have been struggling. Thus, short-term gain by companies impacted on pensions much later. Fourth, one of the most prevalent forms of creative accounting has been the capitalisation of expenses. This perennial creative accounting technique was adopted by 27 % of UK companies. Some of them, such as Greycoat and Next, were found to have capitalised over 100 % of pre-tax profits. In other words, without such capitalisation, they would have made a loss. The sixth accounting technique highlighted is perhaps more a symptom of creative accounting than an actual technique. It was the presence of a low corporate tax charge. Some UK companies were paying hardly any tax at all. In some cases this was perfectly legitimate and the result of the company's good tax planning. However, the report cautions that many low tax charges are created by deferring tax liabilities into the future rather than dispensing with them altogether. Thus, when there is a downturn in a company's fortunes, these tax liabilities crystallise and the company will suffer. The seventh accounting technique involved off-balance sheet debt. This is where the company's true borrowings are concealed and not reflected in the balance sheet of the group. UBS Phillips & Drew identified 23 incidences of this.

The remaining four creative accounting techniques were adopted by less than 20 % of companies. The eighth technique was the lengthening of asset lives. This resulted in less depreciation being charged every year and thus higher profits. As the authors point out, this is perhaps ironic as, with the growth of technology, one would expect asset lives to be shortening rather than lengthening. In the book, this irony is exemplified by the case of the British Airports Authority (BAA). This changed the life of some of its assets from 23.5 years in 1988 to 100 years in 1990. Terry Smith comments, perhaps tongue-in-cheek: 'The sums involved are smaller for runway resurfacing, but it is worth bearing in mind with a shift in economic life from 23.5 to 100 years that 100 years ago man had not achieved powered flight. So will BAA be deriving economic benefit from aircraft using its runways in 2091?' (Smith, 1991, p. 130). The ninth technique was currency mismatch. As already seen, this was exemplified by Polly Peck where a strong currency borrowed was deposited in a weak currency. The tenth technique concerned brand names. In the UK, in 1988 Grand Metropolitan capitalized £588 million of brands. Since then, many brand-rich companies have also capitalized their brands. UBS Phillips & Drew identified 14 companies that had done so. The eleventh technique, identified in their blob index, was deferred consideration or earnouts. This involved an acquiring company making an acquisition and then paying for it later. Earnouts can cause future problems meeting the consideration. UBS Phillips & Drew also recorded a twelfth technique in their report, although they did not include it in their blob index: convertibles with puts. A convertible put bond forces companies to redeem a bond at a premium after a number of years if the investor so wishes. These bonds were issued with a low interest rate in the belief that the share price would rise so that the bonds would be converted into ordinary shares and the put option would not be exercised. However, a weak stock market led to many put options looking likely to be exercised. This made the true cost of the bond more than originally anticipated. This meant an increased charge to the income statement. UBS Phillips & Drew found 12 companies with such bonds.

When I analysed the Phillips & Drew report I found some interesting findings Jones (1992). First, I found that in many cases accounting techniques were used by the majority of companies in a particular stock market sector. Thus, 100 % of brewers and distillers used provisions. Second, I found that three companies used seven techniques and two used six. Of these five companies one was Maxwell Communications, a company that was subsequently the cause of a major accounting scandal (i.e. part of the Mirror Group). And third, banks were the least creative accounting sector with water, engineering and stores being the most creative.

The book *Accounting for Growth* provided numerous examples of creative accounting techniques. It covered the same general techniques as the report. However, in the appendix it looked at three UK companies in more detail: Coloroll, British and Commonwealth and Polly Peck. All three companies collapsed and are examples of UK accounting scandals. As Polly Peck is dealt with elsewhere in the book, particularly in Chapter 18, it is not considered further here. Coloroll was very acquisitive; in a period of 30 months, 13 acquisitions were made. It showed substantial apparent growth in profits. Most of this growth was caused not by actual growth, but through aggressive acquisition-type accounting techniques. In particular, Coloroll used provisions on acquisition. Coloroll collapsed in May 1990. British and Commonwealth was also extremely acquisitive. Once more the company used acquisition accounting. This led to it carrying too much goodwill. A final purchase of Atlantic Computers proved too much for the company. Atlantic Computers, a US company, ran into trouble. As pointed out in Chapter 4, it used a flex lease policy. Under this policy customers could either flex and return the equipment after three years, providing they leased replacement equipment of greater value or walk, which is terminate the lease by returning the equipment after five years. More and more customers flexed or handed their equipment back after five years. As a result, the higher lease payments in later years of a lease were never met. The result of all this was that huge liabilities built up. These liabilities were guaranteed by British and Commonwealth. As Smith points out, this was set out in an innocent-looking note in British and Commonwealth's 1988 annual report, which is set out below.

---

**26. Contingent Liabilities**

'The company has guaranteed bank overdrafts and other substantial trading liabilities of certain subsidiaries which have arisen in the normal course of their business and which are not expected to give any financial loss.'

---

In actual fact, honouring this legal obligation brought the company down.

### 5.2.4  Trevor Pijper, *Creative Accounting* (1993)

This book was written just after a spate of accounting scandals in the UK at the start of the 1990s. A new regulatory regime, consisting of the Accounting Standards Board, the Financial Reporting Review Panel and the Urgent Issues Task Force, had just been introduced. The book investigated creative accounting in the UK in this context. It produced some interesting data on the view that the stock market has of borrowing versus profits and on the most important of the UK's accounting scandals, Polly Peck. On pages 116–123, Pijper focused on the accounting practices of four UK companies. His general conclusion, by looking at their accounts in the financial press in the early 1990s, is that 'what is of interest, is that the stock market seemed unconcerned about changes in borrowing levels for as long as the companies were able to report healthy increases in earnings and dividends per share' (Pijper, 1993, p. 1190). This was taken to its extreme by Polly Peck, which demonstrated a 17-fold increase in borrowings from 1985 to 1989 compared with a doubling in trading profit. Pijper (1993, p. 122) also pointed to the quite legitimate treatment of redeemable subsidiary preference shares by Saatchi and Saatchi. If they were counted as part of the borrowings these would have increased the company's borrowings substantially. In his view, this would have been more reflective of their true nature.

Pijper has a chapter discussing Polly Peck, a notorious UK accounting scandal. Polly Peck collapsed in September 1990. A flavour of the Polly Peck scandal is given here, but more detail is provided in Chapter 18 on the UK, where it is covered in much more depth. It was one of the UK's fastest growing industrial and commercial companies in the 1980s. It was involved in food and electronics. Its 1989 annual report showed that sales had increased by 53 %, profit before tax by 44 % and earnings per share by 16.4 % over 1988. From the end of December 1988 to the end of November 1989, Polly Peck showed a spectacular increase in its share price of 120 545 %.

Since Pijper's book, what happened at Polly Peck has become a lot clearer. Asil Nadir, the charismatic chairman of Polly Peck, fled to northern Cyprus in 1993. He faced 66 charges of theft and fraud totalling £34 million. He has, however, always protested his innocence and in August 2010 returned to face trial. However, there has been an investigation by the Accountants Joint Disciplinary Scheme into complaints about the auditors, Stoy Hayward, that has brought certain facts to light (Accountants Joint Disciplinary Scheme, Polly Peck Investigation Statement of Facts, March 2002).

The report of the joint disciplinary tribunal pointed to a fundamental failure of internal controls at Polly Peck. It gave this damning indictment in paragraphs 8 and 9 of its report: 'The unfettered power of this individual [Asil Nadir] over the group's most significant activities was a key contributory factor in the difficulties that ensued. Of even more significance, however, was the lack of any meaningful high level control environment or system of detailed control procedures within PPI's Head Office in London. This fundamental weakness included the absence of even the most basic control, namely the requirement for dual signatures on all substantial bank disbursements.'

As well as these questionable activities, Polly Peck was argued to have indulged in various potentially creative accounting techniques. First, as pointed out earlier, it was involved in currency mismatching. It borrowed in hard currencies and invested in soft ones. It was then able to book interest receivable in the income statement as soft currencies have higher interest rates than hard currencies. However, it suffered capital losses in the balance sheet as soft currencies depreciate against hard ones. These losses went undetected. Second, although it appeared from the accounts that it had millions of pounds in the bank, much of this was actually stranded in Turkish banks and could not be remitted to the UK. Third, it included brands in its balance sheet. And, finally, as pointed out by the Accountants Joint Disciplinary Scheme investigation (2002, paragraph 50), there was a change in the group's accounting policy which may have been made solely to keep the firm in profit:

> The change in accounting policy, whereby the value of tangible fixed assets in areas of exceptional inflation (chiefly Turkey and the TRNC) were indexed upwards before translation to Sterling in order to reduce the impact on retained profits of the losses on exchange on translation of the year end balance sheets. This change in accounting policy was acceptable, but it should have reminded Stoy Hayward of the very serious impact which the devaluation of the Turkish Lira was having on the group's affairs.

### 5.2.5 Frank Clarke, Graeme Dean and Kyle Oliver, *Corporate Collapse: Accounting, Regulatory and Ethical Failure* (2003, first issued 1997)

This book provides a comprehensive look at Australian corporate collapses from the 1960s onwards. It was first issued in 1997 and then updated to include more recent scandals from 1997–2001. The book is set in the context of creative accounting. It begins by stating: 'conventional accounting produces institutionalised window-dressing. Arguably, the overall quality of GAAP-based accounting is poorer than before the advent of mandatory "compliance standards regime"' (2003, p. 25). Nine major Australian corporate collapses are covered in this book from the 1960s, 1970s and 1980s. These include Reid Murray

Holding, H.G. Palmer, Minisec and Cambridge Credit, which are covered in some detail in Chapter 7.

From 1990 onwards, there was a stream of other scandals such as Adsteam, Bond, One-Tel and, most importantly, HIH, which are covered in Chapter 8 on Australia. Overall, the Australian cases show a wealth of creative accounting, and occasionally, fraud. In particular, Clarke, Dean and Oliver (2003, p. 247) draw attention to the Byzantine structures of groups of related companies. 'From its introduction, giving special status to a group of related companies and methods of consolidating its accounts has facilitated financial deception. Equally paradoxical, rather than abandoning it as its role in corporate crises has become obvious, both the regulatory bodies and the accounting profession have preferred "patching up" consolidation accounting.'

### 5.2.6  Frank Clarke and Graeme Dean, *Indecent Disclosure: Gilding the Corporate Lily* (2007)

This book builds on the previous book by Clarke, Dean and Oliver (2003). However, it is different in that it is more advocatory, using the recent accounting scandals in the USA to promote attitudinal change in regulation. A central tenet of the book is that the current debate on corporate governance may be doing more harm than good. It takes a historical view and shows that current 'corporate shenanigans' bear a similarity to those following the 1929 crash.

In essence, the authors believe that perhaps the modern corporate is 'ungovernable' in its present form and they advocate:

- Less detailed regulation of the integrity of processes and more effective consideration of serviceable outcomes.
- Regulatory mechanisms should emphasise ex-ante protection rather than ex-post penalty.
- Accounting standards should be more principles-based and less rules-compliant.
- There is a need to address the fundamental structure of accounting and auditing for the corporation.

### 5.2.7  McBarnet and Whelan, *Creative Accounting and the Cross-eyed Javelin Thrower* (1999)

This book was written in 1999 and looked at the creative accounting environment after almost 10 years of the new regulatory regime in the UK. Its title was inspired by a remark of David Tweedie's (Head of the UK's Accounting Standards Board) who, when asked if the new regime would win the battle against creative accounting, reportedly replied: 'We're like a cross-eyed javelin thrower competing at the Olympic Games; we may not win but we'll keep the crowd on the edge of its seats!' (McBarnet and Whelan, 1999, p. 30). The book investigated issues such as creative compliance and the steps which the UK's Accounting Standards Board had taken to tighten up UK financial reporting.

Of particular interest is an investigation of the activities of the Financial Reporting and Review Panel. This body is the UK's accounting standards enforcement agency. It investigated a number of cases in which the panel thought there was a danger that accounting standards were not being followed. Several cases discussed by McBarnet and Whelan are worthy of interest: three of them are discussed below. First, British Gas had presented their profit and loss account from 1 January to 31 December after they had changed their year end from 31 March to 31 December. The profit and loss, therefore, included three months of already published results. The effect was to boost profits from £496 million to £1.47 billion. The directors agreed to restate their accounts (McBarnet and Whelan, 1999, pp. 52–53). Second, in 1992, the panel investigated the accounts of Trafalgar House, a large UK company. Trafalgar House had reclassified commercial properties from current to fixed assets. The effect of this reclassification was to turn a £19.7 million pre-tax profit into a £122.4 million pre-tax profit. In the end, after disputing the case, Trafalgar House restated its accounts (McBarnet and Whelan, 1999, pp. 60–62). Third, Butte Mining had rendered services to Gem River Corporation (GRC) and, in return, received shares in payment. Butte Mining booked the whole profit. However, some of the shares had restricted trading rights. The Financial Reporting and Review Panel, therefore, thought only some of the profit should be booked. As a result, a profit of £339 500 was turned into a loss of £967 000 (McBarnet and Whelan, 1999, pp. 62–63).

### 5.2.8 Charles Mulford and Eugene Comiskey, *The Financial Numbers Game* (2002)

This authoritative book looked at the state of creative accounting in the USA pre-Enron. It used a wide definition of creative accounting to include accounting techniques that were both within and beyond US GAAP and fraudulent accounting. The book is packed with specific examples of creative accounting and is a recommended read for all those who wish to have a detailed look at creative accounting in the USA. It shows that, in effect, Enron and WorldCom were not isolated examples. The book uses a fivefold classification of creative accounting practices: recognising premature or fictitious revenue; aggressive capitalisation and extended amortisation policies; misreported assets and liabilities; getting creative with the income statement; and problems with cash flow reporting. The chapter written by Mulford and Comiskey in this book (Chapter 19) effectively updates this book.

#### 5.2.8.1  *Recognising Premature or Fictitious Revenue*

The authors point out that 'premature revenue recognition refers to recognising revenue for a legitimate sale in a period prior to that called for by generally accepted accounting principles' (Mulford and Comiskey, 2002, p. 9). They point out that it is often difficult to distinguish between premature and fictitious revenue recognition. Goods may be ordered but not shipped at the time of recognition. Or goods may be shipped in advance of an expected order. In some cases, companies will ship goods for which no orders are expected or make non-existent shipments. Mulford and Comiskey (2002, p. 162) cite Boston Scientific Corp. In 1997 and 1998, managers were desperate to meet sales goals. Therefore, they shipped 'fictitious' goods to leased commercial warehouses. However, there were no customers. The company, therefore, later issued credit notes and resold the goods. These sales irregularities were revealed by the company publicly in 1998 after they were detected in an internal audit (Johannes, 2000).

### 5.2.8.2  Aggressive Capitalisation and Extended Amortisation Policies

Both aggressive capitalisation and extended amortisation reduce expenses and thus boost profits. This is a common creative accounting technique. Mulford and Comiskey (2002, pp. 11–12) cite the examples of American Software, Inc. and Waste Management, Inc. American Software, Inc. is an example of a company that traditionally capitalised its software development costs. The company capitalised huge amounts of software development costs over the years 1997, 1998 and 1999. However, in the year to 30 April 1999 the company wrote off $24 152 000 in capitalised costs as a result of a review of the recoverability of those costs. Mulford and Comiskey (2002, p. 11) comment 'the company had capitalized more software development costs than could be realized through operations, and it therefore became necessary for the company to write those costs off. In the intervening years leading up to the write-off, however, the company's capitalization policy had boosted its reported earnings and its apparent earning power.' Waste Management, Inc. appears to have been charging too little depreciation on its fixed assets. As a result they were valued too highly. It then took a $3.5 billion write down of fixed assets and other items to correct this. However, in the intervening period its profits had been boosted.

### 5.2.8.3  Misreported Assets and Liabilities

A general category is the misreporting of assets and liabilities. Mulford and Comiskey (2002, p. 12) cite the example of Centennial Technologies, Inc. In 1996, the company had overstated its trade receivables, its inventory and its investments. In their book, the authors cite many more examples of these practices.

### 5.2.8.4  Getting Creative with the Income Statement

Under this heading, Mulford and Comiskey discuss the way in which the format of the income statement can be used creatively. Generally, this is used when companies wish to record higher ongoing earnings than they would otherwise. The authors discuss the well-known example of IBM, which in its 1999 interim report netted a $4 billion gain from sale of an investment against expenses. As a result, ongoing earnings were boosted (Mulford and Comiskey, 2002, p.13).

### 5.2.8.5  Problems with Cash Flow Reporting

The final area that Mulford and Comiskey looked at was the cash flow statement. This subject is discussed in much more detail in their later book, *Creative Cash Flow Reporting* (Mulford and Comiskey, 2005). Readers who want to look at creative accounting and the cash flow statement in more depth are referred to this book. Essentially, cash flow is much harder to manipulate than profit. Indeed, a careful study of cash flow can often detect creative accounting. The trick in creative cash flow accounting is to report higher and more sustainable operating cash flows. This will be at the expense of minimising the investing or financing cash flows. Mulford and Comiskey cite software development costs as a good example of this. The authors suggest that companies may try to report capitalised software development costs as an investing cash outflow rather than as an operating cash flow. This will have the effect of increasing operating cash flows, while decreasing investing cash flows.

### 5.2.9 Beasley, Carcello and Hermanson, *Fraudulent Financial Reporting 1987–1997: An Analysis of U.S. Public Companies* (1999)

The report, commissioned by the US Treadway Commission, had three specific objectives:

(a) To identify instances of alleged fraudulent financial reporting by registrants of the US Securities and Exchange Commission.
(b) To identify key company and management characteristics for a sample of these companies.
(c) To provide a basis for recommendations to improve corporate financial reporting in the USA.

They analysed fraudulent financial reporting in the USA from January 1987 to December 1997, and their research identified nearly 300 companies involved in alleged instances of fraudulent financial reporting. They then sampled 20 financial statement fraud cases. Their main findings concerned the nature of the companies involved, the nature of the control environment, the nature of the frauds, issues relating to the external auditor, and consequences for the company and individuals involved. They then summed up the implications for the companies for each category.

#### 5.2.9.1  Nature of the Companies Involved

The typical size of these companies was small, less than $100 million total assets with 78 % not listed on US Exchanges. Some companies were experiencing net losses or were close to break-even positions. As a result, they were facing financial strain which may have provided incentives for fraud. The implications of these findings were that internal controls needed to be improved and there needed to be effective monitoring of a company's going concern status.

#### 5.2.9.2  Nature of the Control Environment

Top senior executives were frequently involved. In 72 % of the cases, the CEOs were named and 43 % of CFOs were named (combined 83 %). Most audit committees met only once per year, with 25 % of companies not having an audit committee. Most of the directors were also not independent of the company, with family relationships being particularly strong. The implications of these findings are that pressures on senior executives ought to be monitored and that the number of audit committee meetings and financial expertise of the audit committee members deserves closer attention. There should also be a particular emphasis on director independence and expertise, with audit committee members having access to reliable financial and non-financial information. Investors should also be aware of the possible complications arising from family connections.

### 5.2.9.3  Nature of the Frauds

The average financial misstatement or misappropriation was $25.0 million. The mean misappropriation of assets was $71.5 million. Most frauds were not isolated to one financial period. The main methods used to misstate financial statements were improper revenue recognition (50 %) and overstatement of assets (50 %). The overstated revenues involved variously sham sales, premature revenues, conditional sales, improper cut-offs, improper use of contract completion methods, unauthorised shipments and consignment sales. The asset accounts most typically overstated were inventory, trade receivables and property, plant and equipment. The implications of these frauds were that the importance of interim financial statements should be highlighted and there should be enhanced controls at transaction cut-off and asset valuation.

### 5.2.9.4  Issues Related to the External Auditor

The sample fraud companies were audited as follows: 56 % by a Big Eight/Six auditor and 44 % by a non-Big Eight/Six auditor. Fifty-five % of auditor reports were unqualified, with the remainder raising substantial doubts across a range of issues. In 29 % (56 out of 195) of the cases, auditors were involved either through alleged involvement (30 cases) or negligent auditing (26 cases). Just over 25 % of companies had recently changed their auditors. The implications of this are that the auditor needs to look more widely beyond the financial statements to, for example, the client's industry, management motivation towards aggressive reporting, and internal control. The auditor should recognise the greater audit risk potential in cases of poor corporate governance.

### 5.2.9.5  Consequences for Company and Individuals

For the company the consequences often included bankruptcy, significant changes in ownership and delisting. For individuals the consequences were often class action legal suits and personal fines or resignation. Very few individuals were, however, jailed.

### 5.2.10  Joseph Wells, *Principles of Fraud Examination* (2005)

This book focuses on fraud in organisations; it uses as a working definition: 'The use of one's occupation for personal enrichment through the deliberate misuse or misapplication of the employing organisation's resources or assets', which was taken from a US Association of Certified Fraud Examiners Report (2002). The book was written using the author's experience in investigating fraud since the 1980s.

The main part of the book examines how employees can defraud their employers. It details a wide variety of methods such as skimming, where cash is stolen before its entry into an accounting system; cash larceny, where cash is intentionally stolen; or billing, where the fraudster causes the victim organisation to issue a fraudulent payment by submitting invoices for fictitious goods or services, inflated invoices or invoices for personal purchases.

As well as dealing with these individual instances of fraud, the book, in Chapters 11 and 12, covers fraudulent financial statement schemes. Financial statement fraud, defined as preparing false financial statements, is committed mainly by senior management. Wells argues that the senior management commit financial statement fraud to conceal the true business performance, to preserve personal status and to maintain personal income/wealth.

As Wells (2005, p. 322) comments in the US context: 'Financial statement fraud has become a hot subject in the daily press, as recent scandals and criminal actions have challenged the corporate responsibility and integrity of major companies. All of whom have been alleged by the SEC to have committed fraud.' Wells included in his list well-known companies such as Rite Aid, Tyco International, WorldCom, Adelphia and Enron.

Wells identified five major methods of financial statement fraud.

### 5.2.10.1  Fictitious Revenues

This involves the recording of sales of goods and services that did not occur. For example, a fictitious sales invoice could be raised (but not mailed) to a legitimate customer although no goods are sent or services rendered. At the beginning of the next period, the sale might be reversed. Wells cites a case where a publicly traded firm made sham transactions for seven years. These transactions served to increase both assets and revenues. In this case, the company's books were inflated by more than $80 million.

### 5.2.10.2  Timing Differences

Under this method, a company will not correctly record its revenues and corresponding expenses in the same accounting period as it should do under correct accounting principles. So, for example, a company accurately records sales in December, but does not record associated expenses until January. Wells (2005, p. 332) details a US case where management enhanced their earnings by recording unearned revenue prematurely. As a result, its drugstores appeared more profitable than they actually were.

### 5.2.10.3  Concealed Liabilities and Expenses

Underestimating liabilities and expenses will make a company appear more profitable than it actually is. One way of doing this is to fail to record them. For example, purchase invoices might simply not be entered. In the case of WorldCom, expenses were simply improperly capitalised. For example, $3.35 billion in fees paid to lease phone networks were reclassified as assets.

### 5.2.10.4  Improper Disclosures

Management should disclose all significant information. However, they may not. For example, they might omit details of contingent liabilities or omit to record transactions. In the case of Tyco, the SEC charged the CEO Dennis Kozlowski with failure to disclose to shareholders hundreds of millions of dollars of low-interest and interest-free loans. In addition, the SEC alleged that Tyco had paid for the personal expenses of Kozlowski, such as a $16.8 million apartment in New York City, $13 million in original art and half of a $2.1 million birthday party for his wife. In 2005, Kozlowski was sentenced to $8\frac{1}{3}$ years in prison and paid a huge sum in restitution to Tyco and a $70 million criminal fine (Paiste, 2009).

### 5.2.10.5 *Improper Asset Valuation*

Many schemes are used to inflate assets. The most common asset to be inflated is inventory. Inventory can be improperly stated through a manipulated stock-take, or by, for example, inflating the costs of inventory. Wells (2005, p. 343) cited the case of a large cannery and wholesaler in the South West USA where the inventory was sold twice.

# 5.3 THE STATISTICAL STUDIES

The academic studies generally have two main features: they use a large number of company accounts and they estimate, in aggregate, whether creative accounting has taken place. Very few of these statistical studies deal specifically with fraud, probably because fraud studies do not naturally lend themselves to aggregation. However, there are a group of studies that seek to relate certain corporate governance characteristics to the existence of fraudulent financial statements. They are dealt with at the end of the earnings management literature. As these academic studies use the term 'earnings management' or 'income smoothing', these are the terms that will be used in this section. However, these terms are broadly synonymous with creative accounting. The researchers use a large number of accounts so that they can collect sufficient data to run sophisticated statistical tests. The approach they use is to focus on what they call the accruals element of the accounting numbers. Essentially, accruals represent non-cash flow elements of the accounts and can often be manipulated by management. These accruals represent items such as depreciation, inventory, trade receivables and trade payables. Total accruals are estimated as the difference between reported accounting earnings and cash flows from operations. These accruals are then often divided into discretionary and non-discretionary accruals. Management can alter the discretionary accruals but not the non-discretionary accruals. This basic approach thus does not investigate specific items of creative accounting, but infers that creative accounting is going on by the total changes in accruals.

### 5.3.1 Earnings Management Studies

This basic approach has been used in many studies. Over the years these studies have become more sophisticated. In Figure 5.2, I list eight different sets of studies. The first set of studies establishes in general terms that income smoothing or earnings management does occur. The next seven sets of studies look at specific aspects of earnings management such as meeting management or analysts' earnings forecasts, maximising bonuses, maintaining debt covenants, reducing government interference, changes of top management, acquisitions and share issues, and avoidance of earnings surprises. Essentially, the methodologies followed in these studies are similar. First, a hypothesis about a particular form of earning management is posited, data are then collected, the hypothesis is tested and the hypothesis is either confirmed or not. In most cases, evidence consistent with the hypothesis is found.

**(i) Early studies**

The early studies were generally termed "income smoothing" studies. They were first of all concerned with establishing the incentives that managements have for creative accounting. They then tested and found evidence of income smoothing (increasing profits in bad years or reducing them in good years) in general terms. These studies took place in the 1970s, usually on US data sets.

**(ii) Meeting management or analysts' forecasts**

These studies hypothesised that there were incentives for managers to meet their own annual earnings forecasts and also those of stock market analysts. In general, they found evidence of earnings management.

**(iii) Maximizing bonuses**

This set of studies looked at earnings management from the perspective of managers managing earnings so that they could receive higher bonuses. The evidence was generally consistent with this expectation.

**(iv) Maintaining debt covenants**

This research examined accounting income changes associated with maintaining or not breaching loan covenants. They found that managers did indeed attempt to manipulate earnings and the balance sheet so as not to breach their debt covenants.

**(v) Reducing government interference**

These studies looked at a specific subset of companies which had incentives to decrease earnings (such as regulated industries) so as to ward off government interference. Evidence consistent with this was found both in the UK and the USA.

**(vi) Changes of top management**

These studies investigated what happened when a new management took over a company, especially when the previous manager had been underperforming. They found that there was evidence of the so-called "big bath" approach, where managements decreased income in the year of changeover so that future profits could be enhanced.

**(vii) Acquisitions and share issues**

These studies looked at the incentives which surround the acquisition of one company by another. They found that, as expected, the earnings of acquiring firms increased prior to the takeover. In addition, they found that companies' earnings increased just before they issued shares.

**Figure 5.2**   Academic earnings management studies

---

**(viii) Avoidance of earnings surprises**

It was hypothesized that those firms which failed to meet analysts' expectations would be more likely than those who did to issue discretionary disclosures prior to the publication of the earnings announcement. This hypothesis was confirmed. Such firms were more likely to make disclosures so as to manage stock market reactions.

---

**Figure 5.2**    Academic earnings management studies (*Continued*)

### 5.3.1.1    Academic Earnings Management Studies

*Early Studies*

The first studies into earnings management concentrated upon demonstrating that earnings management occurred. Trueman and Titman in 1988 wrote a theory paper which argued that managers wanted to smooth reported income so that they could influence debtholders' perceptions of the firm's earnings (Trueman and Titman, 1988). In particular, managers were seeking to make the firm appear less risky than it otherwise might appear. In this case, the cost of capital would fall. Companies could also raise more money from debtholders as the debtholders would be prepared to pay more. As a result, the share price would rise. This paper thus provided a general rationale which would underpin earnings management. In essence, earnings management would increase share prices. Following on from this, and extending Trueman and Titman's argument, earnings management incentives for managers would arise in situations where managers might gain from share price rises, such as where managerial remuneration consisted of shares or share options.

Two relatively early studies on income smoothing are presented by Dascher and Malcolm (1970) and Moses (1987). Dascher and Malcolm (1970) looked at how companies manipulated four variables: pension costs; dividends from unconsolidated subsidiaries recorded at cost; extraordinary (one-off) expenses and incomes; and research and development costs. They looked at a six-year and then an 11-year period. Their results were consistent with the view that income smoothing had taken place.

Moses (1987) investigated 231 discretionary changes over a five-year period. He found that there was evidence that firms were using non-mandatory accounting changes, such as changes in pension costs, inventory, depreciation and capitalisation, to income smooth. In particular, he found that income smoothing was associated, in general, with company size, the existence of bonus compensation plans and the divergence of actual earnings from expected earnings. Moses, by isolating bonus compensation plans and earnings expectations as reasons for income smoothing, opened the way for further more detailed studies of these areas.

*Meeting Management or Analysts' Forecasts*

Several studies have looked at whether earnings are managed so as to meet earnings forecasts. There are two sorts of earnings forecasts: those provided by management themselves voluntarily and those furnished by analysts. Both help to determine a company's share price. Earnings are one of the, if not the, most important drivers of share price. Consequently, if either the management's own or the analysts' expected earnings forecasts are not met then usually the market punishes the company by marking the shares down in price. There are thus great pressures on management to make not only their own forecasts but also the analysts' forecasts.

Kasnik (1999) investigated the general question of whether managers who issued annual earnings forecasts managed reported earnings to meet those forecasts. He suggested that they might do this to avoid litigation by investors and because they were concerned about losing a reputation for accuracy. Kasnik looked at 499 earnings forecasts.

He used the amount of accruals as a way of detecting whether earnings management had taken place. His overall conclusion was that: 'This paper provides evidence consistent with the prediction that managers use positive discretionary accruals to manage reported earnings upwards when earnings would otherwise fall below management's earnings forecasts' (Kasnik, 1999, p. 79). These results were in line with managers attempting to avoid litigation by disgruntled shareholders. He also found that managers who had overestimated earnings were not likely to manage their reported earnings downwards. As a result of managing earnings upwards, share prices reacted favourably and there was increased following of shares by market analysts.

There have been a considerable number of studies on meeting or beating analysts' expectations. Payne and Robb (1999) use anecdotal evidence as the motivation for their study: 'Anecdotal evidence indicates that there are strong incentives to achieve analysts' earnings forecasts to protect a company's stock price' (p. 371). In particular, they cited a speech by SEC chairman Arthur Levitt, in 1988, denouncing the problem of earnings manipulation. They looked at 13 532 cases of analyst forecast information over the period 1986–97. They found that, as predicted, managers moved earnings towards analysts' forecasts when pre-managed earnings were below market expectations. When pre-managed earnings exceeded analysts' forecasts, they found that managers used income-decreasing accruals so as to lower reported profits to match analysts' forecasts more closely. This was particularly true when there was a low dispersion in the analysts' forecasts. Brown (2001), for example, in the USA finds that there are a disproportionate number of cases where earnings per share figures reported by companies beat analysts' forecasts by a few cents. This is consistent with the view that managers are using earnings management to achieve this result.

Bartov, Givloy and Hayn (2002) investigate the rewards for companies meeting or beating analysts' expectations. They find that their results are consistent with expectations management in that the relative frequency of negative earnings surprises is less than the relative frequency of negative forecast errors. This leads them to conclude that companies have dampened down earnings expectations. This they see as consistent with the view that management has successfully managed the expectations of analysts' forecasts so that reported earnings will exceed them. They also find (2002, p. 202) that although the future performance of firms that 'managed' their MBE [meet or beat current analysts' earnings expectations] is inferior to that of firms that did not manage their MBE, they still fared better than firms that failed to meet or beat their earnings expectations.

*Maximising Bonuses*

Bonus schemes are common. In effect, managers are rewarded if a firm meets or exceeds certain earnings figures. These bonuses will vary in type. They may, for example, just depend on reaching a certain earnings figure, or alternatively be more open-ended and relate to a certain proportion of profit or to a profit escalator. In these more sophisticated cases, the more profit earned, the higher the bonuses. However, whatever the exact form of the bonus, there are obvious incentives for managers to try to achieve these bonuses. If the actual profits do not warrant the payment of the bonuses, there are obvious incentives for managers to indulge in earnings management to reach them.

With such powerful managerial incentives at stake it is probably no surprise that many researchers have been keen to test whether there is indeed evidence of earnings management in order to achieve bonus payouts. Probably the most influential study was by Healey (1985). Healey's motivation for his study was that earnings-based bonus schemes were a popular form of managerial reward. He pointed out that almost all US manufacturing firms used bonuses based on earnings to reward their employees. Such schemes are also extremely common in other countries and in other stock market sectors. Healey looked at cases where there were incentives for managers to manipulate earnings upwards so as to meet earnings thresholds for the payment of bonuses. However, he also looked at cases where there were no incentives for managers to manipulate earnings. For example, where earnings already exceeded the threshold for the payment of bonuses, and bonuses were fixed and not related to further improvements in profit performance. He used a standard accruals-based methodology to attempt to detect earnings management. His findings were consistent with earnings management. He states that the existence of bonus schemes appeared to influence the decisions that managers take when choosing accounting policies. In particular, he found: 'There is a strong association between accruals and managers' income-reporting incentives under their bonus contracts. Managers are more likely to choose income-decreasing accruals when their bonus plan upper or lower bounds are binding, and income-increasing accruals when these bounds are not binding' (Healey, 1985, p. 106). In other words, managers will use earnings management strategies commensurate with maximising their bonuses. The exact nature of these strategies will be dependent on the exact nature of the bonus schemes.

Several later studies have built on Healey's work. Broadly, they have confirmed his findings. Gaver, Gaver and Austin (1995) looked at bonus plans for 102 firms across the period 1980–90. They, like Healey, used an accruals-based methodology. Their results are not consistent with a bonus maximisation hypothesis. However, they are consistent with income smoothing. They summarise their results: 'Under this scenario, managers smooth performance to the financial goal established for the target payout from their bonus plan. This typically implies earnings increases in poor performance years, and earnings decreases in exceptionally good years to avoid an increase in their target for the following year' (Gaver, Gaver and Austin, 1995, p. 27). Holthausen, Larcker and Sloan (1995) looked at mainly US manufacturing firms from 1982 to 1983 and then from 1987 to 1990. They found evidence that was consistent with the manipulation of earnings by managers. In particular, they found that managers manipulated earnings downwards when their bonuses were at a maximum.

The final and most recent study is consistent, and finds robust evidence to support Healey (1985). Guidry, Leone and Rock (1999) state that the prior research suggests that reputation, share ownership and bonus compensation induce managers to adopt a variety of earnings management strategies. The authors looked at the results from business units comprising the individual, disaggregated companies rather than the consolidated company results. They took 103, 135 and 115 independent business units during 1995, 1994 and 1993, respectively. They again used an accruals-based approach but at the level of the individual operating unit, rather than at the level of the overall firm. Several alternative strategies to manage earnings were tested, such as income smoothing and bonus maximisation. Their evidence is consistent with business unit managers manipulating earnings so as to maximise their short-term bonuses.

## Maintaining Debt Covenants

When companies borrow money then the lenders often insist that the companies sign debt covenants. These covenants aim to protect the lenders against the borrower getting into difficulties and, therefore, not being able to repay the debts or service the interest repayments. Often there are penalties if the borrower violates these loan covenants. There are thus incentives for managers to avoid breaching the loan covenants.

These incentives have been investigated by many accounting researchers. Two studies are used for illustration here. Defond and Jiambalvo (1994) looked at 94 US firms that had reported violations of their debt covenants. They looked at voluntary manipulations of total accruals (difference between net income and operating trade cash flows) and working capital accruals (sum charged in inventory, trade receivables less accounts payables and other current liabilities). They found substantial evidence of positive earnings management in the year before violation as firms attempted to manipulate their accounting numbers so as to avoid breaching their loan covenants. In the year in which the debt covenants were breached, they found that firms where management had changed or where there was a 'going concern' qualification were significantly more likely to use special items, such as write-downs of fixed assets, goodwill, inventory and accounts receivables. There was thus evidence of 'big bath' accounting.

Sweeney (1994) also examined US companies that had reported violations of their debt covenants. She found that 'managers of firms approaching violations of accounting-based restrictions are more likely to make income-increasing discretionary accounting changes and early adopt income-increasing mandatory accounting changes' (p. 282). She found that these changes were both cash-increasing, but also income-increasing without boosting cash. In five out of the 22 cases that she examined, managers were able to delay default by one accounting period.

## Reducing Government Interference

In certain circumstances, firms may seek to manage their earnings downwards rather than upwards. A good example of this is where firms fear that governments will intervene so as to reduce their long-term earnings. It is, therefore, better in these circumstances for firms to forego short-term profits so that they can maximise long-term profits. I will look at three examples of this: two related studies on regulated industries in the UK by McInnes and the special case of import relief investigations in the USA. McInnes (1990a, b) conducted a longitudinal study of two regulated UK industries. The first one was of the UK gas industry from 1969–74. This study looked at accounting changes and their effects on income in the year of change and also cumulatively. He examined, for example, the depreciation and amortisation policies relating to plant and the non-capitalisation of interest, salaries and loan interest. His findings were consistent with the gas industry attempting to head off government regulation. Thus, he states: 'Nevertheless, the study has provided evidence which is consistent with the argument derived from the positive accounting literature that when there were incentives to provide an improved justification for a price rise in order to increase the gas industry's cash inflows, income-decreasing accounting changes were made and where these incentives did not exist income-decreasing accounting choices were not made' (McInnes, 1990a, p. 326).

In a further study, McInnes (1990b) investigated the South of Scotland Electricity Board (SSEB) from 1978–88. The SSEB had to notify the UK Price Commission at this time if it wanted to increase prices. The Price Commission considered that certain of the SSEB's accounting procedures, such as conservative asset lives, method of depreciation, treatment of interest on borrowings to finance construction work, additional and supplemental depreciation and historical costs, were inappropriate. The accounting policies that were criticised had major income-decreasing effects over the next 10 years. McInnes concludes that: 'the evidence is consistent with the arguments of the positive accounting theorists that firms which are subject to regulation of their prices have incentives to adopt income-decreasing accounting procedures in order to provide a stronger argument for a price rise' (McInnes, 1990b, p. 66).

The third study concerning possible government intervention comes from the USA. It concerns firms that would benefit from import relief (such as tariff increases or quota reductions). Jones (1991) tests whether firms which were being investigated by the US International Trade Commission (ITC) attempted to decrease their earnings through earnings management. The incentives for these firms were that they might increase the likelihood of obtaining import relief or maximise the amount of that relief if they demonstrated poorer results. Jones tested the broad hypothesis that managers of domestic producers that would benefit from import protection make accounting choices that reduce reported earnings during ITC investigation periods as compared to non-investigation periods. Twenty-three firms were studied, using an accruals-based method. Jones found that her results supported the earnings management hypothesis. Managers did make income-decreasing accruals during import relief investigations. In particular, she found that more income-decreasing discretionary accruals were made in the year in which the ITC completed its investigation than might otherwise be expected.

*Changes of Top Management*

When a company's top management changes, there are incentives for the new managers to want to do well. It may, therefore, be in the new managers' interests to blame the outgoing managers and paint them in as black a light as possible. This will have the effect of making the present management look better. The incentives are particularly great when the departing managers are reporting a loss. If the incoming management can make that loss as big as possible, then it will make the incoming management's intended improvements even better. If, in addition, the incoming management can write off future expenses against the loss or write down assets, it can inflate future profits. This strategy of maximising the current year's loss so as to benefit future profits is known as taking a 'big bath'.

Several researchers have looked for empirical evidence of such 'big bath' accounting. We will look at three studies: two from the USA and one from Australia. The first study is by Murphy and Zimmerman (1993), who look at several discretionary variables such as research and development, advertising, capital expenditures and accounting accruals. They find no evidence of earnings management in strongly performing firms. However, where the CEO's departure is preceded by poor performance, they do find that incoming managers use earnings management, in particular, adopting 'big bath' accounting. The second US study was by Pourciau (1993). She looked at 73 changes of CEO in the USA. She hypothesised that CEOs will indulge in earnings management so that profits in the year of the takeover would decrease and that subsequent years' earnings would increase. Her results were consistent with this. In addition, she found that incoming CEOs adopted accounting changes that increased the size of the current year's loss. In particular, they recorded large write-offs and special items in the year of managerial change. This was consistent with the idea of 'big bath' accounting. In an Australian study, Godfrey, Mather and Ramsay (2000) looked at CEO changes in 63 firms. They used the accruals method to determine whether earnings management had taken place. In the year of CEO change, they found evidence consistent with downwards earnings management as expected. They also found evidence in later years of income-increasing strategies, which was also in line with expectations.

*Acquisitions and Share Issues*

When one firm tries to take over another there are incentives for both the bidder and the target to use earnings management. If the target company can demonstrate higher than anticipated earnings, this will mean that the price at which it will be acquired will rise. This will either deter a takeover or ensure that existing shareholders receive more money. For the bidder, there are also incentives. Many companies plan to finance their acquisitions by issuing shares. It is better for a number of reasons if those shares are highly priced. It enables the bidder to finance its acquisition by issuing fewer shares. In effect, this means that the target firm can be acquired more cheaply. In addition, it means that there is less dilution of the current shareholders' voting power and control. Erickson and Wang (1999) explore this issue by looking at the acquisitions of 55 US companies from 1985 to 1990. In all cases, the acquisitions were funded by shares. The authors used an accruals methodology. These results are consistent with earnings management. In the period just before the acquisition, they find evidence that the acquiring firms manage their earnings upwards. This would reduce the number of shares which the acquiring company has to issue.

Another situation in which managers might have incentives to increase earnings so as to increase the share price is where a listed company is making a new equity issue. The company is, in effect, trying to raise money. The incentives are similar to those in takeover situations. If the price of the shares is higher, then it will have to issue fewer shares to raise the same amount. Or alternatively it can issue the same number of shares, but raise more money. Either way it is in the company's interests to have a higher share price. This issue has been investigated in the USA by Shivakumar (2000). The author's sample consisted of 1222 equity offerings from 1983 to 1992. As with most of the earnings management studies, Shivakumar used an accruals-based methodology. The author finds evidence of earnings management at around the time of the equity offer, with net income being abnormally high. In addition, he finds a subsequent decline in net income. However, Shivakumar also finds that investors unravel earnings management before the equity offering by discounting the share price. He concludes that investors, therefore, expect firms to use earnings management and are, therefore, sceptical of pre-issue earnings. If that is so, he argues, then it is logical for companies to inflate their earnings before an equity issue. If they did not they would lose out as investors would discount their shares anyway.

### Avoidance of Earnings Surprises

If a firm has made an unexpectedly large profit or loss it may need to signal that result to the stock market. The incentives for action would seem to be stronger for firms with unexpectedly large losses as the stock market might severely punish the firm's share price. This issue was investigated in the USA by Kasnik and Lev (1995). They looked at 565 companies with earnings surprises in 1992. There were 171 positive earnings surprises and 394 negative earnings surprises. They found evidence that firms attempted to manage the presentation of the news. Firms with negative earnings surprises were more likely to make disclosures. In particular, they found that larger earnings surprises were more likely to be associated with more quantitative and earnings-related warnings.

### 5.3.1.2 Financial Statement Fraud and Corporate Governance Characteristics Studies

#### Effective Internal Controls

The presence of strong controls reduces the possibility of financial malpractice. Brennan and McGrath (2007), for example, found that weak internal control was a factor in all of the 14 European and US scandals which they studied. Bell and Carcello (2000) also found that across 77 fraud cases in the USA, a weak internal control environment was a significant risk factor.

#### Division of Responsibility between Chief Executive and Chairman

Persons (2005) found that fraud likelihood was lower when the chief executive is not chairman of the board across a matched sample of 111 fraud and non-fraud firms. This finding was confirmed by Farber (2005), who found that fraud firms had a higher percentage of CEOs who combined the roles of chairman and board of directors.

#### Audit Committee

The presence of an effective audit committee has also been found to be important in many studies of fraud firms (e.g. Beasley *et al.*, 2000; Brennan and McGrath, 2007; Crutchley,

Jensen and Marshall, 2007; Farber, 2005; Persons, 2005). In particular, a less independent audit committee is less effective at reducing fraud. Beasley *et al.* (2000) find this across three US volatile industries: technology companies, health care and financial services. Crutchley, Jensen and Marshall (2007) found that fewer outsiders on the audit committee increased the chances of an accounting scandal for 97 firms investigated by the SEC. Farber (2005) finds that in 87 fraud firms there are fewer audit committee meetings, and fewer financial experts on the committee. Persons (2005) finds that fraud likelihood across 111 fraud and non-fraud matched firms is lower when the audit committee has a longer tenure, when the audit committee is solely comprised of independent directors and when they have a smaller number of other directorships. Finally, Brennan and McGrath (2007) find that a weak audit committee was implicated in the 14 frauds they investigated. The only doubting voice was Beasley (1996), who only tested the presence or not of an audit committee. He found that it did not significantly affect the likelihood of financial statement fraud. However, this study is much older than the others and much more basic in its approach. Collectively, the evidence clearly does suggest that the presence of an effective audit committee (i.e. longer tenure, independent, less burdened, staffed with finance experts and meeting regularly) does reduce the likelihood of a major accounting scandal.

### Independent Boards of Directors

The higher the number of outside, non-executive directors the more independent a company's board of directors is perceived to be. Several studies have found a statistical relationship between the presence of external board members and the likelihood of fraud (Beasley, 1996; Beasley *et al.*, 2000; Brennan and McGrath, 2007; Farber, 2005). Beasley (1996) and Beasley *et al.* (2000) found that non-fraud firms had a significantly higher percentage of outside members than fraud firms. Meanwhile, Farber (2005) found that fraud firms had both a small number and a lesser percentage of outside board members than non-fraud firms. Finally, Brennan and McGrath (2007) found that a weak board of directors was a factor in 21 % of the financial statement frauds they studied.

## 5.4 CONCLUSION

This chapter looks at the evidence for creative accounting both in the descriptive studies, which looked at instances of creative accounting in individual companies, and statistical studies that investigated creative accounting using large data sets.

The descriptive studies were found to:

- give frequent examples of creative accounting techniques;
- document actual companies that had used specific techniques;
- show that in many high-profile corporate collapses creative accounting had played a major role;
- fraud was frequent, with financial statement fraud being less common, but greater in magnitude. Financial statement fraud was carried out mostly by relatively small companies, often by senior management, and these companies were characterised by poor corporate governance and complicit or lax auditors.

The statistical studies demonstrated that creative accounting, or earnings management as these studies prefer to call it, occurred across a range of situations:

- Companies were found to income smooth (i.e. increase profits in bad years, but decrease them in good years).
- Managers used earnings management to meet their own earnings forecasts and those of analysts. This happened particularly when companies' actual earnings were low.
- Companies were shown to manage their earnings so that they could maximise their bonuses.
- Managers manipulated company earnings and balance sheets so as not to breach legal covenants.
- Those companies that were subject to government regulations were more likely to decrease earnings so as to ward off government price controls.
- Where top management changed, incoming managers were likely to decrease income in the year of the takeover so that future profits could be enhanced.
- When one company took over another it was likely that earnings of both the acquirer and the target would increase. In addition, new share issues were likely to occur when a company's earnings were high.
- Firms that failed to meet analysts' expectations were most likely to issue discretionary disclosures prior to publication of the earnings announcement.

Generally, therefore, there is comprehensive evidence both from the study of individual companies and also from the study of companies, in aggregate, of the existence of creative accounting. In addition, the findings from an investigation of the relationship between financial statement fraud and corporate governance characteristics found that effective internal controls, a division of responsibility between chief executive and chairman, an effective audit committee and an independent board of directors all reduced the risk of fraud.

# REFERENCES

Accountants Joint Disciplinary Scheme, Polly Peck Investigation (2002), *Statement of Facts*, March.

Association of Certified Fraud Examiners (2002), *Report to the Nation on Occupational Fraud and Abuse*, ACFE, Austin, TX.

Bartov, E., Givoly, D. and Hayn, C. (2002), 'The rewards to meeting or beating earnings expectations', *Journal of Accounting and Economics*, **33**, 173–204.

Beasley, M.S. (1996), 'An empirical analysis of the relation between the board of director composition and financial statement fraud', *The Accounting Review*, **71**(4), 443–465.

Beasley, M.S., Carcello, J.V. and Hermanson, D.R. (1999), *Fraudulent Financial Reporting 1987–1997: An Analysis of U.S. Public Companies*. Research commissioned by the Committee of Sponsoring Organizations of the Treadway Commission.

Beasley, M.S., Carcello, J.V., Hermanson, D.R. and Lapides, P. (2000), 'Fraudulent financial reporting: consideration of industry traits and corporate governance mechanisms', *Accounting Horizons*, **14**(4), 441–454.

Bell, T.B. and Carcello, J.V. (2000), 'A decision aid for assessing the likelihood of fraudulent financial reporting', *Auditing: A Journal of Practice and Theory*, **19**(1), 169–184.

Brennan, N.M. and McGrath, M. (2007), 'Financial statement fraud: some lessons from US and European case studies', *Australian Accounting Review*, **17**(2), 49–61.

Brown, L.D. (2001), 'A temporal analysis of earnings surprises: profits versus losses', *Journal of Accounting Research*, **39**(2), 221–241.

Clarke, F.L. and Dean, G.W. (2007), *Indecent Disclosure: Gilding the Corporate Lily*, Cambridge University Press, Melbourne.

Clarke, F., Dean, G. and Oliver, K. (2003), *Corporate Collapse. Accounting, Regulatory and Ethical Failure*, Cambridge University Press, Cambridge.

County Natwest WoodMac (1991), *Company Pathology*, County Natwest WoodMac, London.

Crutchley, C.E., Jensen, M.R.H. and Marshall, B.B. (2007), Climate for scandal: corporate environments that contribute to accounting fraud, *The Financial Review*, **42**, 53–73.

Dascher, P.E. and Malcolm, R.E. (1970), 'A note on income smoothing in the chemical industry', *Journal of Accounting Research*, Autumn, 253–259.

DeFond, M.L. and Jiambalvo, J. (1994), 'Debt covenant effects and the manipulation of accruals', *Journal of Accounting and Economics*, **17**(4), 145–176.

Erickson, M. and Wang, S. (1999), 'Earnings management by acquiring firms in stock-for-stock mergers', *Journal of Accounting and Economics*, **27**, 149–176.

Farber, D.B. (2005), 'Restoring trust after fraud: does corporate governance matter?', *The Accounting Review*, **80**(2), 539–561.

Gaver, J.J., Gaver, K.M. and Austin, J.R. (1995), 'Additional evidence on bonus plans and income management', *Journal of Accounting and Economics*, **19**, 3–28.

Godfrey, J., Mather, P. and Ramsay, R. (2000), 'Earnings and impression management in financial reports: the case of CEO changes', School of Accounting and Finance, Working Paper No. 68.

Griffiths, I. (1986), *Creative Accounting*, Sidgwick and Jackson, London.

Griffiths, I. (1995), *New Creative Accounting*, Macmillan, London.

Guidry, F., Leone, A.J. and Rock, S. (1999), 'Earnings-based bonus plans and earnings management by business-unit managers', *Journal of Accounting and Economics*, **26**, 113–142.

Healey, P.M. (1985), 'The effect of bonus schemes on accounting decisions', *Journal of Accounting and Economics*, **7**, 85–107.

Holthausen, R.W., Larcker, D.F. and Sloan, R.G. (1995), 'Annual bonus schemes and the manipulation of earnings', *Journal of Accounting and Economics*, **19**, 29–74.

Johannes, L. (2000) 'SEC says managers at Boston Scientific created fake sales', *The Wall Street Journal*, August 22.

Jones, J.J. (1991), 'Earnings management during import relief investigations', *Journal of Accounting Research*, **29**(2), 193–227.

Jones, M.J. (1992), 'Accounting for growth: surviving the accounting jungle', *Management Accounting*, February, 20–22.

Kasnik, R. (1999), 'On the association between voluntary disclosure and earnings management', *Journal of Accounting Research*, **37**(1), 57–81.

Kasnik, R. and Lev, B. (1995), 'To warn or not to warn: management disclosures in the face of an earnings surprise', *The Accounting Review*, **70**(1), 113–134.

McBarnet, D. and Whelan, C. (1999), *Creative Accounting and the Cross-eyed Javelin Thrower*, John Wiley & Sons Ltd, Chichester.

McInnes, W.M. (1990a), 'A longitudinal study of accounting changes: the UK gas industry 1969–1974', *Accounting and Business Research*, **20**(80), 315–327.

McInnes, W.M. (1990b), 'Further evidence on accounting choices: the South of Scotland Electricity Board, 1978–1988', *Accounting and Business Research*, **21**(81), 57–66.

Moses, O.D. (1987), 'Income smoothing and incentives: empirical tests using accounting changes', *The Accounting Review*, **LXII**, 358–379.

Mulford, C. and Comiskey, E. (2002), *The Financial Numbers Game. Detecting Creative Accounting Practices*, John Wiley & Sons, Inc., New York.

Mulford, C. and Comiskey, E. (2005), *Creative Cash Flow Reporting. Uncovering Sustainable Financial Reporting*, John Wiley & Sons, Inc., New York.

Murphy, K.J. and Zimmerman, J.L. (1993), 'Financial performance surrounding CEO turnover', *Journal of Accounting and Economics*, **16**, 273–315.

Paiste, D. (2009), 'SEC issues final order in Tyco case', *New Hampshire Union Leader*, 15 July.

Payne, J.L. and Robb, S.W.G. (1999), 'Earnings management: the effect of ex ante earnings expectations', *Journal of Accounting, Auditing and Finance*, 371–392.

Persons, O.S. (2005), 'The relation between the new corporate governance rules and the likelihood of financial statement fraud', *Review of Accounting and Finance*, **4**(2), 125–148.

Pijper, T. (1993), *Creative Accounting. The Effectiveness of Financial Reporting in the UK*, Macmillan, London.

Pourciau, S. (1993), 'Earnings management and non-routine executive changes', *Journal of Accounting and Economics*, **16**, 317–336.

Shivakumar, L. (2000), 'Do firms mislead investors by overstating earnings before seasoned equity offerings?', *Journal of Accounting and Economics*, **29**, 339–371.

Smith, T. (1991), *Accounting for Growth. Stripping the Camouflage from Company Accounts*, Century Books, London.

Sweeney, A.P. (1994), 'Debt covenant violations and managers' accounting responses', *Journal of Accounting and Economics*, **17**(1), 281–308.

Trueman, B. and Titman, S. (1988), 'An explanation for income smoothing', *Journal of Accounting Research*, **26**, 127–143.

UBS Phillips & Drew (1991), *Accounting for Growth*, UBS Phillips & Drew, London.

Wells, J.T. (2005), *Principles of Fraud Examination*, John Wiley & Sons, Inc., New Jersey.

# 6

## Impression Management

### Michael Jones

## 6.1 INTRODUCTION

A company's financial statements are presented to the shareholders in an annual report. This annual report provides ample opportunity for management to package the numbers and to present them in a way that gives users a particular impression of the firms' results. This management of the presentational aspects of the annual report (such as accounting narratives, graphs and photographs) is called impression management. Like creative accounting, impression management is not illegal.

Impression management can be seen as a basic human trait. When we go for an interview or go on a date we try to give a favourable impression of ourselves. After all, we want the job or a second meeting. As Schlenker (1980, p. v) put it: 'Impression management, or image control, is a central aspect of interpersonal relations. Consciously or unconsciously, people attempt to control images in real or imagined social interactions.' Impression management can be traced back to the work of Goffman (1959).

Managers thus try to present their results in the most favourable light. Three major methods by which they do this, as Figure 6.1 shows, are accounting narratives, graphs and photographs. Accounting narratives are the written parts of the annual report, such as the Chairman's Statement (or President's Letter in the USA) or the Business Review (Management Discussion and Analysis in the USA) where managers can discuss the events of the year.

There is ample opportunity for managers to use these accounting narratives in a biased or selective way. They are the way in which managers tell the story. Graphs are popularly used in annual reports as they enrich the content and provide a quick overview of what has happened. They may also be used to convey a certain impression of a company through selectivity or bias. And, finally, photographs can be used to enliven an annual report and to 'set the scene'. They provide the background 'mood music' against which the report can be judged.

### 6.1.1 Accounting Narratives

Over the last 20 years, accounting narratives have steadily grown in importance. In many countries, such as the UK and the USA, the narrative sections of the annual report (such as the Chairman's Statement and Business Review (BR) in the UK and the President's Letter

*Creative Accounting, Fraud and International Accounting Scandals*    Edited by Michael Jones
© 2011 Michael Jones. Published by John Wiley & Sons, Ltd

---

**(i) Accounting narratives**

These are the written, qualitative parts of the annual reports. Managers may use bias or selectivity to convey their desired impression of the year's results.

**(ii) Graphs**

Graphs are a popular method of displaying data. Management may use selectivity, measurement distortion or presentational enhancement to convey their desired impression of the year's results.

**(iii) Photographs**

Photographs can help to contextualise a firm's performance. They can be used to convey the manager's desired impression of the firm through image management.

---

**Figure 6.1**   Methods of impression management

and Management Discussion and Analysis (MDA) in the USA) now take up more space than traditional financial information (Arthur Andersen, 2001). These narratives are very influential. They enable management to tell the story of the company's year to shareholders. Not only are they widely used by both private and institutional investors (see, for example, Bartlett and Chandler, 1997), but they have been shown by Abrahamson and Amir (1996) to influence investors' decisions.

Accounting narratives are particularly easy to use for impression management because typically they are not audited. It is thus easy for managers to manage their presentation. At most, these sections are reviewed by auditors to see that the text is materially consistent with the accounts. In addition, accounting narratives typically give a managerial assessment of the financial statements. Such assessments are inherently subjective.

As Figure 6.2 shows, there are several ways in which management may use accounting narratives for impression management. In essence, they seek to emphasise good news, but de-emphasise bad news. This can be done in a variety of ways. First, managers may seek simply to report more positive news items than negative news items. Thus, managers might report a new sales contract in Japan, but omit to mention that they have lost a contract in Germany. Second, managers may baffle readers by their use of language. Good news may be reported in a straightforward way such as 'we have made a record profit'. However, bad news may be reported less clearly, such as 'This year we have not performed as well as we would have anticipated'. Third, profitable and unprofitable companies may use different reporting strategies. For example, well-performing companies may use more 'hard numbers' to reinforce their 'stories' than poor performers. And, finally, managers may use attribution in order to attribute good news to themselves, but attribute bad news to the environment. Thus, good news may be attributed to the hard work of the management team, but bad news attributed to a world recession.

Below I look at some of the academic research into accounting narratives. I concentrate on a few studies so as to give a flavour of the nature of the impression management.

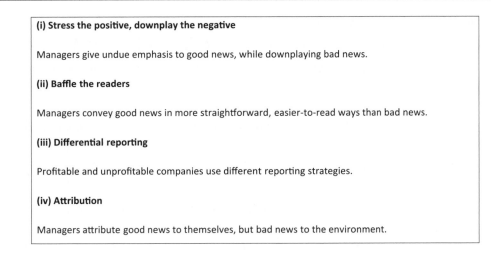

**(i) Stress the positive, downplay the negative**

Managers give undue emphasis to good news, while downplaying bad news.

**(ii) Baffle the readers**

Managers convey good news in more straightforward, easier-to-read ways than bad news.

**(iii) Differential reporting**

Profitable and unprofitable companies use different reporting strategies.

**(iv) Attribution**

Managers attribute good news to themselves, but bad news to the environment.

**Figure 6.2**    Methods of impression management in accounting narratives

Typically, these studies look at a sizeable number of companies and then statistically test the aggregated data.

### 6.1.1.1    *Stress the Positive, Downplay the Negative*

This basic theme underpins most studies into impression management in annual reports. It is a common management technique of presenting both past and predicted events. Pava and Epstein (1993) look at the management discussion and analysis sections of US corporate annual reports in 1989. They find that companies are more than twice as likely correctly to predict positive future anticipated results rather than negative ones. In another example, in the UK, Morrow (2005) looked at narrative reporting in 30 football clubs' annual reports. Despite poor financial performance by many clubs, he found that only 14 % of 3317 textual units were coded as negative. One club, Leeds United, was in deep financial trouble in 2002, yet there were twice as many positive as negative statements. Morrow comments: 'In view of the financial position and performance being reported, it is somewhat difficult to comprehend on what basis the directors saw so many opportunities for positive narrative comments' (Morrow, 2005, p. 39).

Meanwhile, in Australia, Deegan and Gordon (1996, p. 198) found that the environmental disclosure practices of Australian companies 'are typically self-laudatory, with little or no negative disclosures being made by all firms in the study'.

In particular, as Figure 6.3, on the next page shows, they found that 25 randomly selected Australian companies were more inclined to use positive than negative words. In 1991, for example, companies used 105 mean positive words, but only seven mean negative words. Across the five years 151 mean positive words were used, but only seven negative ones. In a related study, Deegan and Gordon found that 71 Australian companies used 4.4 mean positive words, but only 0.7 negative words. They felt that these firms considered 'the benefits from being objective were more than offset by potential negative effects' from the disclosure of bad news.

The number of positive and negative words disclosed in the annual reports of 25 Australian companies was recorded by two Australian researchers (Craig Deegan and Ben Gordon) from 1980 to 1991. As the figures below show, they found scarcely any evidence that bad news was disclosed.

|                            | 1980 | 1985 | 1988 | 1991 |
|----------------------------|------|------|------|------|
| Mean positive disclosure   | 12   | 14   | 20   | 105  |
| Mean negative disclosure   | 0    | 0    | 0    | 7    |

They conclude: "The environmental disclosures are typically self-laudatory, with little or no negative disclosures being made by all firms in the study."

**Figure 6.3**  Environmental accounting in Australia

*Source:* Deegan and Gordon (1996, p. 198). Adapted from Jones (2006, p. 323).

### 6.1.1.2  *Baffle the Readers*

This general category covers two main ways in which managers convey their accounting messages: technical language and language that is difficult to read.

*Technical Language*

The company may present bad or unpleasant news in less than transparent technical language. Enron's (2000) accounts demonstrate this.

Figure 6.4 shows it is not obvious from this note that Enron had built up huge debts amounting to $80 billion. The language used is rather complex, and buried on page 48 of the accounts. It would have taken a very astute investor to detect that Enron had substantial, undisclosed off-balance sheet liabilities which would contribute to the company's demise.

Enron is a guarantor on certain liabilities of unconsolidated equity affiliates and other companies totalling approximately $ 1,863 million at December 31, 2001, including $ 538 million related to EOTT trade obligations [EOTT Energy Partners]. The EOTT letters of credit and guarantees of trade obligation are secured by the assets of EOTT. Enron has also guaranteed $ 386 million in lease obligations for which it has been indemnified by an "Investment Grade" company. Management does not consider it likely that Enron would be required to perform or otherwise incur any losses associated with the above guarantees. In addition, certain commitments have been made related to capital expenditures and equity investments planned in 2001.

**Figure 6.4**  Extract from Enron's Notes to the Accounts

*Source:* Enron, Annual Report (2000), Notes to the Accounts, p. 48.

Several authors have drawn attention to the use of technical language by companies which appears to distract readers' attention away from their poor performance. We take two examples. First, Aerts (1994) studied Belgian annual reports. He shows that, in general, managers use technical accounting terms to explain negative performance, but express positive performance in more clear, cause-and-effect terminology. Second, Courtis, in a series of articles, argues that narratives are used for obfuscation (i.e. burying adverse or negative news through more difficult writing styles).[1]

*Difficult to Read Language*

Companies with poor results have been found to have less readable accounts than those with better results. Smith and Taffler (1992), for example, compare the readability of failed and non-failed companies. They find that company failure is significantly correlated with more difficult language. Overall, they find that 'poor readability is associated with poor performance and ease of readability with financial success' (1992, p. 86).

### 6.1.1.3  Differential Reporting

Profitable firms that have good results report in different ways from companies that are unprofitable and have bad news to report. They tend to concentrate on different things and to present their news in different ways. Thus, Clarke (1997, p. 36) finds that companies with negative results focus on the environment, target markets and emotive words rather than on company action and performance indicators.

Meanwhile, Clatworthy and Jones (2006) focus on the Chairman's Statements of 50 UK listed companies which reported improved performance and 50 UK listed companies with declining performance. They investigate a range of textual characteristics such as length of narrative, number of key performance indicators, number of quantitative references, number of personal references, number of passive sentences and number of future-orientated words. They find that managers are selective in their narratives and, in particular, that profitable companies more clearly and specifically report their past results whereas unprofitable companies prefer to focus on the future rather than dwell on the past. These results confirm Thomas's (1997) finding that in their written texts, companies reporting success use the active voice whereas companies reporting failure use the passive voice.

### 6.1.1.4  Attribution

Attribution studies began in the 1980s. They investigated the tendency of managements to take credit themselves for good news, but to blame external factors for any bad news. Thus, increased profits are attributed to management's efforts whereas decreased profits are attributed to the environment. Many studies have demonstrated this attribution effect. Two studies are illustrative: one from the 1980s and one from 2003. Staw, McKechnie and Puffer (1983) looked at the annual reports of 49 US companies, reporting increases of more than 50 % in earnings per share and of 32 firms with a decrease of more than 50 % in earnings per share. They then investigated the causal attributions made by these companies in their

---

[1] See, for example, Courtis (1998).

letters to shareholders. They attributed the explanations which companies gave to either internal or external factors.

**Internal Credit:** 'Our U.S. earnings advanced primarily because we did what we knew we had to . . .' (Johns-Manville Corporation, 1978).

**External Blame:** 'Questor Education Products turned in disappointing results, partially due to the erratic purchasing pattern which emerged in the toy industry' (Questor Corporation, 1978).

In the first case, Johns-Manville Corporation is taking credit for a good performance (internal attribution) while in the second case, Questor Corporation is blaming the environment for bad news (Staw, McKechnie & Puffer, 1983, p. 587).

Overall, high- and low-performing companies were found to take the credit for any good news, but blamed the environment for bad news. The overall finding was expressed thus: 'Letters to shareholders were found to show strong evidence of self-serving attributions, and these attributions took both an enhancing and defensive form. Self-serving attributions appeared to be convincing to the investing public, since the use of these attributions was associated with subsequent improvements in stock price. It also appeared that self-serving attributions were a form of impression management rather than a genuine expression of optimism, since enhancement was associated with subsequent selling of stock by corporate officers' (Staw, McKechnie & Puffer, 1983, p. 582).

Clatworthy and Jones (2003) was a more recent study, which once more tested attribution theory. They looked at the 50 top UK and 50 bottom UK companies as ranked by percentage change in profit before taxation. The companies' Chairman's Statements were analysed into good news and bad news using keywords and sentences. They found that top-performing companies and bottom-performing companies reported more good keywords than bad keywords. In fact, despite their poor performance the bottom 50 companies reported twice as many mean positive keywords as negative ones. Good performers were 10 times more likely to credit good news to themselves not the environment, but three times more likely to attribute bad news to the environment not themselves. This pattern was repeated for bad performers, with poor performers seven times more likely to take the credit for any good news and 1.4 times more likely to blame the environment for bad news.

They conclude as follows: 'The findings suggest that both groups of companies prefer to emphasise the positive aspects of their performance. In addition, both groups prefer to take credit for good news themselves, while blaming the external environment for bad news. Thus, despite reporting on markedly different financial performance, management approach it in the same self-serving way' (Clatworthy and Jones, 2003, p. 171).

### 6.1.2 Graphs

Most modern annual reports contain graphs. These graphs may present a company's key financial variables (such as sales, profits, earnings per share or dividends per share). Or alternatively they may present other financial or non-financial variables. These graphs are very effective methods of presenting financial data. They are more user-friendly than the traditional table. They provide oases of colour and interest in what otherwise would be fairly staid financial documents. In addition, they are eye-catching and synthesise data effectively.

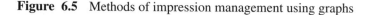

**(i) Selectivity**

This involves deliberately choosing graphs which will give a favourable impression of a company. For example, graphs of profit may be included when the company makes a profit but omitted when it makes a loss.

**(ii) Measurement distortion**

This is where graphs are drawn so as not to accurately represent the underlying numbers. Generally, the graph trend will be exaggerated to produce a graph which presents the company's performance in a more favourable way than is warranted.

**(iii) Presentational enhancement**

The way in which the graph is designed serves to give a more favourable impression of a company's performance than is warranted.

**Figure 6.5**   Methods of impression management using graphs

For the creative manager two key advantages of graphical presentation are that graphs are non-audited and that they present opportunities for creative management. Typically, most graphs are presented by management voluntarily. They are not, therefore, part of a company's mandatory disclosures. These graphs are not, therefore, prescribed nor are they audited.

This presents management with opportunities to indulge in impression management. There are three main types: selectivity, measurement distortion and presentational enhancement (see Figure 6.5). Examples are presented later in this section where management quite legally use the opportunities presented by graphs to portray their financial performance in a flattering way. Selectivity occurs when a company chooses to include, or not include, a graph in its annual report contingent upon the company's underlying performance. So, for example, a company may have included profit graphs when profit increased over the year, but excluded them when profit decreased. Measurement distortion is where the graphs are included, but the figures on the graphs do not accurately represent the underlying financial data. And, finally, presentation enhancement occurs when graphs are constructed so as to emphasise certain design features so as to present a company's performance in a more favourable way than warranted. These three forms of graphical impression management are discussed below. Illustrative examples are presented and, then, some academic evidence is discussed. The academic studies typically use large samples of companies, analyse the way in which these companies use graphs and then statistically test whether impression management has occurred.

### 6.1.2.1  Selectivity

Selectivity is where companies deliberately choose graphs so that they will convey a favourable impression of the company. A simple example of graphical selectivity is given

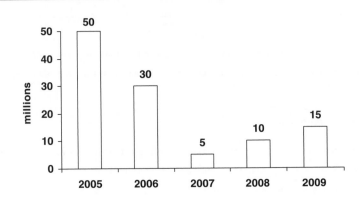

**Figure 6.6a**

below. Usually, companies present five years' graphs in their annual reports. When they use other reporting patterns, then selectivity may be present. In this example, Graphco has the following set of profits for the last five years. Under Figure 6.6a, there is no selectivity and all five years' graphs are presented. Under Figure 6.6b, however, Graphco only present three years' graphs.

    2009    £15 million profit
    2008    £10 million profit
    2007    £5 million profit
    2006    £30 million profit
    2005    £50 million profit

When we include all five years in Figure 6.6a, the company's performance does not look impressive. Indeed, it is clear that the company is doing less well in 2009 than it did in 2005 and 2006.

The company might, therefore, prefer to be selective and only draw three years 2004–6 to present a better trend as in Figure 6.6b.

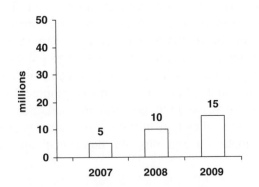

**Figure 6.6b**

Now, if Graphco produced a loss in 2009, it might be tempted not to include a graph at all!

Selectivity of graphs in annual reports has been the topic of many academic studies. Three are illustrative. First, Beattie and Jones (1992a) look at the annual reports of 240 large UK companies for 1989. They find that the decision to use graphs is significantly associated with the increase or decrease in earnings per share over the current year and over five years. This was true for the use of sales, profit before tax, earnings per share and dividend per share graphs. They also find that the decision to use profit before tax, earnings per share and dividend per share graphs is significantly associated with the change in that particular variable. This pattern of results has proved reasonably robust across countries and across time.

Second, the same authors conduct a six-country study of graph usage in annual reports of the top 50 companies in Australia, France, Germany, the Netherlands, the UK and the USA. The authors find: 'some evidence that Australian, French, German, U.K. and U.S. companies were more likely to include graphs when they had "favourable" rather than "unfavourable" financial performance' (Beattie and Jones, 1996, p. 54). This was particularly true in France, Germany and the Netherlands.

Finally, Beattie and Jones (2000) look at the annual reports of 137 top UK companies that were in continuous existence from 1988 to 1992. They 'find strong evidence that the selective use of graphs (the primary graphical choice) is related to corporate performance, especially income and EPS, measured in terms of both the direction of change and the percentage change in the latest year. This finding is consistent with the manipulation hypothesis that financial graphs in corporate annual reports are used to "manage" the impression of company performance portrayed' (Beattie and Jones, 2000, pp. 224–225). An investigation of earnings per share graphs gives a flavour of their results. In 78 cases where companies started or stopped reporting earnings per share graphs, there were 29 starts and 49 stops. While 26 out of the 29 starts showed an increase in EPS, 37 out of the 49 stops were related to decreased EPS.

### 6.1.2.2 Measurement Distortion

Measurement distortion occurs when the graph's physical dimensions do not accurately reflect the underlying numerical data. This may lead to a rising trend in a graph's performance being exaggerated or a declining trend being understated. If a company's results, for example, rise from 10 to 50 over five years (see Figure 6.7) then one would expect

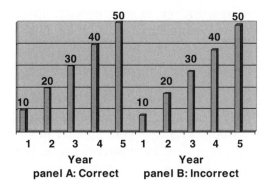

**Figure 6.7**   Illustration of measurement distortion

the columns to increase fivefold; if they increase by more, graphical distortion will have occurred. In the case of Figure 6.7 this distortion is +25 %.

With reference to panel B:

$$\text{Graph Discrepancy Index (GDI)} = \left(\frac{a}{b} - 1\right) \times 100\,\%$$

$$a = \left(\frac{4.8 - 0.8}{0.8}\right) (\text{cm}) \times 100\,\% = 500\,\%$$

$$b = \left(\frac{50 - 10}{10}\right) (\text{cm}) \times 100\,\% = 400\,\%$$

$$\text{thus, GDI} = \left\{\frac{500}{400} - 1\right\} \times 100\,\% = +25\,\%$$

In Figure 6.8, on the next page, three examples are taken from a UK company, Morgan Crucible's 1989 report. In each case, there are measurement distortions: for sales it is +100 %, for profit before tax +6 % and for EPS +23 %.

Once more academics have looked at the topic of measurement distortion in annual reports and have found it to be pervasive. Two illustrative examples will suffice. Beattie and Jones (1992a) looked at measurement distortion in 240 large UK companies' annual reports. Over 465 graphs, they found a mean measurement distortion of +10.7 %. Based on material distortions (distortions over 5 %), they found a discrepancy of +34.3 %. Beattie and Jones (1996) looked at measurement distortion across six important countries. They found material distortions in every country, particularly in France, the UK and the USA.

Measurement distortions can be caused by poor draughtsmanship, but also by the use of certain graphical techniques, such as a non-zero axis. This truncates the Y axis and makes graphical trends look more pronounced than they actually are. The example of earnings per share for T.I.P. Europe is given from its 1989 annual report (see Figure 6.9 on p. 108). This non-zero axis causes T.I.P. Europe's EPS graph to have a +720 % measurement distortion. The actual increase in EPS has thus been grossly exaggerated.

### 6.1.2.3  *Presentational Enhancement*

Presentational enhancement is where undue prominence is given to a particular aspect of the graph. So, for example, colour might be used on the final year's column in a five-year time series trend in order to highlight that particular year's performance. There are many other different types of presentational enhancement. I illustrate three different types below.

In Figure 6.10 on p. 109, there is an example from Devenish (J.A.) 1989 annual report. If we take earnings per share, for example, it has increased from 8.54p to 24.65p. This is an increase of 189 %. In other words, EPS have gone up three times. However, because a 3D pictorial symbol of a lager bottle is used, the apparent increase is much more dramatic. The reader is led to believe that the increase in the variables is much more impressive than it actually is.

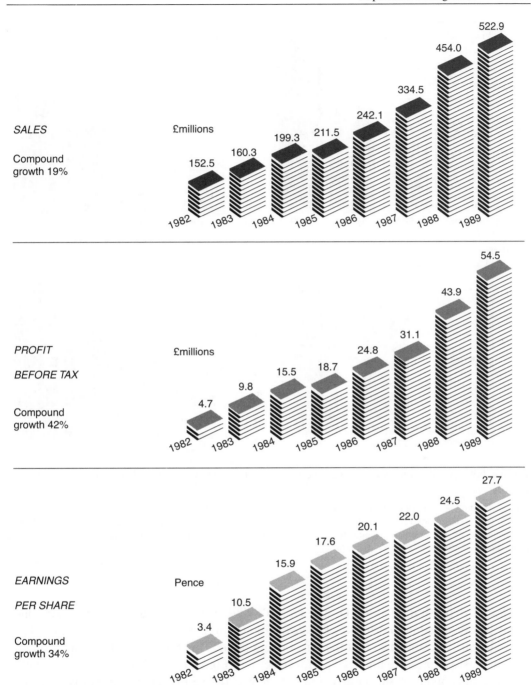

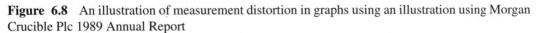

**Figure 6.8** An illustration of measurement distortion in graphs using an illustration using Morgan Crucible Plc 1989 Annual Report

*Source:* Beattie, V. and Jones, M.J. (1992b), *The Communication of Information using Graphs in Corporate Annual Reports*, The Chartered Association of Certified Accountants, Reference Report 31. This research was funded and published by the Certified Accountants Educational Trust (CAET). Extracts are reproduced with ACCA's kind permission.

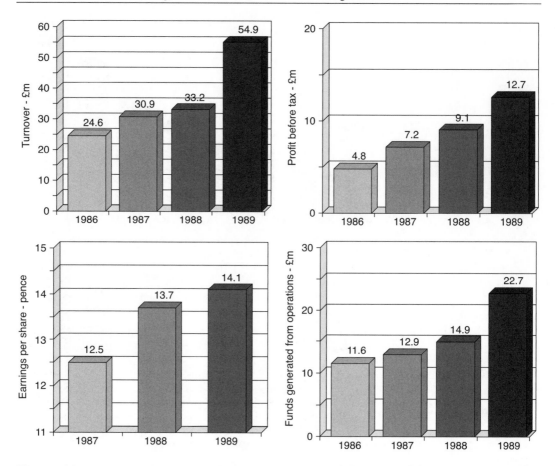

**Figure 6.9**   An illustration of measurement distortion in graphs using T.I.P. Europe's 1989 Annual Report

*Source:* Beattie, V. and Jones, M.J. (1992b), *The Communication of Information using Graphs in Corporate Annual Reports*, The Chartered Association of Certified Accountants, Reference Report 31. This research was funded and published by the Certified Accountants Educational Trust (CAET). Extracts are reproduced with ACCA's kind permission.

The third illustration is of Dowty Group's dividends per share, earnings per share, profit before taxation and turnover (sales) graphs for 1989 reproduced on p. 111. They are judiciously arranged so that there is a rising trend. This reinforces the impression of a tremendously impressive financial performance (see Figure 6.11). There is also a conflation of pence and pounds. A substantive impression of a 20-year trend in the graphs is presented. If, however, the graphs were arranged in reverse order, the performance would look far less impressive!!

Finally, in Figure 6.12 on p. 111 I present the example of an Australian company, Homestate Gold of Australia Ltd. This company uses gold coins to present its operating profit. However, naturally the eye is attracted upwards. As a consequence, we look at the top of the 1991 pile of coins. The loss is thus de-emphasised.

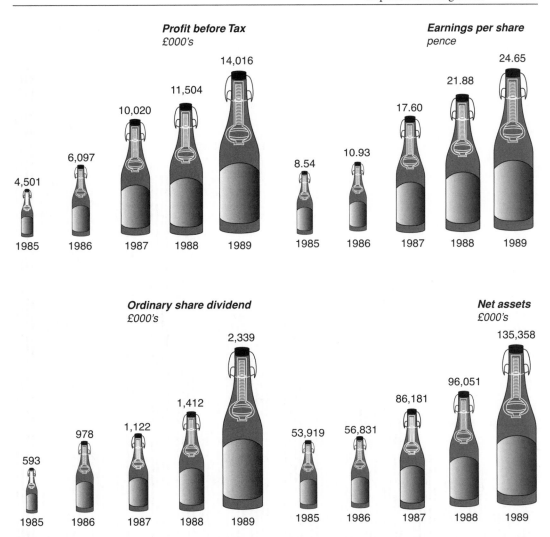

**Figure 6.10** An illustration of presentational enhancement in graphs using Devenish (J.A.) 1989 Annual Report

*Source:* Beattie, V. and Jones, M.J. (1992b), *The Communication of Information using Graphs in Corporate Annual Reports*, The Chartered Association of Certified Accountants, Reference Report 31. This research was funded and published by the Certified Accountants Educational Trust (CAET). Extracts are reproduced with ACCA's kind permission.

Overall, presentational enhancement is common in annual reports. For example, in a study of the graphical reporting practices of 240 corporate annual reports, in 1989, Beattie and Jones (1994) found that, out of 129 companies, in eight cases (6 %) the colour of the columns progressively darkened with time, in 16 cases (12 %) the colour of the last year's individual column was darker than the prior years, all of which were the same colour and in 18 cases (14 %) the colour of the last year's column was a different hue to the other years. In all these cases, the effect was to draw attention to the last year's results.

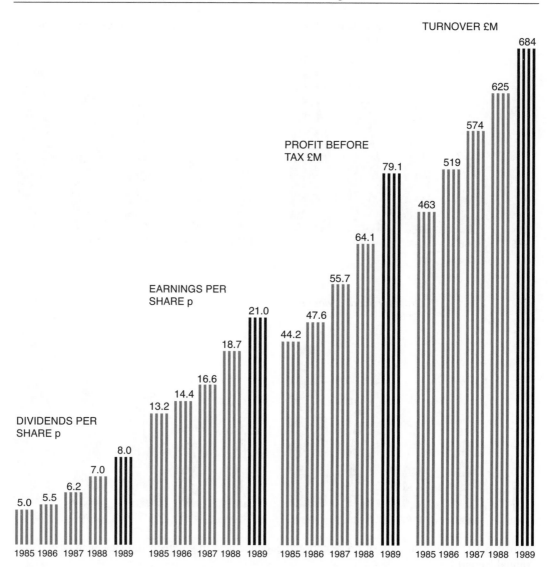

**Figure 6.11** An illustration of presentation management in graphs using Dowty Group's 1989 Annual Report

*Source:* Beattie, V. and Jones, M.J. (1992b), *The Communication of Information using Graphs in Corporate Annual Reports*, The Chartered Association of Certified Accountants, Reference Report 31. This research was funded and published by the Certified Accountants Educational Trust (CAET). Extracts are reproduced with ACCA's kind permission.

### 6.1.2.4 *Photographs*

Photographs are a bit like mood music: they set the tone of the annual reports. Lee (1994, p. 216) observed, after studying 25 British industrial companies in 1965 and 1988, that annual reports 'have become mechanisms to communicate stylish images of corporate identity' instead of being merely vehicles which communicated messages about corporate financial performance. The provision of financial data Lee believed had taken second place to the

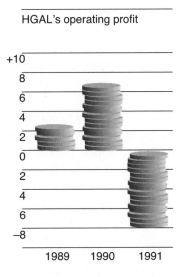

**HGAL's operating profit**

**Figure 6.12**   An illustration of presentational enhancement using HGAL's 1991 Annual Report

*Source:* Beattie, V. and Jones, M.J. (1996), *Financial Graphs in Corporate Annual Reports: A Review of Practice in Six Countries.*

disclosure of voluntary information. As such, there was a danger that the annual report had become part of the 'public relations arm of the very large corporations' (Lee, 1994, p. 231).

The basic idea is to convey a certain impression of the company by the use of photographic imagery. Thus, a company selling alcohol or soft drinks is likely to have photographs of young people in its annual report. There is thus an 'active management of the corporate image' (Hopwood, 1996, p. 56).

Several studies in 1996 demonstrate the growing importance of photographic imagery in annual reports. First, McKinstry (1996) examined the annual reports of Burton's plc, a UK company, from 1930 to 1994. From 1981 to 1994 Burton's used photographs and other design features to increase the attractiveness of its annual report. McKinstry comments (1996, p. 107) that 'every conceivable design device has been used by the company and its design contractors to portray it and its top managers in the best possible light, and to influence the perceptions of the City and the individual investor'. Meanwhile, Graves, Flesher and Jordan (1996) investigate the way in which US annual reports since the 1960s have included colour photographs and other novelty formats. They suggest that the modern age is dominated by television, and television advertising. In such a world, it is natural for companies to adopt similar visual symbols. Finally, Preston, Wright and Young (1996) explicitly link photographs and impression management, suggesting that photographic imagery is a useful tool to be manipulated by managers. It conveys an intended corporate message.

## 6.2 CONCLUSION

The financial statements are presented to the shareholders in an annual report. Managers have every incentive, in theory, to manage the presentation of this annual reporting package.

They can then influence the impression of the firm which users will gain. There is ample evidence that they do so in regards to accounting narratives, graphs and photographs. These represent important constituents of the annual reporting package.

Impression management in accounting narratives consists of four elements. First, stressing the positive and downplaying the negative. Managers have been shown to over-emphasise good news while downplaying bad news. They may, for example, stress their financial successes while downplaying or ignoring completely their financial disasters. Second, managers may baffle the readers by using technical language to convey bad news or by using less readable language to obfuscate their presentation of bad news. Third, managers may use differential reporting. Thus, bad news companies may focus less on the actual results than good news companies, and may prefer to focus on the future rather than the past. And fourth, companies use attribution to ensure that they take the credit for good news, while they blame the environment for bad news.

Impression management using graphs focuses on three aspects. First, companies are selective in their use of graphs. They tend to present graphs when the underlying financial performance is good, but omit them when the underlying financial performance is bad. Second, there is evidence of measurement distortion across time and across countries. In other words, in a variety of settings, companies have been found to draw graphs which present an enhanced picture of the company's underlying performance. These measurement distortions are caused both by poor draughtsmanship so that, for example, a rising trend in a graph's performance is exaggerated or a declining trend is understated and by specific design features such as a non-zero axis. And, finally, companies have been shown to use a variety of graphical design techniques to present the actual graphs in a more flattering way than is actually warranted. This may involve the judicious presentation of graphs or the highlighting of the final year's results.

Photographs are used to set an overall impression of the company. They may, for example, seek to convey the impression of a young, vibrant company by including photographs of only young people. Therefore, they set the 'mood music' for the company.

Collectively, therefore, accounting narratives, graphs and photographs are used by companies for presentational enhancement. In other words, by themselves or in combination these three presentational formats convey a certain image and create a more favourable impression of the company than may be obtained from studying the financial results on their own. Combined with earnings management they may give a false impression of the company's achievements.

# REFERENCES

Abrahamson, E. and Amir, E. (1996), 'The information content of the president's letter to shareholders', *Journal of Business Finance and Accounting*, **23**(8), 1157–1182.

Aerts, W. (1994), 'On the use of accounting logic as an explanatory category in narrative accounting disclosures', *Accounting, Organizations and Society*, **19**(4/5), 337–353.

Arthur Andersen (2001), *Spice up the Story: A Survey of Narrative Reporting in Annual Reports*, Arthur Andersen, London.

Bartlett, S. and Chandler, R. (1997), 'The corporate report and the private shareholder: Lee and Tweedie twenty years on', *British Accounting Review*, **29**, 245–261.

Beattie, V. and Jones, M.J. (1992a), 'The use and abuse of graphs in annual reports: theoretical framework and empirical study', *Accounting and Business Research*, **22**(88), 291–303.

Beattie, V. and Jones, M.J. (1992b), *The Communication of Information using Graphs in Corporate Annual Reports*, The Chartered Association of Certified Accountants, Reference Report 31, ACCA, London.

Beattie, V. and Jones, M.J. (1994), 'Information design and manipulation: financial graphs in corporate annual reports', *Information Design Journal*, **7**(3), 211–226.

Beattie, V. and Jones, M.J. (1996), *Financial Graphs in Corporate Annual Reports: A Review of Practice in Six Countries*, Institute of Chartered Accountants in England and Wales, London.

Beattie, V. and Jones, M.J. (2000), 'Changing graph use in corporate annual reports: a time series analysis', *Contemporary Accounting Research*, **17**(2), 23–26.

Clarke, G. (1997), 'Messages from CEOs: a content analysis approach', *Corporate Communication: An International Journal*, **2**(1), 31–39.

Clatworthy, M.A. and Jones, M.J. (2003), 'Financial reporting of good and bad news: evidence from accounting narratives', *Accounting and Business Research*, **33**(3), 171–185.

Clatworthy, M.A. and Jones, M.J. (2006), 'Differential patterns of textual characteristics and company performance in the chairman's statement', *Accounting, Auditing and Accountability*, **19**(4), 493–511.

Courtis, J. (1998), 'Annual report readability variability: tests of the obfuscation hypothesis', *Accounting, Auditing and Accountability Journal*, **11**(4), 59–71.

Deegan, C. and Gordon, B. (1996), 'A study of the environmental disclosure practices of Australian companies', *Accounting and Business Research*, **26**(3), 187–199.

Goffman, E. (1959), *The Presentation of Self in Everyday Life*, Doubleday Anchor Books, New York.

Graves, O.F., Flesher, D.L. and Jordan, R.E. (1996), 'Pictures and the bottom line: the television epistemology of U.S. annual reports', *Accounting, Organizations and Society*, **21**(1), 57–58.

Hopwood, A.G. (1996), 'Editorial', *Accounting, Organizations and Society*, **21**(1), 55–56.

Jones, M.J. (2006), *Accounting*, John Wiley & Sons Ltd, Chichester.

Lee, T.A. (1994), 'The changing form of the corporate annual report', *Accounting Historians Journal*, June, 215–232.

McKinstry, S. (1996), 'Designing the annual reports of Burton's plc from 1930 to 1994', *Accounting, Organizations and Society*, **21**(1), 89–111.

Morrow, S. (2005), *The Business of Football: Image Management in Narrative Communication*, ICAS Research Report, Edinburgh.

Pava, M.L. and Epstein, M.J. (1993), 'How good is MD&A as an investment tool?', *Journal of Accountancy*, **175**(3), 51–53.

Preston, A.M., Wright, C. and Young, J.J. (1996), 'Imag[in]ing annual reports', *Accounting, Organizations and Society*, **21**(1), 113–137.

Schlenker, B.R. (1980), *Impression Management*, Brooks Cole, Monterey, CA.

Smith, M. and Taffler, R. (1992), 'The chairman's statement and corporate financial performance', *Accounting and Finance*, 75–90.

Staw, B.M., McKechnie, P.I. and Puffer, S.M. (1983), 'The justification of organisational performance', *Administrative Science Quarterly*, **28**, 582–600.

Thomas, J. (1997), 'Discourse in the marketplace: the making of meaning in annual reports', *Journal of Business Communication*, **34**, 47–66.

7

# Taking the Long View: Accounting Scandals over Time

Michael Jones

## 7.1 INTRODUCTION

Human nature does not change. Therefore, the hopes and desires of people living in ancient, medieval or modern times remain very similar. As long as there has been accounting, therefore, there have been temptations for individuals creatively to use that information and to indulge in fraud. Interestingly, the boundaries between creative accounting and fraud have been fairly flexible. In other words, one period's creative accounting becomes the next period's unacceptable accounting, which if followed may be judged fraudulent. This is because creative accounting often contributes to accounting scandals. After these accounting scandals the accounting rules and regulations are often changed to prevent these same creative accounting practices reoccurring.

It is obviously not possible to discuss all the past accounting scandals and the part that creative accounting and fraud have played in them. There are simply too many. The aim of this chapter is just to discuss some of the most famous and interesting ones. Also, the aim is to look across time to show the universality of accounting scams. In Figure 7.1, there is a list of major accounting scandals and scams that have been covered. These are divided into five time periods: the ancient and medieval period, the seventeenth and eighteenth centuries, the nineteenth century, the twentieth century up to 1945 and, finally, the twentieth century from 1945 to the 1980s. The country chapters in the book deal with the main scandals in individual countries since 1980. In the ancient and medieval period, I look first at a one-off fraudulent alteration of an accounting record in the form of a cuneiform monument. I then look at creative accounting as practised by Italian merchants and a fraud perpetrated by English wool merchants.

In the second period, the seventeenth and eighteenth centuries, I look at two trading scandals. In the first, the Africa and India Company of Scotland, there appears to be general mismanagement of the accounts rather than fraud. However, I have included it as it is an interesting, early example of a corporate failure. In the second, the infamous South Sea Bubble, England, 1720 there appears to have been a deliberate and sustained effort to deceive investors. In the third period, the nineteenth century, we look at two famous *causes célèbres*: the railway accounting scandals of Victorian England and the collapse of the City of Glasgow Bank, Scotland, 1878. Moving on to the first half of the twentieth century, I investigate the case of secret reserve accounting in the accounts of P&O and of the Royal

*Creative Accounting, Fraud and International Accounting Scandals*   Edited by Michael Jones
© 2011 Michael Jones. Published by John Wiley & Sons, Ltd

**(i) Ancient and medieval**

1. Cruciform monument, Mesopotamia, third millennium BC.

2. Medieval merchants, Italy, fourteenth century.

3. Cely family, England, late fifteenth century.

**(ii) Seventeenth and eighteenth centuries**

4. Africa and India Company of Scotland, Scotland, 1695.

5. South Sea Bubble, England, 1720.

**(iii) Nineteenth century**

6. Railway scandals 1840s–1860s, England.

7. City of Glasgow Bank, Scotland, 1878.

**(iv) Twentieth century: before Second World War**

8. P&O, New Zealand, 1917–36.

9. Royal Mail Steam Packet Company, UK, 1931.

10. Kreuger & Toll, Inc., USA, 1932.

11. McKesson & Robbins, USA, 1937.

**(v) Twentieth century: 1945–80s**

12. Reid Murray, Australia, 1963.

13. H.G. Palmer, Australia, 1965.

14. Associated Electrical Industries takeover by General Electric Company, UK, 1967.

15. Minisec, Australia, 1971.

16. Equity Funding Corporation of America, USA, 1973.

17. Cambridge Credit, Australia, 1974.

18. Renouf and Judge Corporations, New Zealand, 1980s.

**Figure 7.1**   A selection of major scams and scandals across time

Mail Steam Packet Company. In addition, for the first time I move across the Atlantic to look at two famous US scandals: McKesson & Robbins and Kreuger & Toll, Inc. In the final period, from 1945 to the 1980s, I look at six cases. First of all I investigate two Australian cases: Reid Murray and H.G. Palmer. I then move back to the UK to look at the Associated Electrical Industries (AEI) takeover by General Electric Company (GEC) in 1967. This case appears to have involved the managers using the flexibility in the accounts to boost their profits so as to avoid a hostile takeover. I then return to Australia in 1971 to witness the collapse of Minisec. The fourth case involves the rather spectacular fraud at Equity Funding Corporation of America, where there was the wholesale creation of false insurance documentation. I then revisit Australia to look at the collapse of Cambridge Credit, in 1974. Then, finally, I look at the creative accounting practices of the Renouf and Judge Corporation in New Zealand. These cases, thus, demonstrate examples of creative accounting and fraud; with the possible exception of the Africa and India Company of Scotland in 1695, which is interesting in itself as it is a case of spectacular financial mismanagement.

### 7.1.1 Ancient and Medieval

There are fewer examples of creative accounting and fraud from this period. This does not mean that it does not exist, merely that given the passage of time it is more difficult to find the evidence. Chatfield (1973) states that fraud was common in fifth century Athens and the prevention of fraud was one of the main reasons that Zenon (manager of the finance ministry of Ptolemy II of Egypt) kept accounting records. The Romans were equally keen to stop fraud. In the treatises on estate management written in the thirteenth and fourteenth centuries, potential fraud by agricultural workers was also a very real concern (Jones, 2008). The main evidence for creative accounting at this time comes from an entertaining article written by Robert Parker, entitled 'Misleading accounts: pitfalls for historians'. He demonstrates that both fraudulent and creative accounting have been common occurrences over time. Parker (1991), drawing on other authors, looks at three examples of dubious accounting from Mesopotamia and from Medieval Europe.

#### 7.1.1.1  *Cruciform Monument, Mesopotamia, Third Millennium BC*

This cruciform monument is in the British Museum. It is covered with inscriptions which concern the renovation of a temple and the revenues that the King gave to the temple. Although the inscriptions appear to date from the period c.2276–2261 BC, these inscriptions are probably a later addition. They seem to have been made in the first half of the third millennium BC to bolster the claims of the temple to its revenues.[1]

#### 7.1.1.2  *Medieval Merchants, Italy, Fourteenth Century*

An early example of systematic creative accounting is that practised by medieval Italian merchants. At that time the Christian church banned usury. This essentially meant the prohibition of interest. However, the Italian merchants found ways around this prohibition.

---

[1] Parker cites Sollberger, E. (1968), The Cruciform Monument, *Jaarbernicht Ex Oriente Lux*, Vol. 20 and Jones, M. (1990), *Fake? The Art of Deception*, p. 60.

There were three main ways. The first involved the creative use of language. De Roover (1956) gives an example of ingenious substitute words for interest such as 'cost,' 'gain,' 'gift,' 'gratuity,' 'reward' and 'yield'. A second method according to de Roover (1956) was to buy goods on credit and then sell them for less cash. This can be construed as, in effect, a disguised loan.

Parker (1991, p. 11) comments on the Commune of Genoa: 'The commune, for example, purchased quantities of pepper on credit at £24.5.0 Genoese currency per quintal, but sold them later for cash at £22.14.6 and £22.10.0 per quintal. While the form of this transaction was a loss-making trading venture, the substance according to de Roover was the raising of an interest-bearing loan by the municipality from the local merchants.' Edwards (1989) confirms that Italian merchants were familiar with accounting creativity. He cites Pacioli, an Italian, who wrote the first book on accounting in 1494 as stating that merchants kept two sets of books: one to show customers and one to show suppliers.

### 7.1.1.3   Cely Family, England, Late Fifteenth Century

This example is one of what appears to have been a successful and undetected fraud (Hanham, 1973). One of the UK's main exports in the fifteenth century was wool. The Cely family were English wool merchants. 'The fraud involved the falsification of both the weights and prices of bales of wool, ingeniously and deliberately confusing the different Calais and English systems of weights and measures' (Parker, 1991, p. 10). The idea was apparently to avoid the restrictive trading regulations of the Calais authorities. In particular, the fraud was designed so that payment for the goods could be made in England.

The records appear to have been compiled to put investigators off the scent if an official enquiry was made (Hanham, 1973). However, no enquiry was ever made. These falsifications remained undetected at the time. They were uncovered after the death of George Cely, when investigators were called in to draw up a set of accounts to sort out a legal dispute on the estate. They found a 'curious case of "cooking the books"' (Hanham, 1973, p. 315). The investigators appear not to have fully understood what had happened, with the possibility that George's widow may have lost part of her inheritance.

### 7.1.2  Seventeenth and Eighteenth Centuries

I discuss two examples of this below: the Africa and India Company of Scotland, Scotland, 1695 and the South Sea Bubble in 1720. Lee (2004) provides the basic details for both. In many ways they are similar. Both involved gullible investors from Great Britain who were persuaded to invest in joint-stock trading companies. In both cases the companies collapsed in what were the biggest accounting scandals of their time. However, while in the Scottish example mismanagement was the main cause of corporate collapse, in the English case it was fraud.

### 7.1.2.1   Africa and India Company of Scotland, Scotland, 1695

This case is an early company scandal. The Africa and India Company of Scotland was set up by William Paterson. Paterson was an important figure in the City of London in the late seventeenth century. Indeed, he founded the Bank of England in 1691. He subsequently founded a trading company and many leading citizens joined the venture. The public subscribed £400 000 to the venture, which was said to represent one-half of the available Scottish cash at the time (Lee, 2004, p. 9). The aim was to found a colony on the Darien Peninsula in Panama, Central America. The venture went horribly wrong. 'The project quickly failed, however, due to a disastrous combination of mismanagement, politics at home in Scotland, English refusal to trade with Darien, pressure on government from the venture's main competitor (the East India Company), the climate and terrain of Panama, and military opposition from Spain which claimed ownership of Panama' (Lee, 2004, p. 9). As a result, many Scots lost all their money. The failure essentially happened because a lot of investors saw the chance to earn a lot of money. They did not, therefore, fully evaluate the financial riskiness of the venture. Rather than creative accounting or fraud, this venture failed on financial mismanagement.

### 7.1.2.2  South Sea Bubble, England, 1720

By contrast, the South Sea Bubble was an example of an accounting scandal which involved substantial fraud. The South Sea Company was set up by Robert Harley, Earl of Oxford and leader of the Tory party. It was supported by leading figures of the day, such as Jonathan Swift and Daniel Defoe. It was given a charter in 1711 and had a monopoly to trade with the Spanish colonies in South America, with the condition that it took on some of England's national debt.

The company then took on the whole of the UK's national debt. It was paid for by an issue of shares. 'Almost because it was so brilliant as a financial and political stroke, the scheme as a business proposition was from the first a sham ... Its promoters valued it not for its own sake, but for the advantage it gave them in other capacities in the creation of credit and the management of financial operations for the government' (Carswell, 1960, p. 56). The company bribed politicians with shares. Robert Knight, cashier of the South Sea Bubble, made fraudulent entries to conceal this, keeping a green ledger. Bogus sales to peers and politicians of £574 400 were treated as loans to sundry in the books in 1720 (Carswell, 1960, p. 125). The shares were deliberately talked up in the coffee shops of the City of London. As a result there was a frenzy of buying. The company itself was not very active at trading. As a result there was nothing to support the share price. As with other speculative situations, a bubble was created which subsequently burst. More and more stock needed to be issued just to raise money to pay the current shareholders their dividends. The shares rose from 130 to over 1000 in 1720 before falling back to 190 (Edwards, 1989) before the company collapsed. Many investors were bankrupted. Indeed, the Duke of Portland, one of the richest men in England, was almost bankrupted (Carswell, 1960). As a result of the South Sea Bubble, Charles Snell, a writing master and accountant, was employed to audit the records of a public company. He was possibly the first accountant to conduct a corporate fraud investigation. He discovered false entries, but gave no opinion as to why (Chatfield, 1973).

### 7.1.3 Nineteenth Century

In the nineteenth century, company legislation was just starting. I look at railway scandals and the well-known City of Glasgow bank failure. The railway companies were more of a series of scandals than any one particular episode.

### 7.1.3.1   Railway Scandals 1840s–1860s, England

The first half of the nineteenth century marked the development of the railways in England. The first railway was from Liverpool to Manchester in 1830. This was followed by many other lines. These individual railway lines were run by individual companies. As a result, these companies needed to raise finance to fund the construction of the railway lines. They thus had to persuade individual investors to buy shares. As Lee (2004) points out, individual entrepreneurs such as George Hudson, Leopold Redpath and Richard Hodgson were prominent in the financing of these ventures.

In a pattern that is often repeated across time, the pressure upon companies to raise money and the eagerness of investors to make money caused a relaxation of the normal rules of prudent financing. The need to raise finance and the consequent potential rich rewards led to many accounting abuses. George Hudson, who by 1848 controlled more than one-third of the UK railway network, adopted many dubious practices. Lee comments (2004, p. 11): 'These include false reporting of the financial results of his railway companies, bribery of politicians, insider information to manipulate railway share prices, and sale of railway land he did not own. For example, in 1849, he paid for 900 shares in the Newcastle & Berwick Railway Company. He registered the purchase as 10,000 shares and sold them for a profit of £145,000.' A favourite practice of Hudson was to purchase rails and other parts privately and then sell them to his companies for inflated prices. In 1845, he purchased 10 000 tons of iron at £6.10s per ton and then supplied the Newcastle & Berwick line he owned with 7000 tons at £12 per ton (Evans, 1859, p. 54). This was a practice Hudson was guilty of on the East Counties line. In other words, there was an entanglement of his private money and publicly provided funds. On the East Counties line, a 10 % dividend was maintained by raiding capital. 'Out of £545,714 distributed in dividends, from the 4th of January, 1845, to the 4th of July, 1848, £320,572 was procured by the alteration of traffic accounts and improper charges to capital' (Evans, 1859, p. 54). In the end, Hudson was jailed for failing to repay the shareholders.

A key practice that the railway companies indulged in was the payment of dividends out of capital (Bryer, 1991). The problem with this is that it disguised the fact that the companies were not making healthy profits. In addition, it encouraged the railway companies to raise more capital so that they could use this to pay their current shareholders. Bryer cites The Monteagle Committee, which in 1849 investigated the railway scams. William Quilter, a leading accountant of the day, said in his testimony that the public was being deceived because it was paying higher prices for shares as it thought that the dividends were being paid out of bona fide profits. However, the commissioners were also somewhat sceptical of the shareholders themselves; 'Shareholders, in past years, have proved but too ready to acquiesce in any course of policy which produces a probable augmentation of Dividend' (Monteagle Committee, 1849, third report, pp. x–xi).

Lee (2004) cites two other railway frauds. In the first case, Leopold Redpath was convicted of defrauding the shareholders of the Great Northern Railway Company in 1857. The way in which he did this was to create false shares in the company. He could do this as he was the company's registrar. Not only did he receive dividends, but he also then sold the shares. The situation was discovered only when the maximum allowed shareholding was exceeded. In the second case, Richard Hodgson, an MP, defrauded the North British

Railway Company. 'In 1866, a shareholder investigation of concerns about the financial statements of the North British Railway Company disclosed a complex accounting fraud involving the inflation of sales revenue by transfers from suspense accounts created in previous periods, the understatement of operational expenses by charging railway maintenance and replacement costs to a capital account, and failure to depreciate capital expenditure. Profits stated were, in reality, insufficient to support the declared dividends. Motivation for the fraud lay with the need to maintain dividends because of stock market expectations' (Lee, 2004, p. 12). The accounting scandal was particularly shocking as it affected what was probably, at nearly £13 million, the largest Scottish company of the time. The company was unable to legally pay dividends. However, it did so by illegally distributing £300 000 out of capital. 'The annual accounts for at least three and a half years had been systematically faked to allow the payment of whatever dividend Hodgson desired' (Vamplew, 1974, p. 308).

The *Railway Times* on 25 August 1866 reported a remarkably frank exchange between the Committee of Investigation into the affairs of the North British Railway Company and its company accountant in 1866:[2]

> Question: Have the annual accounts as laid before the shareholders been systematically cooked so as to mislead them as to the true position of the revenue and expenditure of the company, and simply to exhibit an ability to pay the dividend desired by Mr Hodgson (the chairman), regardless of the free revenue of the company being adequate for the purpose?
>
> Answer: Yes, that has been the plan.

This latter scandal has a contemporary feel about it. Not only is the motive of meeting stock market expectations a common reason for creative accounting today, but some of the methods – such as inflating sales and capitalising costs – are reminiscent of companies like Enron and WorldCom.

### 7.1.3.2 City of Glasgow Bank, Scotland, 1878

The City of Glasgow Bank collapsed in 1878. Its collapse came as a great shock to contemporaries. To the outside world it had appeared stable, well managed and profitable. Its dividend had increased from 3 % in 1859 to 12 % in 1878, and its shares from £88 to £243. It had more branches than any other Scottish bank, and gross assets of £12 million (French, 1984).

As Lee (2004) indicates, this was a fraud that took place through the collusion of seven directors, with two directors, Robert Stronach and Lewis Potter, actually perpetuating the fraud. The seven directors were charged with producing fraudulent balance sheets for 1876, 1877 and 1878. When the trustees investigated the bank's affairs, instead of an equity surplus of £1 592 000, they found a deficit of £6 190 000. The directors were found guilty of falsifying balance sheets, of obtaining advances from the bank and embezzling them, and of using bills of exchange improperly to pay the debts of the bank. The directors were

---

[2] As cited in Vamplew (1974).

specifically found guilty of:

- understating deposits by £1 006 217;
- understating drafts outstanding by £973 300;
- understating advances by £2 698 539;
- overstating cash by £29 095;
- overstating government stocks and debentures by £753 211;
- overstating earnings by £125 763;
- stating there were reserves of £450 000 when there were none.

In addition, at the annual general meeting in July 1876, seven directors did 'wickedly and feloniously, and falsely and fraudulently represent, and pretend that the said company was in a sound and prosperous condition, and capable of paying to its members a dividend at the rate of 11 per centum per annum, free of income-tax, and of carrying forward to the credit of next year's profit and loss account a sum of £21,365,105 and 3d, and by thereafter causing the said report and abstract balance sheet or statement of affairs to be printed and published and circulated throughout Scotland' (Couper, 1879: City of Glasgow Bank Trial, 1878, p. 28).

'The fraud took place over a number of years and involved a combination of fictitious accounting entries to understate assets and liabilities, overvaluation of irrecoverable banking assets and other investments, and purchases of the bank's shares to maintain its market valuation' (Lee, 2004, p. 14). By 1878, the bank held 15 % of its own shares. The bank got into difficulties by loaning half its assets to just four firms with inadequate security. In 1875, a new bank manager attempted to rescue the bank through investing in land in Australia. Funds were obtained through discounting bills of exchange. New bills were discounted as old bills fell due. By doing this, the bank survived, but after the collapse of a London bank, the discount market became more cautious, and this led to problems with the bank's credit and it collapsed (French, 1984). A particularly unpleasant consequence of the bank's collapse was that the bank had unlimited liability. The shareholders, therefore, not only lost the money they had invested, but were also expected to cover the bank's debts. Most of them could not do this and eight out of ten were made bankrupt.

### 7.1.4  Twentieth Century: Before Second World War

We will now look at four examples of accounting creativity and fraud in the early twentieth century. For P&O, the main issue was that P&O used secret reserves, which understated the assets of the company, so as to extract dividends from New Zealand and remit them to the UK. These secret reserves were also a key issue for the Royal Mail Steam Packet Company in England. Essentially, secret reserves are created when a company uses accounting techniques to reduce the value of its assets. For example, a company may use accelerated depreciation or set up generous provisions for liabilities. The result of secret reserve accounting is that the net asset value of the company is lower than it would otherwise be. The secret reserves can then be used to profit smooth either by boosting profits in years when they are low or decreasing them when profits are high. Smoothing profits helps to ensure that dividends paid are relatively stable. In addition, they can be paid out of past years' accumulated profits. This, at the time, was seen as prudent: using the fat built up over the good years to see companies through the bad years. In the case of McKesson & Robbins and Kreuger & Toll, Inc., there were spectacular frauds. In McKessen & Robbins, Donald Coster constructed a totally fictitious Canadian subsidiary. While in Kreuger & Toll, Inc., Ivan Kreuger built up an apparently successful company by paying dividends out of capital.

### 7.1.4.1  P&O, New Zealand, 1917–1936

P&O was a major shipping company based in the UK, but with numerous overseas subsidiaries. Founded in 1875, by 1914 it owned 75 ships with 232 147 tons. The P&O example is one where a company used creative accounting for many years to achieve a specific purpose. This was to remove from its New Zealand subsidiary, The Union Steam Ship of New Zealand Limited (Union), £8 million in dividends with no public disclosure of what it was doing. Union was acquired in 1917 and was exploited by P&O. This exploitation was facilitated by the widespread use of secret reserves. As we shall see in the Royal Mail Steam Packet Company case, secret reserves were commonly used in this period.

Napier (1995) details a number of methods by which Union contributed to P&O's well-being. First, Union loaned P&O money, which totalled £5.4 million by 1929. For example, on the merger Australian and New Zealand shareholders were paid by Union, and this was accounted for as a £600 000 loan. Second, Union gave P&O rebates. Third, P&O received undisclosed bonus dividends from Union. 'The effect of these undisclosed transactions was that Union transferred a total of over £3.5 million to P&O between 1922 and 1931' (Napier, 1995, p. 148). If these disclosures had been known, it is probable that there would have been pressure for the company to reduce its freight rates.

However, these transfers were not enough to help P&O, which was in some financial difficulty. P&O wished to remit money back to the UK but not to alert the New Zealand government to what it was doing. It therefore devised complicated schemes to do this. Napier (1995) details how an intermediary company domiciled in New Zealand was to be set up. Union then paid this company an undisclosed bonus dividend and debited the dividend to its secret reserves. 'The new company would then be liquidated, and its assets distributed to P&O. As this would represent a capital distribution on liquidation, there would be no United Kingdom tax to pay' (Napier, 1995, p. 151). An inactive company, Land and Mortgage Securities Limited, was used as the intermediary company and a secret dividend of £4.5 million was paid. This constituted a loan of £3 500 000 Union owed to P&O and £1 000 000 in New Zealand government securities. By careful negotiations, the company managed to conceal from the New Zealand authorities what was actually happening. 'Probably fewer than a dozen people in New Zealand, all Union insiders, were aware of the full arrangements, while in the United Kingdom details of the scheme were kept just as confidential' (Napier, 1995, p. 153). Using this scheme and in other ways, at least £8 million was withdrawn from New Zealand. These withdrawals enabled P&O to survive a difficult economic trading position in 1930–31. However, the withdrawals may have harmed the New Zealand economy. 'P&O was assisted in grabbing Union's surplus resources by the flexibility of accounting regulation at the time. The maintenance of secret reserves was encouraged by lax laws and judicial approval' (Napier, 1995, p. 155).

### 7.1.4.2   *Royal Mail Steam Packet Company, UK, 1931*

The First World War was a good time for the UK shipping industry. They were very profitable and built up secret reserves through accelerated depreciation charges. However, after the First World War there was a downturn in the shipping market as well as a rise in the replacement cost of ships. As a result, the shipping industry ran into problems. Lord Kylsant was found guilty of publishing false accounts in a prospectus to shareholders in 1928.

Lord Kylsant of the Royal Mail Steam Packet Company sought to try to cover up the poor state of his company by 'extending his financial ingenuity to the development of dangerous and misleading reporting practices' (Edwards, 1975, p. 298). These involved different companies in the group paying dividends to each other, by the payment of dividends from excess tax provisions, by the inclusion of non-trading incomes in profits, and probably the use of transfers in and out of secret reserves to bolster profits. These practices 'distorted the trend of [the company's] trading results' and 'disguised the lack of current operating profitability' (Arnold, 1991, p. 203). Lee (2004) states that about £5 million was paid as dividends from non-existent profits. In essence, there was the use of accounting techniques to smooth profits in the hope that the company would return to profitability.

Lord Kylsant was charged on three counts. The first two charges concerned the 1926 and 1927 balance sheets. The published accounts, it was alleged, were false as in those two years it appeared from the accounts that the company had made large trading profits whereas it had actually made serious losses. It was further alleged that the auditor had condoned the deception. The third charge covered the issuance of a false prospectus by Lord Kylsant in 1928 which induced people to lend or entrust money. In particular, the prospectus stated that: '[a]lthough this company in common with other shipping companies has suffered from the depression in the shipping industry, the audited accounts of the company show that during the past ten years the average balance available, including the profits of the insurance fund, after providing for depreciation and interest on existing stock, has been sufficient to pay interest on the present issue more than five times over' (Brooks, 1933, reprinted 1980).

The facts were reasonably clear. It was revealed, to much public consternation, that the existing law allowed 'a great company, in which the money of the public had been ventured and to which new money had been invited, to publish over a period of seven years balance sheets and profit and loss accounts which did not show whether profit had been earned or not, and during these years to pay in dividends the sum of £5,000,000 which had not been found from current earnings, but from non-recurring items of revenue and undisclosed transfers of secret reserves' (Brooks, 1933, reprinted 1980, p. xiii).

On the first two charges, Lord Kylsant was found not guilty. The case hinged on the fact that the balance sheets contained no statements which were actually false. They had concealed, but not misstated, a position. The law was at fault, but Lord Kylsant had acted within the law. The prospectus charge was, however, upheld. Lord Kylsant was sentenced to 12 months. Even here, there was some popular sympathy for Lord Kylsant. Prospectuses were well known for exaggerating the excellence of the offer, and Brooks quoted a popular writer of the time (Withers in *Stocks and Shares*, a contemporary magazine) as stating: 'All prospectuses should be scanned in a spirit of jaundiced criticism, and with the most pessimistic readiness to believe that they are speciously alluring traps laid by some designing financier to relieve the reader of some of his money' (Brooks, 1933, reprinted 1980).

As a result of the Royal Mail case there was a reappraisal by the accounting profession of the use of special reserves and special credits. Brooks (1933, reprinted 1980) discussed this issue. He cited a head of a banking company who wrote down his gilt-edged investments when the market fell at the balance sheet date, but did not write them up when the market recovered. In this way, he could prudently and legally build up substantial hidden reserves. The key question, he considered, was how far such concealment is proper and for what purposes the reserves can be applied. A UK Company Law Amendment Committee in a 1932 report recommended that the profit and loss account for a period should show a true balance for the year and that special credits should be separately stated. No government legislation was actually forthcoming. However, secret reserve accounting was no longer an accepted accounting practice.

### 7.1.4.3   *Kreuger & Toll, Inc., USA, 1932*

Kreuger & Toll, Inc. was a Swedish match company whose shares were the most widely held in the USA in the 1920s. Although apparently successful the company, as Flesher and Flesher (1986) detail, was unsound. The company was led by Ivan Kreuger. He sold the shares in small denominations and paid over 20 % dividends for both stocks and bonds.

Kreuger was Swedish, but came to the USA in 1900. He returned to the USA and built up a substantial company trading in matches through a series of mergers and acquisitions. He loaned governments money in return for a monopoly to sell matches in the country. Kreuger raised the capital for the loans from the US public. Essentially, Kreuger operated a pyramid scheme. There was a continual need to sell new stocks and shares so as to obtain new capital to pay out dividends to existing shareholders. 'Neither the investing public nor financial analysts were aware of the extent of Kreuger's manipulations because corporate secrecy was practiced by many firms at that time. In fact, Kreuger often stated that all an investor needed to know was a company's dividend policy; nothing else mattered' (Flesher and Flesher, 1986, p. 423). As with the Royal Mail Company, limited mandatory disclosure led to the investing company being left in the dark about the company's true trading position.

The scam was maintained successfully while Kreuger was alive through the use of some dubious accounting methods. The company balance sheet was heavily laden with debt. Kreuger & Toll's balance sheets, unusually for the time, included intangible assets such as monopoly rights. These intangible assets were more subjective to value than tangible assets and harder to realise into cash. There were also forgeries, such as $140 million Italian bonds.

The accounting scandal only came to light when Kreuger died. Price Waterhouse investigated the company. They found that nearly a quarter of a billion dollars in reported assets did not exist. Three-quarters of a billion dollars had been dissipated over time. And 'Ivan Krueger had stolen and spent over one hundred million dollars' (Flesher and Flesher, 1986, p. 432). On the day Kreuger died, the shares were worth $5 per share. Within weeks the price fell to 5 cents. It was the biggest bankruptcy the USA had ever had. It also led to numerous changes in financial reporting after a Senate and Congressional hearing and contributed to the introduction of the 1933 US Securities Act. One result was the introduction of mandatory audits.

### 7.1.4.4  McKesson & Robbins, USA, 1937

McKesson & Robbins was a US wholesale drugs company. The company traded in both Canada and the USA. The firm grew rapidly in the 1920s and 1930s, and by 1937 had 70 branches and sold 48 000 items. It was run by Donald Coster. On the surface it seemed that McKesson & Robbins was very successful (Shaplen, 1955). However, as Baxter (1999) documents, all was not as it seemed. Donald Coster was actually a convicted swindler.

The problem was the Canadian subsidiary. It was set up by Coster in 1927. He sold a million dollars of shares to investors. It was then under the direct and exclusive control of Coster. It dealt with the international buying and selling of crude drugs. The way in which the operation worked was that when a purchase was considered, five Canadian companies were asked for a quote. Documentation, including duplicate purchase orders and stock records, was completed. This was processed through the normal bookkeeping and accounting channels. All sales were handled by the Montreal office of W.W. Smith and Co. Ltd. Sales were always made to foreign companies.

The only problem was that the Canadian trade did not actually exist. It was all imaginary. It was controlled by Coster, who used a few employees who reported directly to him and some accommodation addresses. As Baxter comments: 'Coster was an astonishing man who, not content with building a real empire in the US, conjured up a phantom one in Canada' (Baxter, 1999, p. 162). There was a mass of paperwork, but there were no underlying transactions. Baxter (1999, p. 162) comments 'One cannot but be impressed with the immense care and skill with which Coster ran the Canadian mirage. Not only accounts but imposing legal papers, reports to manager etc., were elaborate and life-like. Each company's invoices and other papers, were printed with utmost realism. In 1937, fictitious sales totalled over $180,000,000, yielding a fictitious gross profit of over $1,800,000.' There were non-existent trade receivables of $49 million and inventory of $10 million.

How much Coster himself gained from this fictitious enterprise is unclear. It took 146 000 man hours to establish that Coster had passed $135 million through 158 accounts. He withdrew $25 million and returned $21.8 million. The difference was the amount that went missing and was booked as profit. However, what actually happened to this $3.2 million is unclear. Some was paid as commission to W.W. Smith ($150 000), some paid to an intermediary, Manning and Co. ($12 000), and some was paid to blackmailers (Shaplen, 1955).

The scam was only detected in 1937, when the directors of McKesson wanted to reduce their bank borrowings and ordered that $4 million of drugs should be turned into cash. However, the Canadian drugs did not exist and so could not be turned into cash. Coster was in trouble and tried to get out of it by raising a loan. However, the treasurer of McKesson's, Thompson, was by now suspicious. He was disbelieving and amazed. The sheer scale of the fraud and its complexity meant that it took him a long time to realise his suspicions. This led to an emergency board meeting. As a result, the company's shares were suspended. Coster committed suicide.

The company itself was reorganised and still survives. The fraud by Coster led to a questioning of the role of the auditor. When Price Waterhouse took on the audit in 1924 they agreed not to do a physical stock-take or to circularise debtors. They never did either. Ritts, a senior accountant at Price Waterhouse, indeed commented: 'Accountants are not competent to judge physical inventory. They could show me a barrel of drugs and say it was thus and so, but I wouldn't know' (Shaplen, 1955, p. 41). There was an investigation into Price Waterhouse's audit by the Securities and Exchange Commission (SEC). The SEC concluded that although Price Waterhouse had done what was mandatory, they had not exercised sufficient vigilance. The result was that the American Institute of Certified Public Accountants published a report stating that auditors should examine inventory and circularise debtors.

### 7.1.5 Twentieth Century: 1945–1980s

In this section, we look at seven examples. Four are Australian: Reid Murray, H.G. Palmer, Minisec and Cambridge Credit. These examples are taken from *Corporate Collapse* (Clarke, Dean and Oliver, 2003). This book outlines a series of high-profile Australian corporate collapses and demonstrates the central role played by creative accounting in them. In the case of Reid Murray, there were concerns about the overvaluation of land, the capitalisation of interest and bad debt provisions. For H.G. Palmer, the main concern was the improper recording of bad debts. For Minisec, the main issues were the treatment of share-trading losses, back-to-back loans and its accounting treatment of investments. With Cambridge Credit there was conflation between the Cambridge group and various private companies owned by Hutcheson who also controlled Cambridge Credit. The other three examples covered are the AEI takeover by GEC, Equity Funding Corporation of America and Renouf and Judge Corporations, two New Zealand companies. The case of the GEC takeover is one where by using different accounting principles and creative accounting, in a contested UK takeover, it was possible to arrive at very different profit figures. In the case of Equity Funding, we see how there was a massive fraud while in the Renouf and Judge Corporations there was widespread use of creative accounting and the manipulation of accounting information.

#### 7.1.5.1   Reid Murray, Australia, 1963

Reid Murray was a large Australian retailing company. It unexpectedly went into receivership in May 1963. Clarke, Dean and Oliver (2003) show how the company was involved in aggressive takeover activity and used dubious accounting methods. From 1958 to 1962, the company raised £43 million in nine share issues. The company's expansion depended on the amount the company could borrow. The terms of the trust deed allowed Reid Murray Acceptance (RMA), a related company and effectively the group's banker, to borrow up to five times its shareholders' funds. The book value of RMA in turn depended on the value of the assets of Reid Murray Holdings (RMH). If RMA defaulted then the guarantor company was bizarrely RMH. As Clarke, Dean and Oliver (2003, p. 58) put it: 'RMA could lend, and could thus increase by a factor of five what it could borrow on the strength of new capital. RMA could issue shares to RMH, which could draw its cheque and pay it to RMA. RMA could then lend the same amount to RMH by return cheque, and then borrow forthwith five times that amount on the market. Facilitating this was resort to a now common commercial device – the cheque round robin, a circuitous routing of cheques through related companies so as to obscure the real source of payment and legitimize its ultimate destination – often one of the entrepreneur's family companies.'

In the early 1980s in Australia the government introduced a credit squeeze. The result was that the company ran into difficulties with the downturn in the market. It was heavily geared and, in effect, was carrying too much debt. When the company collapsed the reasons for its collapse were investigated. The accounts were found to be deceptive. The accounts in 1961 showed a profit of £895 892. However, the inspectors looking into the company found that this profit was boosted by several dubious accounting policies such as changes to the methods of calculating unearned income and accounting for rental income and the profit on land sales. In addition, stock provisions and unappropriated profits were used creatively. If these policies had not been followed, then the company would have made a loss of £67 120.

In addition, the inspectors were concerned with the overvaluation of land and the improper capitalisation of interest. In particular, the inspectors disliked the reporting of real estate investment projects as current assets. This type of asset is normally classed as a fixed asset. By classifying them as inventory the effect was to increase closing stock and thus profit.

Overall, therefore, Reid Murray used some dubious accounting practices. The result of these was to disguise the extent of the company's financial difficulties. However, their use only postponed the company's collapse, it did not prevent it.

### 7.1.5.2 *H.G. Palmer, Australia, 1965*

H.G. Palmer was another Australian retail company that collapsed in the 1960s. The company grew rapidly and was financed by debt. Like Reid Murray, it expanded through acquisition. It expanded too quickly and got into problems. However, its troubles only became public when it was itself acquired by a large life assurance company, Mutual Life Corporation Ltd.

Palmer was able to borrow because it gave the appearance of a profitable company and enjoyed a good reputation. The more companies it acquired and the quicker it grew, the greater was its reputation. Its share price rose steadily. Goods were sold on credit and, in turn, Palmer was given credit by its suppliers. All this was apparently underpinned by an impressive growth in sales and profits. However, all was not as it seemed. The company had severe liquidity problems. In particular, there was a complete failure in credit control. In essence, money was not being collected from customers. From 1961 to 1965 the outstanding debtors balance exceeded the annual sales. For example, in 1964 sales were about £15 million while outstanding debtors were about £24 million. This failure of credit control eventually proved fatal for the company.

It was caused by mismanagement and the failure to properly account for bad debts. There was an absence of effective credit control so the debts kept piling up. An extravagant credit policy was adopted so as to maximise sales. Once the debts had built up, the accounting treatment was woefully inadequate. In effect, the bad debts were simply ignored. This had the effect of boosting profit. In effect, if the bad debts had been correctly reported then Palmer would never have made any profits throughout its existence. 'It was a victory for "accounting fiction" over "financial facts"; fiction that was duly audited and presumably passed on to the market as if it were fact' (Clarke, Dean and Oliver, 2003, p. 80).

### 7.1.5.3  Associated Electrical Industries Takeover by General Electric Company, UK, 1967

The GEC takeover of AEI is not a matter of accounting fraud. However, it did provoke much concern at the time as it stretched the flexibility of accounting to its limits. The takeover is discussed by Rutherford (1996). Essentially, late in 1967 GEC bid for AEI. Both companies were in the British heavy electrical engineering field and might, therefore, be expected *prima facie* to follow similar accounting practices. The bid was a contested takeover, with the directors of AEI resisting the takeover. Ten months into their financial year they issued a profit forecast of £10 million for the year. The bid was, however, successful. However, the results for AEI when published, instead of showing a £10 million profit, showed a £4.5 million loss.

There was a joint report into the loss by the two auditors involved with the company: Deloitte Plender Griffiths & Co. and Price Waterhouse & Co. Most of the shortfall came from five operating divisions. This came to £13.8 million. The main items causing the difference were that £4.3 million was written off stocks, £4.4 million was set aside for estimated losses on contracts and £0.5 million was provided against debts. The report stated that of the total shortfall of £14.5 million, £5 million were matters of fact and £9.5 million matters of judgement.

There was speculation that management used the flexibility in the allowable accounting system to maximize profits. As a result the share price would have been inflated, making the company much more difficult to take over. These suspicions are aired by Rutherford (1996, p. 155): 'Managerial optimism affects judgements about the value of stock and work in progress as well as forecasts. AEI's general position may well have caused it to lean towards the optimistic side well before the bid was announced and the factors outlined earlier in relation to the bullishness of AEI and the conservatism of GEC as a result of the bid situation would have applied equally to the valuation of stock and work in progress.' In addition, it is possible that the incoming management wished to write down the assets of AEI. This 'big bath' accounting would reduce the profits in the year of acquisition, but boost profits in subsequent years.

The difference between the actual and expected profits caused a furore in the accounting world. There was intense press criticism. Academics joined the debate with influential articles, such as that by Professor Edward Stamp. The accounting profession was very much on the defensive. It is probably no coincidence that in 1969 in the UK the Accounting Standards Steering Committee was set up with the aim of improving financial reporting in the UK.

### 7.1.5.4  Minisec, Australia, 1971

Minisec was an Australian share trading company that had a spectacular rise and then an equally spectacular fall. It only lasted five years. At first, Minisec booked substantial profits. However, by 1970 the Australian stock market began to wane. As a result, Minisec then started to incur losses. In order to try to retrieve the situation, Minisec adopted three rather dubious accounting practices: the backdating of share-trading losses, back-to-back loans and creative treatment of its investments.

First, Minisec backdated $2.1 million of losses on share trading to the prior year's accounts. It mentioned this in notes to the accounts, but the amount was not specified nor was the effect on profit outlined. Readers of the accounts would thus not have been aware of the effect of the write-off. Non-transparent reporting was thus used to hide creative accounting. Second, Minisec used a subsidiary company, Robe River Limited, to indulge in back-to-back loans. Robe River was not allowed by the terms of its trust deeds to lend more than 5 % of its total tangible assets to related companies. Minisec used creative accounting to circumvent this inconvenient restriction. Robe River made loans to investment banks which then, in turn, made equivalent loans to Minisec. By using intermediary companies the actual transactions of Minisec were disguised. Third, Minisec reclassified some of its investments. It had purchased $30 million worth of investments in Queensland Mines, Kathleen Investments and Thiess. These stocks were, and should have been, classified as trading stocks. They should, therefore, have been valued at the lower of cost and market value. As their value had fallen, Minisec was supposed to take a loss on them. However, what Minisec actually did was to reclassify them as long-term investments. They did not, therefore, have to be marked-to-market. The result of this was that there was no need for Minisec to have to report a loss. If the normal accounting treatment had, however, been followed then Minisec would have reported a loss not a profit. By this creative classification Minisec was, therefore, able to manipulate its operating profits. 'Clearly it is non-sense to claim that assets are worth more or less, have greater or less value, according to how directors *classify* them' (Clarke, Dean and Oliver, 2003, p. 101).

Minisec, therefore, used creative accounting practices to manufacture profits. However, it failed to survive when legal advice forced it to exclude from its income the profits it had made on its back-to-back share deals. Once these intra-group profits were excluded the company quickly collapsed.

### 7.1.5.5  *Equity Funding Corporation of America, USA, 1973*

Equity Funding Corporation of America is one of the most spectacular frauds. Lee (2004) analyses the case. Equity Funding was founded in 1959. In 1969, Stanley Goldblum became its chairman. The company then expanded rapidly to become one of the 10 largest insurance companies in the USA. Fred Levin was appointed President of Life Insurance Operations. The company flourished. By 1972, it apparently had assets of $500 million and profits of $26 million.

However, all was not what it seemed. Two-thirds of the more than $3 billion life insurance policies were fraudulent. Goldblum and Levin had created a detailed file for each false policy to fool both the insurance inspectors and the auditors. The auditors' rooms were bugged and phone calls about the non-existent policies were taken by Goldblum and Levin. In addition, loans were not recorded as liabilities but were treated as reductions in the trade receivables from policy holders.

The fraud had been going on for 18 years. Gradually, it grew from a small deception into a massive fraud. The internal controls of the company were overridden by senior executives. The fraud was not discovered by the auditors, it only came to light through a whistleblower.

In total, the fraud involved more than $60 million of inflated mutual fund assets and more than $80 million of other fictitious inflated assets. Goldblum and Levin were convicted of fraud and jailed for four years and two-and-a-half years, respectively.

### 7.1.5.6  Cambridge Credit, Australia, 1974

Cambridge Credit was a fast-growing Australian company in the 1970s. It was set up and controlled by a charismatic individual, Mort Hutcheson. Hutcheson also owned some private family companies. Cambridge Credit was involved in land development. This was a long-term business and the company experienced liquidity problems. It, therefore, needed to borrow money. The ability to borrow was dependent on satisfactory profits. The network of public and private companies was used to disguise the true profitability of the group. For example, Hunter, a private company, was used to hide the bad debts of the group.

Overall, Clarke, Dean and Oliver (2003, p. 113) comment: 'Inspectors alleged that the Hutcheson family companies were vehicles used to manipulate the profits of Cambridge so as to preserve borrowing rights. Capital structures were devised to avoid consolidation as Cambridge subsidiaries, yet they operated on funds originating in Cambridge. Eventually group profits were achieved primarily from profits on "front-end" sales and non-recognition by Cambridge of bad debts in loans to its subsidiaries.'

Cambridge took advantage of the flexibility of the accounting regulations concerning when to take profit. It took profit from real estate development projects at the earliest possible moment. Typically, companies in which Cambridge had an interest would sell undeveloped land to joint ventures in which Cambridge also had an interest. Cambridge would then include a full share of profits from the deal without disclosing Cambridge's share in the purchasing company. Often Cambridge would have originally financed the purchase by lending the purchaser the money. The sale was, therefore, not really a true sale.

Another technique which Cambridge used was to use other companies as stores for losses on investments. These losses were not then consolidated into the accounts. In addition, Cambridge loaned amounts to family companies. When the auditors doubted the recoverability of these loans, the debts were eliminated by inter-group transfers of profits.

In essence, therefore, Cambridge was using creative accounting techniques to manufacture profits and hide debts. By reporting profits the group was able to keep paying dividends and look healthy. It was, therefore, able to raise new loans. However, eventually the game could go on no longer. Creative accounting only postponed the inevitable and the company went into receivership in 1974.

### 7.1.5.7  Renouf and Judge Corporations, New Zealand, 1980s

The Renouf and Judge Corporations were two New Zealand companies. Their tale is told by Hooper and Kearins (1995). In 1986, two international companies had merged their New Zealand operations to form a Renouf/Judge group. Both the Renouf Corporation and the Judge Corporation recorded excellent results in 1987. However, they subsequently collapsed without warning. Their story is one of using the inherent flexibility within New Zealand's accounting rules in the late 1980s rather than indulging in any illegal activities.

The Renouf/Judge group used a variety of accounting strategies and techniques to create profits. First, it sold assets and investments to related companies, often for shares. This created paper profits, but generated no cash. The group would also use techniques such as warehousing where wealthy associates bought shares temporarily on the understanding that the shares would be bought back at a later date. This was usually through a put option at a pre-fixed price. When the stock market fell, these put options were exercised and the profits which the group had already booked proved illusory.

Second, the Renouf/Judge group used fixed asset revaluations to boost its asset valuations in the balance sheet. As a result, its balance sheet and thus gearing ratios were both improved. Third, the Renouf/Judge group selectively used equity accounting. For example, in the Judge Corporation's 1987 accounts a loss on a subsidiary was omitted. Similarly, losses made by Impala Pacific were excluded from the Renouf Corporation accounts, while profits were taken. Finally, assets were classified as either fixed or current depending on the needs of the situation rather than on the normal accounting treatment. This permitted a great deal of flexibility when determining the asset figures and also had knock-on effects for the profit and loss account.

With the collapse of the stock market in October 1987, the two companies' share prices collapsed. Judge Corporation went into receivership while the Renouf Corporation continued to trade but at a very low share price.

In this example, the two companies were able to use creative accounting until the stock market's collapse. They used a variety of techniques to increase profits, but most of these involved one-off transactions and were dependent on a rising stock market. When the stock market fell then the creative accounting practices became unsustainable.

## 7.2 CONCLUSION

In this chapter, we looked at 18 examples of fraud, creative accounting and financial mismanagement. These stretched across both time and space. The earliest major scam was the doctoring of the cruciform monument in the third millennium BC; while the latest was the Renouf and Judge Corporations in the 1980s. Geographically, these case studies cover Australia, Italy, Mesopotamia, New Zealand, the UK and the USA. These scandals are not meant to be exhaustive of past scandals, but illustrative. However, some of the world's most notable scandals are covered, such as the South Sea Bubble. More recent scandals are discussed in the country chapters of the book in the next section, Part B.

Fraud and creative accounting play a major part in these accounting scandals. Indeed, the African and India Company of Scotland is probably the only corporate scandal which did not involve financial malpractice. The earliest two frauds involved the falsification of accounting numbers. In the case of the cruciform monument, this involved tampering with the inscriptions so as to boost revenues while in the Cely case it involved the falsification of weights and measures. In the South Sea Bubble investors were misled by false statements and politicians were bribed. A common fraudulent practice was to pay dividends out of capital. New capital was continually raised to supply the money for dividends. This occurred not only in the nineteenth century railway scandals but also in the USA in the 1930s, where Ivan Kreuger successfully paid dividends from capital until he died and the scam was finally uncovered.

The three remaining financial frauds were all complex and substantive, occurring over many years. In the City of Glasgow Bank in the 1870s in Scotland, the bank's directors fictitiously invented financial transactions over several years so that the balance sheets bore no relation to reality. In McKesson & Robbins, in the USA, Donald Coster, a businessman and ex-swindler not content with a flourishing US trading operation, invented a substantial fictitious Canadian business. He successfully maintained this fictitious enterprise for many years. Finally, in the Equity Funding Corporation of America, Stanley Goldblum and Fred Levin gradually built up a fictitious edifice of false documentation over a series of years to make Equity Funding one of the leading US insurance companies.

The earliest example of creative accounting that we discuss is of fourteenth-century Italian merchants who used creative accounting to bypass the strict regulations of the Catholic Church on usury. From then on examples of creative accounting abound. As accounting evolved so did creative accounting. In the period between the two World Wars, the main example of creative accounting was the use of secret reserves. In the case of P&O, these secret reserves appear to have been used to transmit money secretly from New Zealand to the UK. In the case of the Royal Mail Steam Packet Company, there was an attempt to use the previously built up reserves of the company to ease the company through the bad times until the expected good times reappeared. The four Australian cases of creative accounting of the 1960s and 1970s (Reid Murray, H.G. Palmer, Minisec and Cambridge Credit) all shared certain characteristics. The companies involved were fast growing and acquisitive. They all used a variety of accounting techniques such as round-robin cheques, provision accounting, not recording bad debts, retrospective accounting, back-to-back loans, misclassification of assets and 'front-end' sales to manufacture earnings and assets. In the case of the Associated Electrical Industries takeover by General Electric Company in 1967, creative accounting seems to have been used by AEI to increase their profits so as to raise the company's share price in an unsuccessful attempt to ward off the takeover. It may also have been used by the incoming management to depress the current year's figures at the expense of future years' profits. Finally, in the Renouf and Judge Corporations a range of creative accounting techniques appears to have been used to sustain the profits of the companies.

Creative accounting and fraud have, therefore, been used for a variety of purposes. Generally, they have come to light when the companies have run into trouble or, most commonly, have collapsed. However, in some cases (the cruciform monument, the Cely merchants and Kreuger & Toll), the perpetrators appear to have been undetected in their lifetimes. However, more commonly companies have collapsed and then an enquiry has been instigated. The enquiry established that creative accounting and/or fraud have been implicated in the company's collapse. However, the interesting and unanswerable question remains: how many cases of creative accounting and fraud have been successfully accomplished without detection?

## REFERENCES

Arnold, A.J. (1991), 'Secret reserves or special credits? A reappraisal of the reserve and provision accounting policies of the Royal Mail Steam Packet Company, 1915–1927', *Accounting and Business Research*, **21**(83), 203–214.

Baxter, W.T. (1999), 'McKesson & Robbins: a milestone in auditing', *Accounting, Business and Financial History*, July, 157–174.

Brooks, C. (1933), 'The Royal Mail Case 1931'. Reprinted in *Dimensions of Accounting Theory and Practice*, ed. R.P. Brief, Arno Press, New York, 1980.

Bryer, R.A. (1991), 'Accounting for the "railway mania" of 1845 – a great railway swindle?', *Accounting, Organizations and Society*, **16**(5/6), 439–486.

Carswell, J. (1960), *The South Sea Bubble*, The Cresset Press, London.

Chatfield, M. (1973), *A History of Accounting Thought*, The Dryden Press, IL.

Clarke, F., Dean, G. and Oliver, K. (2003), *Corporate Collapse: Accounting, Regulatory and Ethical Failure*, Cambridge University Press, Cambridge.

Couper, C.T. (1879), 'City of Glasgow Bank Trial, 1878', in *Accounting History and the Development of a Profession*, ed. R.P. Brief, Garland Publishing, Inc., New York, 1984.

de Roover (1956), 'The development of accounting prior to Luca Pacioli according to the account books of Medieval merchants', in A.C. Littleton and B.S Yamey, *Studies in the History of Accounting*.

Edwards, J.R. (1975), 'The accounting profession and disclosure in published reports, 1925–1935', *Accounting and Business Research*, **6**, 289–302.

Edwards, J.R. (1989), *A History of Financial Accounting*, Routledge, London.

Evans, D.M. (1859), *Facts, Failures and Fraud: Revelations, Financial, Mercantile, Criminal*, Groombridge and Sons, London.

Flesher, D.L. and Flesher, T.K. (1986), 'Ivar Kreuger's contribution to U.S. financial reporting', *The Accounting Review*, **LXI**(3), 421–434.

French, E.A. (1984), *Introduction to City of Glasgow Bank. Report and Trial of the Directors and Managers of the City of Glasgow Bank*, Yale, USA.

Hanham, A. (1973), 'Make a careful investigation: some fraudulent accounts in the Cely papers', *Speculum*, **98**(2), 313–324.

Hooper, K. and Kearins, K. (1995), 'The rise and fall of the Judge and Renouf Corporations: extravagant reporting and publicity', *Accounting, Business and Financial History*, **5**(2), 187–209.

Jones, M.J. (2008), 'Internal control, accountability and corporate governance: medieval and modern Britain compared', *Accounting, Auditing and Accountability Journal*, **21**(7), 1052–1075.

Lee, T.A. (2004), 'The dominant manager in the history of auditing', *Accounting Business and Financial History Conference*, Cardiff, September.

Monteagle Committee (1849), *House of Lords Select Committee on the Audit of Railway Accounts. First, Second and Third Report, Minutes of Evidence and Appendix*, British Parliamentary Papers.

Napier, C. (1995), 'Secret accounting in New Zealand: P&O and the Union Steam Ship Company, 1917–36', in A. Tsuji and P. Garner (eds), *Studies in Accounting History: Tradition and Innovation for the Twenty-First Century*, Greenwood Press, Westport, CT, pp. 135–157.

Parker, R.H. (1991), 'Misleading accounts: pitfalls for historians', *Business History*, **33**(4), 1–18.

Rutherford, B.A. (1996), 'The AEI–GEC gap revisited', *Accounting, Business and Financial History*, **6**(2), 141–161.

Shaplen, R. (1955), 'The metamorphosis of Philip Musica', *The New Yorker*. Reprinted in *Great Business Disasters, Swindles, Burglaries and Frauds in American History*, ed. I. Barmarsh, Playboy Press Book, Chicago, IL, 1972.

Vamplew, W. (1974), 'A careful and most ingenious fabrication of imaginary accounts: Scottish Railway Company Accounts before 1868', *The Accountants' Magazine*, August, 307–312.

# Part B

# Accounting Scandals in Australia since the Late 1980s

Garry D. Carnegie and Brendan T. O'Connell

## 8.1 INTRODUCTION

Corporate failures and accounting scandals are often interrelated. History has repeatedly shown that accounting failure is frequently a determinant of unexpected corporate collapses. As sharply illustrated in the early 2000s with Enron and WorldCom in the United States and with HIH Insurance in Australia, such a phenomenon is not ancient or quaint. In response to instances of accounting failure, legislative and other reforms are typically adopted to ensure that such instances do not arise again in future. Notwithstanding these reforms, corporate failures are perennial, especially during periods of economic downturn, and typically leave the accounting profession defending itself, repeatedly, leading to yet further governance reforms that are intended to ensure, as far as possible, that errors, misjudgements and negligence of the past do not recur.

Corporate scandals up to the time of writing in Australia have not been unusual in the sense that such failures reflect the excesses of human behaviour, specifically in the commercial/corporate world, where greed and hubris can assume prominence, especially during periods of rapid economic development or transformation or extended economic growth. Such conditions are exacerbated during times when there is little or no effective company regulation, especially when the accounting and audit provisions of relevant company legislation, if any, are shown to be inadequate. Such circumstances were evident in Eastern Australia during the early 1890s major economic depression which brought the boom time that had been experienced since the 1870s to an abrupt end. Since that time other rounds of corporate failure have been experienced in Australia, most notably during the 1960s, 1970s, late 1980s/early 1990s and early 2000s. The early 2000s corporate failures did not necessarily arise as a consequence of tight or severe general economic conditions, but have occurred largely due to poor or ineffective management, including inadequate corporate governance and accounting and financial reporting, combined with concerns about the lack of perceived independence of auditors, in general, and about the perceived lack of independence of certain audit practitioners, in particular.

Australia is part of the developed world as a resource-rich industrial country. It is known as the 'lucky country'. As Australia once comprised six British colonies until Federation took place on 1 January 1901, Australian institutions and legislation were

*Creative Accounting, Fraud and International Accounting Scandals*   Edited by Michael Jones
© 2011 Michael Jones. Published by John Wiley & Sons, Ltd

shaped by Britain as the 'mother' country. Its regulation of companies across time has been specifically influenced by spates of corporate collapses in Australia. In addition, major corporate failures in Britain, which have often resulted in the passage of corrective laws in that country, have subsequently influenced the form of Australian laws on companies. More recently, US legislative reforms have impacted developments in Australia, particularly the Sarbanes-Oxley Act of 2002, while International Accounting Standards/International Financial Reporting Standards of the International Accounting Standards Board have been adopted in Australia, since 2005, as Australian International Financial Reporting Standards (AIFRS).

The remainder of this chapter is structured as follows. First, there is an overview of corporate and accounting scandals in Australia during particular periods, as outlined above, dating from the 1890s economic depression. In the next section, further attention is placed on four specific corporate scandals, namely Adelaide Steamship, Bond Corporation, Harris Scarfe and One.Tel that occurred either during the late 1980s and early 1990s or in the early 2000s. A detailed examination of the collapse of HIH Insurance, which collapsed in 2001, and the aftermath of that major company collapse follows. Thereafter, the implications of such scandals for corporate governance oversight and regulation in Australia are briefly examined. The conclusion then follows.

## 8.2 OVERVIEW OF ACCOUNTING SCANDALS DURING AND SINCE THE 1890s

According to Sykes (1998, chapter 2), the first major corporate collapse in Australia, when known as New South Wales, was the Australian Auction Company, which failed in Sydney in 1841 due to mismanagement and a lack of commercial prudence. This collapse came during the country's earliest economic downturn after European settlement and followed a major speculative land boom and excessive consumer spending during the 1830s. While there were a number of other major corporate collapses during the period until the early 1890s, such as the Royal Bank of Australia in 1849 (Sykes, 1998, chapter 3), the Bendigo Waterworks Company in 1860 (Sykes, 1998, chapter 4), the Bank of Queensland in 1866 (Sykes, 1998, chapter 5) and the Provincial and Suburban Bank in 1879 (Sykes, 1998, chapter 6), the first major calamitous period in Australian corporate and accounting history came in the early 1890s. This dramatic decline followed a spectacular land boom, where optimism and speculation reached almost staggering heights during the 1880s (see, for example, Blainey, 1958, chapter 10; Boehm, 1971; Butlin, 1961, chapter 12; Butlin, 1964; Cannon, 1967).

The Colony of Victoria was made prosperous by the gold rush of the 1850s and, following mass immigration and rapid pastoral industry expansion, boom times were experienced. Victoria's capital, Melbourne, became known as 'Marvellous Melbourne' during the 1880s and, by 1892, it was Australia's largest city with half a million inhabitants (Briggs, 1977, p. 278). Eastern Australia of the period has been described as one of the most concentrated examples of the *laissez-faire* 'boom and bust economy' (Cannon, 1967, back cover). The year 1888 is recognised as the 'insane miraculous year' (Serle, 1971, p. 247). The inevitable economic depression that followed a silver boom and a period of excessive land speculation was catastrophic and gripped Eastern Australia during the early 1890s. This period brought havoc and witnessed the collapse of many banks, building societies and land finance companies. Briefly during this period, two-thirds of the country's banking assets were frozen (Sykes, 1998, p. xi). According to Sykes (1998, p. xi), this crash brought the worst wave of collapses experienced in Australia's history in terms of 'personal grief and economic disruption'. In distributing blame for the collapse, the accounting profession was not immune from harsh criticism.

Particular attention was focused on the state of auditing around the time, which was described by various commentators as a farce. A report in the *Age* newspaper of 14 December 1891, for example, stated '. . . the urgent demand for a better system of audit is conspicuous. Existing auditing arrangements have been proved in numberless instances to be farcical' (p. 4). Commentators were especially critical of the close personal ties between directors and auditors, the incompetence of certain auditors and the focus placed by too many auditors on the arithmetical accuracy of books and the balance sheet (Waugh, 1992, p. 377) rather than exercising their professional judgement on key matters such as the collectability of debts and loans and the dependability of the monetary values attributed to assets (see, for instance, the *Australasian Insurance and Banking Record*, 1891). According to John B.C. Miles, President of the Sydney Institute of Public Accountants (1894), the auditors in many cases were unable or unwilling to provide 'diligent examination of the accounts . . . and they were, in all probability, friends of the directors, whose acquiescent minions they voluntarily became' (Miles, 1895, reproduced in Carnegie and Parker, 1999, pp. 207–226).

The *Australasian Insurance and Banking Record* (*AIBR*) was as scathing as Miles on standards of accounting and audit (Carnegie and Parker, 1999, p. 17). The journal's considered views on the auditing aspects of the 1890s financial crisis are contained in a two-part article in its February and March 1892 issues. It was explained in the first part of the article that:

> [t]he disasters which have recently overtaken some of the financial institutions doing business in Melbourne and Sydney, have caused the subject of audit to be brought more prominently before the public than has hitherto been the case. At some of the meetings of shareholders it has been more than hinted that collapse could have been averted had the auditors appointed to examine and certify to the correctness of accounts performed their duties in a less perfunctory manner.
>
> (*AIBR*, 1892, p. 81, reproduced in Carnegie and Parker, 1999, pp. 182–184; also see Waugh, 1992, pp. 377–388)

While the last two decades of the nineteenth century witnessed increased demand for accounting and audit services due to growth in company formation and the beginnings of the organised accounting profession in Australia (Carnegie and Edwards, 2001, pp. 305–306), the 1890s scandals were a severe test for the fledgling professional accounting bodies and their members. Notwithstanding the impact of these scandals, Davison (1978, p. 112) put the view that 'a popular fear of bad bookkeeping . . . gave accountants their new professional status'. The 1890s scandals also resulted in the passage of the Victorian Companies Act of 1896 which was the first legislation on company auditing in Australia (Chua and Poullaos, 1998; Gibson, 1971, pp. 39–47; 1979, pp. 24–25; 1988, p. 24). This Act required public companies to issue an audited balance sheet which disclosed a minimum range of information.

The 1890s crash demonstrated that 'big crashes follow big booms' (Sykes, 1998, p. xi). This phenomenon was not the case during the Great Depression of the 1930s as Australia had not experienced a sizeable boom during the 1920s. While the Great Depression was the worst ever economic depression to be experienced in Australia, it was not marked by a wave of corporate collapses as companies and other entities as well as individual business operators toughed out the turmoil. The early 1960s witnessed a rapid expansion in consumer spending fuelled by the easiest credit terms in living memory following an influx of European settlers to Australia from 1949 and, ultimately, brought about a Commonwealth government-imposed credit squeeze. Companies which failed during this period included Reid Murray, Stanhill Development Finance, Cox Brothers and H.G. Palmer (Consolidated). Conventional accounting practices, once again, came under strong criticism (see, for example, Birkett and Walker, 1971; Chambers, 1973; Clarke, Dean and Oliver, 2003, pp. 49–50). One commentator stated 'one point that does emerge clearly from these results [i.e. failures] is that several companies have very misleading statements of profits in the previous year's accounts and in interim statements last year' (*Australian Financial Review*, 22 January 1963). It was also indicated that stock exchange officials asserted that 'poor accounting ... brought about these situations' (*Australian Financial Review*, 22 January 1963; also see Birkett and Walker, 1971). A 1966 report of the General Council of the Australian Society of Accountants (ASA), entitled *Accounting Principles and Practices Discussed in Reports on Company Failures*, while responding to criticism of certain accounting practices and of the profession generally following these failures, endeavoured to defend accounting from playing a key role and instead identified management and management practices as the main culprits (ASA, 1966). On the other hand, the Institute of Chartered Accountants in Australia (ICAA) appears to have virtually remained silent in dealing with the specific criticisms made, thus illustrating another form of 'response' to this testing period for the local accounting profession. Notwithstanding the ICAA approach, 'the [accounting] profession was "stirred" by the company failures of the 1960s' (Birkett and Walker, 1971, p. 136).

The next boom in Australia during the early 1970s was led by the mining industry and was known as 'the nickel boom' (Sykes, 1998, p. 384). This period witnessed the demise of Mineral Securities Australia, Mainline Corporation, Cambridge Credit Corporation, Gollin Holdings and Poseidon NL among other failed companies. Following a major share market downturn in October 1987, the 'frantic boom' of the 1980s was over and there resulted the 'second worst' wave of corporate collapses ever to have been experienced in Australia (Sykes, 1998, p. xi) to the time of writing. This pre-recession period has been described as 'the dreamtime casino' (McManamy, 1990) and was fuelled by the notion that 'greed is good' (Barry, 1990, p. 286). The period prior to the 1989–92 economic recession was marked by excessive borrowing, much of which was raised to finance certain takeovers at substantial or excessive prices. Failures included Adelaide Steamship, Ariadne, Bond Corporation, Hooker, Judge Corporation, Parry Corporation, Spedley Securities, Tricontinental and Westmex as well as the State Bank of Victoria and the State Bank of South Australia. According to Green (1991, p. 145) 'everyone had their eyes closed' during the 1980s boom period while Sykes likened the seemingly inevitable collapse to the events of the 1890s in stating 'clearly by the 1980s we had forgotten the lessons of the 1890s' (Sykes, 1998, p. xi).

The early 2000s, especially the year 2001 which shockingly brought global terrorism to the fore, also brought another round of corporate failures in Australia, which included Ansett, Centaur, Harris Scarfe, HIH Insurance, One.Tel and Pasminco (see, for example, Bosch, 2001; Clarke and Dean, 2001; Clarke, Dean and Oliver, 2003, pp. 215–221; Fabro, 2001; Johnson, 2004b, pp. 1–16). Such failures coincided with the shock failure of Enron and WorldCom, which were causing much anxiety in international financial markets and within the worldwide accounting profession (see, among others, Brewster, 2003; DiPiazza and Eccles, 2002; Fox, 2003; Hamilton and Micklethwait, 2006; Jeter, 2003) with implications for popular conceptions of accountants and accounting (Carnegie and Napier, 2010). In January 2002, an Australian press story headline stated 'Judges face busy time as watchdogs pounce' (Hepworth, 2002).

Unlike earlier failures in Australia, as outlined above, this series of collapses did not eventuate in the immediate aftermath of a boom period. Instead, the boom in Australia which commenced following the 1989–92 corporate shakeout has continued virtually unabated since 2001 to the time of writing. Kohler (2001, p. 21), in commenting on the role of auditors in the early 2000s failures, argued:

> Auditors once again have a lot to answer for. Every time there is a wave of collapses, auditors shuffle into the firing line. It has happened again, with auditors once again saying that the problem is not their performance but the 'expectation gap' – this is, we all expect too much of them.

Stephen Harrison, the then Executive Director of the ICAA, defended the accounting profession in stating 'you can change the rules on auditors as much as you like and it's not going to prevent companies collapsing' (Hepworth, 2001, p. 8; also see Harrison, 2001). Furthermore, as Humphrey, Moizer and Turley (1992) suggested, there has probably always been an audit expectation gap of a genre (also see Carnegie and Parker, 1999, p. 11). Notwithstanding such perceptions, within the context of corporate collapse in Australia, accounting has repeatedly shown itself, according to Clarke, Dean and Oliver (2003, p. xxiii) as 'a willing traveller, revealing in many instances surprisingly little along the path to failure' while many failed companies, over the decades, 'collapsed unexpectedly, just after reporting healthy profit figures' (also see Clarke and Dean, 1992; Harris, 2003). According to Gaffikin, Dagwell and Wines (2004, p. 17), 'accounting is not solely responsible for corporate collapse, but if the purpose of accounting is to provide information to users – accountability – then it must accept part of the responsibility'. Auditors have also been subject to multi-million claims for damages due to their actual or perceived negligence in conducting audits of companies which later failed (see, for example, Johnson, 2004a; Lawson, 1993; Pheasant, 1993).

## 8.3 CASE STUDIES OF ACCOUNTING SCANDALS SINCE THE LATE 1980S

As indicated earlier, this section examines four case studies, namely Adelaide Steamship, Bond Corporation, Harris Scarfe and One.Tel, which failed during the periods dating from the late 1980s and early 1990s through to the early 2000s. The first two named companies ultimately collapsed in 1991, while the other two entities failed in 2001. Bond Corporation and Adelaide Steamship were two of the largest corporate failures in Australia during the 1989–92 recession. The failure of Harris Scarfe and One.Tel added to consternation in the Australian share market around the time of the collapse of HIH Insurance (see Clarke, Dean and Oliver, 2003, p. 218 for a tabulation of major company failures in Australia in the early 2000s). The four cases are illuminated in alphabetical order and, for each case, the background, accounting issues and legal outcomes will be addressed on a summarised basis. The section thereafter deals with the demise of HIH Insurance which, as mentioned earlier, collapsed in 2001.

### 8.3.1 Adelaide Steamship

#### 8.3.1.1 Background

The Adelaide Steamship Company Limited ('Adsteam') was one of Australia's oldest surviving industrial companies in the late 1980s. It had operated passenger and cargo ships in Australia since 1875. Under the leadership of entrepreneur John Spalvins, the company divested many of its traditional businesses in the late 1970s and aggressively acquired significant shareholdings in a variety of companies in a number of fields including retailing, hotels, leisure industries and civil engineering. A feature of its structure was a complex web of cross-shareholdings across the group, with many of these shareholdings comprising slightly less than 50 per cent of total issued shares.

Adsteam's share price rose dramatically through much of the 1980s and it was hailed by some commentators as being entrepreneurial, well managed and with a highly-disciplined reporting system (Clarke, Dean and Oliver, 2003, p. 159). Yet by 1990 the company was in poor shape as revelations about suspect or inappropriate financial reporting practices and excessively high debt levels placed strong downward pressure on its share price. In 1991, Adsteam was placed under an informal, receivership-type scheme of arrangement (Peers, 1991, pp. 1 and 2). A newspaper report on its failure carried the sub-headline 'Adsteam a humiliation for the accounting profession' (Kohler, 1991, p. 52; also see Burge, 1991).

#### 8.3.1.2 Accounting Issues

Clarke, Dean and Oliver (2003, p. 158) pointed out that Adsteam was 'an excellent instance of how the rule-book approach to consolidation accounting imposed by the law and the Accounting Standards *at the time* determined managerial actions' (emphasis in original). Prevailing accounting rules for consolidation enabled Adsteam to avoid consolidating the results of entities that were under its effective control (Pierpont, 1992; also see Carnegie, Gavens and Gibson, 1989, pp. 112–113; McCrann, 1986; Sykes, 1989). This is because 'control' under companies legislation in place at that time was based on levels of ownership interest or what was generally known as 'the 50 per cent rule'. Adsteam owned just below 50 per cent of many of its major interests and thus was able to avert the consolidation for financial reporting purposes of certain important strategic interests through a strict application of this rule. This approach was at odds with a 'substance over form' approach to accounting which emphasises reporting on the full dimensions of the controlled entities comprising a corporate group. Concerns were also raised about Adsteam's approach to asset revaluations and the valuation basis for some assets (see next part). When under attack from analysts and commentators, Spalvins 'followed a popular strategy ..., his bellicose remarks aimed directly at those who doubted the financial strength and viability of Adsteam' (Clarke, Dean and Oliver, 2003, p. 162).

### 8.3.1.3  Legal Outcomes

The Australian Securities Commission (ASC) (later known as the Australian Securities and Investments Commission) alleged that related-party transactions between Adsteam and other parties were used to present the Group's affairs in an artificially better state than the underlying conditions justified. It was further alleged that some asset revaluations, related entity profits and dividend transfers were accounted for in ways which did not comply with the (then) existing accounting standards. For instance, it was claimed that the interim dividend for 1990 should not have been paid as directors should have been aware that the Group's profits were grossly overstated. The basis for this allegation was that assets relating to certain loans and future income tax benefits were recorded in the accounts at figures higher than could have been reasonably justified in the prevailing circumstances. Some asset revaluations were also selective and seemingly over-optimistic (Clarke, Dean and Oliver, 2003, p. 161).

The Adsteam saga contributed to major changes to Australian accounting rules pertaining to consolidation and led to the issue of AAS 24 Consolidated Financial Statements by the accounting profession in June 1990 for application from 30 June 1991 (subject to a 'legal impediment,' see Deegan, 2005, p. 880) and the issue of AASB 1024 Consolidated Accounts with statutory backing in 1991 (Walker, 1992; Walker and Mack, 1998, pp. 58–59). Specifically, the definition of 'control' for consolidation purposes was broadened beyond prescribed ownership interests to embrace control over an entity's financial and operating policies, making use of the notion of 'substance over form' in determining the existence of a controlled entity. A decade after the company was placed into receivership, a major out-of-court settlement (reportedly for $20 million) was reached between the directors and auditors of Adsteam and the Australian Securities and Investments Commission (ASIC), thus settling a class action that ASIC had brought on behalf of Adsteam (ASIC, 2000; Johnson, 2004a, p. 19; Maiden, 2000).

## 8.3.2  Bond Corporation

### 8.3.2.1  Background

Bond Corporation Limited ('Bond Corporation') was a diversified industrial company that had a spectacular rise and fall. It had humble beginnings in the 1960s as a sign-writing firm that was owned by Alan Bond. From the 1970s to the 1980s, under the leadership of Alan Bond, a charismatic and overt personality, Bond Corporation expanded aggressively through a series of takeovers and reached its peak in the late 1980s with acquisitions of brewing interests and a major TV network among other interests; it was also a property developer and even owned Australia's first private university, known as Bond University. Towards the end of 1988, Bond Corporation also sought to gain control of the international trading house, Lonrho, which as a defence released an almost 100-page financial analysis of the Bond group that contended it was 'technically insolvent' at the time of its preparation in November 1988 (Anon, 1989; also see Clarke, Dean and Oliver, 2003, pp. 183–186).

The company's share price, which had risen dramatically throughout the 1970s and early to mid-1980s, began to slide in late 1988. The declines in share price were due to concerns about the declining value of some of its investments following the October 1987 share market downturn and as a consequence of its high or excessive debt levels. By 1991 the company was insolvent and Alan Bond had resigned as chairman, effectively leaving the company's creditors to administer its affairs.

### 8.3.2.2   Accounting Issues

Bond Corporation became associated with the 'window-dressing' of accounts (Walker, 1988b; also see Barry, 1990; Gibson, 1990, 1992; Ryan and McClymont, 1992a, b; Walsh, 1992). According to Clarke and Dean (2001, p. 73), 'image-enhancing financial reporting tactics masked the financial impact of [Bond Corporation's] growth by acquisition policy'. More specifically, Walker (1988a), for example, elucidated the treatment of gains and losses on the sale of businesses as part of normal or ordinary operations claiming that its 'primary operations' included 'the disposition of assets acquired during the period or held for trading purposes from prior years'. Walker (1988b) also examined the group's use of tax-effect accounting and its treatment of convertible bonds. Changes to the group's accounting policy for taxes, for instance, meant that during the year 1986–87 there was an effective offset of a current liability (provision for income tax) against a non-current asset (future income tax benefit, which is an accounting entry reflecting the likelihood of future savings in income tax to the company arising under tax-effect accounting) (Walker, 1988b). Convertible bonds were treated as equity rather than as liabilities. In addition, during the financial year ending 30 June 1987, the proceeds of an issue of convertible bonds were applied to reduce the amounts of certain debts as at that year end even though the proceeds were received nine days after financial year end (also see Carnegie, Gavens and Gibson, 1989, pp. 39–41). Walker (1988b) argued that such aggressive accounting treatments maximised 'the impression of growth and liquidity'. Questions were also raised about the company's treatment of foreign exchange translations. In the 1987–88 financial statements foreign exchange gains constituted a significant 38 per cent of the reported consolidated operating profit for the year (Clarke, Dean and Oliver, 2003, pp. 194–195).

### 8.3.2.3   Legal Outcomes

Alan Bond ended up pleading guilty to fraud and was sentenced to jail for a period of four years, later extended to seven years, for transferring £1.2 billion from companies in the Bell Resources group to subsidiaries and related parties of Bond Corporation. At the time of the transfer, Bond Corporation was experiencing serious financial difficulties while Bond Corporation and related parties combined owned 53 per cent of Bell Resources, which was a separately listed holding company. This upstream transfer from Bell Resources 'has been described as Australia's largest corporate fraud' (Clarke, Dean and Oliver, 2003, p. 178). Bond Corporation's auditors, Andersen, settled out of court in 2002, allegedly for approximately $100 million, after legal action was taken over its handling of the company's 1988 audit (Drummond, 2002a, b; Johnson, 2004a, p. 19). Originally known as 'Arthur Andersen & Co.,' the firm gradually dropped parts of this name, becoming 'Arthur Andersen' in the mid-1990s and simply 'Andersen' in 2001 ('Arthur Andersen re-brands … again,' *Accountancy*, April 2001, p. 15). Hereafter, the firm is referred to as Andersen.

### 8.3.3 Harris Scarfe

#### 8.3.3.1 *Background*

Harris Scarfe Limited ('Harris Scarfe') was a publicly-listed discount department store chain at the time of being placed into receivership in April 2001. On entering receivership, the retailer had been operating for a continuous period in excess of 150 years. The company entered receivership as a result of bad management following revelations of serious accounting and financial reporting irregularities arising over a period of six years.

#### 8.3.3.2 *Accounting Issues*

Accounting irregularities which occurred at Harris Scarfe led to the publication of misleading financial statements. Reported profit numbers for many years appeared to be engineered in order to meet the profit expectations of directors. For instance, the consolidated financial statements for year ended 31 December 2000 were found to have overstated the group's net assets. Inventories were deliberately stated in the financial statements at artificially high levels under inappropriate accounting for this class of asset, while liabilities were understated (Clarke and Dean, 2001, p. 75; Debelle, 2001; Johnson, 2004b, p. 7; for a case study on Harris Scarfe's pathway to insolvency, see Whittred, 2005, pp. 720–725).

Discrepancies in accounting for inventories were discovered in March 2001 and the auditors were requested to investigate the deterioration of the group's net asset position. The auditors reported to the board that the irregularities had been occurring for up to six years, suggesting the existence of weaknesses in the internal control system. Evidently, neither the board nor the auditors were aware of the irregularities at any stage during this period. The board announced that it had acted in good faith on financial information received from senior management.

#### 8.3.3.3 *Legal Outcomes*

Various legal actions have been mounted against the former management of Harris Scarfe. The ASIC announced an investigation into possible breaches of the Corporations Act by the company's management. Criminal charges were laid against the former Chief Financial Officer of Harris Scarfe, Allan Hodgson. He pleaded guilty to a total of 32 charges (18 counts of failing to act honestly as an officer, six counts of acting dishonestly as an employee, and eight counts relating to the dissemination of false information to the Australian Stock Exchange) and was sentenced to six years' imprisonment (ASIC, 2002; Clarke, Dean and Oliver, 2003, p. 218). Legal action has also been launched against the former auditors of

Harris Scarfe, Ernst & Young and PricewaterhouseCoopers, for alleged negligence in the conduct of their respective audits (James, 2006). The action for $220 million in damages was, according to Johnson (2004b, p. 4), 'highly likely' to be 'settled out of court,' as turned out to be the case with Ernst & Young which negotiated a confidential settlement with the plaintiffs (Gluyas, 2006).

### 8.3.4  One.Tel

#### *8.3.4.1  Background*

Established in 1995, One.Tel Limited ('One.Tel') operated in the mobile telephone services sector. Essentially, it acted as a reseller of telephone services provided by major telecommunications companies. It focused on signing up new customers on telephone plans for, and on behalf of, the owners of major telephone networks. It had a spectacular rise during the mid to late 1990s as the mobile telephone sector in Australia expanded significantly. It had managed to negotiate an attractive contract with one of Australia's major telecommunications companies, Optus, to receive a set fee for each new customer it signed. It also received revenue from customers' telephone usage. One.Tel was founded by Jodee Rich (Clarke, Dean and Oliver, 2003, p. 16), an individual with very strong self-belief and a dominant personality (Barry, 2002, pp. xv and 38–39), who was adept at selling the virtues of One.Tel to all who would listen.

One.Tel's share price rose significantly from the mid to late 1990s. The company became increasingly ambitious. The sons of two high-profile businessmen, Lachlan Murdoch (son of Rupert) and James Packer (son of the late Kerry), invested considerable amounts into One.Tel and were non-executive directors (Clarke and Dean, 2001, pp. 78 and 82–83). One.Tel's management decided that it would develop its own mobile telephone network rather than continue to rely on being a reseller of telephone services. The cost of this major expansion combined with its inadequate accounting systems, which allegedly 'caused One.Tel to cost its product incorrectly' (Clarke and Dean, 2001, p. 98) and also contributed to debtors' collection problems as outlined below, resulted in the company becoming insolvent and being placed into liquidation in 2001. At the time of its collapse, One.Tel had over 40 subsidiaries in 16 countries (Clarke and Dean, 2001, p. 96).

#### *8.3.4.2  Accounting Issues*

According to Clarke, Dean and Oliver (2003, p. 263), the failure of One.Tel 'epitomises the consequences of overtrading, overcapitalisation, marketing ploys that entailed cash outflows impossible to sustain, and the problems endemic of *recognising* revenues ahead of the likely related cash flows' (emphasis in original). It appears to have grossly overstated its debtors' balances. The company aggressively sold telephone services on street corners, in city shopping centres and in major regional centres across the country. Few or inadequate credit checks were undertaken on the customers who signed up for these services, suggesting a major internal control weakness. As a result of this aggressive marketing campaign, people of all ages and circumstances, such as the unemployed, teenagers and international visitors, seemingly happily signed on as its customers. The result of this aggressive business development strategy was that many of its debtors did not pay their accounts for services provided by the company. Notwithstanding these problems with the collectability of its receivables, the consolidated financial statements showed a fairly modest or even low provision for doubtful debts.

One.Tel recorded as an asset on its balance sheet spectrum licences it had acquired at a cost amount in excess of $500 million (Clarke, Dean and Oliver, 2003, p. 263). These licences were deemed necessary for the company to realise its aim of developing its own mobile telephone network. It was later reported that the price paid was 10 times higher than amounts competitors had paid for the same bandwidth access just a few years earlier (Barry, 2002, p. 178). In addition, a prepaid 'advertising' cost of $90 million was treated as an asset which, reportedly, was written off on One.Tel's demise (Clarke, Dean and Oliver, 2003, p. 263). In April 2000, One.Tel was subject to an ASIC enforcement action in respect to its capitalisation of advertising and staff costs as an asset rather than writing off the costs as expenses (da Silva Rosa, Filippetto and Tarca, 2008).

### 8.3.4.3   Legal Outcomes

Various legal actions have been launched by ASIC and others against the former management of One.Tel, including civil charges for alleged dishonest and misleading acts and fraud (see, for example, Clarke, Dean and Oliver, 2003, p. 218). In particular, the ASIC alleged that former directors, Jodee Rich, Mark Silbermann and Brad Keeling, deliberately withheld information from the rest of the board of directors and investors. ASIC also alleged that a fourth director, John Greaves, breached his duty to exercise the standards of care and diligence required by the law. ASIC reached agreement with Greaves and Keeling after they pleaded guilty. Greaves was prohibited from managing a corporation for a period of four years, and agreed to pay compensation of $20 million to One.Tel as well as ASIC's court costs of $350 000 (ASIC, 2004). Under the terms of the ASIC settlement with Keeling, he was banned from being a director, or otherwise from being involved in the management of any corporation for a period of 10 years and was 'liable to pay compensation of $92 million to One.Tel (ASIC claims that all four defendants are jointly and severally liable for this compensation)' as well as to pay ASIC's costs of $750 000 (ASIC, 2003). In November 2009, ASIC suffered a 'humiliating loss' when the NSW Supreme Court 'threw out' the charges against Rich and Silbermann and 'criticised the watchdog for exaggerating and running a superficial case' (Jacobs and Grigg, 2009, p. 1; also see Chenoweth, 2009).

## 8.4 HIH INSURANCE

The collapse of HIH Insurance Limited (hereafter known as 'HIH') in 2001 was the largest ever collapse in Australia's corporate history (Martin, 2003; Westfield, 2003). Its failure had a profound impact on many parts of industry and commerce. According to the HIH Royal Commission Report (2003):

> Its collapse left the building industry in turmoil. Home owners were left without compulsory home warranty insurance; the owners of residential dwellings have found that cover for defective building work has vanished; builders are unable to operate because they cannot

obtain builders' warranty insurance. The cost to the building and construction industry alone
has forced state governments to spend millions of dollars of public money to prevent further
damage to the industry. (p. xiii)

The following analysis of HIH will provide a background to the company, address why
the collapse occurred, examine the accounting issues emanating from this collapse, provide
a brief postscript of the fallout arising from the collapse for HIH executives and consider
the evidence on the role of the auditor in the decline of HIH.

### 8.4.1 Background

HIH was formed as a small insurance company in 1968 by Ray Williams, who became its
long-serving CEO, and Michael Payne. Ray Williams has been described as a dominating
personality with a 'relentless drive to succeed' (Main, 2003, p. 34). HIH's main business was
to underwrite workers' compensation insurance in Australia as an agent for two syndicates
of Lloyd's of London. The company expanded its operations into property, commercial and
professional liability from the mid-1980s. During this period, it also moved into the UK and
the US insurance markets. In the USA, the focus was on workers' compensation insurance.
Public liability and professional indemnity insurance were its main specialisations in the
UK.

HIH increased its share of the Australian market in 1997 by means of the takeover of
Colonial Mutual General Insurance Company Limited. In 1999, HIH completed another
major acquisition in the form of FAI Insurance Limited (FAI). By the late 1990s particular
segments of HIH's operations, especially the US and UK operations, were not performing
well (see HIH Royal Commission Report, 2003, Section 3.3 for an elaboration of HIH's
poor financial performance in these two geographical areas).

Moreover, the FAI acquisition was also generating some concerns within the board and
management of HIH because of unexpected losses arising from apparent under-reserving in
FAI's professional indemnity portfolios. According to the HIH Royal Commission Report
(2003, p. 56), the actual losses as at 30 June 2000 amounted to more than $530 million
and were either debited to a 'goodwill on acquisition' account or purportedly covered by
reinsurance policies written with other insurers. These issues will be examined shortly in
the 'accounting issues' subsection.

During 2000, HIH exhibited a declining profitability and capital base which management
primarily attributed to low insurance premiums in highly competitive markets (Westfield,
2003, p. 185). The financial media and stock analysts were also questioning the company's
performance and future prospects. At this time, as a consequence of its declining financial
position, HIH signed a joint-venture agreement with Allianz Australia Insurance Limited.
Under this arrangement, HIH transferred its valuable personal lines and compulsory third-
party insurance business to an unincorporated joint venture in return for a payment of
$200 million. The company's share price plunged in reaction to this announcement. In-
vestors evidently viewed this transaction as an act of desperation (Westfield, 2003, p. 181).
Following an adverse review of HIH's financial position by KMPG in early March 2001, a
provisional liquidator was appointed by the HIH board. The issuing of a court order on 27
August 2001 placed HIH into official liquidation.

As a result of HIH's collapse, investors lost millions and many consumers and companies suddenly found they were uninsured. The Australian Commonwealth government announced a Royal Commission into the HIH collapse in response to the public outrage and entered into an arrangement to indemnify HIH policyholders who were able to demonstrate genuine hardship. State governments around the country also took action to mitigate the effects of the collapse and undertook to fulfil many outstanding HIH builders' warranties and third-party obligations (HIH Royal Commission Report, 2003, Section 3.7).

### 8.4.2  Why did HIH Collapse?

In the HIH Royal Commission Report (2003), the Honourable Justice Owen (the Commissioner) noted that:

> ... the shambling journey towards oblivion began a long time before March 2001 ... the corporate officers, auditors and regulators of HIH failed to see, remedy or report what should have been obvious. And some of those who were in or close to the management of the group ignored or, worse, concealed the true state of the group's steadily deteriorating financial position. (p. xiii)

The HIH Royal Commission Report (2003, p. xiii) attributed the failure of the company to two key factors. First, claims arising from insured events in previous years were much greater than the company had provided for in its accounts, thus leading to an overstatement of reported profits. This is known as 'under-reserving' or 'under-provisioning' (see, for example, Main, 2002; Sykes, 2002; Zehnwirth, 2002). Indeed, large claims against previously written insurance policies exceeded present income. Obviously, the company could not trade indefinitely in such adverse circumstances.

The second factor concerns the further mismanagement of HIH through poorly conceived and badly executed acquisitions. Justice Owen summed this up, stating that there was:

> ... a lack of attention to detail, a lack of accountability for performance, and a lack of integrity in the company's internal processes and systems. Combined, these features led to a series of business decisions that were poorly conceived and even more poorly executed. Among such decisions were the ill-fated commitment in 1996 to re-enter the US market (HIH having extricated itself at a profit in 1994); the expansion of the UK operations in about 1997 into previously 'uncharted territory'; and the unwise acquisition of FAI Insurances Ltd in 1998. (p. xiii)

Justice Owen further noted the sub-optimal nature of the corporate culture of HIH, which was characterised by the board's unbending faith in the company's leadership, especially its dominant CEO (p. xiii). This deference to the CEO at HIH has been documented by other commentators (see, for example, Main, 2003; Westfield, 2003). Justice Owen's investigations pointed to the incapacity of the company and its management to see what had to be done and what had to be stopped or avoided in addressing the group's inherent problems (HIH Royal Commission Report, 2003, Section 3). He found that insurance risks were not properly identified and managed (p. xiii). There was an environment where unpleasant information was hidden from the board or filtered or sanitised to reduce discomfort or undue questioning from the board. And there was a lack of sceptical questioning and analysis by senior management, by the board and, arguably, by the auditors (Section 3, p. xiii).

### 8.4.3 Accounting Issues

Attention now turns to evaluating three key accounting issues, among others that were involved, arising from the collapse of HIH:

- provisions for expected future claims;
- earnings management using reinsurance contracts;
- accounting for goodwill.

#### 8.4.3.1  Provisions for Expected Future Claims

Before describing the aggressive approach to provisioning seemingly accepted by HIH, it is important to provide an overview of accounting for insurance contracts in Australia.[1] A deferral and matching method is applied in the recognition of insurance profits. That is, the recognition of premium revenue is deferred and matched to the recognition of liabilities for outstanding claims. Liabilities are estimated as the present value of the expected future cash flows associated with the claims. Insurance assets are valued at present market prices. In providing for possible future claims on insurance policies, actuaries provide an assessment based on their professional judgement. However, the directors of the insurer, not the actuary, are ultimately responsible for the size of this provision (HIH Royal Commission Report 2003, Section 7).

It is critical that the amount ascertained and allocated to the balance sheet as a provision for outstanding claims is appropriate to reflect prevailing circumstances and conditions. An increase or decrease in this provision from one reporting period to the next is an expense item deducted from revenue or an addition to revenue in the profit determination process respectively, thereby underlying periodic profit measurement and reporting. If the provision is understated, profit will be overstated; if the provision is overstated, profit will be understated. A small percentage variation in this provision, because it is usually such a large figure, can have a major impact on the level of reported profit (HIH Royal Commission Report, 2003, Section 5). Further, under-provisioning can overstate solvency in the balance sheet; that is, if provisions are understated this provides a misleading impression of the value of shareholders' funds and threatens the solvency of the insurer.

At the time of the demise of HIH, a general insurer could choose to calculate its provision using a central estimate or by applying a prudential margin. The central estimate is the figure that has an equal chance of being right or wrong. According to AASB 1023, this was described as the mean of the distribution of all possible values of the outstanding

---

[1] The prevailing standard in Australia at the time of writing is entitled *AASB 1023 General Insurance Contracts* (15 July 2004). It supersedes *AASB 1023 Financial Reporting of General Insurance Activities* which became operational on 6 November 1996. The latter standard applied at the time of the HIH debacle and is discussed in the HIH Royal Commission Report (2003).

claims liability. A prudential margin is an amount by which the provision set aside in the accounts for outstanding claims liabilities is greater than the actuarial central estimate of the liabilities.[2] Hence, it is a more conservative approach.

Evidence presented before the HIH Royal Commission indicates that the prudential margin approach is common industry practice due to the inherent uncertainties in predicting claims. Yet HIH almost always employed the central estimate and did not apply a prudential margin. The consequence was not only to take an overly optimistic view of claims provisions, but to continually overstate reported earnings. Accordingly, if one assumes that a lower amount of claims is likely to be made on outstanding policies this will generally make profits look more substantial than would otherwise be the case, given an inverse relationship between profits and provisions for future claims (that is, liabilities). According to Main (2003, p. 107) and Westfield (2003, pp. 38 and 43), the approach to profit determination at FAI and HIH was to choose a targeted profit number and to alter the provisions to effectively arrive at that arbitrary figure. Not only did this approach appear to violate the spirit of the accounting standard, but it would eventually result in large losses being reported should actual claims exceed the amounts that were previously provisioned.

### 8.4.3.2  Earnings Management Using Reinsurance Contracts

HIH appears to have obscured its optimistic provisioning by entering into so-called financial reinsurance arrangements with other parties. Reinsurance is a process 'whereby a second insurer, in return for a premium, agrees to indemnify a first insurer against a risk insured by the first insurer in favour of an insured' (HIH Royal Commission Report, 2003, Section 5.2).

According to AASB 1023, for a transaction to be accounted for as insurance or reinsurance, there must be a transfer of risk to the reinsurer. The standard does not describe, either in qualitative or quantitative terms, what degree of risk transfer is required. This, theoretically, could be interpreted by some individuals as meaning that if there is any risk transfer, however slight, the contract can properly be accounted for as reinsurance. Nevertheless, there was general acceptance among those presenting evidence before the Commission that in order to qualify for accounting treatment as a reinsurance contract under AASB 1023 there had to be a more than minimal risk transfer arrangement put into place (HIH Royal Commission Report, 2003, Section 5.2.3).

Without examining the intricate details of the actual transactions entered into by HIH, these contracts, in effect, 'promised that no claim would be made on a specific reinsurance policy' (Main, 2003, p. 115). The overall objective was to use reinsurance to offset any likely increase in claims liabilities on the balance sheet with an apparent corresponding recovery

---

[2] Under para. 5.1.6 of the 'new' AASB 1023, the outstanding claims liability includes an explicit risk margin to reflect the inherent uncertainty in the central estimate of the present value of expected future payments. However, under the 'old' version, para. 5.1, the outstanding claims liability was simply measured as the present value of expected future payments. In practice, under this version some insurers included a risk management and some insurers reserved at the central estimate (AASB 1023: Section A.2).

under a reinsurance contract. Justice Owen summed up the use by HIH of reinsurance contracts as follows:

> In 1998 FAI negotiated with reinsurers arrangements that were structured in such a way as to give the appearance of a transfer of risk when in fact there was none. A wide array of practices was employed to achieve these ends, among them the use of side letters setting out arrangements that negated the transfer of risk, the backdating of documents, the inclusion of sections of cover not intended to be called upon, and the use of 'triggers' for additional cover that were unrealistic. The word 'audacious' springs to mind. (p. xiii)

Main took the view that these contracts were 'not genuine reinsurance but were accounted for as such, and that the board of HIH and its auditors were deceived' (2003, p. 187). Justice Owen concluded that the HIH management seemed to use reinsurance as a means of solving, or at least as a means of deferring, the problem of under-provisioning in their operations (HIH Royal Commission Report, 2003, pp. xiii–lxv). Westfield took a similar view, stating that 'FAI was using reinsurance contracts to dress up its profits' (2003, p. 69). Clearly, an insurer should not be able to report a more profitable position than is actually the case on the basis of a reinsurance policy that purports to provide cover against future claims but, in substance, does not provide that outcome at all.

### 8.4.3.3  Accounting for Goodwill

In acquiring the shares of FAI, HIH gave consideration which, in total, amounted to $300.5 million. This acquisition was initially recorded in 1999 in the consolidated financial statements of HIH as comprising $25 million of net tangible assets and $275 million of purchased goodwill. Subsequently, another $163 million of FAI-related 'goodwill' was added to this intangible asset account so that by the year 2000 this goodwill account had a balance of $438 million (HIH Royal Commission Report, 2003, Section 7.1.4). Justice Owen contended that the goodwill adjustments (and reinsurance transactions referred to earlier) became techniques for concealing under-reserving problems inherent in FAI's insurance portfolio, and stated '... in the accounting practices of HIH goodwill became something of a repository for the unpleasant and unwanted consequences of poor business judgment' (p. xiii).

In other words, it would seem that the HIH management preferred to charge amounts to the goodwill account rather than to record the underlying losses as expenses in the statement of financial performance. On being quizzed about this seemingly dubious accounting treatment at the HIH Royal Commission, former HIH CEO Ray Williams stated that the treatment adopted of augmenting the goodwill asset account would have 'naturally been discussed and cleared and signed off by Arthur Anderson [the auditors]' (cited in Main, 2003, p. 181). Westfield (2003, p. 178) also refers to the accumulation of FAI-related 'goodwill' as a type of earnings management device.

### 8.4.4  Legal Outcomes Arising from the HIH Collapse

In March 2002, former directors of HIH, Rodney Adler and Ray Williams, were found guilty on civil charges of breaching their directors' duties over the payment by HIH of $10 million into a trust controlled by Adler. These findings were upheld by the New South

Wales Court of Appeal in July 2003. Adler was banned from acting as a company director for 20 years, fined $900 000 ($450 000 of which was payable by Adler Corporation Pty Ltd), and ordered to pay compensation jointly with Adler Corporation Pty Ltd and Williams of approximately $7 million (ASIC, 2005a). In addition to sharing this cost, Williams was banned from being a company director for 10 years and ordered to pay a pecuniary penalty of $250 000 (ASIC, 2005b).

In addition, Adler was sentenced in 2005 to four and a half years in jail, with a non-parole period of two-and-a-half years, on four charges arising from his conduct as a director of HIH in 2000. These charges consisted of two counts of disseminating information knowing it was false in a material way and which was likely to induce the purchase by other persons of shares in HIH contrary to Section 999 of the Corporations Act 2001, one count of obtaining money by false or misleading statements, and one count of being intentionally dishonest and failing to discharge his duties as a director of HIH in good faith and in the best interests of that company (ASIC, 2005a). Adler served the minimum jail term.

Williams was convicted of three criminal charges and sentenced to four and a half years in jail with a non-parole period of two years and nine months. The court held that Williams was reckless in carrying out his duties and failed to properly exercise his powers and discharge his duties for a proper purpose as a director when he signed a letter that was misleading in October 2000. The court also found that Williams authorised the issue of a prospectus by HIH in 1998 that contained a material omission. Finally, the court held that Williams made a statement in the 1998–99 HIH Annual Report which he knew to be misleading and which had the effect of overstating the operating profit before abnormal items and income tax by $92.4 million (ASIC, 2005b). Williams also served the minimum jail term.

The investigation of HIH by the ASIC also led to criminal prosecutions of three other former senior executives of HIH for breaches of the Corporations Law and the Crimes Act. Terry Cassidy, the former Managing Director of HIH, pleaded guilty to criminal charges that he made misleading statements to the Australian Prudential Regulation Authority about the financial position of HIH subsidiaries CIC Insurances Ltd and HIH Investment Holdings Ltd. He was sentenced to 15 months' imprisonment (ASIC, 2005c). Bradley Cooper, the former chairman of the FAI Security Group, was convicted on six charges of corruptly giving a series of cash benefits to influence an agent of HIH and on seven charges of publishing false or misleading statements with intent to obtain a financial advantage. He received a sentence of eight years in jail (ASIC, 2006c). Tony Boulden, a former Financial Controller of FAI General Insurance Company Ltd, was sentenced to 12 months' imprisonment after pleading guilty to one count of being privy to the fraudulent altering of the general ledger of that company with the effect of reducing claims estimates by $5.5 million (ASIC, 2006a).

Dominic Fodera, the former Chief Financial Officer of HIH, was found guilty in the Supreme Court of New South Wales in April 2007 of authorising the issue of a prospectus which contained a material omission. The omission related to a transaction between HIH and Société Générale Australia where HIH carried the real risk from a swap derivatives transaction yet the prospectus indicated that Société Générale Australia bore that risk (Moran, 2007; see also ASIC, 2006b). Fodera received a two-year prison sentence for this offence. His term was later increased by another year for failing to disclose to directors and auditors of HIH the full details and risks of certain reinsurance contracts entered into by the company (Moore, 2007).

### 8.4.4.1  Role of the HIH Auditor

HIH's auditor, Andersen, was criticised in the report of the Commission for the way it undertook the audit but has not been implicated in any criminal action (Main, 2003, p. 265). Justice Owen commented on the apparent lack of substantive testing undertaken, especially given that Andersen viewed HIH as a high risk audit client:

> Andersen's audit work in relation to the 1999 and 2000 audits was characterised by a lack of sufficient audit evidence to support its conclusions. It is surprising that Andersen was so willing to accept positions put by HIH management without obtaining sufficient appropriate audit evidence in respect of those positions.
>
> (HIH Royal Commission Report, 2003, Section 21.6.3)

Justice Owen was also critical of the perceived lack of independence of Andersen from HIH. He highlighted the issues as being: the presence of three former Andersen partners on the board of HIH; HIH's dealings with the audit committee and non-executive directors; and intense pressure placed on Andersen partners to maximise fees from non-audit work available at HIH (HIH Royal Commission Report, 2003, Section 21.4.7). Each of these shall briefly be considered in turn.

From 1998 onwards the HIH board included three former Andersen partners, Geoffrey Cohen, Dominic Fodera and Justin Gardener (HIH Royal Commission Report, 2003, Section 21.4.3). Cohen was also chairman of the board from January 1992 and chaired the HIH audit committee from August 1999 until the demise of HIH. Justice Owen was especially critical of an ongoing consultancy arrangement that Cohen had in place with Andersen whilst he was a director of HIH. The Commission highlighted that this consultancy arrangement was not disclosed to the HIH board nor was it reported in HIH's annual report (HIH Royal Commission Report, 2003, Section 21.4.3). Justice Owen concluded that 'the professional antecedents and continuing links with Andersen ... gave rise to a perception that Andersen was not independent of HIH' (HIH Royal Commission Report, 2003, Section 21.4.3).

Turning to the second issue, the Commission heard evidence from a Senior Manager of the Andersen audit team for HIH, Jonathon Pye, that it was the normal practice for members of the audit committee to meet HIH management prior to audit committee meetings to discuss agenda items in the absence of the auditor. Pye contended that he was uncomfortable with that approach because he felt that the non-executive directors were forming views before coming to audit committee meetings and before hearing Andersen's position. He felt that the non-executive directors of HIH should have met with the auditor in the absence of the management of HIH. Moreover, he observed that HIH directors, as a group, seemed to rely heavily on HIH's management to consider and resolve issues (HIH Royal Commission Report, 2003, Section 21.4.4).

Referring to the third issue, the Commission noted that the criteria by which Andersen partners were appraised and remunerated encouraged them to focus on increasing fees from non-audit services (HIH Royal Commission Report, 2003, Section 21.4.4). The Commission Report referred to an Andersen 'action plan' which had been prepared by Pye, and had been in place from 2000, as follows:

Historically we have had very low success at gaining penetration into the client from other divisions ... The key will be to 'partner' them in and manage the relationships and delivery of the product in the 'HIH way' to maximise our opportunities for success.

(HIH Royal Commission Report, 2003, Section 21.4.5)

This quote suggests that Andersen considered the HIH relationship as undeveloped in terms of the potential to generate even higher non-audit service fees and a solution may have been to become closer to the client as a means of increasing total fee revenue from this client.

Counsel assisting the Commission submitted that the reduced satisfaction of an audit client, as a result of an auditor exhibiting strong professional scepticism, might result in the relevant Andersen partners having difficulty in cross-selling Andersen's non-audit services. This was seen by Justice Owen to be a major independence threat because 'HIH management had demonstrated a tendency to be upset easily' (HIH Royal Commission Report, 2003, Section 21.4.5).

The HIH Royal Commission Report (2003) contained an illuminating statement in relation to the audit of HIH: 'Andersen's approach to the audit in 1999 and 2000 was insufficiently rigorous to engender in users confidence as to the reliability of HIH's financial statements' (Section 7.2). In November 2002, the HIH liquidator took legal action against the auditor for alleged negligence in the conduct of the HIH audit (Main and Fabro, 2002; Sexton, 2002). In July 2007, the liquidator entered into a confidential settlement with Andersen and dropped a damages suit against 180 former partners of Andersen. In addition, the liquidator settled with the HIH directors and the actuary. Of the total settlement amount that was estimated at approximately $80 million, the bulk of the sum was reported to have come from Andersen (Sexton, 2007).

## 8.5 CORPORATE GOVERNANCE REFORMS FOLLOWING THE ACCOUNTING SCANDALS OF THE EARLY 2000s

A series of governance reforms most typically follows each round of major corporate failures. Such reforms embrace financial reporting and auditing reforms which are intended to ensure, as far as possible, that the errors, misjudgements and negligence of the past are not repeated in the future. Following the corporate failures in Australia and elsewhere in the early 2000s, Australia, like the USA and the UK, enacted major corporate laws in order to address the key deficiencies identified. The Corporate Law Economic Reform Program (Audit Reform and Corporate Disclosure) Act of 2004 was the Australian government's primary response to the accounting and corporate governance scandals of the recent past (Dellaportas et al., 2005, p. 21). This new legislation followed a major review of auditor independence, the Ramsay Report (Ramsay, 2001) and the HIH Royal Commission Report. Some of the key changes included in this complex piece of legislation were to: require rotation of audit partners of publicly listed company clients every five years; heighten legal protection of whistleblowers; increase disclosure requirements pertaining to executive remuneration; mandate CEO and CFO certification of financial statements; introduce legal underpinning of auditing standards; and expand the role for the Financial Reporting Council to take responsibility for the auditing and accounting standard-setting regime as well as oversight of auditor independence. This legislation, whilst significant in terms of scope and volume, is less draconian than the US Sarbanes-Oxley Act of 2002 (O'Connell, Webb and Schwarzbach, 2005). For example, certain consulting services that were readily provided by auditors to their audit clients were banned in the USA but this has not occurred in Australia.

Apart from the Corporate Law Economic Reform Program (Audit Reform and Corporate Disclosure) Act of 2004, another major reform of recent years is the Australian Stock Exchange (known as the Australian Securities Exchange from December 2006) *Principles of Good Corporate Governance and Best Practice Recommendations* of March 2003 (revised and reissued in 2007 as *Corporate Governance Principles and Recommendations*). The key corporate governance principles for publicly listed companies relate to areas such as ensuring a balance of executive and non-executive directors on the board of directors, maintaining well-documented risk management processes and ensuring proper oversight by management, and ensuring the adoption of a properly constituted and well-qualified selection process in appointing individuals to the audit committee. These guidelines, while not mandatory for publicly listed Australian companies, are highly influential as any companies which decide not to follow aspects of these principles are required to outline in their annual report the reasons they have chosen not to adopt the guidelines.

## 8.6 CONCLUSION

Corporate failures in Australia have tended to follow in the immediate aftermath of boom time periods. Such circumstances were evident in Eastern Australia during the early 1890s major economic depression which brought a long-lived boom to an abrupt end. Since that time other rounds of corporate collapses have occurred in Australia, specifically during the 1960s, 1970s, late 1980s/early 1990s and early 2000s. The early 2000s corporate failures did not necessarily arise as a consequence of tight or severe general economic conditions. Rather, poor or ineffective management, including inadequate corporate governance and accounting and financial reporting failure have been shown to be contributors to corporate demise, especially unexpected corporate collapses. Concerns about the perceived lack of independence of auditors have also been a feature of many of the contributions on the corporate failures of the early 2000s.

While it is difficult to generalise on why management of some companies choose to employ misstatement strategies in their financial reports, it would seem apparent from addressing cases of failed companies, such as Bond Corporation and HIH, that desperation to portray a false or incomplete view of the financial performance and position of a company in the face of the reality of declining financial fortunes tends to be at the forefront of such accounting and financial reporting. While accounting practices and financial reports seem to become more complex as the decades pass by – fuelled by, among other things, the ever-expanding number of accounting standards on issue and the often-increasing word length of most accounting standards – the overall effects of misstatement strategies remain relatively simple to comprehend. Failed companies are often found to have overstated income or understated expenses or both, or to have otherwise disclosed total assets and net assets at inflated levels in audited financial reports given the particular market conditions which prevailed at the specific time of reporting. The misleading disclosures that are fuelled by such high-powered optimism, in retrospect, often appear to have been misguided at best or fraudulent at worst.

Following each series of corporate collapses, corporate governance reforms are enacted to rein in the excesses of corporate behaviour and address perceived deficiencies in governance mechanisms and processes in the hope that they may not arise, at least in the same form, in the future. Notwithstanding the adoption of such measures, corporate failures and accounting scandals in Australia will undoubtedly recur after the time of writing and will continue to reflect the excesses of human behaviour, specifically in the commercial/corporate world, where greed and hubris have been shown to assume prominence, especially during periods of extended or rapid economic development. History has a habit of repeating itself, thus confirming the need for chapters of this genre to continue to be written to reflect unknown yet anticipated events that will unfold.

# ACKNOWLEDGEMENTS

The authors gratefully acknowledge financial assistance for this project in the form of an Australian Research Council Discovery Grant (No. DP0452053). Leona Campitelli and Jenny Cave provided valuable research assistance, while the assistance of Jill Bright and Lauren Carroll of the CPA Library, CPA Australia is also appreciated. Appreciation is also expressed to Robert W. Gibson, Lúcia Lima Rodrigues, Brian West and Graeme Wines for their helpful comments on early drafts of this paper. The editor, Michael Jones, also provided valuable comments on further developed drafts of the paper.

# REFERENCES

*AIBR* (1891), 'The duties of auditors – The Anglo-Australian Bank', *Australasian Insurance and Banking Record*, **XV**(5), 18 May, pp. 314–315.

*AIBR* (1892), 'Audit', *Australasian Insurance and Banking Record*, **XVI**(2), 18 February, pp. 81–82.

Anon (1989), 'Bond to sell stake in Lonrho', *The New York Times*, 9 March, p. 4.

ASA (1966), *Accounting Principles and Practices Discussed in Reports of Company Failures*, Australian Society of Accountants General Council, Melbourne.

ASIC (2000), 'Adsteam settlement'. Australian Securities and Investments Commission, *Media Release No. 00-452*, 2 November.

ASIC (2002), 'Former Harris Scarfe officer jailed. Australian Securities and Investments Commission', *Media Release No. 02-229*, 26 June.

ASIC (2003), 'Brad Keeling settles in ASIC One.Tel proceedings'. Australian Securities and Investments Commission, *Media Release No. 03-099*, 21 March.

ASIC (2004), 'ASIC reaches agreement with John Greaves in One.Tel proceedings'. Australian Securities and Investments Commission, *Media Release No. 04-283*, 6 September.

ASIC (2005a), 'Rodney Adler sentenced to four-and-a-half years' jail'. Australian Securities and Investments Commission, *Media Release No. 05-91*, 14 April.

ASIC (2005b), 'Ray Williams sentenced to jail'. Australian Securities and Investments Commission, *Media Release No. 05-94*, 15 April.

ASIC (2005c), 'Former HIH managing director pleads guilty'. Australian Securities and Investments Commission, *Media Release No. 05-72*, 24 March.

ASIC (2006a), 'Former FAI officer sentenced. Australian Securities and Investments Commission', *Media Release No. 06-417*, 1 December.

ASIC (2006b), 'Dominic Fodera to stand trial on criminal charge concerning HIH insurance'. Australian Securities and Investments Commission, *Media Release No. 06-257*, 28 July.

ASIC (2006c), 'Bradley Cooper sentenced to eight years' jail'. Australian Securities and Investments Commission, *Media Release No. 06-210*, 23 June.

Barry, P. (1990), *The Rise and Fall of Alan Bond*, Bantam Books, Sydney.

Barry, P. (2002), *Rich Kids*, Bantam Books, Auckland.

Birkett, W.P. and Walker, R.G. (1971), 'Response of the Australian accounting profession to company failures in the 1960s', *Abacus*, **7**(2), 97–136.

Blainey, G. (1958), *Gold and Paper: A History of the National Bank of Australasia Limited*, Georgian House, Melbourne.

Boehm, E.A. (1971), *Prosperity and Depression in Australia, 1887–1897*, Oxford University Press, London.

Bosch, H. (2001), 'Introduction', in *Collapse Incorporated: Tales, Safeguards & Responsibilities of Corporate Australia*, CCH Australia, Sydney, pp. 71–98.

Brewster, N. (2003), *Unaccountable: How the Accounting Profession Forfeited a Public Trust*, John Wiley & Sons, Inc. Hoboken, NJ.

Briggs, A. (1977), *Victorian Cities*, Penguin Books, Harmondsworth.

Burge, G. (1991), 'Adsteam's $4.49 billion loss is biggest ever', *Sydney Morning Herald*, 1 October, p. 25.

Butlin, N.G. (1961), *Australia and New Zealand Bank*, Longmans, London.

Butlin, N.G. (1964), *Investment in Australian Economic Development*, Cambridge University Press, Cambridge.

Cannon, M. (1967), *The Land Boomers*, Melbourne University Press, Melbourne.

Carnegie, G.D. and Edwards, J.R. (2001), 'The construction of the professional accountant: the case of the Incorporated Institute of Accountants, Victoria (1886)', *Accounting, Organizations and Society*, **26**(4/5), 301–325.

Carnegie, G.D. and Napier, C.J. (2010), 'Traditional accountants and business professionals: portraying the accounting profession after Enron', *Accounting, Organizations and Society*, **35**(3), 360–376.

Carnegie, G.D. and Parker, R.H., (eds) (1999), *Professional Accounting and Audit in Australia, 1880–1900*, Garland Publishing, New York.

Carnegie, G.D., Gavens, J. and Gibson, R.W. (1989), *Cases in Financial Accounting*, Harcourt Brace Jovanovich, Sydney.

Chambers, R.J. (1973), *Securities and Obscurities: A Case for Reform of the Law of Company Accounts*, Gower Press, Melbourne.

Chenoweth, N. (2009), 'Rich kids in One.Tel tangle', *Australian Financial Review*, 19 November, pp. 60–61.

Chua, W.F. and Poullaos, C. (1998), 'The dynamics of "closure" amidst the construction of market, profession, empire and nationhood: an historical analysis of an Australian accounting association, 1886–1903', *Accounting, Organizations and Society*, **23**(2), 155–187.

Clarke, F. and Dean, G. (1992), 'Chaos in the counting-house: accounting under scrutiny', *Australian Journal of Corporate Law*, **2**(2), 177–201.

Clarke, F. and Dean, G. (2001), 'Corporate collapses analysed', in *Collapse Incorporated: Tales, Safeguards & Responsibilities of Corporate Australia*, CCH Australia, Sydney, pp. 71–98.

Clarke, F., Dean, G. and Oliver, K. (2003), *Corporate Collapse: Accounting, Regulatory and Ethical Failure*, 2nd edn, Cambridge University Press, Cambridge.

da Silva Rosa, R., Filippetto, J. and Tarca, A. (2008), 'ASIC actions: canaries for poor corporate governance', *Accounting Research Journal*, **21**(1), 67–86.

Davison, G. (1978), *The Rise and Fall of Marvellous Melbourne*, Melbourne University Press, Melbourne.

Debelle, P. (2001), 'Harris Scarfe creative accounting revealed', *The Age,* Business Section, 7 August, p. 1.

Deegan, C. (2005), *Australian Financial Accounting*, 4th edn, McGraw-Hill, Sussex.

Dellaportas, S., Gibson, K., Alagiah, R., Hutchinson, M., Leung, P. and Van Homrigh, D. (2005), *Ethics Governance and Accountability: A Professional Perspective*, John Wiley & Sons Australia Ltd, Milton, QLD.

DiPiazza, S.A. and Eccles, R.G. (2002), *Building Public Trust: The Future of Corporate Reporting*, John Wiley & Sons, Inc., Hoboken, NJ.

Drummond, M. (2002a), 'Andersen to settle $1bn Bond claim', *Australian Financial Review*, 26 April, pp. 1 and 8.

Drummond, M. (2002b), 'Bond case: Andersen's $100m', *Australian Financial Review*, 22 May, p. 9.

Fabro, A. (2001), 'Insolvencies up as business feels the GST pinch', *Australian Financial Review*, 22 May, p. 3.

Fox, L. (2003), *Enron: The Rise and Fall*, John Wiley & Sons, Inc., Hoboken, NJ.

Gaffikin, K., Dagwell, R. and Wines, G. (2004), *Corporate Accounting in Australia*, 3rd edn, UNSW Press, Sydney.

Gibson, R.W. (1971), *Disclosure by Australian Companies*, Melbourne University Press, Melbourne.

Gibson, R.W. (1979), 'Development of corporate accounting in Australia', *Accounting Historians Journal*, **6**(2), 23–38.

Gibson, R.W. (1988), 'Two centuries of Australian accountants', *Accounting Historians Notebook*, Spring, 17–26.

Gibson, R.W. (1990), 'Bond: a commentary on accounting issues discussed', *Accounting History*, **2**(2), 136–142.

Gibson, R.W. (1992), 'Review of Barry (1990)', *Accounting History*, **4**(2), 65–67.

Gluyas, R. (2006), 'Big shot', *The Australian*, 20 October, p. 18.

Green, J. (1991), ' "Fuzzy law" – a better way to "stop snouts in the trough"?' *Company and Securities Law Journal*, **9**(3), 144–157.

Hamilton, S. and Micklethwait, A. (2006), *Greed and Corporate Failure: The Lessons from Recent Disasters*, Palgrave Macmillan, Basingstoke.

Harris, T. (2003), 'Accounting for corporate collapse', *Australian Financial Review*, 23 May, p. 9.

Harrison, S. (2001), 'Auditing the auditor', *Business Review Weekly*, Letter, 16 August, p. 14.

Hepworth, A. (2001), 'Auditors face conflict crackdown', *Australian Financial Review*, 12 June, pp. 1 and 8.

Hepworth, A. (2002), 'Judges face busy time as watchdogs pounce', *Australian Financial Review*, 11 January, p. 8.

HIH Royal Commission Final Report (2003), *The Failure of HIH Insurance,* The HIH Royal Commission (The Honourable Justice Owen Commissioner), Commonwealth of Australia, Canberra, April.

Humphrey, C., Moizer, P. and Turley, S. (1992), 'The audit expectations gap – plus ça change, plus c'est la meme chose?', *Critical Perspectives on Accounting*, **3**(2), 137–161.

Jacobs, M. and Grigg, A. (2009), 'ASIC slated in One.Tel court defeat', *Australian Financial Review*, 19 November, pp. 1 and 10.

James, C. (2006), 'Your shares are worth 5c', *The Advertiser*, 3 October, pp. 1 and 4.

Jeter, L.W. (2003), *Disconnected: Deceit and Betrayal at WorldCom*, John Wiley & Sons, Inc., Hoboken, NJ.

Johnson, R. (2004a), 'Corporate collapses of the 1980s and early 1990s: unresolved auditor business', in *Readings in Auditing*, ed. R. Johnson, John Wiley & Sons Australia Ltd, Milton, QLD, pp. 18–30.

Johnson, R. (2004b), 'Introduction', in *Readings in Auditing*, ed. R. Johnson, John Wiley & Sons Australia Ltd, Milton, QLD, pp. 1–16.

Kohler, A. (1991), 'In the bad books', *Australian Financial Review*, 2 April, pp. 1 and 52.

Kohler, A. (2001), 'Why they didn't see it coming', *Australian Financial Review*, 21 December, pp. 19 and 21.

Lawson, M. (1993), 'Accountants "top for claims" ', *Australian Financial Review*, 2 August, p. 3.

Maiden, M. (2000), '$20m deal settles Adsteam saga', *The Sydney Morning Herald*, 3 November, p. 22.

Main, A. (2002), 'The geometry of HIH's problems', *Australian Financial Review*, 14 December, p. 8.

Main, A. (2003), *Other People's Money: The Complete Story of the Extraordinary Collapse of HIH*, Harper Collins Publishers, Sydney.

Main, A. and Fabro, A. (2002), 'HIH liquidator takes aim at regulator, Andersen', *Australian Financial Review*, 14 November, pp. 1 and 6.

Martin, W. (2003), 'HIH Royal Commission Speech', 4 June, downloaded on 28 October 2006 from the website of the Attorney-General's Department of the Australian Commonwealth Government, http://www.tisn.gov.au.

McCrann, T. (1986), 'DJ's pumps $28m into Adsteam's Christmas present', *The Age*, 30 December, p. 17.

McManamy, J. (1990), *The Dreamtime Casino*, Schwartz and Wilkinson, Melbourne.

Miles, J.B.C. (1895), *Concerning Auditing*, Sydney Institute of Public Accountants, Sydney, 28 November, 21 pp.

Moore, A. (2007), 'Former HIH chief gets extra year of jail', Australian Broadcasting Corporation, transcript of the *Lateline* programme, last downloaded on 18 March 2008 from http://www.abc.net.au/lateline/business/items.

Moran, S. (2007), 'HIH's Fodera faces jail after guilty verdict', *The Australian*, 5 April, pp. 1 and 19.

O'Connell, B., Webb, L. and Schwarzbach, H.R. (2005), 'Batten down the hatches! Lessons for Australian regulators and the accounting profession from the reactions of their US counterparts to the recent accounting scandals', *Australian Accounting Review*, **15**(2), 52–67.

Peers, M. (1991), 'Adsteam disaster – the next phase', *Australian Financial Review*, 2 April, pp. 1–2.

Pheasant, B. (1993), 'Auditors in danger from $2.5bn claims', *Australian Financial Review*, 30 June, pp. 1 and 6.

Pierpont (1992), 'Adsteam accounting made clear', *The Bulletin*, 14 April, p. 93.

Ramsay, I. (2001), *Independence of Australian Company Auditors: Review of Australian Current Requirements and Proposals for Reform*, Report to the Minister for Financial Services and Regulation, Canberra.

Ryan, C. and McClymont, K. (1992a), 'Alan Bond: the untold story', *The Sydney Morning Herald*, 1 August, pp. 35 and 38.

Ryan, C. and McClymont, K. (1992b), 'Bond's round robin cheques disquieted ANZ', *The Sydney Morning Herald*, 3 August, pp. 21 and 23.

Serle, G. (1971), *The Rush to be Rich*, University of Melbourne, Melbourne.

Sexton, E. (2002), 'HIH auditor, actuary negligent', *The Age,* Business Section, 15 November, p. 3.

Sexton, E. (2007), 'HIH liquidator drops damages claim in secret deal', *The Age*, 12 July, p. 3.

Sykes, T. (1989), 'Adsteam unmasked', *Australian Business*, 19 April, pp. 1619.

Sykes, T. (1998), *Two Centuries of Panic: A History of Corporate Collapses in Australia*, Allen & Unwin, Crows Nest.

Sykes, T. (2002), 'Resurrected report raises doubts about HIH's insolvency', *Australian Financial Review*, 22–23 June, p. 12.

Walker, R.G. (1988a), 'Brought to account: normal items? extraordinary!' *Australian Business*, 10 February, pp. 95–96.

Walker, R.G. (1988b), 'Window-dressing at Bond Corp', *Australian Business*, 24 February, pp. 77–78.

Walker, R.G. (1992), 'Consolidation standard – in practice', *New Accountant*, **5**(10), 24.

Walker, R.G. and Mack, J. (1998), The influence of regulation on the publication of consolidated statements, *Abacus*, **34**(1), 48–74.

Walsh, M. (1992), 'Morality wanes the more the law waxes', *The Sydney Morning Herald*, 4 August, p. 29.

Waugh, J. (1992), 'Company law and the crash of the 1890s in Victoria', *UNSW Law Journal*, **15**(2), 356–388.

Westfield, M. (2003), *HIH: The Inside Story of Australia's Biggest Corporate Collapse*, John Wiley & Sons Australia Ltd, Milton, QLD.

Whittred, G. (2005), 'The road to insolvency', in *Financial Accounting: An Integrated Approach*, 3rd edn, eds T. Trotman and M. Gibbons, Thomson, South Melbourne, pp. 720–725.

Zehnwirth, B. (2002), 'HIH fails short on technicals', *Australian Financial Review,* Letter, 9 December, p. 50.

# 9

# Corporate Accounting Scandals in China

Catherine Huirong Chen, Yuanyuan Hu and Jason Zezhong Xiao

## 9.1 INTRODUCTION

The objectives of this chapter are to examine Chinese accounting scandals, identify their causes, discuss their consequences and explore their implications for accounting, law and corporate governance. Although there were scandals before the 1990s, most significant Chinese scandals have occurred since then.

Since the introduction of economic reforms and 'open door' policies in 1978, China has been in transition from a centrally planned to a market economy, achieving a 73 % degree of marketization in 2003 (Institute for Economic and Resource Management Research, 2005) and achieving the world's fourth largest GDP in 2005.

China's modern legal system was built from scratch in the late 1970s and did not embrace the concept of property rights until 2004 (Pistor and Xu, 2005). Its legal protection of shareholders is poor (Allen, Qian and Qian, 2005; Pistor and Xu, 2005). This is evidenced by the virtual absence of investor lawsuits. Administrative enforcements by regulators, such as the China Securities Regulatory Commission (CSRC), are also limited (Pistor and Xu, 2005).

China's stock market has developed rapidly, with over 1400 listed firms. However, its share price and investor behaviour do not reflect listed firms' fundamental values (Allen, Qian and Qian, 2005) and there are many accounting frauds and scandals, as shown in this chapter. Further, the banking sector is dominated by state-owned banks, which results in ineffective monitoring and management of loans to state-owned enterprises (SOEs).

The Company Law lays down a hierarchy of internal corporate governance mechanisms: the shareholders' general meeting, the board of directors (BoD), the supervisory board (SB) and senior company managers. However, as many companies are state-owned or controlled, government agencies might still intervene in corporate decision-making and most SBs are more 'decorative' than functional (Tenev and Zhang, 2002; Xiao, Dahya and Lin, 2004). Further, independent directors are normally nominated by executive directors and thus rarely vote against board resolutions. As a result, Chinese listed companies quite often fall under control of a few key board members or executive officers, which facilitates such immoral and self-serving opportunist behaviours as collusion between government and managers; channelling company's profit and assets to large shareholders through unfair related-party transactions and excessive dividends; engaging in self-dealing in pursuit of private gains; earnings management for meeting share listing requirements; manipulating Initial Public

Offering (IPO) and secondary market prices; and trading on insider information (Lee and Hahn, 2001; Qian, 1995).

Although Chinese accounting regulations have become increasingly harmonized with international practices (Ezzamel, Xiao and Pan, 2007; Li, 2001; Xiao, Zhang and Xie, 2000), their effectiveness has been weakened by many factors such as insufficiently trained accountants, inadequate market demands for high quality accounting and auditing, weak corporate governance mechanisms and ineffective legal enforcement (Xiao, Dahya and Lin, 2004). In particular, auditor independence is severely impaired by government influence (Xiao, Zhang and Xie, 2000) due to a high proportion of state ownership and the close government–auditor relationship (Hao, 1999).

A series of listing requirements[1] and regulations on listed firms' disclosures stipulated by the CSRC since 1993 (Xiao, 1999) have also had a profound impact on accounting, auditing and reporting (Chen and Yuan, 2004; Zou and Xiao, 2006). One of the impacts has been to induce listed companies to comply 'creatively' with the listing requirements by fabricating their accounts.

Although the establishment of stock markets has relieved the government from financing SOEs, intervention from the government and the reliance of companies on favourable governmental treatments still exist due to the traditional close ties between the government and SOEs and the dominance of state ownership.[2] Government, rather than the market, controls the number and frequency of companies which go public. As a result, SOEs stand a better chance of being selected than private companies. These firms are well protected by their local governments, even in the event of accounting frauds, because being listed, they symbolize the prestige of the local governments (Chen, Chen and Su, 2001) and their performance plays an important role in the assessment of government officials' performance.

Despite the introduction of recent reforms, there are still loopholes in the Chinese system, which have allowed scandals to occur. Table 9.1 summarizes the cases discussed in this chapter. The rest of this chapter is organized as follows. The next section focuses on six scandals: Shenzhen Yuanye, Great Wall Fund Raising, Hongguang, Daqing Lianyi, Kangsai and Lantian Gufen, and shows how accounting creativity and fraud have played a large part in the scandals. The following section analyses the Zhengzhou Baiwen scandal in depth and discusses the aftermath. The final section provides implications and conclusions.

## 9.2 SUMMARY OF CORPORATE SCANDALS

### 9.2.1 Shenzhen Yuanye

Shenzhen Yuanye Industrial Corporation Limited (hereafter Yuanye) was the first case in which a Chinese listed company was de-listed from the stock exchange due to financial fraud

---

[1] For example, a company is qualified to apply with the CSRC for listing as well as rights issues when it has recorded three consecutive years of profit (at least 10 % annual return on equity). The CSRC stipulated that IPO prices should be a fixed multiple of EPS reported in the prospectus (Aharony, Lee and Wang, 2000; Chen, Chen and Su, 2001; DeFond and Park, 1997), which gives company management incentives to boost short-term profit prior to IPO.

[2] Over 64 % of shares in listed firms in 2003 were owned by the state or state-controlled SOEs. By law, these shares are not publicly tradable, leaving only about one-third of shares publicly tradable.

**Table 9.1**  Summary of scandals discussed in this chapter

| Scandal | Year | Company | Issues of creative accounting and/or fraud |
|---|---|---|---|
| 1 | 1992 | Shenzhen Yuanye | Falsifying capital contributions; inflating profits and assets appreciation; fraudulent applications for listing; management embezzlement |
| 2 | 1993 | Great Wall Fund Raising | Financial statement misrepresentation; management embezzlement of raised funds |
| 3 | 1997 | Hongguang | Fraudulent applications for listing by inflating profits and misrepresentations in the prospectus |
| 4 | 1997 | Daqing Lianyi | Bribery and corruption; fraudulent applications for listing; forging documents and statements |
| 5 | 1998 | Kangsai Group | Bribery; financial statement misrepresentations; inflating profits by related-party transactions |
| 6 | 1999 | Lantian Gufen | Falsified assets and manipulating profits; fraudulent applications for listing |
| 7 | 2000 | Zhengzhou Baiwen | Inflated profits for listing; management embezzlement; creative accounting through related-party transactions; fraudulent applications for listing |

to meet listing requirements and individuals seeking personal gains. This involved falsifying the capital contribution, inflating profits and assets, fraudulent applications for listing, and management embezzlement (Huang, 2001). The scandal also caused the Shenzhen Special Economic Zone Accounting Firm to shut down, which was the first case of this nature in Chinese accounting history. The firm's key CPAs were disqualified for material negligence and committing wrongdoings (Huang, 2001; Xiao, Zhang and Xie, 2000).

Originally established in 1987 as an SOE in the textile manufacturing sector, Yuanye was transformed into a Sino-foreign, joint-venture shareholding company in February 1989, with a registered capital of RMB 1.5 million (about £0.11m)[3], of which 60 % of shares were held by two SOEs, 20 % by Hong Kong Kaisheng Company, 10 % by Jiandong Peng, and the remaining 10 % by another individual. In 1988, Hong Kong Kaisheng company transferred its shares that it did not actually purchase (actually paid for by one of the SOEs) to a Hong Kong company, Runtao. In 1990, when Yuanye listed on the Shenzhen Stock Exchange, Runtao became its largest shareholder, holding 51 % of the firm's shares.

Yuanye was later discovered by the Shenzhen Intermediate People's Court to have committed the following financial frauds (Huang, 2001; Xie, 2001). First, it had misrepresented financial reports before its listing. Since the establishment of the joint venture in 1989, a controlling company Runtao and two other individuals had been counterfeiting capital contributions without investing actual capital. In 1988, Runtao illegally inflated the company's capital to RMB 4.2 million (or £0.3m) from RMB 1.5 million (or £0.11m) with a fake capital contribution certificate to become the largest shareholder. In March 1988,

---

[3] The exchange rate at the time of writing (spring 2008) between Renminbi (RMB, the Chinese currency) and US dollars is about 7 and that between RMB and British pounds is about 14. Thus, RMB 1.5 million equals US$214 286 or sterling £107 143.

Yuanye reported an asset appreciation of RMB 23 million (about £1.64m) that was not independently verified by an asset valuation firm as required by the law. Further, before listing, Runtao forged sales of three million shares to four companies to meet the listing requirement. Yuanye also profited from selling these shares to the public in 1990 (Huang, 2001). Second, Yuanye counterfeited a cumulative profit of RMB 77.4 million (around £5.53m) between 1990 and 1992, by forging assets, inflating sales revenue and misstating management costs, while it actually suffered cumulative losses of over RMB 113 million (about £8.07m) (Huang, 2001). Third, the chairman of Yuanye at that time, Jiandong Peng (an Australian Chinese), who was also the chairman of its controlling company Runtao, had illegally tunnelled about US$9.2 million and HK$0.46 million from Yuanye into Runtao or its overseas branches by June 1992, partly to meet his personal desires, according to the court.[4] As a result, Yuanye was de-listed from the stock exchange in July 1992 and Jiandong Peng was given a 16-year sentence and expelled from China (Huang, 2001; Xie, 2001). The audit firm, Shenzhen Special Economic Zone Accounting Firm, was found guilty by the court of helping the client to falsify accounts by providing 10 false capital contribution certificates[5] and unqualified audit reports for the client (Xiao, Zhang and Xie, 2000).

### 9.2.2  Great Wall Fund Raising

The 'Great Wall Fund Raising' scandal involved illegal fund raising, account fabrication, management embezzlement and bribery. It implicated the Zhongcheng Accounting Firm (Xiao, Zhang and Xie, 2000; Zheng and Chen, 1993). In this case, a loss-making firm, the Great Wall Electrical Engineering Science and Technology Co., illegally raised RMB one billion (about £0.07b) in a few months between 1992 and 1993 by issuing very high coupon securities (at 2 % interest per month) to over two million private investors in 17 large Chinese cities to develop an allegedly energy-saving electrical product without obtaining proper authorization from the financial authority. The money raised was partly embezzled (e.g. the company President, his wife and a Vice-President took RMB one million (about £0.07m) into their own possession) and partly used to establish over 20 subsidiaries and 100 branches throughout the country (Zheng and Chen, 1993). The successful fund-raising activity was essentially attributed to its promotion by several major mass media and a then Deputy Minister of the National Commission for Science and Technology. In addition, a branch of Zhongcheng Accounting Firm also played a key role in the fraud. Its three CPAs provided an unjustified certificate confirming RMB 300 million (about £21.43m) capital of the company (Wang, 1993). No accounting number in the client's financial statements was verified through any due auditing process. The bank account balance was not checked against the bank statements, the cash balances were not based on counting cash, nor was the stock value based on stock-taking. The CPAs did not issue any inquiry letters concerning accounts receivables and long-term investments. Moreover, the Great Wall Company's fixed asset of RMB 187 million was based on a fake invoice. Besides, the company also reported

---

[4] For example, Jiandong Peng liked to gamble and once was in debt to the tune of RMB 290 000. He borrowed money from Yuanye to pay back the debt. This was published by the court in 1994 (http:my.tdctrad.com/airlaws/index.asp?id=14452).

[5] The capital contribution certificates are audit documents issued by auditors according to Chinese law to represent the truthfulness and legality of capital contributions as well as related assets and liability from investors.

the raised fund as equity (Sun, 2000). None of these dubious activities were discovered by the CPAs. The CPAs' involvement in the case gained nationwide exposure. For example, the *People's Daily* published an article entitled 'An unjust CPA firm' on 29 July 1993.

Obviously, the fraud caused a huge stir (Sun, 2006). While the investors were the first victims, five CPAs from Zhongcheng were disqualified and the whole firm was dismantled (Xiao, Zhang and Xie, 2000). The President of the 'Great Wall,' Taifu Shen, was found guilty of embezzlement and bribery and received the death penalty, carried out in April 1994 (Gao, 2003).[6] A journalist for the *China Science and Technology Daily* was jailed for seven years and deprived of political rights for one year for accepting bribes and bribing the Deputy Minister while another journalist from the China Central Broadcast Station was also imprisoned for six years for accepting bribes (Gao, 2003; Sun, 2006). The Deputy Minister was sentenced to jail for 20 years for accepting bribes and the appropriation of public money, and was deprived of political rights for four years (Gao, 2003; www.wst.net.cn, 2007).

### 9.2.3 Hongguang

Hongguang was the first listed Chinese company to announce a loss in its first year of listing (Xie, 2001), and was sued by individual shareholders (Huang, 2001). This is a case of fraudulent application for listing by inflating profits and misrepresentation in the prospectus (Xie, 2001).

Originally an electronic SOE in Sichuan Province, Hongguang was transformed into a shareholding company in May 1993, and made its IPO on the Shanghai Stock Exchange in May 1997, raising RMB 410 million (about £29.29m). Its prospectus disclosed that the firm had an EPS of RMB 0.38, 0.49 and 0.40, respectively, in the three years prior to the IPO. The Chengdu Zhudu Accounting Firm provided a clean audit opinion, confirming that the company's financial statements for the three years were legal and reliable. The company's underwriters and legal advisors all provided unqualified underwriting or legal reports. However, it was discovered later by the CSRC that the company had inflated its profit by RMB 150 million (about £10.71m) by forging sales, manipulating depreciation, overstating inventory, and using other unlawful accounting treatments. In particular, the company actually made a loss of over RMB 100 million (about £7.14m) in 1996 instead of a reported profit of RMB 63 million (about £4.5m). It later reported a profit of RMB 16.74 million (about £1.20m) rather than the actual loss of RMB 65 million (about £4.64m) in its 1997 interim report; and the company once again understated its actual loss by RMB 31.52 million (about £2.2m) in its 1997 annual report.

The prospectus stated that the funds raised would be used to expand the colour kinescope production lines, which would increase the company's revenues by RMB 2.292 billion (about £0.16b) and the profit after tax by RMB 285 million (about £20.15m) upon completion by 1998. It also forecast that the profit of the company would be RMB 70.55 million (about £5.04m) (an EPS of RMB 0.31) in 1997. However, the company announced an EPS of only RMB 0.07 in its interim report for 1997, warning investors that the firm was suffering operational difficulties. In January 1998, the BoD of the firm announced that the production capacity had dropped because some main production facilities were obsolete

---

[6] http://www.china.com.cn/aboutchina/txt/2009-04/08/content_17571861.htm (last accessed on 22 October 2009).

and required major maintenance and technical improvement, which should have been disclosed in the prospectus issued six months ago. Hongguang then revealed a loss of RMB 0.198 billion in its 1997 annual report (an EPS of RMB –0.863) and became the first listed firm in China to report a loss and be designated a 'Special Treatment' (ST) company in the first year of listing.[7] A further loss of RMB 144.2 million (about £10.03m) was announced in 1998, resulting in the company's share price dropping sharply from RMB 14 per share on its first day of listing to RMB 5.90 per share at the end of 1999.

In November 1998, the CSRC published a statement revealing the company's illegal activities which had included forging its profits to meet listing requirements; understating losses to deceive investors; masking material events; and misappropriating publicly raised funds for share trading. The CSRC imposed a penalty of RMB one million (about £71 429) as well as penalizing the related accounting firm, law firm and asset verification firm and other intermediaries and their employees involved in the fraud (Xie, 2001).

In December 1998 and 1999, the company was sued by private shareholder(s), as the first securities lawsuit in China (Liu, 2001). The lawsuit was first dismissed by the court because the shareholders' loss could not be attributed directly to the company's misrepresentations. In 2002, the case was settled out of court with a compensation of RMB 225 000 (about £16 071) paid by Hongguang and its underwriter to 11 investors (*International Finance Newspaper*, 2006). This was the first securities civil suit that had been settled out of court with claimants.

### 9.2.4 Daqing Lianyi

This case involved bribery and corruption, fraudulent application for listing and forged documents and statements in order to meet listing requirements (*International Finance Newspaper*, 2006; Shi, 2004). Daqing Lianyi was first established as an SOE in 1985, and was transformed into a shareholding company in 1996. It acquired a listing on the Shanghai Stock Exchange in 1997 with 55 million ordinary A-shares, including five million employee shares, at a price of RMB 9.87 per share. In 1999, the company published a statement that it was being investigated by securities regulatory authorities. It was discovered later by the investigation team from the CSRC, the Supreme People's Procuratorate and the National Audit Office of the People's Republic of China that the company had committed several material frauds. First, it had systematically forged the application documents to meet the listing requirements (Shi, 2004). For example, it modified the time of acquiring a business licence (i.e. a licence provided by the government so a company can trade) as a shareholding company back from 1 January 1997 to 20 December 1993, the timing of which was crucial for obtaining a listing. It also inflated its profits from 1994 to 1996 by RMB 161.76 million (about £11.55m) by not recognizing expenses, overstating sales and not offsetting intra-group transactions as well as modifying a deferred tax payable statement from RMB 4 million (about £0.29m) to RMB 4.4 million (about £0.31m) issued by Daqing Tax Bureau

---

[7] A listed company will be classified by the CSRC as a 'Special Treatment' (ST) company if it has encountered losses in two consecutive years. Any change in the share price of a ST company is limited to 5 % both ways. If an ST company fails to become profitable in the following year, it will be labelled 'Particular Transfer' (PT); its shares are then temporarily suspended from trading except via the stock exchange's Special Transfer service. The firms will be de-listed if failing to improve in the next two or three years.

(Huang, 2001). However, according to the final Decision of Punishments issued by the Heilongjiang Intermediate People's Court in 2004, Harbin Accounting Firm and Wanban Law Firm, being aware of this, still provided clean audit and legal opinions; similarly, the company's main underwriter, Shenyin Securities Company, and the Heilongjiang Province Securities Registration Company also provided a series of forged documents to the CSRC.[8]

Second, the company misappropriated current assets and diverted the raised funds to trade shares on the stock market. The company opened 28 securities trading accounts using fake names to buy all the five million employee shares, which should have been distributed to its employees, with the funds raised from the IPO (Huang, 2001). Third, it channelled a large amount of the funds raised from the IPO premium to central and local government officials. It carved out two million employee shares for this purpose. It was revealed by the investigation team that 179 officials from 76 central or local government departments purchased 941 500 employee shares from Daqing Lianyi, and profited by earning a total share premium amounting to RMB 10.94 million (about £0.78m). The remaining 1.06 million employee shares were purchased by the firm itself and the related IPO premium was misappropriated and embezzled by the officials of the company (Huang, 2001; Xie, 2001). For example, the chairmen of the BoD and supervisory board took RMB 210 000 (about £15 000) and RMB 610 000 (about £43 571), respectively (Huang, 2001; Xie, 2001[9]). The Director of the company's Beijing Office gave RMB 520 000 (about £37 143) to his girlfriend and other friends, while his deputy put RMB two million (about £0.14m) into his own pocket (Huang, 2001; Xie, 2001).

As a result, 39 officials of the Party, the government or the company were given Party or administrative disciplinary punishments by the Party or the CSRC, and 10 were brought to court (Huang, 2001; Xie, 2001). Harbin Accounting Firm was warned and two CPAs who signed the audit reports were disqualified for securities-related auditing and another CPA was fined RMB 30 000 (about £2143). In 2004, Daqing Lianyi's main officials, and its IPO underwriter, Shenyin Wanguo Securities Company, were sued and brought to court by its 679 investors for misrepresentations and deceit in the IPO (*International Finance Newspaper*, 2006). Two defendants were found guilty and ordered to compensate the investors with RMB 12 million (about £0.86m). This was the first Chinese securities lawsuit in which the victimized investors successfully sued the company and were compensated (*International Finance Newspaper*, 2006).

### 9.2.5 Kangsai Group

This case involved the Kangsai Group in bribery, misrepresentation of financial statements and manipulation of profits with related-party transactions in order to obtain and maintain a stock exchange listing (Lu and Hua, 2003). Kangsai Group was a garment manufacturing company in Hubei Province. In 1993, its capital increased by RMB 10.29 million through an asset revaluation. This was in turn 'distributed' to shareholders as 52.79 million additional shares based on the pre-asset valuation shares. In 1996, the company obtained a listing on the Shanghai Stock Exchange. In 1999, the company's annual report showed a loss of

---

[8] http://antifraud.12312.gov.cn/typicalcase/4_article_DX2007060105441.jsp (last accessed on 22 October 2009).

[9] See also: http://www.hnaudit.gov.cn/info/read.asp?newsID=84 (last accessed on 22 October 2009).

RMB 62.03 million (about £4.43m). In April 2000, the company was publicly reprimanded by the Shanghai Stock Exchange.

A series of wrongdoings were subsequently exposed by the CSRC, the Huangshi Intermediate People's Procuratorate and Huangshi Intermediate People's Court. First, the company had obtained its listing through severe bribery and corruption by giving officials and their families free employee shares. For example, the company bribed a Deputy Minister of the State Economic and Trade Commission and an ex-Mayor of Huangshi, who helped the company obtain a priority ticket for entering the stock market in 1993 (Huang, 2001; Lu and Hua, 2003). Second, the firm provided a series of fraudulent financial statements to the market from 1996 to 1998, with consecutively reported earnings of RMB 42.4 million (about £3.03m), RMB 57.64 million (about £4.12m) and RMB 37.35 million (about £2.68m), respectively. However, it was discovered that the company had continuously made a loss since 1997 (i.e. RMB 5.13 million or about £0.37m in 1997, RMB 76.50 million or about £5.46m in 1998, and RMB 62.03 million or about £4.43m in 1999) (Huang, 2001; Lu and Hua, 2003). A major method used by the company was related-party transactions. For example, some reported sales were 'made' to subsidiaries while the stock remained in the company's own warehouse (Huang, 2001; Lu and Hua, 2003). Third, it undertook fraudulent related-party transactions with its large shareholders. For example, its largest shareholder, Kangsai Industry Ltd borrowed from Kangsai Group RMB 68 million (about £4.86m) raised from the 1998 share issue and this was treated as Kangsai Industry Ltd's contribution to the capital of Kangsai Group. However, the capital verification report prepared by the Hubei Accounting Firm (later renamed the Hubei Lihua Accounting Firm) stated that the net fund of RMB 203.85 million (about £14.56m) raised from the share issues was true and legal[10] (Huang, 2001; Lu and Hua, 2003). Fourth, the company used the money raised from investors to trade shares on the stock market. From these, Shijian Tong, the chairman of the BoD and also the CEO, gained RMB 15.85 million (about £1.13m); while Jianping Zhang, the deputy CEO and also the Party chief of the company, benefited to the tune of RMB 11.86 million (about £0.85m) (*Zhonghua Gongshang Times*, 2003). They were both charged with bribery and corruption and jailed for 15 and 10 years respectively (Lu and Hua, 2003).

The central and local government officials who accepted bribes and colluded with the company were all sentenced (Lu and Hua, 2003). It is worth noting that Hubei Accounting Firm, which provided a clean capital verification statement, not only played an important role in this scandal, but also provided unqualified audit opinions for forged financial statements prepared by at least seven other listed companies (Jiang, Li and Pi, 2001). The accounting firm was penalized by the MoF for its wrongdoings in a series of scandals and was later taken over by a Beijing-based accounting firm after the exposure of the Kangsai Group scandal (Huang, 2001; Lu and Hua, 2003).

### 9.2.6 Lantian Gufen

The Lantian Gufen case involved falsifying assets and manipulating profits and fraudulent applications for listing (Luo, 2005; Xinhua, 2002a; Xinjingbao, 2005). Lantian Gufen was

---

[10] Hubei Accounting Firm's wrongdoings were investigated and proved by the CSRC and punished by the MoF (http://media.news.sohu.com/39/69/news146306939.shtml. Last accessed 28 October 2009.)

established by a merger of three firms in Shenyang, comprising 18.28 million state shares, 35.25 million legal person shares[11] and 13.42 million employee shares. Its businesses included pharmacy and agricultural and aquatic products. Lantian Gufen made an IPO of 30 million shares in 1995 and was listed on the Shanghai Stock Exchange in June 1996, at 8.38 RMB per share.

The company disclosed a continued and rapid (more accurately, magic) growth from 1996 to 2000, with total assets surging from RMB 266 million (about £19m) to RMB 2.84 billion (about £0.2b), EPS ranged from RMB 0.6 to RMB 1.15 (Xinjingbao, 2005), and capital increased from 9.7 million shares in 1996 to 446 million shares in 2000, a growth of 4500 % (Xinhua, 2002a).

In October 1999, the CSRC disclosed that the company had fabricated listing application documentation. Lantian Gufen had fabricated an intangible asset of RMB 11 million by forging a land use approval by the Shenyang Land Bureau, a certificate of land use rights[12] and a price verification of the land[13] by the Shenyang Municipal Government. The CSRC also discovered that the company had inflated its bank account balance by RMB 27.79 million (about £2m) by forging bank statements. The company also altered the total shares from 83.70 million shares to 66.96 million shares, by reducing the number of state shares and employee shares. The hidden employee shares were then traded, although forbidden by the then prevailing securities regulations. As a result, Lantian Gufen was given a warning by the CSRC and fined RMB one million (about £71 429). The chairman, who had direct responsibility, was also given a warning and fined RMB 100 000 (about £7143) (Xinjingbao, 2005). The company applied for rights issues three times between 1999 and 2001, but the applications were all rejected by the CSRC, indicating that the CSRC had no faith in the company.

A further investigation into Lantian was carried out by the CSRC in September and October 2001. In October 2001, a short article by an academic, published in *Internal References on Finance* (an internal magazine for banking officials in China), pointed out that Lantian Gufen's magic relied not on real rapid growth but on bank loans and that the company would be in no position to repay its debts amounting to RMB two billion (about £0.2b). The article urged Chinese banks to stop lending money to Lantian Gufen, which effectively cut off the company's financing sources. Several facts were subsequently disclosed by the CSRC. First, the company had borrowed over RMB three billion (about £0.21b) from various banks by August 2002. The borrowed money, together with the firm's operating income, was claimed to have been used to build fixed assets. By 2000, the reported fixed assets reached RMB 230 billion (about £14.43b), but most of the assets were the underwater facilities for producing aquatic products in a lake, which could not be verified. This unverifiability about the true value of the fixed assets can be illustrated by one fixed asset project,

---

[11] A legal person is an artificial entity in China through which the law allows a group of natural persons (individuals) to act as if it were a single composite individual for certain purposes, or in some jurisdictions, for a single person to have a separate legal personality other than their own. This legal fiction does not mean these entities are human beings, but rather means that the law recognizes them and allows them to act as natural persons for some purposes – most commonly lawsuits, property ownership and contracts.

[12] 'Land use rights' is used in China to describe the leasehold and is distinct and separate from land ownership.

[13] The price of land requisition is normally decided by the local government (e.g. Land Administration Authority), based on the guidelines from a higher authority. For a large amount of land, the price has to be verified by the higher governmental authority.

which although started in 1996 was still not completed by 2000, even though its spending was already twice over budget. This implied that the money might not have been utilized as it was claimed (Xinhua, 2002a; Xinjingbao, 2005). Second, one of its large shareholders shouldered many types of expenses for Lantian Gufen, for example, advertising expenses amounting to RMB 0.2 billion, resulting in Lantian Gufen's inflated profits. Third, the facilities for the company's main business had not been in use for some time before the aforementioned CSRC investigation, although the firm claimed to have produced annual revenue of RMB 200 million (about £14.29m) (Xinhua, 2002a; Xinjingbao, 2005).

In May 2001, as a result of retrospective restatement of the financial statements, the company reported losses in the previous three years in succession: RMB 80.34 million (about £5.74m) in 1998, RMB 10.68 million (about £0.76m) in 1999 and RMB 22.87 million (about £1.63m) in 2000. As a result, the company was designated 'ST' on the stock exchange. In January 2002, 10 senior company officials of Lantian were arrested by the police, being involved in the misrepresentations in the company's financial statements (Luo, 2005; Xinjingbao, 2005). The share price dropped from over RMB 20 per share in June 2000 to RMB 12.58 per share on 27 August 2001 and to RMB 5.89 per share on 23 January 2002.

In 2003, the two ex-chairmen of Lantian Gufen's BoD (including Zhaoyu Qu) were sentenced to jail for two and three years, respectively (Luo, 2005; Xinjingbao, 2005). Zhaoyu Qu was sentenced to jail for three years as a result of his company's bribing Heling Sun.[14] Heling Sun, a retired Director General of the Finance Department at the Ministry of Agriculture, was sentenced to jail for eight years in 2007 for accepting bribes from Lantian and for abusing his position of power which enabled Lantian to obtain a stock exchange listing.[15] Also Faxiong Wang, Director of the Research Office and Director General of the Policy and Law Bureau at the Organisational Department of the Central Committee, the Communist Party of China (CPC), was fired by the Organisational Department and the CPC for accepting bribes and assisting Lantian's listing application.[16] In 2005, Lantian Gufen, Lantian Group – one of the large shareholders, the accounting firm and eight company officials were sued by 83 investors for the financial misrepresentations. The verdict was that Lantian Gufen (now renamed Hubei Ecological Agriculture Shareholding Co. Ltd) had to compensate the investors with RMB 5.4 million (about £0.39m) and the accounting firm had to bear joint liability (Mo, 2006).

## 9.3 A CASE IN DEPTH – ZHENGZHOU BAIWEN

### 9.3.1 Background

Zhengzhou Baiwen Co. Ltd (hereafter Baiwen) was located in Zhengzhou, Henan Province. The company dealt in household appliances and department stores. It was originally formed by a merger of Zhengzhou City Department Store and Cultural Products Company and was

---

[14] http://business.sohu.com/20081021/n260152087.shtml (last accessed on 29 October 2009).

[15] http://news.cnnb.com.cn/system/2007/12/21/005425479.shtml (last accessed on 29 October 2009).

[16] http://news.sina.com.cn/c/2005-05-31/07576034514s.shtml (last accessed on 29 October 2009).

listed on the Shanghai Stock Exchange in April 1996.[17] During the year after its listing, Baiwen, with a turnover of RMB 7046 million (about £503m), became the fifth largest of 800 listed companies in 1997. Its reported EPS was RMB 0.45 in 1997, up from RMB 0.37 a year earlier; its return on equity (ROE) increased from 15.88 % in 1996 to 19.97 % in 1997; and its share price surged from RMB 8 in April 1996 to RMB 22.7 in May 1997.

It was discovered later by the CSRC, however, that Baiwen's reported success was based on a combination of creative accounting and fraudulent practices (Huang, 2001). The company obtained a stock exchange listing and maintained its listing status by falsifying financial statements (Ding, Zhang and Zhu, 2005). Specifically, it made up artificial sales records and excluded 22 subsidiaries before its IPO and 23 subsidiaries between 1996 and 1998 in its consolidated financial statements due to their poor performance (Wang, 2006). Baiwen also fabricated accounts to inflate net profits from 1994 to 1997. However, its operating results declined dramatically from 1998, which started to attract public attention.

The first major public sign of trouble appeared in the company's 1998 interim report, with a reported EPS of only RMB 0.07, followed by a loss of RMB 502 million (about £35m), an ROE of –1148.46 % and an EPS of RMB –2.54 in its 1998 annual report. At the end of 1999, Baiwen reported a loss amounting to RMB 956 million (around £68m) and a debt of RMB 2.5 billion (£178m) owed to the China Construction Bank, which was sold to Cinda Assets Management Company.[18] As a result, Baiwen was designated 'ST' and later 'PT' in February 2001.

In March 2000, after assessing Baiwen's operations and its ability to repay its debts, Cinda applied to the Zhengzhou Intermediate People's Court for bankruptcy and liquidation proceedings against Baiwen. But the local government stopped the court from proceeding with the liquidation, resulting in a rejection of the bankruptcy application. The government later worked closely with Baiwen's management to pursue a restructuring plan, which was finally approved at a shareholders meeting in February 2001. On 4 February 2002, Baiwen's entire board resigned and Sanlian Commerce Group Company (hereafter Sanlian), a state-owned retailer of consumer electronics and major appliances in Shandong Province, took control. On 30 April 2002, Baiwen's application for an extension of its 'PT' status to the Shanghai Stock Exchange was granted. In April 2006, the company's net asset per share was RMB 1.57, with an EPS of RMB –0.0002.

An investigation by the CSRC later revealed that Baiwen had inflated its profits by RMB 19 million (£1.4m) by capitalizing expenses, for which the company as well as its board of directors were fined RMB two million (£130 000) by the CSRC. In November 2001, one of the independent directors, Jiahao Lu, who denied his involvement in the Baiwen accounting fraud, sued the CSRC for its unfair punishment. This prosecution has received plenty of attention from the public, being the first lawsuit against the CSRC by a director of a company. In November 2002, the Beijing Municipal Higher People's Court gave the final verdict that Lu Jiahao's appeal was dismissed and that the original verdict should be

---

[17] Baiwen is a subsidiary company. Baiwen's parent company held around 14 % of Baiwen's shares. It is common in China to have a subsidiary company listed on the stock exchange, rather than the entire organization.

[18] Cinda is one of the four asset management companies established by the Ministry of Finance to resolve the non-performing loans of state commercial banks.

**Table 9.2**   Net profits fabricated by Zheng Baiwen (RMB million)

|  |  | Reported net profit | Amount of net profit inflated | Net profit after the investigation |
|---|---|---|---|---|
| Before IPO | 1994 | 25 | 3 | 22 |
|  | 1995 | 27 | 16 | 11 |
| **Total (before IPO)** |  | **52** | **19** | **33** |
| After IPO | 1996 | 50 | 12 | 38 |
|  | 1997 | 78 | 98 | −20 |
|  | 1998 | −502 | 34 | −536 |
| **Total (after IPO)** |  | **−374** | **144** | **−518** |

*Source*: Li (2000).

maintained, which drew the 'Lu Jiahao vs. China Securities Regulatory Commission' case to an end (www.china.com.cn, 2002).[19]

### 9.3.2  Themes of the Scandal

Below we analyse how Baiwen falsified its accounts and employed creative accounting techniques (e.g. related-party transactions and bad debt provision) to report the company's 'success'.

#### 9.3.2.1  Sales Fraud

To fulfil the listing requirements, Baiwen fabricated its financial statements by making fraudulent sales records to create an illusion of a profitable company. The method Baiwen used was to make 'fake' sales to related companies to inflate its profits (Ding, Zhang and Zhu, 2005; Li, 2000; Wang, 2006). For example, Baiwen would sign a sales agreement with a 'friendly company' (a company that was willing to help disguise Baiwen's poor performance), allowing Baiwen to record credit sales from the latter while neither side had any intention of carrying through the sale. Using this method, Baiwen inflated its net profits by RMB 19.08 million (around £1.36m) and RMB 143.9 million (around £10.2m) before and after its listing, respectively (see Table 9.2). Meanwhile, Baiwen's accounts receivable grew dramatically up to RMB 911 million (£63m) in 1997 from only RMB 49 million (£3.4m) in 1995. These accounts receivable increased to 13 % in 1997 from 3.6 % of its sales in 1995. By 1999, Baiwen's accounts receivable had reached 46 % of its current assets.

#### 9.3.2.2  Misused Raised Capital

Baiwen fraudulently inflated its assets by RMB 149 million (around £10.57m) in its 1998 annual report (Ding, Zhang and Zhu, 2005) through a misapplication of its raised capital.

---

[19] http://sientechina.china.com.cn/chinese/FI-c/234008.htm (last accessed on 22 October 2009).

In April 1998, Baiwen undertook a rights issue with three objectives, namely to invest RMB 126 million (around £9m) in 30 new merchandise distribution centres, to merge with Zhengzhou Chemical Material Company, and to provide the company with liquidity. The company raised RMB 155 million (around £11m) from the market in July 1998. However, only RMB six million (around £0.43m), 0.4 % of the raised capital, was used to complete a merger with Zhengzhou Chemical Material Company as promised, while the remainder was used to repay bank loans, but this was neither mentioned in the prospectus nor disclosed in its 1998 annual report (Ding, Zhang and Zhu, 2005).

### 9.3.2.3  Manipulation of Capitalizing Expenses

Baiwen fabricated a profit of RMB 19 million (around £1.4m) by capitalizing expenses of RMB 2.83 million in 1994 and RMB 16.17 million in 1995 (Ding, Zhang and Zhu, 2005), respectively, to meet the listing requirements. Capitalization of expenses represented 23.8 % of Baiwen's net profit in 1996, 125 % in 1997 and 6.8 % in 1998.

### 9.3.2.4  Deferred Recognition of Expenses

Baiwen either deferred or excluded expenses incurred during the current period in order to massage the period's financial statements (Li, 2000). This fraudulent accounting technique was used to defer Baiwen's reported expenses from 1997 to 1998, which led to an increase in profit of RMB 86 million in 1997 (around £6.14m).

### 9.3.2.5  Inflated Asset Value

To hide the loss, Baiwen falsified its accounts by not disclosing an annual loss amounting to RMB 27.63 million (around £1.97m) in 1997 that was made by five departments of Zhengzhou Baiwen's household electrical appliance subsidiary. Instead, the actual loss was booked as assets (Ding, Zhang and Zhu, 2005).

### 9.3.2.6  Related-party Transactions

Baiwen employed creative accounting to turn a three-year loss into a profit of RMB three million (around £214 285), thus avoiding delisting (Li et al., 2002). In its 2001 annual report, Baiwen reported an after-tax profit of RMB 3.82 million (around £263 500) due to an income of RMB 38 million (£2.7m) received through related-party transactions. According to an agreement made in January, Baiwen's parent company would buy Baiwen's assets at book value on 30 June 2000, and would also be responsible for any loss and liabilities arising from disposal of Baiwen's assets and liabilities during the transaction period. In other words, the assets would be sold with a fixed price at a future time, and if the assets depreciated during the transaction period, the parent company would bear the loss, while any gain would be recognized by Baiwen. This led to a very peculiar result that the greater the loss Baiwen incurred, the higher its profit. Following the true and fair principle, any loss or gain from this transaction should have been recognized as capital reserves rather than other income (Li et al., 2002). However, as the then accounting standards did not specify how to account for this 'asset agreement sale,' Baiwen thus creatively recorded this gain as other income to inflate its profit.

### 9.3.2.7  Bad Debt Provision

To polish its accounts, Baiwen did not make a doubtful debt provision in 2001 due to a 'creative judgement' by the firm's board (Li *et al.*, 2002; Wang, 2006). In November 2001, Baiwen sold RMB 856 million (about £61m) of assets at book value to its parent company for RMB 940 million (£67m). The parent company, who held around 14 % of Baiwen's shares, agreed to pay RMB 540 million (£38m) while the difference of RMB 400 million (£29m) would be regarded as Baiwen's accounts receivable. In the meantime, Sanlian agreed to provide the security to Baiwen's parent company.[20] According to Baiwen's then accounting principles, the company should have made a bad debt provision of 10 % of its outstanding accounts receivable falling due within one year, but Baiwen's board believed that Sanlian's security had significantly reduced or even removed the risk of bad debts, thus without consulting the company's shareholders, Baiwen decided not to make a provision.

### 9.3.3  Who is to Blame?

### 9.3.3.1  Auditing

Zhengzhou Auditing Co. Ltd, as Baiwen's auditors, produced misrepresentative auditing reports (unqualified auditing opinions) in both 1996 and 1997. The two CPAs who provided auditing reports with misrepresentations[21] were fined by the CSRC RMB 300 000 (about £21 429) and RMB 200 000 (about £14 286), respectively and their CPA qualifications were suspended.

Between 1998 and 2000, all Baiwen's auditing firms (for example, Beijing Tianjian Auditing Company) provided a disclaimer[22] on their financial statements instead of 'adverse opinion' or 'qualified auditing report,' which is not legally wrong. While this lessened the risk of the audit firm getting a regulatory penalty, the client could still publish the financial statements as if they were 'clean' (see Chen, Chen and Su, 2001; Chen, Su and Zhao, 2000). Only in 2001, after the exposure of the Baiwen scandal, did the new auditor Shandong Tianhengxin Auditing Co. Ltd produce a qualified auditing report with explanatory notes.

---

[20] In the aforementioned plan for restructuring Baiwen, Salian would have become the controlling shareholder of Baiwen. Thus Salian was willing to provide a guarantee concerning the balance of the payment by Baiwen's current parent company.

[21] There are five types of audit opinions in China: unqualified, unqualified with explanatory paragraph(s), qualified, disclaimer and adverse (Chen, Chen and Su, 2001; Chen, Su and Wang, 2005; Chen, Su and Zhao, 2000). Normally, an explanatory note will be given when a modified audit opinion is issued. However, Chinese auditing standards allow auditors to use explanatory paragraphs in unqualified audit opinions when deemed necessary. This is used by many auditors to substitute what would otherwise be a qualified audit opinion.

[22] A disclaimer is issued when an auditor cannot form, and consequently refuses to present, an opinion on the financial statements. To avoid the risk of receiving regulatory penalties, Chinese auditors tend to protect themselves by issuing a disclaimer to clients with financial difficulties.

### 9.3.3.2   Management: BoD and SB

Baiwen was the first listed company whose senior managers faced criminal prosecution for fraudulent accounting practices. There were systematic failures at board level and at supervisory board level. In 1997, both Baiwen and its household electrical appliance subsidiary reported a loss of RMB 275 million (around £19.6m), but the incumbent chairman of the BoD, Fuqian Li; the CEO, Yide Lu; and CFO, Qunfu Du, instructed the chief accountant to fabricate Baiwen's accounts to inflate its revenues and net profits by RMB 78 million (around £5.57m). The subsidiary was also required to revise the report, manipulating the current year's accumulated profit to hide a loss of RMB 255.39 million (£18.24m). The CSRC therefore fined chairman Fuqian Li RMB 500 000 (£35 715), CEO Yide Lu RMB 300 000 (£21 429) and CFO Qunfu Du RMB 300 000 (£21 429), respectively for fraud and conspiracy over the collapse of Baiwen (Ding, Zhang and Zhu, 2005). In 2002, Fuqian Li and Yide Lu were sentenced to imprisonment for three and two years, respectively (Xinhua, 2002b).

Baiwen's SB was also ineffective in playing its monitoring role. In Baiwen's Listing Notice, the SB was composed of the Deputy chairman, Secretary of the Party committee, Director and Deputy Director of the auditing department, Deputy Director of the general manager's office, and Deputy Secretary of the Communist Youth League committee. Such a powerful SB should have monitored the performance of the BoD and required the BoD and management to take remedial action when they acted against the interests of the company, but the SB failed to do any of these. However, there is no publicly available information of any explicit action taken against the SB in this case.

Further, Baiwen's 'independent directors' failed to play a positive role. Jiahao Lu, a Professor of English at Zhengzhou University, was the only independent director from January 1995 to 2001. After the Baiwen scandal broke, Mr Lu was fined RMB 100 000 in 2001. In his interview with China Central Television (CCTV) in 2002, he emphasized that he was a titular director, never received any remuneration, nor did he review annual reports or know any techniques of fabricating accounts. He protested against the CSRC's verdict by claiming that he was more a consultant to the BoD than a real independent director and rarely attended board meetings due to his busy lecture schedule. Although his appeal was rejected by the court on the first and final trial, his argument demonstrated, and started to attract attention to, the defects in the system of independent directors in China.

### 9.3.3.3   Local Government

Baiwen was the first company transformed from an SOE to a listed company in Zhengzhou Province. In Baiwen's Listing Notice in 1996, Zhengzhou State-owned Assets Supervision Council (ZSASC) was shown to be both the largest shareholder (15 %) as a representative of state ownership and Baiwen's asset verification agency (Sina, 2006). Obviously, this dual role might affect ZSASC's position to give a true and fair valuation of Baiwen's assets. Since the state-controlled shares are non-tradable, they are not under stock market pressures or monitoring and are therefore not responsive to the interests of the small shareholders (Ding, Zhang and Zhu, 2005). Moreover, as a state-controlled shareholder (April 1996–June 1998), ZSASC failed to perform its duty to monitor Baiwen's operations. Figure 9.1 illustrates

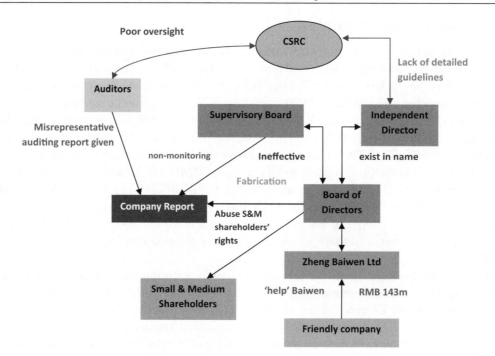

**Figure 9.1**  Zhengzhou Baiwen scandal: who is to blame?

how Baiwen managed to bypass a chain of monitoring devices in manipulating its financial accounts.

### 9.3.4  Consequences of the Baiwen Scandal

The consequences of the Baiwen scandal were serious and extensive. The scandal not only fatally influenced the company, but also adversely affected its investors and auditing firms involved.

#### 9.3.4.1  Market Reaction

The scandal caused a downturn in Baiwen's share price. Its EPS declined from RMB 0.37 in 1996 to RMB –1.52 in December 1998. Accumulated losses by the end of June 2000 amounted to RMB 1.8 billion (£124m), sending Baiwen's share price from RMB 22.70 on 12 May 1997 to RMB 4.01 on 17 May 1999, with its typical price drifting between RMB 4.5 and RMB 5.90 before its reorganization by Sanlian.

#### 9.3.4.2  Reaction of Small Investors

Baiwen's restructuring plan was regarded as having infringed the fundamental rights of small shareholders. A rule of *'implied consent, expressed opposition'*[23] used to vote on

---

[23] 'Implied consent, expressed opposition' means that there is no need for shareholders to indicate their attitudes if they agree to transfer 50 % of their stakes to Sanlian for free. Otherwise, the shareholders must explicitly express their opposing views.

the company's restructuring plan at the shareholder meeting in February 2001 was controversial. Under this rule, shareholders with an opinion other than 'consent' or 'opposition' would be deemed not to participate in the reorganization and the company would repurchase their shares. In March 2001, 32 shareholders submitted a statement that they neither consented to a free transfer of 50 % of their shares, nor agreed with the company's repurchase of their shares. They argued that Baiwen's BoD had no right to order them to transfer their shares for free. In November 2001, eight shareholders took Baiwen to court for the manipulated ballot. However, on 9 November 2001, the Zhengzhou Intermediate People's Court ruled that Baiwen's restructuring plan had been passed in a legitimate fashion and ordered the Shanghai Branch of the China Securities Depository and Clearing Corporation Ltd (CSDCC) to assist Baiwen's BoD in executing the ruling. By the end of June 2003, the CSDCC's Shanghai Branch had helped Baiwen repurchase and write off 38 shareholders' stakes at RMB 1.84 per share.

The rule of *implied consent, expressed opposition* has been hotly debated over Baiwen's reorganization. Some believe that majority shareholders have no right to dispose of the shares held by minority shareholders. The Baiwen scandal has destroyed investors' confidence, particularly that of small shareholders. Baiwen's reorganization exposed a lack of specification of the rights of minority shareholders in Company Law.

### 9.3.5 Aftermath

#### 9.3.5.1 Regulatory Reaction

The Baiwen scandal has once again made the CSRC reconsider the importance of corporate governance and internal control (Ding, Zhang and Zhu, 2005; Green and Ho, 2003; Wang, 2006). In 2001, the CSRC issued the *'Rules on Information Disclosure by Companies Issuing Securities to the Public – No. 14 Non-standard Unqualified Audit Opinion and Treatment of Related Matters'*. This regulation requires auditors not to substitute explanatory notes for modified audit opinions, and not to substitute modified audit opinions for adverse opinions.

As for the problems of independent directors derived from the Baiwen scandal, the CSRC issued *'Corporate Governance Guidelines for Listed Companies'* in 2002. The Guidelines clearly state that at least one of the independent directors should be an accounting professional. The Guidelines also require companies to establish an audit committee to take charge of recommending, hiring or firing external auditors, supervising internal auditing, enabling communications between internal and external auditors, and reviewing a company's internal control system.

#### 9.3.5.2 Legal Reactions

The Baiwen scandal has provided an opportunity to enhance legislation related to private securities litigation. Before 2000, only criminal sanctions and administrative punishment were used to punish listed companies for violating the Securities Law or relevant regulations. In January 2001, the Supreme Court issued the *'Notice Regarding Civil Lawsuits against Listed Companies on the Grounds of a False Statement,'* which allows private securities litigation to be accepted by local courts if an administrative sanction (e.g. a warning or a fine) is given by the CSRC (Li, 2004). In 2003, the Supreme Court specified rules on private securities litigation,[24] enabling investors to sue listed companies if there are criminal verdicts against a company's BoD or administrative sanctions, such as warnings or fines, given by relevant state organizations, such as the Ministry of Finance (Sina, 2005).

In addition, a derivative suit[25] mechanism was incorporated into the Company Law 2006 to give minority shareholders a statutory right to bring legal proceedings on behalf of the corporation against directors and senior management who fail to comply with the laws and regulations or fail to perform their duties, causing harm to the company. Although a class action is still unavailable to shareholders, by 2007, around 22 listed companies had been sued by individual investors for their management misrepresentations in financial statements.

## 9.4 CONCLUSION

Despite its rapid economic development over the last two decades, the Chinese system is embedded with financial scandals and creative accounting practices. This chapter reviews seven typical scandals of Chinese listed firms: six of them were presented only as snapshots while the case of Zhengzhou Baiwen was analysed in depth. The common themes of these seven scandals include:

- fraudulent applications for listing, e.g. Yuanye, Hongguang, Daqing Lianyi, Kangsai Group, Lantian Gufen and Baiwen;
- creative accounting, e.g. Baiwen;
- financial statement misrepresentations, e.g. Yuanye, Great Wall Fund Raising, Kangsai and Baiwen;
- related-party transactions, e.g. Yuanye, Kangsai, Lantian Gufen and Baiwen;
- bribery and corruption, e.g. Daqing Lianyi, Great Wall Fund Raising and Kangsai Group;
- management embezzlement, e.g. Yuanye and Baiwen.

The emergence of financial scandals has revealed the existing problems and weaknesses in China's financial system, including but not limited to: a weak corporate governance system, the lack of effective accounting and auditing professions, weak regulations in terms of IPOs, and poor information disclosure and protection of investors' rights. Lessons should be learned and accordingly several implications are elicited below for policy-makers and business practitioners.

First, Chinese listed firms suffer from serious insider control problems. As a result, the interests of shareholders and other stakeholders depend largely on the moral standards of their top management. To limit financial scandals, a more balanced governance structure should be established, and the independence of the BoD and roles of the SB should be stressed. Besides, more attention should be paid to the nomination, appointment, training, authorization and incentives of independent directors.

---

[24] On 9 January 2003, the Supreme Court promulgated detailed rules on private securities litigation, 'Several Rules on Adjudicating Civil Lawsuits against Listed Companies on the Ground of False Statements'.

[25] A derivative suit is a civil lawsuit where the shareholder brings an action in the name of the corporation, not on behalf of the shareholders, against the parties allegedly causing harm to the corporation. Often derivative suits are brought against officers or directors of a corporation who are alleged to have breached their fiduciary duties.

Second, accounting and auditing quality should be strengthened. The most damaging piece of evidence from these cases is that the accounting manoeuvres used are common and unsophisticated (even by China's standards). How could the auditing firms fail to spot the frauds? If they did spot them, why did they not report them? The independence, and moral and professional ethics of auditors should be emphasized and mass media should be encouraged to play an active role in monitoring accounting and auditing quality. Moreover, the role of auditing committees should be strengthened.

Third, timely and reliable information disclosure and investors' lawsuit legalization are two important premises which protect investors' rights. Improved financial transparency helps investors to fulfil their monitoring and oversight roles, particularly important in China where insider transactions are prevalent (Lin, 2004). The law should prescribe more clearly the types of punishment applicable to those providing false financial statements and more efforts need to be made to enforce it. Also, Chinese law-makers would benefit from carefully studying and learning from some Western rules, such as the Sarbanes-Oxley Act (2002). Currently, shareholders' lawsuits are either rejected or processed after a prolonged delay by courts, as in the case of Kangsai. To avoid shareholders' voting rights being abused by a few large shareholders, the possibility of class action and collective voting should be seriously considered.

Last, the regulations relating to IPOs, listing and de-listing should be reformed. Chinese regulators should consider modifying the compulsory profitability requirements for listing, to allow the market to decide whether a firm should be listed or not. A 'hard to get in, easy to get out' system should be introduced. Only when well-performing, high-quality firms are selected for listing can financial frauds be substantially reduced. The handover of power from government officials to the market would also largely reduce government intervention in the financial market and in turn reduce the corruption by government officials shown in some of the above financial scandals, e.g. the Great Wall Fund Raising case. In this sense, the government should gradually relinquish certain roles to the market, which in turn should require reforms in the ownership rules for listed firms.

In conclusion, by analysing the typical financial scandals in China's stock markets, and exploring their causes and consequences, this chapter provides enriched evidence on creative accounting practices in China for international researchers and business practitioners. Chinese financial scandals share similar themes and symptoms to international creative accounting and fraud, but their specific causes relate to China's specific institutional settings.

# REFERENCES

(For convenience, articles in Chinese have been translated into English.)

Aharony, J., Lee, C.J. and Wang, T.J. (2000), 'Financial packaging of IPO firms in China', *Journal of Accounting Research*, **38**(1), 103–126.

Allen, F., Qian, J. and Qian, M. (2005), 'Law, finance, and economic growth in China', *Journal of Financial Economics*, **77**(1), 57–116.

CCTV (2002), 'Baiwen's reorganisation legal barriers and its outlook'. CCTV Economic News, 8 August, http://www:financ.sina.com.cn, accessed on 18 June 2006.

Chen, K. and Yuan, H. (2004), 'Earnings management and capital resource allocation: evidence from China's accounting-based regulation on rights-issuing in China', *The Accounting Review*, **79**(3), 645–665.

Chen, J.P., Chen, S.M. and Su, X.J. (2001), 'Profitability regulation, earnings management, and modified audit opinions: evidence from China', *Auditing: A Journal of Practice and Theory*, **20**(2), 9–30.

Chen, S., Su, X. and Wang, Z. (2005), 'An analysis of auditing environment and modified audit opinions in China: underlying reasons and lessons', *International Journal of Accounting*, **9**(3), 165–185.

Chen, J.P., Su, X.J. and Zhao, R. (2000), 'An emerging market's reaction to initial modified audit opinions: evidence from the Shanghai Stock Exchange', *Contemporary Accounting Research*, **17**(3), 429–455.

DeFond, L.M. and Park, C. (1997), 'Smoothing income in anticipation of future earnings', *Journal of Accounting and Economics*, **23**(2), 115–139.

Ding, Y., Zhang, H. and Zhu, H. (2005), 'Accounting failures in Chinese listed firms: origins and typology', *International Journal of Disclosure and Governance*, **4**(2), 395–412.

Ezzamel, M., Xiao, Z. and Pan, A. (2007), 'Political ideology and accounting regulation in China', *Accounting, Organizations and Society*, **32**(7), 669–700.

Gao, J. (2003), 'An analysis of paid news reporting over the last 20 years', http://home.donews.com/donews/article/4/43834.html, accessed on 16 August 2007.

Green, S. and Ho, J. (2003), 'Old stocks, new owners: two cases of ownership change in China's stock market', *Asian Programme Working Paper*, No. 9.

Hao, Z.P. (1999), 'Regulations and organisation of accountants in China', *Accounting, Auditing and Accountability Journal*, **12**(3), 286–302.

Huang, X.Y. (2001), *Hedong Jiemi (Exposure to Corporate Scandals)*, Zhuhai Publishing, Guang-dong. http://www.newsgd.com/business/enterprise/200601240031.

Institute for Economic and Resource Management Research (2005), *Report on Marketisation in China*, Beijing Normal University, Beijing.

*International Finance Newspaper* (2006), '30 Lawyers declare war against Deloitte & Touche by signing an Action Manifesto', 11 April.

Jiang, S., Li, P. and Pi, S. (2001), 'Investors shocked by the mad falsification by Hubei Lihua Accounting Firm', XinhuaNet, 19 August.

Lee, K. and Hahn, D. (2001), 'From insider–outsider collusion to insider control in China's SOEs', *Working Paper Series No. 44*, Institute of Economic Research, Seoul National University.

Li, R. (2000) 'Legal thinking on accountant responsibilities of ZhengZhou Baiwen Ltd', *Accounting World*, http://www.e521.com/cksj/2/0201165935, accessed 14 June 2006.

Li, R.S., Fang, J.X., Jin, H.F., Feng, M. and Jiang, W.P. (2002), 'An analysis of PT Baiwen's Annual Report', http://www.people.com.cn/GB/jinji/35/161/20010206/390089, accessed 10 June 2006.

Li, Y. (2001), 'A major measure for developing an accounting system suitable for China – the issuance of the Enterprise Accounting System', *China Finance and Economics Newspaper*, http://www.e521.com/cksj/yjyw/0036, accessed 10 January 2007.

Lin, T.W. (2004), 'Corporate governance in China: recent development, key problems, and solutions', *Journal of Accounting and Corporate Governance*, **1**, 1–23.

Liu, W.D. (2001), 'Ten biggest corporate scandals in China's stock market', *China Economic Times*, 27 February, http://www.cg.org.cn/practice/pra19.asp, accessed 8 June 2006.

Lu, C. and Hua, H. (2003), 'The inside story of Gangsai Gufeng that stirred up the whole country', *Democracy and Law*, Vol. 19, http://www.zydg.net/magazine/article/1003-1723/2003/19/184163.html, accessed 16 August 2007.

Luo, C. (2005), 'The story of the downfall of the Director-General of the Finance Department at the Ministry of Agriculture in the Lantian case', *Xinjingbao*, 21 September, p. 12.

Mo, D. (2006), 'The Shengtai Nongye case opened yesterday', *Shanghai Securities Newspaper*, 30 May.

Pistor, K. and Xu, C. (2005), 'Governing stock markets in transition economies: lessons from China', *American Law Economics Review*, **7**(1), 184–210.

Qian, Y. (1995), 'Reforming corporate governance and finance in China', in *Corporate Governance in Transition Economies: Insider Control and the Role of Banks*, eds M. Aoki and H. Kim, The World Bank.

Shi, J. (2004), 'Back dating documents: an insight into the methods used in the Daqing fraud', *Securities Market Weekly*, 7 December.

Sina (2005), 'Several rules on adjudicating civil lawsuits against listed companies on the ground of false statements', 12 December, http://finance.sina.com.cn/stock/otheran-nouce/20051212/13102191011.shtml, accessed 5 December 2006.

Sina (2006), 'Background information on Lantian Gufen', http://money.finance.sina.com.cn/corp/view/vISSUE_MarketBulletinDetail.php?stockid=600898&end_date=19960311, accessed 5 December 2006.

Sun, L.R. (2000), 'A study of the establishment of an accounting monitoring system under the market economy conditions', Jilin Planning Office for Philosophy and Social Science, http://www.jlpopss.gov.cn/newscontent.asp?id=554, accessed 28 September 2006.

Sun, W.Y. (2006), 'What the fallen "Great Wall" company told us?' *Law Weekly*, 24 November.

Tenev, S. & Zhang, C. (2002), *Corporate Governance and Enterprise Reform in China: Building the Institutions of Modern Markets*, World Bank Publications.

Wang, X. (2006), 'The kinds, causes of frauds and its treatment: research on the accounting frauds in listed companies', *Journal of Modern Accounting and Auditing*, **2**(1), 71–77.

Wang, Z.Y. (1993), 'Thoughts on the lessons of the Zhongcheng case', in *Some Thoughts on Social Audit*, ed. Z.Y. Wang, Olympic Publishing, Beijing, pp. 193–207.

www.china.com.cn (2002), 'The appeal from Zhengzhou Baiwen's Independent Director was dismissed', http://sientechina.china.com.cn/chinese/FI-c/234008.htm, accessed 22 October 2009.

www.wst.net.cn (2007), 'The main fraudster in the "Great Wall Fund Raising Fraud" sentenced to death on 11 April 1994', http://www.wst.net.cn/history/4.11/041118.htm, accessed 18 July 2007.

Xiao, Z. (1999), 'Disclosures made by Chinese listed companies', *International Journal of Accounting*, **34**(3), 349–373.

Xiao, Z., Dahya, J. and Lin, Z. (2004), 'A grounded theory exposition of the role of Supervisory Board in China', *British Journal of Management*, **15**(1), 39–55.

Xiao, Z., Zhang, Y. and Xie, Z. (2000), 'The making of independent auditing standards in China', *Accounting Horizons*, **14**(1), 69–89.

Xie, Y.D. (2001), 'Taking stock of the top ten frauds on the Chinese stock market', Dadi, No. 24, http://www.people.com.cn/GB/jinji/222/3466/3468/20010201/386575.htm, accessed 18 January 2007.

Xinhua (2002a), 'Background information on Lantian Gufen', http://news.xinhuanet.com/fortune/2002-01/25/content_257401.htm, accessed 5 September 2006.

Xinhua (2002b), 'Former Chairman of Zhengbaiwen committed the crime to provide false accounting reports was sentenced', 14 November, http://news.xinhuanet.com/newscenter/2002-11/14/content_630091.htm, accessed 8 September 2006.

Xinjingbao (2005), 'The truth about Lantian legacy: the protagonists were four officials', 27 September, http://www.sconline.com.cn/economics/qyxw/20050927/200592792139.htm, accessed 15 November 2006.

Zheng, Q.D. and Chen, W.W. (1993), 'The failure of a one billion Renminbi fraud', *The People's Daily* (Overseas Edition), 24 June, p. 3.

*Zhonghua Gongshang Times* (2003a), 'Insane share dealings leading to 15 years in jail', 11 August.

Zou, H. and Xiao, Z. (2006), 'The financing behaviour of listed Chinese companies', *British Accounting Review*, **38**(2), 239–258.

# Accounting Scandals in Germany

Hansrudi Lenz

## 10.1 INTRODUCTION

In this chapter I describe important accounting scandals in Germany with respect to their motives, structure of accounting transactions, with related balance sheet and profit and loss items, and the reactions of concerned parties (supervisory board, regulatory agencies, management, auditors, the public).

Accounting scandals occur where companies have adopted questionable accounting practices in quarterly or annual reports characterized by high media coverage. I distinguish between creative accounting and fraudulent reporting.[1] Misstatements can arise directly from fraudulent financial reporting (e.g. the booking of fictitious receivables), or indirectly in conjunction with the misappropriation of assets (e.g. theft of inventory which is falsely recognized in the accounts as depreciation of damaged inventory) (see for details ISA 240, redrafted 2006).

When there are material misstatements due to fraud, then three conditions are generally present: (i) incentives or pressure; (ii) perceived opportunities to commit the fraud; and (iii) inner attitudes to rationalize or justify the fraud. Generally, risk factors are grouped into these three categories (see, for example, ISA 240; Loebbecke *et al.*, 1989). This concept can also be applied to legal, but in the eyes of the public questionable, earnings management or creative accounting. In the following description of accounting scandals I try to identify risk factors relating to these three conditions. These conditions can also be understood as the causes of creative accounting and/or of financial statement fraud.

Furthermore, it is also interesting to determine potential failures of internal and external control institutions which make possible creative or fraudulent reporting. In German joint stock corporations, the supervisory board has the task of monitoring the management and the financial reporting process (Art. 111 Stock Corporation Law). If the top management, which can override internal control mechanisms, is involved in creative accounting or fraudulent financial reporting, a potential safeguard for the prevention and detection of such behaviour could be a pro-active supervisory board. Another central safeguard is the auditor, whose responsibility is to obtain reasonable assurance that the financial statements

---

[1] *Creative accounting* is characterized by using the flexibility within the applicable reporting framework to manage the measurement and presentation of the accounts so that they give primacy to the interests of the preparers not the users. *Fraudulent financial reporting* is when management step outside the rules and regulations that govern accounting (for a fuller discussion of these terms see Chapter 1).

are free from material misstatement, whether caused by fraud or error (Art. 317 Commercial Code).

Accounting scandals are major drivers of the regulatory development. In response to accounting scandals, the legislative landscape in Germany has been changed fundamentally in the period between 1980 and 2006. For example, in 2005 the Financial Reporting Enforcement Panel, a new enforcement institution, was created responsible for the correctness of financial statements.

I have used case studies based on an analysis of a variety of documents from different sources (e.g. books about accounting scandals, press articles, investigation reports). All information in this chapter is based on publicly available sources and it should be mentioned that the reliability of the sources varies. Court decisions directly concerned with fraudulent financial reporting are rare events in Germany, so the analysis cannot be based on such documents (Wulf, 2005, p. 214). Prosecutors focus on other offences, like the deception of creditors or the forgery of documents, because it is easier to prove them than to prove fraudulent financial reporting. The consequence is that in Germany very few trials relating to financial statement fraud end in a conviction.

The next section discusses four high-profile cases of accounting scandals in more detail (Co op, Balsam, BVV, Philipp Holzmann). In the following section I provide details of the two most important German scandals, Flowtex and ComRoad. Then I give a short overview of the regulatory responses to the accounting scandals, and briefly discuss the investigations concluded by the new German Financial Reporting Enforcement Panel. Finally, I summarize and conclude.

## 10.2 ACCOUNTING SCANDALS BETWEEN 1985 AND 2006

### 10.2.1 Co op AG (1988)

The former owner of the Co op AG, a retail chain, was the German trade unions. The sale of Co op AG resulted in an opaque and complex ownership structure and thereafter in one of Germany's most spectacular cases of economic crime (see for the latter: *Spiegel* No. 42/1988, pp. 142–155; No. 10/1989, pp. 122–125; No. 36/1989, pp. 124–133; Peemöller and Hofmann, 2005, pp. 85 *et seq.*; Student and Garding, 1992). Even though Co op AG was in a bad financial condition before 1987, an Initial Public Offering (IPO) of the Co op shares in the year 1987 was successful. The dominating figure was Bernd Otto, who acted as CEO.

In 1988, a long and detailed article in the influential political magazine *Der Spiegel* claimed that the financial leverage of the group was much higher than the official figure in the financial statements, and criticized the opaque ownership structure with firms mainly domiciled in offshore countries like the Cayman Islands. The business activities abroad were mostly organized as entities under common control (e.g. the management board of those entities comprised Co op management without a majority equity investment of Co op AG). Such a structure enabled Co op not to consolidate these entities. Furthermore, the article showed evidence of numerous dubious related-party transactions (e.g. firms which were controlled by the management of Co op AG, wrongfully owned shares of Co op[2] and conducted other transactions relating to property and equipment which were not properly

---

[2] Wrongfully, as a company should not own shares in itself above a 10 % threshold together with certain other conditions.

reported in the financial statements). The financial press suspected that the pension fund of Co op also wrongfully acquired Co op shares (see Peemöller and Hofmann 2005, p. 85, with further references) although this was never actually proved in court. The article guessed that Co op AG was in large part monitored by the management itself with no independent effective oversight. As a result of this article some directors seen to have left the board and this article almost resulted in the insolvency of Co op AG. Despite a long-lasting trial against the top management and some members of the supervisory board most of the accusations, especially those relating to financial statement fraud, were never substantiated. Bernd Otto, the former chief, confessed to some charges (such as misappropriation of 21 million German marks)[3] and was sentenced to four and a half years in jail for financial malpractice. Other top executives got even milder punishments (*Spiegel* No. 9/1994, pp. 130–134).

The last published financial statement of the firm in the years before the crisis depicted a highly leveraged firm, but with a good Return on Equity (ROE in 1997 = 10%). The 1987 annual report stated that Co op AG had been successfully reorganized in the past years and that the equity ratio had been increased and was a sound basis for future growth. Absolutely no clues relating to potential future risk for the firm could be found in the financial statements. For example, in the notes no details about other material operating expenses or related-party transactions were given. The auditors issued an unqualified report in 1986 and 1987. It was virtually impossible to decipher the true picture of the group from the published financial statements.

The Co op case showed that pressure to be creative in the financial statements was caused by the bad financial condition of Co op (i.e. high leverage and low profitability). Some dominating members of the top management appear to have tried to gain near total control of the firm to enrich themselves via high salaries and other monetary benefits (e.g. Co op shares). Opportunities were given because a lax supervisory board and lenient auditors did not adequately discharge their monitoring function. The German legal system proved to be ineffective in this case because the conjectured financial statement fraud and other allegations relevant to the issues were never clarified definitively. Shareholders and creditors lost billions of German marks.

### 10.2.2 Balsam AG (1994)

The non-listed joint stock corporation Balsam AG was initially a medium-sized successful manufacturer and distributor of synthetic floors for sports stadiums with approximately 1000 employees founded by Friedel Balsam in 1973 (see for the latter: *Spiegel* No. 15/1994, pp. 81–82; No. 24/1994, pp. 102–104; 17/1996, pp. 112–120; No. 36/1999, pp. 108–109; Hennes and Henry, 1994; Henry and Hennes, 1994; Peemöller and Hofmann, 2005, pp. 92 *et seq.*; Westerburg, 2002, pp. 45–88). An excessive focus on turnover growth and market share, neglecting liquidity and profitability, led to serious financial troubles in the mid-1980s for the market leader in this special business segment. The financial problems intensified because of an economic downturn in the market for synthetic stadium floors. The CFO

---

[3] €1 equals 1.96 German marks (DM), i.e. one million German marks = €511 292. This exchange rate was fixed at 31 December 1998.

began to use factoring to reduce the cash cycle, therefore reducing liquidity problems. The factor was Procedo GmbH, which refinanced itself using various banks. After a while the CFO sold – with the knowledge and active participation of the CEO – fictitious receivables to the factor. This started with the selling of receivables with inflated amounts and also receivables which did not yet exist from subsidiaries of Balsam AG. The fraud scheme worked for over 10 years because Balsam AG collected the (sold) receivables and not the factor. There was no direct contact between the factor and the debtor (i.e. a so-called hidden factoring where the debtor is not informed that the right has been transferred to the factor). The factor checked the existence of the receivables only through copies of the order confirmation and the invoice. So it was possible to pay the older faked receivables which were sold to the factor with new money stemming from the selling of new fictitious receivables to the factor ('Ponzi scheme'). Due to the strong increasing volume of the factoring business, the factor later demanded an independent confirmation of the account balances. The CFO falsified a confirmation and wrongly used the name of the audit firm Arthur Andersen. The auditor of Balsam relied on these (false) confirmations too.[4]

The fraud (forgery of documents) was connected with the booking of some of the fictitious receivables and revenues in the financial statements of Balsam AG and therefore caused a material misstatement in the individual and group accounts. In 1992, the group turnover of Balsam AG was only 364 million German marks, but the volume of the factoring amounted to 1975 million marks, fivefold the sales. This apparent disparity – clearly a potential 'red flag' – had to be explained by the CEO and CFO to the factor and the auditor. The CFO explained that Balsam sells receivables from third parties (i.e. firms engaged in consortiums together with Balsam). In reality, Balsam had no right to sell these receivables. The factor relied on this explanation without demanding reasonable evidence. No direct contact with the postulated third parties was sought. With respect to the cash flows between Balsam and Procedo, a clearing account was set up which was closed at year end with fictitious receipts of payments from Arabian and Asian clients. The zero balance account was not checked by the auditor (see Westerburg 2002, p. 71; Regional Court Bielefeld, 20.9.1999, Az 9 KLs 6 Js 415/92 – K 2/95 IX, p. 40). With hindsight it can be said that since 1991 the factoring fees paid (i.e. the discounts with which the receivables were sold) were higher than the real revenues of the firm. Furthermore, taxes had to be paid on the basis of non-existing incomes. The necessary cash flow for these expenses had also been created by the selling of new fictitious receivables. It should be mentioned that the auditor of Balsam was also the auditor of Procedo, the factor, too. So the auditor had information from both sides, actually an ideal situation for an auditor. Because Balsam AG was the main client of Procedo, which delivered up to two-thirds of its sales, the auditor should have devoted a considerable portion of attention to this business relationship. Actually, the auditor failed to do so.

Central statements in the 1992 annual report were that the outcome of the 1992 financial year was a satisfactory net income, that the leading position on the world market was strengthened and that an adequate net income was expected for the coming financial year (1993). No risk factors were mentioned in the annual report. Instead, the financial statements

---

[4] Factoring is a common source of financing where a firm agrees to sell some of its account receivables, at a discount, to a financial institution with the aim of obtaining the cash more quickly. Hidden factoring means that the debtor is invoiced by the firm and is not informed about the selling of the receivable to the factor. Debt is first collected by the firm and then the money transferred to the factor.

showed a firm with high liquidity, an equity ratio of 26 % in 1992 (1991: 30 %) and a ROE in 1992 of 17.5 %.

The fraud was detected by a whistleblower who informed the public prosecutor's office in 1993, which did not react immediately. After a television report in 1994 the factor, other banks and the prosecutor's office reacted. Only 10 days after the report, bankruptcy proceedings were opened. In the end, 1.8 billion German marks of fictitious receivables led to the bankruptcy of Balsam AG and to huge losses for the factor and some banks. The trial against the CEO and CFO ended with long periods of imprisonment (eight and 10 years) for these executives. The auditor was on remand for two years, but in the end was acquitted. The audit firm was a subsidiary of Price Waterhouse which paid an out-of-court settlement of approximately 60 million German marks. The vice-chairman of the supervisory board, although there were hints of potential irregularities, failed to clear up inconsistencies in the numbers and in the explanations from the board of directors. He was sentenced to pay damages of about 5 million German marks due to a breach of monitoring duties according to Art. 111, 116 Stock Corporation Law (see Westerburg, 2002, p. 82). To sum up, control failure of the supervisory board made the financial statement fraud easier. 'Red flags' were apparently ignored by the auditor.

### 10.2.3 Bremer Vulkan Verbund AG (1995)

Bremer Vulkan Verbund AG (BVV AG) was a shipyard with a long-lasting tradition dating back to the nineteenth century (see for the latter: *Spiegel* No. 18/1996, pp. 118–121; No. 51/1993, pp. 86–87; No. 45/2000, pp. 150–152; Investigative Committee 'Bremer Vulkan', 1998; Westerburg, 2002, pp. 89–135). After World War II, BVV was booming but in the 1970s, insolvency could only be avoided with the help of the federal government and the City of Bremen. Between 1987 and 1993, BVV developed a diversified holding of dockyards (shipbuilding), electronics and manufacturing engineering systems. The aim was to create a leading 'maritime technology group'. The diversification would help to minimize its dependency on shipbuilding. Following this strategic goal, BVV mainly bought firms in a bad financial condition which needed an all-embracing organizational and financial reorganization. This diversification strategy, in conjunction with competitive pressure on the shipbuilding market, led to a chronic strained liquidity of BVV AG in the 1980s and the beginning of the 1990s. Because BVV was a huge employer, the City of Bremen over the years entered into debt guarantees and bought, via a city-owned holding, overpriced ship investments from BVV. Over and over again BVV successfully used political pressure – the potential layoff of employees in a city with a high unemployment rate – to get state aid. A subsidy mentality and a close link between city, political system and corporation developed over time. The CEO at that time was a former high-ranked city civil servant with excellent political connections. Up to the insolvency in 1995, a total amount of 1.5 billion German marks came from the City of Bremen.

After the reunification of Germany in 1989, BVV bought the large and most important former East German shipyards in 1992 and 1993. The eastern shipyards got large state aid in the form of restructuring and operating aid to finance investments, layoffs and operating losses (see for the following: European Commission, 1999). This money – over 800 million German marks (€408 million) – paid not in instalments due to liquidity needs, but as a lump sum – flew into the central cash concentration system of BVV created in October

1993. Under European law, Germany had to provide evidence in the form of annual reports by an independent accountant that the aid was benefiting only shipyards in the former German Democratic Republic. With respect to BVV, these reports were provided by the same audit firm (Coopers & Lybrand, now PricewaterhouseCoopers) who audited BVV's annual accounts. Later on, a special audit conducted by another audit firm, Susat & Partner, a middle-tier audit firm, concluded that the authors of these reports did not perform their mandate properly because they had not examined in detail the placement of funds in the cash concentration system (European Commission 1999, p. 36). However, it is open to question whether this criticism was actually justified. In fact, BVV used the state aid for the eastern firms to cover operating losses in the western part of the group. Later, the European Commission (European Commission, 1999) initiated proceedings against the German government and decided that the total amount of misused funds was approximately 790 million German marks (€403 million).

In 1995, BVV slipped into a severe liquidity crisis which ended with bankruptcy at the start of 1996. The last published annual group report for the financial year 1994, however, showed a group which had significantly increased equity, reduced provisions and liabilities, and turned a previous loss into a positive net income. Coopers & Lybrand, one of the leading international firms, issued a clean opinion. In the middle of 1995, the CEO of BVV explained at the annual meeting that he expected a positive net income and the payout of dividends in 1995. It is perhaps surprising that the CEO did not know that his statements at that time were incorrect because of mounting liquidity problems and operating losses. Later, in the special audit conducted by Susat & Partner, it turned out that operating results in nearly all the business segments in 1994 and 1995 were negative (Investigative Committee 'Bremer Vulkan,' pp. 436–439). The same was the case for the net income of the group. The losses were compensated mainly by the use and release of provisions. The external reader of an annual report could not prove if only expenses that related to the original provision were set against it. Generally, professional discretion relating to valuation judgements was strained to the limit. A report from the above-mentioned special audit summarized and evaluated the quality of the financial statement for 1994 as follows:

> In a juridical sense a financial statement fraud could not be detected but there were strong evidence for extreme creative accounting policies and a too optimistic description of the business situation in the management report. Insofar as the understanding and the interpretation of the accounting principle of true and fair view is incompatible with creative window-dressing then the board violated its respective duties. (see Investigative Committee 'Bremer Vulkan,' 1998, p. 429)

An investigation committee appointed by the parliament of the City of Bremen concluded in its report:

> A major cause for the crisis at the BVV was the widespread inability to tell the truth. This inability had diverse shades. With respect to the board it reached from 'positive influence on press' and visions not grounded on facts, and from concealment to untruthfulness; by the auditors and members of the supervisory board from trust over loyalty, blind confidence to cronyism; by the government from illusionary hope to the politically motivated angst to hear the truth. In the face of the significance, the hopes and the tradition of the BVV it was obviously difficult to tell the truth. (Investigation Committee Report, 1998, p. 817)

Critical words about the auditor of BVV can also be found in the report because the audit firms worked at the same time for the City of Bremen to evaluate the potential risk of guarantees that the city had granted to BVV. In this function, the audit firm had to evaluate whether the guarantees were justified based on the business plans stemming from BVV. Applying common sense, the Committee came to the result that 'this accumulation of tasks – at the same time auditor and consultant, simultaneously working for the state-aid donor and the direct beneficiary – will lead and in this case has led even by diligent task separation to a certain blindness and mutual reciprocity because the audit results should in the end fit together' (Investigation Committee Report, 1998, p. 795). Despite this harsh criticism, no disciplinary proceedings against the auditor took place. In criminal proceedings, members of the board were originally sentenced because of the misuse of state funds from the eastern shipyards. This can be seen as an extreme example of creative accounting rather than as financial statement fraud. However, later, the Federal Court of Justice repealed the judgment and recommitted the proceedings to the lower courts. A final decision is pending and even an abatement of action seems to be probable now (see Jahn, 2010). In this case, therefore, the board members appear to have successfully denied the charges and may get their names cleared of fraud.

With respect to the supervisory board, the information flow from the executive board to the supervisory board was fragmentary and the supervisory board failed to take strong measures to obtain full information. The supervisory board only mildly criticized the executive board. Critical inquiries were rare because even the supervisory board trusted in the state aid and guarantees from the City of Bremen (see Westerburg, 2002, pp. 119–130). Personal ties between the charismatic CEO, Friedrich Hennemann, and the president of the supervisory board were not conducive to tough monitoring. According to the Investigative Committee Report, Dr Hennemann was also the centre of power who, over a long time, unfavourably dominated the supervisory board (Investigative Committee Report, 1998, p. 815).

Overall, therefore, this case, despite the widespread criticism of both the auditors and directors, can be seen as an extreme example of creative accounting rather than as financial statement fraud. Certainly nothing illegal has been proved against either the auditors or the directors.

### 10.2.4 Philipp Holzmann AG (1999)

Philipp Holzmann AG was one of Europe's largest construction and engineering companies. It constructed and built bridges, tunnels, industrial facilities, public and commercial buildings (see Lenz, 2004b; Westerburg, 2002, pp. 136–184). Holzmann was also engaged in property and facility development. The main shareholders at January 1999 were one of the leading German banks (Deutsche Bank AG) with a share of 20.9 % and a holding company (Gevaert N.V.) of the Belgian industrialist André Leysen with 30.4 %. In 1998 and 1999, Gevaert N.V. bought a 30.4 % share of Holzmann for 400 million German marks. The Belgian company took over an interest of about 10 % from Deutsche Bank at year end 1998 and another 5 % with the help of Deutsche Bank. The residual 15 % were bought via an exchange of shares from the construction company Hochtief AG. At this time the chairman of the supervisory board was Boehm-Bezing (member of the management board of Deutsche Bank). Another member was the Belgian industrialist and owner of Gevaert, André Leysen.

The management report for the year 1998 contained the following forecast for the subsequent year: 'The financial year 1999 will be characterised by further restructuring measures in conjunction with an unchanged difficult market condition. The operating profits will further improve. We expect a slightly positive result.'[5] The management report does not contain any suggestions about significant risks for the company. The auditor (KPMG) issued an unqualified auditors' report, signed on 22 April 1999.

Dr Heinrich Binder, the then chairman of the management board of Holzmann AG, declared in his speech at the annual general meeting of the company on 30 June 1999 that the turnaround of the company through a reorganization in the preceding years had been achieved. After the 'cleaning up of the legacy of previous failures' the company would be profitable in the future. He argued: 'In the past financial year and on the way to forming a new group we made considerable progress. The turnaround is achieved, the restructuring is on schedule and the financial situation has clearly become easier. The annual report received a clean opinion from the auditor and is more transparent and direct than before and therefore provides a basis for profitable growth in the future.'[6] Binder announced at the annual shareholders' meeting a 'moderate profit for the current financial year'. This speech by the chairman at the annual meeting thus further reinforced the positive forecast in the management report.

Four and a half months after the shareholders' annual general meeting, the company informed the public on 15 November 1999 about a probable loss in 1999 of about 2.4 billion German marks leading to an almost total loss of equity. According to the management the huge losses were caused by transactions for which the former management board bore responsibility and which could not have been detected earlier. This so-called 'legacy' could not have been foreseen and shown in the preceding financial statements because these losses had been systematically disguised and kept secret by former representatives.

At this moment, intensive negotiations started with bank and credit insurers about the further proceedings. The question was: insolvency or financial restructuring? The negotiations failed and Holzmann AG opened bankruptcy proceedings. The share price fell by 80 %. In November 1999 the then German Chancellor Gerhard Schröder talked with the banks and reached an agreement. The 10 largest German banks were engaged by Holzmann AG to the extent of over 5 billion German marks and the financial restructuring required further aid of about 2 billion German marks (e.g. increased share capital, new loans) (€1.02 billion). The supervisory board instructed the audit firm Ernst & Young to carry out a special audit and the chairman Binder declared his resignation on 14 December 1999. The company issued the following ad-hoc release on that day:

> The supervisory board discussed in today's meeting of Philipp Holzmann AG the report and the statements therein of the special auditor Ernst & Young and the conclusion to be drawn from it. The results of the statements and the juridical appraisal reveal without doubt considerable breaches of duty of former board members and representatives . . . In addition, the supervisory

---

[5] Philipp Holzmann AG, Annual Report, 1998, p. 17.

[6] Speech by Dr Heinrich Binder, chairman of the management board, at the annual general meeting of Philipp Holzmann AG on 30 June 1999.

board discussed the reasons which have led to a probable loss of 2.4 billion German marks. In this context the special auditor and the auditor of the financial statements KPMG gave these comments. The potential losses of 600 million German marks stemming from a selection of projects and transactions mentioned in the report of the special auditor as well as the overall evaluation of the management board of Philipp Holzmann AG are based to a large extent on an end-of-year related new evaluation of transactions initiated in former periods (the so-called 'legacy'). The total amount of losses will be recognised in the financial statements 1999 and will not be corrected by retrospective restatements. The auditors' opinions about former periods are therefore not questioned.

At the extraordinary shareholders meeting on 30 December 1999, a capital reduction with a subsequent capital increase was decided. The audit firm Ernst & Young was elected as an additional auditor (i.e. KPMG and Ernst & Young had to perform a joint audit). The financial press raised many questions about the auditor KPMG (i.e. why had KPMG accepted a management report in the financial statements 1998 without any remarks about possible material risks?). A detailed report of the financial magazine *Capital* (No. 1/2, 2000) used citations from the long-form auditors' report. The citations revealed a lot of critical remarks about the internal control and risk management system and the recognition and measurement of provisions and construction contracts. In particular, many project calculations were inadequate and overly optimistic, resulting in an overvaluation of unfinished building contracts and an underestimation of provisions for onerous contracts.[7] In the end, however, the auditors argued that the recognition and measurement decisions were at the limits of the accounting rules but justifiable. Therefore, an unqualified auditors' report was possible. An example taken from the long-form auditors' report shows the auditors' arguments: 'Overall the provisions for rental risks (i.e., risks arising from rental contracts) are quite low. Insofar as the assumptions used to calculate the provisions are not realistic, significant increases may be necessary.' The auditor KPMG defended itself against the questions with arguments mainly relating to the difficulties of property valuations and to changing assumptions over time which could not have been anticipated.

The Holzmann case can be seen as an example of creative accounting because of the probable overvaluation of unfinished building contracts, the missing or underestimated provisions for onerous contracts and the insufficient reporting about risk factors in the management report. These creative, but not illegal, accounting techniques were used by prior management to cover up the company's bad situation. This case is arguably also an example of an auditor who did not draw the line clearly enough at central recognition and measurement questions.

## 10.3 MOST IMPORTANT CASES: FLOWTEX AND COMROAD

### 10.3.1 Flowtex Gmbh & Co. KG (2000)

Flowtex was a mid-sized, non-listed owner-dominated company. Flowtex developed and distributed a new horizontal drilling system. The system allowed pipes to be moved underground without drilling down into the soil. The dominating and charismatic person who

---

[7] A contract where, according to IAS 37, para. 68, the unavoidable costs of meeting the obligations exceed the contract's expected economic benefits.

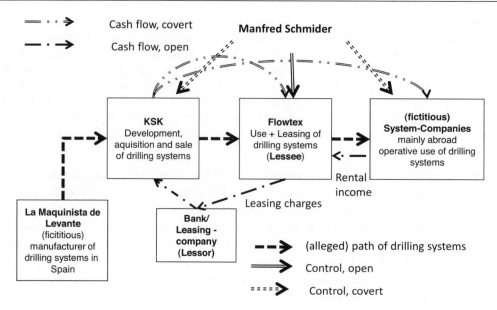

**Figure 10.1**    The Flowtex Ponzi scheme

was the founder of the company, Manfred Schmider, had excellent connections politically. The fraud scheme used by Schmider and other executives and confidants was a classical Ponzi scheme (see Figure 10.1 and Heck, 2006; also Martens and Pauly, 2000; Schwab and Sturm, 2000) and led to one of the largest creditor frauds in post-war Germany. Creditors lost approximately 2 billion German marks (€1.02 billion) in this fraud. A bank or leasing firm bought (basically non-existent) drilling systems from a corporation named KSK and these systems were to a lesser extent used or to a greater extent rented to other (fictitious) firms (so-called 'system companies') by Flowtex. In theory, the 'system companies' would use the drilling equipment and they would earn the necessary cash flows to finance the leasing charges. KSK and the 'system companies' were formally economic and legal autonomous entities but in reality they were controlled by Schmider, the Flowtex owner. He used dummies as executives and drew a curtain over the real control situation. The (fictitious) main manufacturer of the drilling system (La Maquinista de Levante, Spain) and the so-called 'system companies' predominantly operated abroad. Because only minor real revenues were earned by Flowtex and the system companies, the money which KSK got from selling the machines was covertly transferred to Flowtex and the system companies, and thereafter was used to pay the leasing charges. So in effect the banks paid their own leasing charges. Obviously this system needed more and more cash. In the end, Flowtex argued that 3400 drilling systems were operating all over the world but only 250 drilling systems really existed. One real drilling system was sold 13 times. A handful of people participated in this fraud scheme. Obviously, the balance sheet and profit and loss account of KSK and Flowtex were manipulated to conceal the fraud. For example, KSK had to falsify invoices about drilling systems bought from La Maquinista and Flowtex used forged leasing and rental agreements to create the illusion of a growing and prosperous business with the system companies. The auditor of Flowtex was the Big 4 firm KPMG and Flowtex received unqualified opinions on its accounts. A KPMG subsidiary acted as a consultant on behalf of Flowtex (Heck, 2006, p. 125). Furthermore, Schmider misappropriated approximately €350 million by tunnelling money to covert accounts in tax-haven countries to finance his luxurious lifestyle. He also falsified bank accounts to increase his creditworthiness.

The auditor of Flowtex, KPMG, and the banks and leasing companies who bought the (nonexistent) drilling machines did some sample inspections with the aim of ensuring the existence and completeness of the drilling systems. For this purpose, the same drilling machines were always prepared and the identification plates were replaced as needed with every new contract (Heck, 2006, pp. 112–115). KPMG verified the existence of the drilling systems at the end of 1998 and certified the existence of 2139 systems (Heck, 2006, p. 124). Banks and rating agencies counted on the KPMG report.

The fraud scheme was detected by tax auditors[8] in 2000. There was an ongoing criticism that state tax auditors had had some information about irregularities since 1996. However, a lawsuit against the state was not successful. In effect, the state and communities benefited from the fraud because Flowtex always fulfilled its tax duties on time and for this reason paid taxes on non-existent profits and revenues. It has been estimated that the state received 320 million German marks in taxes over the years (Heck, 2006, p. 194), which were actually paid by the financing banks. The fraud detection took place a few days before the placement of a 300 million German mark bond on the capital market. Flowtex had received a really good rating ('BBB,' investment grade) from the renowned credit rating agency Standard & Poor's. The fraud could easily have been detected using information from Spanish authorities showing that the supposed manufacturer of thousands of drilling systems was in fact a non-operating company with no revenues and employees. Non-announced inspections of drilling machines and analytical procedures to reconcile the revenues from 3500 drilling systems with external sources (e.g. information from competitors) would also have been helpful. In this large-scale fraud no independent control (e.g. supervisory board) except the auditor existed. The auditor paid 100 million German marks to banks in an extrajudicial settlement without admitting any wrongdoing: this was the largest sum so far paid by a German audit firm. The executives, e.g. Manfred Schmider, involved in this fraud, which included fraudulent financial reporting, were imprisoned for between six and 12 years.

### 10.3.2 ComRoad AG (2001)

ComRoad AG, a supplier of so-called telematik traffic systems (i.e. GPS-based onboard units in cars which can be used for different applications), was listed in November 1999 on the former German New Market (Neuer Markt), a specialized exchange market for technology firms (see for the latter: Daum, 2003; Lenz, 2004a; Weber *et al.*, 2008). The company's principal activities were the development and marketing of traffic telematic applications, in particular, the in-car computer, using Global Transport Telematic Systems (GTTS). The applications also used Global Positioning Systems, Global Systems Mobilcommunications (GSM), voice portals and the internet. The company sold the software to telematic service centre operators for fleet management, vehicle security, dynamic off-road navigation,

---

[8] Tax auditors are employees of the government's financial authorities whose task is to verify the tax declarations.

**Table 10.1**    Selected income statement and balance sheet items for ComRoad AG

**Com Road**

| Income statement (in thousand €) | 1998 | %Sa | 1999 | %Sa | 2000 | %Sa | 1.1.−30.9.2001* | %Sa |
|---|---|---|---|---|---|---|---|---|
| Sales (Sa) | 2 335 | | 10 235 | | 43 870 | | 61 812 | |
| thereof domestic | n.a. | | 162 | | 122 | | n.a. | |
| thereof abroad | n.a. | | 10 073 | | 43 748 | | n.a. | |
| thereof VT Electronics | 1 471 | | 8 802 | | 42 554 | | n.a. | |
| Cost of materials | 1 659 | 71 % | 7 676 | 75 % | 32 406 | 74 % | 45 042 | 73 % |
| Net income/loss | −150 | | −346 | | 4 152 | 9 % | 9 125 | 15 % |

| Cash flow statement (in thousand €) | | | | | | | | |
|---|---|---|---|---|---|---|---|---|
| CF from operating activities | −166 | | −1 668 | | −1 781 | | −11 100 | |

| Balance sheet (in thousand €) | 1998 | %TA | 1999 | %TA | 2000 | %TA | 1.1.−30.9.2001 | %TA |
|---|---|---|---|---|---|---|---|---|
| Payments in advance | 0 | 0 % | 1 633 | 7 % | 14 153 | 15 % | 14 342 | 14 % |
| Accounts receivable | 1 561 | 73 % | 1 449 | 6 % | 1 487 | 2 % | 20 538 | 21 % |
| Accounts payable | 1 432 | 67 % | 668 | 3 % | 1 720 | 2 % | 1 059 | 1 % |
| Total assets (TA) | 2 140 | | 24 670 | | 93 511 | | 99 501 | |

*Unaudited third-quarter interim report.

mobile internet access, road assistance, etc. The issue price for one ComRoad share was €20.5 and the subsequent first market price €29, resulting in an underpricing of 41 %. The IPO proceeds amounted to €26 million. The prospectus contained the audited financial statements and the management report and reviewed reconciliations to US-GAAP. In 1999 to 2001 ComRoad reported rapidly increasing sales and profits (see Table 10.1). The financial statements for 1999 and 2000 both received unqualified auditor's reports.

In Spring 2001, questions about the business model and reported figures of ComRoad became public. Actual and planned sales volumes released by ComRoad were contradictory to the numbers reported by the British client Skynet. The journalist Renate Daum visited a ComRoad subsidiary in Hong Kong and the local official in charge guessed the share of the sales of ComRoad in Asia at less than 2 % of total sales. However, in the 2000 annual report ComRoad declared that approximately one-half of its total sales stemmed from Asia. This apparent contradiction prompted Daum to intensify her search for the 'phantom partners' of ComRoad in Asia. First of all she examined press releases, marketing brochures and annual reports. In an article in June 2001 entitled 'Asia sales in the dark' she hypothesized that the reported sales from Asia in the 2000 annual report were too high (see Daum, 2001; 2003, p. 69). In further inquiries, Daum used information from the commercial register (i.e. a state-operated data bank with company information) and trade associations abroad. The existence of only two out of eight ComRoad customers in Asia could be proved. In a further article, Daum wrote that this confirmed the suspicion of inflated Asian sales in the audited financial statements (Daum, 2003, p. 71). A further inquiry in Asia in January 2002 confirmed that the ComRoad statements about business partners in Asia could not be true and led to a further article in which the amount of sales in 2000 and 2001 was seriously questioned (see Daum, 2002). The journalist also visited one of the manufacturers of ComRoad car onboard units (VTech Holdings). The actual production numbers – together with the figures from a German manufacturer – were too low in comparison with the reported sales figures. An attempt to find the purported third supplier of ComRoad products was not successful and raised another question in the press: 'In addition to phantom customers had ComRoad a phantom supplier too?' In the KPMG-audited management report 1999 and 2000 only two suppliers were mentioned (BvR in Germany and VTech in China). In the notes relating to accounts payable in the annual report 1998 the following sentence appeared: 'The accounts payable were confirmed by a list of account balances and relate to diverse domestic suppliers and with an amount of 2,454,800.00 German marks to the firm VT Electronics Ltd., Hong Kong.'

The ongoing critical press reports caused the auditors of ComRoad, KPMG, to dig deeper into the speculations concerning inflated sales. However, before that KPMG declared on 5 February 2002, in response to a request from the chairman of the supervisory board, that the audit firm had no concrete findings with respect to the suspicions. Shortly thereafter, on 19 February 2002, KPMG laid down their audit mandate. Under German rules an auditor can only terminate an audit if there is an important cause (e.g. deception by the client). At this moment it was clear that KPMG had detected a financial statement fraud. In an ad-hoc release from 23 April 2002 ComRoad disclosed:

> A special audit done by the audit firm Rödl & Partner commissioned by the supervisory board of ComRoad concerning the sales of ComRoad via VT Electronics Ltd., Hong Kong, in 1998 to 2000 has led to the following provisional result: In 1998, reported sales from 4.567 million DM[9] stem 63 % from VT Electronics Ltd. In 1998, reported sales were 20 million DM, thereof 86 % (17 million DM) from VT Electronics. In the financial year 2000 the reported sales amounted to 85 million DM, thereof 97 % (83.2 million DM) from VT Electronics. The audit firm Rödl & Partner pointed out that for all these years they could find no evidence that actual business transactions took place and the customer really existed.

### 10.3.2.1  Detailed Reconstruction of the Financial Statement Fraud

Based on Daum (2003) the financial statement fraud conducted by the CEO Bodo Schnabel and his spouse can be reconstructed as follows (see Lenz, 2004a, pp. 221–227 and Figure 10.2).

The CEO and his spouse prepared falsified accounts concerning the manufacturing of equipment from a non-existing supplier, VT Electronics, in Hong Kong. The fictitious units were delivered directly to similarly fictitious customers. VT Electronics took over the collection procedure for ComRoad, therefore simulating fictitious payments. Real payments did not come in at ComRoad because VT Electronics simulated a quarterly offsetting of payments from ComRoad customers with outstanding debits from VT Electronics concerning ComRoad. Balances for the benefit of ComRoad were booked mainly as payments in advance for new equipment and the residual amounts as trade receivables. This scheme

---

[9] DM = German marks.

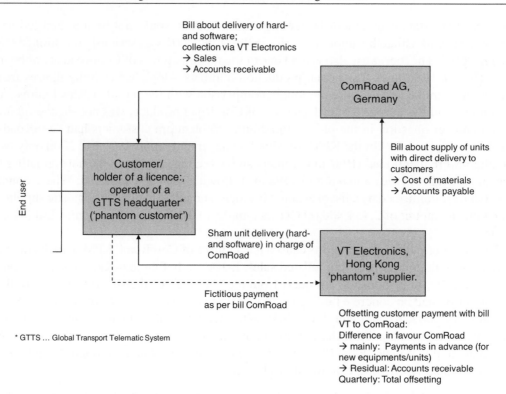

**Figure 10.2**   Financial statement fraud ComRoad AG

made it possible to conduct both the sales and the cost of materials via VT Electronics, simulating fictitious cash flows without real cash transactions at ComRoad accounts. An example with hypothetical numbers exemplifies the modus operandi. Sales of €100 million result in cost of materials of €80 million, which is offset against the sales leading to the recognition of payments in advance of €15 million and receivables of €5 million. The example results in a net income of €20 million and a cash flow statement produces a cash flow from operating activities of zero. An incomplete offsetting of the cost of materials would lead to an additional corresponding increase in trade payables.

### 10.3.2.2  *Role of the Auditor and the Supervisory Board*

The numbers in Table 10.1 provide plausible support for the process described above. In 2000, when nearly the whole sales volume was with VT Electronics, the sales figure corresponds approximately to the sum of the cost of materials plus increase of advance payments minus increase in trade payables. Furthermore, the table shows the development of net income and cash flow from operating activities in the opposite direction.

Beyond question, the balance sheet and profit and loss statement items 'sales, cost of materials, payments in advance, account receivables and account payables' should have been audited with special emphasis and intensity. The description of the ComRoad case in Daum (2003) contains some evidence which raises questions as to whether KPMG acted according to professional standards (see Daum 2003, pp. 105–127). In the ComRoad case, a lot of 'red flags' were present and were arguably disregarded by the audit firm, falling short of its duty of 'professional scepticism'. According to German professional standards,[10] the auditor should always be aware that errors or fraud could lead to material misstatements in the financial statements and the management report. Therefore he/she cannot trust in explanations of the management board without further evidence. Instead, he/she should seek reasonable evidence (former IDW auditing statement HFA 7/1997). However the auditors denied they had done anything wrong.

The prospectus itself had contained information about support services for customers. Analytical audit procedures could have been used to check if support services had increased together with increasing sales. Real customers sometimes complain about deficient products, but not fictitious ones. The non-existence of customer complaints should have been a red flag for the auditor. Obviously, such customer complaints did not exist in the ComRoad case. An instructive example of a possible audit failure is the procedure concerning confirmation of accounts receivable. The auditors were satisfied with a fax confirmation which they received from the spouse of the CEO, Ingrid Schnabel. Reportedly, Ingrid Schnabel had sent a letter with the request for a confirmation to VT Electronics in Hong Kong. She gave the auditors the sham fax with a fax number from Hong Kong and a confirmed balance (Daum 2003, p. 115). According to professional standards the selection, transmission and return of confirmations should be under the control of the auditor. Simple audit procedures (e.g. a phone call to Hong Kong) should have been sufficient to detect this fraud.

To sum up, in this case a journalist acted like an auditor and applied a risk-oriented audit strategy. The journalist tried to understand in detail the strategy, business activities and processes of ComRoad. She applied analytical audit procedures (e.g. she tried to reconcile available information about sold units and prices with reported sales, and she compared internal information with information from external sources).

According to the German Stock Corporation Law, the supervisory board has to check the financial statements. In the ComRoad case, an independent control could not be expected because one of the board members was Ingrid Schnabel, the spouse of the CEO Bodo Schnabel. She also performed bookkeeping, personnel and marketing services for ComRoad. Another board member prepared the annual and interim statements of ComRoad and acted as a tax advisor on behalf of ComRoad. This was criticized by the auditor KPMG. An active and independent oversight role for the supervisory board as required by the German Stock Corporation Law could not therefore be expected to exist in the ComRoad case.

The CEO Bodo Schnabel was sentenced to seven years in jail for criminal fraud and market manipulation and his spouse received two years on remand. Due to a special law, the state of Bavaria seized Mr Schnabel's personal wealth. Civil liability suits were not successful (i.e. the shareholders got no compensation for their near total losses). Up to now, there have been no successful law suits concerning the role of the auditor of ComRoad, which denied any wrongdoing.

---

[10] See, for details of the German audit standard-setting process, Köhler *et al.* (2008).

## 10.4 ACCOUNTING SCANDALS AND REGULATORY RESPONSES

Since 1985, the major drivers of accounting and auditing requirements for German firms were directives of the European Union. With the European Accounting Directives Act (Bilanzrichtliniegesetz, BiRiLiG) of 1985 the 4th, 7th and 8th European Community Directives were implemented into German law (Eierle, 2005; Fey and Fladt, 2006). Since then all major accounting and auditing requirements for German firms can be found in the Third Book of the German Commercial Code. A detailed description of the German accounting system is given in Leuz and Wüstemann (2004) and Fey and Fladt (2006). According to Leuz and Wüstemann (2004, p. 453) the German financial system can be characterized as a 'relationship-based' or an 'insider system' in which

> firms establish close relationships with banks and other financial intermediaries and rely heavily on internal financing, instead of raising capital in public equity or debt markets. Corporate ownership is mainly in the hands of insiders with privileged access to information ... Given the nature of the system, information asymmetries are resolved primarily via private channels rather than public disclosure. Thus, the key contracting and financing parties are reasonably well informed, while outside investors face a lack of transparency. However, opacity is an important feature of the system because it provides barriers to entry and protects relationships from the threat of competition.

With respect to financial statement fraud it follows that insiders (e.g. controlling shareholders in the Balsam, ComRoad and Flowtex examples) can misuse their strong position in the German financial system to expropriate outside investors (Enriques and Volpin, 2007). Strengthening internal governance, empowering shareholders, enhancing disclosure requirements and tougher public enforcement are possible legal remedies. The German corporate governance system is characterized by its two-tier board structure (see for details Köhler *et al.*, 2008). The 'managerial board' is responsible for the management of the company (including the reporting systems and the financial statements) and the 'supervisory board' is responsible for the monitoring of the managerial board. For example (Köhler *et al.*, 2008, p. 115):

> the supervisory board has to examine the annual financial statements for which the executive board is responsible. This audit is usually based on the findings of the statutory auditor (i.e., the auditor not only contributes to the credibility of financial statements from an external stakeholder perspective but also enhances the monitoring function of the supervisory boards). Consequently, auditor selection, auditor engagement (subsequent to auditor election by the general assembly or Annual General meeting) are the responsibility of the supervisory board. It is also the supervisory board – not the executive board – that is the addressee of the long form audit report.

In 1998, the 'Act on Corporate Control and Transparency' (Gesetz zur Kontrolle und Transparenz im Unternehmensbereich, KonTraG) was adopted. This Act was a direct regulatory response to accounting scandals. With respect to auditors and the supervisory board, the Act required that the auditor of a company – after election by the shareholders in the annual general meeting – be engaged by the supervisory board. Before this Act the board of directors (the management) authorized the auditor and negotiated the audit fee. The long form audit report is to be submitted to the supervisory board, which is the principal for the audit. Furthermore, regulations concerning the subject and the scope of the audit have been clarified and intensified. For example, Art. 317 I Commercial Code requires that an audit shall be planned and performed so that misstatements and violations of statutory provisions materially affecting the presentation of a true and fair view are detected if professional diligence is exercised. Art. 317 II Commercial Code introduced tougher rules concerning the audit of the management report (e.g. the auditor has the responsibility to examine whether the risks of future developments have been suitably presented in the report). According to Art. 317 IV Commercial Code for a listed company, the auditor shall evaluate within the scope of the audit if the executive board of the company has set up a monitoring system to detect material risk which could put at risk the existence of the firm (Art. 91 II Stock Corporation Law). In the explanatory notes of the law, the legislature explicitly refers to accounting scandals and trying to improve the auditor's role, strengthening the function of the supervisory board and improving the disclosure of potential future risks in the management report. This can be seen as a direct response to the control failures of the supervisory board and the auditor in these German accounting scandals.

Recent important revisions in response to the need to adopt new EU legislation were the 'Financial Reporting Enforcement Act' (Bilanzkontrollgesetz, BilKoG) and the 'Act on the Introduction of International Accounting Standards and to Safeguard the Quality of Audits of Financial Statements' (Bilanzrechtsreformgesetz, BilReG) in 2004 (see Ernst & Young, 2004). The BilKoG established a two-tier enforcement regime. The Financial Reporting Enforcement Panel (FREP, Art. 342b *et seq.* Commercial Code) is responsible, as an institution organized under private law, for the first level of enforcement. To monitor accounting (see FREP, 2006), the Panel enforces the applicable accounting standards. It has to examine whether the most recently published individual or consolidated financial statements and the related respective management reports of companies listed on capital markets comply with the applicable regulations and principles, including the accounting standards permitted by law. The Panel will initiate an examination if:

- there are concrete indications of an infringement of financial reporting requirements (*examination with cause*);
- *at the request of the Federal Financial Supervisory Authority (BaFin)*, when concrete indications exist; or
- without any concrete indications based on *random sampling* (FREP, 2007, p. 3).

The Panel only examines financial statements if the company under examination is willing to cooperate with the Panel. If the company declares its willingness to cooperate, the legal representatives of the company, and the other persons assisting the legal representatives in their cooperation with the Panel's examination, are obliged to provide accurate and complete information and to submit accurate and complete documents (FREP, 2006, p. 17). If the company refuses to cooperate, the Federal Financial Supervisory Authority (BaFin) takes over the examination at the second level. The BaFin as a state agency has the authority to enforce an examination. If misstatements are found, the BaFin will order the publication of the results of the examination. The establishment of this two-tier enforcement system is the most obvious legal reaction to deficiencies in the financial statements of listed firms in Germany.

Among other things the BilReG tried to strengthen the independence of auditors, therefore implementing some of the EC recommendations (European Commission, 2002). For example, Art. 319 para. 2 states: 'German public auditors ... may not audit financial statements if there are reasons, in particular business, financial or personal relationships, that indicate that their independence may be impaired.' Art. 319 para. 3–5 specifies conditions that impair auditor independence and which are therefore not allowed (e.g. bookkeeping or preparing financial statements, actuarial or valuation services which materially impact annual accounts). Art. 319a contains even more restrictions for auditors of public-interest clients (i.e. firms which issue securities on a regulated market). These restrictions cover services such as legal or tax advisory services or the development, establishment and implementation of accounting information systems (for details, see Köhler *et al.*, 2008). To increase transparency, audit and non-audit fees had to be disclosed in the notes of individual and consolidated accounts (Art. 285 sentence 1 No. 17, Art. 314 para. 1 No. 9 Commercial Code) from 2005. Furthermore, the BilReG requires more detailed disclosures in the management report.

Most important with respect to accounting is Art. 315a Commercial Code. Para. 1 rules that parent companies which are required to prepare consolidated statements under Art. 4 of Regulation (ED) No. 1606/2002 of the European Parliament and of the Council of 19 July 2002, on the application of international accounting standards, are exempted from German GAAP. Other companies may voluntarily prepare their consolidated accounts in accordance with IFRS.

Other recent acts established an external quality control system (from 2001) and tried to strengthen the disciplinary oversight of the audit profession in Germany. For example, since 1 January 2005 the independent Auditor Oversight Commission (AOC) is responsible for the public oversight of the German Chamber of Public Accountants (see, for details, the Annual Reports of the AOC, www.apak-aoc.de). All these measures can be interpreted as a reaction to insufficient audit quality in past years, as evidenced by the documented accounting scandals (for details, see Köhler *et al.*, 2008).

## 10.5 EXAMINATIONS OF THE GERMAN FINANCIAL REPORTING ENFORCEMENT PANEL 2005–2006

The Financial Reporting Enforcement Panel began in July 2005 (see Annual Activity Reports 2005 and 2006 of the FRRP, www.frep.info). In the period July 2005 to December 2006, the Panel completed 116 examinations, of which 102 were randomly selected, 13 were examinations initiated for a concrete reason and one was requested by the Federal Financial Supervisory Authority (BaFin). The task of the Panel is to examine whether the financial statements comply with the respective accounting standards (Art. 342b paras 2 and 5 Commercial Code). Of the Panel's 116 completed examinations, in 21 cases the financial statements were determined to contain misstatements. That gives an astonishing overall error rate of over 18 %. Erroneous financial statements were determined at two MDAX companies, two SDAX and 16 non-indexed companies.[11] The errors relate primarily to

---

[11] MDAX and SDAX are medium (MDAX) and smaller (SDAX) companies which are part of the Prime Standard of the German Exchange (Deutsche Börse). Non-indexed companies are not included in such stock market categories.

small or mid-sized firms. In 11 cases the relevant companies agreed with the examination results, the other 10 cases will be reviewed at the second enforcement level by BaFin (most of them were pending at the date of the publication of the FRRP Annual Report). I searched in the electronic version of the *Federal Gazette* over the period July 2005 to November 2007 and found 25 cases of published accounting irregularities over this period (in one case in 2005 the BaFin did not order publication of the error).[12] Table 10.2 shows the main misstatements of these cases and gives information about the auditor in the year under consideration. Of particular interest is where the accounting irregularities led to an auditor change in the following year. However, it should be mentioned that an auditor change does not imply that the replaced auditor was at fault and that an auditor change may be caused by other reasons.

Some tentative conclusions can be drawn from Table 10.2. At the moment, smaller companies are more likely to have accounting irregularities and the cases are approximately evenly distributed between the more demanding Prime Standard (52 %) and the General Standard (48 %).[13] The misstatements found are not representative because they clearly reflect the main audit focus of the FREP in the period under study (e.g. deferred tax assets and liabilities, business combinations, disclosures).

With respect to the auditors involved, 79 % can be classified as small or middle-sized auditors and 21 % belong to the Big 4. The dominance of the small and middle-sized audit firms and the five observed auditor changes in the following periods to a Big 4 audit firm can tentatively be interpreted as companies choosing to move because of the perceived superior audit quality of Big 4 audits. It should be mentioned that in only three out of 25 cases had the auditors qualified their reports with respect to the misstatement mentioned by the FREP. In all other cases, the auditor either did not detect or did not report the misstatement in the audit opinion. This can be seen as preliminary evidence of insufficient audit quality and as a justification for the establishment of the FREP. From the outside, there is no easy way to decide if the detected misstatements are caused by non-intentional acts (simple errors due to the complexity of IFRS or unqualified staff) or intentional acts (creative accounting). The first case (Arques) was clearly a case of questionable creative accounting rather than illegality because both the board and auditors were aware of the material missing disclosures (see press release Arques 2005). In other cases, the question cannot be answered definitively but we can conjecture that there are many more cases of creative accounting in the sample.

## 10.6 CONCLUSION

What can we learn from these accounting scandal case studies? Case studies have a didactic value for education purposes. Student interest is much higher in comparison to other parts of accounting education. Case studies can also be used to study specific technical aspects of accounting standards. Furthermore, accounting scandals have an 'educative function'

---

[12] It should be mentioned that in 2007 new examinations started or previous examinations were completed. Therefore, the 25 cases are more than the above-mentioned 21 cases.

[13] The General Standard is subject to the minimum statutory requirements for the Regulated Market (regulated according to EU laws). Above and beyond the requirements of the General Standard, the Prime Standard requires companies to meet international transparency standards (e.g. quarterly reports in German and English, at least one analyst conference per year).

**Table 10.2** Misstatements detected by the Financial Reporting Enforcement Panel in Germany

| Company name<br>Date of publication<br>Exchange index<br>Total assets | Misstatement found | Auditor in misstatement year | Auditor change in the following year |
|---|---|---|---|
| 1. Arques AG<br>03.02.2006<br>SDAX/Regulated Market<br>€142 million | Missing disclosures and other errors relating to acquisitions/business combinations (IFRS 3) in FY 2004 | Single auditor (sole proprietorship) | Change to Big 4 firm (PwC) |
| 2. Allgeier Holding AG<br>04.08.2006<br>General Standard/Regulated Market<br>€46 million | Misstatements relating to business combinations and diverse missing information in notes to accounts in FY 2004 | Small audit firm | No change |
| 3. PC-Ware Information Technologies AG<br>06.09.2006<br>Prime Standard/Regulated Market<br>€139 million | Missing information in notes to accounts; no provision for losses from derivatives in FY 2005 | Mid-sized audit firm | Change to Big 4 firm (Deloitte Touche) |
| 4. Haitec AG<br>20.09.2006<br>General Standard/Regulated Market<br>€5 million | Overvalued loan and missing notes to accounts; errors relating to valuation of financial instruments and stock option and respective missing notes to accounts in FY 2005 | Small audit firm | No change |
| 5. MTU Holding AG<br>22.01.2007<br>MDAX/Prime Standard/Regulated Market<br>€2553 million | Irregular purchase price allocation and depreciation of immaterial assets in FY 2005 | Big 4 auditor (Deloitte & Touche) | No change |

| Company | Issue | Auditor | Change |
|---|---|---|---|
| 6. Interhyp AG<br>15.02.2007<br>SDAX/Prime Standard/Regulated Market<br>€53 million | Incorrect recognition and valuation of deferred tax assets in FY 2005 | Big 4 auditor (Ernst & Young) | No change |
| 7. Zapf Creation AG<br>27.02.2007<br>SDAX/Prime Standard/Regulated Market<br>€148 million | Incomplete provisions; incorrect revenue recognition; overvaluation of assets and incorrect currency translation in FY 2004 | Middle-tier firm (Rödl & Partner) | Joint audit with KPMG in FY 2005; change to KPMG in FY 2006 |
| 8. Agor AG<br>27.02.2007<br>General Standard/Regulated Market<br>€262 million | Incorrect revenue recognition from sale-and-lease-back-transaction; irregular cash flow statement in FY 2004 | Small audit firm | No change |
| 9. S&R Biogas Energiesysteme AG<br>27.03.2007<br>General Standard/Regulated Market<br>€2.5 million | Missing disclosures about risk management system in FY 2005 | Small audit firm | No change |
| 10. Mensch und Maschine Software AG<br>17.04.2007<br>Prime Standard/Regulated Market<br>€66 million | Overvaluation of financial assets and goodwill; irregular cash flow statement in FY 2005 | Small audit firm | No change |
| 11. Neue Sentimental Film AG<br>19.06.2007<br>Prime Standard/Regulated Market<br>€19 million | Overvaluation of deferred tax assets and goodwill; missing disclosure assets held for sale in FY 2005 | Small audit firm | No change |
| 12. DEAG Deutsche Entertainment AG<br>26.06.2007<br>Prime Standard/Regulated Market<br>€105 million | Incorrect disclosure of discontinued operations; overvaluation of deferred tax assets; no separate presentation of investment properties; incorrect purchase price allocation in FY 2005 | Middle-tier firm (BDO) | No change |

(Continued)

**Table 10.2** Misstatements detected by the Financial Reporting Enforcement Panel in Germany (*Continued*)

| Company name<br>Date of publication<br>Exchange index<br>Total assets | Misstatement found | Auditor in misstatement year | Auditor change in the following year |
|---|---|---|---|
| 13. OHB Technology AG<br>18.07.2007<br>Prime Standard/Regulated Market<br>€266 million | Missing disclosures; incorrect classification of cash equivalent in cash flow statement in FY 2005 | Middle-tier firm (BDO) | No change |
| 14. AWD Holding AG<br>20.07.2007<br>Prime Standard/MDAX/Prime Standard/Regulated Market<br>€426 million | Missing disclosures about risk factors in FY 2004 | Middle-tier firm (BDO) | No change |
| 15. Württembergische Lebensversicherung AG<br>20.07.2007<br>Non-listed firm; bond issuer<br>€29 203 million | Long list of accounting irregularities in FY 2005 | Big 4 firm (Deloitte & Touche) | Change to Big 4 firm (PwC) |
| 16. Schön & Cie AG<br>20.07.2007<br>(insolvency) | Overvaluation of deferred tax asset; overvaluation of investment in affiliate in FY 2005 | No information | No information available |
| 17. Süd-Chemie AG<br>02.08.2007<br>General Standard/Official Market<br>€828 million | False presentation of minority interest in balance sheet in FY 2005 | Big 4 firm (Ernst & Young), qualified opinion with respect to the misstatement the auditor had detected | No change |
| 18. Vivacon AG<br>06.08.2007<br>SDAX/Prime Standard/Regulated Market<br>€421 million | Incorrect fair value of stock options; missing disclosures; incorrect revenue recognition in FY 2005 | Small audit firm | Change to Big 4 (Ernst & Young) |

| Company | Finding | Auditor | Outcome |
|---|---|---|---|
| 19. Gesco AG<br>08.08.2007<br>Prime Standard/Regulated Market<br>€174 million | Missing disclosures with respect to business combinations in FY 2005/06 | Small audit firm; qualified opinion with respect to irregularity | No change |
| 20. GAG Immobilien AG<br>22.08.2007<br>General Standard/Regulated Market<br>€1.944 million | Overvaluation of deferred tax assets; recognition of non-existent liability in FY 2005 | Small audit firm | No change |
| 21. Action Press Holding AG<br>11.09.2007<br>General Standard/Regulated Market<br>€5.7 million | Missing disclosures; incorrect presentation of balance sheet, etc. in FY 2006 | Small audit firm | No change |
| 22. Dom Brauerei AG<br>26.09.2007<br>General Standard/Regulated Market<br>€13.8 million | Missing disclosures with respect to financial situation; overvaluation of subsidiaries; diverse missing disclosures in FY 2005 | Small audit firm | No change |
| 23. Piper Generalvertretung AG<br>19.10.2007<br>General Standard/Regulated Market<br>€9.7 million | Consolidated financial statements in accordance with German GAAP instead of IFRS in FY 2005/06 | Small firm, qualified opinion with respect to the misstatement the auditor had detected | No information available |
| 24. Indus Holding AG<br>24.10.2007<br>SDAX/Prime Standard/Regulated Market<br>€915 million | Missing disclosures with respect to business combinations; false hedge-accounting; sale of ABS-transaction not realized in FY 2005 | Small firm | No change but qualified opinion in the following year |
| 25. Jil Sander AG<br>07.11.2007<br>General Standard/Regulated Market<br>€97 million | Overvaluation of deferred tax assets; overvaluation of a US subsidiary in FY 2005/06 | Big 4 firm (Deloitte & Touche) | No information available |

for preparers, auditors and regulators. They are like 'warning signs' or 'red flags' serving to keep up professional scepticism and a proper ethical orientation. In some cases, they demonstrate more that audit quality should be improved. Furthermore, publicly discussed accounting scandals are important drivers of regulatory activity.

Control failure of the supervisory board and the auditors has been found as the main reason for German accounting scandals. The legislative authorities have tried consequently in recent years to strengthen the responsibilities of the supervisory board and the auditor. In the cases of Co op, Balsam, ComRoad and Flowtex, dominant insiders tried to expropriate outside investors. These examples are typical for an insider-oriented financial system. Enriques and Volpin (2007, p. 122) point out that families or controlling shareholders, like managers in a widely held company, 'can abuse their power and use corporate resources to their own advantage. When this happens in a family-controlled firm, things are even worse than in a widely held corporation, because controlling families cannot be ousted through a hostile takeover or replaced by the board of directors or by the shareholders' meeting.'

The most critical points in the eyes of the public and the press were:

- The annual report of insolvent companies often gave no hint about critical risk factors; the management report and the forecast outlook showed too optimistic a picture of the financial condition of the firm in the face of near crisis.
- Too often the auditors issued an unqualified audit report and did not discuss the risks that seriously jeopardized the existence of the company or the group, even in cases where 'red flags' were present. The public did not criticize the competence but rather the independence of the auditors.
- In large part the public, the press and academics (Theisen, 1998) evaluated the monitoring task of the supervisory board in the German two-tier system as ineffective.

The public debate following the real and alleged accounting scandals has resulted in regulatory consequences. The major legal accounting and auditing changes in the past two decades have been motivated by the desire to prevent future accounting scandals. Examples are rules which increase auditors' responsibilities with respect to material misstatements in financial statements and the establishment of a new two-stage enforcement institution in Germany.

# REFERENCES

(For convenience, articles in German are also translated into English.)

Daum, R. (2001), 'Asian revenues in the dark' (Asienumsätze im Dunkeln verborgen), *Börse Online*, **25**, 30–31.
Daum, R. (2002), 'Navigation into nowhere' (Navigation ins Nirgendwo), *Börse Online*, **6**, 24–25.
Daum, R. (2003), *Out of Control (Außer Kontrolle)*, FinanzBuch-Verlag, München.
Eierle, B. (2005), 'Differential reporting in Germany – a historical analysis', *Accounting, Business & Financial History*, **15**, 279–315.
Enriques, L. and Volpin, P. (2007), 'Corporate governance reforms in Continental Europe', *Journal of Economic Perspectives*, **21**, 117–140.
Ernst & Young (2004), *Reform of the Stock Corporation, Accounting and Corporate Governance Law 2004* (Reform des Aktien-, Bilanz- und Aufsichtsrechts 2004), Stuttgart.

European Commission (1999), 'Commission decision of 22 July 1998 on the misuse of restructuring aid for MTW-Schiffswerft and Volkswerft Stralsund, two companies formerly belonging to Bremer Vulkan Verbund, and the unauthorised loan of DEM 112,4 million to MTW-Schiffswerft', *Official Journal of the European Community*, L108/34–43, 27 April.

European Commission (2002), 'Commission recommendation of 16 May 2002, Statutory Auditors' Independence in the EU: A Set of Fundamental Principles', *Official Journal of the European Community*, L191/22–57, 19 July.

Fey, G. and Fladt, G. (2006), *German Accounting Legislation*, 4th edn, IDW Verlag, Düsseldorf.

FREP (2006), *2005 Annual Activity Report for the Period from January 1 to December 31* (Tätigkeitsbericht für den Zeitraum vom 1. Januar bis 31. Dezember), Financial Reporting Enforcement Panel, Berlin, 5 February.

FREP (2007), *2006 Annual Activity Report for the Period from January 1 to December 31* (Tätigkeitsbericht für den Zeitraum vom 1. Januar bis 31. Dezember), Financial Reporting Enforcement Panel, Berlin, 22 February.

Heck, M. (2006), *Der Flowtex-Skandal (The Flowtex Scandal)*, 2nd edn, Fischer Verlag, Frankfurt am Main.

Hennes, M. and Henry, A. (1994), 'To lull everybody' (Einlullen lassen), *Wirtschaftswoche*, **26**, 42–45.

Henry, A. and Hennes, M. (1994), 'To make things worse' (Noch schlimmer), *Wirtschaftswoche*, **25**, 49–50.

Investigative Committee 'Bremer Vulkan' (1998), *Report of the Investigative Committee into 'Bremer Vulkan'* (Bericht des Parlamentarischen Untersuchungsausschusses Bremer Vulkan), Vols I, II, Bremische Bürgerschaft Drucksache 14/1147, 16 October.

Jahn, J. (2010), 'Criminal judges let Bremer Vulkan go unpunished' (Strafrichter lassen Bremer Vulkan ungesühnt), FAZ net, http://www.faz.net, 26.01.2010.

Köhler, A., Marten, K.-U., Quick, R. and Ruhnke, K. (2008), 'Audit regulation in Germany', in *Auditing, Trust and Governance*, eds R. Quick, S. Turley and M. Willekens, Routledge, London, pp. 111–143.

Lenz, H. (2004a), 'Financial statement audit and enforcement according to the Financial Statement Control Law' (Abschlussprüfung und Enforcement nach dem Bilanzkontrollgesetz – Zwei Fallbeispiele), *Betriebswirtschaftliche Forschung und Praxis*, **3**, 219–238.

Lenz, H. (2004b), 'Financial Statement Audit of the Philipp Holzmann AG or "Don't Blame Us, We're Only Accountants" – A Case Study with respect to the Function of Auditors', (Abschlussprüfung der Philipp Holzmann AG-Ein Fallbeispiel zur Funktion von Wirtschaftsprüfern) in *International Accounting, Auditing and Analysis – Exercises and Solutions (Internationale Rechnungslegung, Prüfung und Analyse – Aufgaben und Lösungen)*, eds G. Brösel and R. Kasperzak, Oldenbourg Verlag, München/Wien, pp. 231–252.

Leuz, C. and Wüstemann, J. (2004), 'The role of accounting in the German financial system', in *The German Financial System*, eds J.P. Krahnen and R.H. Schmidt, Oxford University Press, Oxford, pp. 450–477.

Loebbecke, J.K., Eining, M.M. and Willinghan, J.J. (1989), 'Auditors' Experience with Material Irregularities: Frequency, Nature, and Detectability', *Auditing: A Journal of Practice & Theory*, **9**, 1–28.

Martens, H. and Pauly, Ch. (2000), 'Wondrous increase' (Wundersame Vermehrung), *Der Spiegel*, **7**, 102–103.

Peemöller, V.H. and Hofmann, St. (2005), *Accounting Scandals (Bilanzskandale)*, Erich Schmidt Verlag, Berlin.

Schwab, F. and Sturm, C. (2000), 'Fictitious drilling' (Luftbohrungen), *Focus*, **7**, 250–251.

Student, D. and Garding, C. (1992), 'Great high bar exercises' (Große Reckübungen), *Wirtschaftswoche*, **8**, 128–132.

Theisen, M.R. (1998), 'Empirical evidence and economic comments on board structure in Germany', in *Comparative Corporate Governance: The State of the Art and Emerging Research*, eds K.J. Hopt, H. Kanda, M.R. Roe and S. Prigge, Oxford University Press, Oxford, pp. 259–265.

Weber, J., Willenborg, M. and Zhang, Jieying (2008), Does Auditor Reputation Matter? The Case of KPMG Germany and ComROAD AG, *Journal of Accounting Research*, **46**, 951–972.

Westerburg, J. (2002), *Control of the Management Board through Supervisory Board and Auditor. A Study with Cases (Balsam AG, Bremer Vulkan Verbund AG, Philipp Holzmann AG and Metallgesellschaft AG) before and after the KonTraG (Die Kontrolle des Vorstandes durch Aufsichtsrat und Abschlussprüfer. Eine Studie anhand von Fallbeispielen (Balsam AG, Bremer Vulkan Verbund AG, Philipp Holzmann AG und Metallgesellschaft AG) zur Rechtslage vor und nach dem KonTraG)*, Verlag Dr Kovac, Hamburg.

Wulf, M. (2005), 'Risks of criminal proceedings by preparation and auditing of financial statements' (Strafrechtliche Haftungsrisiken bei Abschlusserstellung und Abschlussprüfung), in *Bilanzreform und Bilanzdelikte (Financial Statement Reform and Fraudulent Financial Reporting)*, ed. C.-Ch. Freidank, Deutscher Universitäts-Verlag, Wiesbaden, pp. 211–239.

# 11

# Creative Accounting and Fraud in Greece

George Kontos, Maria Krambia-Kapardis and Nikolaos T. Milonas

## 11.1 INTRODUCTION

Fraud, embezzlement, side payments, insider trading, creative accounting and creative transactions are all evidence of the same human behavioural trait of bypassing a set of rules to advance one's own objective. This behaviour is not confined to certain periods of time, a particular country or to a specific area of activity. The behaviour of individuals in charge of decision-making or in control of operations has caused multinational companies from different national origins like Barings, Enron, Siemens, Société Générale, Parmalat and Sumitomo Corporation, to mention but a few, to either go bankrupt or lose a significant part of their value.

Despite sophisticated auditing and computer information systems, human minds can find the way to overcome security controls and act on their own. In 2008, according to press reports, the case of Jerome Kerviel – who seems to have bet on the stock market rising using derivatives without hedging his positions but instead falsifying hedge documentation (and in the process losing €4.9 million for Société Générale) – may prove to be an example of such human behaviour (Cimilluca, 2008). Usually and in general, excessive trading positions beyond authorized levels, and against the rules and procedures, are discovered only when markets turn against such positions. At other times, such behaviour may not be discovered or the individual may turn out to be a very successful trader.

When Greece joined the European Union (formerly the European Economic Community) in 1981, economic scandals became the order of the day as many cashed in on the opportunities presented. According to Kourakis (2001, p. 327), membership of the European Union (EU) meant a lowering of border controls, and the illegal importation of cigarettes, alcohol, food and petrol became rampant. Of particular interest are cases involving the fictitious supply of duty-free petrol to ships and fishing vessels under foreign flag. Large supplies of duty-free petrol were acquired by companies (supplying petrol to petrol stations) by the presentation of fictitious documents showing foreign ships and foreign fishing vessels that supposedly docked in Greek ports to take on supplies, including petrol for their own needs. The petrol was then sold to Greek petrol stations at much higher prices (*Eleftheros Typos/Free Press*, 14 January 2000, p. 25). Also the EU provided subsidies to companies which created new positions for employment. Exploiting the opportunity, nine light ready-garment industries in northern Greece applied for and were paid the financial subsidies for having created new employment opportunities – they fired their personnel and re-employed them under a different company name (*Ta Nea/Τα Νέα*, 19 May 1999, p. 51).

*Creative Accounting, Fraud and International Accounting Scandals*   Edited by Michael Jones
© 2011 Michael Jones. Published by John Wiley & Sons, Ltd

The literature on creative accounting and financial fraud in Greece is scant. However, Baralexis (2004) points out that the legal framework in Greece within which the financial statements are prepared in fact encourages creative accounting (p. 442). This is especially the case with tax law and economic development law. To illustrate, Law 2238/1994 provided that annual depreciation charges as well as provisions for doubtful debts (i.e. 0.5 % of annual sales) were not compulsory and, consequently, a firm may choose 'to make such charges in one accounting period but not in another'. On the basis of a questionnaire survey of senior auditors and independent accountants in Greece, Baralexis provides seven examples of earnings management opportunities within the Greek law that are conducive to creative accounting. More specifically, he found that large Greek firms prefer to overstate profit more readily to obtain external funds whereas small Greek firms prefer to understate profits in order to reduce income taxes (p. 452).

Baralexis (2004) states that motives of profit overstatement are: (a) borrowing from banks, (b) increasing share prices, (c) improving the company's image and (d) getting funds from the EU economic development programmes (p. 450). Reasons for profit understatement are: (a) payment of fewer dividends, (b) to pressurize partners to leave the company, (c) competition and (d) planning of fictitious bankruptcy. He concluded that, with the blessing of the law, creative accounting is a frequent occurrence in Greece and on a significant scale, estimated to be about 25 % of pre-managed earnings. However, it should be noted in this context that since his research was carried out, a number of measures have been introduced to limit creative accounting in Greece (see the 'Aftermath' section).

Misleading potential investors, insider trading and share manipulation produced other types of scandal. An interesting stock exchange scandal in Greece is described by N. Frantzi in the newspaper *To Vima/To Βήμα* (26 January 2000, p. B5). Eleven persons connected with the company 'Lavreotiki'/'Λαυρεωτική,' including businessmen, stockbrokers and shareholders (some of whom were later convicted and sentenced), tried to utilize confidential information and spread misinformation in order to increase the value of the company's shares on the Athens Stock Exchange. However, ironically, their efforts resulted in the shares taking a big drop in value because the false claims being made were contradicted by the reported financial information of the company.

Another scandal involving share price manipulation was with Ipirotiki Software & Publications SA, which produced software and published all kinds of books of a legal, financial, tax and accounting nature. The Capital Market Commission imposed fines amounting to a total of €900 000 on three brokerage firms and five individuals proved to have manipulated the share price of the company. The investigation started in April 2005, after the suicide of its main shareholder, entrepreneur Babis Maniotis. From February 2004 to April 2005, five individuals carried out transactions through three brokerage firms (Midas Financial Services, Olympia Financial Services and Megatrust Financial Services) and artificially influenced the price and marketability of Ipirotiki share prices. The share price manipulation took place through systematic buying and selling just prior to the end of the stock market session, as well as via transactions among the individuals involved that moved the price to where they wanted. Such manipulative schemes were possible because Ipirotiki shares lacked sufficient liquidity. On 4 April, the Capital Market Commission decided to suspend trading on Ipirotiki Software shares.[1]

---

[1] See announcement in the Athens Stock Exchange website www.ase.gr.

The absence of corporate governance in Sex Form SA, a listed company specializing in the manufacture of underwear, led to the company's bankruptcy and left hundreds of employees unpaid. The Capital Market Commission asked the Athens Stock Exchange to suspend trading in Sex Form shares on the grounds that the company had not informed the investing public of (a) the fate of €5 million paid to the vice president and managing director of the company (according to the company this was for his services in 'conducting negotiations') and (b) the reasons why it had not used part of this sum to immediately pay wages for its employees and honour the remaining company obligations. Both these points were noted by the auditor, who qualified the financial statements of 2004. The company did not provide an adequate explanation for the above issues and the investigation by the Capital Market Commission confirmed the disappearance of the €5 million, which led to the dismissal of hundreds of employees, the delisting of the company on November 2006 and the eventual closure of its operations.[2]

The purpose of this chapter is to provide a brief account of some important Greek accounting scandals, which have been publicized in the media and by academic articles where either the persons responsible have been tried and a verdict has been reached or supervisory authorities (such as the Capital Market Commission) have imposed fines after completing an investigation. In the second section we present two cases of rather recent scandals, one in financial services (ETBA Finance) and one in the field of health clubs (Dynamic Life). In these two cases, the auditors did not identify the transgressions either explicitly or implicitly.

The third section deals extensively with the most important recent scandal in Greece, the Bank of Crete scandal in the 1980s. This scandal had a profound effect on economic and political life in Greece. George Koskotas had exploited the significant gaps in the information systems in the banking sector and from a mere employee he became the owner of the Bank of Crete within a short period of time. In the process, he embezzled more than 30 million dollars.

In the 'Aftermath' section, we discuss the fallout after the Bank of Crete scandal, paying special attention to the political turmoil and the change of government. Also, we discuss the new set of rules that has been instituted since then to prohibit the use of creative accounting and associated fraud.

In the final section, we provide a brief summary of the chapter and raise the expectation that the emergence of new scandals will be limited by the institution of many mandatory rules for reporting.

## 11.2 TWO ACCOUNTING SCANDALS[3]

### 11.2.1 ETBA Finance

The Hellenic Bank of Industrial Development SA (ETBA Bank) was established in 1964 as a state bank. The purpose of the bank was to promote industrial, handicraft, tourist, shipping, mining and commercial activities, and generally any activity that could contribute to the financial development of the country and the promotion of the capital market in Greece.

---

[2] On 27 November 2006 and according to the decision 404/22.11.2006 of the Hellenic Capital Market Commission, shares of the SEX FORM SA company that were suspended from trading till then, were purged from the Athens Stock Exchange.

[3] For a more extensive discussion of the two scandals, see Papakyrillou (2006).

ETBA Finance was a subsidiary of ETBA Bank, and its objective was to finance companies. The fraud orchestrated by company executives was revealed towards the end of 2001. These executives had embezzled 11 billion drachmas (about €32 million) from the company. This revelation began with the 1998 report made by Grant Thornton, who carried out a special investigation of ETBA Finance for 1993–97 (*Kathimerini*, 2002a).

The auditing firm highlighted the weaknesses of internal audit and the lack of rudimentary operational rules within the company. Grant Thornton indicated that there was an urgent need to describe the responsibilities of every member of the personnel so that each individual's duties and roles were clearly defined and stated in writing. In particular, every phase of the transactions must correspond to a different employee to facilitate audit procedures. At the time of the Grant Thornton report, company employees were allowed to handle on their own all phases of a transaction or any other financial activity. Such practice imposed great financial risks on the company since, by controlling all phases of a transaction, high-level employees could hide fraudulent activities. In fact, Grant Thornton had expressed its fear that the company's organizational weaknesses might legitimize the €32 million embezzlement (*Kathimerini*, 2002b).

One of ETBA Finance's activities was the management of companies in distress and under liquidation. In the latter case, among other things, ETBA Finance undertook the management of its available cash. To achieve better returns, this cash was usually invested in fixed deposits or in repurchase agreements[4] along with the cash of other companies and that of ETBA Finance itself in one unified account. Then the earned interest was allocated to one account for the firms under liquidation and one account for ETBA Finance. This led to misallocations. The allocation to each account was supposed to be proportional. Yet, this process allowed the individuals involved to keep for themselves the additional interest income earned from having combined all cash into one deposit account relative to what it would have earned, had each account been invested separately. During the period 1993–97 the cash invested in repurchase agreements amounted to several billion drachmas and yielded a large amount of interest, aided by the high interest rates in Greece at that time. However, the process was characterized by a complete lack of transparency. ETBA Finance proceeded to correct the situation by establishing a committee to supervise the process. Yet, those appointed were the same persons performing the operations, which in a way legitimized the entire process that led to the embezzlement.

Another aspect of inappropriate accounting was when ETBA Finance's income appeared reduced due to a delay in the liquidation procedures of companies; there were provisions made for the liquidation fees through a decision by the board of directors without the issuance of invoices or the collection of fees within the financial period. In other words, when provisions were made, ETBA Finance's income was credited and the provisional account of the liquidated company was debited. This accounting tactic resulted in the payment of VAT on income at a different time, since it was paid when the invoice was finally issued, that is, in later financial periods. On one occasion in 1995, the income

---

[4] Banks offer to sell, usually overnight, short-term treasury debt to an investor at a specific price and agree to repurchase from the same investor the same debt at a specific but higher price. The difference in the prices amounts to the interest earned by the investor. This investment is called a repurchase agreement (or repo) and is similar to depositing money with a bank. However, usually, funds invested in repos earn higher interest than bank deposits.

provision was 126 billion drachmas while the collected fees barely amounted to 20.8 billion drachmas.

In the expenses section, the investigatory report mentions occasions said to concern fees for 'fictitious services'. There is also the impressive case of liquidation expenses of a particular company amounting to 3.9 million drachmas, for which no voucher or proof existed. Company executives justified these expenses as either a 'bonus' to the staff of the company under liquidation or advertisement fees for newspaper announcements which, however, were never actually made. It is, therefore, unknown why such expenses were permitted by ETBA Finance in the absence of receipts for services rendered. Also, the report mentioned that the travelling allowances and fees of ETBA Finance employees were 'disproportionately high and lacking supporting documents'. Finally, Grant Thornton found that there were cases of employees who had been promoted two or three levels in the managerial hierarchy within a single year and received benefits from all position levels (i.e. two or three benefits for all their promotion grades), held without presenting the required vouchers. Lawyers' fees were characterized as high. However, these were accompanied by supporting documents and subjected to due tax deductions.

Despite the specific findings and suggestions made in the report about the framework of cash audit, the shortcomings of the company's internal audit procedures and the lack of effective organization, there were no measures taken to avoid the financial scandal which would break out at the beginning of 2002 during the process of ETBA Bank's privatization.

Fourteen individuals were indicted in this case for fraud, forgery and embezzlement: five company executives, four employees of Avax Securities SA, three branch managers of Eurobank SA and two owners of companies facilitating stock orders.[5] One of the 14 individuals charged, namely George Dimitriadis, owned a small brokerage firm named Europrofit and transmitted stock orders via Avax Securities on behalf of his clients. According to the charges, he took advantage of his acquaintance with the ETBA Finance executives from his former employment as a bank manager and collaborated with them. The plan was for him to appear as a representative of Eurobank, one of the large Greek banks, and to submit interest rate offers to ETBA Finance to deposit their available cash with Eurobank. Spyros Stefanatos, Georgia Smbarouni and Dimitrios Fragkodimitropoulos were the three members of the ETBA Finance committee who evaluated the offers on the basis of the level of interest offered and the safety of the investment, and decided if the money should be deposited with Eurobank. In this way, large sums of money were sent to Eurobank – to the Dimitriadis account. However, instead of being deposited to earn interest, Dimitriadis transferred the money either to offshore companies (from 1996 to 1999) or to the bank account of an old lady (who has since died) – the grandmother of Dimitrios Kampanellis, one of the 14 persons charged and a close associate of Dimitriadis. Then, the money from these accounts (i.e. either the offshore accounts or the grandmother's account) was deposited in a brokerage account with Avax Securities to be invested in the stock market. The purpose of this scam was for those involved to share the profits from the stock market after they had returned to ETBA Finance the interest that would have been earned had the money been

---

[5] Small brokering firms who invest in the stock market. These companies receive orders from customers which they then transmit to a stockbroking firm which enters the order into the stock market system.

deposited in the bank. The fraud did not come to light until a decline in the stock exchange prevented the five company executive accomplices from returning the cash assets they had been using for their own profit.

The racket was organized in 1997. In 1999, when discussions started for the privatization of ETBA Finance, those who were in on the scam suspended their activities for fear the fraud might be exposed following the assets inspection of the group of companies. After one year, however, they resumed unimpeded. In total, they invested 26 billion drachmas (about €75 million), 11 billion drachmas (about €32 million) of which never returned.

The trial of 13 individuals lasted nine months and the verdict was reached in February 2008. Reading the court's decision,[6] life terms in prison were given to three senior managers of ETBA Finance: Spyros Stefanatos, former CEO, Georgia Smbarouni, former CFO and Dimitrios Fragkodimitropoulos, former chief accountant. The chartered accountant received a prison term of 11 years and six months. Ten years in prison were given to Dimitrios Kampanellis. Prison terms of ten years and six years were given to two former Avax executives. Finally, prison penalties of 20 months were given to three officers of Eurobank. Three bank employees were also given prison sentences. Three other individuals were freed from their charges. The fourteenth individual is George Dimitriadis, who has not been convicted as yet – from 2001 he still remains at large. The ten convicted individuals have appealed and a five-member appellate court reached its verdict in July 2009. The court upheld the convictions for Stefanatos, Smbarouni, Fragkodimitropoulos and Kampanellis but reduced their life term in prison to 17 years in prison for the first two individuals and nine years in prison for the third individual, while it reduced the conviction of the fourth individual by one year. The two former Avax executives and a bank employee were found innocent. Because of the statute of limitation, charges were dropped against the chartered accountant and two other individuals.

It is worth adding that many believed that the way the company was managed and the extent of the fraud could not possibly have gone unnoticed by the chartered accountant if he had properly planned the inspection and had indeed been working to high quality standards. Initially, the chartered accountant was sentenced to 11 years. Then at the appeal trial charges were dropped because of the statute of limitation. Observing the shortcomings in the detection of fraud and the accounting errors highlighted by the Grant Thornton report and the efforts made by top management to legitimize the firm's irregularities, any chartered accountant should not have relied on the company internal audit system. Judging from that, the Association of Chartered Accountants referred the chartered accountant to the Disciplinary Committee. The strictest disciplinary penalty was imposed on him (i.e. definitive dismissal and striking off the register of the Chartered Accountants Association). The chartered accountant lodged an appeal against the decision of the Disciplinary Committee, claiming that company top management was involved in the fraud and therefore obstructed the proper performance of his auditing work. His penalty was reduced to six months' disciplinary suspension. Afterwards, the chartered accountant appealed to the State Council, requesting that the Disciplinary Committee judgment be revoked.

---

[6] See Pathfinder News at the internet site: http://news.pathfinder.gr/greece/news/456085.html (in Greek).

### 11.2.2  Dynamic Life[7]

Dynamic Life SA began business in 1996. It was established to carry on the work of Dynami Zois, which in 1994 was the first company in Greece to start up and establish the practice of franchising gyms. According to Natasha Bougatioti, chairwoman of the company, the objective of Dynamic Life was to create the appropriate conditions that would turn gyms into dynamic businesses and generally boost the culture of sports and exercise in Greece. Natasha Bougatioti was a determined, marketing-oriented person. In implementing its objectives, on the one hand, the company focused its know-how on facility specifications and infrastructure and, on the other hand, on changing the mentality of both gym owners and gym employees, aiming in the long run at the improvement of the image of exercising and fitness among Greek people. In addition, she branched out into marketing of sports equipment and collaborated with the biggest firms abroad, therefore achieving the best terms of trade.

The registered company trademarks were: Universal Studios by Natasha, Vis Vitalis, Universal Ladies by Natasha, Vis Vitalis Ladies, Natasha's VIPS and The Club by Natasha. The company was listed in the special segment of dynamic and fast developing companies on the Athens Stock Exchange in September 2002, with an initial share price of €1.40. Both sales and profits of the company exhibited fast growth, but it was not long before problems began.

Dynamic Life had mainly focused its development on a three-year programme of services provided (exercising, solarium, hair salon services, etc.). The 'Club by Natasha' programme had a temporary duration of one or two months, during which the customer could walk away before the three-year programme started. However, after the lapse of this provisional time the customers could not in effect terminate their subscription because they were charged by credit card to be paid in 36 interest-free monthly instalments. In contrast, Dynamic Life had been paid by the credit company for the entire three-year membership programme up-front. After strong reaction from consumer associations against the company's misleading practice, the company discontinued the gym subscription programme and established a payment scheme per use. However, the interruption of the subscription programme brought about the eventual collapse of Dynamic Life. After the termination of the subscription programme, the company turned to an annual membership fee and launched a new programme called 'Being Best,' aimed to be the spring board that would allow the owner to branch out internationally as she claimed. The programme was launched in spring 2004 and coincided with the first deplorable incidents that led franchisee gyms to start loosening their ties to the company as their owners found ways to subscribe new members without reporting to Dynamic Life.

Towards the end of 2004, and following an investigation carried out by the Capital Market Commission, it was revealed that the company was involved in improper accounting practices. The Commission imposed a fine of €1.5 million on Natasha Bougatioti

---

[7] See newspaper stories: *Imerisia* (2005), 'Investors against the management of Dynamic Life', *Imerisia* (4 January 2005), 'Dynamic life under the microscope', *Imerisia* (13 January 2005), 'The big trick of Dynamic Life', (16 January 2005).

because she had published and distributed inaccurate and misleading information through accounting statements (both holding company and consolidated) which the company released for the first half of 2004. In particular, in the consolidated financial statements dated 30 June 2004, financial figures were falsified as the company turnover was increased by a non-existent €3 million. The falsification was done through a transaction of €3 million with a wholly owned subsidiary abroad and, in effect, concerned future receipts and not income pertaining to the current financial year. By this method, the consolidated turnover presented an apparent increase of 62% in comparison with the first period of 2003, while the actual turnover increase was only 15%. For the same reason, and because they concealed from the public the worsening of the financial condition of the company in the third quarter of 2004, a €500000 fine was imposed on Mr Leonidas Goumas, president of the board of directors of Dynamic Life SA and a €100000 fine on Mrs F. Zagoudi, company chief accountant. In addition, a €500000 fine was set on the company itself due to the fact that it had issued misleading and inaccurate information regarding its financial condition in the first half of 2004. It had concealed the considerable deterioration of its financial figures during the third quarter of its financial year 2004, and failed to inform the investing public in time of important corporate events. Finally, there was a €350000 fine set for Egnatia Financial Services SA, which had acted as an underwriter for Dynamic Life SA because, among other things, it had not ensured that the investing public were informed in time about the changes in company activities.

Despite the fines imposed by the Capital Market Commission, the picture regarding the activities of the company on the stock market is rather foggy. What seems certain is that management had persuaded many institutional investors to invest in the shares by offering significant discounts on the market price of the stock. Nine months later the company showed almost stagnant sales compared with those of the first quarter of 2004. The company acquired a mere 5000 new members in the third quarter, which corresponds to 45 new members per gym. These new members in Greece and abroad were registered in its 100%-owned foreign subsidiary, which managed Being Best and was not consolidated.[8] The story is more complicated if we also take into consideration the company's intention to proceed with a new share issue that followed the purchase of the company's shares by a former ship-owner who seemed to have played the role of a strategic investor. All this happened before 12 December 2004, when the Capital Market Committee decided to suspend trading of the shares, based on the argument that the company top management had failed to give satisfactory explanations regarding the company's activities. On 14 January 2005, the Capital Market Committee decided to file a petition to the Athens Court of First Instance requesting a cash audit of the listed company 'Dynamic Life SA'.

---

[8] Since the subsidiary was owned 100% by the company, one would expect the parent company to consolidate its financial results. It is therefore a mystery why the company would intentionally reduce its revenues by not consolidating its subsidiary. The reduced results would have had a negative impact on share prices. So perhaps the planned new share issue could be made at a lower price, thus encouraging investors. Consolidating the financial results of the subsidiary in the next financial period would, however, have a strong positive impact on next year's share prices. This was perhaps the plan which, however, was left unfinished.

The chartered accountant who audited the 2004 financial statements qualified the accounts for the reasons set out in the notes below. These notes were attached to the financial statements:

1) The 'Long-term Investments' account included: a) the sum of 1,679,000 euros invested in a 100% wholly-owned non-listed foreign company with a negative internal accounting value, b) the sum of 3,620,000 euros concerned the 19.98% of a non-listed company whose internal accounting value is 3,039,787.08 euros, c) the sum of 2,000,000 euros, which pertains to the cost value of an investment in a non-listed company whose internal accounting value amounted to 412,080.88 euros. For the aforementioned cases there should have been provisions for losses of an amount totalling 3,847,132.04 euros, which should equally reduce revenues of the financial period.

2) In the 'Deferred Expenses' account the following are included: a) items, which should be amortised and which should reduce the results of the present financial year by 350,000 euros, b) items amounting to 2,265,000 euros pertinent to the costs of writing of manuals. This was treated as a deferred expense (i.e., as an asset) as it was incurred this period, but would benefit future periods (Papakyrillou, 2006, p. 45). (Up until the moment when the audit certificate was granted this item was not verified and may not, therefore, actually have existed), c) the sum of 354,000 euros regarding services which the parent company performed for the subsidiary and which should have been paid by the subsidiary were a claim against its subsidiary. Yet this was treated as an expense reducing the operational results with an amortisation of 70,880 euros.

3) The 'accounts receivable' company account also includes old receivables amounting to 3,638,580.10 euros for which the company had made past provisions in the financial statements amounting to a total of 54,795.59 euros. However, this was an insufficient loss provision. The correct provision should have reduced operating results by 2,683,580.10 euros for 2004 and by 900,000 euros for previous fiscal years.

4) The company income included a sum of 3 million euros, which came from the sale of the right to use software to a wholly-owned foreign subsidiary and according to the existing contract the collection of the revenues should take place in the period from January 2005 to December 2007. Up until the date of the auditor's report, the first instalment amounting to 83,333.33 euros had not been collected. The sum of 3 million euros, therefore, pertains to receipts of future fiscal periods and should not have been acknowledged as revenue for the present financial year, which was 2004.

Overall, the remarks made by the auditor do not allude to a healthy business. Furthermore, the company's ability to carry on its activities was doubtful and it faced a huge problem of liquidity. If the auditor's comments were reflected in the company's financial statements, the whole picture would be entirely different. In that case, the company would have shown a loss of €6 million instead of €560 413.51 pre-tax profit. Also, if loss provisions were made for the pending lawsuits against the company of €23 700 000, the income losses would have been even more.

Given all the above, it is reasonable to wonder why the chartered accountant finally signed the auditor's report and let the company continue its fragile operations. The aftermath of this was that the Accounting Standardization Committee ordered an examination of the audit quality performed by the chartered accountant and for his possible omissions during the audit of the company's financial statements. Special mention was made of the

€3 million included in the company's income statement relating to the income of future fiscal periods and not the one which was audited. Overall, there seems to have been a plan to go international with the 'Being Best' programme to make up for losses incurred in Greece. As this plan did not seem to be working, efforts were made to convince investors to hold onto their shares, otherwise the share prices would collapse. The improper accounting practices appear to have been adopted as a last resort to cover up the company's problems.

## 11.3 THE BANK OF CRETE SCANDAL

The Bank of Crete scandal is synonymous with the Koskotas scandal. The ingredients that make it of interest are: Koskotas's background and meteoric rise to wealth and power in Greece; the frauds he committed and the bravado with which he did so; how he managed to conceal them for a period of time even though so many knew about them; his deep involvement as a supporter of the Socialist Party; the live broadcast of his trial and, finally, the crisis into which the Koskotas scandal plunged the Socialist Party, culminating in the Greek Prime Minister, the deputy Premier and three ministers being prosecuted for a number of offences.

The Koskotas scandal was facilitated by the following: (1) inadequate internal controls and lack of segregation of duties – there was a lack of corporate governance and no audit committee; (2) Koskotas was in charge and had employed people willing to do what he wanted; (3) Koskotas had government officials 'helping him out'; (4) at the time there were no applicable International Accounting Standards (IFRS) and, finally, (5) the existence of legislation providing for the confidentiality of bank accounts prevented Koskotas from being found out for a period of time.

According to Demetriou (1996), Koskotas was born in Athens in 1954 to poor uneducated parents. In 1969, at the age of 15, he migrated to the USA with his parents and brother Stavros where he worked in his father's business – painting, decorating and renovating houses. At the same time, he attended classes at Fordham University and Lehman College in New York. However, the tertiary qualifications he later claimed to have acquired from those two, and other tertiary institutions in the States, were false because he had himself forged the academic transcripts concerned. Koskotas was to stay a total of 10 years in the USA, the first six of them as a minor. However, in addition to forging his academic qualifications, he committed 64 other offences, mainly deception offences involving forging signatures and assuming false identities in the context of his father's renovating business, for which he was charged in the USA (Demetriou, 1996, p. 115). Thus, before returning to Greece financially well off, he had an accomplished record as a fraudster.

At the trial, Koskotas was described by some of those who testified as 'silly'. In his article, Demetriou (1996) described him as follows: not university educated on the one hand but, on the other, as someone who would not stop at anything to achieve his goals; daring and cunning; and, also, as having a pronounced proclivity for perpetrating economic crimes. One may say Koskotas was an example of an overstrong personality. He worked behind the scenes as a mastermind to implement his plans with the support of a dedicated group of people. He was very clever at finding and exploiting the gaps in the reporting system. In addition, his meteoric rise from a junior position in the accounting department to the Bank's CEO was very impressive.

### 11.3.1 Koskotas's Employment with the Bank of Crete

On 3 July 1979 Koskotas commenced employment in the Bank's financial administration department, which consisted of the accounting and computing sections. On 26 June 1980, he was assigned control of the Bank's foreign currency officers; in other words, he was in charge of the internal audit team of the Bank's foreign currency reserves and the Bank's reserves in the Bank of Greece. On 7 April 1981, he was promoted to deputy-head of the accounting section but was, at the same time, carrying out the duties of the head of the same section. He was now in a position, in the name of the Bank's needs and interests, to take the initiative and authorize at his own risk and personal responsibility, transfers of payments of money in Greece or overseas as the Bank's authorized legal representative. Being in such a privileged position, he conceived the idea of misappropriating money belonging to the Bank in the belief that he would not be found out. Only 22 days after he was appointed head of the Bank's internal audit section, on 18 July 1980, he stole for himself cheques that belonged to customers of the Bank's branch in Piraeus – amounting to \$US 1 155 000 – and were part of the Bank's foreign currency (Dermitzakis, 1999, p. 1222). More specifically, being in charge of managing the said amount, he deposited it in his Bank's current account with 'Westminster Bank Ltd' but without making the relevant entries in the Bank's accounting books (p. 1223). On the same day, he authorized by fax (but without any reference number being stated on the fax) the transfer of that amount to his father-in-law's account at the same bank in London.

Encouraged by his successful misappropriation of that amount, about four weeks later, on 26 August 1980 and in exactly the same way, he stole \$US 1 507 515 from customers' cheques paid into the Bank's Piraeus branch (p. 1223). His father-in-law subsequently withdrew the money involved from his account with Westminster Bank in London and gave it to Koskotas. In 1981, he started misappropriating large amounts of drachmas, too, from the Bank's reserves and, in due course, he managed to own 95 % of the Bank's shares. By 18 January 1985, at 31, he became President of the Bank's board and executive director of the Bank, thus acquiring complete control of the Bank and its management, which he himself represented. At the same time, he employed individuals in the Bank's various departments and, also, had appointed to the Bank's board of directors, persons who would unquestionably carry out his instructions (p. 1223). In total,[9] according to Dermitzakis (1999), he misappropriated the incredible amount of \$US 30 718 190. The accounting irregularities used to conceal his fraudulent activities were not to be discovered for a number of years.

When in January 1987 the Bank of Greece decided to audit a number of the Bank's branches, transactions involving accounts held by some companies owned by Koskotas at the Bank's main branch came under suspicion. In an apparent over-reaction and fearing that the Bank of Greece might carry out audits of his Bank's accounting section, he decided to replace a number of documents by forged ones retrospectively for the period 1 January 1986 until 30 November 1986. In fact, the false documents showing the money paid into

---

[9] The reader should note that different authors on the Koskotas scandal (e.g. Demetriou, 1996; Dermitzakis, 1999) provide somewhat different figures regarding the total amount of money misappropriated by Koskotas. This is why the present authors give different figures depending on the source. Demetriou (1996), for example, quotes the total amount misappropriated as being 32 million US dollars.

his fictitious account could not be accessed by the auditors of the Bank of Greece in view of existing confidentiality legislation safeguarding the privacy of personal bank accounts. In order to arrange the creation of the necessary false documents, on a Sunday early in February 1987 Koskotas called a meeting at a particular branch of the Bank of Crete where he cajoled some of the senior staff of the Bank to carry out the forgeries he wanted (Dermitzakis, 1999, p. 1223). The group of forgers comprised the head of accounting, the departmental head of accounting and a third senior employee. The team of forgers then proceeded to systematically identify all the documents that had to be replaced by forged ones in order to ensure the cover-up.

The media in Greece on 17 June 1988 reported that in November 1987 authorities in the USA had arrested Koskotas and the Bank of Greece ordered an ad-hoc general audit of the Bank of Crete. Faced with the danger of such an audit unearthing evidence that Koskotas had misappropriated for himself large amounts of money that should have been paid to the Bank of Crete, Koskotas, once freed from the US authorities, assembled a number of his Bank employees whom he pressurized into forging during the period 12–20 June 1988 a number of documents held in the accounting department of the Bank which the Bank had entrusted to them and to which they had access. In addition, the same bunch of accomplices falsely certified to numerous others the legality of moneys credited to Koskotas's fictitious personal account (Dermitzakis, 1999, p. 1223).

Regarding the forgeries, on 5 October 1988 Koskotas authorized one of his own senior Bank employees to hand over to the external auditors of the Bank of Greece from the ad-hoc general audit two uncertified photocopies of two letters in English, dated 26 May 1988 that were addressed to Koskotas (Dermitzakis, 1999, p. 1223). One of the letters had been sent from New York by the well-known stockbroking firm Merrill-Lynch and the other from the Irving Trust Company bank, also in the USA. The first letter, signed by the deputy-president of the company, stated that the Bank of Crete had GNMA (Ginnie Mae) investments of $US 13 718 190 in debentures of the US National Union as security. The second letter, signed by the deputy director of the Irving Trust Company Bank (Dermitzakis, 1999, p. 1223) confirmed that on 31 December 1987 the Bank of Crete had (a) in one foreign currency account with the said US bank $US 15 000 000 in bonds of the US Ministry of Finance with interest at 11.25 % and payable on 15 February 1994 and (b) in another fixed-term deposit account $US 2 000 000 payable with interest on 30 June 1988. Both letters were in fact false and had been forged in May 1988 under the guidance of Koskotas who, stating a pack of lies, drafted their content and also forged the signature on each of them (p. 1223). Koskotas provided the two false letters to mislead the auditors of the Bank of Greece. He believed he had thus covered his tracks and was able to continue his illegal activities (Dermitzakis, 1999, p. 1224) because the external auditors had not detected the forged documents.

Meanwhile, in 1982 Koskotas set up the company 'Line' as a mass media company with himself elected the following year as chairman of the board. Into that company he diverted approximately 12 500 000 000 drachmas ($US 84 317 032) of the 32 000 000 000 drachmas ($US 215 851 602) he misappropriated. Koskotas had by then managed to get full control of his media company's board after forcing two of its founding members and major shareholders to withdraw from the company. In order to increase his position in the Greek press, in May 1987 he bought the newspaper *Kathimerini* for 280 million drachmas ($US

1.8 million) as well as the newspaper *Evdomi*, and in June 1988 the newspaper *Vradini* for 430 million drachmas ($US 172 million). Both newspapers had until then been critical of PASOK and the Papandreou government. Koskotas's media company published six magazines and one newspaper that expressed positive views about Papandreou's socialist government. However, Koskotas had already upset many people and he was soon to be exposed for his fraud.

Before describing the charges for which Koskotas was convicted, it is important to understand the state of the inadequate accounting information systems and the Greek economic environment at that time, which Koskotas fully exploited for his own advancement, along with the way he did it.

### 11.3.2 The Accounting Information Systems of the Time

To fully understand the reasons that led to the accounting frauds, it is necessary to understand the shortcomings of the accounting information systems in the 1980s, which Koskotas spotted and shrewdly exploited.

The architecture of the accounting information systems was based on the idea that every branch of the bank was an autonomous accounting entity. Every branch therefore set up its own ledgers and finally its own general ledger, which together with the ledgers of the rest of the branches was the basis for the creation of the balance sheet and the results of every bank. At the time, the accounting information systems of the banks could not meet the needs of the emergent economy and as a result, accounting events that affected two or more branches could not be processed simultaneously. This, in turn, led to the accumulation of problems in the reconciliation of inter-branch accounts. When, for example, Branch A received from an importer the equivalent of the foreign exchange which was granted to it through the correspondent Bank X, the branch had to make the following entry:

$$\text{Dr (debit)} \quad \text{Cash}$$
$$\text{Cr (credit)} \quad \text{Inter-branch account/Head Office} \quad\quad (11.1)$$

Together with the entry, the branch ought to send to Head Office details of the event so that they could go ahead with the entry:

$$\text{Dr} \quad \text{Inter-branch account/Branch A}$$
$$\text{Cr} \quad \text{Correspondent bank/X} \quad\quad (11.2)$$

This entry sets up the Head Office account with Bank X.

If the two entries do not take place simultaneously, there will remain a balance at the inter-branch account, which reveals the weakness of the information system. In other words, the initial cash will have been recorded, but no corresponding liability to the corresponding bank will have been set up. As seen from Table 11.1 and the corresponding Figure 11.1, all big Greek banks at the time faced a similar problem of large inter-branch account balances as a percentage of their assets. These percentage balances were gradually reduced for all banks except the Bank of Crete. The latter had much larger percentage balances after 1980 when Koskotas's involvement was increased.

**Table 11.1**  Inter-branch account balances analysis of major Greek banks for the period 1980 to 1990 (billions of drachmas)

| | National Bank of Greece | | Credit Bank | | Ionian Bank | | Bank of Crete | |
|---|---|---|---|---|---|---|---|---|
| Year | Balance | % of Assets | Balance | % of Assets | Balance | % of Assets | Balance | % of Assets |
| 1980 | 8.0 | 1.4 | 2.9 | 4.5 | 1.1 | 1.5 | 0.1 | 0.8 |
| 1981 | 13.9 | 1.8 | 4.2 | 5.1 | (1.2) | 1.2 | (0.1) | 1.2 |
| 1982 | 12.8 | 1.3 | 6.1 | 5.6 | (1.5) | 1.1 | (0.2) | 1.5 |
| 1983 | 20.5 | 1.6 | 6.8 | 5.4 | 0.9 | 0.6 | (0.3) | 2.3 |
| 1984 | 23.0 | 1.3 | 7.7 | 4.4 | 1.1 | 0.5 | (0.5) | 2.7 |
| 1985 | 21.9 | 1.0 | 8.3 | 3.8 | (1.0) | 0.4 | 2.9 | 8.6 |
| 1986 | 39.3 | 1.5 | 1.0 | 0.3 | (2.7) | 0.9 | 1.8 | 2.7 |
| 1987 | 53.9 | 1.8 | 0.3 | 0.1 | 5.2 | 1.3 | 0.4 | 0.5 |
| 1988 | 38.6 | 1.1 | 0.0 | 0.0 | (3.6) | 0.7 | 5.6 | 5.8 |
| 1989 | 29.8 | 0.7 | 0.0 | 0.0 | (7.5) | 1.2 | 5.8 | 5.2 |
| 1990 | 75.5 | 1.6 | 0.0 | 0.0 | (4.9) | 0.8 | 4.2 | 2.7 |

*Source:* Financial statements of banks.
*Note:* Numbers in brackets represent credit balances (i.e. liabilities).

The reconciliation problem was not limited to the inter-branch accounts. It extended to other important accounts of assets, mainly to 'deposits with correspondent banks' and to the 'Bank of Greece – current account'.

For reasons that we will mention later, there was such a great increase in the foreign exchange transactions of the banks that the computerized systems were not in a position to deal with them effectively and, as a result, the situation was getting progressively worse.

From the correspondence between the big commercial banks at the time and the foreign correspondent banks, we can see that the reconciliation of their deposit accounts with the

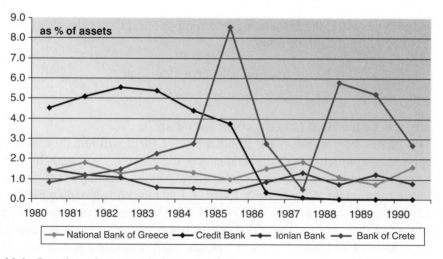

**Figure 11.1**  Inter-branch account balances analysis

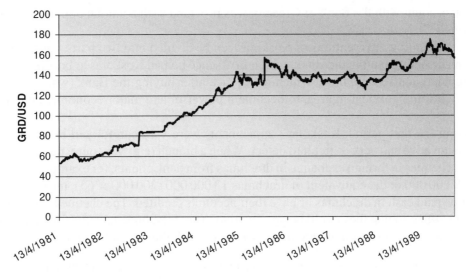

**Figure 11.2**  Evolution of GRD/$US exchange rate from 1981 to 1989

*Note*: The above exchange rates are certified by the Federal Reserve Bank of New York for customs purposes as required by section 522 of the amended Tariff Act of 1930. These rates are also those required by the SEC for the integrated disclosure system for foreign private issuers. The information is based on data collected by the Federal Reserve Bank of New York from a sample of market participants.

foreign banks was delayed by five to ten years. We can also see a delay, to a smaller extent, in the reconciliation of their deposit account with the Bank of Greece.

### 11.3.3  The Economic Environment at that Time

The collapse of the system of fixed exchange rates of Bretton Woods in August 1971 and the successive oil crises that followed in the 1970s had a serious influence on foreign exchange rates and interest rates. Countries with weak currencies, such as Greece, saw their currency devalue continuously, which created a climate of insecurity for those who participated in international trade and substantial profit opportunities for those who had long foreign exchange positions. Figure 11.2 shows the exchange rate evolution of the Greek drachma per US dollar. From about 55 drachmas per US dollar in 1981, the drachma had gradually devalued to about 158 drachmas per US dollar in 1989 – that is almost 300 % in just nine years. This continuous appreciation of the dollar attracted the attention of Koskotas, who duly took advantage of it, as described below.

#### 11.3.3.1  The 'Interventions' of Koskotas

From the day Koskotas was appointed to the Bank, his main purpose was to buy the Bank from its major shareholder at the time, Ioannis Karras, who had expressed a wish to sell his shares. Koskotas, by having under his immediate and exclusive supervision the basic operations of the Bank (accounting, foreign exchange, reconciliation of the deposit account with the Bank of Greece), was provided with a unique opportunity to fulfil his aims.

The accounting interventions of Koskotas can be divided into two parts. First, those that were made before buying the Bank, which in essence helped Koskotas to become the major shareholder, and second, those which took place after buying the Bank, where he sought, through bribing political figures, to become a powerful and major economic and political figure.

During the first period, Koskotas's movements were very careful and his interventions were innovative and very difficult to detect. When a branch (e.g. Voucourestiou str., Athens) bought cheques in foreign exchange in drachmas from bank clients, for example, the amount of $US 200 000 or the equivalent of drachmas 13 000 000 (200 000 × 65), the clients would either be paid cash in drachmas or have their accounts credited. The cheques were then sent to Head Office so that they could be presented to the correspondent banks for payment. The branch, say Voucourestiou, would have proceeded with the following entry:

| Dr | Inter-branch account/Head Office | 13 000 000 |
| Cr | Deposits in foreign exchange/clients' accounts | 13 000 000 |

The Head Office entry was supposed to be:

| Dr | Foreign banks/NatWest |
| Cr | Inter-branch account/Voucourestiou branch |

The Bank of Crete kept a foreign exchange account with NatWest/Piraeus branch where it deposited to its credit all cheques in foreign currency received from its clients. So that when the inter-branch accounts were eliminated, the only entries left in the books should have been:

| Dr | Foreign banks/NatWest |
| Cr | Deposits in foreign exchange/clients' accounts |

However, as Koskotas's intention was to embezzle the amounts deposited with NatWest he did not put these entries through the books. Koskotas made sure that the cheques were sent to National Westminster – Piraeus branch and duly credited the sending branches, but instead of debiting National Westminster, he credited and debited other accounts in foreign exchange at a different rate (for example, 70 in debit and 65 in credit) so as to create corresponding differences in drachmas as the debit of National Westminster.

In our example, Koskotas proceeded with the following entry:

| Dr | Foreign banks/Citibank  182 000 000 | | Difference 13 000 000 (the |
| | ($US2600 000 × 70) | | amount to be embezzled) |
| Cr | Foreign banks/Citibank  169 000 000 | | |
| | ($US2600 000 × 65) | | |
| Cr | Inter branch account/Athens  (Voucourestiou branch)    13 000 000 | | |

In effect, Koskotas inflated the balances in drachmas in existing accounts with foreign banks without affecting the balances in foreign currencies. He thus actually discounted the devaluation of the drachma. In this way the investments in National Westminster did not show in the books, and so Koskotas as the administrator of the foreign exchange gave orders to credit accounts abroad in his name or the name of relatives, mainly his wife.

Citibank did not get involved in the transaction at all. However, the Bank of Crete had a $US deposit account with Citibank, the balance of which is $US 10 000 000. This amount had been translated to 650 000 000 drachmas, using 1 $US to 65 drachmas as an exchange rate. Since Koskotas had the intention of abusing $US 200 000, which is translated to 13 000 000 drachmas, he had to increase the exchange rate accordingly. Therefore, he increased the exchange rate of the deposit amount from 1 $US to 65 drachmas to 1 $US to 66.3 drachmas. As a result, to maintain the total amount of the deposit of $US 10 000 000 the entry is now translated as follows:

$$\begin{array}{ll}
\text{\$US rate to drachmas} \\
2\,600\,000 \times 70 & = 182\,000\,000 \\
7\,400\,000 \times 65 & = 481\,000\,000 \\
\hline
10\,000\,000 \times 66.3 & = 663\,000\,000 \\
\end{array}$$

Thus, 663 000 000 drachmas less 650 000 000 drachmas leaves an exchange rate difference, equivalent to the fraud of 13 000 000 drachmas.

As can be seen from Figure 11.2, the drachma constantly depreciated and as a result Koskotas managed to reap the benefit, in advance, from the exchange differences which were created both from the long position in $US that the Bank of Crete had and from the constant depreciation of the drachma. In this way the investments in National Westminster did not show in the books and so Koskotas, as the administrator of the foreign exchange, gave orders to credit accounts abroad in his name or the name of relatives, mainly his wife.

As the drachma was continuously devalued, the inflated sums in drachmas in the foreign exchange accounts were covered by the devaluation of the drachma. In this way, Koskotas misappropriated the exchange rate differences which were provoked by the devaluation of the drachma, due to long positions in foreign exchange that the Bank held. This strategy was, however, not enough to satisfy the 'ambitious' plans of Koskotas and he was forced to resort to the easy way, which is the use of the inter-branch account as well as the current account of the Bank of Greece.

These two accounts, which are very important to every bank, had not been reconciled for many years throughout the banking system, so no auditing could detect the great secret that Koskotas hid in those accounts.

Koskotas, having taken over the bank on December 1984, became completely insolent and made extensive use of the above-mentioned foreign exchange accounts, but the majority of the embezzlements were hidden in the inter-branch accounts. It is worth mentioning that from the total of the embezzlement amounting to 31.9 billion drachmas, 30.3 billion was hidden in these inter-branch accounts.

Given that such a huge amount was likely to be picked up during auditing, Koskotas made sure that when publishing the annual balance sheet these large sums were provisionally transferred to deposit accounts so that Koskotas could exploit the law of confidentiality and hence avoid auditing. For example, on 31 December 1987 he reduced the balance of the inter-branch account by 5.9 billion drachmas with a simultaneous reduction in deposits (Audit Report of Bank of Greece auditors, No. 1/16.11.88).

In order to prevent such transactions from showing up as outstanding for a long time, he would debit and credit the same accounts at regular intervals so that the transactions actually appeared to be outstanding for a much shorter period of time.

It was never actually revealed how the total misappropriated amount was used. What is certain is that the money was used to buy the Bank of Crete, the publishing company GRAMMI and the famous Greek football club Olympiakos Piraeus. Large sums were also used to bribe important political figures of the time and to carry out football player transfers, while the remainder found its way into Koskotas's own personal accounts as well as those of other members of his family.

Koskotas's attempt to enter and control the press was ultimately what led to his demise. The continuous efforts of other publishing tycoons to unveil the Koskotas mystery proved successful and his 'reign' finally came to an end on 19 October 1988, with the appointment of a provisional general manager and an auditing team of the Bank of Greece.

### 11.3.3.2  The Indictable Offences for which Koskotas was Convicted

Koskotas was charged that, while being the Executive Director of the Bank of Crete, he misappropriated assets of the Bank by paying sums into and transferring sums to the accounts of his relatives in banks overseas without making the necessary entries into the books of accounts of the bank concerned. The Court found him guilty of having persuaded certain persons in the employment of the Bank to (a) create, retrospectively, on a number of occasions fictitious transactions in his personal account with the Bank and, also, (b) forge documents on a number of occasions to support the fictitious transactions appearing in his account. He also forged two photocopies of credit letters by overseas financial institutions in order to acquire for himself an amount of money greater than 50 000 000 drachmas ($US 337 268) and 25 000 000 drachmas ($US 168 634), respectively, even though the same money had already been paid to the Bank of Crete. Koskotas's three accomplices, who conspired with him to forge Bank documents to cover his criminal trail in breach of their Bank's trust, were convicted by the three-member Criminal Court of Athens. The High Court of Greece subsequently quashed their appeal against conviction to the five-member Court of Appeals. The chartered accountant auditing the Bank of Crete at the critical Koskotas period was Anastasios Palliarakis. He was sentenced by the Greek justice system to 12.5 years in prison. Even before the Court's decision, the Greek Chartered Accountants Association dismissed him from its membership for inappropriate behaviour.

### 11.3.3.3  What Happened to Koskotas?

On 16 March 2001, George Koskotas was released from prison on parole, after serving 12 years of a 25-year sentence for a plethora of felonies as CEO of the Bank of Crete, including embezzlement to the tune of $US 206 million, forgery and obstructing the course of justice. A mitigating factor taken into account by the five-member Court of Appeal imposing the sentence was the defendant's remorse. He had fled to the United States, was arrested in Massachusetts on 23 November 1988, and was held in custody there until he was extradited to Greece in 1991 to face trial. The trial, conducted by a Special Court that consisted of 13 Justices of the Supreme Court of Greece ['Arios Pagos'], lasted 10 months and has been called the 'trial of trials' and the most significant since the trial in 1922 of some of the protagonists of Greece's national catastrophe in Asia Minor (Tzifras, 2001, p. 10).

## 11.4 THE AFTERMATH

In ancient Greek theatre, tragic events are always followed with 'catharsis',[10] that is, cleansing is established and things get back to normal either with the help of the gods or with the victory of virtue over evil or with the institution of law and order. The aftermath of the scandals discussed here could not have been more different. Catharsis followed each scandal under the full investigation, although the fate of the protagonists varied in each case from receiving monetary fines (Natasha Bougatioti) to becoming a fugitive (George Dimitriadis, Natasha Bougatioti), to serving terms in prison (G. Koskotas, S. Stefanatos, G. Smbarouni, D. Fragkodimitropoulos, A. Palliarakis) or at the extreme, to committing suicide (Babis Maniotis).

The scandals described earlier had a twofold character: they involved creative accounting, fraud or alleged fraud. In all cases, the masterminds had the help of associates and especially company accountants and even chartered accountants. In fact, even the presence of well-written audit reports by internationally known auditors (such as Grant Thornton), as with ETBA Finance, was not enough to change the course of a scandal. Only when the Capital Market Commission became involved, did its investigations reveal the real story, although most often such investigations were conducted ex post when the damage to shareholders, employees and creditors had already taken place. Yet, very often those fined by the Capital Market Commission succeed in having such fines reduced or even dropped when contested in the court. One reason for that is that the Capital Market Commission lacks the uncontested authority on imposing fines much like other Commissions do (e.g. the US Security and Exchange Commission).

The aftermath of the small-scale scandals mainly affected the person(s) involved: the shareholders and the employees most of all. This was the case with Ipirotiki Software, where the owner committed suicide and the rest of the company was in limbo, with shareholders losing money and the company's assets under pressure from various interested parties. In the case of Sex Form, the main figure responsible for their scandal left the country and employees were unpaid and lost their jobs. In the case of ETBA Finance, five people were found guilty while the chartered accountant was stripped of his licence. The company was eventually absorbed by the Bank of Piraeus which acquired ETBA Bank, the parent company of ETBA Finance. Dynamic Life was another case whereby the owner left the

---

[10] A purifying or figurative cleansing of the emotions, especially pity and fear, described by Aristotle as an effect of tragic drama on its audience (see *The Free Dictionary*, Farlex, 2008, www.thefreedictionary.com/catharsis).

country as a fugitive and the company does not exist any more, leaving all franchisee gyms to operate on their own.

As expected, the aftermath of the Bank of Crete scandal was not as limited as in the other scandals just mentioned. It rocked the country, and its political life. The Koskotas financial scandal resulted in the resignation of a few government ministers and, eventually, in the fall of the socialist government in 1989. Prime Minister Andreas Papandreou himself was charged with a number of offences and on 27 September 1989 the Greek Parliament committed him to trial by a Special Court, as provided by Article 86 of the Greek Constitution, together with his Deputy Premier Agamemnon Koutsogiorgas and ex-ministers Dimitri Tsovolas, George Petsos and Panagiotis Roumeliotis. The trial commenced on 11 March 1991. The Court was in session 42 times and a total of 199 witnesses testified. Papandreou was acquitted on 17 January 1992 by a majority decision (seven Justices in favour, six against). The deciding vote was that of Justice Parmenion Tzifras, the most senior of the Justices who comprised the Special Court constituted by the Greek Parliament to try the Prime Minister. The rationale of the majority decision was articulated in 20 pages and that of the minority in 152 (for the rationale of the latter see Demetriou, 1996, p. 14).

Law 2298 of 1995 was enacted in an attempt to, *inter alia*, limit the fallout for the socialist government from the Koskotas scandal. In other words, the legislation was passed in order to put an end to any 'outstanding' cases emanating from the scandal, in breach of Art. 4 (para. 4) of the Greek Constitution (Demitzakis, 1999). However, the High Court was of the view that while Parliament had decided not to allow the prosecution of politicians involved in the Koskotas scandal, it did not apply to non-politicians like Koskotas and his accomplices.

Since the Koskotas scandal many things have changed. First of all, the information systems run by the banks have been modernized and information between branches and central offices is online, each entry must now balance in the entire system, and banking supervision is stricter and more effective so that the former infrastructure does not exist for a scandal like that of Koskotas to recur. As is the practice in EU Member States, Greek banks and all companies listed in the Athens Stock Exchange adhere to International Financial Reporting Standards and a mandatory code of corporate governance, and must have an internal auditor who reports to the audit committee made up of members of the board of directors. The corporate governance code was made mandatory in 2002 after a voluntary code published in 1999, the Principles of Corporate Governance, was not complied with. While there was no special law emanating from the Koskotas scandal, the Association of Chartered Accountants had issued a Directive that required special attention to be paid in the case of outstanding balances in inter-branch accounts. Also, because of the Bank of Crete scandal it became obvious that changes needed to be made in the auditing profession: new auditing firms were created along with the Accounting Standardization Committee, a public body that ensures the quality of the auditing reports in Greece and takes disciplinary action against those chartered accountants who do not serve the profession well.

Of particular interest to the accounting profession are some new measures that were introduced in Greece to limit the scope for creative accounting. Baralexis (2004) mentions that annual depreciation charges were made compulsory in 2000, while the law no longer permits additional depreciation charges and, finally, Article 38 of Law 2873/2000 provides that starting in 2000, an accountant in Greece is now responsible for the financial statements signed by him (p. 454). Furthermore, since January 2006 companies listed in EU Member States have to comply with IFRS, thus limiting the scope for creative accounting in Greece as the IFRS are stricter than local accounting standards. Finally, the Bank of Crete that shot to fame, or perhaps infamy, thanks to Koskotas was eventually privatized and merged into other banking institutions in Greece (www.//wiki.phantis.com/index.php/Bank_of_Crete/).

In the aftermath of the scandals, one interesting development that should be mentioned is the institution of Presidential Decree 340/1998 that regards a chief accountant of a company as co-responsible with its CEO. Until this law, accountants were considered as employees and the responsibility of their actions rested with the CEO of the company.

## 11.5 CONCLUSIONS

In this chapter some of the most important accounting and fraud scandals in the last two decades in Greece have been presented. The cases include: a finance company, an accounting software company, an underwear clothier, a health club chain and for Greece the mega scandal of all time, the Bank of Crete. All the facts presented here refer to cases that have already been investigated with a verdict having been reached by the courts or the Capital Market Commission.

In most scandals, it was fraud that made the central figures conceal their wrongdoings, always with the help of associates and in some cases with the great tolerance of the chartered accountants whose certificates gave the companies clean bills of health.

Monetary fines were imposed on all individuals involved after the authorities concluded their investigations. To avoid trial, one owner committed suicide, two became fugitives and Koskotas, the main figure in the Bank of Crete scandal, served a 12-year prison term in the United States and Greece. One may argue that it was pure luck that only the Koskotas scandal took place at that time. The inadequate information system in the banking sector at a time of economic growth could have allowed a similar type of scandal in any other bank.

While specific laws have not been enacted in the aftermath of the scandals, financial reporting is now more trustworthy since accountants are responsible for the statements they sign, reporting follows IFRS, mandatory corporate governance has been introduced, and internal auditors and audit committees are in place to serve shareholders' interests. All these measures, along with the supervision of the Capital Market Commission, are likely to limit the scope for creative accounting and accounting fraud in Greece. However, whether the stated aim has been achieved remains to be seen, and future empirical research of the kind reported by Baralexis (2004) could provide some answers. After all, scandals emerge not only from a lack of proper legislation but also from a socio-politico-economic environment that tolerates lower standards when applying the law. This tolerance may be blamed for the fact that accounting scandals in Greece are ongoing.

## REFERENCES

(For convenience, titles of articles written in Greek have been translated into English.)

Baralexis, S. (2004), 'Creative accounting in small advancing countries', *Management Auditing Journal*, **19**(3), 440–461.

Capital Market Commission (2006), *Decision on Technical Olympic*, 377/5.4.2006 (in Greek).

Cimilluca, D. (2008), 'Who are you Jerome Kerviel?' *Deal Journal – The Wall Street Journal*, 24/1/2008, http://blogs.wsj.com/deals/2008/01/24/who-are-you-jerome-kerviel/?mod= homeblogmod_dealjournal.

Demetriou, M. (1996), 'Why did we vote K?' *Eleftheros Typos*, 12 February, pp. 14–15 (in Greek).

Dermitzakis, S. (1999), II Penal Code. Special Section (Embezzlement) AP. 899/1999 Vol. E, 1220, *Pinika*, Vol. 12 (Year 2), Nomologia, pp. 1220–1225 (in Greek).

*Eleftheros Typos* (2000), 14 January (in Greek).

Grant Thornton (1998), *Audit Report for ETBA Finance* (in Greek).

Greek Body of Certified Public Accountants, Professional Code of Conduct of Members of the Body of Certified Public Accountants (in Greek).

*Imerisia* (2005), 'Investors against the management of Dynamic Life', 4 January (in Greek).

*Imerisia* (2005), 'Dynamic life under the microscope', 13 January (in Greek).

*Imerisia* (2005), 'The big trick of Dynamic Life', 16 January (in Greek).

*Kathimerini* (2002a), 'ETBA under persecution', 4 January (in Greek).

*Kathimerini* (2002b), 'Since 1998 Grant Thornton rang the bell for ETBA Finance', 2 April (in Greek).

Kourakis, N. (2001), 'Economic crime in Greece today', in *Economic Crimes in Cyprus: A Multi-Disciplinary Approach*, eds M. Krambia-Kapardis, A. Kapardis and N. Kourakis, A.N. Sakkoulas Publishers, Athens, pp. 323–353 (in Greek).

Naftemporiki (2006), 'A big fine on Technical Olympic', 5 April (in Greek).

Papakyrillou G. (2006), *Economic Scandals in the Last Twenty Years in Greece and the Role of Auditing*, Master's Thesis, Athens University of Economics and Business (in Greek).

TA NEA (19/5/1999), p. 51 (in Greek).

TO VIMA (26/1/2000), p. B5 (in Greek).

Tzifras, P. (2001), *My Acquitting Vote for Andreas Papandreou*, Livanis-Nea Sinora, Athens (in Greek).

www.ase.gr, *Athens Stock Exchange Company Notifications*, 04/04/2005.

www.euro2day.gr, 14/04/2005, *Sex Form: A Family Change of Guard* (in Greek).

www.presspoint.gr, *Notification on Ipirotiki Software and Publications S.A.* (in Greek).

www.xrhmatistirio.gr, *Lawsuit against BoD of Sex Form* (in Greek).

## 12

# Corporate Creative Accounting in India: Extent and Consequences

Bhabatosh Banerjee

Gain all you can
But not at the expense of your conscience.
John Wesley[1]

## 12.1 INTRODUCTION

India started liberalising its economy in 1991 and since then a number of measures have been adopted by the federal and state governments to make India a key player in the global market.[2] A notable feature of the current growth phase is the sharp rise in the rate of investment in the economy.[3] Over recent years, India has developed its corporate sector, stock markets and accounting profession (Banerjee, 2005). The growing importance of the corporate sector calls for its efficient working and greater transparency (about 34 000 new companies are added annually). However, the prevalence of creative accounting and fraud in Indian companies hinders this.

The Indian regulatory environment comprises five parts. First, the Companies Act, modelled on the British Companies Act, lays down provisions regarding company formation, capitalisation, accountability, mandatory reporting, audit, liquidation, etc. (Banerjee, 2002; Das Gupta, 1977). Second, the Ministry of Corporate Affairs (MCA), Government of India (www.dca.nic.in), is responsible for the collection, compilation, maintenance and dissemination of basic statistics on the Indian corporate sector. Registered companies are required to file certain documents and returns under the provisions of the Companies Act, 1956. The most important of these are the annual reports, company balance sheets and returns on share capital. Third, the Institute of Chartered Accountants of India (ICAI) issues accounting standards for measurement and reporting of financial data by companies (www.icai.org). Compliance is checked through the audit of accounts by the members of the Institute. Fourth, the Securities and Exchange Board of India (SEBI) is empowered to regulate the capital markets and protect the interests of the investors (www.sebi.gov.in). Fifth, there are

---

[1] Quoted from John Hancock (ed.), *Investing in CSR*, Kogan Page, 2005, p. 2.
[2] The growth rate in GDP in 2006–7 was 9.6 %.
[3] In 2005–6, it was 33.8 % (Government of India, *Economic Survey*, 2006–7).

regulatory mechanisms to control the accounting profession (e.g. the Companies Act, 1956 and the Rules of Conduct laid down by the ICAI).

In spite of all these checks and balances, there have been a number of accounting scandals since the 1980s. Firms adopt accounting procedures that minimise unfavourable economic effects and enhance favourable ones. Such creative accounting is attributed to the flexibility provided by the accounting system (Mulford and Comiskey, 2002). The accounting system in Anglo-Saxon countries has been designed to be flexible enough to accommodate a variety of situations and present them 'fairly' in the accounts (Coopers and Lybrand, 1993). In India, the Companies Act (section 211) requires that accounts must be 'true and fair'. Sometimes, however, management abuses the freedom of choice in the accounting system. Methods are adopted to hide the true picture, and show an improved performance of the firm.

The main objective of the present chapter is to examine the extent and consequences of creative accounting in India since 1980. The chapter also examines to what extent constraints on creative accounting, both internal and external, could work and the reasons for any failure. This study is exploratory in nature. This chapter is based not only on published articles and books, but also on press releases and newspaper reports.

The rest of the chapter is designed as follows: the next section deals with a few cases of creative accounting in India. This is followed in the third section by reference only to a few high-profile cases, viz. JVG, The Unit Trust of India (Lakshminarayan, 2003) and the Global Trust Bank (Jaganathan, 2003) where legal cases have been pending. However, Satyam Computer Services Pvt. Ltd is covered in detail because a confessional statement was made to the media on 7 January, 2009 by its promoter (i.e. the person in overall charge of a company)-chairman. The Satyam case is the latest and the largest scandal in the corporate sector in India. We then examine the aftermath of the scandals, before a summary and conclusions are given in the last section.

## 12.2 SOME EXAMPLES OF CREATIVE ACCOUNTING IN INDIA

Company management may adopt methods to dress up financial statements to show improved performance. Accounting risk may be different for different financial statements. In respect of the profit and loss account, the accounting risk is usually the overstatement of income and understatement of expenses. For the balance sheet, it may exist in three areas: the correct valuation of the company's assets, accounting for all liabilities, and over- or understatement of net worth.

Accounting methods can have a significant impact on the balance sheet valuations of an asset. Valuation methods for stocks, choice of depreciation method and decisions on the capitalisation of expenses related to fixed assets can affect reported profits. The effect of creative accounting may thus defeat the very purpose of presentation of 'true and fair' financial statements. It should be stressed that these companies have done nothing illegal but merely used the flexibility permitted by Indian law to present their view of their companies' financial statements.

Some examples of creative accounting (Global Data Services of India Ltd, 2006) are given below from 1994–95 to 2004–5. Table 12.1 contains the names of the companies,

**Table 12.1** Impact on profit due to changes in policies, methods of stock valuation or depreciation, etc.

| Company | Years | Nature of transaction | Impact on financial statements |
|---|---|---|---|
| WIPRO Ltd | 1996–97 to 1999–2000 | Transfer of land to stock creating capital reserve with the fair value and using it to neutralise the effect on profit of reduction of land value. | In 1994–95, Wipro Ltd, one of the successful companies in the IT sector, transferred land of Rs.197 million from fixed assets to current assets, pending its sale. The asset was transferred at the fair market value of Rs.4500 million and the surplus of Rs.4303 million was transferred to capital reserve.[4] In subsequent years (1996–97 to 1999–2000), reduction in the value of land was charged to the profit and loss account and an equivalent amount was withdrawn from the capital reserve to offset the impact on the profit and loss account. |
| Bombay Dyeing and Manufacturing Company | 2003–4 and 2004–5 | Creating provisions for possible loss on firm purchase contract and subsequent write-back of such provision thereby converting operating losses into operating profit. | In 2003–4, the company had entered into a firm purchase contract for the import of raw materials (paraxylene). On conversion of this raw material into its finished product (viz. DMT), it was expected that the net realisable value would be substantially lower than cost, compared with reference to estimated selling price of DMT. Accordingly, a provision for the loss was made in the accounts.<br><br>This was reversed in 2004–5. The reversal in the profit and loss account formed nearly 25 % of the reported profit after tax for 2004–5. |
| Larsen & Toubro Ltd | 1999–2000 and 2001–2 | Income recognition through transfer of loan liabilities at a lower consideration. | In 1999–2000 and 2001–2, Larsen and Toubro (L&T) assigned some of its outstanding debt to one of its subsidiaries and reported the difference between the outstanding loan amount and the transfer value as 'income' in its profit and loss account with a note to accounts. L&T continued to show this amount under 'contingent liability'. |

*(Continued)*

---

[4] In order for readers to gain some idea of the scale of the currency charges: 1 pound = INR 80.5; 1 USD = INR 44 (as at June 2004).

**Table 12.1** Impact on profit due to changes in policies, methods of stock valuation or depreciation, etc. (*Continued*)

| Company | Years | Nature of transaction | Impact on financial statements |
|---|---|---|---|
| Apollo Tyres Ltd | 2004–5 | Debiting profit and loss account with additional excise duty payable to the government and transferring equivalent amount from general reserve to neutralise the effect. | The company charged additional excise duty refundable to the Government of India and interest thereon aggregating to Rs.320.85 million (net of tax, Rs.140.81 million) to the profit and loss account and transferred an equivalent amount to the profit and loss account from the general reserve resulting in nil impact on the profit for the year. Had the charge not been set off against transfer from general reserve (a) the profit for the year after tax would have been lower by Rs.320.85 million with a corresponding increase in general reserve and (b) earnings per share would have been Rs.9.07 against Rs.17.64, as shown in the financial statements. |
| Asian Electronics Ltd | 2004–5 | Impairment of assets: treatment of deferred tax. | In 2004–5, Asian Electronics Ltd recognised impairment on fixed assets and capital work in progress. This impairment of Rs.170.09 million was deducted from the general reserve. If this had been expensed in the profit and loss account, the company would have reported a loss of Rs.60.32 million as against a reported profit of Rs.100.78 million. While the expense was deducted from reserves, a deferred tax asset of Rs.61.31 million created on impairment was credited to the profit and loss account, leading to an increase in profit by the same amount. |
| Oil & Natural Gas Commission, Mukund Ltd, Torrent Power AEC Ltd and Tata Motors Ltd | 2004–5 | Capitalisation of interest as well as other intangible assets to show fixed assets value upward and understating revenue expenses. | These companies had capitalised the interest on loans as well as other intangible assets and then written off the same through depreciation over the life of the asset. Since the life of the fixed asset is generally longer than the duration of the loan, the annual write-off works out lower than normal interest write-off and hence profits were overstated. |

| Company | Year | Practice | Description |
| --- | --- | --- | --- |
| Hindustan Zinc Ltd | 2003–4 and 2004–5 | Reclassifying assets in the balance sheet. | Hindustan Zinc Ltd's marketable investments represented an investment of Rs.6193.3 million in mutual funds as at 31 March 2004 and Rs.687.90 million as at 31 March 2005. Apart from those marketable securities, the company invested Rs.830.4 million in shares of Andhra Pradesh Gas Power Corporation Ltd. This investment entitles the company to draw power in Andhra Pradesh from its Vishakapatnam unit. The investment was made in the year 2000–1 and was disclosed as an investment. However, the company changed the classification of these investments to intangible assets from the year 2003. |
| Tata Motors, Bombay Dyeing, Mahindra and Himachal Futuristic | 2001–2 | Direct write-offs from reserves | In the accounts for the year ended 31 March 2002, companies like Tata Motors, Bombay Dyeing, Mahindra and Mahindra wrote off large amounts of miscellaneous expenditure and other forms of direct deferred expenditure directly through securities premium accounts with the approval of the High Court as part of 'financial restructuring'. There is specific provision in sections 78 and 100 of the Companies Act regarding 'application of securities premium' and 'reduction of share capital', respectively. In the above cases, annual write-offs in the profit and loss account have been avoided to show a significant increase in the subsequent years' profits, other things remaining constant.<br><br>In subsequent years (from 2002–3 to 2004–5), many more companies made similar write-offs and some, without High Court approval. The more worrying trend is that the companies which undertook 'financial restructuring' in 2001–2 have continued to make direct write-offs in subsequent years as well.<br><br>Himachal Futuristic Communications Ltd wrote off 'goodwill on acquisition' directly from reserves in the year 2002–3 instead of amortising through the profit and loss account. The amount of goodwill written off directly from the reserves constituted about 50 % of its reserves and surplus. |

nature of the transaction and financial year, and the impact of the transactions on the financial statements. Some comments indicating how rules and regulations were bent without being broken in each of the above cases now follow.

Wipro Ltd had converted fixed assets to stock. As the conversion was made at market price, not cost, the difference was credited to reserves, improving the net worth per share and current ratio. The actual sale of the land took place after five years from the date of conversion, which means they held the stocks for a considerable period. Thus, the company subtly bent the requirements of AS 10. Further, the requirements of AS 2 on 'inventories' have not been followed in spirit. The 'cost or net realisable value whichever is lower' principle was flouted by drawing an amount equivalent to the loss arising out of reduction in value of stock from the capital reserve account created at the time of conversion. Even in the year of sale, the remaining amount of capital reserve was written back by crediting the value of opening inventories. In effect, the capital reserve was treated as the revaluation reserve.

In the case of Bombay Dyeing and Manufacturing Company, it may be stated that making of the provision itself was debatable in view of the fact that production was yet to take place using those raw materials and creation of such provision was to take care of a *notional loss*. Accounting based on an uncertain future allowed the company to move profits back and forth, from one year to another. This practice defeated the purpose of preparing periodical financial statements.

Larsen & Toubro Ltd had transferred some of its loan liabilities to one of its subsidiaries and reported the difference between the loan amount and transfer value as 'income'. This was thus a related-party transaction. This is not conventionally regarded as income and so may be classified as creative. It is interesting to note that the company remained contingently liable for the repayment of such a loan. There is a problem in accepting such a practice. First, it is an income recognised through exchange between the holding company and the subsidiary. Second, if the subsidiary fails to repay the loan, the burden would fall on the holding company. Consequently, there may be a problem of maintenance of capital if a subsidiary's financial position is not good and it fails to honour its commitments. Third, the holding company may have paid dividends out of such profits.

The treatment of additional excise duty in the case of Apollo Tyres Ltd amounted to bending GAAP. There should have been no transfer from general reserves. The auditors accordingly qualified the accounts.

In respect of Asian Electronics Ltd, it should be stated that accounting standards in India require companies to carry productive assets at the lower of fair value and cost price in their accounts from 2004–5. AS 28 (effective from 1 April 2004) requires impairment to be recognised as an expense in the income statement which ultimately reflects the net worth. Any impairment loss arising after 1 April 2004 should be recognised in the profit and loss account unless an asset is carried at a revalued amount. An impairment loss on a revalued asset should be treated as a revaluation decrease. Asian Electronics, however, deducted the impairment loss from reserves rather than from the profit and loss account. In addition, the company did not comply with AS 28 regarding treatment of deferred tax and auditors qualified the accounting treatment for deferred tax on impairment. In effect, the company creatively credited the deferred tax asset to the profit and loss account, but took the related impairment to reserves.

The practice followed by Oil & Natural Gas Commission, Mukund Ltd, Torrent Power AEC Ltd and Tata Motors Ltd of capitalising interest as well as other intangible assets and writing off the same interest through depreciation over the life of the asset is questionable. The important question is: should the value of an asset be dependent on its source of finance?

In the case of Hindustan Zinc Ltd (HZL), it may be stated that, conceptually, the share-holding should be treated as 'investment' if it was a financial asset that was not subject to any condition regarding its disposal. In this case, Hindustan Zinc Ltd was free to divest its holding in Andhra Pradesh Gas Power (APGP) Corporation Ltd and yet retain all its rights to draw power. It, therefore, should be treated as investment instead of an intangible asset. HZL had treated its investment in shares of APGP Corporation as an intangible asset instead of as an investment. Hence, it was a case of creative accounting. There was, therefore, no need to reclassify the investment as an intangible asset. The motive behind such reclassification might be to avoid the requirements of providing for losses in the value of investment as provided in AS 13. The company did not comply with the provision of AS 13. The auditors qualified the accounts for the years 2002–3, 2003–4 and 2004–5 in respect of the investments disclosed by the company as intangible assets.

Accounting Standard 14, dealing with amalgamations and mergers, specifies that good-will arising on acquisition should be amortised to income on a systematic basis over its useful life but not exceeding five years unless a longer period can be justified. Thus, in the case of Tata Motors, Bombay Dyeing, Mahindra and Himachal Futuristic, by writing off the goodwill directly through reserves, reported profits or losses were quite legally increased.

In short, it can be said that management of the firms could indulge in the above-mentioned practices because of flexibility in accounting standards and other regulatory provisions.

## 12.3 SOME IMPORTANT CORPORATE CASES IN INDIA

Creative accounting is a by-product of flexibility in the accounting system. However, when the regulatory system is lax, managers may indulge in manipulation by bending all sorts of regulatory requirements (Mulford and Comiskey, 2002). In India over recent years there have been several prominent cases where there have been suspicions that companies might have crossed that line. Three important cases have attracted media and regulatory attention. These cases are referred to below. However, it is important to stress that although legal cases are pending there have so far been no convictions for any improprieties.

(1) *The JVG Group of companies* – JVG Finance, JVG Leasing and JVG Securities *(1997–8)* – where investors lost their money and there were speculations that regulatory provisions were by-passed (icmr.icfai.org, ICMR FINC 007 ECCH 102-027-1).

(2) *The Unit Trust of India (1999–2003)*: The US 64 scheme of this public sector biggest mutual fund lost its significance and UTI was split into two separate entities – UTI Mutual Fund and Specified Undertaking of the Unit Trust of India (www.icmr.icfai.org, ICMR FINC 003:ECCH 102-0241-1). There was widespread speculation in the Indian press of improper reporting and financial mismanagement.

(3) *The Global Trust Bank (2000–5):* Global Trust Bank, a private sector bank, was forced to merge with Corporation Bank, a public sector bank, at the instance of the Government

of India to protect the interests of bank depositors, creditors and other stakeholders (icmr.icfai.org, ICMR FINC 004 ECCH 302-044-1).

The above three cases attracted media and government attention. Since there has been multiplicity of legal cases and many of them are pending due to a number of reasons, we refrain from dealing with them in this paper. However, the most recent case in point is Satyam Computer Services Ltd (started in January 2009). Since in this case the promoter-chairman, who is the prime accused, made a confessional statement, we deal with some aspects of this scandal in detail in the next section.

## 12.4 THE SATYAM COMPUTER SERVICES LTD SCANDAL (2009)

### 12.4.1 Background

On 7 January 2009, Mr B. Ramalinga Raju, chairman of Satyam Computer Services Ltd (hereinafter referred to as Satyam), admitted in a Press Conference in Hyderabad to a 'Rs.78 000 million' fraud weeks after a bid to acquire the two Maytas firms failed. He also admitted that he had been 'cooking the books of Satyam since 2001 to inflate profits and cash flows and the Maytas acquisition bid was an attempt to fill fictitious assets with real ones' *(The Statesman*, Kolkata, 8 January 2009, p. 1*)*. A glance at the reported and actual figures for the 2nd quarter ending 30 September 2008 will indicate the nature of the fraud (Table 12.2):

**Table 12.2**   Some reported and actual financial figures of Satyam for the 2nd quarter ending on 30 September 2008 (Rs./million)

| Particulars | Reported amount | Actual amount | Fictitious amount |
|---|---|---|---|
| Revenue | 27 000 | 21 120 | <u>5880</u> |
| Operating margin | 6490 | 610 | <u>5880</u> |
| Cash balance | 53 610 | 3210 | 50 400 |
| Debtors | 26 510 | 4900 | 21 610 |

*Source*: *The Statesman*, Kolkata, 8 January 2009, p. 1.

### 12.4.2 Satyam: A Global Organisation

Satyam, the fourth ranking company in the IT sector in India, was founded by Mr B. Ramalinga Raju on 24 June 1987 and Mr Raju, a graduate from Ohio University, became its founder chairman. Since inception the company had grown in terms of lines of business and subsidiaries and also in terms of accounting numbers. Over time, its services included: Application Services, BI & PM, BPO, Business Value Enhancement, Consulting and Enterprise Solutions, MES and LIMS, Oracle Solutions, Product and Application Testing, Product Life Cycle Management, SAP Solutions, Six Sigma Consulting, Supplier Relationship Management, and Supply Chain Management. In the process, it invested in various subsidiaries like Satyam BPO, Citisoft, CA Satyam, SFI China, and Bridge Consultancy.

**Table 12.3**    Operating performance of Satyam (Rs./million)

| Particulars | Financial Year End | | | | | Average growth rate (%) |
|---|---|---|---|---|---|---|
| | 2003–04 | 2004–05 | 2005–06 | 2006–07 | 2007–08 | |
| Net Sales | 25 415.4 | 34 642.2 | 46 343.1 | 62 284.7 | 81 372.8 | 38 |
| Operating Profit | 7743 | 9717 | 15 714.2 | 17 107.3 | 20 857.4 | 28 |
| Net Profit | 5557.9 | 7502.6 | 12 397.5 | 14 232.3 | 17 157.4 | 33 |
| Operating Cash Flow | 4165.5 | 6386.6 | 7868.1 | 10 390.6 | 13 708.7 | 35 |
| ROCE (%) | 27.95 | 29.85 | 31.34 | 31.18 | 29.57 | 30 |
| ROE (%) | 23.57 | 25.88 | 26.85 | 28.14 | 26.12 | 26 |

*Source*: www.geogit.com

Mr Raju also formed two companies – Maytas Properties and Maytas Infrastructure – in the names of his family members.

In its annual report (2008), it is mentioned, *inter alia*, that this global organisation has more than 51 000 associates covering 60 nationalities, has revenue in US$ exceeding 200 million, has more than 654 customers including one-third of the Fortune Global & US 500 companies, and operates in 63 countries and 31 global solution centres. Its shares are listed on NYSE, US & Euronext, Amsterdam, Europe, BSE and NSE.

In financial terms, Satyam displayed, in its reported statements, spectacular results in all key operating parameters (Table 12.3).

Despite the company's reported best performance on all fronts, this was not reflected in its share price performance (Mr Krishna Pelepu, Director, reported to have observed in the Audit Committee Meeting held on 17 October, 2008). He advised a review to see 'if the company is lacking in communication front to the market' (*The Statesman*, Kolkata, 18 January 2009).

Some distress signals came to light at the end of 2008. For a month or so, the company had been in the news for all the wrong reasons. For example, the acquisition of Maytas Infrastructure and Maytas Properties (real estate companies promoted by Raju's sons) was postponed in the face of stiff resistance from the shareholders, resignations of four non-executive and independent directors, etc. But no one ever suspected that a fraud of this scale would take place in a concern which had won so many laurels for itself and for the country as a whole.

As the promoter of the company, Mr Raju, admitted that he had been cooking the books since 2001, on 14 January, the new board[5] appointed Deloitte and KPMG 'to assist the Board in the *restatement* of financial numbers of Satyam'.

### 12.4.3 Alleged Possible Processes and their Impact

The most important question is: how could this scandal happen in the Indian corporate sector in spite of checks and balances in the regulatory system? The alleged

---

[5] Within a few days of the confession of fraudulent practices by Mr Raju, the Government of India superseded the Board and appointed a new board of directors.

processes were:

- 'Cooking the books of accounts' – window-dressing, fudging or creative and fraudulent accounting (Mr Raju himself admitted this in a press conference);
- Information asymmetry – insider trading;
- Corporate misgovernance.

What is the possible impact of the scandal? Apart from the amount of Rs.78 000 million, to which Mr Raju confessed, there are many other aspects of the scandal viz.

- Promoters' holding went down from 25.6% (31.3.01) to 8.79% (31.3.06) to 3.6% (6.1.09). There is speculation that Raju made money by off-loading shares.
- Share price plunged 77.6% on the Bombay Stock Exchange to close at Rs.39.95 as of 6 January 2009 (Rs.100000 m estimated loss in market cap). On the NYSE Satyam's share price plunged by over 90% to $0.85. So, millions of shareholders in India and abroad lost their money.
- Uncertain fate of the employees (53 000 less a number of fake employees);
- Bond money (i.e. deposits against contractual non-fulfillment) of 10 000 new employees at stake;
- Huge loss to the economy including loss to the exchequer;
- Threatened to damage India's image as one of the important outsourcing hubs of the world, and
- Hurt FDI flows into Asia's third largest economy.

The country's largest ever corporate fraud is akin to the energy giant Enron case in the US in 2001 (Reuters, 7 January 2009). The revelation shocked India Inc., Indian capital markets, regulators and the auditing profession across the world. At a time when the country was struggling with the impact of the world economic crisis and the stock markets were recovering slowly, the timing could not have been worse. Some consider it as a system failure, others are of the view that it is nothing but an isolated case. Consider the following two important views on the subject.

Dr Manmohan Singh, Prime Minister of India, while addressing the captains of industry in the CII's meeting at Mumbai on 18 February 2009, observed as follows:

> The Satyam episode is a blot on our corporate image. It indicates how far malfeasance in one company can inflict suffering on many and also tarnish India's image.

In an editorial in *The Chartered Accountant* (February, 2009), the editor made the following observations:

> Although the Satyam episode is not a system failure and an aberration, still, it poses a danger of domestic and overseas investors losing confidence in Indian corporate governance and related oversight mechanisms.

### 12.4.4 Good Guy, Bad Choices[6]

In the history of corporate scandal it is not difficult to find a disgraced person like Mr Raju. In July 2005, the former chief executive, Mr Bernard J. Ebbers of WorldCom, whose $11b fraud dumped the telecommunication company into bankruptcy (Weston *et al.*, 2008*)*, was sentenced to serve 25 years in prison. The former financial chief officer of the company, Scott Sullivan, who pleaded guilty and testified against his former boss, told the jury that he had warned Ebbers that accounting adjustments, creative accounting or cooking the books could not be justified. But Ebbers told him to achieve the financial revenue targets by any means. Wall Street analysts and financial journalists went along with the web of lies woven by the WorldCom team until the whole edifice began to collapse in 2000, and the share price crashed.

It seems that Satyam was re-enacting the WorldCom play. 'A circus man riding a tiger may be fun to watch but not when a company CEO does it' (Batra, 2009).

### 12.4.5 Role of the Auditors

PricewaterhouseCoopers (PwC), a global name, was the auditor of Satyam from June 2000 to September 2008. PwC operates in 150 countries employing 155 000 people with the job of channelling knowledge and value through their lines of service and 22 industry specialised practices. The website of PwC (www.PwC.com) describes its functions and objectives as follows:

> Our Global Annual Review details how our industry-focused *services in the fields of assurance, tax, human resources, transactions, performance improvement and crisis management* have helped address client and stakeholder issues. Our success in meeting today's business challenges rests on the way we approach our work. We call that approach *Connected Thinking*.
>
> Sound governance and transparency form the bedrock of leadership. We are committed to serving as a force for integrity, good sense and wise solutions to the problems facing businesses and the capital markets today. Transparency and good standards of corporate governance – both in our clients' businesses and in our own – are central to our ability to achieve those objectives. And we aim to continue to achieve them from our position of strength and professional leadership.

As against the above, let us now examine the role of the auditor in the Satyam scandal. Mr Srinivas Talluri, Partner, signed the audited accounts on 21 April 2008. On Mr Raju's admission that books of accounts were cooked to inflate profits and cash flows and PwC's contention that it found nothing wrong in auditing the books of accounts of Satyam, the role of the auditor came to the surface and the Institute of Chartered Accountants of India issued a show cause notice to PwC on 10 January and asked it to reply within 21 days. The case is pending with the Institute.

While Raju in his statement to the board and the SEBI disclosed that he was quitting because of the failure in bridging the gap between fictitious and real assets, the auditor's report said that the company was maintaining proper records (www.business-beacon.com).

---

[6] Mr Barack Obama, while making comments on the policies and actions of former US President, George Bush, a few days before his swearing-in ceremony as the US President.

**Table 12.4**  Satyam's total income and audit fees (Rs./million)

| Year | 2004–5 | 2005–6 | 2006–7 | 2007–8 |
|---|---|---|---|---|
| Total Income (A) | 35 468 | 50 122.2 | 64 100.8 | 83 944.8 |
| Audit Fees (B) | 6.537 | 11.5 | 36.7 | 37.3 |
| % of B to A | 0.0184 | 0.0229 | 0.0573 | 0.0444 |

*Source*: Annual Reports. Percentage computed.

Interestingly, the auditor 'found no significant risks and exposures during its audit of the financial statements for the quarter ended September 30, 2008', as per the Minutes of the Audit Committee dated 17 October 2008. The auditor also noted that 'there have been no disagreements with management and their audit is designed to obtain reasonable assurance that the *financial statements are fairly stated*'. (*The Statesman*, Kolkata, 18 January).

A spokesperson of PwC defended the audit report on 11 January in the following words:

> We have neither come across any instance of fraud on or by the company, noticed or reported during the year, nor have we been informed of such case by the management.—Mr Srinivas Talluri (*The Statesman*, Kolkata, 12 January).

But on 14 January PwC said its audit of the IT company's financials could be 'inaccurate and unreliable' in view of the financial irregularities disclosed by Mr Raju. It also said in a letter to the newly constituted board that PwC would like to work with the company and 'provide assistance to the new board of directors to address any issues that arise in the course of such investigations . . .'

A point has also been raised about the increase in audit fee. A reference to the figures of audit fee in comparison with total income over a period of time may be pertinent (Table 12.4).

Table 12.4 shows that over a period of four years, 2004–5 to 2007–8, audit fee increased by 5.7 times whereas total income increased by 2.47 times during the same period. Nevertheless, it is difficult to draw any conclusion at this point as to whether the increase in audit fee was justified or not.

Another important question in this case is: was the auditor, PwC, guilty of professional misconduct? Since the case is under consideration by the Institute of Chartered Accountants of India (ICAI) and in many other forums, it is difficult to jump to any hasty conclusion.

The provisions for professional misconduct are contained in Part I of the Second Schedule to the Chartered Accountants Act 1949, and Chartered Accountants Regulations 1988. If the Council of the Institute *prima facie* is of the opinion that the auditor concerned is guilty of professional and/or other misconduct, the case is referred to the Institute's disciplinary committee for enquiry. Next the disciplinary committee's findings go to the Council. The Council then gives its verdict after giving the respondent/accused an opportunity of being heard. Finally, the matter has to go to the High Court, having jurisdiction in the matter, for review. The entire process followed in the Institute is quasi-judicial.

In relation to timeliness, a reference to one of the earlier cases also involving PwC may be made. In the Global Trust Bank (GTB) case (2000–5), some questions arose regarding the audit of the financial position of the bank for the year 2002–3. The financial results of GTB were not properly reported. The auditors, PwC, were under investigation for professional misconduct. The Council of ICAI very recently held two Indian audit partners of PwC 'guilty of audit negligence' (Bloomberg UTV) and the case is now (at the time of writing, May 2010, pending before the Bombay High Court). The Parliamentary Committee, formed to probe the case and recommend measures, criticised both RBI and ICAI for failure to take action against the auditors (www.parliamentofIndia.nic.in).

### 12.4.6 Institution of Legal Proceedings

In this extraordinary case, Mr B. Ramalinga Raju, chairman, Raju's brother and managing director, Mr B. Rama Raju, were arrested on 9 January 2009. Mr Vadlamani, chief finance officer, was arrested on 10 January 2009. All the three accused have been booked under various sections of the Indian Penal Code for criminal conspiracy (sec. 120-B), criminal breach of trust (sec. 406), cheating (sec. 420), forgery (sec. 468) and showing forged documents as genuine (sec. 471). It is important to mention that none of the accused except Mr B. Ramalinga Raju have admitted their guilt. Mr B Ramalinga Raju's bail petition was rejected by the Andhra Pradesh High Court and the Supreme Court of India on 19 February and 15 March 2010 respectively (http://thehindubusinessline.com and timesofindia.indiatimes.com).

On 24 January, two of the partners of PwC, Mr S Gopalakrishnan (chief relationship partner) and Mr S. Talluri (engagement leader) were arrested by Andhra Pradesh Police and 'slapped with charges of cheating, forgery, criminal breach of trust and criminal conspiracy' (*The Statesman*, Kolkata, 25 January 2009). It may be stated that in India giving a misleading or defective audit report amounts to a criminal offence. The statutory auditor, Mr Telluri Srinivas, was however granted bail by the Supreme Court of India on 5 February 2010 (http://economic times.indiatimes.com).

There appears to be multiplicity of court cases and the legal battle is likely to continue for a long time.

### 12.4.7 Salvaging Satyam

Should Satyam be allowed to fail? There was no difference of opinion regarding the brand image created by Satyam. Therefore, we quote two views in favour of salvaging Satyam:

> 'No one has questioned the quality of products and services that Satyam provides to the corporate global. Its intellectual and technical foundation is strong' (Batra, 2009).
> 'Satyam has a value; it has intellectual property rights; it has trained manpower and world's good clients' (Prem Chand Gupta, Union Corporate Affairs Minister, 19 January 2009).

The Department of Company Affairs and other regulatory bodies handled the survival issue very carefully and finally allowed it to be taken over by another company based on competitive bids. The present status (www.ndtv.com; 14 April 2009) of Satyam may be summarised in brief:

- Months-long speculation came to an end with the announcement of the highest bidder for Satyam. The highest three bidders were Tech Mahindra (Rs.58 per share), L&T (Rs.46) and WL Ross (Rs.20). [Spice Corpn, IBM and iGate had earlier withdrawn from the race.]
- Tech Mahindra, an M&M-promoted company, would pay Rs.17 570 million for 31% stake.
- The Satyam board selected Venturbay Consultants, a subsidiary of Tech Mahindra, to acquire the controlling stake subject to approval of the Company Law Board.
- Tech Mahindra will run Satyam as an independent company with separate liabilities. The new company is known as Mahindra Satyam Ltd (www.mahindrasatyam.net). A six-member board has been constituted with Mr C.P. Gurnani as CEO of Mahindra Satyam Ltd.

The next important issue is: what immediate measures need to be taken by the acquiring firm to bring the tainted IT company back to normal health? This is a critical issue and may involve opinions of all sorts. We, however, suggest the following:

- stricter management control and continuous monitoring by the regulatory bodies;
- restoring confidence of the stakeholders by good governance;
- the granting of working capital loans by public sector banks and financial institutions;
- focusing on the unexplored home market along with export markets;
- developing innovative services;
- enforcing strategic cost management in all of its value chain;
- the leadership issue however remains uppermost. For Satyam an honest, dedicated, exemplary CEO with a towering personality and vision is the most pressing necessity.

### 12.4.8 Rebuilding the Corporate Image

There is no doubt that the image of the corporate sector in India has been tarnished due to recent developments relating to Satyam. Therefore, the important task would be to rebuild the corporate image. How to achieve it? The most critical aspect would be to enforce the regulatory mechanism effectively and companies must comply with them in letter and spirit. Consider the following suggestions in this context:

- 'The industry captains should look closely into their operations to ensure that their systems are fully operational and fraudulent activities are effectively prevented. Actions of corporate leaders and management have reputational impact much beyond the reputation of the companies' (Prime Minister, 18 January at a meeting of the captains of Industry in Mumbai).
- To comply with Clause 49 of the Listing Agreement, they should adopt appropriate strategies at the company level. For example, to deter possible corporate frauds, many companies have started re-codifying their risk management policies.
- Nearly 90% (of 400 companies affiliated to ASSOCHAM) said that companies henceforth would spend enormous amounts of money, maybe 30% of their overhead expenses, on implementing and complying with Clause 49 of the Listing Agreement as these provided

for enough regulations to prevent corporate frauds (*The Statesman*, Kolkata, 12 January 2009).

### 12.4.9 Some Antidotes

Perhaps Satyam is an isolated case. Even then occurrence of such fraud speaks of the hollowness of the regulatory mechanism. Hence, efforts should be made to maintain the robustness of the regulatory system. The following are some of the suggestions:

- Ensure the robustness of the regulatory system as good governance is a *sine qua non* for healthy continuation.
- Maintain the independence of directors and auditors. For the latter, *inter alia*, introduce rotational audit and peer review.
- Speed up the legal and quasi-legal trials.
- Both internal and external auditors have to act as bloodhounds nosing for the curious smells (Chattopadhyay, 2008).
- Recognise and reward the efforts of the whistle-blowers.
- News media through investigative reporting should assume the role of outside auditors (Batra, 2009).

## 12.5 AFTERMATH

The examples given in the second section generally relate to creative accounting. However, an analysis of the three cases referred to on page 239, Section 12.3, will show that most of them, with the lone exception of Satyam, were stock market-related rather than resulting directly from fraudulent accounting although, in some form or another, dubious accounting and reporting were also involved in the process. In Satyam, the processes involved were fraudulent accounting practices, insider trading and alleged involvement of the promoter-chairman. These cases took place during the period 1985 to 2009 (e.g. JVG, 1997–98; UTI, 1999–2003; GTB, 2000–5 and Satyam Computer Services Ltd, 2009–). India started liberalising its economy in 1991 and many steps were taken to attract foreign capital, introduce reforms in banking and the financial sector, streamline the corporate sector through better standards of governance and make the companies competitive in the global economy. Thus, many measures have been taken to improve the functioning of banks, financial institutions and corporate enterprises and to enhance the effectiveness of checks and balances of accounting and reporting systems. However, it has generally not been possible to tie up regulatory changes to specific cases. We discuss the regulatory consequences below.

### 12.5.1 Changes in the Companies Act

As mentioned earlier, the Companies Act 1956 contains provisions relating to general administration, financing, accounting, reporting and audit (GOI, 1956). Many of the provisions of the Companies Act had, however, fallen behind international practice. So, pending the revamping of the Act, the Government of India amended it. The Companies (Amendment) Act 1998 relates to the Disclosure of Accounting Policies and Compliance with

Accounting Standards (section 211(3A)). Every profit and loss account and balance sheet of the company shall comply with the accounting standards. In case of non-compliance, the deviation from the accounting standards and the reasons for such deviation and the financial effect of the deviation, if any, need to be disclosed. Similarly, subsection 3(1)(d) of section 227, dealing with powers and duties of auditors (also introduced by the same Ordinance), requires an auditor to state whether, in his opinion, the profit and loss account and balance sheet complied with the accounting standards. A new Bill (2009) on company legislation is now under active consideration by the Government of India. It is likely to streamline various provisions relating to company management. Against the backdrop of the Satyam scam, the government is to frame new legislation to address the regulatory loopholes in the existing Companies Act (*The Statesman*, Kolkata, 4 July 2010, p. 9).

### 12.5.2 Measures Taken by the SEBI

With the liberalisation of the economy, corporate governance also started changing (Das, 2007). In the late 1990s and early 2000s, the Ministry of Corporate Affairs (MCA) of the Government of India and the SEBI appointed several expert committees to suggest improvements in the standards of the corporate governance system. These were set against the background of failures of corporate governance in India. Consequently, the SEBI introduced a new Clause 49 of the Listing Agreement in 2000, applicable to all listed companies. In 2004, the Listing Agreement was again revised based on the recommendations of the Narayan Murthy Committee, which reflected many of the provisions of the US Sarbanes-Oxley Act.

In addition to prescribing the code of conduct for better standards of corporate governance, the SEBI introduced many other important measures to safeguard the interests of the stakeholders (Bose, 2005). Some of the recommendations of the Naresh Chandra Committee (on corporate governance) e.g. rotation of audit among the firms rather than among partners are under consideration by the regulatory body. The ICAI has already recommended Peer Review of audit to enhance the effectiveness of audit.

### 12.5.2.1  Registration, Listing and Disclosures by Market Participants and Anti-fraud Laws

A new section added to the SEBI (Amendment) Act in 2002 prohibits manipulative and deceptive devices. It prohibits any device, scheme or artifice to defraud or any act or business that could be considered deceitful. The SEBI Prohibition of Fraudulent and Unfair Trade Practices (FUTP) laws relating to Securities Market Regulations 1995, brought into force after the scandals of the early 1990s, were repealed in 2003. According to the new laws (SEBI, 2003), the scope of the definition of 'fraud' was broadened comprehensively (Regulation 12A).

### 12.5.2.2  Price Manipulation

In the amended FUTP regulation (2003) (www.dca.nic.in), an all-encompassing definition of 'fraudulent or an unfair trade practice' was given as 'any act or omission amounting to manipulation of the price of a security'. This will be considered an offence whether or not there is any wrongful gain or avoidance of any loss in such dealings. The Amendment Act (2002) also covers frauds involving the provision of misinformation to the public which can cause fluctuations in prices by inducing others to buy or sell. Penalties have been revised and increased substantially.

### 12.5.2.3  Insider Trading

Prohibition of insider trading has been within the purview of the SEBI's duties since its inception. However, new regulations were made in 2002 based on the recommendations of the Kumar Mangalam Birla Committee (2000) (www.dca.nic.in). These regulations now seek to govern the conduct not only of *insiders* but also *connected persons*. There is a new definition of price-sensitive information, and a model code to prevent insider trading.

### 12.5.2.4  Investigation Powers

The SEBI (Amendment) Act, 2002 enhanced the powers of the SEBI substantially in respect of inspection, investigation and enforcement. For example, the SEBI is now empowered to suspend trading of the security *prima facie* found to be involved in fraudulent and unfair trade practices.

The ICAI has taken a decision to converge its accounting standards with International Financial Reporting Standards (IFRS) with effect from April 2011. Listed companies will then be required to prepare their financial statements based on 'Indian-equivalence' of IFRS. This step is likely to improve the quality of accounting information. Transparency and accountability are expected to be enhanced.

### 12.5.2.5  Corporate Disclosure Practices

Listed companies are now required to give price-sensitive information to stock exchanges and disseminate it on a continuous and immediate basis.

### 12.5.3  Prudential Norms of the RBI

Following the UTI and GTB banking cases, the RBI amended prudential norms for income recognition, asset classification and provisioning for the advances portfolio of banks in order to reflect a bank's actual financial health in its balance sheet as per the recommendations made by the Committee on Financial Systems (Narasimham Committee). If the interest and/or instalment of principal have remained overdue for a specified period of time, it is called an NPA (non-performing asset). Bearing in mind the international practices and the scandals that took place (e.g. the GTB case), the RBI has reduced the concept of 'specified period of time' from 270 to 90 days (RBI, 2005). This change in the concept of the NPA, and guidelines detailing their accounting and reporting, has tightened the management of banks' assets.

With *internal control*, the surveillance and monitoring of investment in shares/advances shall be done by the company's audit committee, which shall review in each of its meetings the total exposure of the bank to capital markets, ensure that the guidelines issued by the RBI are complied with, and that adequate risk management and internal control systems are adopted.

Regarding *disclosure*, banks have to make appropriate disclosures in the 'Notes on Account' to the annual financial statements in respect of those cases where the bank had exceeded the prudential exposure limits during the year.

The developments above suggest that more and more requirements have been included in the regulations and laws in order to ensure full disclosure and transparency by Indian corporate organisations, stock exchanges and banks. These requirements are aimed at, among others, plugging the loopholes in the management of the corporate and the banking and financial sectors with a view to curbing creative accounting and scandals.

## 12.6 CONCLUSION

India, following the economic reforms in 1991, is growing fast with an estimated growth rate in GDP at 8.7 % (Economic Survey, 2006–7)[7]. There has been a sharp rise in foreign direct investment and foreign institutional investment. Over the years, India has developed its corporate sector, accounting profession and stock markets. The GAAP in India comprise, apart from general principles, the provisions of the Companies Act 1956 and accounting and auditing standards issued by the Institute of Chartered Accountants of India (ICAI). The standard-setting board of the ICAI predominantly follows IFRS in formulating Indian accounting standards. The accounting and auditing system plays a strong role in corporate governance and reporting. However, despite this there have been many examples of creative accounting.

In this chapter, a few cases of creative accounting have been examined that have stretched the flexibility of rules and regulations but not specifically broken them: WIPRO Ltd (1996–97 to 1999–2000), Bombay Dyeing and Manufacturing Company (2003–4 and 2004–5), Larsen & Toubro Ltd (1999–2000 and 2001–2), Apollo Tyres Ltd (2004–5), Asian Electronics Ltd (2004–5), Oil & Natural Gas Commission, Mukund Ltd, Torrent Power AEG Ltd and Tata Motors (2004–5), Hindustan Zinc Ltd (2003–4 and 2004–5), Tata Motors, Bombay Dyeing, Mahindra & Mahindra and Himachal Futuristic (2001–2). The nature of these creative transactions ranges from: (i) the transfer of land to stock in trade, creating a capital reserve with the fair value and using it to neutralise the effect on profit of the reduction of land value; (ii) creating provisions for a possible loss on purchase contract and subsequent write-back of such provisions, thereby converting operating losses into operating profit; (iii) income recognition through the transfer of loan liabilities to a subsidiary; (iv) debiting profit and loss account with additional excise duty payable to the government and transferring an equivalent amount from the general reserve to neutralise the effect; (v) the impairment of assets; (vi) the capitalisation of interest and other intangible assets to inflate fixed assets and understate expenses; (vii) reclassifying assets in the balance sheet; and (viii) direct write-offs from reserves. The impacts of such transactions were to overstate profit or understate losses, enhance the value of assets and/or reduce the

---

[7] For the remaining period of the 11th Five Year Plan (2007–12), the revised average rate of GDP growth, because of world economic crisis, is announced at 7.8 % for the next three years (*The Statesman*, Kolkata, 2 September 2009, p. 9).

value of liabilities in the balance sheet. In some, but not all, of these cases the auditors qualified their audit reports.

The chapter then referred to three cases viz. (i) JVG Group of companies, (ii) The Unit Trust of India and (iii) Global Trust Bank. Since legal battles have been going on, these cases have not been dealt with individually. But some aspects of the most recent (coming to the surface in January 2009) and biggest scandal in the corporate sector in India have been dealt with in detail because of the confessional statement made by the promoter-chairman and managing director of Satyam Computer Services Ltd, even though court cases are likely to continue for quite some time.

Although the economy has been able to overcome the shock caused by these corporate scandals, regulators have taken some preventive measures. They range from amending the Companies Act, introducing a code of corporate governance for listed companies, amending the SEBI Act 1992, introducing the Prohibition of Fraudulent and Unfair Trade Practices laws with consequential changes in SEBI regulations to tighten the prudential norms for income recognition, asset classification and provisioning, and issuing guidelines for better risk management on the part of commercial banks.

It is worth mentioning that the impact of creative and fraudulent accounting can be reduced by streamlining the accounting and auditing system and more effective corporate governance. The quality of accounting information is influenced by the state of corporate governance. In the Indian context, creative and fraudulent accounting may be reduced by:

- reducing the alternative choices of accounting treatment in accounting standards;
- revamping the Companies Act;
- enhancing the quality of corporate governance;
- enforcing regulation;
- increasing the effectiveness of audit;
- speeding up the trials of the accused, and
- incorporating a suitable provision in the Companies Act to protect the financial statement analysts, in line with the provisions of the SOX Act. Such a provision may promote their true and faithful analysis of financial health of companies.

Both the Ministry of Corporate Affairs and SEBI should review the corporate governance standards and practices in India in the light of the Satyam case so as to plug the loopholes therein.

Lastly, the regulatory authorities in India may have seriously to reconsider whether an Oversight Board, akin to the Public Company Accounting Oversight Board in the USA, should also be formed in addition to the existing governmental and institutional oversights.

## 12.7 ACKNOWLEDGEMENTS

The author thanks Dr Satyajit Dhar, Reader, Department of Business Administration, University of Kalyani and Guest Lecturer in Commerce, University of Calcutta, for his helpful comments on earlier drafts of the chapter. Special thanks are due to Professor Mike Jones (the editor) for providing detailed comments for revision. The author, however, remains responsible for any errors and omissions.

# REFERENCES

Banerjee, B. (2002), *Regulation of Corporate Accounting and Reporting in India*, World Press, Kolkata.

Banerjee, B. (2005), 'India', in *Asian Accounting Handbook: A Users Guide to the Accounting Environment in 16 Countries*, ed. S.M. Saudagaran, Thomson, Singapore.

Batra, N.D. (2009), 'Salvaging Satyam', *The Statesman*, Kolkata, 14 January, p. 7.

Bombay Stock Exchange of India (BSE), http://www.bseindia.com.

Bose, S. (2005), 'Securities market regulations – lessons from US and Indian experience', *Money & Finance*, January–June.

Chattopadhyay, P. (2008), *Corporate Mis-governance*, IAA Research Foundation.

Coopers & Lybrand (1993), *International Accounting Summaries*, John Wiley & Sons, Inc., New Jersey.

Das, S.C. (2007), *Corporate Governance in India: An Evaluation*, Unpublished PhD Dissertation, University of Calcutta.

Das Gupta, N. (1977), *Financial Reporting in India*, Sultan Chand & Sons, Delhi.

Department of Company Affairs (DCA), *Government of India*, http://www.dca.nic.in.

Global Data Services of India Ltd (2006), *Accounting & Analysis: The Indian Experience*, Professional Version, Vol. 1.

Government of India (GOI), *Companies Act, 1949, 1956* (as amended up to date).

Government of India (2007), *Economic Survey,* 2006–7, p. 3.

Institute of Chartered Accountants of India (ICAI), http:/www.icai.org.

Institute of Chartered Financial Analysts of India (ICFAI), ICFAI Centre of Management Research, Tripura University, http://www.icmr.icfai.org. [For Global Trust Bank (GTB), JVG Group (JVG) and Unit Trust of India (UTI).]

Jaganathan, V. (2003), *A Crisis Tale and Two Banks: Global Trust Bank and ICICI Bank, PTI Report.*

Kumar Mangalam Birla Committee (2000) (http://www.dca.nic.in).

Lakshminarayan, T.V. (2003), 'UTI fiasco stirs up political cauldron', Tribune News Service, 15 July, New Delhi.

Mulford, C.W. and Comiskey, E.E. (2002), *The Financial Numbers Game: Detecting Creative Accounting Practices*, John Wiley & Sons, Inc., New York.

Parliament of India, http://www.parliamentofindia.nic.in.

PricewaterhouseCoopers(PwC), http://www.PwC.com.

Reserve Bank of India (RBI) (2005), *Prudential Norms*, Master Circular, 13 August, http://www.rbi.org.in.

Reuters, News Service (2009), 'Satyam Scandal could be India's Enron', MSNBC, 7 January.

Saudagaran, S.M. (ed.) (2005), *Asian Accounting Handbook: A User's Guide to the Accounting Environment in 16 Countries*, Thomson, Singapore.

Securities and Exchange Board of India (SEBI), http://www.sebi.gov.in.

*The Statesman,* Kolkata, 2009 (8 January, 12 January, 18 January, 25 January).

*The Statesman*, Kolkata, 2010 (4 July, p. 9).

Weston, J.F., Mitchell, M.L. and Melherin, J.H. (2008). *Takeovers, Restructuring and Corporate Governance*, Pearson Education, New Delhi, pp. 617–622.

# 13

# Creative Accounting and Accounting Scandals in Italy

Andrea Melis

## 13.1 INTRODUCTION

Italy has had a long tradition of creative accounting. Greco (1933) and Della Penna (1942) described many creative accounting practices used in the financial statements of Italian listed and unlisted companies during the first decades of the last century. Such creative accounting practices included premature recognition of revenues from sales due to recording revenues before goods were shipped, compensation between credits to customers and debts to suppliers (which became illegal in the 1940s), unrealized equity increment (i.e. the reporting of equity before the shares were actually sold to the investors), as well as several practices of creating hidden reserves in order to smooth future reported income, such as the manipulation of the inventory valuation, of the depreciation costs of tangible assets, and of the probability of uncollectible trade debtors.

Masini (1947) reported that during the 1930s, the practice of preparing multiple financial statements for the same year was widespread. Italian companies used to prepare and present two different financial statements: (a) the one which got published (the annual report), which was prepared by the board of directors to safeguard the interests of the owners (or major shareholders); and (b) internal (non-published) financial statements, which correctly represented the patrimonial (i.e. assets, liabilities and equity) and financial position of the company. There were relevant differences in the information provided, in terms of lack of correspondence between the reported values of assets and liabilities (revenues and expenses) and the actual ones.

Amaduzzi (1949) conducted the first systematic study to explain the rationale for creative accounting practices among Italian companies, pointing out that in financial statements 'the appraisal process is not necessarily based on objective norms [...] The actual appraisal process in financial statements shows that it is the outcome of an interests' game between different corporate stakeholders' (Amaduzzi, 1949, pp. 12–13). In his view, the content of financial statements was the equilibrium outcome of the conflict of interests between different stakeholders.

Until the introduction of a set of accounting standards in 1974 creative accounting practices were, to some extent, widely accepted among practitioners and even among accounting scholars. During the 1960s and 1970s, the debate about the legitimacy of creative accounting (named *politiche di bilancio*) was intense within the accounting profession and academia. While some influential scholars (e.g. Coda, 1966; Dezzani, 1974) argued against creative accounting practices; some other mainstream accounting scholars (e.g. Amodeo, 1964; Onida, 1974) argued that creative accounting practices were not necessarily bad, especially when they were aimed at smoothing income and reported 'distributable' income (i.e. the income that could be distributed to shareholders without hurting the company's ability to operate over time).[1]

Although the debate within the Italian accounting academic community about creative accounting died down with the introduction of a set of generally accepted accounting standards in 1974, and eventually ended with the endorsement of the 4th European Directive in 1991, creative accounting practices have not ceased. In particular, the influence of tax on Italian financial statements has been so widely observed that Italian GAAP (see CNDCR 11, 1994) felt the need to state that the neutrality principle was aimed at avoiding the influence of the Tax Authority on the measurements and reporting of transactions in financial statements. Until 2006, Italian tax law used to require that the same accounting method be employed in the financial statements issued to shareholders as in the financial reports on which taxes were based. However, as tax profits are no longer strictly linked to the corporate financial statements, tax-related creative accounting practices should cease to exist (Dezzani, 2006).

Italian listed companies used to adopt Italian GAAP for the preparation and presentation of their financial statements and, when there were gaps in the former, international financial reporting standards (IFRS). Both GAAPs (i.e. Italian and IFRS) are generally considered 'principles-based' accounting standards (i.e. broadly applicable accounting rules that derive from basic accounting principles, see e.g. Alexander and Jermakowicz, 2006; Tweedie, 2002). Principles-based GAAPs tend to temper Enron-like 'aggressive' accounting practices (i.e. the creation of complex transactions only designed to elude accounting standards rather than for business purposes; see Palepu and Healy, 2003). However, they cannot eliminate the risk of accounting fraud or creative accounting. In fact, in principles-based GAAPs the key issue is the actual enforcement of the true and fair overriding principle, rather than adherence to the letter of the accounting standards (Melis, 2005a).

Some creative accounting practices are due to the influence of business law, which sometimes requires companies to record a transaction in accord with its legal form, no matter what its economic substance. A good example is provided by the accounting for leases. Leases have been a convenient source of off-balance sheet financing for Italian companies. Until the mandatory adoption of IFRS, which makes companies record finance leases as assets and liabilities in their balance sheets (see IAS 17), Italian companies could commit themselves to a financial lease – just as they would if they had used a loan to purchase an asset – but they would not have to capitalize the lease (i.e. to record the asset and its corresponding liability on the balance sheet). The only requirement was to report the details regarding the lease in the footnotes of the corporate financial statements. This accounting practice was widespread and creative, as it was in accord with tax and business law. Leases were treated in accordance with their legal form rather than their economic substance, thus improving corporate debt-to-equity ratios.

---

[1] See D'Oriano (1990) for an in-depth review of the 1960s and 1970s debate among Italian accounting scholars concerning creative accounting.

The last decades have been characterized by several cases of fraudulent financial reporting that have concerned listed companies, including, just to name a few of the most recent cases: Finmatica, Giacomelli Sport, Freedomland and, of course, Parmalat, which represents the most spectacular and important recent case of accounting fraud in Italy.

With the exception of the Parmalat case, which will be examined in detail in this chapter, all the other cases of accounting frauds were relatively 'simple'. Very basic fraud techniques were employed by the key actors in order to conceal the true and fair financial position and economic performance of the company. Finmatica, a software developer, recorded fictitious gains in its profit or loss as well as artificially inflating intangibles as assets on its balance sheet. Giacomelli Sport, a sportswear store chain, inflated reported income by recording fictitious revenues from phantom sales to related parties (which were not consolidated), as well as inflating assets by overstating inventories, which were deliberately reported in the annual report at artificially high levels using improper accounting for inventories. Freedomland, an internet service provider, 'aggressively' recorded revenues from its satellite internet services. They gave out free trial (six months or one year) packages to customers and recorded them as sales. In other words, they recorded as actual revenue fictitious revenues derived from sales to phantom customers.

The remainder of this chapter is structured as follows. The second section describes some examples of creative accounting practices that have recently occurred among Italian non-financial companies. The third section focuses on the most important case of financial reporting fraud that occurred in Italy during the last two decades: Parmalat. It illustrates the key accounting issues as well as briefly describing the role of the key actors either directly involved in the accounting fraud as preparers of the financial statements or indirectly as gatekeepers.[2] The fourth section briefly illustrates the impact on business and society of the Parmalat scandal. A final section concludes.

## 13.2 CREATIVE ACCOUNTING PRACTICES IN ITALY: A CASE STUDY ANALYSIS

Below, I look at some examples of recent company cases that were concealed from the public as well as some creative accounting practices that are widespread either among all Italian companies or within a specific industry.[3]

### 13.2.1 The Choice of Consolidation Technique

The choice of consolidation area for the preparation of group financial statements may give birth to creative accounting practices. As argued by McCoy and Hoskins (2006), creative accounting in the choice of consolidation techniques is not ruled out by principle-based GAAPs, as the preparers of the consolidated financial statements who intend to conceal the 'true' economic result and financial position can claim that, in their judgement,

---

[2] Gatekeepers have been defined as reputational intermediaries who provide verification and certification services to investors, including auditors and financial analysts. See Coffee (2002) on the Enron fraud case.

[3] The practices mentioned were not illegal (unless clearly stated otherwise), but did not represent the company's real economic position.

consolidation of a particular entity is not necessary. The Pirelli case provides an interesting example of such a perfectly legal creative accounting practice. Pirelli was a major multinational conglomerate, and substantially controlled Telecom Italia group (hereafter TI) via a non-listed company named Olimpia SpA Pirelli owned over 50 % of the voting shares at Olimpia. In addition, it had signed a shareholders' agreement with the other four minor shareholders. Although Olimpia only owned approximately 18 % of TI voting shares, it was able to appoint the majority of the company directors at TI (15 out of 19) (see Melis, 2006a).

Despite the fact that in TI's US form 20-F it was stated that Olimpia was indirectly controlled by Pirelli, Pirelli decided not to consolidate Olimpia and TI in its Italian consolidated financial statements. Although Pirelli actually controlled TI, it was not required to do so as Italian GAAP did not make consolidation compulsory when a company does not exercise sole control over another, but jointly with other shareholders. Pirelli had signed a shareholders' agreement with four other minority shareholders that it controlled TI with these shareholders. Pirelli's management decided to make form prevail over substance as the choice of non-consolidating TI had an important economic consequence: Italian bank regulation requires banks to spread their risk by avoiding financial exposure concentration over a single client. More specifically, an Italian bank is not allowed to give loans to a single company or a corporate group for an amount that exceeds 25 % of the bank's capital for supervisory purposes (*patrimonio di vigilanza*).[4] If Pirelli had consolidated TI, thus considering it as part of its group, the exposure of some Italian banks to the Pirelli group (including Telecom Italia's debts) would have exceeded the 25 % threshold, so that Pirelli would have had to reduce its debt exposure to those banks. The net effect of this creative accounting practice was to expand Pirelli's ability to access the debt market, thus bypassing the national bank regulation. The auditors were not criticized as Pirelli complied with the letter of the law.

### 13.2.2 The Accounting of Stock Options

A widespread creative accounting practice concerns accounting for stock options. Italian GAAP has never included any standard on employee share-based payments. The diffusion of stock options in Italy is relatively recent and seems to be explained by the 'perceived-cost view' (Murphy, 2002), according to which the popularity of stock options depends mainly on an accounting treatment which conceals their 'true' economic cost and on a favourable fiscal treatment.

Since 1998[5] Italian law has stated that the issuance of new shares to employees by an employer (or a company belonging to the same group) does not constitute in-kind compensation for tax-related income (Di Pietra and Riccaboni, 2001). The stock options are not taxed as income, but only at a low rate of capital gain when they are sold.[6] The accepted financial reporting practice was driven by a 1998 CONSOB recommendation. CONSOB (*Commissione Nazionale per le Società e la Borsa*), the public authority that is responsible for regulating and controlling the Italian securities markets, required Italian listed companies to disclose in their notes to the accounts the details of the stock options to

---

[4] This is part of the capital that the bank cannot lend freely to safeguard its own solvency.

[5] Before 1998, information regarding stock options was not publicly available.

[6] Tax law changed in 2008: since then stock options are taxed as income.

directors and senior managers as well as to credit equity when the options were exercised by the holders.

Before 2005, when the mandatory adoption of IFRS obliged listed companies to recognize the cost of the stock options in the corporate income statements (IFRS 2, 2004), stock options were thus basically an off-balance-sheet operation, as almost none of the listed companies that gave stock options to its senior management (or other employees) as part of their compensation recognized such costs in their profit or loss accounts. This creative accounting practice affected the balance sheet only when the options were exercised as the credit to equity was usually balanced by debiting reserves. The unrecognized cost of stock options was not included in the reported income and was thus not included in the profit and loss account. The adoption of IFRS 2 has shown that in some companies, such as Fullsix and Safilo, the impact of the cost of stock options represented approximately 124 % and 27 %, respectively, of their reported income (Melis and Carta, 2008).

Some listed companies (such as ERG, ACEA, De Longhi, Datalogic and Dataservice) used the option given by IFRS 2 (2004, para. 58), which did not require companies to restate comparative information to the extent that the information related to a period or date earlier than 7 November 2002. This creatively improved their reported performance for these earlier periods.

### 13.2.3 The Accounting of 'Creative Gains' in Football Club Companies

A specific industry sector where creative accounting practices are widespread and well known is the football industry, which includes both listed and unlisted companies. Most Italian football clubs struggle to report a profit in their financial statements, due to the high cost of the salaries of the football players (Lago, Simmons and Szymanski, 2006). The incentive for creative accounting may be strong as reporting a loss has strong economic consequences on a club: its licence to participate in the national football league depends on some financial covenants, including ratios such as income/debts and equity/assets (Bianchi and Corrado, 2004).

Football clubs acquire the rights to hold the registration of a player for a specific number of years. If another club wishes to acquire that player during the period of his contract, a fee (hereafter transfer cost) is usually required to facilitate the transfer of that registration. The registration right of a player is usually treated as an intangible asset of the football club, as it is assumed to provide benefits over its useful life. Thus, the transfer cost incurred is usually capitalized and amortized (written off) in accordance with the duration of the contract signed by the football player (i.e. the number of years that the football player commits himself to play for the club; Teodori, 1995). If the registration right is transferred to another club within the contract period, the club that sells it may record a gain or a loss, depending on the difference between the book value (i.e. the purchase cost less amortization) and the selling price obtained.

A widespread creative accounting practice concerns the accounting of 'creative gains' derived from the sale of players' registration rights. For example, if two clubs A and B needed to manage their earnings in order to respect their financial covenants, they used to sell each other, at inflated prices, the registration rights concerning two players. Club A sold Club B the rights regarding football player 1 at a price much above its historical cost, and recorded a gain in its accounts. At the same time, Club B sold the registration rights regarding football player 2 to Club A at the same price, again above its net book value. As the two prices were equal, each club could match the debit with the credit and no cash payments occurred. Both the clubs recorded a gain. Such transactions occurred frequently. For example two 'rival' clubs such as Internazionale Milan F.C. and A.C. Milan used to sell each other the registration rights of young 'home-grown' players, whose historical cost was either irrelevant or even null (as no purchase cost has occurred), at the price of approximately €3 million in order to avoid reporting losses. Almost none of the exchanged players ever played in the first team. Although the transaction was legal, their value was clearly inflated. Such creative (yet legal) accounting practices occurred in almost all top league Italian football clubs, including two listed companies.

In addition, in 2003, Italy issued a law (the so-called *save football law*) containing measures on accounting rules for professional sports clubs. The law permitted football clubs to lengthen the period over which the transfer cost was able to be amortized, from the duration of the contract to the fixed length of 10 years. More precisely, the carrying value of the intangible asset of the players' contracts was to be written down to a realizable value as a one-off valuation in 2003 certified by an independent expert. This figure was then still written off over the period of the contract. However, the difference between the unamortized cost prior to the write down and the realizable value was allowed to be transferred to a new intangible asset (named 'the *save football* asset') rather than written off as an expense in the profit or loss. This asset was then amortized over an arbitrary period of 10 years rather than over the length of a player's contract, which rarely exceeds five years. There was thus a reduced charge to the profit and loss accounts. This creative practice was adopted by 15 top league football club companies, including two listed companies (S.S. Lazio and A.S. Rome), which were allowed to understate their reported losses (Morrow, 2006).

Another creative accounting practice which inflates reported income concerns the sale of the football club's 'brand' to a controlled company. Although football club brands, used for advertising and marketing, may have a high market value, the value recorded in the company accounts as an asset is often very low (even zero). Italian GAAP allow internally generated brands to be recognized as assets only as far as the amount of the direct costs incurred in the production of the brand (OIC 24, 2005). In order to increase their reported assets, some top league clubs (e.g. A.C. Milan, Internazionale F.C., U.C. Sampdoria, Brescia Calcio and A.C. Chievo Verona) sold their brand, at market value, to a company that belonged to the same group. As the clubs do not prepare consolidated financial statements (otherwise the effect of the transaction would have been zero), they recorded the gain in their profit or loss statement, improving their reported income.

So, for instance, in September 2005, A.C. Milan sold its brand to Milan Entertainment Srl, a related party owned by the same shareholders, at a price of €183.7 million and recorded a gain of €181.7 million in its profit or loss. The club then leased back its brand from Milan Entertainment Srl. As the club does not prepare consolidated financial statements, the net effect was to inflate its reported income, while maintaining the control of its asset. The accounting of this transaction was creative, in the sense that it was legal as it did reflect the form of the transaction (the sale of the brand) but not its substance (the sale could be said to be fictitious as the club maintained the use and, in substance, the ownership of the brand).

## 13.3 THE MOST IMPORTANT ACCOUNTING FRAUD IN ITALY: THE PARMALAT CASE

Parmalat represents the most spectacular and important recent case of accounting fraud in Italy. Founded in 1961 in Italy, Parmalat quickly expanded internationally and became a major multinational group (see Figure 13.1) with multiple interlocking subsidiaries. In fact, Parmalat was technically insolvent since 1990 when the company was listed on the Milan Stock Exchange. This insolvency may also have provided a motive for the fraud. Greed also played a key role in shaping the behaviour of the key actors involved in the Parmalat fraud, as most of them benefited personally. Apart from the Tanzi family, which was able

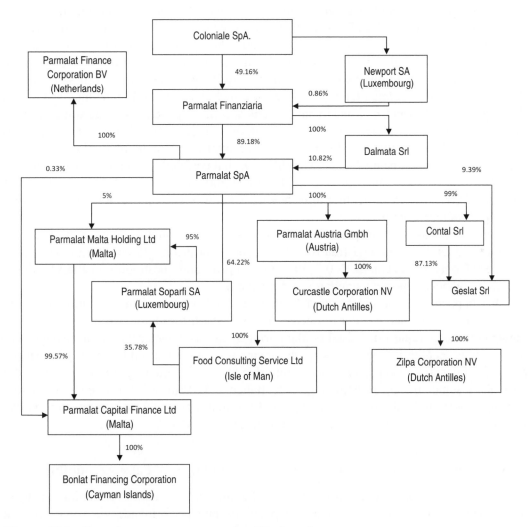

**Figure 13.1** Parmalat group structure: a simplified version

*Source:* Compiled from company reports. Due to the complexity of the Parmalat group, only the companies that are relevant to understand the issues discussed in this paper are considered. Companies are based in Italy, except when a different country is expressly mentioned.

to funnel significant resources to its own private companies, the Parmalat CFO, Tonna, admitted to deriving personal gains from the fraud. Other players received substantial amounts of money for their services. It seems logical that the key rationale behind the Parmalat accounting fraud was to try to keep the company afloat (Storelli, 2005).[7]

In 1998, Parmalat's financial situation worsened dramatically, and Parmalat decided to create a Cayman Islands subsidiary, Bonlat, and use it as an 'accounting dump' to avoid going bankrupt. In fact, Tonna, Parmalat's CFO, testified that Bonlat was conceived as a temporary remedy, in the search for a more stable solution to the financial problems of the group.

The Parmalat fraud was unveiled at the end of 2003, when Parmalat defaulted on a €150 million bond. Parmalat senior management claimed that this occurred because one of its customers, a speculative fund named Epicurum, defaulted on its bill. In October 2003, CONSOB had required Parmalat to clarify some balance sheet items before Parmalat published its third-quarter results. In November 2003, Parmalat disclosed the nature of CONSOB's request and its reply, revealing details surrounding Epicurum (which was soon discovered to be a fictitious hedge fund created by Parmalat itself), as well as details of some of Parmalat's Cayman Islands subsidiaries, including Bonlat Financing Corporation (hereafter Bonlat), which claimed to have a bank account deposit containing some millions of euros. In December 2003, however, the Bank of America's New York branch informed the auditors of Bonlat that it did not have any account in the name of Bonlat and denied authenticity of a document (dated 6 March 2003) that certified the account's existence. In fact, there was no such bank account. In December 2003, Parmalat was declared insolvent and entered bankruptcy protection after having acknowledged that billions of euros were missing from its accounts.

Often labelled as the 'European Enron,' such a sizeable accounting fraud, approximately twice as big as the combined frauds at Enron and WorldCom (PricewaterhouseCoopers Advisory Crisis Management, 2004), has led to a profound questioning of the soundness of Italian financial reporting standards and regulation.

What happened at Parmalat was a deliberate misstatement of information shown on the financial statements in order to deceive users of the information. From an accounting viewpoint, the first question raised by the Parmalat case is whether its senior management used various accounting tricks to avoid disclosing relevant debts and losses or whether the corporate financial misreporting was simply due to false accounting. In other words, did Parmalat's senior managers exploit gaps in Italian GAAP in order to manage corporate earnings, assets and liabilities or did they falsify company accounts so as to manage assets, liabilities and earnings which could not be managed otherwise?

### 13.3.1 Parmalat: Was it a Case of Creative Accounting or of False Accounting?

Rather than an exploitation of loopholes of the Italian GAAP that allowed senior managers to conceal the 'true' corporate financial positions and performance via some creative

---

[7] Newspapers, academic papers and books have widely discussed the Parmalat fraud. CONSOB declared Parmalat's 2002 financial statements as void because of the existing fraud. However, the trial is still underway and key people have yet to be declared guilty.

accounting techniques, what emerges at Parmalat is indeed a major falsification of corporate accounts. As a matter of fact, Parmalat's former CFO Tonna did acknowledge to Italian prosecutors a systematic falsification of accounts within the corporate group that dated back over 15 years before the bankruptcy. That is to say, the fundamental nature of the Parmalat case is about the fraudulent accounting practices which have violated both fair and faithful presentation of corporate financial reports (Melis and Melis, 2005). Non-etheless, as we see below, there were also incidences of creative accounting, for example, in accounting for preference shares.

According to PricewaterhouseCoopers, which served as external auditor after the Tanzis stepped down and nominated a turnaround expert as CEO in December 2003, Parmalat's financial statements included created assets and revenues, overstated earnings and under-reported debts. Parmalat had overstated assets and understated liabilities by approximately €14.5 billion (PricewaterhouseCoopers Advisory Crisis Management, 2004). The actual net worth of Parmalat Finanziaria was a deficit of approximately €11 billion (Hamilton, 2005).

An analysis of Parmalat Finanziaria's and Parmalat SpA's consolidated and separate financial statements shows relatively little evidence that the accounting fraud involved either really complex accounting techniques, sophisticated earnings management or financial engineering techniques specifically designed to get around accounting standards.

One example of creative accounting practices offered by the Parmalat case concerns accounting for preference shares. At the end of the 1990s, Parmalat Corporation Finance Ltd, a subsidiary of Parmalat SpA (see Figure 13.1), issued preference shares for approximately €477 million to some banks (including Merrill Lynch International, Credito Italiano SpA and Cariplo SpA). The value of the shares was recorded as equity in the Parmalat financial statements. Such shares provided the holder with mandatory dividends calculated on the London Interbank Offered Rate (LIBOR) plus 2.5 %. Although the shares had no maturity date, they were 'redeemable' (i.e. they gave the holder the right to require the issuer to redeem the shares after a particular date for a fixed amount). In other words, the preferred shareholders' relationship with Parmalat could terminate if the holder exercised its call privilege at a given future, unspecified date. Future, unspecified transactions took the legal form of equity, but were liabilities in substance as they were redeemable. Thus, in accordance with the substance over form principle, their value should have been recorded as debt. The net effect of such a transaction was to significantly improve the reported gearing ratio of the Parmalat group.

### 13.3.2 Key Accounting Issues at Parmalat: Some Examples of the Accounting Fraud

Some uncertainty still surrounds (as at the time of writing, February 2010) the Parmalat fraud in the absence of a final verdict from the courts. It will be the task of judges to reconstruct exactly what happened and decide who is to be held responsible for the fraud. Nevertheless, it is possible to provide a summary account of the ways in which the accounting fraud was perpetrated. In order to conduct its fraudulent financial reporting practices, Parmalat created wholly fictitious transactions as well as misreported actual transactions. Parmalat used various wholly-owned 'nominee' entities, i.e. companies that had no commercial activities or purposes and no real assets. The nominee entities entered fictitious assets and revenues on their accounts to provide factual support for the fabrication of non-existent financial operations aimed to offset the debts and losses of Parmalat SpA as well as other operating subsidiaries. They also helped to disguise the intra-group loans from one subsidiary to another subsidiary which was experiencing operating losses.

Fraudulent financial reporting practices at Parmalat included both the falsification of earnings as well as the overstatement of assets and the understatement of liabilities.

### 13.3.2.1   The Falsification of Earnings

The Parmalat fraud involves a major falsification of earnings. Table 13.1 reports the significant difference that exists between the reported earnings and EBITDA (Earnings Before Interest, Taxes, Depreciation and Amortization) of Parmalat Finanziaria and the actual numbers. Parmalat Finanziaria should have reported losses, rather than profits, in every period since 1990 (except 1991 and 1998) until it went bankrupt in 2003. Overall, cumulative reported EBITDA was €6099 million, whereas cumulative actual EBITDA was €2440 million. Similarly, cumulative reported earnings were €1513 million as opposed to an actual cumulative loss of €3694 million.

In order to manage earnings that could not be managed otherwise, Parmalat used various fraudulent techniques, most of which were aimed at inflating revenues. The most relevant schemes for the magnitude of the amount involved include the following.

**Table 13.1**   Reported and actual earnings of Parmalat

| | Parmalat Finanziaria | | | |
|---|---|---|---|---|
| Period | Reported EBITDA | 'Actual' EBITDA | Reported Earnings | 'Actual' earnings (before taxes) |
| 1990 | 88 201 989.91 | 78 336 813.78 | 3 006 832.72 | −28 243 128.07 |
| 1991 | 104 674 306.27 | 89 353 177.29 | 21 792 002.15 | 12 421 039.89 |
| 1992 | 129 619 131.63 | 11 058 165.48 | 26 670 699.85 | −77 732 149.31 |
| 1993 | 160.935.460 45 | 53 056 426.46 | 41 519 888.76 | −114 479 088.10 |
| 1994 | 213 890 150.65 | 106 699 385.77 | 52 625 238.22 | −72 534 630.85 |
| 1995 | 267 480 774.89 | 145 889 535.38 | 69 986 107.31 | −136 684 238.47 |
| 1996 | 324 517 241.91 | 128 843 503.23 | 98 106 152.55 | −108 392 255.17 |
| 1997 | 387 830 726.09 | 202 743 232.95 | 104 649 145.01 | −90 017 255.00 |
| 1998 | 536 683 417.09 | 339 762 417.09 | 135 442 371.16 | 37 922 797.61 |
| 1999 | 722 155 000.00 | 434 144 000.00 | 173 983 000.00 | −161 667 538.25 |
| 2000 | 870 764 000.00 | 365 546 000.00 | 194 733 000.00 | −419 486 254.44 |
| 2001 | 948 141 000.00 | 409 758 111.00 | 218 493 000.00 | −481 830 889.00 |
| 2002 | 931 270 000.00 | 143 004 000.00 | 252 102 000.00 | −917 581 000.00 |
| 30.06.03 | 412 918 000.00 | −68 398 180.97 | 119 917 000.00 | −1 135 698 180.97 |
| **Total** | **6 099 081 198.89** | **2 439 796 587.46** | **1 513 026 437.73** | **−3 694 002 770.13** |

*Source:* Elaborated from Chiatturini (2004). Reported data in euros are based on the consolidated financial statement of Parmalat Finanziaria. 'Actual' data in euros are based on the estimates of the accounting expert of the Milan Court.

*Recording Fictitious Revenues from Sales of Goods (that Never Occurred) to Phantom Customers*

One of the most significant (fictional) transactions involved the sale of powdered milk to Empresa Cubana Importadora de Alimentos, a Cuban state-owned importer. From 1999 to 2003, Bonlat recorded sales of powdered milk to this company for an overall amount of over €2 billion. The sales were allegedly executed through a Singapore-based shell company, which had 'sold' the powdered milk to Bonlat, which then allegedly shipped it from Singapore to Cuba. The Singaporean company never recorded the sale in its accounts (Chiatturini, 2004).

*Double Billing*

Parmalat issued duplicate invoices to its distributors and supermarkets in Italy. These duplicate invoices allowed Parmalat to book fictitious sales to obtain liquidity, in the form of credit, from banks. The net effect was to improve its reported income, which allowed Parmalat to access the credit markets more easily.

*Fabrication of Fictional Revenues by Parmalat's Operating Subsidiaries through Sales to Controlled Nominee Entities at Inflated or Entirely Fictitious Amounts*

For example, some of the reported income derived from the sale of fictitious trademarks or technologies to nominee entities incorporated in fiscal havens, such as the Dutch Antilles (e.g. Curcastle Corporation N.V. and Zilpa Corporation N.V., see Figure 13.1) was fabricated. Despite the fact that the assets sold did not exist or were nearly worthless, the prices recorded were extremely high. The net effect was not neutral: such transactions improved the reported income of Parmalat's operating companies, while most of the costs of the nominee entities were not included in Parmalat Finanziaria's consolidated financial statements, as some of these companies remained unconsolidated.

*Overbilling*

Parmalat used to buy services from Tanzi's privately owned companies (such as HIT SpA and Parmatour) at prices above the fair market value. These related-party transactions reduced Parmalat's reported income by inflating Parmalat's expenses. However, they were crucial in funnelling relevant resources to the Tanzi family as well as covering losses in Tanzi's privately owned business, such as one of the Italian leading travel agencies, Parmatour.

### 13.3.2.2   *The Falsification of Assets and Debts*

Not only were earnings falsified at Parmalat, but also assets and debts were, respectively, overstated (or created) and understated (or eliminated), in order to report a 'balanced' financial structure. Melis and Melis (2005) point out that in fact, although Parmalat's reported net debt position had improved since 1999, this was not due to debt repayments,

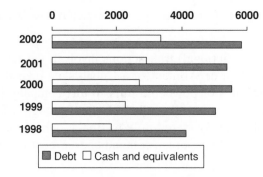

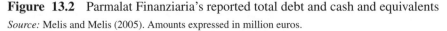

**Figure 13.2**  Parmalat Finanziaria's reported total debt and cash and equivalents

*Source:* Melis and Melis (2005). Amounts expressed in million euros.

rather to the rising amounts of reported cash and equivalents (see Figure 13.2). These amounts were, in fact, fictitious.

In order to improve its reported financial structure, an assortment of 'tactics' was employed by Parmalat's senior management, including the following.

### Not Recording Debts in its Books

Debt was either simply written off or improperly removed from the consolidated financial statements. For example:

- Approximately €200 million of Parmalat SpA payables were simply written off as though they had been paid when, in fact, they were still due (Chiatturini, 2004).
- Still uncertain (but undoubtedly material) amounts of bank debt were mischaracterized as inter-company debt when consolidating the company's financial statements. Since inter-company loans do not appear on consolidated financial statements, the net effect was to understate Parmalat's debt.

### Improperly Recording Debt as Equity

The net effect was to overstate Parmalat's equity and to understate its debt. For example:

- The use of 'partnerships' to hide debt as equity. The so-called 'Buconero (black hole) deal' provides an excellent example of this fraudulent practice undertaken by Parmalat. Buconero LLC (hereafter Buconero) was a Delaware (USA) subsidiary unit set up in compliance with US regulations and controlled by Citigroup bank, an independent US banking group. In fact, Buconero was designed to serve as a special financing vehicle for Parmalat. Buconero signed a joint venture agreement with the Swiss branch of Geslat Srl (hereafter Geslat), a consolidated Parmalat subsidiary (see Figure 13.1). Buconero contributed €117 million to a partnership with Geslat, which intended to use such funds to make loans to other companies belonging to the Parmalat group. Geslat agreed to give Buconero a predetermined fixed amount as dividends, no matter what its economic results. The Buconero deal helped to report the €117 million loan as an equity investment on the Parmalat balance sheet. Since Geslat was officially receiving funds from a partner, Parmalat recorded the amounts received by Buconero as equity. In fact, Citigroup structured the transaction to give itself a bond-like rate of return, and correctly reported the amount of money that Buconero contributed to Geslat as a credit or loan advance towards the Parmalat group in the Italian bank credit database register (*Centrale Rischi*) (Chiatturini, 2004). Thus, in accord with the substance over form principle, the amounts received by Geslat from Buconero should have been recorded as debt, rather than equity.[8]

*Overstating its Assets*

Assets were either improperly measured or simply created:

- The use of nominee entities allowed Parmalat to transfer uncollectible and/or impaired receivables to them from Parmalat SpA (or one of its operating subsidiaries), in order to conceal their diminished or non-existent value.
- The use of a forged depository account to increase reported liquidity. Parmalat Finanziaria's consolidated financial statements reported a cash equivalent asset of approximately €3.95 billion deposited in a Bank of America account in the name of Bonlat. Bonlat was in fact a nominee entity with no real business activity. It served as a vehicle to hide the fact that the credits derived from the fictitious sales could not be turned into cash, and to conceal the forged assets reported in other nominee entities, such as Zilpa and Curcastle (see Figure 13.1). In December 2003, Bank of America informed Grant Thornton, auditors of Bonlat, that there was no account in the name of Bonlat and denied authenticity of a document that endorsed its existence. Later, Tonna, Parmalat's former CFO, confessed that he had forged the Bank of America document on behalf of the chairman/CEO Tanzi. The reported account did not exist.

### 13.3.3 The Role of Corporate Governance Actors

When a significant fraud is disclosed, one of the key issues (apart from identifying and punishing the fraudulent behaviour and actors) is to understand how it was possible for a fraud to remain concealed for so long and how to prevent a similar fraud reoccurring. If you want to prevent fraud you have to know how it happened and what has caused it (Hodson, 2005). The role of the actors involved in the financial reporting system at Parmalat will therefore be examined in order to understand why such a large accounting fraud was possible in the first place and remained disguised for over a decade. The key actors involved in the financial reporting system on the information supply side include corporate senior management (CEO and CFO, above all), external auditors and internal corporate governance bodies, such as the board of directors (including its audit committee) and the board of statutory auditors.

---

[8] Although Parmalat used the Buconero transaction improperly, Citigroup has not been implicated in any malpractice.

### 13.3.3.1  The Role of the Tanzis

Parmalat's ownership and control structure was characterized by a large shareholder (the Tanzi family) that, via two non-listed companies (Coloniale SpA and NewPort SA), controlled the majority of voting shares of the holding company of the Parmalat group (50.02 %) (see Figure 13.1).

Senior management was accountable to the Tanzi family, who also held the positions of CEO and chairman as well as other executive and non-executive director positions within the board. Thus, the Tanzi family had sufficient power to exploit private benefits from the Parmalat group to manage the measurement and presentation of the financial statements so that they gave primacy to the family's own interests rather than the information needs of the users. Members of the Tanzi family did indeed exploit such power in order to funnel corporate resources to themselves directly. For example, Parmalat used to be able to arrange a discounted price in its dealings with key suppliers. However, Parmalat would often record the full price as paid, while the total amount of the discount was deposited via a bank transfer into Tanzi's personal accounts.

Significant resources were funnelled to the Tanzis indirectly, via an overbilling scheme, with some related-party transactions with various companies privately owned and operated by some Tanzi family members. The latter did not perform any equivalent services for the amount of money received by Parmalat. For example, there is evidence that Parmalat was usually overcharged for travel agency services rendered by HIT SpA, a Tanzi privately owned company. These related-party transactions were not disclosed in either Parmalat Finanziaria's or other subsidiaries' financial statements or other information provided to prospective investors in connection with debt issues.

### Parmalat's Fraud: sed quis custodiet?

In order to try to counterbalance the power of the Tanzi family and have adequate information to make their economic decisions, minority shareholders and other stakeholders (including investors and creditors) would have needed well-functioning internal governance systems and an external auditor able and willing to safeguard the enforcement of the principle of 'true and fair view' in Parmalat's financial statements.

Such a sizeable accounting fraud could only come about if the systems, checks and balances, in place to try to prevent such failures, have themselves failed to work. In fact, they all failed to ensure corporate financial reporting quality.

### 13.3.3.2  The Role of the Board of Directors

Listed companies with more independent boards have a significantly lower likelihood of financial statement fraud (Beasley, 1996). The board of directors of Parmalat Finanziaria was dominated by corporate insiders. There were 13 members, only five of whom were non-executive directors. Such a low presence of non-executive directors is rather uncommon in Italy (see e.g. CONSOB, 2003). Four members of the Tanzi family sat on the board: one non-executive director and three executive directors, including the CEO/chairman. None of the minority shareholders was able to appoint any director on the board.

Parmalat Finanziaria claimed that three of its non-executive directors were independent directors. However, further analysis based on data not provided by the company (see Melis, 2005b) showed that one of the alleged independent directors, Silingardi, who was also the chairman of the audit committee, had significant business relationships with the Tanzis, as well as being an old personal friend of the chairman/CEO/controlling shareholder, Callisto Tanzi. Thus, his independence should have been questioned. Eight of the Parmalat Finanziaria directors also sat on the board of directors of Parmalat SpA, the key manufacturing company, including all the executive directors and Silingardi.

The boards of directors of the key companies of the Parmalat group were clearly dominated by the senior management and the Tanzi family. No surprise, then, if they fostered or, at least, allowed the preparers of the financial statements to manage the measurement and presentation of the accounts so that they gave primacy to the interests of the corporate insiders, at the expense of the users (minority shareholders and creditors). The boards of directors had no interest in ensuring corporate financial reporting quality, thus they did not foster the enforcement of the 'true and fair view' accounting principle.

### 13.3.3.3  The Role of the Audit Committee

The role of the audit committee is central to effective internal control systems (DeZoort *et al.*, 2002). In fact, in many of the US corporations involved in financial reporting fraud during the last decades, the audit committee was either non-existent or dysfunctional (COSO, 1999). Parmalat's audit committee was similarly lacking in independence. Audit committee effectiveness is usually evaluated according to the following criteria: financial literacy, independence and frequency of meetings (see e.g. Krishnan, 2005; Windram and Song, 2004).

Parmalat Finanziaria set up its audit committee in 2001. Since then, its frequency of meeting and directors' financial literacy have been acceptable: the majority of the members of the audit committee had an accounting background and the committee used to meet bimonthly. The problem was, again, the lack of independence of the audit committee from the corporate insiders. The audit committee was composed of only one non-executive director (Silingardi), who, as mentioned before, was close to the Tanzis, and two executive directors, one of them being the CFO (Tonna). No actual independent director sat on the audit committee. Such composition did not comply with the recommendations of the Italian code of corporate governance best practice (Preda Code of Conduct, 1999, para. 10). Dominated by corporate insiders, the role of the audit committee as a monitor was clearly flawed.

### 13.3.3.4  The Role of the Board of Statutory Auditors

The board of statutory auditors is a typical Italian device. Basically, all Italian listed companies are characterized by a particular board structure, a sort of 'half-way house' between the British unitary board and the German two-tier board structure (i.e. executive and supervisory) consisting of a board of directors and a board of statutory auditors. The latter is not part of the board of directors, and its members are all independent auditors directly elected by the annual shareholders' meeting every three years, rather than being nominated by the board of directors. Although it differs significantly from the audit committee in relation to its composition and nomination process, the board's duties overlap somewhat with those of the audit committee.

The duties of the board of statutory auditors include, *inter alia*, the review of the adequacy of the corporate organizational structure for matters such as the internal audit system, the administrative and accounting system as well as the reliability of the latter in correctly representing any company's transactions. In other words, the board of statutory auditors is supposed to detect any sizeable or systematic corporate governance failure or accounting fraud.

Nonetheless, Cardia (2004), chairman of CONSOB, noted that there was no record that the board of statutory auditors of Parmalat Finanziaria ever warned shareholders about what was happening at Parmalat or reported anything to the courts or to CONSOB.

For example, in December a UK minority shareholder (Hermes Focus Asset Management Europe Ltd) asked the board of statutory auditors to investigate some accounting issues such as: (a) the related-party transactions between Parmalat Finanziaria and a Tanzi-owned company that operated in the tourism sector (HIT SpA); (b) the accounting of some intangible assets of Parma Football Club (a subsidiary of Parmalat Finanziaria) and (c) the disclosure of some put options related to Parmalat Administracao Ltd (a Brazilian subsidiary of Parmalat). The board of statutory auditors responded by denying that any irregularity ('atypical and/or unusual related party or inter-company transaction'), either *de facto* or *de jure*, was happening. However, investigators found that Tanzi was able to funnel important resources from Parmalat to HIT despite the fact that Parmalat always claimed to treat related-party transactions according to criteria of 'substantial' and 'procedural' fairness. Besides, the accounting of some intangible assets at Parma F.C. seems to imply that some creative accounting had occurred in order to report increased assets (Chiatturini, 2004).

The board of statutory auditors was clearly unable to detect, or at least report, what was happening at Parmalat. There are several reasons for its ineffectiveness as a gatekeeper; most of them derive from more general issues concerning the actual role of the board of statutory auditors.

The inefficiency of the boards of statutory auditors of Italian listed companies as gatekeepers has been attributed to (a) their lack of access to information related to controlling shareholder activities, and (b) their lack of independence from the controlling shareholders, as statutory auditors need their votes in order to be reappointed (see Melis, 2004). Indeed, in a corporate governance system characterized by the presence of a strong controlling shareholder, like the Tanzis in Parmalat, the board of statutory auditors seems to provide a legitimating device, rather than a substantive monitoring mechanism (Melis, 2004).

However, its capability as an effective monitor was further underscored by some issues that are specific to the Parmalat case. The Draghi law requires corporate by-laws to ensure that minority shareholders are allowed to appoint one (or two, when the board of statutory auditors is composed of more than three members) of the statutory auditors.[9] Parmalat Finanziaria's board of statutory auditors was composed of three members. Corporate

---

[9] The Draghi law (1998) has regulated the financial markets and corporate governance in listed companies, with the main purpose of 'strengthening investors' by protecting all minority shareholders.

by-laws set up a threshold of 3 % of company voting shares to appoint a statutory auditor (i.e. a minority shareholder was required to have, at least, 3 % of the company shares to be able to vote for a statutory auditor. This rule made appointing a statutory auditor difficult for minority shareholders, as none of the existing minority shareholders at Parmalat Finanziaria owned more than 2.2 % of the share capital. In fact, there is no evidence that any of the statutory auditors was appointed by the minority shareholders. Again, there was a problem in the enforcement of the law (Benedetto and Di Castri, 2005). Either because of a lack of resources, or of independence from the controlling shareholders, the board of statutory auditors failed to ensure corporate financial reporting quality.

### 13.3.3.5   *The Role of the External Auditors*

External auditors at Parmalat failed to exercise their role as monitors. Not only did they fail to ensure that the corporate financial reporting gave a true and fair view of Parmalat's financial situation and performance, but they also did not detect the accounting fraud that had gone on for approximately 15 years until the very last moment.

Before its bankruptcy, Parmalat's accounts had been audited by three auditing firms during the last two decades: one Italian auditing firm, named Hodgson Landau Brands (until 1989) and the Italian branches of two well-known international auditors, Grant Thornton (1990–98) and Deloitte & Touche (1999–2003). Parmalat Finanziaria was required to change auditors relatively often because of the Italian regulation that mandates lead auditor rotation for listed companies (see Draghi law, 1998, art. 159).[10]

The aim of mandatory auditor rotation is clearly to foster auditors' independence from their clients, thus reinforcing the auditors' role as a gatekeeper. However, in the Parmalat case auditor rotation was not in fact fully adopted. Penca and Bianchi, who audited Parmalat on behalf of Hodgson Landau Brands until 1989, then kept on auditing Parmalat. Italian law did not forbid an auditor to continue to audit the same company if s/he changed the auditing firm in which s/he worked. Penca and Bianchi had jointed Grant Thornton.

In 1999, when Deloitte & Touche replaced Grant Thornton as chief auditor, Grant Thornton (specifically Penca and Bianchi) continued to audit the financial statements of Parmalat SpA as well as some of Parmalat's off-shore subsidiaries, including Bonlat, from which a significant part of the group's reported total assets and consolidated revenues derived (see Table 13.2). The 1998 company law had a loophole in the auditor rotation rule that allowed an incumbent auditor to remain as a 'subcontractor' even after the permitted engagement period.

Deloitte & Touche never accepted overall responsibility for Parmalat's consolidated financial statements, stating in their auditors' reports that their opinion as chief auditors was basely solely upon other auditors' reports with regard to the part of the group's total assets and consolidated revenues which came from Parmalat's subsidiaries whose financial statements were audited by other auditors (that is Grant Thornton).

Deloitte & Touche did not report any warnings, either in their auditors' reports, or directly to CONSOB until eight weeks before Parmalat's insolvency. Only on 31 October

---

[10] At that time Italian law made chief auditor rotation compulsory after three engagements, leading to a maximum of nine years for audit engagement. Italy was the only large economy to have made auditor rotation mandatory at that time.

**Table 13.2**    Total assets and revenues audited by 'subcontractors'

| Year | 1999 | 2000 | 2001 | 2002 |
|---|---|---|---|---|
| Total assets of the Parmalat group not audited by the chief auditor | 22 % | 40 % | 42 % | 49 % |
| Consolidated revenues of the Parmalat group not audited by the chief auditor | 16 % | 23 % | 23 % | 30 % |

*Source:* Elaborated from data based on Deloitte & Touche reports.

2003 was a review report issued on the interim financial information for the six months ended June 2003 in which Deloitte & Touche auditors stated they were unable to verify the carrying value of Parmalat's investment in the Epicurum Fund, which is now known to have never operated. Parmalat's participation in the fund was obtained by 'investing' in Epicurum approximately €500 million of Bonlat's credits, derived from Tanzi's privately owned Parmatour. In other words, there was no investment at all and the whole transaction was fictitious as Epicurum never existed in the first place. Only on 11 November 2003 was a public signal sent to investors when Deloitte & Touche refused to sign off Parmalat Finanziaria's half-year financial statements. Cardia (2004) points out that the decision to publicly question Parmalat originated not within Deloitte & Touche, but as a direct consequence of CONSOB's pressure on the auditor.

Although the auditors claimed to be victims of the fraud perpetuated by Parmalat's senior management, it seems reasonable to argue, as pointed out in Melis (2005b), that this is not wholly true. Although the main aim of the external audit process is not to detect fraud, auditors arguably should have discovered the fraud if they had acted according to the generally accepted auditing standards and exhibited the proper degree of professional 'scepticism' required of auditors in executing their audit procedures.

For example, bank deposits are not complicated items to audit. They should be matched to a bank statement as part of a company's reconciliation procedures in order to ensure that bank statements received by the client and used in the reconciliation process have not been altered. If Grant Thornton auditors had followed such a procedure, they would have discovered that Bonlat did not have any cash deposited, as reported.

As a matter of fact, Italian prosecutors reported that Grant Thornton as auditors relied on Parmalat's internal mail system, rather than getting in direct contact with the Bank of America, to receive and accept a verification letter, allegedly from the Bank of America, confirming that Bonlat held €3.95 billion in cash and investments in an account at the bank. That document had been taken as the basis for the certification of Bonlat's – and Parmalat Finanziaria's – 2002 accounts.[11]

Moreover, Grant Thornton auditors in Italy seemed to be not independent from their client, as noted by Parmalat's former CFO (Tonna), who reported to Italian prosecutors that the idea of setting up Bonlat was proposed by Grant Thornton auditors in order to

---

[11] Testimony of Bianchi M., partner of Grant Thornton (Italy), at the judicial hearing in front of prosecutor F. Greco (Il Sole 24 Ore, Date 22 May 2008).

conceal Parmalat's financial crisis from the incoming chief auditor Deloitte & Touche. Italian auditors are accused of collusion with Parmalat by Italian prosecutors.[12]

Deloitte & Touche, which relied heavily on Grant Thornton's report accepting the Bank of America's forged verification letter, arguably might have failed to exercise the proper degree of 'scepticism' as they decided to rely on Grant Thornton without sufficient monitoring and so failed to pick up the fact that Grant Thornton were, in fact, auditing transactions that were fictional (i.e. made up by Parmalat's senior management only for financial reporting purposes).

### 13.3.4 The Role of Information Demand-side Actors: Institutional Investors, Financial Analysts and Banks

Very little was heard from institutional investors about Parmalat's financial statements publicly before the collapse. The only exception was a British-based institutional investor (Hermes Focus Asset Management Europe Ltd), which, in December 2002, filed with Parmalat Finanziaria's board of statutory auditors a request that it investigate specific potential accounting irregularities.

It is not clear yet to what extent institutional investors had their potentially active role of monitoring Parmalat's corporate governance hampered by the misleading information provided by the corporate financial reporting, or by their preference for 'voting with their feet' (rather than with their voice) or by their ties with banks, which either sold Parmalat's bonds or helped Parmalat to obtain financing.

Some banks, for example, were earning high fees from dealing with Parmalat (Sale, 2004). The key problem with such banks is that they were major long-term lenders of Parmalat. A Parmalat lender who learned of the senior management's actions was likely to have incentives to keep it secret because as a major lender it had much to lose if the management actions became public (Diamond, 2004).

As with Enron, financial analysts seem not to have detected any of the structural deficiencies within Parmalat until the very last moment (Melis and Melis, 2005). Only on 5 December 2002 (i.e. approximately a year before the collapse) did one financial analyst (Merrill Lynch's London office) downgrade Parmalat to a sell rating. Merrill Lynch issued seven other public reports in 2003 reinforcing its sell recommendation. Nevertheless, the rest of the financial analysts' community seems to have been unaware of what was going on at Parmalat (see Melis and Melis, 2005).

A simple explanation of their behaviour is the lack of financial reporting quality which hampered them. When financial statements are false, as in the Parmalat case, financial statement analysis techniques are intrinsically flawed. In fact, Parmalat's 'numbers' were forged to portray a 'rosy' picture of the group's financial situation and performance. However, using financial statements analysis techniques on data publicly available at the time, Chiaruttini (2004) and Melis and Melis (2005) found some evidence that might have led a

---

[12] See the testimony of Bianchi M., partner of Grant Thornton (Italy), at the judicial hearing in front of prosecutor F. Greco (Il Sole 24 Ore, Date 22 May 2008). Grant Thornton expelled the Italian auditors who were dealing with Parmalat from its network.

sophisticated analyst to have some doubts about Parmalat's reported financial situation and performance.

It is unclear whether sell-side financial analysts did not raise the alarm because of their lack of competence (analysts are often trained more in finance than in accounting) or their herding mentality (analysts find it easier and more convenient to follow their peers, rather than beat them), or because they did detect the issues but did not release any report because of their close links with the banks which had relevant stakes in Parmalat as creditors and suppliers of highly lucrative services (see Di Castri, 2004).

## 13.4 THE AFTERMATH OF THE PARMALAT SCANDAL AND ITS IMPACT ON BUSINESS AND SOCIETY

The collapse of Parmalat has had a wide-reaching impact on business and society. First of all, it has caused significant damage to the personal reputations of the Tanzis, former CFOs, internal accountants, external auditors and legal counsel of Parmalat, who have variously been questioned, arrested and had their personal assets impounded by Italian courts. The reputational damage to Grant Thornton has had a similar effect to that of Arthur Andersen in the USA: Grant Thornton does not operate in Italy any more. Deloitte & Touche's acceptance of the information provided to them also raised questions about the professionalism and business practices of some of its auditors.

Italian regulation and national standards on external auditing were questioned after the Parmalat scandal, which led to a change in the external auditor's engagement rules. This happened despite the fact that Italian regulation at the time of the Parmalat scandal was one of the strictest in Europe.

In Italy the external auditing firm was already appointed by the shareholders' annual general meeting, which took into account whether the board of statutory auditors approved the appointment or not. Auditor rotation was already mandatory before the Parmalat scandal: after three appointments (i.e. nine years, as each appointment lasts three years) a listed company was required to rotate its lead auditing firm. Given these strict regulations, in this author's opinion, the emphasis on flaws of Italian auditing regulation is misplaced; nor can the evidence from the Parmalat case be catalogued as 'country-specific' (Ferrarini and Giudici, 2006; Melis, 2005b).

However, the Parmalat case did show some flaws existing in the auditing regulation in Italy. For example, there is no point in requiring mandatory chief auditor rotation if the chief auditing firm relies significantly on 'subcontractors' (i.e. other auditing firms which audit subsidiary firms of the group, which are not obliged to rotate) without being held responsible for their work. In addition, mandatory auditing firm rotation may be flawed if the law does not require the audit partners to rotate as well after a reasonable period of time. As in the Parmalat case with the two Grant Thornton partners (formerly auditors at Hodgson Landau Brands), auditors could change the auditing firm in which they work and remain auditing the same company even after the three engagements' limit.

In January 2006, the Italian Parliament acted and issued a law (named 'Saving law') which tightened auditor rotation rules in order to prevent future Parmalat-like scandals. The length of the engagement period of the auditing firm was extended to six years (it was previously three years), but it may only be renewed once (rather than twice as in the past). The rotation of the audit partner is now mandatory for the second engagement. The extension of the engagement period is aimed at fostering the continuity necessary to an auditing firm to carry out its work efficiently, while the mandatory rotation of the audit partner should foster its independence.

The 2006 law also prescribed that the chief auditing firm is allowed to rely on 'sub-contractors' to audit companies that have subsidiaries operating in countries in which the former does not operate. However, in this case the chief auditing firm is compelled to take responsibility for the actions of the 'subcontractor'.

In order to ensure the representation of minority shareholders on the board of directors, so as to make it less dependent on corporate insiders, the 2006 law has also proscribed the use of 'slates' for directors' nomination, forbidding the 'winner-takes-all' procedure, which allows the majority shareholder to appoint all the directors in the board.

The evidence from the Parmalat case has also had an impact on European auditing policy-making. The key flaws that allowed the Parmalat fraud have led to the changes to the 8th Directive in 2006, approved by the European Parliament. The revised European Directive has recommended that Member States adopt mandatory audit partner rotation as well as stricter rules on auditor independence and responsibility. It also makes the establishment of an independent audit committee compulsory for listed companies.

In addition, the Parmalat case, along with other Italian corporate scandals, put the whole Italian corporate system under pressure. Despite the fact that Parmalat is not necessarily a particularly Italian case, it has been perceived as such by a large part of the Anglo-Saxon business media (e.g. Heller, 2003; Lyman, 2004; Mulligan and Munchau, 2003). The collapse of Parmalat has had a wide-reaching impact on the ability of Italian companies to access international capital markets. For example, Ferrarini and Giudici (2006) report that the number of Italian companies accessing the international bond markets has collapsed since the Parmalat scandal.

Despite the empirical evidence that the Parmalat case was not due to a failure or weakness of the Italian GAAP, but rather because of a lack of their enforcement (see Melis and Melis, 2005), the quality of Italian GAAP was questioned after the Parmalat scandal, especially internationally by financial analysts and finance academics. For instance, a Citigroup analyst report (2003, p. 3) noted that there was 'little doubt that Italian GAAP accounting has fostered a lack of transparency which we hope will be resolved over the next few quarters as Parmalat shifts towards reporting under tighter IAS accounting standards from 2005'. In their investigation of the Parmalat case, Buchanan and Yang (2005) argued that Italy has always had a bad reputation regarding its GAAP, implying that this played a role in the Parmalat case.

The Parmalat scandal had a significant impact on the Italian political agenda, which switched from relaxing company regulations (e.g. the 2004 Company Act) to tightening regulation and controls (the 2006 Saving law). For example, when the Parmalat scandal occurred, the Italian Parliament had just introduced laws to make false accounting a civil rather than a criminal offence, thereby downplaying the seriousness of such behaviour, and was working on a company law reform (eventually released in January 2004) aimed at allowing Italian companies to choose between three different board structures (Italian, British and German). Despite this great innovation in regulation, hardly any of the listed companies have changed their board structures, given the increased scrutiny of corporate governance procedures after Parmalat (Melis, 2006b).

## 13.5 CONCLUSION

Italy is characterized by a principles-based GAAP environment, and this chapter has shown that creative accounting practices are by no means limited to a rules-based GAAP environment. When the preparer of the financial statements is opportunistic, principles-based GAAPs are no defence against creative accounting as the Pirelli case illustrated.

This chapter has also analysed the evidence from a recent major case of financial reporting fraud: Parmalat. The key accounting techniques employed by Parmalat senior management, as well as the relationship with the corporate governance structures that allowed and/or did not hamper the fraud, were investigated in order to outline the key characteristics of the accounting fraud. Accounting issues at Parmalat included creative accounting practices (such as the creative practice of 'redeemable' preference shares recorded as equity) but, mostly, the accounting practices used went well beyond the boundaries of conventional GAAP. Fraudulent accounting at Parmalat was significant, and included the falsification of earnings, assets and liabilities, via a great variety of techniques.

The collapse of Parmalat has indeed had a wide-reaching impact on Italian business and society. This has led to changes in regulation regarding the external auditor's engagement rules, and the mandatory representation of minority shareholders on the board of directors. Since 2005 Italy has complied with the EU requirement to adopt IFRS for the preparation and presentation of consolidated financial statements by listed companies. In addition, the Italian Parliament has also required the mandatory adoption of IFRS by listed companies for the preparation and presentation of their non-consolidated (i.e. separate and single) financial statements since 2006.

The mandatory adoption of IFRS should enhance the quality or, at least, the reputation of the financial reporting system of the Italian listed companies. Listed companies should find it less difficult to gain access to the international capital markets. However, this does not mean that future financial reporting fraud will not occur. The adoption of IFRS per se would not have avoided the accounting fraud that occurred at Parmalat.

## REFERENCES

(For convenience, articles in Italian have also been translated into English.)

Alexander, D. & Jermakowicz, E. (2006), 'A true and fair view of the principles/rules debate', *Abacus*, **42**(2), 132–164.
Amaduzzi, A. (1949), *Conflicts and Equilibrium of Interests in Corporate Financial Statements* (Conflitto ed equilibrio di interessi nel bilancio dell'impresa), Cacucci, Bari.
Amodeo, D. (1964), *The Administration of Industrial Firms* (Le Gestioni Industriali Produttrici di Beni), UTET, Turin.
Beasley, M. (1996), 'An empirical analysis of the relation between the board of director composition and financial statement fraud', *The Accounting Review*, **71**(4), 443–465.

Benedetto, F. and Di Castri, S. (2005), 'The "Parmalat case" and the independence of the monitors: directors, statutory auditors and external auditors, (Il 'caso Parmalat' e l'indipendenza dei controllori: amministratori, sindaci e revisori alla prova del crack)', *Banca Impresa Società*, **24**(2), 211–246.

Bianchi, L. and Corrado, D. (2004), *Financial Reporting in the Football Club Industry* (I bilancio delle società di calcio), Egea, Milan.

Buchanan, B. and Yang, T. (2005), 'The benefits and costs of controlling shareholders: the rise and fall of Parmalat', *Research in International Business and Finance*, **19**(1), 27–52.

Cardia, L. (2004), 'The relationship between non-financial companies, financial markets and investors' protection' (I rapporti tra il sistema delle imprese, i mercati finanziari e la tutela del risparmio). Testimony of the CONSOB President at Parliament Committees VI 'Finanze' and X 'Attività produttive, commercio e turismo' della Camera and 6° 'Finanze e tesoro' and 10° 'Industria, commercio e turismo', del Senato, 20 January.

Chiatturini, S. (2004), *Report on the Parmalat group. Issues on Fraud in Financial Statements* (Consulenza tecnica Gruppo Parmalat. Profili di falsità dei bilanci), Procura della Repubblica – Tribunale di Milano, Milan.

Citigroup analyst report (2003), *Parmalat*, 17 November.

CNDCR (1994), *Principio Contabile n. 11 – Bilancio d'esercizio – Finalità e postulati* (Financial statements: objectives and postulates), Fondazione OIC, Rome.

Coda, V. (1966), *The Audit of Financial Statements* (La certificazione dei bilanci d'impresa), Giuffrè, Milan.

Coffee, J. (2002), 'Understanding Enron: it's about the gatekeepers, stupid', *The Business Lawyer*, **57**, 1403–1420.

CONSOB (2003), *Annual Report 2002* (Relazione Annuale 2002), CONSOB, Rome.

COSO (1999), *Fraudulent Financial Reporting 1987–1997: An Analysis of U.S. Public Companies*.

D'Oriano, R. (1990), *On the Developments of Financial Statements* (Sugli sviluppi dell'informazione di bilancio), Editoriale scientifica, Naples.

Della Penna, F. (1942), *Corporate forms* (Le forme aziendali), Muglia Editore, Catania.

DeZoort, F.T., Hermanson, D.R., Archambealt, D.S. and Reed, S.A. (2002), 'Audit committee effectiveness: a synthesis of the empirical audit committee literature', *Journal of Accounting Literature*, **21**, 38–75.

Dezzani, F. (1974), *The External Audit of Financial Statements* (La certificazione del bilancio d'esercizio), Giuffrè, Milan.

Dezzani, F. (2006), 'The adoption of IAS/IFRS and tax effects' (Introduzione degli IAS/IFRS ed effetti fiscali), in *L'evoluzione del bilancio d'esercizio e l'introduzione dei principi contabili internazionali (IASB)*, Pula-Cagliari Conference Proceedings, 28 October.

Diamond, D. (2004), 'Presidential address, committing to commit: short-term debt when enforcement is costly', *Journal of Finance*, **59**(4), 1447–1479.

Di Castri, S. (2004), 'Financial analysts' conflict of interests: US regulation, trends in E.U. and perspectives in Italy' (I conflitti di interesse degli analisti finanziari: disciplina statunitense, evoluzione della normativa comunitaria e prospettive nell'ordinamento italiano), *Banca Impresa Società*, **23**(3), 477–514.

Di Pietra, R. and Riccaboni, A. (2001) *Reporting of Stock Options: Creative Compliance in a Regulated Environment*, University of Siena, Quaderni Senesi di Economia aziendale e di Ragioneria, Serie interventi, No. 72.

Draghi law (1998), *Company Act* (Testo Unico delle Disposizioni in Materia di Intermediazione Finanziaria), Legislative decree No. 58/1998.

Ferrarini, G. and Giudici, P. (2006), 'Financial scandals and the role of private enforcement: the Parmalat case', in *After Enron. Improving Corporate Law and Modernising Securities Regulation in Europe and the US*, eds J. Armour and J. McCahery, Hart Publishing, Oxford, pp. 159–215.

Greco, E. (1933), *Essays and Jokes on Financial Accounting* (Scritti e Scherzi di Ragioneria Professionale), LIR, Milan.

Hamilton, S. (2005), 'How going global compromised Parmalat', *European Business Forum*, **21**(Spring), 65–69.

Heller, R. (2003), 'Parmalat: a particularly Italian scandal', *Forbes*, 30 December, available at http://www.forbes.com.

Hodson, N. (2005), 'Detecting fraud and managing the risk', in *Governing the Corporation: Regulation and Corporate Governance in an Age of Scandal and Global Markets*, ed. J. O'Brien, John Wiley & Sons, Inc., Hoboken, NJ, pp. 185–204.

IAS 17 (2006), *Leases*, International Financial Reporting Standards, IASCF, London.

IFRS 2 (2004), *Share-based Payment*, International Financial Reporting Standards, IASCF, London.

Krishnan, J. (2005), 'Audit committee quality and internal control: an empirical analysis', *The Accounting Review*, **80**(2), 649–675.

Lago, U., Simmons, R. and Szymanski, S. (2006), 'The financial crisis in European football: an introduction', *Journal of Sports Economics*, **7**(1), 3–12.

Lyman, E. (2004), 'Parmalat's problems: an Italian drama', *The Washington Times*, 12 January.

Masini, C. (1947), *The Administration of Industrial Firms and Financial Accounting* (Economia delle Imprese Industriali e Rilevazioni D'azienda), Giuffrè, Milan.

McCoy, T. and Hoskins, M. (2006), 'Alza Corporation: an illustration of form over substance', *Journal of Accounting, Ethics & Public Policy*, **6**(1), 31–48.

Melis, A. (2004), 'On the role of the board of statutory auditors in Italian listed companies', *Corporate Governance – An International Review*, **12**(1), 74–84.

Melis, A. (2005a), 'Critical issues on the enforcement of the "true and fair view" accounting principles'. *Learning from Parmalat, Corporate Ownership and Control*, **2**(2), 108–119.

Melis, A. (2005b), 'Corporate governance failures: to what extent is Parmalat a particularly Italian case?' *Corporate Governance – An International Review*, **13**(4), 478–488.

Melis, A. (2006a), 'Strong blockholders and corporate governance structures that improve minority shareholders' protection. The case of Telecom Italia', in *International Corporate Governance. A Case Study Approach*, ed. C. Mallin, Edward Elgar, Cheltenham, UK, pp. 57–81.

Melis, A. (2006b), 'Corporate governance developments in Italy', in *Handbook of International Corporate Governance. Country Analyses*, ed. C. Mallin, Edward Elgar, Cheltenham, UK, pp. 45–68.

Melis, A. and Carta, S. (2008), 'The impact of expensing stock options in blockholder-dominated firms. Evidence from Italy', *Corporate Ownership and Control*, **6**(2), 107–114.

Melis, G. and Melis, A. (2005), 'Financial reporting, corporate governance and Parmalat. Was it a financial reporting failure?' in *Governing the Corporation: Regulation and Corporate Governance in an Age of Scandal and Global Markets*, ed. J. O'Brien, John Wiley & Sons, Inc., Hoboken, NJ, 233–254.

Morrow, S. (2006), 'Impression management in football club financial reporting', *International Journal of Sport Finance*, **1**, 96–108.

Mulligan, M. and Munchau, W. (2003), 'Comment: Parmalat affair has plenty of blame to go round', *Financial Times*, 29 December.

Murphy, K. (2002), 'Explaining executive compensation: managerial power versus the perceived cost of stock options', *University of Chicago Law Review*, **69**, 847–869.

OIC 24 (2005), *Intangibles* (Immobilizzazioni immateriali), Fondazione OIC, Rome.

Onida, P. (1974), 'Nature and limits of creative accounting' (Natura e limiti della politica di bilancio), *Rivista dei Dottori commercialisti*, **25**(6), 895–937.

Palepu, K. and Healy, P. (2003), 'The fall of Enron', *Journal of Economics Perspectives*, **17**(2), 3–26.

Preda Code of Conduct (1999; 2002), *Code of Conduct* (Codice di Autodisciplina), Borsa Italiana, Milan.

PricewaterhouseCoopers Advisory Crisis Management (2004), *2004 Foreign Securities Litigation Study*.

Sale, H. (2004), 'Banks: the forgotten(?) partners in fraud', *University of Cincinnati Law Review*, **73**, 139–177.

Storelli, C. (2005), 'Corporate governance failures. Is Parmalat Europe's Enron?' *Columbia Business Law Review*, **20**(3), 765–824.

Teodori, C. (1995), *Business Administration and Financial Accounting in the Sport Industry. The Case of Football Clubs* (L'economia ed il bilancio delle società sportive. Il caso delle società di calcio), Giapichelli, Turin.

Tweedie, D. (2002), *Statement of Sir David Tweedie, Chairman, International Accounting Standards Board before the Committee on Banking, Housing and Urban Affairs of the United States Senate*, Washington DC, 14 February.

Windram, B. and Song, J. (2004), 'Non-executive directors and the changing nature of audit committees: evidence from UK audit committee chairmen', *Corporate Ownership and Control*, **1**(3), 108–115.

# 14

# Creative Accounting and Accounting Scandals in Japan

Kazuyuki Suda

## 14.1 INTRODUCTION

In Japan, there have been several high-profile accounting scandals in recent years (e.g. the Livedoor case, which caused the Tokyo Stock Exchange to shut down entirely for trading on 18 January 2006 and the Kanebo case, which has been referred to as a Japanese-style Enron accounting scandal). These followed a long history of creative accounting and accounting frauds in Japan. However, as there is insufficient space here to trace the long history of Japanese accounting, this chapter will mainly look at accounting scandals that have occurred since the 1980s.

This chapter focuses on individual accounting scandals. However, there is also aggregate evidence of creative accounting in Japan. Suda and Shuto (2007) investigate *whether* and *how* Japanese companies manage reported earnings to avoid earnings decreases and losses. They examine earnings distribution and study *whether* earnings management exists for Japanese companies. They then estimate discretionary accruals and investigate *how* company managers engage in earnings management. Their evidence suggests that the Japanese companies which reported small earnings or small earnings increases tend to engage in creative accounting.

The accounting scandals investigated in this chapter are characterized by their motivation and divided into three groups (i.e. accounting scandals to maintain high share price, accounting scandals designed to fulfil contractual arrangements, and accounting scandals to avoid bankruptcy). This chapter shows the content of these accounting scandals and how they influenced the accounting institutions in Japan.

The remainder of this chapter is organized as follows. The second section outlines the accounting regulation and standards in Japan. The third section gives a short history of accounting scandals before 1980. The fourth section looks at three types of accounting scandals post-1980s. The fifth section presents the institutional consequences of accounting scandals. A final section summarizes and concludes.

*Creative Accounting, Fraud and International Accounting Scandals*   Edited by Michael Jones
© 2011 Michael Jones. Published by John Wiley & Sons, Ltd

## 14.2 ACCOUNTING REGULATIONS AND STANDARDS IN JAPAN

### 14.2.1 Accounting Regulations

The legally authorized forms of companies named *Kaisha* in Japanese consist of *Godo-kaisha*, *Gomei-kaisha*, *Goshi-kaisha* and *Kabushiki-kaisha*. The *Kabushiki-kaisha*, or joint stock company, is the most common type of company in Japan and the type related to the accounting frauds discussed here. The total number of registered joint stock companies exceeds 2.5 million and makes up more than 96 % of all registered companies in Japan (National Tax Agency, 2009).

Three principal laws regulate and influence company accounting practice in Japan: the Corporation Law, the Financial Instruments and Exchange Act and the Corporation Tax Law.[1] The Corporation Law is administered by the Ministry of Justice and imposes restrictions on the activities and decisions of the management of a company in order to ensure the safety and reliability of commercial transactions and to protect the interests of the company's owners and creditors.[2] The Financial Instruments and Exchange Act is administered by the Financial Services Agency, an external organ of the Cabinet Office, and concerned with providing information to securities investors for their decision-making and maintaining the integrity of the securities exchange markets. While the Corporation Law governs all companies, the Financial Instruments and Exchange Act only applies to particular companies, such as those that have raised more than a hundred million yen in the securities markets or whose shares are listed on stock exchanges. The total number of Japanese listed companies was 3869 as at 31 December 2008 and the Tokyo Stock Exchange (TSE) is the biggest stock exchange. The Corporation Tax Law requires the computation of taxable income in conjunction with accounting income calculated under the Corporation Law. That is to say, the Corporation Tax Law requires conformity between financial reporting and tax reporting and provides rules about income adjustments calculated under the Corporation Law to reconcile it with taxable income.

The above three laws regulate and influence Japanese accounting practice for joint stock companies. The three laws are not in conflict but connected and interrelated, constituting what has been referred to as a triangular legal accounting system (Ministry of Economy, Trade and Industry, 2004; Shiba and Shiba, 1997).

### 14.2.2 Accounting Standards

Japanese accounting standards are issued by the Accounting Standards Board of Japan (ASBJ), which superseded the Business Accounting Deliberation Council (BADC) in 2001. While BADC was an advisory body of the Ministry of Finance, ASBJ is a core organization within the Financial Accounting Standards Foundation (FASF), which was established by contributions of private capital. It means that the accounting standard-setting responsibility has been moved from a government body to a private-sector organization. Accounting

---

[1] The Corporation Law was enacted, separately from the Commercial Code, in 2006. The Financial Instruments and Exchange Act was enacted in 2006 and before that it was the Securities and Exchange Law. Choi and Hiramatu (1987), Cooke and Kikuya (1992), Shiba and Shiba (1997), JICPA (1998) and Koga (2006) explain the laws and accounting regulations in further detail in English.

[2] Toda and McCarty (2005) and Buchanan (2007) study Japanese corporate governance in detail.

standards developed by the ASBJ are authorized by the Financial Services Agency as part of generally accepted accounting principles applicable to companies.

Accounting standards issued by the BADC fitted the needs of Japanese companies well and did not give rise to any inconvenience in the past. However, in the late 1990s, concerns were raised about the soundness and reliability of financial statements in light of international developments. In response to these concerns, action was initiated in 1998 to improve accounting standards and rapidly achieve international harmonization. These changes were termed the 'accounting big bang'.[3]

### 14.2.2.1  Disclosure of Financial Statements

According to accounting standards and regulations of the Corporation Law and the Financial Instruments and Exchange Act, Japanese listed companies disclose financial statements for the individual company and, if the company has a subsidiary, consolidated financial statements. Annual individual and consolidated financial statements include a balance sheet, income statement, statement of changes in shareholders' equity and cash flow statement. While listed companies must submit financial statements to the Financial Services Agency in conformity with the Financial Instruments and Exchange Act, the companies submit financial statements by using the electronic disclosure system, EDINET (Electronic Disclosure for Investors' NETwork: www.fsa.go.jp/edinet/edinet.html).

In addition to the regulations of the Corporation Law and the Financial Instruments and Exchange Act, Japanese share exchanges request the listed companies to submit condensed financial reports to the exchanges immediately upon approval of a draft of the financial statements by the board of directors. The TSE listed companies usually submit them within 45 days after the end of the accounting period by the use of the TDnet system (http://www.tse.or.jp/english/index.html); that is, the timely disclosed information dissemination system of the stock exchange. The condensed financial reports are the most timely disclosed accounting information which general investors can access.

## 14.3  SHORT HISTORY OF ACCOUNTING SCANDALS BEFORE THE 1980S

The current regulatory environment of accounting in Japan was shaped after World War II. Responding to the enactment of the Securities and Exchange Law in 1948, the BADC issued *Financial Accounting Standards for Business Enterprises* in 1949 and *Auditing Standards* in 1950, which were the initial accounting and auditing standards in Japan. These standards were not inductively set, based on general practice of those days, but deductively set, with the political purpose of maintaining the integrity of accounting disclosures and promoting greater efficiency in the securities exchange markets. Therefore, many companies and audit firms were poorly prepared for the standards.

The first, and most influential, accounting fraud was Sanyo Special Steel's case in 1965. Sanyo Special Steel Co. Ltd, a special steel manufacturer whose shares were listed on the TSE, became bankrupt owing debt of 50 billion yen – the largest ever failure at that time.

---

[3] The Ministry of Economy, Trade and Industry (2004) shows its process and influence in detail.

After the bankruptcy, it was discovered that Sanyo Special Steel had reported fictitious sales and illegally inflated earnings by 13 billion yen from 1952 to 1965 (Nihon-keizai-shimbun-shokenbu, 1966, p. 23). On the other hand, the contributed capital excluding reserves shown on the balance sheet at the end of the 1964 financial year was 7.4 billion yen. The auditors provided an unqualified opinion of the audit report throughout these periods. Sanyo Special Steel continued to pay a dividend and bonus to the executives during these periods despite the fact that the company would have had a deficit twice as big as the stated capital without earnings manipulation (Nihon-keizai-shimbun-shokenbu, 1966, p. 23).[4]

The way Sanyo Special Steel falsified its financial statements was based largely on making improper sales to subsidiaries. Sanyo Special Steel forced its subsidiaries to buy its products at a high price and recorded fictitious sales transactions on the parent-only individual financial statements[5] (Nihon-keizai-shimbun-shokenbu, 1966, p. 48). Moreover, Sanyo Special Steel falsified its financial statements by understating the cost of goods sold, its selling and administrative expenses, and interest expenses (Nihon-keizai-shimbun-shokenbu, 1966, p. 19). It is said that Mr Hagino, a former president of the company, managed it like an autocrat and internal control of the company, including the board of directors, ceased to function properly. For example, Mr Hagino borrowed 79 million yen from the company to use for private purposes and company-owned land was appropriated for his family use (Nihon-keizai-shimbun-shokenbu, 1966, p. 64).

The Ministry of Finance accused the former executives of violating the Securities and Exchange Law in 1965 and punished the auditor by removing his licence to practice as a certified public accountant. In 1978, while Mr Hagino's participation in a public trial was brought to a halt because of his illness, the Kobe District Court sentenced four former executives to one year and six months, one year and two months, one year, and 10 months in jail with a one-year suspension, respectively for violations of the Commercial Code, i.e. illegal dividend and aggravated breach of trust (*Asahi-shimbun*, 26 December 1978).

The Ministry of Finance took the situation seriously and inspected financial statements of questionable companies, in particular, from 1965 to 1972. It was found that 169 listed companies had padded figures and the auditors of the financial statements had all, without exception, expressed an unqualified opinion. As a consequence, the 169 companies resubmitted restated financial statements to the Ministry of Finance and 52 auditors were deprived of their certified public accountants licence (Nihon-keizai-shimbun-shokenbu, 1977, p. 120).

Following on from this scandal, the *Auditing Standards* were revised to include visits to affiliated companies, an observation of physical inventory and a confirmation of accounts receivable. In 1967, the BADC issued the *Statement of Opinion on Consolidated Financial Statements* to establish a disclosure system for consolidated financial statements. It was necessary to disclose consolidated financial statements to prevent earnings manipulation by using subsidiaries. After considerable deliberation, the BADC issued *Accounting Standards for Consolidated Financial Statements* in 1975 and listed companies with subsidiaries began to disclose consolidated financial statements from 1978.

---

[4] The Commercial Code prohibited a company without sufficient financial resources from paying dividends and had set a ceiling on income available for dividends. The current law, the Corporation Law, also requires a ceiling on the surplus available for dividends.

[5] At this time, Japanese companies did not disclose consolidated financial statements, only unconsolidated individual financial statements. Listed companies with a subsidiary have disclosed both consolidated financial statements and unconsolidated individual financial statements since 1978.

Despite these improvements to accounting standards and auditing procedures, accounting fraud has subsequently occurred repeatedly. The largest ever earnings manipulation at the time, Fuji Sash's, occurred in 1976. Fuji Sash Co. Ltd, a metal products manufacturer, listed on the TSE, illegally boosted earnings from 1973 to 1976 by 42.5 billion yen (three times larger than in the case of Sanyo Special Steel). The technique used was to boost sales by forcing an associated company to purchase Fuji Sash's products at an improper high price and understate cost of goods by overstating obsolete inventories. Fuji Sash illegally paid dividends of 1.5 billion yen and managerial bonuses of 150 million yen despite the fact that the company would have been in deficit without earnings manipulation from 1973 to 1975. After the case, the Ministry of Finance revised the standards of accounting for consolidated financial statements and the equity method was introduced from 1984, which increases (decreases) periodically the investment's carrying amount by the investor's proportionate share of the earnings (losses) of the investee for associated companies including non-consolidated subsidiaries.

The TSE delisted the shares of Fuji Sash Co. Ltd in 1978. The Ministry of Finance accused a former president of violating the Securities and Exchange Law, and punished the two auditors by removing their licences. In 1982, the Tokyo District Court sentenced a former president to three years in jail with suspension for violating the Commercial Code and the Securities and Exchange Law (i.e. illegal dividend, aggravated breach of trust and false financial reporting). Since the sentence was suspended for five years, he actually avoided jail.[6]

## 14.4 THREE TYPES OF ACCOUNTING SCANDAL POST-1980s

Almost all the accounting scandals which occurred in the 1960s and 1970s were motivated by avoidance of bankruptcy. Post-1980s, although there are still many cases of accounting scandals committed to avoid bankruptcy, accounting scandals with differing motives increased in number. Several high-profile accounting scandals and examples of creative accounting post-1980s are shown in Appendix 14.1.

As presented in Appendix 14.1 and discussed in depth later, the accounting scandals by Yaohan Japan, Sawako and Livedoor were all intended to maintain high share prices. In addition, the accounting scandal of Ishikawajima Harima Heavy Industry, IHI, is thought also to be motivated by the need to maintain a high share price (*Nihon-keizai-shimbun*,[7] 12 December 2007 and *Asahi-shimbun*, 3 January 2008). IHI, which makes ships and heavy machinery and was listed on the TSE, restated an originally presented annual operating income of 24.6 billion yen to a loss of 5.6 billion yen in 2007 and restated a semi-annual operating income of 1.06 billion yen to a loss of 8.7 billion yen in 2006 because it had improperly recognized revenue on a long-term construction contract based on the percentage-of-completion method (*Nihon-keizai-shimbun*, 13 December 2007). The TSE moved it to the monitoring post (this means the TSE investigates whether the company should be delisted) and the Securities and Exchange Surveillance Commission (SESC), the Japanese market watchdog, started an investigation in December 2007. The SESC recommended that the Financial Services Agency should impose a record fine of

---

[6] In many cases, in this and in subsequent scandals, suspended sentences were given and their recipients avoided jail.

[7] *Nihon-keizai-shimbun* is a Japanese business newspaper similar to the *Wall Street Journal* or *Financial Times*. *Asahi-shimbun* is a general newspaper, one of the most authoritative newspapers in Japan.

1595 million yen on IHI for falsifying financial statements, in violation of the Financial Instruments and Exchange Act. As a result of the recommendation, the Financial Services Agency ordered IHI to pay the fine of 1595 million yen on 9 July 2008 and IHI paid the fine without appealing to the law. The amount of the fine was the largest ever at that time.

Since IHI had issued new shares amounting to 64 billion yen in January and February 2007 and new bonds amounting to 30 billion yen in June 2007, it was reported that the improper accounting procedure might be motivated mainly by the need to maintain high share prices in order to issue the new securities favourably (*Nihon-keizai-shimbun*, 12 December 2007 and 20 June 2008; *Asahi-shimbun*, 3 January 2008). After moving to the special monitoring post of the TSE, IHI submitted reports to ensure appropriate internal control systems to the TSE by rule. While the TSE may delist companies if it concludes that their internal control systems are inappropriate, the exchange removed IHI from the special monitoring post on 12 May 2009 because it believed that IHI had fully resolved the problems in its internal communications, monitoring and other systems that resulted in the huge restatement of income (*Jiji Press America*, 11 May 2009 and *Nihon-keizai-shimbun*, 12 May 2009).

As presented in Appendix 14.1, the accounting scandals of Morimoto-gumi and Nikko Cordial Co., Ltd were thought to be motivated by contractual considerations. Morimoto-gumi is related to a public construction contract and Nikko Cordial is related to a managerial compensation contract (*Nihon-keizai-shimbun*, 13 May 2004 and 19 February 2007). The Japanese government agency in charge of public construction ranks the construction companies into various size categories. Companies can bid for construction contracts within their allocated categories. Morimoto-gumi falsified its financial statements to maintain its ranking and bid for larger public construction contracts. Nikko Cordial set up a management compensation scheme linked to consolidated net income just before the period when the company manipulated earnings.

On the other hand, the accounting scandals of Riccar Co. Ltd, Yamaichi Securities Co. Ltd, Long-Term Credit Bank of Japan and Kanebo Co. Ltd were traditional ones motivated by the avoidance of bankruptcy. For example, the Long-Term Credit Bank of Japan went bankrupt in October 1998 and, after the injection of 7 trillion yen worth of public funds to clean up the mess, restarted as Shinsei Bank in 2000. The Tokyo District Court and the Tokyo High Court sentenced three top executives to prison for violation of the Commercial Code and the Securities and Exchange Law because they had falsified its financial statements and paid dividends illegally worth about 7.1 billion yen for 1998 by failing to write off 313 billion yen in irrecoverable loans using lax assessment standards. However, on 18 July 2008, the Supreme Court delivered a judgment of acquittal because a rational estimation of irrecoverable loans is very difficult and the executives did not act illegally when estimating irrecoverable loans. The acquittal did not mean that there had been no creative accounting which was mainly motivated by the need to avoid bankruptcy.

Although these post-1980s accounting scandals in Japan can be classified into three motivational types (i.e. to maintain a higher share price, to implement contracts favourably and to avoid bankruptcy), some accounting scandals, such as Sanyo Electric Co., had more complicated motivations. Sanyo Electric restated its financial statements for the parent company on 25 December 2007. The company restated an originally presented net income of 17.6 billion yen to a loss of 90.8 billion yen for 2001. The dividend it paid between 2003 and 2004, totalling 28 billion yen, was higher than legally allowed given its restated loss.

Sanyo Electric failed to record properly an impairment loss of subsidiaries' shares in its financial statements for the parent company. According to the Japanese accounting standards, equity investments in subsidiaries should be valued at historical cost but, after a significant drop, fair value should be used as the new book value, unless the fair value is expected to recover. The valuation differences have to be treated as impairment loss for the accounting period (JICPA, 2000; Koga, 2006). Sanyo Electric did not record properly an impairment loss of subsidiaries' shares on the parent financial statements and it was speculated that this would enable it to continue to pay dividends (*Asahi-shimbun*, 26 December 2007). The company said that the losses did not affect the consolidated financial statements. On 25 December 2007, the Securities and Exchange Surveillance Commission recommended that the Financial Services Agency should fine the company 8.3 million yen. As a result of the recommendation, the Financial Services Agency ordered Sanyo Electric to pay the fine of 8.3 million yen on 18 January 2008 and the company paid the fine without appealing to the law. While the TSE moved Sanyo Electric to the monitoring post for possible delisting on 25 December 2007, the exchange removed the company from the monitoring post on 9 February 2008 (*Nihon-keizai-shimbun*, 9 February 2008).

Since the improper treatment of the impairment loss of subsidiaries' shares on the financial statement for the parent company did not affect the consolidated financial statements, these dubious accounting practices are unlikely to have been directly motivated by the need to maintain high share prices. Sanyo Electric was neither financially distressed nor were any of its contracts affected by its accounting treatment. Thus, the case of Sanyo Electric does not correspond exactly to the three types of accounting scandals below. It is said that the dubious accounting practices might be motivated by the need to continue dividend payments (*Asahi-shimbun*, 26 December 2007).

### 14.4.1 Accounting Scandal to Maintain High Share Prices

This subsection presents chronologically three accounting scandals motivated by the need to maintain a high share price (i.e. Yaohan Japan, Sawako Corporation and Livedoor).

#### 14.4.1.1 *Yaohan Japan*

Yaohan Japan Co. Ltd ran a chain of supermarkets consisting of more than 400 stores in 15 countries around the world and its shares were listed on the TSE. The company collapsed in September 1997 leaving more than 185.5 billion yen in debts, the biggest in the Japanese retail industry.

Yaohan Japan issued convertible bonds from 1990 to 1994 amounting to about 47 billion yen. Although the second issue of convertible bonds was due for redemption by 20 May 1997, the company was low in funds and sold 16 stores in May 1997 to raise the redemption money (*Nihon-keizai-shimbun*, 16 May 1997). However, since the other convertible bonds would fall due for redemption in September 1998, May 1999 and September 2001, the company made desperate efforts to maintain a higher share price in order to stimulate bond-holders to convert their convertible bonds into common shares (*Nihon-keizai-shimbun*, 16 December 1998).

The company rigged its earnings by understating cost of goods sold, overstating obsolete inventories and booking gains on sales of real estate to a dummy company while the real estate was repurchased after the end of the financial year. The company illegally paid dividends worth about 1.4 billion yen as it had losses worth about 12.6 billion yen in 1996 without earnings manipulation (*Nihon-keizai-shimbun*, 31 March 1999).

A former president, Mr Terumasa Wada, a member of the founding family, was arrested on 9 November 1998 for violating the Commercial Code and the Securities Exchange Law. The prosecutor alleged that Mr Wada had falsified the financial statements of the company in 1996 in order to maintain its credibility and stimulate bond-holders to convert their convertible bonds into common shares (*Nihon-keizai-shimbun*, 16 December 1998). On 31 March 1999, the Shizuoka District Court sentenced him to three years in prison suspended for five years for violating the Commercial Code and the Securities Exchange Law (i.e. illegal dividends and false financial reporting). The accounting fraud of Yaohan Japan was mainly motivated by maintaining a high share price.

The Ministry of Finance punished the auditors who had expressed an unqualified opinion on the financial statements of Yaohan Japan with three months' cessation of business (*Nihon-keizai-shimbun*, 21 June 2000). The 143 investors of the convertible bonds, having made decisions based on the false financial statements, filed a lawsuit against the former executives and Chuo Audit claiming about 420 million yen damages. On 21 July 2004, they agreed in settlement that the former executives and Chuo Audit would pay about 190 million yen (*Nihon-keizai-shimbun*, 22 July 2004). The company obtained court approval in December 1997 and is now restructuring with support from the major supermarket chain, Aeon Co. Ltd.

### 14.4.1.2 *Sawako Corporation*

Sawako Corporation, a medium-sized general construction company whose shares were traded on the over-the-counter market in Japan and the Nasdaq in the USA, reported operating income of 1.65 billion yen in 1998, which was 7 % growth year-on-year and the highest ever for the company. The share prices correspondingly soared. However, it was revealed that Sawako Corporation had boosted its sales by the fraudulent application of the percentage-of-completion basis for construction in 1998 and 1999. The *Nihon-keizai-shimbun* reported that Sawako Corporation had inflated earnings illegally by 4.6 billion yen in total and the company would have reported a decrease in sales and operating income without manipulation in 1998 (*Nihon-keizai-shimbun*, 26 December 2001).

Sawako Corporation had issued convertible bonds of 3 billion yen and bonds with share purchase warrants[8] of 500 million yen. If bond-holders did not exercise the conversion rights, Sawako Corporation needed redemption funds, but its cash flow became worse and it had negative working capital of 7.5 billion yen in 1998. Therefore, the company was making desperate efforts to maintain a higher share price so as to stimulate bond-holders to exercise their conversion rights.

Sawako Corporation recognized sales on a long-term construction contract based on the percentage-of-completion method. Under this method, the amount of sales to be recognized

---

[8] Share purchase warrants are a type of security entitling the holders to buy a proportionate amount of common shares at a specified price.

each year is equal to the total contract price multiplied by the percentage of the contract completed. The percentage completed is estimated as a rule by the ratio of costs incurred during the period to total estimated costs. Sawako Corporation rigged the period's incurred costs by forcing a co-worker in the construction project to make out a false invoice and boosted the period's sales by 6 billion yen (*Nihon-keizai-shimbun*, 26 December 2001). Sawako Corporation illegally paid dividends worth about 320 million yen in 1998 and 1999.

A former president of Sawako Corporation, Mr Ohira, was arrested on 4 December 2001 for violating the Commercial Code and the Securities and Exchange Law (i.e. paying illegal dividends and false financial reporting). It is reported that Mr Ohira was an overstrong personality and internal control of the company ceased to function properly. For example, while Mr Ohira held shares in the company and received dividends paid illegally, he erected a new three-storey house in 1998 and used the proceeds from the illegal dividends for a loan (*Nihon-keizai-shimbun*, 26 December 2001).

He was eventually sentenced by the Nagoya High Court to one year and two months in prison suspended for four years. According to the judgment, Mr Ohira made substantial efforts to maintain the share price and directed an employee to make out a false invoice to boost the period's sales (*Nihon-keizai-shimbun*, 29 March 2005). The accountant who audited the financial statements of Sawako Corporation was punished by the Japanese Institute of Certified Accountants by one month's cessation of business.

### 14.4.1.3  Livedoor

The accounting scandal of Livedoor, an internet conglomerate company, whose shares were traded on the TSE, was large-scale and had a very substantial impact upon the Japanese economy and society. While traditional Japanese companies focused on increasing sales as a business objective, Mr Horie, a president of Livedoor, kept his eyes on increasing the company's market capitalization. He assembled a company with a market value of 700 billion yen (about $US 7 billion) in just 10 years through more than 30 acquisitions of businesses ranging from software to internet connections and online financial services. This expand-by-acquisition strategy is common in the UK and USA, but still relatively new to Japan, where companies usually expand into new fields more cautiously (*Wall Street Journal*, 18 January 2006). Consecutive increases in earnings helped to bolster the company's share price and allowed it to make acquisitions with inflated shares.

Mr Horie suddenly became famous in June 2004, when he announced that he wanted to buy a corporation owning a professional baseball team, Kintetsu Buffalos. Mr Horie also tried to acquire a Japanese major television network, Fuji Television Network, Inc., in April 2005. He was a hero of the times and enjoyed widespread popularity among young people (Okumura, 2006, p. 20).

In 2004, Livedoor reported four times more consolidated operating income than in 2003. However, it was revealed that Livedoor had reported fictitious revenue of 5.2 billion yen and the company would have reported a consolidated operating loss without manipulation. Livedoor used off-balance sheet vehicles, special purpose entities (SPE), to hide losses and to illegally book capital gains in its accounts. This worked as follows.

Livedoor Marketing, a publicly traded online advertisement and marketing company, was a subsidiary of Livedoor. Livedoor Marketing announced its intention of acquiring Money

Life, a publishing and advertising company, in a share-exchange deal. An appraising and consulting company, Livedoor Finance, had been asked to establish a purchase price for Money Life. However, the acquisition was a camouflage because prior to the announcement of the deal, Livedoor Marketing had already purchased the shares of Money Life in cash for a lower amount via the SPE, VLMA No. 2 Investment Business Partnership. Moreover, Livedoor Finance was a subsidiary of Livedoor and had inflated Money Life's estimated value to an unreasonable amount. When Livedoor Marketing announced it would acquire Money Life with the more highly valued shares, the shares of Livedoor Marketing were transferred into the SPE instead of to Money Life's shareholders. The SPE then sold the shares of Livedoor Marketing to foreign investors at a highly valued amount and booked the gains on the share sales of 600 million yen. Since Livedoor Marketing was a subsidiary of Livedoor, Livedoor should have reported these share disposals as a capital transaction in the consolidated financial statements. However, recording multiple capital transactions as sales, Livedoor boosted operating income by 5.3 billion yen altogether on consolidated financial statements in the 2004 financial year (*Nihon-keizai-shimbun*, 16 March 2006 and *Wall Street Journal*, 24 January 2006).

As soon as the news spread that prosecutors had raided Livedoor's headquarters and Mr Horie's home on suspicion of Securities and Exchange Law violations, a sell-off of Livedoor's shares was sparked and the benchmark Nikkei 225 declined by 5.4%. The TSE then shut down its entire trading system on 18 January 2006 after the news prompted a sell-off threatening to crash its computer system. The event rattled confidence in the stock market and became known as the 'Livedoor Shock'.

The founder and charismatic president of Livedoor, Mr Horie, was arrested for alleged accounting fraud on 23 January 2006. TSE moved Livedoor Co. Ltd to the monitoring post and decided to delist Livedoor's shares on 14 April 2006. After the raid in January, more than 500 billion yen (about $US 5 billion) was wiped off Livedoor's share value before delisting.

On 5 June 2006, more than 1600 shareholders filed a lawsuit against Livedoor and Mr Horie for damages incurred from accounting manipulation that had inflated share prices. The plaintiffs seek 10.1 billion yen in damages (*Nihon-keizai-shimbun*, 6 June 2006). Fuji Television Network Inc., a large shareholder of Livedoor, with 130 million shares, also filed a lawsuit against Livedoor in the Tokyo District Court and claimed 34.5 billion yen damages because of accounting fraud (*Nihon-keizai-shimbun*, 27 March 2007).

The Tokyo District Court sentenced Mr Horie, 34 years old, to two-and-a-half years in jail on 16 March 2007 for violating the Securities and Exchange Law. The Chief Justice read out the reasons for judgment: Mr Horie had violated the need to disclose accounting information fairly and increased the company's market capitalization by sacrificing the investors. This sentence is harsher than usual in Japan, where executives found guilty are often given suspended sentences (*Wall Street Journal*, 16 March 2007). While the Tokyo High Court delivered the same sentence, Mr Horie has appealed against the Judge's decision to the Supreme Court. The lawsuit is still proceeding at the time of writing (May 2010).

Koyo Audit Corporation had audited the financial statements of Livedoor. It is noteworthy that the Tokyo District Court sentenced an accountant of Koyo Audit Corporation to 10 months in prison on 23 March 2007. This is the first case where a certified public accountant was sentenced to prison without a suspended sentence. The Chief Justice criticized him for giving an unqualified opinion on the audit report in spite of his recognition of accounting irregularities and for the way he had reported the capital transaction for the shares of Livedoor Marketing as a sale (*Nihon-keizai-shimbun*, 24 March 2007).

Livedoor's case raised questions about Japanese accounting standards for special purpose entities. Just as Enron and other US companies used them to keep certain financial deals off their books, Livedoor also relied on a similar vehicle to falsify financial statements. As a result, the ASBJ issued *Practical Solution on Investors' Accounting for Limited-Liability Partnerships and Limited-Liability Companies* in September 2006, which requires companies to include special purpose entities in their consolidated financial statements as subsidiaries if an entity is substantially controlled by another entity which is the parent. Whether an entity is substantially controlled is judged by criteria such as the percentage of share ownership, contribution of funds or earnings distribution.

### 14.4.2 Accounting Scandal Related to Contracts

This subsection presents two accounting scandals motivated by business contracts. The Morimoto-gumi case relates to public construction contracts, but the case of Nikko Cordial is related to managerial compensation contracts.

#### 14.4.2.1 *Morimoto-gumi*

The Japanese governmental budget for public construction in the 2007 financial year was more than 6.9 trillion yen, corresponding to 3.6% of Japanese GDP (*Nihon-keizai-shimbun*, 5 September 2007). There is fierce competition between construction companies in this huge market. The government agency in charge of public construction ranks the construction companies into several categories and then relates the scale of construction to the ratings. Ranked companies put in a bid for construction within the respective scale of construction. For example, in 2004, a company ranked *AA* is approved to put in a bid for public construction for more than 1.35 billion yen and a company ranked *A* can put in a bid for public construction for more than 0.35 billion yen but less than 1.35 billion yen (*Nihon-keizai-shimbun*, 13 May 2004).

The ranking is conducted based on the following criteria: (1) size of operation, (2) state of management, (3) technical capabilities and (4) other evaluation items. The first and second items are mainly evaluated in accordance with the figures from the company's financial statements (e.g. construction revenue, return on assets and operating income to construction revenue ratio).

Morimoto-gumi Co. Ltd, a long-established midsize construction company, illegally manipulated earnings amounting to 98 billion yen from 1999 to 2003. The objective of this manipulation was to maintain its ranking and put in a bid for larger public construction contracts (*Nihon-keizai-shimbun*, 13 May 2004). Morimoto-gumi understated its cost of goods sold by deferring expenses to the next financial year so as to boost the ratio of operating income to construction revenue. Morimoto-gumi also paid illegal dividends as the company would have had a deficit without earnings manipulation.

On 18 April 2006, the Osaka District Court sentenced a former president, Mr Morimoto, a member of the founding family, to six years in jail for violating the Securities and

Exchange Law (i.e. false financial reporting) and the Commercial Code (i.e. paying illegal dividend), and for cheating a bank out of a loan on the basis of a fraudulent construction contract. It is said that Mr Morimoto managed like an autocrat and internal control of the company did not operate normally. According to the judgment of the Chief Justice, Mr Morimoto directly required subordinates to falsify the financial statements in order to maintain the company's construction rating so as to bid for larger public construction contracts (*Nihon-keizai-shimbun*, 18 April 2006).

### 14.4.2.2 Nikko Cordial

A Japanese company generally does not have an explicit earnings-based compensation contract with its managers. The sum of compensation paid to managers is reported in the annual report, but more detailed information on compensation, either by kind or by person, is seldom disclosed. Since some empirical studies of Japanese managers' compensation have presented evidence that the correlation between a manager's compensation and the profitability of the company is statistically significant (Kang and Shivdasani, 1995; Kaplan, 1994; Shuto, 2007; Otomasa, 2004), it is believed that the relation between a manager's compensation and company performance is similar to that in the UK and USA (even though explicit earnings-based compensation contracts are not widely used).

However, the number of companies with explicit managerial earnings-based compensation contracts has recently increased. Nikko Cordial, one of the three biggest securities houses in Japan, listed on the TSE, has changed its managerial compensation system to a performance-based one and disclosed information about the compensation by kind and by person since 2004. The new managerial compensation system of the company triggered creative accounting. This worked as follows.

In September 2004, Nikko Principal Investments (NPI), a subsidiary of Nikko Cordial Co. Ltd, acquired share-exchangeable bonds fluctuating in line with the share price of a call-centre company, Bell System 24, issued by NPI Holdings (NPIH), which is a special purpose company. As the share price of Bell System 24 rose, NPI recognized a valuation gain and NPIH recognized a valuation loss on the bonds. However, Nikko Cordial consolidated NPI's financial statements, but did not consolidate NPIH's financial statements and, therefore, reported a valuation gain of 18.7 billion yen (about $US 155.8 million at that time) as operating income in the consolidated income statement for 2005.

Moreover, NPI adjusted the date of the bond issue to the lowest price of the day to record more valuation gain and more operating income. Although the share price of Bell System 24 at the decision date of issuing the share-exchangeable bonds was 26 540 yen, NPI adjusted the date of the bond's issuance to the lowest share price of the day, 24 480 yen. Since the market value at the end of 2005 was 28 100 yen, NPI could book more valuation gain than the real gain (*Nihon-keizai-shimbun*, 31 January 2007; *Wall Street Journal*, 2 February 2007).

The Securities and Exchange Surveillance Commission (SESC), the Japanese market watchdog, investigated the transactions and alleged that Nikko Cordial had manipulated its consolidated income by including false valuation gains and losses on the bonds and by changing the date of the bonds issued. The SESC recommended that the Financial Services Agency should fine Nikko Cordial on 18 December 2006. The Financial Services Agency fined Nikko Cordial 500 million yen (about $US 4.2 million) for manipulating earnings in 2007, the biggest penalty ever levied by the Financial Services Agency (*Nihon-keizai-shimbun*, 31 January 2007; *Wall Street Journal*, 6 January 2007).

On 19 December 2006, Nikko Cordial announced corrected earnings for the years ended March 2005 and March 2006 and the TSE moved Nikko Cordial to the monitoring post on the same date to investigate whether the company should be delisted. The chairman of Nikko Cordial, Mr Kaneko, and the president, Mr Arimura, resigned on 25 December 2006. Nikko Cordial then established an investigation committee which consisted of outside experts and undertook to give a clear picture of the accounting scandal.

On 27 January 2007, the investigation committee reported that Nikko Cordial should have consolidated NPIH's financial statements. Moreover, the investigation committee found that accounting manipulation had been conducted intentionally and was an organization-wide attempt. Nikko Cordial had originally said that the accounting manipulation was caused by an employee who had made a mistake and top management was not aware of any manipulation. By contrast, the investigation committee stated that Mr Yamamoto, a former chief financial officer of Nikko Cordial, was directly involved in the manipulation so as to boost earnings while Mr Arimura, the former president, was in a position to know the details of what was happening. Furthermore, Mr Kunihiro, a lawyer and a member of the investigation committee, stated that the performance-related compensation of the management seemed to be one of the most important motivations for the earnings manipulation.

Nikko Cordial had set up a management compensation scheme linked to annual consolidated net income just before the period in which the company illegally manipulated earnings. NPI, a subsidiary of Nikko Cordial, contracted with the executives to pay a bonus of 3 % of the annual operating income (*Nihon-keizai-shimbun*, 19 February 2007). According to the 2005 annual report, Mr Arimura's compensation consisted of 71 million yen fixed payment and 88 million yen performance-related pay. Moreover, he was given 186 share options[9] whose total market price was about 150 million yen at the end of the year. His compensation was much better than the average amount of other companies and the proportion of performance-based compensation was very high. This scheme of compensation was very infrequent in Japan.

Nikko Cordial reported officially that the company had found inappropriate procedures in its bond valuation, resulting in consolidated operating income being boosted by 19.1 billion yen, and submitted restated consolidated financial statements to the Financial Services Agency on 27 February 2007 (*Nihon-keizai-shimbun*, 28 February 2007). The TSE removed Nikko Cordial from the monitoring post on 13 March 2007 because it lacked any conclusive evidence that Nikko Cordial had conducted accounting manipulation intentionally and that the manipulation was an organization-wide attempt (*Nihon-keizai-shimbun*, 13 March 2007).

However, on 23 April 2007, Nikko Cordial filed a lawsuit against Mr Arimura, Mr Yamamoto and Mr Hirano (a former chairman of NPI) in the Tokyo District Court, claiming about 3.4 billion yen damages because of improper huge compensation caused by accounting manipulation. The three men appealed at the Tokyo District Court (*Nihon-keizai-shimbun*, 24 April and 6 July 2007). Finally, it was reported that Nikko Cordial and the

---

[9] One option consists of 1000 shares with each share being worth about 800 yen at the end of the year.

former managers had agreed to accept a settlement whereby the former managers would pay 300 million yen (*Nihon-keizai-shimbun*, 18 June 2009).

Misuzu Audit Co., formerly ChuoAoyama PricewaterhouseCoopers, audited the financial statements of Nikko Cordial. ChuoAoyama PricewaterhouseCoopers was broken down into Misuzu and Arata after the Kanebo accounting scandals. However, Misuzu, under pressure after the accounting scandal at Nikko Cordial, was forcibly dissolved in July 2007. The accounting scandals of Kanebo and the dissolution of Misuzu are explained in the following subsections.

### 14.4.3 Accounting Scandal to Avoid Bankruptcy

The accounting scandals of Riccar, Yamaichi Securities and Kanebo were traditional ones motivated by the avoidance of bankruptcy. However, the influence of these scandals upon the Japanese accounting institution was enormous.

#### *14.4.3.1 Riccar*

Riccar Co. Ltd was a leading Japanese sewing machine manufacturer whose shares were listed on the TSE. Riccar had been suffering from excessive debt and applied for court protection from creditors under the Corporate Rehabilitation Law in August 1984. The accounting fraud by Riccar was discovered after the application for the Corporate Rehabilitation Law.

Riccar reported fictitious revenue of 53.6 billion yen in total and boosted earnings by 32.9 billion yen from 1976 to 1984. Since the actual revenue for 1984 was 48 billion yen, Riccar's accumulated fictitious revenue accounted for more than one year's normal revenue. Moreover, it was revealed that Riccar had a negative net worth of close to 14 billion yen at the end of 1984 without earnings manipulation (*Nihon-keizai-shimbun*, 21 April 1985). In spite of a negative net worth and huge deficit without earnings manipulation, Riccar continued to pay dividends and a bonus to the directors. In 1985, Riccar's accounting frauds were said to be the second largest value of fictitious earnings, after the Fuji Sash case, at the time in Japan (*Nihon-keizai-shimbun*, 11 April 1985).

The method of earnings manipulation was very simple. Riccar had bad inventory but issued a fictitious sales invoice to false customers and hid the corresponding merchandise in a warehouse. These were treated as sold merchandise and the inventory was thus not recorded in the books and was, in effect, an off-balance sheet asset. The newspaper reported that the off-balance sheet assets, sewing machines, constituted more than 170,000 machines in warehouses across the country (*Nihon-keizai-shimbun*, 21 April 1985). Mr Hiraki, a member of the founding family, held the positions of president and chairman of the board for 14 years. It is said that he insisted on reporting earnings to maintain dividends and exercised such strong powers to manipulate earnings that the chiefs of the finance division could not act counter to him even if they recognized that the accounting treatment was illegal (*Nihon-keizai-shimbun*, 22 May and 1 November 1985).

On 12 March 1987, the Tokyo District Court gave Mr Hiraki a three-year jail sentence (suspended for four years) for violating the Commercial Code and Securities Exchange Law (i.e. illegal dividends of about 1.43 billion yen in 1980 and 1982, illegal payments of bonuses to managers of 20 million yen, embezzlement of corporate funds and false financial reporting). Two ex-presidents, Mr Yoshida and Mr Nakayama, were sentenced to two years and six months in jail (suspended for four years) for violating the Commercial Code and Securities Exchange Law. A former president, Mr Ishii, was given a 10-month jail sentence (suspended for two years) for violating the Securities Exchange Law.

As a result of Riccar's case, the *Auditing Standards of Field Work* were revised in May 1989 to require customer visits and the collection of documentary evidence to confirm accounts receivable and inventories.

### 14.4.3.2  Yamaichi Securities

Yamaichi Securities, Japan's fourth-largest brokerage house, shut down in November 1997 after 100 years in business with debts of about three trillion yen, which was the largest financial failure since World War II. After the closure, accounting fraud was detected and a former chairman of the board, Mr Yukihira, was sentenced to two years and six months in prison (suspended for five years) by the Tokyo District Court and a former president, Mr Miki, was sentenced to three years in prison (suspended for five years) by the Tokyo High Court for hiding losses of more than 200 billion yen and paying illegal dividends (*Nihon-keizai-shimbun*, 28 March 2000 and 25 October 2001).

The massive losses were incurred through years of dubious 'tobashi' securities deals, in which shares with market value sinking below their book value were valued at historical cost based on the accounting standards at that time and shuffled through a complex web of Yamaichi's customers with a pledge that the unrealized losses would be covered. Shares with unrealized losses were rotated among the customers with different accounting periods to prevent the losses from surfacing. However, in November 1991, Yamaichi decided to shift the loss-carrying shares to dummy companies and overseas subsidiaries, and began to dispose of the losses in December 1991. Pressured by funding difficulties amid revelations of the off-the-book losses, Yamaichi announced its closure late in November 1997 (*Japan Times*, 28 September–4 October 1998; *Jiji Press*, 4 March 1998; *Nihon-keizai-shimbun*, 26 December 1997).

The newspaper indicates that the closure of Yamaichi shows the weakness of the Japanese style of corporate governance (*Nikkei-sangyo-shimbun*, 16 June 1997). Cross-shareholding between banks and corporations, and among corporations, was extensive for Japanese companies. Cross-shareholders do not usually meddle in each other's company management. For Yamaichi, the high level of ownership by banks and other corporations had a significant negative influence on the monitoring of the executives. The newspaper reported that nobody monitored executives of Yamaichi and their illegal accounting and business (*Nikkei-sangyo-shimbun*, 16 June 1997).

The receivers sued Chuo Audit, which was affiliated to PricewaterhouseCoopers, for failing to spot these off-the-book losses. Although the receivers claimed about 6 billion yen damages, they agreed to accept a settlement whereby Chuo Audit would pay about 166 million yen (corresponding to five years' audit fee) on 19 November 2003 (*Nihon-keizai-shimbun*, 20 November 2003).

### *14.4.3.3  Kanebo*

While the accounting scandal of Kanebo Co. Ltd was provoked by the same motivation of bankruptcy avoidance as in the Riccar and Yamaichi Securities cases, the influence of Kanebo's case upon accounting institutions in Japan was much greater. Kanebo's case is referred to as a Japanese-style Enron accounting scandal because Kanebo's case was the largest ever amount of earnings manipulation and its audit firm, ChuoAoyama Pricewater-houseCoopers, was forcibly broken up – as was Arthur Andersen in Enron's accounting scandal. Furthermore, after the accounting scandal of Kanebo, the Corporation Law and Financial Instruments Exchange Law in Japan required large companies, for the first time, to establish internal control systems to prevent accounting frauds and management problems similar to the Public Company Accounting Reform and Investor Protection Act of 2002 (Sarbanes-Oxley Act) in the USA.

Kanebo was once a leading textile and cosmetics company, established more than a hundred years ago. Kanebo's shares were listed on the TSE. In 1994, Kanebo reported an operating loss for the first time in 15 years and failed to pay dividends for the first time in 11 years. The operating performance of the company remained poor after that and the consolidated balance sheet in 1997 showed a negative net worth close to 24 billion yen.

Mr Hoashi took up the post of president and Mr Miyahara became a vice-president in 1998 when the company was restructured. The cosmetics division made good progress following their appointment and Kanebo reported consolidated net income of 11.6 billion yen and positive consolidated net worth in 2001. However, the textile division performed very badly and consolidated net income fell to 70 million yen in 2002. With failing performance and additional bank loans, Kanebo was close to having a negative consolidated net worth again in 2003.

It was revealed in April 2005 that the true financial position was much worse than that presented in the balance sheet. Kanebo executives, including Mr Hoashi and Mr Miyahara, had hidden losses of 81.9 billion yen in 2001 and 80.6 billion yen in 2002. Kanebo had illegally boosted earnings of 215 billion yen in total from 2000 to 2004 (*Nihon-keizai-shimbun*, 27 March 2006).

The methods of illegally boosting earnings were diverse. For example: (a) Kanebo sold unsaleable merchandise just before the end of the financial year with a covering contract and then bought them back at the beginning of the next financial year; (b) Kanebo did not record inventory loss for obsolete inventories; (c) Kanebo deferred its advertising and sales promotion expenses to the next financial year and accelerated next year's sales to the current year; (d) Kanebo sold a subsidiary's shares to a business partner just before the end of the financial year with a covering contract, whereby the shares would be bought back later, in order temporarily to remove the loss-making subsidiary from the consolidation and boost that period's consolidated earnings (*Nihon-keizai-shimbun*, 16 April, 29 July, 19 August and 30 November 2005).

After Kanebo announced that it would restate financial statements for the five years from 2000 to 2004, the TSE decided to delist its shares in June 2005. Mr Hoashi and Mr Miyahara were arrested for alleged accounting fraud in July 2005. The Tokyo District Court sentenced Mr Hoashi to two years in prison and Mr Miyahara to 18 months on 27 March 2006. Both sentences were suspended for three years. The Chief Justice stated that the reason for the 'suspended' sentences was that Kanebo had begun to falsify its financial statements from the middle of the 1970s, long before they took up the posts of president and vice-president, and they – as executives of the company – had tried hard to restructure the organization. In fact, they explained in the course of the trial that the company's negative net worth was 250 billion yen without manipulation when they were appointed and they were left to choose either a bankruptcy or window-dressing (*Nihon-keizai-shimbun*, 27 March 2005).

Kanebo sought support from the Industrial Revitalization Corporation of Japan (IRCJ), a government-sponsored bailout agency, set up in April 2003 under Prime Minister Koizumi. The IRCJ buys loans from an ailing company's non-prime lenders and then works with its main bank to help the troubled company get back on its feet. Under the IRCJ, Kanebo's profitable cosmetics division was spun off into a separate company, Kanebo Cosmetics Co. Ltd. In January 2006, Kao, Japan's biggest maker of personal care and cleansing products, acquired Kanebo Cosmetics and turned it into a wholly owned subsidiary.

Three certified public accountants, Mr Sato, Mr Kanda and Mr Tokumi, who were employed by ChuoAoyama PricewaterhouseCoopers and had audited the financial statements of Kanebo, were arrested for conspiring with Mr Hoashi and Mr Miyahara to falsify Kanebo's financial statements in September 2005. ChuoAoyama PricewaterhouseCoopers was one of the biggest four audit firms in Japan and had audited the financial statements of Kanebo since 1973. Mr Sato had been an auditor of Kanebo for 12 years (*Nihon-keizai-shimbun*, 14 September 2005). The Financial Services Agency removed their licences as certified public accountants and ordered ChuoAoyama PricewaterhouseCoopers to halt auditing services for its clients in July and August of 2006 as a penalty for its role in Kanebo's accounting fraud.

Mr Sato was sentenced to 18 months and the other auditors, Mr Kanda and Mr Tokumi, were sentenced to one year. All sentences were suspended for three years. The Chief Justice stated that they had damaged the social trust of certified public accountants and their crimes deserved to be severely criticized. However, the Justice said the reason that he had suspended their sentences was because the auditors only played a passive role in the crime, which was actually perpetrated by Kanebo's executives. The Judge also said that the auditors had been aware of Kanebo's history of accounting fraud since 1998, but could neither expose nor stop the falsification because Kanebo's executives threatened to reveal past improper accounting treatments committed by ChuoAoyama PricewaterhouseCoopers (*Knight Ridder Tribune Business News*, 10 August 2006).

Although the sentences were suspended, the accounting frauds dealt a fatal blow to ChuoAoyama PricewaterhouseCoopers. ChuoAoyama PricewaterhouseCoopers was broken down into the Misuzu Audit Corporation and PricewaterhouseCoopers Arata after the Kanebo accounting scandal. ChuoAoyama PricewaterhouseCoopers was not a full member firm within PricewaterhouseCoopers's global network. It was rather a junior affiliate, even though it was able to use the PricewaterhouseCoopers brand (*Wall Street Journal*, 13 May 2006). ChuoAoyama PricewaterhouseCoopers resumed full operations under a new name, Misuzu Audit Corporation, on 1 September 2006. Misuzu had 2506 personnel, including 1354 certified accountants. Meanwhile, Arata, set up by PricewaterhouseCoopers of the USA, also became fully operational on the same day with 931 personnel. Most of the certified accountants belonging to Arata came from ChuoAoyama (*Knight Ridder Tribune Business News*, 1 September 2006). After the dismantling of ChuoAoyama

PricewaterhouseCoopers, Misuzu encountered new problems due to an accounting scandal by one of its clients, Nikko Cordial Co. Ltd. Finally, Misuzu asked three other major audit firms to take over its audit operations and its certified public accountants. It was formally dissolved in July 2007.

# 14.5 CONSEQUENCES OF THE ACCOUNTING SCANDALS

Accounting scandals that have occurred since the 1980s have heavily influenced accounting institutions. In particular, they have caused new accounting standard setting, the reorganization of audit firms and the establishment of internal control systems. This section presents the relation between some accounting scandals and the change of accounting institutions.

### 14.5.1 Revision of Accounting Standards for Consolidated Financial Statements

Although the accounting scandals of Livedoor, Nikko Cordial and Kanebo were induced by different motivations, they had a common effect on accounting standard setting. That is to say, these accounting scandals led to the realization of the necessity of setting more sophisticated accounting standards for consolidated financial statements. Livedoor and Nikko Cordial had used special purpose entities (SPE) to boost earnings, and Kanebo discretionarily removed a loss-making subsidiary from the consolidated financial statements.

The ASBJ issued two accounting statements in September 2006 after the accounting scandals (Practical Solution on Investors' Accounting for Limited-Liability Partnerships and Limited-Liability Companies and Practical Solution on Application of the Control Criteria and Influence Criteria to Investment Associations). These require SPE to be included in consolidated financial statements as subsidiaries if one entity is substantially controlled by another entity which is the parent. Whether an entity is substantially controlled is judged by such criteria as the percentage of share ownership, contribution of funds or earnings distribution. If entity X borrows from entity Y more than 50 % of all contributed funds, X is judged as a subsidiary of Y and included in the consolidated financial statements. If entity X distributes earnings to entity Y of more than 50 % of all earnings, then X is judged as a subsidiary of Y and included in the consolidated financial statements.

Furthermore, the ASBJ issued *ASBJ Guide No. 15: Implementation Guide on Disclosure about Certain Special Purpose Entities* in March 2007. This requires disclosure of certain information about SPE judged as a non-subsidiary (i.e. the number of SPE, transaction amounts between the entities, current net income and financial position of the SPE, and so on).

### 14.5.2 Reorganization of Audit Firms

The notable second consequence of the accounting scandals is that Japanese economic society has reconfirmed the significance of audit and a reorganization of audit firms has occurred. A certified public accountant who audited financial statements of Livedoor was sentenced to prison without suspension for the first time, and the Koyo Audit Corporation was dissolved. The Financial Services Agency ordered ChuoAoyama Pricewaterhouse Coopers to halt auditing services for its clients in July and August of 2006 as a penalty for its role in accounting fraud at Kanebo.

The influence of these penalties upon the business community was enormous because, under the Corporation Law, companies must terminate their contract with an auditor who has received a business suspension order. More than 2000 companies which ChuoAoyama PricewaterhouseCoopers audited had to find a new auditor in a short time. Some companies, including Toyota Motor Corporation and Sony Corporation, found a new auditor but many companies could not find a new auditor at a time of year when other auditors were also stretched. Consequently, many companies retained ChuoAoyama PricewaterhouseCoopers for the time being and named a temporary alternative auditor for the two months (*Financial Times*, 11 May 2006).

ChuoAoyama PricewaterhouseCoopers was broken down into Misuzu and Arata after the Kanebo accounting frauds. However, Misuzu, under fire due to the accounting scandal at Nikko Cordial, was forcibly dissolved in July 2007. While about 1000 personnel including CPA of Misuzu moved to Ernst & Young ShinNihon, about 500 moved to Deloitte & Touche Tohmatsu Japan, and about 300 moved to KPMG Azsa & Co (*Nihon-keizai-shimbun*, 13 April 2007). It was not necessarily easy for the client companies to move to a new audit firm because audit firms tended to inspect new clients carefully. As some companies could not find a new auditor, the Japanese Institute of Certified Public Accountants helped them.

Moreover, the accounting scandals led to the amendment of the Certified Public Accountants Law in Japan on 20 June 2007. In order to urge auditors to scrutinize financial statements more strictly and stamp out accounting fraud, the amended CPA Law delegated power to the Financial Services Agency to impose new penalties on auditors involved in illegal accounting practices. Before this, the Financial Services Agency was allowed to implement only three penalties against problematic auditors (i.e. giving a reprimand, issuing a business suspension and issuing a dissolution order). Under the amended CPA Law, the Financial Services Agency has been empowered to fine auditors involved in accounting frauds, to issue business improvement orders to audit firms and to fire company executives involved in illegal accounting practices (*Jiji Press News Service*, 26 February 2007; *Nihon-keizai-shimbun*, 16 and 21 June 2005).

### 14.5.3 Establishing Internal Control Systems

The third noteworthy consequence of the accounting scandals is that these have facilitated Japanese companies in establishing internal control systems to prevent accounting problems. The Japanese Corporation Law, starting in May 2006, has for the first time required large companies, with stated capital of more than 500 million yen or liabilities of more than 20 billion yen, to establish internal control systems. The Financial Instruments and Exchange Act, enacted in June 2006, has required listed companies to establish an internal control reporting system in order to prevent companies making false financial statements and to maintain the integrity of the securities exchange market.

In the USA, compliance with some provisions of the Sarbanes-Oxley Act has been criticized as vague and expensive. Companies have largely been left on their own to determine whether they are in compliance, costing them a huge amount of time and money (*Knight Ridder Tribune Business News*, 29 December 2006). In Japan, to avoid such problems and ease the burden, the Financial Services Agency introduced mitigated rules.

According to the rules, the internal control system should cover divisions with approximately two-thirds of a company's consolidated sales. For the internal control system, all accounting processes have to be documented, a system of double-checking of external transactions must be provided, and due processes for important decisions by executive managements should be prepared. The internal control system should be checked by an audit firm or certified public accountant. An executive of the company is required to compile an internal control report each year along with annual financial statements, and to obtain approval by an audit firm or certified public accountant before releasing it publicly. Listed companies should comply with the new rules at the start of their respective financial years beginning on or after 1 April 2008.

## 14.6 CONCLUSION

This chapter has reviewed accounting scandals and creative accounting in Japan, especially post-1980s, which were divided into three types by the underlying motivation for the scandals (i.e. accounting scandals to maintain high share price, accounting scandals designed to implement contracts favourably and accounting scandals to avoid bankruptcy).

The accounting scandals of Yaohan Japan, Sawako Corporation and Livedoor were all motivated by the desire to maintain high share prices. Yaohan Japan and Sawako Corporation had issued convertible bonds and wanted to maintain a high share price so as to encourage bond-holders to exercise their rights. Livedoor window-dressed its earnings so as to bolster the company's share price and allow it to make mergers and acquisitions with inflated shares. It is said that the dubious accounting by IHI was mainly motivated by the need to maintain a high share price so as to issue new securities on more advantageous terms.

The accounting scandals by Morimoto-gumi and Nikko Cordial were motivated by the execution, maintenance and performance of contracts. Morimoto-gumi is related to a public construction contract. Morimoto-gumi falsified its financial statements to maintain its rating for public construction contracts, thus enabling it to bid for larger construction contracts. The case of Nikko Cordial is related to managerial compensation. Nikko Cordial set up a management compensation scheme linked to an annual consolidated net income just before the period when the company began to manipulate its earnings.

The accounting scandals of Riccar, Yamaichi Securities and Kanebo were induced by a more traditional motive: the avoidance of bankruptcy. However, the influence of their scandals upon Japanese accounting institutions was enormous. Kanebo's case is referred to as a Japanese-style Enron accounting scandal because the case was the largest ever amount of earnings manipulation and after the scandal its audit firm, ChuoAoyama PricewaterhouseCoopers, was broken up in a similar way to Arthur Andersen in Enron's accounting scandal.

Although the accounting scandals of Livedoor, Nikko Cordial and Kanebo were induced by different motivations, these accounting scandals exerted a great influence on Japanese accounting institutions in three main ways. The first was the development of more elaborate accounting standards for consolidated financial statements. The second was that the importance of auditing was re-emphasized and audit firms were reorganized. The third was that companies were required to establish internal control systems in order to prevent companies from making false financial statements and to maintain the trust of the securities exchange markets.

However, it is not so easy to eliminate accounting scandals and creative accounting by way of improving accounting standards, auditing or internal control systems. The accounting scandals of Sanyo Electric and IHI occurred after these reforms. Throughout Japanese history, the difficulty of eliminating accounting scandals by reforming accounting institutions has been appreciated. However, what is needed to prevent companies from committing accounting frauds is not only the reform of accounting institutions, but also investors themselves acting as a watchdog for creative accounting.

# REFERENCES

(For convenience, articles in Japanese have been translated into English.)

Buchanan, J. (2007), 'Japanese corporate governance and the principle of internalism', *Corporate Governance*, **15**(1), 27–35.

Choi, F. and Hiramatu, F. (eds) (1987), *Accounting and Financial Reporting in Japan*, Van Nostrand Reinhold, London.

Cooke, T.E. and Kikuya, M. (1992), *Financial Reporting in Japan: Regulation, Practice and Environment*, Blackwell Publishers, Oxford.

Financial Accounting Standards Foundation (2003), *FASF Japanese Accounting Standards on CD-ROM: Release 2002 – Selected Accounting Standards of Japan and other Japanese Accounting Pronouncements translated into English as at December 31, 2000*, Financial Accounting Standards Foundation, Tokyo.

JICPA (1998), *Corporate Disclosure in Japan*, 4th edn, Japanese Institute of Certified Public Accountants, Tokyo.

JICPA (2000), *Practical Guidelines on Accounting Standards for Financial Instruments*, Japanese Institute of Certified Public Accountants, Tokyo (in Japanese).

Kang, J.-K. and Shivdasani, A. (1995), 'Firm performance, corporate governance, and top executive turnover in Japan', *Journal of Financial Economics*, **38**, 29–58.

Kaplan, S.N. (1994), 'Top executive rewards and firm performance: a comparison of Japan and the United States', *Journal of Political Economy*, **102**, 510–546.

Koga, C. (2006), *CCH Japan GAAP Guide*, CCH Asia Pte. Ltd.

Ministry of Economy, Trade and Industry: Study Group on the Internationalization of Business Accounting (2004), *Report on the Internationalization of Business Accounting in Japan*. (Electronic copy available at: http://www.meti.go.jp/english/report/downloadfiles/IBAreporte.pdf).

National Tax Agency (2009), *Results of the Corporation Sample Survey*. (in Japanese) (Electronic copy available at: http://www.nta.go.jp/kohyo/tokei/kokuzeicho/kaishahyohon2007/00.pdf).

Nihon-keizai-shimbun-shokenbu (1966), *Window-dressing*, Nihon-keizai-shimbun-sha, Tokyo (in Japanese).

Nihon-keizai-shimbun-shokenbu (1977), *Disclosure*, Nihon-keizai-shimbun-sha, Tokyo (in Japanese).

Okumura, H. (2006), *Fraudulent Capitalism*, Toyokeizai-shinpo-sha, Tokyo (in Japanese).

Otomasa, S. (2004), *Mechanism of Balancing the Interests of Firms and Accounting Information*, Moriyama-shoten, Tokyo (in Japanese).

Shiba, K. and Shiba, L. (1997), 'Japan', in *Financial Reporting in the Pacific Asia Region*, ed. R. Ma, World Scientific, Singapore.

Shuto, A. (2007), 'Executive compensation and earnings management: empirical evidence from Japan', *Journal of International Accounting, Auditing and Taxation*, **16**, 1–26.

Suda, K. and Shuto, A. (2007), 'Earnings management to meet earnings benchmarks: evidence from Japan', in *Focus on Finance and Accounting Research*, ed. M.H. Neelan, Nova Science Publishers, New York, 67–85.

Toda, M. and McCarty, W. (2005), 'Corporate governance changes in the two largest economies: what's happening in the U.S. and Japan?', *Syracuse Journal of International Law and Commerce*, **32**(2), 189–231.

**Appendix 14.1** Creative Accounting and Accounting Scandals post-1980s

| Company | Industry | Year | Auditor | Description |
|---------|----------|------|---------|-------------|
| Riccar | Sewing machine manufacturer | 1976–84 (two auditors) | Joint audit | The company issued a fictitious sales invoice and hid corresponding merchandise in a warehouse to treat it as sold merchandise. The accounting scandal was the second largest in terms of the value of fictitious earnings at that time in Japan and mainly motivated to avoid bankruptcy. |
| Yamaichi Securities | Securities | 1995–97 | Chuo (after ChuoAoyama) | Japan's fourth largest brokerage shut down with debts of about three trillion yen, which was the largest financial failure. Two top executives were sentenced to prison for hiding losses of more than 200 billion yen and paying illegal dividends, mostly the result of 'tobashi' securities deals, in which shares with market value sinking below book value were shuffled through a complex web of clients, affiliates and dummy firms to keep the losses from appearing on their balance sheets. The scandal was mainly motivated to avoid bankruptcy. |
| Yaohan Japan | Supermarket | 1996 | Chuo (after ChuoAoyama) | The company collapsed in 1997 leaving more than 185.5 billion yen in debts, which was the biggest in the retail industry. It was revealed afterwards that the company illegally paid dividends worth about 1.4 billion yen. It had losses worth about 12.6 billion yen in 1996 without earnings manipulation. The company rigged earnings by booking gains on sales of real estate to a dummy company. The scandal was mainly motivated by maintaining a high share price in order to encourage convertible bond-holders to exercise their rights. |

*(Continued).*

**Appendix 14.1**  Creative Accounting and Accounting Scandals post-1980s (Continued)

| Company | Industry | Year | Auditor | Description |
|---|---|---|---|---|
| Long-Term Credit Bank of Japan | Bank | 1998 | Showa Ota (after Ernst & Young ShinNihon) | The bank went bankrupt in October 1998 and, after an injection of 7 trillion yen worth of public funds to clean up the mess, restarted as Shinsei Bank in 2000. The Tokyo District Court and the Tokyo High Court sentenced three top executives to prison for violation of the Commercial Code and the Securities and Exchange Law because they had falsified its financial statements and illegally paid dividends worth about 7.1 billion yen for 1998 by failing to write off 313 billion yen in irrecoverable loans using lax assessment standards. However, the Supreme Court delivered a judgment of acquittal because a rational estimation of irrecoverable loans is very difficult and the case was not concerned with the use of unfair assessment standards at that time. The creative accounting was mainly motivated by the need to avoid bankruptcy. |
| Sawako | Construction | 1998–99 | Tohmatsu (after Deloitte & Touche Tohmatsu) | Under the percentage-of-completion method for the revenue recognition on long-term construction contracts, the company rigged the cost incurred by forcing a co-worker of the construction project to make out a false bill and boosted periodic sales. The scandal was mainly motivated by the need to maintain a high share price in order to stimulate convertible bond-holders to exercise their rights. |
| Morimoto-gumi | Construction | 1999–2003 (one auditor) | Individual audit | Understating cost of goods sold by deferring expenses to the next financial year, the company boosted the operating income to construction revenue ratio. The scandal was mainly motivated by the need to get a good ranking to put in a bid for larger public construction contracts. |
| Livedoor | Internet conglomerate | 2004 | Koyo | Using special purpose entities, the company hid losses and illegally booked capital transaction as income in its accounts. The scandal was mainly motivated by the need to maintain high share prices in order to do a favourable finance and share swap merger |

| Kanebo | Textile and cosmetics | 2000–4 | ChuoAoyama Pricewaterhouse-Coopers | The company sold merchandise just before the end of the financial year with a covering contract and did not record inventory loss for obsolete inventories. It also removed temporarily a loss-making subsidiary from the consolidation. The scandal is the largest ever amount of earnings manipulation and mainly motivated by the need to avoid bankruptcy. |
| Sanyo Electric | Electronics manufacturer | 2001–6 | ChuoAoyama Pricewaterhouse-Coopers | The company restated a net income of 17.6 billion yen in the 2001 financial year to a loss of 90.8 billion yen because it did not properly record an impairment loss of subsidiary stocks. The dividend between 2003 and 2004, totalling 28 billion yen, was higher than legally allowed. The creative accounting was probably mainly motivated by the need to continue dividend payments. |
| Nikko Cordial | Securities | 2005–6 | Misuzu (former ChuoAoyama) | Booking a false valuation gain and loss on the stock-exchangeable bond which was issued by the special purpose company, the company manipulated its consolidated net income. The creative accounting was probably mainly motivated by the income-based executive compensation contracts. |
| IHI | Ships and heavy machinery manufacturer | 2006–7 | Ernst & Young ShinNihon | The company restated an operating income of 24.6 billion yen in the 2007 financial year to a loss of 5.6 billion yen because it had recognized improper revenue on a long-term construction contract based on the percentage-of-completion method. The creative accounting was probably mainly motivated by the need to maintain a high share price in order to issue shares on favourable terms. |

# Financial Accounting Scandals in the Netherlands

Henk Langendijk

## 15.1 INTRODUCTION

The accounting profession in the Netherlands is partially founded on a large financial fraud in the 1870s in Rotterdam (the so-called Pincoffs affair). Before 1879, the Rotterdam merchant Pincoffs had achieved high esteem both economically and politically. In one of his companies, the Afrikaansche Handelsvereeniging, which was converted to an NV (limited company) in 1869, management falsified the books and the balance sheet. This was to conceal the fact that the company's West African operations were failing. The withdrawal of foreign short-term credit by Pincoffs led the supervisory board of the Afrikaanse Handelsvereeniging in Spring 1879 to suspect a financial fraud and the subsequent investigation revealed a fraud of DFL 2.8 million (which was a large amount in those days). It would be about 100 million US dollars today.

In the criminal case in 1880 against Pincoffs amongst others, it came to light that a falsified profit of DFL 2 million was in fact a loss of DFL 8 million. Two bookkeepers of the Afrikaansche Handelsvereeniging had been forced by Pincoffs to cook the books. The supervisory board had also failed in its duties. They had neither checked the books, nor compared the balance sheets with the books. The supervisory board had not found it necessary to check the books as there was an atmosphere of dignity, decency and friendship between them and Pincoffs. Consequently, Pincoffs could do whatever he liked. Pincoffs was sentenced by default to eight years in prison (Beckman, 2007, p. 28).

The first Dutch auditor was appointed, in 1879, at the newly founded Nieuwe Afrikaanse Handelsvereeniging as a reaction to the Pincoffs affair. This auditor can be regarded as the first Dutch auditor and so as the start of the accounting profession in the Netherlands (De Vries, 1985, pp. 34–36).

There have not been many cases of fraudulent reporting and creative accounting in the Netherlands. This can be explained partially by the fact that the Netherlands uses 'principle-based' accounting. This is shown by the wording of art. 2:362 sections 1 and 4 of the Dutch Civil Code.

> Section 362.1. 'The annual accounts, prepared in accordance with generally acceptable accounting principles, shall provide such a view as enables a sound judgement to be formed of the assets and liabilities and results of the legal person.' [...]

*Creative Accounting, Fraud and International Accounting Scandals*  Edited by Michael Jones
© 2011 Michael Jones. Published by John Wiley & Sons, Ltd

Section 362.4. 'In its annual accounts the legal person shall include information supplemental to the requirements of the special provisions set out in or pursuant to this Part if required in order to give the view referred to in subsection 1. The legal person shall not apply such provisions to the extent necessary to provide such view and the reason for not applying such provisions shall be set out in the notes.' [...]

It can be argued that the true and fair view allows management ample opportunity to provide their own interpretation of the accounts. Management of companies in the Netherlands have traditionally been able to use creative accounting and then sometimes argue that they have done this to give a true and fair view. The Dutch Civil Code permits this. The introduction of IFRS for listed companies in the Netherlands from 1 January 2005 has restricted the ability of companies to hide creative accounting behind the mantle of a true and fair view, although there is some discussion in the Netherlands about the difference (if any) between the true and fair view according to art. 2:362 Section 1 and IAS 1 (Verdict Supreme Court AFM/Spyker case, April 2009). So, it is possible that the introduction of IFRS has not or only partially restricted the possibilities to apply creative accounting behind the curtain of a true and fair view.

The relatively low status of the private standard-setting in the Netherlands (set by the Council of Annual Reporting (CAR)) also gives management a lot of opportunity to interpret the particular contents of the true and fair view. The low status of the CAR was confirmed by the verdict of the Supreme Court in the KPN-SOBI case of February 2006. Furthermore, the judges in the criminal case against members of the former management of Royal Ahold in January 2009 argued that the management of companies in the Netherlands are able to interpret Dutch accounting rules flexibly (using the true and fair view).

There was also no active enforcement body in the Netherlands which regulated the quality of financial statements. However, this changed in 2006. The Authoriteit Financiële Markten (The Netherlands Authority for the Financial Markets (AFM)) investigates the financial statements of listed companies in the Netherlands according to the Wet Toezicht Financiële Verslaggeving (Law on Supervision of Financial Reporting). The AFM has a limited arsenal of sanctions and administrative measures if it finds that consolidated financial statements of listed companies in the Netherlands do not comply with IFRS. One of these measures is that the AFM can start a financial statements procedure at the Ondernemingskamer (Enterprise Court) in Amsterdam.

Despite the prevalence of the true and fair view, there are companies in the Netherlands which have been creative with their financial statements in the past, for instance RSV, Fokker and Landis. These examples relate to creative accounting in the sense that the companies were using flexibility in accounting within the regulatory framework to manage the measurement and presentation of the accounts. There was, therefore, *no* financial fraud (or fraudulent reporting) at these companies.

The three cases which are discussed in this chapter in depth are RSV and Fokker, then more particularly, Royal Ahold.

Members of former management of Royal Ahold have been convicted in a criminal case in the Netherlands with respect to the financial fraud at Royal Ahold (January 2009). Royal Ahold is the largest retail company in the Netherlands. On 13 October 2004, the SEC filed fraud and other charges in the US District Court of Columbia against Royal Ahold and three former top executives: Mr van der Hoeven, Mr Meurs and Mr Andreae.[1] This filing concerned the joint venture sales and operating income fraud at Royal Ahold. Royal Ahold agreed to settle the SEC's action, without admitting or denying the allegations in the complaint, by consenting to the entry of a judgment permanently enjoining the company from violating the antifraud, reporting, books and records, and internal control provisions of the federal securities laws in the US. Royal Ahold did not have to pay a fine to the SEC.

The financial statements of Royal Ahold have been restated as a consequence of the accounting irregularities (restatement annual accounts 2002), mainly because of the accounting scandal at the head office concerning consolidation and at the American subsidiary US Foodservice (USF) concerning vendor allowances and other minor errors.

I only look at fraudulent reporting and creative accounting in financial accounting. So fiscal frauds and other financial frauds unrelated to financial accounting are excluded. Also, the irregularities and violation of cartel and competition laws in the Dutch construction sector, which have led to a Parliamentary Inquiry by the Second Chamber in the Netherlands (2003), are not discussed in this chapter. This is because the financial accounting part of these irregularities is quite modest.

In Section 15.2, I first look at two cases of creative accounting in the Netherlands by relatively smaller companies: RSV and Fokker. Then in Section 15.3, I provide an overview of the consolidation fraud and the vendor allowances fraud at Royal Ahold. In Section 15.4, I present some overall conclusions. This chapter was written in May 2010.

## 15.2 SOME MINOR ACCOUNTING SCANDALS

In this section, I deal with two other less important accounting scandals in the Netherlands: RSV and Fokker.

### 15.2.1 Creative Accounting at Rijn-Schelde-Verolme (RSV)

In 1971, RSV was formed by a merger of Rijn Schelde Machinefabrieken en Scheepswerven N.V. and Verolme N.V. Both companies were shipbuilders. RSV was listed on the Amsterdam Stock Exchange. At 31 December 1971, the equity of RSV was 390 million Dutch florins (DFL) and the profit for the financial year 1971 was 26 million DFL.[2] However, after a decade this large company went bankrupt.

The first four financial years after the merger were quite profitable with a stable growth of both profit and equity (from 26 million DFL profit in 1971 to 65 million DFL in 1974 respectively from 390 million DFL equity in 1971 to 478 million DFL equity in 1974).

1975 represented a turning point in the history of this company: net profit decreased by 23 % to 50 million DFL and according to Hoogendoorn (1987), the first signals of creative accounting were visible in the 1975 annual report of RSV with regard to accounting for deferred taxes. The company had debited a deferred tax asset. However, prudence would

---

[1] Mr van der Hoeven and Mr Meurs have agreed to settle the SEC's action without admitting or denying the allegations in the complaint. Mr van der Hoeven and Mr Meurs have consented to orders barring each of them from serving as an officer or director of a public company. The SEC has not reached a settlement with Mr Andreae (SEC, 2004a; Verdict Criminal Court Amsterdam, 2009, para. 4.5.1).

[2] The equivalent of one Dutch Florin is €0.45 and £0.36.

have dictated that they should not have done so as the future prospects for the company were unfavourable. According to the Dutch Council for Annual Reporting, it is only permissible to debit the deferred tax asset with regard to a deferred tax carry forward if there is reasonable assurance that there will be sufficient taxable profit before the carry forward expires. So there were serious doubts whether the deferred tax asset should have been recognised. The amount was approximately 40 million DFL, so without this creative gain the reported profit would have been just 10 million DFL instead of the 50 million DFL actually reported in 1975. The decrease in the net profit would have been 84 % instead of 23 %.

RSV went from bad to worse. In 1976, RSV reported losses for the first time (34 million DFL) and equity decreased to 457 million DFL. However, the losses would have been much larger, as restructuring costs (30 million DFL) were neither recognised as costs in the profit and loss account nor written off to reserves. In addition, the deferred tax asset was debited with respect to a non-recognised carry forward of 65.5 million DFL. However, the prospects for 1977 were unfavourable. According to Hoogendoorn (1987, p. 14) more prudent annual accounts would have led to the presentation of a loss of 148 million DFL.

In 1977, the reported loss was 50 million DFL and equity decreased to 408 million DFL. In that year RSV received for the first time a government grant in the form of a special subordinated loan for 37.3 million DFL. This government grant was not recorded as a liability, but directly credited in the profit and loss account as income. However, the conditions for non-repayment had not yet been fulfilled. In this respect, the management of RSV was very pessimistic, because it was only if RSV was in a permanent loss situation in the foreseeable future that RSV was not required to pay the grant back to the Dutch government. Directly recording the gain cast serious doubt on RSV as a going concern.

However, at other places in the 1977 annual report RSV management is much more optimistic about the financial future (e.g. reasonable assurance that there is sufficient taxable profit before the deferred tax carry forward expires, no need for an impairment on property, plant and equipment to lower value in use because of the expectation of higher returns on these fixed assets in the coming years). The prospects for 1978 and 1979 were also favourably reported in the directors' report according to the management. In addition, in 1977, the pension obligation had not been recorded. At a minimum it would have been 60 million DFL. So, the reported loss would have been at least 106.6 million DFL if management of RSV had been less creative and more prudent.

In 1978, RSV reported a loss of 60 million DFL, so the results were deteriorating instead of improving as suggested by the 1977 directors' report. In 1978, RSV again received a government grant (160 million DFL in four years: 45 million DFL in 1978, 1979 and 1980 and 25 million DFL in 1981). This grant had to be paid back from 1982 to 1991 depending on the magnitude of the profits in those years. The full amount of 160 million was recorded as a gain in 1978. Moreover, RSV received a government grant in the form of a special subordinated loan for the amount of 62 million DFL which was also recorded directly as a gain in 1978.

As in 1977, management was quite pessimistic with regard to the accounting treatment of the government grant, but not with respect to the accounting treatment of the deferred taxation carry forward and the impairment of property, plant and equipment. So, if the management of RSV had been more cautious and less creative the loss for the financial year 1978 would have been approximately 289 million DFL.

In 1979, RSV reported a loss of 22 million DFL. In 1979, RSV received another government grant of 225 million DFL which was recorded as 204 million DFL in the profit and loss account and the rest (21 million DFL) direct in equity. This government grant was approved by the European Union (EU) in 1980 and had to be paid back if there were sufficient profits in the future. A more prudent accounting treatment would have resulted in a loss of 226 million DFL in 1979. In 1980 and 1981, RSV showed comparatively low losses (29 million DFL and 8 million DFL respectively).

In December 1982, RSV collapsed and went bankrupt because of an acute liquidity crisis. A large project, the manufacturing of huge coal diggers, failed completely. The coal diggers were fully capitalised as work in progress (and not impaired) on the balance sheet of RSV. However, there was no market for them.

To conclude, RSV showed too high profits in 1975 and too low losses in the financial years 1976 to 1979. The recognition of carry forward, restructuring costs, pension obligations, valuation of property, plant and equipment and especially government grants was quite creative and not prudent. From 1978, the equity of the company, if recorded in the annual reports more correctly, would have been negative (between 13 million and 299 million DFL) rather than positive (between 428 million and 391 million DFL) (see Hoogendoorn, 1987, for a detailed analysis of this case).

### 15.2.2 Creative Accounting at Fokker

Fokker was a Dutch aircraft manufacturer (listed on the Amsterdam Stock Exchange), which went bankrupt in 1996. In the aircraft industry, companies have to make huge investments in the development of new prototypes of aircrafts (development costs, series production start-up costs and the development of specific tools for the building of specific aircraft). These investments are made in the expectation that these costs in combination with the direct production costs will be covered by the profitable sale of aircraft of the specific prototypes. The payback period of these development costs in this industry is approximately six to 10 years. After this period, the specific aircraft will be in production for another 10 to 14 years. For the capitalisation of these high amounts of costs for such a long period the starting point should be very prudent. For Fokker this was further emphasised by the severe problems in the airline industry in the 1990s (much lower demand for aircraft and a very competitive environment with rivals having much more capital, e.g. Boeing and McDonnell Douglas). This meant that Fokker had to price their aircraft quite low. Further, their aircraft were priced in US dollars which depreciated to a large extent against the Dutch florin (DFL) in the early 1990s. The DFL was the reporting currency of Fokker and much of the development and production costs of Fokker were in DFL. Also, Fokker did not hedge their position in US dollars. Moreover, there were overruns with respect to the development costs of new prototypes of aircraft by Fokker. In general, total costs of Fokker aircraft were higher than the revenues. These programme losses were also capitalised as work in progress. This was approximately 1 billion DFL from 1988 till 1992 (Deterink *et al.*, 1997, p. 62; Langendijk, 1998, p. 32). This capitalisation was not very prudent.

Because of the unfavourable market conditions and higher development and production costs, the management of Fokker had to postpone the break-even point in their planning. According to Deterink *et al.* (1997, p. 57), there was a pattern of planned profits under conditions of great uncertainty in the last part of the planning period with much too favourable assumptions. The capitalised amounts of development costs should have been impaired. McDonnell Douglas fully impaired their development costs for the MD-11 programme in 1995 (recorded in the profit and loss account). The management of McDonnell Douglas came to the conclusion that they would never reach the break-even number of sales of the MD-11 aircraft in the future.

The long-term development costs including programme losses are a discretionary accrual of a huge size, which have to be capitalised on a very prudent basis, especially with Fokker. In the case of Fokker, these costs were capitalised in a very optimistic way with the hope that the distant future would bring prosperous times without any clear present evidence. In addition, as well as being capitalised, they were not written down or impaired when there was little hope of their recovery.

# 15.3 ROYAL AHOLD

## 15.3.1 Consolidation of Joint Ventures at Royal Ahold

In 1989, the former management of Royal Ahold started an ambitious growth strategy. The ambition was to be in the same league as Wal-Mart and Carrefour, the number one and number two internationally-ranked retail companies. Royal Ahold planned to accomplish this ambition by maintaining its dominant position in the Netherlands, developing a critical mass in the US and seizing international opportunities (De Jong *et al.*, 2005, p. 5; Knapp and Knapp, 2007, pp. 643, 646–648). Royal Ahold's growth strategy differed from that of Wal-Mart and Carrefour. Royal Ahold grew via acquisitions of store chains and then continued to operate these chains under their own name, local management and local identity. Carrefour and Wal-Mart had very different strategies. Carrefour expanded both nationally and internationally under one name with a large international presence. Wal-Mart did the same but particularly in the US (Coriolis Research, 2001).

The former management of Royal Ahold was ambitious; they pointed out in the 1996 and 1997 annual reports that they wanted to become the best and *largest* retail company in the world (Royal Ahold Annual Report 1996, p. 2; Royal Ahold Annual Report 1997, p. 3). In later years, they became more modest and said that they wanted to become a very large retail player.

The size of a retail company is measured by the consolidated sales (and to a lesser extent the consolidated gross profit). Royal Ahold had five major joint ventures (ICA Ahold AB (ICA), Disco Ahold Int. Holdings N.V. (DAIH), Bompreco S.A. (Bompreco), Jeronimo Martins Retail (JMR) and Paiz Ahold N.V. (Paiz Ahold). Full consolidation led to higher consolidated sales for Royal Ahold than either proportionate consolidation or the equity method (or according to Dutch GAAP: net equity value (nettovermogenswaarde)).

There was thus an incentive for the former management of Royal Ahold to 'enlarge' the consolidated sales by full consolidation of particular joint ventures (instead of applying proportionate consolidation or the equity method). Although it was not permitted by the special provisions of the Dutch Civil Code (Section 2:409), full consolidation of the joint ventures was argued by Royal Ahold's former management to give a true and fair view.

So, full consolidation of joint ventures could reinforce the growth strategy of the former management of Royal Ahold. The key issue in the Royal Ahold case is thus whether under Dutch GAAP and US GAAP (Royal Ahold was listed in the US) the five joint ventures could be fully consolidated and treated as part of the group or not.

### 15.3.2 Consolidation Accounting in the Netherlands

According to the special provisions of the Dutch Civil Code, it is permissible to consolidate joint ventures proportionally or to account for joint ventures according to the net equity value in the consolidated financial statements (see Section 2:409 Dutch Civil Code). Full consolidation is, in general, required for *group* companies. The definition of a group company is set out in Section 2:24b of the Dutch Civil Code: a group is an economic entity in which legal entities and companies are affiliated in organisational terms. The term group, in relation to financial statements, is set out in CAR 214. CAR 214.103a explains that whether or not a group or group company is involved must be determined in all cases on the basis of the actual situation. There is a group relationship if one company actually exercises dominant influence over another company. Overall, according to Dutch GAAP, professional judgement is needed to determine that a group company is involved. In effect, dominant influence means that a company exercises dominant influence over another company in both a *financial* and *operational* way and/or a company has the ability to exercise the majority of the voting rights at the General Assembly of Shareholders or the ability to appoint and dismiss the board members of another company (CAR 214.103a). See Verdict Criminal Court Amsterdam, 2009, chapter 3 for an in-depth analysis of Dutch GAAP in relation to this particular case.

### 15.3.3 Consolidation Accounting under US GAAP

Consolidation under US GAAP depends on substantive control. Substantive control is where more than 50 % of the shares are held by the parent company (see Accounting Research Bulletin (ARB) 51 and FAS 94). However, this is not necessarily true in all cases. For example, if the shareholder holding more than 50 % of the shares is only entitled to appoint half of the directors, no substantive control is involved. On the other hand, if 50 % or less of the shares are held, substantive control can nevertheless occur. This depends on the control that arises from the shareholders' agreement (and the control letter) or the articles of association. In all cases, the rights of the other (minority) shareholders should also be taken into account (see Emerging Issues Task Force (EITF) 96-16). According to Accounting Principles Board (APB) Opinion No. 18, para. 16 a corporate joint venture should be accounted for according to the equity method in the consolidated financial statements. It is not allowed to proportionally (or fully) consolidate corporate joint ventures according to US GAAP. In essence, therefore, under US GAAP, Royal Ahold would have to demonstrate that it *exercised substantive control* over the five joint ventures. This proved difficult for Royal Ahold to do (see Verdict Criminal Court Amsterdam, 2009, chapter 4 for an in-depth analysis of US GAAP in this area and chapter 2.6.8 for the importance of control letters with respect to full consolidation on the basis of US GAAP).

### 15.3.4 The Control and Side Letters

Central to the consolidation abuses are the facts and circumstances surrounding certain letters that were the basis for the full consolidation of the joint ventures (other than JMR) (the control letters) and certain previously undisclosed related letters that nullified the control letters (the side letters). The disclosure of the side letters resulted in the decision to deconsolidate the four joint ventures (Koninklijke Ahold N.V. 2002 Consolidated Financial Statements, p. F-26).

The increasing importance of joint ventures in Royal Ahold's growth strategy and the relative importance of Royal Ahold's international operations led to the commencement of a discussion between Royal Ahold and the auditor, Deloitte & Touche (D&T, nowadays called Deloitte), on the consolidation of the joint ventures.

The discussion centred on whether Royal Ahold complied with the criteria enabling it to fully consolidate or continue to fully consolidate the joint ventures. Royal Ahold's former management was convinced that although 50 % of the management of the joint ventures always consisted of representatives of Royal Ahold and 50 % of the representatives of the joint ventures partner(s), in practice Royal Ahold always made all the important operational and financial decisions. Consequently, Royal Ahold's former management believed that it was unacceptable if it could not fully consolidate these joint ventures. D&T requested Royal Ahold to gather evidence in this respect. Certain members of Royal Ahold's former management indicated that it intended to adjust the joint venture agreements (either through modification of the joint venture agreements itself, or by using control letters) (Koninklijke Ahold/De Brauw Blackstone Westbroek, 2004, pp. 28–33) (see Verdict Criminal Court Amsterdam, 2009, chapter 2.6 for an in-depth analysis of the realisation, meaning and consequences of the control letters and side letters).

There were four pairs of almost completely similar control letters and side letters with respect to the four joint ventures (ICA, DAIH, Bompreco and Paiz Ahold).

The contents of the control letters were as shown in Figure 15.1. This control letter was handed over to the auditors with respect to three joint ventures. On the basis of this document, other evidence and audit procedures the auditor decided, it seems, that Royal Ahold was allowed to fully consolidate the joint ventures according to US GAAP.

However, members of former management of Royal Ahold were also involved in the so-called side letters. These side letters were *not* handed over by former management of Royal Ahold to the auditors of Royal Ahold, which constituted a breach of the Letters of Representation (LORs).

The contents of the side letters were as shown in Figure 15.2.

Former management of Royal Ahold, therefore, did include these joint ventures in its consolidated accounts. This resulted in an overestimation of the consolidated net sales and consolidated gross profit for US GAAP reporting purposes.

A whistleblower sent an anonymous letter to the press on 21 February 2003 with a description of irregularities in the financial accounting of Royal Ahold (amongst others the full consolidation of ICA and the existence of control and side letters for ICA). Further, in this anonymous letter it was stated that there were large disagreements between Royal Ahold and their auditors Deloitte. An anonymous source had already phoned *Het Algemeen Dagblad* (a Dutch newspaper) on 10 February 2003 with the message that there was a

---

Letterhead Royal Ahold

Date

Dear contract partner(s) in the joint venture,

Our auditors have requested us that we be more specific with regard to the interpretation of the shareholders' agreement for the joint venture.

The shareholders' agreement stipulates that all (major) decisions with regard to the joint venture will be made in consensus between you on one side and Royal Ahold on the other side. This is the basic understanding of the partnership. However, Royal Ahold understands that according to the best interpretation of the shareholders' agreement in the case that we reach no consensus decision on a certain issue, which we are unable to resolve to shareholders' mutual satisfaction, Royal Ahold's proposal to solve that issue will in the end be decisive. In the unlikely event that this occurs, Royal Ahold will always act in such a way that the interests of the joint venture contract partner(s) are (is) best protected.

Yours sincerely,                                    Agreed*:

Signature                                           Date:

Member Executive Board Royal Ahold                  Signature(s) contract partner(s) joint
                                                                                    venture

---

*In the Bompreco control letter the word   Aware appeared instead of Agreed and the control letter was restricted to the foreseeable future. This was not the case with the other three control letters.

**Figure 15.1**  Control letter

*Source*: in revised form derived from Verdict Criminal Court Amsterdam LJN: BH 1789 28 of January 2009, chapter 2.6.

conflict between Royal Ahold and Deloitte with respect to the way ICA was recognised in the consolidated financial statements of Royal Ahold and that this would cause the then CFO to lose his job. *Het Algemeen Dagblad* confronted Royal Ahold with this message the same day. On 12 February 2003 CEO Mr van der Hoeven was informed by Mr Miller (CEO USF) that there had been irregularities with vendor allowances at USF (Adviescommissie Fondsenreglement, 2004, pp. 3 and 7).

Royal Ahold restated the financial statements of the financial years 2000 and 2001 after the aftermath of the accounting scandals. This was announced by Royal Ahold on 24 February 2003. Royal Ahold indicated that these restatements were primarily related to overstatements of vendor allowance income at USF and the deconsolidation of five current or former joint ventures: ICA, DAIH, Bompreco, JMR and Paiz Ahold. Royal Ahold's then CEO Mr van der Hoeven and CFO Mr Meurs resigned (Adviescommissie Fondsenreglement, 2004, p. 2; Koninklijke Ahold N.V. 2002 Consolidated Financial Statements, p. F-26).

Letterhead(s) contract partner(s)

Date:

Dear member of the Executive Board of Royal Ahold,

I (we) are aware of the contents of your letter of date Control Letter. This is to inform you that I (we) do not agree with the interpretation given by you of our shareholders' agreement.

Yours sincerely,                                                  Agreed:

                                                                Date:

Signature(s) contract partner(s)                                Signature Member

                                                                Executive Board Royal

                                                                Ahold

**Figure 15.2**   Side letter

*Source*: in revised form derived from Verdict Criminal Court Amsterdam LJN: BH 1789 28 of January 2009, chapter 2.6.

The deconsolidation of the five joint ventures only had a very small effect on the previously reported net income under Dutch GAAP for the fiscal years 2000 and 2001 (less than 1 %). There was also only a quite moderate impact on the shareholders' equity under Dutch GAAP at 30 December 2001 with respect to the deconsolidation of the joint ventures (less than 1 %).

However, the impact on the net sales and gross profit was huge in both 2000 and 2001. Deconsolidation of the joint ventures led to downward corrections of net sales in 2000 of €10.6 billion (20.6 % of net sales as previously reported) and of gross profit of €2.2 billion (18.4 % of gross profit as previously reported). Deconsolidation of the joint ventures led to downward corrections of net sales in 2001 of €12.2 billion (18.3 % of net sales as previously reported) and of gross profit of €2.5 billion (17 % of gross profit as previously reported) (Koninklijke Ahold N.V. 2002 Consolidated Financial Statements, pp. F-34–35). The announcement of the accounting scandals by Royal Ahold on 24 February 2003, led to enormous losses for shareholders as the price of common stock on foreign exchanges dropped by approximately 63 % and the price of the American Depository Receipts of Royal Ahold trading on the NYSE fell by approximately 61 % (Adviescommissie Fondsenreglement, 2004, p. 2).

In January 2009, in a criminal case, Mr Meurs, former CFO was sentenced for forgery (Section 225 Dutch Criminal Law) with respect to false control letters and false LORs handed over to the auditors Deloitte. In those LORs, the former management of Royal Ahold declared that all financial records and related data had been handed over to the auditor.

Mr Andreae (former member of the board of Royal Ahold) was sentenced for forgery with respect to the ICA control letter and because Ahold had not informed Deloitte in the proper way.

Further, the criminal court concluded that the consolidation of three joint ventures was not in line with US GAAP and so the Form 20-F reconciliations of Royal Ahold were false for the years 1999, 2000 and 2001. Mr Meurs was sentenced in this respect for the years 1999, 2000 and 2001 and Mr Andreae for the years 2000 and 2001. However, the criminal court did not reach the conclusion that the consolidation of the five joint ventures led to untrue financial statements under Dutch GAAP (Section 336 Dutch Criminal Law).

According to the Criminal Court Amsterdam Mr van der Hoeven, former CEO, had a limited role in this financial fraud. The court gave Mr Meurs a suspended prison sentence (voorwaardelijke gevangenisstraf) of six months, a task sentence (taakstraf) of 240 hours and a fine of €100 000; Mr. Andreae a suspended prison sentence of three months and a fine of €50 000 and Mr van der Hoeven a fine of €30 000 (Verdict Criminal Court Amsterdam, 2009).

As mentioned in the introduction, the judges in the criminal case argued that management of companies in the Netherlands had ample scope to interpret Dutch accounting rules (in the light of the true and fair view and consolidation criteria). Therefore, the judges did not reach the conclusion that the consolidation of the five joint ventures led to untrue financial statements under Dutch GAAP (Section 336 Dutch Criminal Law).

### 15.3.5  Accounting for Vendor Allowances at US Foodservice (USF)[3]

USF is a food-service distributor and supplies food and related products in the US to restaurants, hotels, care institutions, government services, universities, stadiums and catering companies. USF was the second-largest food service distributor in the US in 2003 (29 500 employees and net sales of $15.8 billion). USF has 250 000 customers spread across the US.

Vendor allowances can be described as the purchase discounts distributors get from their suppliers on condition that they purchase a certain amount of goods in a certain time period: this could be up to a couple of years. In the case of USF, these discounts were received quite often upfront as cash.

### 15.3.6  Proper Accounting Treatment Vendor Allowances

Royal Ahold received various types of vendor allowances in the form of upfront payments, rebates (in the form of cash or credits) and other forms of payments that effectively reduced Royal Ahold's cost of goods purchased from the vendor or reduced the cost of promotional activities conducted by Royal Ahold on behalf of the vendor. Most common allowances offered by vendors are (i) volume allowances, which are off-invoice or amounts billed back to vendors based on the quantity of products sold to customers or purchased from the

---

[3] Further coverage of this issue can be found in the US chapter, Chapter 20.

vendor and (ii) promotional allowances, which relate to cooperative advertising and market development efforts. Vendor allowances are only recognised in income if evidence of a binding arrangement exists with the vendor.

Slotting and stocking allowances that are paid by vendors in return for introducing their new products in a store and upfront payments by vendors and rebates received relating to volume allowances are recognised on a systematic basis as a reduction of the purchase price of the related products as they are purchased or sold. If these volume allowances are contingent on achieving certain minimum volume targets, the allowances are recognised only to the extent it is probable that the minimum volume targets will be achieved and the amount of the allowance can be reasonably estimated.

Payments from vendors for promotional activities are initially deferred and subsequently recognised, when the advertising or marketing activities specified in the contract are performed by Royal Ahold for the vendor. If no specific performance criteria are defined in the contract, the allowance is deferred over the term of the contract (Koninklijke Ahold N.V. 2002 Consolidated Financial Statements, p. F-24).

Already at the time of the acquisition of USF by Royal Ahold in April 2000 the internal control system of USF was weak in particular with respect to tracking and calculating vendor allowances. After USF was acquired by Royal Ahold, USF launched a programme to improve its internal control system. USF set up an Internal Audit Department (IAD) to conduct control programmes and make recommendations for the improvement of their internal control systems. USF appointed a Vice-President of Divisional Accounting to monitor the results of the divisions and to supervise and monitor the financial reporting by the divisions. Further, USF initiated four strategic IT initiatives to achieve central corporate control. However, the correction of these deficiencies would take a number of years.

This process was further complicated by the acquisition by Royal Ahold, finalised in December 2000, of PYA (another food service distributor in the US) which had its own central commercial, logistics and tracking system and the acquisition of Alliant Exchange including its subsidiary Alliant Foodservice in December 2001. The former management of USF first wanted to switch to the PYA tracking system, which it partly did. Then after the acquisition of Alliant Exchange USF they wanted to switch to the tracking system of Alliant. The PYA system had to be connected to the Alliant tracking system and the codes used in the PYA system for products, vendors and other relevant data had to be translated into codes compatible with the Alliant system – a process which could take years.

USF's former management each time reported to Deloitte USA that it did not have any written contracts with vendors relating to vendor allowances. During the years 2000 and 2001, the vendors confirmed the balance statements they received to Deloitte USA (Koninklijke Ahold/De Brauw Blackstone Westbroek, 2004, pp. 60–61).

The USF investigations by the new management of Royal Ahold (from March 2003 onwards) identified accounting fraud relating to fictitious and overstated vendor allowance receivables and an understatement of cost of goods sold. The investigation found that certain senior officers of USF and other employees were involved in this fraud. It was also found that such inappropriate vendor allowance accounting had existed at the date of the acquisition of USF in 2000 (Koninklijke Ahold N.V. 2002 Consolidated Financial Statements, p. F-26).

The improper accounting for vendor allowances at USF (and Tops, another US subsidiary of Royal Ahold) led to an overstated net income under Dutch GAAP in 2000 and 2001.

The overstatement in 2000 was €103 million (9.2 % of net income as previously reported) and in 2001 it was €215 million (19.3 % of net income as previously reported).

The overstatement of shareholders' equity under Dutch GAAP for December 2001 was €418 million (7.1 % of shareholders' equity under Dutch GAAP as previously reported).

The net income from vendor allowances was overstated, due to the intentional and unintentional misinterpretation of Dutch GAAP. Moreover, there was the intentional inappropriate accounting for, and mischaracterisation of, cash receipts, which led to the premature recognition of vendor allowances according to Dutch GAAP. Furthermore, certain vendor allowances were misclassified as revenue instead of a reduction of cost of sales as required under Dutch GAAP (Koninklijke Ahold N.V. 2002 Consolidated Financial Statements, pp. F-27–28).

The accounting fraud relating to vendor allowances at USF was covered up by USF employees, who prepared incorrect balance statements relating to the auditors' confirmation of balance procedure. These incorrect statements were sent to vendors and these vendors subsequently confirmed the incorrect balance statements to Deloitte USA. Deloitte USA used the so-called confirmation of balance procedure. Deloitte USA sent a letter to USF vendors in which these vendors were requested to confirm, among other things, to Deloitte USA the amount owed to USF by the vendor at the end of the previous financial year, less the repayments made or reductions given by the vendor during the financial year in question, plus the vendor allowances that the vendor had granted during the year and to specify what part of the amount owed was paid after the end of the financial year. Further, the vendors were asked to confirm the percentage of vendor allowances to which USF was entitled with respect to the vendor in conformity with the base programme.

However, before the vendors received these balance statements, the vendors to whom they were sent were called by certain employees of USF (those who were involved in the fraud). If employees of the vendor had any questions, they called those USF employees. Employees of USF (who were involved in this matter) would then inform them by telephone or in writing that the balance statement they received was only an internal estimate of USF that was not actually payable and/or that USF would not try to collect the balance that the vendor had to pay to USF according to the statement. Employees of the vendors, including those who asked for and who received information from USF employees, confirmed the incorrect balance statements to Deloitte USA (SEC, 2004b, pp. 4–9).

The irregularities were revealed because Deloitte USA received two replies from one vendor in conducting the confirmation of balance procedure in their 2002 audit. One reply came from the vendor's CEO, who confirmed the balance specified by USF. The other reply came from the vendor's CFO. This reply showed that the amounts specified by USF were incorrect, that (contrary to what USF had always told Deloitte USA) there was a written contract between the vendor and USF and that (also contrary to what USF had always told Deloitte USA) this contract included stipulations regarding substantial pre-payments. Further, Deloitte USA received a confirmation from another vendor, which stated:

> Based on the conversations held with US Foodservices about this letter and subject to the interpretation given by them of the amounts shown, we agree with the interpretation presented in the preceding letter.

Finally, USF's former management informed Deloitte USA that with regard to one vendor, the amounts that this vendor had to pay USF according to the balance statement sent to this vendor were grossly overstated (Koninklijke Ahold/De Brauw Blackstone Westbroek, 2004, pp. 61–64).

In detail, the effect on the consolidated income statement of Royal Ahold for the fiscal year 2001 and 2000 was as follows (in millions of euros) (Koninklijke Ahold N.V. 2002 Consolidated Financial Statements, p. F-29).

| | 2001 | 2000 |
|---|---|---|
| Net sales | (80) | (44)[i] |
| Cost of sales | (214) | (104)[ii] |
| Selling, general and administrative expenses | (2) | – |
| Tax effect | 118 | 56[iii] |
| Share in income (loss) of joint ventures and equity investees | (37) | (11)[iv] |
| Net impact of vendor allowance adjustments on net income | (215) | (103) |

Notes: Explanation of the effect of the restatement on the consolidated income statement of Royal Ahold 2001 and 2000.
(i) the net sales were *over*stated by the misclassification of vendor allowances; so the correction was to reduce profit by (€80 million) in 2001 and (€44 million) in 2000.
(ii) the cost of sales was *under*stated by the misclassification of vendor allowances; so the correction was to reduce profit by (€214 million) in 2001 and (€104 million) in 2000.
(iii) the tax expense with respect to the misclassification of vendor allowances was *over*stated; so the correction was to increase profit by €118 million in 2001 and €56 million in 2000.
(iv) the share in income (loss) of joint ventures and equity investees related to the misclassification of vendor allowances at USF was *under*stated; so the correction was to reduce profit by (€37 million) in 2001 and (€11 million) in 2000.

### 15.3.7 Measures Taken by Royal Ahold after Discovering the Fraud

Shortly after this fraud was discovered, the Audit Committee called in White & Case LLP and the forensic accountants of Protiviti, Inc. to investigate. Following this investigation, Morvillo and the forensic accountants of PWC were called in to investigate the fraud further. Royal Ahold took many measures after the discovery of this particular fraud, amongst others:

a) the employees of USF that were involved in the unlawful interference in the confirmation of balance procedure were dismissed;
b) the CEO, the then CFO and the then Executive Vice President, at that time also General Counsel of USF, resigned;
c) the financial figures of USF and Royal Ahold for the years 2000–2 were restated;
d) the Alliant tracking system was implemented for the whole of USF;
e) pending the implementation of the Alliant system for USF, USF has installed a manual system to track the vendor allowances (Koninklijke Ahold/De Brauw Blackstone Westbroek, 2004, pp. 63–66). (See Royal Ahold Annual Reports 2002 and 2003 for other measures taken by the new management of Ahold and more details in this respect.)

One of the major findings of the forensic investigations was that a number of USF divisions incorrectly claimed allowances from vendors within the scope of their vendor allowance schemes, for example by reporting incorrect volumes of goods sold. USF divisions also used a 'broad' interpretation of the agreements regarding allowances. As a consequence, USF had overbilled different vendors.

In July 2004, the SEC announced that it had filed charges against four former executives of USF. These individuals included the company's former CFO, former chief marketing officer, and two former executives in the company's purchasing division. The two former purchasing executives settled the charges by agreeing to permanent injunctions that prohibited them from being officers or directors of public companies and by forfeiting stock market gains they had earned on the sale of Royal Ahold's common shares during the course of the fraud. In September 2006, the former CFO pleaded guilty to one count of conspiracy and was given three years' probation by a federal judge in the US. In November 2006, a federal jury found the USF former chief marketing officer guilty of conspiracy and federal securities fraud. In 2007, he was sentenced to seven years in federal prison in the US (Knapp and Knapp, 2007, p. 653; see also Buckley and Michaels, 2004; *Het Financieele Dagblad*, 2006a and b).

Ms Chatman Thomsen, deputy director of enforcement at the SEC said: 'Executives at US Foodservice went to extraordinary lengths to perpetuate the illusion of stellar financial performance. Their fraud created the appearance that they had met their budgets and allowed them to line their own pockets with unearned bonuses' (Buckley and Michaels, 2004, p. 25).

Other accounting irregularities at Royal Ahold were detected after the discovery of the accounting fraud at USF.

### 15.3.8 Acquisition Accounting

#### 15.3.8.1  *Acquisition of USF*

According to the USF investigations after the discovery of the accounting fraud at USF, net receivables from vendors which were on the books of USF at the moment of acquisition of USF did not exist at the time of the acquisition in 2000. At the date of acquisition, a liability for deferred revenue related to promotional allowances, that were not yet earned, was not recorded. Furthermore, Royal Ahold determined that a liability should have been recognised at the date of acquisition for amounts that were overbilled to vendors for promotional allowances. The total amount of these adjustments led to an overstatement of net assets acquired by €70 million. This error was recorded as a retroactive adjustment to the goodwill recorded upon acquisition of USF according to Dutch GAAP and IFRS Exposure Draft 3 Business Combinations. Accordingly, shareholders' equity as of 30 December 2000 under Dutch GAAP was reduced by €70 million (Koninklijke Ahold N.V. 2002 Consolidated Financial Statements, p. F-29).

#### 15.3.8.2  *Acquisition of Superdiplo and Taking an Interest in ICA*

In connection with the acquisition of Superdiplo and taking an interest in ICA (joint venture of Royal Ahold) in December 2000 and April 2000, respectively, Royal Ahold did not properly allocate purchase consideration to certain acquired real estate properties at the respective acquisition dates. The restated consolidated financial position and results for

2000 and 2001 reflect adjustments to record such assets at their fair values at the acquisition date and their subsequent depreciation. In certain instances, this affected the gains made on the subsequent disposal of these assets. In addition, Royal Ahold failed to allocate purchase consideration correctly to certain identifiable intangible assets in 2001. The effect of these accounting irregularities on equity and net income was modest.

### 15.3.9  Reserves, Allowances and Provisions

Prior to 2002, Royal Ahold recorded certain reserves, allowances and provisions related to income taxes, pensions and restructuring expenses. Royal Ahold subsequently determined that these reserves, allowances and provisions, and releases thereof, should not have been recorded under Dutch GAAP, since the documentation available was not adequate to support the amounts recorded, or the reserves, allowances and provisions were of a non-specific nature. In addition, certain pension and early retirement provisions had not been accounted for as defined benefit plans and the charges and accruals related to certain health and welfare plans were not calculated appropriately. As a result of these adjustments, shareholders' equity as of 30 December 2001 decreased by €105 million and net income decreased by €33 million, for the financial year 2001 and €38 million, for the financial year 2000.

### 15.3.10  Lease Accounting

Finally, Royal Ahold identified a number of sale-leaseback transactions that occurred in 2000 and 2001, under which certain leases that had been classified as operating leases should have been classified as capital leases or financing arrangements. The effect of these accounting irregularities on equity and net income was modest (Koninklijke Ahold N.V. 2002 Consolidated Financial Statements, pp. F-29–32).

On 11 March 2003 Mr Eustace was appointed as interim CFO at Royal Ahold. On 5 May 2003 Mr Moberg started as CEO of Royal Ahold. On 19 June 2003 Ahold announced the appointment of Mr Ryöppönen as new CFO of Royal Ahold (Verdict Enterprise Court, 2005). This new management team implemented many changes such as setting up a new task force reporting to the Audit Committee. It improved its trading system for vendor allowances.

New management also formulated a new strategic direction. It abandoned its ambition to become one of the world's greatest retailers. It now has four key priorities. The first is restoring financial health, the second is re-engineering the retail business, the third is recovering the value of USF and the fourth is reinforcing accountability, controls and corporate governance (Royal Ahold Annual Report 2005, p. 8).

In July 2007 USF was sold by Royal Ahold for a purchase price of $7.1 billion (Royal Ahold Annual Report 2007, p. 6).

## 15.4  CONCLUSION

Although the Dutch accounting profession has been grounded partially on a large financial fraud there have not been many accounting scandals in the Netherlands (until recently). This can be explained in part by the fact that the Netherlands is an arena of 'principle-based' accounting. In a way, the 'true and fair view,' in combination with the necessary professional judgement can hide creative accounting under the surface. The relatively low status of the Dutch standard setter (the CAR) also contributes. Until recently there was no enforcement body active in the Netherlands with respect to the financial statements of listed companies. However, this changed in 2006. The Netherlands Authority for the Financial Markets (AFM) investigates the financial statements of listed companies in the Netherlands from 2006 on. This could lead to the detection of more accounting scandals in the future.

The most prominent recent accounting scandal from the Netherlands has been Royal Ahold. In less detail we have also discussed some minor accounting scandals in the Netherlands (RSV: mainly a case of the optimistic debiting of deferred tax assets on the basis of a carry-forward estimation of future profits and a pessimistic view related to the ability to pay back received government grants, and Fokker: creative accounting with development costs and capitalising of programme losses). At Royal Ahold there were two major accounting scandals: the consolidation scandal and the vendor allowances scandal. The consolidation accounting scandal was in fact the full consolidation of joint ventures where proportional consolidation or the equity method was appropriate according to US GAAP. The effect on net income was almost nil. However, the effect on consolidated net sales and gross profit was huge.

Mr Meurs, former CFO, was sentenced for forgery with respect to false control letters and false LORs handed over to the auditors Deloitte. Mr Andreae (former member of the board of Royal Ahold) was sentenced for forgery with respect to the ICA control letter and because Ahold had not informed Deloitte in the proper way.

Further, the criminal court concluded that the consolidation of three joint ventures was not in line with US GAAP and so the Form 20-F reconciliations of Royal Ahold were false for the years 1999, 2000 and 2001. Mr Meurs was sentenced in this respect for the years 1999, 2000 and 2001 and Mr Andreae for the years 2000 and 2001. However, the criminal court did not reach the conclusion that the consolidation of the five joint ventures led to untrue financial statements under Dutch GAAP (Section 336 Dutch Criminal Law). According to the Criminal Court Amsterdam Mr van der Hoeven, former CEO, had a limited role in this financial fraud.

The accounting scandal at Ahold also had an impact on Dutch society. Management, auditors and supervisory boards have become more sensitive to creative accounting and fraudulent reporting in the Netherlands. To a certain extent this attitude has been stimulated by the new oversight role of the Netherlands Authority for the Financial Markets (AFM) with respect to financial reporting by listed companies. Also, the Dutch financial press has become more alert regarding financial frauds. The Ahold scandal and scandals abroad have also greatly reinforced the need for a corporate governance code in the Netherlands. After these accounting scandals the former CEO of Unilever, Mr Tabaksblat, was invited to lead a group of professionals from business and society to develop a Dutch corporate governance code which was implemented for 2004. There have also been changes to the criminal law. The term of imprisonment for an untrue financial statement has been raised from one year to two years (art. 336 Dutch Criminal Law). Further, the Dutch Civil Code has been revised partially as a reaction to the accounting scandals in the Netherlands and abroad.

# REFERENCES

Adviescommissie Fondsenreglement (2004), *Advice regarding the Request of Euronext Amsterdam N.V. with respect to Royal Ahold N.V. in Zaandam (Advies in zake het Verzoek van Euronext Amsterdam N.V. ten aanzien van Koninklijke Ahold N.V. te Zaandam)*, 7 May.

American Institute for Certified Public Accountants (AICPA) (1959), *Consolidated Financial Statements, Accounting Research Bulletin No. 51*, (AICPA: New York).

American Institute for Certified Public Accountants (AICPA) (1971a), *APB Opinion No. 18, The Equity Method of Accounting for Investments in Common Stock*, (AICPA: New York).

American Institute for Certified Public Accountants (AICPA) (1971b), *Accounting Interpretations of APB Opinion No. 18*, (AICPA: New York).

Annual Report Ahold 1996 (Jaarrapport Ahold 1996).

Annual Report Ahold 1997 (Jaarrapport Ahold 1997).

Beckman, H. (2007), *Financial Statements and Accountability (Jaarrekening en Verantwoording)*, inaugural speech, (Kluwer: Deventer).

Buckley, N. and A. Michaels (2004), 'Ahold US chiefs accused of fraud', *Financial Times*, 28 July, p. 25.

Coriolis Research (2001), *Retail Supermarket Globalisation: Who's Winning?*, (Coriolis Research: Auckland).

Council of Annual Reporting (CAR) (2001), *Guidelines for annual reporting Year edition 2001 (Richtlijnen voor de jaarverslaggeving Jaareditie 2001)*, (Kluwer: Deventer).

Criminal Court Amsterdam (Gerechtshof Amsterdam) (2009) (LJN: BH1789, 1790, 1791 and 1792), *Verdict in higher appeal regarding Royal Ahold case (Uitspraak in hoger beroep in de Ahold zaak)*, 28 January.

Deterink, A. A. M., B. F. M. Knüppe, A. L. Leuftink and R. J. Schimmelpenninck (1997), *Investigation into the causes of the bankruptcy of FOKKER (Onderzoek naar de oorzaken van het faillissement van FOKKER)*, (N.V. Koninklijke Nederlands Vliegtuigenfabriek Fokker, Amsterdam/Oude Meer).

Dutch Civil Code (*Burgerlijk Wetboek Titel 9*, revised by law of 18 April 2002).

Dutch Criminal Law (*Wetboek van Strafrecht*, revised 2002).

Enterprise Court Amsterdam (Ondernemingskamer Gerechtshof Amsterdam) (2005), *LJN: AR8831*, Verdict regarding Royal Ahold N.V. (*Uitspraak inzake Koninklijke Ahold N.V.*), January 6.

Financial Accounting Standards Board (FASB) (1987), *FASB No. 94 Consolidation of All Majority-Owned Subsidiaries*, (FASB: Norwalk).

Financial Accounting Standards Board (FASB) (1996), *EITF No. 96-16 (1996), Investor's Accounting for an Investee When the Investor Has a Majority of the Voting Interest but the Minority Shareholder or Shareholders Have Certain Approval or Veto Rights*, (FASB: Norwalk).

Gray, K. R., L. A. Frieder and G. W. Clark, Jr (2005), *Corporate Scandals: The Many Faces of Greed: The Great Heist, Financial Bubbles and the Absence of Virtue*, Paragon House: St Paul, Minnesota.

Het Financieele Dagblad (2006a), *Hedge funds enlarge pressure on Ahold (Hedge funds voeren druk op Ahold op)*, 18 September.

Het Financieele Dagblad (2006b), *Ahold-man in US confesses guilty (Ahold-man in VS bekent schuld)*, 20 September.

Hoogendoorn, M. N. (1987), 'Creative accounting at RSV' (*Het creatieve jaarrekeningbeleid van RSV*), *Pacioli Journaal*, November, pp. 13–16.

Inquiry committee OGEM (Enquêtecommissie OGEM) (Van der Hoeven J., Van Putten A. and Slagter W. J. (1986), *Report of the inquiry of the Enterprise Court (Verslag van het onderzoek aan de Ondernemingskamer)*, 31 December.

Koninklijke Ahold/De Brauw Blackstone Westbroek (2004), *Defense against the Request for an Inquiry Pursuant to section 2:345 of the Dutch Civil Code, Enterprise section of the Amsterdam Court of Appeal*, 17 May.

Jong, de, A., D. V. DeJong, G. Mertens and P. Roosenboom (2005), *Royal Ahold: A Failure of Corporate Governance*, (Working Paper Erasmus University: Rotterdam).

Knapp, M. C. and C. A. Knapp (2007), 'Europe's Enron: Royal Ahold, N.V.', *Issues in Accounting Education*, Vol. 22, No. 4, November, pp. 641–660.

Koninklijke Ahold N.V. *Consolidated Financial Statements* 2002.

Langendijk, H. P. A. J. (1995), 'Flexibility and creative accounting' (Flexibiliteit en jaarrekeningbeleid), *Tijdschrift voor Bedrijfsadministratie*, Vol. 99, No. 1180/81, July/August, pp. 259–269.

Langendijk, H. P. A. J. (1998), *The Quality of Profits: An Essay about Income Measurement and the Appropriation of Profits (De kwaliteit van de winst Een Essay over Winstbepaling, Winststuring alsmede Winstbestemming)*, (Nyenrode University Press: Breukelen).

Parliamentary Inquiry Construction Industry (Parlementaire Enquête Bouwnijverheid) (2003), *Final Report: The Building Industry out of the Shadow (Eindrapport De bouw uit de schaduw)*, (Sdu Uitgevers: The Hague).

Royal Ahold Annual Report 2002.

Royal Ahold Annual Report 2003.

Royal Ahold Annual Report 2005.

Royal Ahold Annual Report 2007.

Securities and Exchange Commission (SEC) (2004a), *Litigation Release No. 18929, Accounting and Auditing Enforcement No. 2124, SEC v. Royal Ahold, SEC v. A. Michiel Meurs and Cees van der Hoeven, SEC v. Johannes Gerhardus Andreae*, 13 October.

Securities and Exchange Commission (SEC) (2004b), *Plaintiff, SEC v. Royal Ahold*, 13 October.

Supreme Court Verdict (Hoge Raad) (2009), *AFM/Spyker case Financial accounting law (AFM/Spyker zaak Jaarrekeningrecht)* (LJN BG8790), 24 April.

Vries, de, J. (1985), *History of Accountancy in the Netherlands Start and Unfolding, 1895–1935 (Geschiedenis der Accountancy in Nederland Aanvang en Ontplooiing, 1895–1935)*, (Van Gorcum: Assen).

# 16

# Creative Accounting and Financial Scandals in Spain

Nieves Carrera

## 16.1 INTRODUCTION

Corporate fraud is a serious problem in the Spanish economy that has cost investors millions of euros. Time after time, we are 'surprised' by companies failing 'unexpectedly'. In most cases, however, the evidence suggests the presence of 'red flags' alerting investors to the high probability that a corporate failure was about to occur. Many of the financial scandals have occurred in highly regulated sectors like banking (e.g. the Banesto case); some have had a significant media impact because of the political repercussions (e.g. the Grupo Torras case) and others have been given extra publicity because of the involvement of significant amounts of public funds to ensure that investors were compensated (e.g. the Gescartera case) (Gonzalo and Garvey, 2005, p. 429). Consistently, at times of crisis, many questions arise about the lack of effectiveness of the control mechanisms in detecting and preventing these scandals. Reacting in a similar way to regulators in many other countries (see, for example, Sikka, 1997), Spanish authorities have reacted to corporate scandals by enacting new legislation.

In Spain, accounting professionals and academics '... have generally shown no significant interest in analysing the causes of these scandals in proposing measures and reforms to make sure that they wouldn't happen again' (Gonzalo and Garvey, 2005, p. 430). García-Benau et al.'s (1999) analysis of Banesto and Vico-Martínez's (2002) research on the Gescartera case and its impact on regulation represent the few examples of academic work on Spanish financial scandals.

The role of creative accounting and the significance of fraud in Spain is also an under-researched area. A limited number of studies have provided evidence of the use of creative accounting (e.g. Amat, Perramon and Oliveras, 2003; Blasco-Lang, 1998; García-Benau and Vico-Martínez, 2002; Gay-Saludas, 1997; Oliveras and Amat, 2003; Villaroya and Rodríguez, 2003). Oliveras and Amat (2003), for instance, analyse the impact of alternative accounting policies for research and development costs on Spanish bank loan officers. In a similar vein, Amat et al. (2003) illustrate some of the creative accounting practices used by the top 35 Spanish listed companies. Villaroya and Rodríguez (2003), using a sample of 61 companies, show that the most frequent accounting manipulations relate to the violation of the principle of prudence, the valuation of inventory and the provision for contingencies. Finally, Gonzalo and Garvey (2005) reflect upon the role of ethics in Spanish accounting education following recent financial scandals.

This chapter focuses on the main financial scandals in Spain during the past 30 years. The evidence derives primarily from press and media information. The press has been identified as a 'watchdog' for accounting fraud, including '... combining public and non-public information with an analysis that highlights potential problems' (Miller, 2006, p. 1006). Although the agendas of journalists and academics can differ significantly (García-Benau *et al.*, 1999), and some systematic biases may exist in the type of companies and issues the media addresses (Miller, 2006), this information is very useful for analysing the causes and consequences of financial scandals. Our analysis also employs official documents and the transcripts of congressional hearings.

The structure of the chapter is as follows. Following a brief description of the Spanish economic environment and accounting framework since the 1980s, the next section then reviews some of the more important financial scandals in Spain during the past 30 years; these are outlined in Appendix 16.1. Then, we focus on several accounting scandals in the philatelic sector. The final two sections reflect upon the aftermath of the scandals and summarize the main issues discussed in the chapter.

## 16.2 ACCOUNTING SCANDALS IN SPAIN SINCE THE 1980s

From the mid-1970s to the first part of the 1980s, Spain suffered a serious economic crisis. However, the country's economic boom in the mid-1980s, the deregulation of the financial system and the entry of Spain into the European Economic Community provided an opportunity for business and a period of economic euphoria characterized by *cultura del pelotazo* ('the culture of the fast buck'). The economic situation changed drastically towards the end of the decade. The early 1990s witnessed a major economic crisis that worsened following the devaluation of the Spanish currency (the peseta) in 1992. A high level of political corruption led to a change in the government in 1996 after 14 years of Socialist government. Several accounting scandals (e.g. the Banesto case) also played a significant role in bringing down the Socialist government (*The Economist*, 1/09/2001). By the end of the 1990s, however, there was a substantial economic recovery. Factors such as the low yields on government bonds and the upcoming switch from the peseta to the euro (effective 1 January 2002) caused a significant amount of 'undeclared money' to come out of the closet, leading many investors to find alternative investments and new financial products for their savings.

Spain lacks a strong tradition of accounting and auditing regulation. The first set of Spanish Generally Accepted Accounting Principles (GAAP) was established in 1973 (Plan General Contable, 1973). Pressure by the European Union (EU) to improve and modernize the Spanish accounting framework led to the significant development of accounting and auditing regulation during the 1980s. For instance, Spanish companies were required to audit their financial statements for the first time following the approval of the Spanish Audit Law in 1988. In 1990, regulators developed a new Spanish GAAP (Plan General Contable, 1990). During the 1990s and 2000s, EU Directives impelled changes in Spanish auditing and accounting regulation. A new Spanish GAAP conforming to

International Financial Reporting Standards (IFRS) was passed on November 2007 (Plan General Contable, 2007).

Since the 1980s, there have been a significant number of financial scandals in Spain, many of which were front-page news. At the beginning of the 1990s, cases such as Grupo Torras and Ibercorp[1] acquired a significant public dimension because of the involvement of prominent members of Spanish society, such as the Governor of the Bank of Spain. More recently, Spanish financial authorities received strong criticism after cases such as Gescartera, Afinsa and Fórum Filatélico. Companies in difficult financial and economic situations used creative accounting practices to escape the control of the Spanish authorities (e.g. Banco de Navarra), while managers had incentives to obtain personal benefits (e.g. Caja Rural de Jaen, Banesto, Gescartera, Afinsa and Fórum Filatélico). In the following sections, we describe the most important financial scandals that have occurred in Spain in the banking sector, the investment services sector and the real estate industry.

### 16.2.1 The Banking Sector

The crisis of the Spanish economy from 1975 to 1984 affected the banking sector profoundly. During this time, more than 50 banks experienced financial difficulties (e.g. Banco de Navarra and Banca Catalana; see Fernández-Navarrete, 1999). Traditionally, the Spanish industrial sector has been very close to banks. During the period 1975–84, 50 % of the investments made by banks were used to finance their industrial arms. Many banks undertook suspicious activities – such as the revaluation of assets, the recording of fictitious profits and other accounting irregularities – to escape the control of the Bank of Spain (Fernández-Navarrete, 1999). As a result, thousands of millions of pesetas (Pts) in deposits vanished or changed hands (Galindo, 2006).

Some of the bankrupt banks were also involved in creative accounting and accounting manipulation (e.g. Caja Rural de Jaen (see RJ 1994\1121, 1994) and Fidecaya (see Congreso de los Diputados, 1982)). In 1984, the directors of Caja Rural de Jaen and related entities (e.g. Uteco) were accused of accounting manipulation in their 1981 financial statements with the aim of hiding their high level of indebtedness from the authorities. The company recorded fictitious profits and attempted to reduce an 'accounting hole' of around Pts 3500 million (€21 million). The reasons behind these manipulations were managers' incentives to obtain personal benefit. In 1984, the Audiencia Nacional (National Court) sentenced the managers to three years in jail, though the penalties were repealed three years later by the High Court (RTC 1987\122, 1987). The case continued in the courts and in 1992 the Court of Jaen sentenced the managers for fraud and forgery. The appeal lodged by the managers against this decision was rejected by the Supreme Court in 1994 (RJ 1994\1121, 1994).

---

[1] The Group Torras case is related to the Kuwait Investment Office (KIO) affair in courts in the United Kingdom (Reuters, 26/11/1992; JUR 2006\200237, 2006; RJ 2007\5374, 2007). Ibercorp was a financial group that faced allegations of improper transactions with treasury stocks and the use of insider and privileged information for the personal benefit of certain shareholders (Argandoña, 1999). In the case of Ibercorp the prosecutor and the defendants agreed the judgment based upon a plea bargain (*sentencia de conformidad*). Several individuals were found guilty of price-fixing and management misbehaviour and sentenced to 12 months in prison (García-Abadillo, 1999).

The period 1985–91 witnessed more accounting scandals in the banking sector (e.g. Caja Previsora Andaluza and Caja de Crédito Andaluza).[2] The most important, however, was still to come. Banesto, one of Spain's leading domestic banks, was the protagonist in one of the most important scandals in the country's history (see García-Benau et al., 1999 for a detailed analysis). In December 1993, the Bank of Spain seized control of Banesto to '. . . prevent the situation endangering the entire Spanish banking system' (García-Benau et al., 1999, p. 704). At the time of its collapse, Banesto had more than 278 000 shareholders, of whom about 90 % owned fewer than 1000 shares (García-Benau et al., 1999). The Bank of Spain estimated the accounting deficit to be about Pts 605 000 million (€3.6 million). Banesto's management board was subsequently replaced, with chairman Mario Conde, an emblematic figure of the Spanish economic boom of the late 1980s, as the principal suspect in the fraud. In July 2002, the Supreme Court sentenced Conde to 20 years in prison following convictions for misappropriation, fraud and forgery (Remírez de Ganuza, 2002). The senior management team was also charged with illegal activities.

The Spanish courts found that Conde, whom the *Institutional Investor* had named banker of the year in 1989, had manipulated the accounts using a range of questionable accounting practices, finding evidence of manipulation in the company's income statement and balance sheet positions, and non-compliance with the matching and accruals principles (see García-Benau et al., 1999; Vázquez, 1996; ARP 2000\107, 2000; RJ 2002\6357, 2002). For example, the expenses related to the initial public offering (IPO) of Corporación Industrial Banesto (Banesto's industrial arm), amounting to Pts 4122 million (€24.78 million), were recorded in Banesto's financial statements as assets in the balance sheet rather than as current expenses in the income statement (RJ 2002\6357, 2002). Investigation also found that Banesto had incurred significant losses through excessive payments for some investments and by selling assets at artificially low prices. Banesto's executives used creative accounting techniques to justify some of these transactions. One example was the acquisition of land from Promotora de Obras. Banesto paid Pts 800 million (€4.8 million) – including commissions to its executives – but the asset was recorded in the financial statements for only Pts 105 million (€631 063). The difference between the price actually paid and the book value of the asset (€4.17 million) appeared in Banesto's balance sheet as 'Sundry expenditures relating to land purchase from Promotora de Obras, SA' (RJ 2002\6357, 2002, p. 25). There was also evidence of questionable transactions for Conde's personal benefit. For example, in 1989 Conde unilaterally – without the authorization of the Banesto administration – disposed of Pts 300 million (€1.8 million) for purposes other than the proper business of Banesto (RJ 2002\6357, 2002). The transaction was justified by Mario Conde as an amount to be paid to the ex-Prime Minister of Spain, Adolfo Suárez, for mediation services with the Bank of Spain relating to problems resulting from the merger agreement between Banesto and Banco Central in 1988.[3]

---

[2] Caja Previsora Andaluza and Caja de Crédito Andaluza operated as savings banks even though they were not authorized to do so (RJ 2008\2151, 2004). In the Registro Mercantil (Mercantile Register), Caja de Crédito Andaluza was registered as a 'consulting firm' and Caja Previsora Andaluza as a coin and stamp dealer (see the section 'Investments in Stamps' for more details about scandals related to stamp dealers). The directors of both companies were found guilty of fraud.

[3] There were serious disagreements among the members of the board of directors during the merger process. The combined financial statements for 1988, which contained information about the merger process, were approved by only 11 of the 21

According to the final report prepared by the Spanish High Court, these facts were never proven (RJ 2002\6357, 2002). Although the transaction took place in a branch located in Madrid, it was recorded in the accounting books of a branch located in another city (Pamplona). In 1994, following the existing accounting regulation for banks, Banesto's accountants created a provision to remove the account related to this transaction from the balance sheet. The board of directors never approved this transaction. The Supreme Tribunal found Mario Conde not guilty of misappropriation for this particular offence. The court took the view that an offence of misappropriation had been committed, but because of the expiry of the statute of limitations, which was five years for fraud or misappropriation of assets, Mario Conde incurred no criminal liability (RJ 2002\6357, 2002, p. 38).

The Bank of Spain and Banesto's auditors (Price Waterhouse; PW) were fiercely criticized because four months before the collapse, Banesto had completed the first two parts of the largest share issue in Spanish banking history. Neither the Bank of Spain nor PW raised concerns about Banesto's financial condition (García-Benau et al., 1999). PW was fined Pts 127 million (€763 285) by the Instituto de Contabilidad y Auditoría de Cuentas (ICAC), the Spanish body in charge of accounting and auditing issues. Arthur Andersen was also fined in relation to Corporación Banesto as Banesto's industrial arm. At the time, there was also strong criticism of the activities of the financial community and the effectiveness of the auditors and the regulators:

> [I]t would be imprudent to forget the mistakes of the institutional control mechanisms … the Bank of Spain, whose negligence in not detecting the entity's situation and approving the share issue is undeniable. In the second place, the Comisión Nacional del Mercado de Valores (CNMV; the Spanish Stock Exchange Commission), which didn't protect shareholders by saying that information was good when it wasn't. And in third place, the actions of the company's auditors, that approved accounts which did not reflect the net worth of the bank.
>
> (*El Mundo*, 24/12/1994, p. 3; quoted in García-Benau et al., 1999, p. 704)

Problems in the banking sector continued in the years that followed. The most recent scandal occurred in 2003, when the Bank of Spain seized control of Eurobank del Mediterráneo, SA, after the directors of the company filed for bankruptcy protection (Valero, 2003; see also www.bde.es/clientebanca/noticias/18-03-2005_liquidacion_Eurobank.htm). Eurobank executives faced allegations of misrepresentation, misappropriation and fraud (Cortes, 2003). In March 2007, the bank's ex-president and two of his colleagues were acquitted of fraud charges (ABC, 3/03/2007). The company and its directors were punished for breaking the Law 26/1988 de Disciplina e Intervención de Entidades de Crédito (Law 26/1988 of 29 July on Discipline and Intervention of Credit Institutions).[4] The appeal lodged by the directors against this decision was rejected by the Audiencia Nacional (National Court) in 2008 (RJCA 2008/664, 2008).

---

members of the board of directors (five members voted against, another five abstained). The division in the board of directors was a major issue of concern for the Bank of Spain given the potential impact on the Spanish banking system. Ultimately, the merger did not take place, and Banco Central and Banesto filed individual annual statements. Mario Conde argued that ex-Prime Minister Suárez mediated on behalf of Banesto by helping the bank to achieve authorization for the demerger and the approval of the 1988 financial statements by the Bank of Spain.

[4] The company and its directors received monetary fines for failing to comply with the applicable rules and requirements (e.g. providing services prohibited by the law).

## 16.2.2 Investment Service Firms

Several investment service firms have also been involved in accounting scandals during the past two decades (e.g. Brokerval, AV; Sistema de Ahorro Multiple; AVA Asesores de Valores and Socimer España, SA). In the case of Brokerval VA, several directors were found guilty of embezzlement by the Spanish High Court in 2005 (RJ\2005\1938, 2005). In the case of Sistema de Ahorro Multiple, the National Court sentenced the owners of the company to two years in prison for fraud (AP Magistratura, 1998; JUR\2000\291257, 2000). The case of AVA-Socimer is still in the court system (Audiencia Nacional). Four ex-directors of AVA and the auditor were acquitted of mismanagement and criminal act of bankruptcy in a separate trial at the Zaragoza Provincial Court (*El Economista*, 8/04/2008).

The most important scandal involved Gescartera, a brokerage house. Gescartera collapsed in July 2001, and its main shareholder, Antonio Camacho, was jailed after €100 million was found to have disappeared (*Expansión*, 10/05/2006). Camacho was said to be a man of strong personality who delighted in showing off (García-Abadillo, 2001). The history of the company and the events surrounding the case – for example, evidence of the use of company assets for personal ambitions – suggest that greed led Gescartera's principal shareholder and other executives to manipulate the company's financial information. The Spanish High Court sentenced Camacho to 11 years in prison: eight years for embezzlement and three years for forgery. Another seven people, including the managing director, were also convicted (*Expansión*, 28/03/2008, p. 37). The two saving banks which handled Gescartera's transactions (La Caixa and Caja Madrid) were also found liable and required to reimburse their clients €87.99 million plus accrued interest (*El País*, 28/03/2008).

The Gescartera case illustrates '... a complex tale of greed, nepotism and fraud that cast a vivid light on Spain's traditional old-boy network in business' (*The Economist*, 1/09/2001, pp. 45–46). Gescartera was founded in 1992 as a portfolio management company (Sociedad Gestora de Cartera). In 1994, the Spanish Stock Exchange Authority, Comisión Nacional del Mercado de Valores (CNMV), imposed a fine on Gescartera for providing certain financial services without authorization. The fine was not made public, and it did not have any impact on the capacity of Camacho to continue providing services as a manager in the brokerage house. In 1999, Gescartera was again fined by the CNMV for resistance to being supervised. The internal investigation undertaken by the CNMV pointed out that the company '... did not have the required accounting entries ...'[5] and had '... weak internal controls ...' (Comisión Gescartera, 2001, pp. 8952–8970). All decisions were made by Camacho and all of the bank accounts were held under his name (*El Mundo*, 30/03/2008, p. 18). According to the CNMV, the 'accounting hole' of the company in 1999 was around Pts 1000 million (€6 million). In spite of the findings of the CNMV's internal investigation, the members of the supervisory body's board did not agree on the need to take control of the company. Moreover, the CNMV authorized Gescartera to become a securities broker, raising the status of the company (Vico-Martínez, 2002). As a securities broker, Gescartera was able to attract a significant roster of clients.

---

[5] Unfortunately, I did not have access to information concerning details of the problems with Gescartera's accounting entries.

The concerns about Gescartera's activities and its lack of cooperation with the CNMV continued. In 2001, the CNMV seized control of the company '... given the impossibility of knowing the economic and financial situation of the firm' (Vico-Martínez, 2002, p. 29). At 30 June 2001, the estimated deficit of the company was Pts 14 641 million (€87 996 million). According to the sentence issued by the Audiencia Nacional, at June 2001 the firm had no cash and no assets to meet creditors' demands due to the 'irregular and inexplicable' disappearance of resources (RJ\2008\1893, 2008, p. 49). The court's investigation showed that Gescartera did not invest its clients' money; rather, money was 'siphoned off' to 'unknown' places.[6] There was also evidence of the falsification of documents (e.g. certificates from banks such as La Caixa), and the information given to investors was scarce and unclear (JUR 2008\112612, 2008). Gescartera provided a summary of the amount invested without any information about the investments undertaken (Aparicio, 2001). In addition, there were concerns about the excessive number of intraday transactions made by Gescartera. Indeed, according to some Gescartera employees, the only activities performed by the company in the previous few years were intraday transactions (Marcos, 2001). Apparently, the main objective of these transactions was to demonstrate to the authorities and the auditors that the company carried out a certain level of investment activity. Typically, Gescartera contacted two financial intermediaries and opened a buy-and-sell position for the same amount of shares in a given company. Because they were intraday transactions, capital gains and losses were compensated for and Gescartera only had to pay the brokerage fee. The capital gains and losses were then discretionally allocated to clients in the absence of any rational criteria (Marcos, 2001).

The scandal had a significant media impact with severe consequences for the Spanish financial community and politicians.[7] The case also had important implications for the future of the financial sector in Spain (see below). The auditing firm Deloitte & Touche (D&T), which had given a clean audit report for the 2000 financial statements and had sent a favourable report about Gescartera just six months before the CNMV seized control of the company, was accused by the ICAC of not gathering enough audit evidence to support their findings (RJ\2008\1893, 2008). D&T argued that, given the rules at the time, they were not required to analyse the portfolios Gescartera managed on behalf of their clients (Comisión Gescartera, 2001). The auditors admitted that given the 'sophistication' of the irregularities in Gescartera, it was not possible for them to detect that something was wrong (Gómez, 2002). D&T was subsequently fined by the ICAC (Gómez, 2002). Even though the audit firm lodged an appeal against the fines imposed on the company and on the partner in charge of Gescartera audits for the financial years 1999 and 2000, the Supreme Court rejected the appeal and ratified the fines (RJ\2008\1892, 2008; RJ\2008\1893, 2008).[8]

---

[6] The experts of the Spanish Tax Agency could not find a significant amount of money (approximately €6.5 million) provided by the clients (JUR 2008\112612, 2008, p. 187). Investigations also showed that Gescartera had companies in Delaware in the United States (JUR 2008\112612, 2008).

[7] A junior minister at the Finance Ministry, whose sister was the managing director of Gescartera, was forced to resign. The president of the CNMV stepped down two months after the scandal.

[8] For the audits of financial year 1999, the fines amounted to €685 432 and €6 010, for the audit firm and the partner in charge respectively (RJ 2008\1892, 2008). For the audits of the financial year 2000, the fines amounted to €632 707 and €6 010 respectively (RJ 2008\1893, 2008).

### 16.2.3  The Real Estate Sector: The Case of PSV and IGS

Several real estate and housing cooperatives have also been involved in financial scandals in recent years (e.g. Grupo Brokers and Caja Hipotecaria de Valores). In 1993 a court of first instance of Barcelona announced the bankruptcy of Grupo Brokers – the Provincial Court of Barcelona ratified such decision in May 1994. Both judgments argued that 'the firm suffered from a severe lack of control over accounting and financial matters' (*La Vanguardia*, 10/5/1994). The managers, however, were found not guilty of fraud (JUR 2006\87009, 2005). In the case of Caja Hipotecaria de Valores several directors were sentenced to prison for fraud (JUR 2000\308779, 2000; RJ 2004\459, 2003; RTC 2006\328, 2006).

One of the most significant cases involved the companies Promotora Social de Viviendas (PSV) and Iniciativas de Gestión de Servicios (IGS). The events surrounding this case had a significant media impact because the two companies were owned by Unión General de Trabajadores (UGT), at the time the largest trade union in Spain. This scandal brought into question the credibility of UGT and its role in Spanish society (Vitzthum, 1994).

PSV was founded as a housing cooperative to provide low-cost housing for its members. It was estimated that around 20 000–50 000 people had begun either paying or saving for their houses with PSV (Bruce, 1993). IGS was the holding company that managed the cooperative. In December 1993, PSV suspended payments to suppliers and made public the fact that the company would need around Pts 100 billion (€601 million) to meet its financial obligations (Vitzthum, 1994, p. A7D). Two years later, the court declared PSV bankrupt because the liabilities of the company exceeded its assets by Pts 14 176 million (€85 million).

According to PSV's by-laws, IGS was in charge of managing the housing cooperative. PSV had no *de facto* autonomy over its resources as they were all transferred to IGS's accounts. There was, therefore, no independent control by PSV. IGS could use these resources at its convenience. At the year-end, IGS prepared two sets of accounting books: IGS's and PSV's financial statements. IGS was most concerned with maximizing its own income and liquidity rather than that of PSV. The accounting irregularities in PSV and IGS included non-compliance with the matching principle. In 1993, IGS recorded in PSV's financial statements expenses related to future services to be provided by IGS, leading to an overestimate of current expenses. The cash receipts from these expenses significantly improved IGS's liquidity position (most of which – €61 million out of €108 million – PSV paid immediately). There was also evidence of the double recording of certain expenses and a lack of documentation supporting many transactions (*Cinco Días*, 25/06/1997).

IGS also made use of creative accounting techniques involving intracompany transactions. For example, on 30 December 1992, just one day before 'closing the books,' IGS recognized a gain on sale of assets amounting to Pts 207 million (€1.24 million) for the sale of a building to one of its subsidiaries (IGS de Mercado Hipotecario SCH, SA. (IGS owned 99.99 % of IGS de Mercado Hipotecario SCH, SA)). The gain significantly improved IGS's net income: instead of reporting a net loss of Pts 52.6 million (€316 132), IGS now reported a net profit of Pts 105.6 million (€634 669) (RJ 2003\7233, 2003). The sale was cancelled in April 1993. IGS, however, did not reverse the journal entry for the sale of the asset and the gain was never removed from IGS's financial statements (RJ 2003\7233, 2003).

PSV's manager, who controlled 53 % of IGS (the remaining 47 % was in the hands of UGT), was sent to prison immediately after the bankruptcy of IGS with allegations of fraud and the misappropriation of funds (Sampedro, 1994). He was in prison for 13 months. In July 2001, the Audiencia Nacional sentenced PSV's manager to prison for two years and four months (JUR 2001\205441, 2001). Two years later, the Spanish High Court confirmed the sentence (RJ 2003\7233, 2003). PSV's auditor, Ernst & Young (E&Y), was fined €426 720. In 1995, the auditor also faced a civil lawsuit filed by a group of members of the cooperative. They argued that E&Y had failed to detect and show the accounting irregularities in the 1991 and 1992 financial statements (*El Mundo*, 28/01/1995). However, in July 1999, the judge concluded that the audit partner in charge of PSV's audit was not responsible for the accounting irregularities in the PSV case.

## 16.3 INVESTMENTS IN STAMPS: THE LATEST SERIES OF FINANCIAL SCANDALS IN THE COUNTRY. AFINSA AND FÓRUM FILATÉLICO

The popularity of investment in stamps in Spain is unique in the world (Segovia, 2006). Spanish investors are generally attracted to these investments not for love of philately but for their higher than average investment returns. Indeed, many consider stamps part of their long-term saving and investment plan. This popularity may be partially explained by the marketing strategies employed by two of the more important stamp traders in the world, Afinsa SA and Fórum Filatélico SA (hereafter, Afinsa and Fórum). For years, these companies attracted thousands of investors thanks to marketing based on a 'word-of-mouth' strategy and sponsorship of cultural and sporting events (Calvo, 2006).[9]

In the past few years, thousands of Spanish investors have lost millions of euros invested in stamps. Doubts about stamp investments were raised in 2002, when the Spanish financial authorities intervened in Banco Filatélico Español SA (Banfisa) because of the estimated embezzlement of €1.2 million (*Expansión*, 10/05/2006). Banfisa was accused of defrauding around 200 investors who bought stamps with the promise of getting high returns for a 10-year investment at the end of the 1980s. When the clients tried to recover their investments, the company gave them some African stamps that were worth far less than the company had promised (Barroso, 2002). After some negotiation, the company promised to repurchase the stamps after three years if the investors were unable to sell these stamps in the market. In October 2002, only days before Banfisa needed to make full payment, it closed without any prior notification. Hundreds of investors sued the firm and the case is still in court (as at August 2009). In 2006 the Provincial Court of Madrid rejected an appeal lodged by a former director of the company, in which he claimed that he should not be included as a defendant in the case because he did not have a working relationship with Banfisa since 1990 (JUR 2007\61172, 2006). At the time the scandal broke, several consumer lobby associations (e.g. ADICAE) warned about the problems of investing in stamps:

> [N]one of the supervisory bodies ... has given an answer to investors because the firm is not under the supervision of any regulatory body ... investors are completely abandoned.
> (Fernando Herrero, Coordinator of ADICAE, Europa Press, 12/01/2002)

---

[9] Fórum had a very strong brand name because for many years it sponsored one of the major basketball teams in the country, Fórum Valladolid. Afinsa was also very active in promoting cultural events and exhibitions throughout Spain. Both companies possessed an extensive network of commercial agents that attracted relatives, friends and neighbours.

Different lobby groups pressured the government to pass new regulations for stamp trading companies. In particular, there were concerns about Afinsa and Fórum. The following subsection analyses these cases in detail.

### 16.3.1 Background of the Cases of Afinsa and Fórum Filatélico

For several years, the Agencia Tributaria (the Spanish Tax Agency) had concerns about the activities of Afinsa and Fórum. These concerns forced an investigation that eventually led authorities to open criminal investigations against both companies. On Tuesday 9 May 2006, Spanish police raided and sealed off the premises of Afinsa and Fórum following instructions by the Audiencia Nacional, the highest Spanish court on criminal matters. The companies were accused of embezzling around €4.2 billion in a massive pyramid scheme affecting about 400 000 investors – nearly 1 % of the Spanish population. The prosecutors (Ministerio Fiscal) argued that the alleged fraud was of such magnitude that it could have serious consequences for the Spanish economy (Querella Afinsa, 2006; Querella Fórum, 2006). The allegations against Afinsa, its two owners and three executives were the following: embezzlement, forgery, money laundering, breach of trust, tax evasion, and fraudulent bankruptcy (Querella Afinsa, 2006, p. 9). The lawsuit against Afinsa included as defendants Francisco Guijarro and two of his companies (Guijarro Lázaro, SL and Francisco Guijarro Lázaro Filatelia SL). Fórum and five members of the board including its chairman faced allegations of embezzlement, money laundering, breach of trust and fraudulent bankruptcy (Querella Fórum, 2006, p. 6). As a result, both companies were closed and their assets frozen.[10]

Afinsa was founded in 1980. At the time of the fraud allegations, the company was the world's largest stamp dealer and the third largest player in collectibles after Sotheby's and Christie's (Brewster and Crawford, 2006). At the 2003 year-end, the company reported an operating turnover of €411 million. At the end of 2004, its outstanding contracts with 142 697 clients totalled €1.75 billion. Afinsa had a significant network of direct investments in national and international companies and was the main shareholder of Escala Group Inc., a NASDAQ-listed auction house and stamp and coin dealer.

Fórum was founded as a stamp trading company in 1979. The operational performance of Fórum in recent years has been impressive: €884 million turnover in 2004 and profit after taxes of €135 million. At the end of 2004, the company had €3.8 billion in outstanding contracts. Like Afinsa, Fórum had a diversified portfolio with interests in 29 companies in different sectors. The criminal proceedings also required the investigation of some of its affiliates, such as Creative Investments SL, Stamp Collectors SL and Atrio Collections SL among others (Diligencias Previas Fórum, 2006, p. 3).

Both companies offered investment plans backed by the revaluation of stamps. These investments were very attractive for a number of reasons. First, they allowed retail investors to invest their savings – the minimum investment amount was just €300. Second, the plans offered high liquidity and high returns, with guaranteed annual returns of between

---

[10] In February 2010 the Litigation-Administrative chamber of the Spanish National Court said that the Spanish state was not responsible for the damages caused by the companies Afinsa and Fórum Filatélico (JUR 2010\67490, 2010). In April 2010, the court dismissed the appeal filed by the appellants against this decision. Investigations in relation to this case are still ongoing.

6% and 10%. These were significantly higher than comparable investments: Spanish government bonds, for example, yielded just 3.5%. Third, the plans were attractive from a fiscal viewpoint because they were not subject to *retención fiscal* (tax withholding). The popularity and success of these investments was supported by a powerful network of salespeople and by a 'word-of-mouth' marketing strategy. In addition, the Spanish press backed such investments, arguing that: (a) the revaluation of the stamps over time explained the high returns, (b) the companies promised to buy back the stamps at the end of the period so the level of risk was minimal, and (c) the investments were unaffected by shocks in the economy (Relaño, 2002). Indeed, it was argued that '... right now, stamps are the most secure bet' (Morán, 2002, p. 63).

According to prosecutors, both companies had to '... necessarily fool investors using a double fiction ... [The companies] created the illusion that the stamps acquired were valuable and rare (when in fact they were extraordinarily overvalued ...), and that the interest paid to investors was from generated revenues (when in fact it was from funds from new investors)' (Querella Afinsa, 2006, p. 2; Querella Fórum, 2006, p. 2). That is, the investment schemes worked essentially as a pyramid scheme. In this manner, the businesses could only survive by reproducing *ad infinitum* the same mechanism with new clients, whose investments were used to sustain the dynamics of the system.

### 16.3.2 The Nature of the Businesses and the Accounting for Investment Contracts

Afinsa and Fórum's primary business line was the wholesale and retail trade in stamps and other collectibles. They were also authorized to trade investment contracts where the underlying assets were stamps. As stamp dealers, they sold the stamps – usually the companies were in charge of the custody and security of the assets – promising to buy back the assets after a certain period of time for the initial amount of the investment plus an additional minimum guaranteed return.

There are doubts, however, about the nature of such transactions. According to some experts, the investment schemes were contracts of a financial nature rather than of a trade nature for two reasons. First, the revaluation of the investment was agreed upon in advance – the repurchased price of the assets was fixed at the inception of the contract. Second, the revaluation depended on the length of the contract and on the minimum guaranteed annual return from capital, not on the variations in the value of the underlying asset. That is, in the event of a reduction in the value of the stamps, the clients would be unaffected (Informe Afinsa, 2007). Therefore, taking into consideration the economic substance rather than the legal form of the transaction, it could be argued that the investment contracts should be considered as loans from the clients to Afinsa and Fórum, i.e. a financial activity where the underlying assets were irrelevant (Informe Fórum, 2006; Informe Afinsa, 2007).

Under Spanish law, trading activities in collectibles such as stamps and coins are regulated by Law 35/2003 *Ley de Instituciones de Inversión Colectiva*, Additional Disposition No. 4.[11] This legislation explicitly prohibits companies, such as Afinsa and Fórum, from supplying

---

[11] These companies are not subject to the supervision of Spain's financial authorities (the CNMV, the supervisory body of listed companies; the Bank of Spain, in charge of supervising financial services institutions; or the *Dirección General de Seguros y Planes de Pensiones*, the body in charge of supervising insurance and pension plans).

financial services similar to those provided by financial institutions. If activities by Afinsa and Fórum were categorized as financial services, then both companies were breaking the law. In June 2005, Afinsa made public a report about the nature of its activities. The report concluded that Afinsa's activities should not be considered as financial activities (Rojo, 2005). At the time of the fraud allegations, both companies strongly denied the financial nature of their activities (*El Mundo*, 12/05/2006).

The categorization of the transactions as trading activities had important implications for their accounting treatment. Afinsa and Fórum used the accounting procedures of a retailer selling stamps. Typically, clients signed three contracts at the time of the agreement: in the first contract they agreed to the purchase of the stamps; the second contract contained the companies' offer to provide custody for the stamps free of charge and the third contract contained the companies' promise of buying back the stamps after a given period of time for the original price plus a given amount of interest (*El Mundo*, 11/05/2006; Informe Afinsa, 2007). The companies recorded the amount of the investment as revenue and removed the stamps from the inventory. When the contracts matured, they recorded the stamps as inventory for the amount promised to the clients, leading to an 'artificial' revaluation of the stamps. It is noteworthy that they did not recognize the liability related to the repurchase agreement (see below).

Under Spanish GAAP, '... the economic substance rather than the legal form of the transaction should prevail' (BOICAC No. 6, 1991). Specifically, a transaction involving the sale of an asset and a repurchase agreement requires the write-off of the asset and simultaneously the recognition, for the original value, of the asset to be repurchased. A liability for the repurchase price should be recorded at the inception of the contract. The difference between the liability and the cash received at the time of the sale of the asset will be recorded as accrued expenses (BOICAC No. 6, 1991; also, Norma de Valoración 5.g).

Neither Afinsa nor Fórum recognized the liability of the repurchase agreement. Concerns about this issue were raised on several occasions. In 1996, the Dirección General de Tributos (a body under the Ministry of Economy) recommended that Afinsa recognize these promises as liabilities on the balance sheet. Afinsa, however, did not follow this recommendation, arguing instead that investors could choose between keeping their stamps until maturity or, alternatively, selling them on the open market. According to Afinsa, the repurchase agreement was '... a residual question' (Crawford, 2005b, p. 34), and the recognition of a liability was not justified. In 2004, Afinsa hired KPMG to prepare a report about the accounting treatment of the contracts. KPMG's report clearly stated that the investment plans should be treated as financial contracts as their main purpose was to obtain financial resources to invest in other assets. Accordingly, their accounting treatment should be in conformity with its financial nature (Informe Afinsa, 2007). For example, Afinsa should not recognize the sale of the stamps as revenue. Revenue recognition would be possible if, and only if, there was certainty that the client would not exercise the repurchase option. KPMG also argued that the company should recognize a liability for the repurchase agreement. Afinsa, however, did not follow the KPMG recommendations (Informe Afinsa, 2007, p. 245).

Afinsa and Fórum also failed to recognize in their balance sheets the assets to be repurchased at the inception of the contract (Informe Afinsa, 2007, p. 48; Informe Fórum, 2006,

p. 206). The companies recognized these stamps at the maturity of the contract – once they had repurchased the stamps from the clients – by the amount promised to shareholders. This amount was significantly higher than the selling price as both companies promised returns of around 7–10 %. *Prima facie*, this implies a violation of the Spanish GAAP, which explicitly prohibits the revaluation of a repurchased asset (BOICAC No. 6, 1991; Norma de Valoración 5.g).

The evidence suggests that the ambiguous nature of the activities carried out by the two companies allowed them to create an 'artificial' set of accounts that did not reflect economic reality (Informe Afinsa, 2007; Informe Fórum, 2006). Both companies showed resistance to changing their accounting model, as suggested by both regulators and experts, because of the unfavourable effect this would have had on their financial statements. Their financial statements failed to comply with several accounting principles. For instance, they did not comply with the prudence principle because they recognized the revenues derived from an apparent sale that at the same time implied the obligation of repurchasing the stamps in the future. This obligation, however, was not recognized as a liability in the companies' balance sheet. Fórum and Afinsa also failed to comply with the historical cost principle because the repurchased stamps were added back to the balance sheet at the maturity date at a value significantly higher than the acquisition price.

### 16.3.3 The Suppliers

The reports produced by the administrative receivers of Afinsa and Fórum showed that both companies displayed irregularities in their transactions with suppliers (Informe Fórum, 2006; Informe Afinsa, 2007). Afinsa's problems were related to Francisco Guijarro, the main supplier to Afinsa before 2003 through different companies (e.g. Guijarro Lázaro SL). As mentioned above, the lawsuit against Afinsa included as defendants Francisco Guijarro and two of his companies (Guijarro Lázaro SL and Francisco Guijarro Lázaro Filatelia SL). He faced allegations of embezzlement, forgery, money laundering, breach of trust, tax evasion and fraudulent bankruptcy (Querella Afinsa, 2006, p. 9). Mr Guijarro was under arrest for a month before being released by the judge on pre-trial release (subject to certain conditions such as the obligation to report every three days to a pre-trial officer) (*Auto Audiencia Nacional*, 7/7/2006). Although his testimony before the judge was not made public, a press article reported that he admitted he did not have invoices for most of the transactions 'because of ignorance and because I was poorly advised' (López, 2006). From 1998 to 2002, Afinsa bought Guijarro Lázaro SL stamps for €58 million. These stamps were sold to clients for €724 million. The purchase price of these stamps was around 8–20 % of the catalogue price. The stamps were sold to clients at 100 % or even 200 % of the catalogue price, depending on the kind of contract (Informe Afinsa, 2007). Besides, it was expected that the value of the stamps would increase by around 6–10 % by the end of the contract.[12]

---

[12] The companies offered a fixed annual return during the investment period and promised to buy back the stamps at the original sale price at the end of the contract.

The Spanish tax authorities found several irregularities in the transactions between Afinsa and Guijarro's companies (Informe Afinsa, 2007, p. 191). First, no evidence was found of most of the transactions, neither invoices nor receipts, between Afinsa and Guijarro's companies. Second, Afinsa detected important irregularities in the stamps sold by Guijarro. As a consequence, Afinsa had to replace a large amount of stamps – a loss of €55 million according to the company's estimation (Informe Afinsa, 2007). Afinsa, however, did not undertake any action against the supplier. Third, the authorities detected a significant and unjustified increase in Guijarro's wealth. According to the prosecutors, these accounting irregularities provided evidence that these transactions were allegedly used to siphon off money from Afinsa (Querella Afinsa, 2006).

After 2003, Escala Group Inc., a NASDAQ-listed auction house and stamp and coin dealer, became the main stamp supplier to Afinsa. From 2005, Afinsa was the main shareholder of Escala. Although Escala argued that all intracompany transactions took place at independently established prices, analysts noted that 'Escala's gross margins on sales to Afinsa are above 50 per cent, compared with gross margins of only 8 per cent on stamp sales to other clients' (Crawford, 2006c, p. 6). The experts did not understand why in 2003 Afinsa gave Escala $3.5 million in advance to purchase inventory to be sold to Afinsa at a 10 % mark-up in accordance with the supply contract signed between the two companies (Martin, 2004). US hedge funds also had serious concerns about the value of the transactions between the two companies (Hill, 2006). A US hedge fund manager noted that '[t]he whole edifice is coming down like a house of cards, because Escala's business was totally dependent on Afinsa, and Afinsa's business depended on the confidence of its Spanish and Portuguese investors' (Crawford, 2006a, p. 10). Escala Group acknowledged the possible negative effects of Afinsa's problems on its own business. In the Form 10-Q for the period ended March 31, 2006, the company stated that '[T]he effect of these developments on the business and financial condition of Escala cannot be determined at this time. A significant portion of the Company's collectibles revenue and gross profit are attributable to sales to Afinsa. Unless offset by increases in other areas of the Company's business, a significant decrease in the level of sales to Afinsa, or the termination of the supply arrangements with Afinsa, would have a material adverse effect on the Company's financial condition and results of operations' (Form 10-Q Escala Group, 2006: 25).

Fórum operated with different suppliers, mainly foreign companies. From 1998 to 2001, Fórum purchased stamps for a total amount of around €133.5 million from a network of 14 international suppliers (*El Mundo*, 25/05/2006). The price paid by Fórum to the suppliers was higher than the catalogue prices. Specifically, the average price paid by Fórum in 2005 was 73.17 % above the catalogue price[13] (Informe Fórum, 2006). It is difficult to understand why Fórum, which had significant negotiating power with its suppliers given the amount of stamps acquired and its position as unique client for some of them, paid more than the catalogue price (Informe Fórum, 2006). One of the arguments given by Fórum to justify the difference between the catalogue value of the existing inventory and the value of the purchases was that the company destroyed part of the purchases because some stamps did not pass quality control (Diligencias Previas Fórum, 2006). The information given by Fórum

---

[13] Percentage calculated using the Yvert-Tellier catalogue, which provides reference prices for retailers (Informe Fórum, 2006).

to the tax authorities indicates that in 2001, they bought stamps for a value of Pts 8444 million (€50.75 million) and destroyed around 38 % of them – €18.34 million (Diligencias Previas Fórum, 2006). As even the judge commented, the explanation given by Fórum 'is completely illogical' (Diligencias Previas Fórum, 2006, p. 5). According to the prosecutors, '... the over-invoicing and the payment of prices that were far higher than those in the open market provide evidence of money laundering' (Querella Fórum, 2006, p. 6).

It is worth mentioning that the two companies had significant problems with their internal control systems. As pointed out by the administrative receivers appointed by the courts, there were serious breaches in the system of controlling transactions with suppliers (e.g. no control of invoices and receipts). The internal control of inventory was also limited (e.g. no records of the flow of stamps in and out of the companies). Accordingly, investigators could not find information about the costs related to the custody and movement of the inventory, or information about the inventory costing method used by the companies (Informe Fórum, 2006; Informe Afinsa, 2007). Moreover, the custody of the stamps was not undertaken properly. The administrative receivers found literally hundreds of boxes with stamps that were unclassified, and kept where they could be easily damaged (Informe Fórum, 2006; Informe Afinsa, 2007).

### 16.3.4 Valuation of Stamps

The price of any stamp is related to its singularity and scarcity. From an accounting point of view, the stamps should be valued at the lower of market price and historical cost. Both Afinsa and Fórum recorded the stamps at their historical cost (price paid at acquisition), which was higher than the market price. This was especially problematic in the case of the stamps repurchased from clients, which appeared in the balance sheet at the repurchased price (historical cost plus the promised return of the investment), leading to an artificial revaluation of inventory. The value of the stamps did not increase because of the market, but because of the returns promised to clients over the life of the contract. For example, from 1998 to 2002, Afinsa bought stamps for its short-term investment plans for an amount of about €57 million, which were sold for around €723 million, meaning an artificial increase of the value of the stamps of €666 million (around 1168 % the original cost). Moreover, at the time of selling the stamps Afinsa promised to return at maturity €723 million plus interest (around 7–10 %) (*El País*, 6/2/2007, p. 27). At the maturity of the contracts, these stamps were thus recorded at €723 million plus interest on the balance sheet. As the valuation system for the stamps was linked to the short-term contracts, concerns were raised about the company's ability to continue operations, as such contracts were '... pyramid schemes that relied on a constant influx of new investors to pay interest to older clients' (*El País*, 13/04/2007, p. 3).

Both companies claimed that the valuation of their stamps was based on the reference price established by several well-recognized international and independent (mainly European) catalogues.[14] There are a number of problems with this argument. First, given the

---

[14] Experts argue that European stamp catalogues generally provide only 'reference values' giving dealers ample room for discounting. In contrast, American stamp catalogues use a 'retail value' system closer to market price. According to experts, '... you cannot trust catalogues for stamp pricing' (Martin, 2005, p. 22).

amount of stamps bought by Afinsa and Fórum, they had the power to affect prices in the industry. According to some experts, the principal market maker, Afinsa, dictated these prices (Martin, 2005, p. 22). Second, the independence of some of the catalogues was questionable. From documents found in Afinsa's headquarters, there is evidence of agreements between Afinsa and several catalogues. In fact, some of Afinsa's contracts were valued according to the DOMFIL catalogue, which was 100 % owned by Afinsa (Informe Afinsa, 2007). This led Spanish authorities to question DOMFIL's independence (Diligencias Previas Afinsa, 2007). Afinsa also confidentially acquired the Brookman's catalogue, a US catalogue with a good reputation for independence, in June 2003. Afinsa was very concerned about the confidentiality of such an acquisition as inferred from electronic correspondence between an Afinsa executive and its main supplier Escala asking for 500 copies of the catalogue. Afinsa's executive wrote '... as you are aware, our name must not appear' (Diligencias Previas Afinsa, 2007, p. 7).

Several consumer lobby groups detected problems with the stamp valuation. The Organización de Consumidores y Usuarios (OCU) acquired in 2004 several stamps from Afinsa under short-term contracts. According to several philatelic experts, the catalogue price of these stamps was around 84 % of the investment, and the market price was only one-third of the catalogue price. Afinsa's general manager denied the accuracy of OCU's data (Agencia EFE, 27/02/2004). Problems with the valuation of stamps were also detected by syndicates at Lloyd's of London who '... did not renew Afinsa's €1.2 billion policy in 2006 because of doubts about the true value of the insured stamps' (Crawford, 2006c, p. 6). One additional concern was whether the stamps were faked or had been manipulated. The Spanish authorities subsequently required an examination of some stamps from Afinsa's vaults (Calatrava, 2006).

### 16.3.5 Reflections on the Scandal

The main reasons used to justify the criminal investigation against Afinsa and Fórum were as follows. First, the value of the stamps, as the underlying assets, was very low in comparison with the liabilities of the companies. Second, many purchases of stamps were not registered. Third, there were concerns about the manipulation of stamp prices – through the control of stamp catalogues – and the faking of some stamps. Finally, there was a lack of documentation supporting the cash transactions with suppliers. Because of these irregularities, the prosecutors argued that both companies were bankrupt. Spanish authorities required insolvency proceedings to be enacted, and the judges appointed three trustees for each company to oversee the operations of the companies during the liquidation process.

The liquidators initially estimated that Fórum's deficit as at December 2005 was €2843 million (Informe Fórum, 2006). The assets of the company were estimated as €923 million and the liabilities as €3766 million. In addition, there was €11 million categorized as contingent liabilities (not included in the liabilities) corresponding to those clients who did not provide information to the liquidators (Informe Fórum, 2006). Afinsa's estimated deficit as at December 2004 was €1100 million (*Expansión*, 22/06/2006). The companies denied the wrongdoings and urged their clients to remain calm (*El Mundo*, 9/05/2006), arguing that, as required by the law, they had their financial statements audited and deposited in the Registro Mercantil (Mercantile Register).

### 16.3.6 Where were the Auditors?

Afinsa and Fórum's auditors were concerned about the accounting policies adopted by the firms, and accordingly they issued qualified audit reports in relation to their most recent financial statements (*Tiempo*, 15/05/2006). In the 2004 audit report, Afinsa's auditors, Gestynsa Auditores Externos, raised concerns about the provision of €60.6 million for losses due to the repurchase agreements of a set of stamps for prices higher than market prices. They were also concerned about changes in the value of inventory, as they could not verify their reasonableness and accuracy. Finally, the auditors warned Afinsa that there were no invoices for transactions amounting to €3.42 million (Rodrigo, 2006).

Carrera Auditores SA had acted as Fórum's auditor since 1997. The audit report for 2002 accounts was clean, but Fórum received qualified reports in subsequent years. In 2003, the auditor stated that the financial statements presented fairly the financial position and operating performance of the firm, in conformity with Spanish GAAP 'except for' adjustments required in relation to the financial situation and debts of several companies of the group. The financial statements for 2004 had qualifications for the same reasons. Fórum affiliates' losses were financed by the parent company. According to the auditors, in 2004, Fórum gave loans to affiliates of some €50.8 million, and it was not possible to determine whether a provision was necessary for these loans (Informe Fórum, 2006). Auditors also raised concerns about a provision for the liabilities of the company because '... it is not easy to find a comparable activity and determine whether it is necessary to increase the provision' (Informe Fórum, 2006, p. 16).

Neither Afinsa's nor Fórum's auditors questioned the accounting treatment of the sales and repurchase agreements. Neither did qualification of the financial statements stop investors investing in the schemes. The ICAC (Instituto de Contabilidad y Auditoría de Cuentas), the body in charge of accounting and auditing in Spain, further investigated the auditing work of the auditors and fined both. Carrera Auditores was fined €150,000 for its audit of Fórum's financial statements of 2002. The fine for the partner in charge of the audit work amounted to €3050 (BOICAC No. 68, 2006). Gestynsa appealed against the ICAC's decision (Ministerio de Economía y Hacienda, 25/05/2006).[15] In June 2006 the judge decided to include the two partners in charge of Afinsa and Fórum as defendants (*El Economista*, 06/06/2006).At July 2010 the case remains open.

### 16.3.7 Was it a Surprise?

For many, what happened was not a surprise. In 2001, the Ministry of Economy received an investors' lawsuit against Afinsa claiming that Afinsa was undertaking financial activities for which it had no authorization (Ekaizer and Romero, 2006). The lawsuit was sent to the Spanish financial authorities. In January 2002, the Bank of Spain confirmed that, unless required by the Ministry of Economy, the Bank of Spain was not competent to investigate

---

[15] The case remains open at the time of writing, July 2010. According to the Spanish Audit Law, the limit of a fine for an audit firm in very serious cases (*infracción muy grave*) is between 3 % and 6 % of the audit fees of the last fiscal year. The fine cannot be lower that €24,000. In addition, the partner in charge of the engagement could be fined a minimum of €12,001 and a maximum of €24,000. The individual auditor can also be delisted (temporarily or permanently) from the Official Register of Auditors (ROAC) (Law 12/2010, 2010).

Afinsa (Ekaizer and Romero, 2006). The CNMV (Comisión Nacional del Mercado de Valores), responsible for the supervision of listed companies, and the DGSPP (Dirección General de Seguros y Planes de Pensiones), in charge of the control of pension plans and funds, also concluded that Afinsa was not subject to their supervision (Letter, 2002a, b).

Following Banfisa's bankruptcy in January 2002, ADICAE, a lobby group for consumers' rights, made public comments about Afinsa's and Fórum's similarities with Banfisa (Uriol, 2002; ADICAE, 2002). ADICAE criticized the lack of regulation of this type of investment and sent letters to different regulators such as the CNMV and the Bank of Spain. The response of Fórum and Afinsa to this initiative was very different: while Fórum supported ADICAE's initiative, Afinsa fiercely criticized ADICAE (ADICAE, 2002, p. 43). In 2003, the Spanish government warned investors about companies trading in fine art or stamps (*Expansión*, 29/03/2003). The warning emphasized that these companies were not financial institutions and that the investments were not covered by the same guarantee systems that characterized investments made through banks or brokerage houses. In 2004, the consumer lobby group OCU published a similar warning (Dinero y Derechos, 2004).

In September 2004, *Barron's* published an article questioning the accounting practices of Escala (Greg Manning Auctions at the time). The *Barron's* article argued that '[s]tamps aren't what they used to be, and a number of investors and analysts are raising questions about Manning's operations and accounting' (Martin, 2004, p. 25). One year later, a *Barron's* reporter trapped one of Afinsa's top executives after showing him some stamps bought from Afinsa for €600. When asked what he thought was the value of the stamps, the executive said they were worthless (Martin, 2005). By 2005, the pressure on the two companies by consumer lobby groups had increased. In addition, the insurers of Fórum and Afinsa at the Lloyd's of London syndicate had already realized that all was not well (Crawford, 2005b). In the summer of 2005, Hiscox, a specialist insurer at Lloyd's, cancelled its policies with Afinsa and Fórum because it was unhappy with the '. . . insurance-to-value mismatch, meaning that the sums insured were much higher than the real, open-market value of the stamps' (Crawford, 2005b, p. 34). Other insurers at Lloyd's also reviewed their insurance policies (Crawford, 2005b). In April 2006, the financial press argued that '. . . it is highly unlikely that the other Lloyd's insurers will agree to renew their policies with Afinsa at the annual deadline' (Martin, 2006a, p. 17).

Information was also published by the international financial press about the pressure that consumer groups and the insurance industry were putting on Spanish financial authorities in relation to companies trading stamps (e.g. Crawford, 2005a, p. 34). One year before the Spanish authorities seized control of the companies, commentators described the situation of Afinsa as follows:

> If Afinsa ever ran into financial difficulty and couldn't honour its guarantees, investors might well be unable to recoup their outlays on the open market. And since Afinsa isn't classified as a financial institution, it receives scant government oversight.
>
> (Neil A. Martin, 'Sticky situation,' *Barron's*, 23 May 2005, p. 22)

The events described illustrate Miller's arguments about the role of the press as a '. . . watchdog for accounting fraud' (Miller, 2006, p. 1001), meaning that journalists alert the public to an issue through press coverage by assisting in the early identification of accounting problems. Business-orientated (non-Spanish) press such as *Barron's* and the *Financial Times* developed new information for the market and played an important role as '. . . an independent or information intermediary in financial markets' (Miller, 2006, p. 1003), raising issues about the two companies. The impact of such media reports on Spanish investors, however, was very limited. This may be partially explained by the characteristics of the investors in Afinsa and Fórum – many were financially illiterate and did not have access to the non-Spanish press – and by the role of the Spanish press because it did not broadcast the findings of the international press (Martin, 2006b).

### 16.3.8 Consequences of the Scandal

The primary outcome of the alleged fraud was the dramatic consequences for thousands of small investors. The situation was worse than in many other cases because these investors were not backed by deposit insurance schemes. In addition, because of the 'word-of-mouth' strategy, the investments were usually made by employees and their relatives or friends, leaving many families in a desperate situation (Calvo, 2006). The Ministry of Health and Consumer Affairs and consumer lobby groups have provided some guidance about the procedure for recovering at least part of their investment (De Barrón, 2006).

The scandal led to questions concerning the regulation of these companies and deficiencies in the control mechanisms. The current rules have been subject to strong criticism because of the low protection offered to investors. The scandal also raised questions about the effectiveness of the Spanish financial authorities: despite the mounting danger signs, the Spanish financial authorities failed to alert investors. The Bank of Spain's money-laundering unit investigated Fórum in 2001, 2003 and 2005 but failed to give the necessary warnings. The CNMV warning which cautioned investors was as a general 'caveat emptor' that did not prevent investors investing in these companies (Hill, 2006, p. 21). The Bank of Spain and the DGSPP disclaimed any responsibility for the supervision of these companies. The work done by the auditors was also criticized by the ICAC and the prosecutors. Although they gave qualified reports, they did not give an adverse opinion when, according to the prosecutors, the financial statements did not offer a true and fair view of the financial situation of the companies. Some experts even criticized the way the Spanish authorities decided to take control of the companies because it created significant social alarm and further deteriorated the economic situation of both companies (Rico, 2006).

The scandal also affected the collectible assets industry, especially in the philately sector, because of the dominant position of Fórum and Afinsa. Many other philately firms tried to show that their businesses were secure despite offering similar schemes. It is important to note, however, that the prices of stamps in the philatelic market did not fall significantly, suggesting that these companies had their '. . . own artificial market' (ADICAE, 2006, p. 12). The uncertainty and lack of trust generated by the scandal also affected other companies offering alternative investment products. ING Direct, the global financial institution of Dutch origin that offers insurance, banking and asset management services over the phone and by mail, had in May–June 2006 the worst monthly results in its history in Spain. Although ING Direct's range of services are very different from those provided by Afinsa and Fórum, many investors withdrew their deposits because of rumour and speculation about the credibility of online banking (*El Mundo*, 26/07/2006). ING's clients withdrew around 10 % of their deposits in this period (Andrés, 2006). To recover investors' confidence, ING launched an important marketing campaign and opened an office to the public in Madrid – Spain was the first country where ING had a physical office (*El Mundo*, 21/06/2006).

It is worth mentioning the international dimensions of the scandal. Clearly, the events in Spain had a great impact on Escala, the NASDAQ-listed company. Its share price dropped from \$17.29 to \$14.71 on the day of the police raids (Brewster and Crawford, 2006). A significant portion of Escala's turnover and profits were attributable to transactions with Afinsa. Consequently, the termination of the contract had a materially adverse effect on the company's financial results (Crawford, 2006b). In June 2006, the Securities Exchange Commission launched a formal investigation into the relationship between Afinsa and Escala. The company has since received a delisting determination from NASDAQ because of non-compliance with the continued listing requirements (*Business Wire*, 11/10/2006). In March 2009, the SEC filed a disclosure and accounting fraud case against Escala Group, its founder and former CEO and its former CFO alleging fraudulent related-party transactions between the company and Afinsa. The SEC complaint alleges 'a fraudulent business scheme based upon the secret and dramatic manipulation of collectible stamps values' (SEC vs. Escala Group, Inc. Gregory Manning, Larry Lee Crawford, 2009). At the same time, Escala Group announced that it had reached a settlement with the SEC resolving charges filed against the company in connection with the transactions with Afinsa. The settlement was approved by the Court on March 30, 2009. Under the settlement, Escala 'consented, without admitting or denying the allegations, to a permanent injunction against any future violations of certain provisions of the federal securities laws. No fines, civil penalties or monetary sanctions were assessed against the Company' (From 10-K Spectrum Group International Inc, 2009: 20). In May 2009 the company announced that it changed its corporate name to Spectrum Group International, Inc.

Afinsa and Fórum are currently involved in insolvency proceedings. The courts have appointed trustees to control both companies. The consequences for the executives, who denied the allegations of fraud, are still unknown. The prosecutors are asking for penalties of 14 years in the case of Fórum's executives and 20 years in the case of Afinsa's. The management teams are currently facing a criminal investigation, and, as at July 2010, the outcome is still to be determined.

## 16.4  THE AFTERMATH OF THE SCANDALS

Spanish history shows the decisive influence that financial crises and accounting scandals have on regulation (e.g. Bernal-Lloréns, 2004). As in many other countries, such corporate scandals lead to reinforced regulatory mechanisms (e.g. Sikka, 1997). Spanish regulators and control mechanisms have been subject to a high degree of scrutiny after the financial scandals described in the previous sections. As suggested by the Governor of the Bank of Spain after the Gescartera case:

> What happened in Gescartera raises important questions about the control mechanisms, both private and public, of the Spanish financial market. Such mechanisms are vital for the functioning of the market.
>
> Governor of the Bank of Spain; Special Committee for the Investigation of Gescartera, Session No. 21, 26/10/2001; *Journal of Debates*, Congress, p. 1064

The Gescartera case happened at the very time the Spanish government was working on new regulation for the financial system (Ley de Medidas para la Reforma del Sistema Financiero), popularly known as Ley Financiera (Financial Law). The Gescartera case and other scandals happening abroad at the time (e.g. Enron, WorldCom) pressured the government to develop a stricter framework of corporate governance with the aim of reinforcing the confidence of Spanish investors. While the Financial Law was passed, it was with some delay. It has since been argued that the delay was related to the government's decision to wait for the findings of the Gescartera investigations (Vico-Martínez, 2000). The Bill tabled in March 2002 contained several recommendations derived from the Gescartera case. In particular, it included the necessity of giving publicity to all fines imposed by the CNMV, irrespective of their category. The previous rule, which required that only those sanctions regarded as 'very serious' be made public, was fiercely criticized because although Gescartera was fined several times, investors did not have information about the company's problems. The Financial Law, finally approved in October 2002, included a request for the internal reform of the CNMV because of the failures detected in the Gescartera case and emphasized the need for greater coordination between the different financial authorities.

The recent cases of Afinsa and Fórum raised questions about investor protection. The regulation applicable to companies trading collectibles, such as stamps and coins (Law 35/2003), establishes certain legal requirements (e.g. giving clients information in writing about the rights and obligations arising from contracts) and explicitly prohibits these companies from providing financial services. For many, the root of Afinsa's and Fórum's problems was that the regulation was '. . . deficient and insufficient' (ADICAE, 2006, p. 6). First, these investments were not backed by deposit insurance schemes, similar to those existing for protecting banks' users. Second, some commentators strongly criticized the loose requirements stated in the Law for valuing the underlying assets of the contracts, even when they are the only guarantee investors have in the case of bankruptcy. Third, the Ministry of Health and Consumer Affairs is in charge of supervising these companies. Experts argue that this supervision should instead be in the hands of the financial authorities (e.g. the Bank of Spain). Finally, there were criticisms about the procedures investors had to follow to recover their investments after the companies filed for bankruptcy (ADICAE, 2006). Following the Afinsa and Fórum cases, politicians debated the need to reform the existing regulation (Congreso de los Diputados, 17/05/2006). Given the increasing popularity of other companies offering similar contracts and subject to the same regulation, the pressure to make reforms was significant. In December 2007, the Spanish Parliament passed a new law (Ley 43/2007) to protect customers acquiring collectibles and other similar goods when the contracts include a repurchase agreement.

The Spanish auditing profession has also been under scrutiny in the aftermath of the accounting scandals. In particular, the profession has been criticized because of its lack of response to the crisis produced by the financial scandals, both at national and international level (Gonzalo and Garvey, 2005). García-Benau *et al.* (1999) describe the reaction of the Spanish auditing profession during the 1990s as follows:

> Initially, the profession's reaction to scandals such as Banesto was minimal – not surprisingly, given that much of the early analysis in the press sought to direct attention to the failings of corporate management and the political aspects of the various cases. However, as the realization

grew that firms were likely to be sanctioned for inadequate audit work, the profession assumed a more visible role in debates on the role and responsibilities of auditors with respect to corporate collapses.

García-Benau *et al.*, 1999, pp. 711–712

The accounting scandals of the 2000s prompted debate about auditor independence and auditing quality (Ruiz-Barbadillo, 2003). In particular, because of the Gescartera case, there was renewed interest in the mandatory rotation of auditing firms. Before the parliamentary discussion of the Financial Law in April 2002, the government included an amendment with a requirement for the rotation of auditing firms every 12 years. Although the amendment was finally rejected, the law included a provision for the mandatory rotation of auditing partners and auditing teams every seven years for listed companies, for companies under public supervision and for companies with a turnover higher than €30 million (for more details, see Carrera *et al.*, 2007).

After the Afinsa and Fórum scandals, concerns were raised about auditing quality, especially in relation to the work of small auditing firms.[16] In particular, the debate has focused on the economic dependence of auditors on their clients and the impact it may have on auditor independence. In this regard, the new Spanish Audit Law, approved on June 30 2010, establishes that auditor independence is at stake if the audit-related fees received by the auditor from a particular client are a significant percentage of its average annual turnover over the last three years (Law 12/2010, 2010). The issue is still under discussion, and the ICAC has not yet announced a final decision (at the time of writing this chapter, August 2009). Professional associations representing the interests of small auditing firms and sole practitioners are understandably against the reform because '. . . it would cause the elimination of the small and medium auditor, contributing to the concentration of the market in the hands of the big auditing firms' (Fernández, 2006, p. 23).

## 16.5 CONCLUSION

This chapter has reviewed some of the most significant recent accounting scandals in Spain. During the past 30 years, there have been a significant number of corporate collapses. These have caused thousands of investors to lose millions of euros. As in many other countries (see, for example, Grant and Visconti, 2006), the diagnosis of corporate scandals suggests they are a combination of personal greed and moral laxity, combined with inadequate oversight by auditors, financial authorities and regulators, boards and the media. A characteristic of the scandals in Spain is the media focus on their political implications, as illustrated by the Banesto and Gescartera cases. Regulators and financial authorities have received strong criticism, while the Spanish auditing profession, although subject to scrutiny, has played a secondary role compared with the degree of controversy about auditors' work that has characterized the aftermath of corporate scandals in other developed countries.

The companies involved in the accounting scandals analysed in this chapter have used different creative accounting practices. In all cases, the companies were subject to

---

[16] In spite of the high market share of the biggest auditing firms in the Spanish market (see Carrera *et al.*, 2005), many Spanish companies are audited by small and medium-sized audit firms (78 % of all Spanish auditing firms have an annual turnover of less than €300 000).

investigation because certain practices were considered illegal or fraudulent. We have also seen examples of non-compliance with the matching, accruals and historical cost principles (e.g. Banesto, Afinsa and Fórum), the overestimation of expenses (e.g. PSV), the use of artificial transactions to manipulate the accounts (e.g. Gescartera) and the underestimation of liabilities (e.g. Afinsa and Fórum), among others. Overall, these companies have failed to provide a true and fair view of their economic realities.

To conclude, it is important to note the lack of reaction on the part of the Spanish academic community in the aftermath of these financial scandals (García-Benau *et al.*, 1999; Gonzalo and Garvey, 2005). This behaviour contrasts markedly with the prior involvement of the academic community in the development of the existing legislation (García-Benau *et al.*, 1999). With a few exceptions (García-Benau *et al.*, 1999; Vico-Martínez, 2002), the responsibility for analysing Spanish financial scandals has rested with the Spanish news media and journalists. Although the press can fulfil an important role as an information intermediary in financial markets (Miller, 2006), the agendas of journalists and academics can differ (García-Benau *et al.*, 1999). A more active role of Spanish accounting academics in the analysis of corporate scandals could contribute significantly to international debate on the factors, consequences and potential solutions to corporate scandals.

# REFERENCES

(For convenience, references in Spanish have also been translated into English.)

ABC (2007), 'Eurobank's CEO acquitted of corporate offence and fraud charges' ('Absuelven al ex presidente de Eurobank de un delito societario y otro de estafa'), 3 March, p. 3.

ADICAE (2002), BANFISA, 'Spanish Philatelic "Bank" goes bankrupt. A financial kiosk?' ('BANFISA, "Banco" Filatélico Español, se declara insolvente. ¿Chiringuito Financiero?'), *Revista Usuarios,* Enero–Febrero 2002, pp. 42–43. *ADICAE, Asociación de Usuarios de Bancos, Cajas y Seguros*, Madrid.

ADICAE (2006), 'Philatelic investments: a popular saving scheme without control' ('Inversiones filatélicas: un ahorro popular sin control),' *ADICAE, Asociación de Usuarios de Bancos, Cajas y Seguros*, Madrid.

Agencia EFE (2004), 'The OCU alerts us to the risk of investments in stamps and art works' ('La OCU alerta del riesgo de inversión en sellos y obras de arte'), 27 February.

Amat, O., Perramon, J. and Oliveras, E. (2003), 'Earnings management in Spain. Some evidence from companies quoted on the Spanish Stock Exchange', *University Pompeu Fabra, Economics and Business Working Paper* No. 677, available at ssrn.com/abstract=428262 (accessed 21 July 2007).

Andrés, J.J. (2006), 'ING Direct's volume of deposits increased 4 % in August' ('ING Direct aumenta un 4 % su volumen de depósitos en agosto'), *Expansión*, 18 October, p. 30.

AP Magistratura (1998), 'The National Court sentenced a couple from Seville to two years in prison for defrauding 452 investors of 2.9 million' ('La Audiencia Nacional condena a 2 años de cárcel a un matrimonio sevillano por estafar 2,9 millones de euros a 452 pequeños ahorradores'. Available at http://www.apmagistratura.com/apm/noticias/100504c.htm#c (accessed 28 August 2009).

Aparicio, L. (2001), 'Gescartera managed 10,000 million in undeclared money. The 'hole' is more than twice the resources of the company' ('Gescartera manejaba 10.000 millones en "dinero negro" El "agujero" es más de dos veces superior a los fondos declarados'), *El País*, 29 July, p. 44.

Argandoña, A. (1999), 'Ethics in finance and public policy. The Ibercorp case', *Journal of Business Ethics*, **22**(2), 219–231.

ARP 2000\107 (2000), *National Court (Criminal Division, Section 1), Sentence No. 16/2000, 31 March 2000 (Audiencia Nacional (Sala de lo Penal, Sección 1ª), Sentencia núm. 16/2000 de 31 de marzo)*.

Auto Audiencia Nacional (2006). *National Court (Central Court No. 1), Judicial Decree (D. Previas 134/2006) 7 June 2006 (Audiencia Nacional (Juzgado Central de Instrucción Uno), Auto (D. Previas 134/2006) de 7 de junio*.

Barroso, F.J. (2002), 'The police are searching for the managers of a "stamps bank" that closed with its clients' money' ('La policía busca a los responsables de un 'banco filatélico' que cerró con el dinero de sus clients'), *El País*, 9 January, p. 4.

Bernal-Lloréns, M. (2004), 'Financial crises and the publication of the financial statements of banks in Spain, 1844–1868', *Accounting Historians' Journal*, **31**, 1–26.

Blasco-Lang, J.J. (1998), 'From creative accounting to accounting fraud' ('De la contabilidad creativa al delito contable'), *Partida Doble*, **85**, 33–39.

BOICAC No. 6 (1991), *Official Bulletin of the Spanish Institute of Accounting and Auditing (Boletín Oficial del Instituto de Contabilidad y Auditoría de Cuentas)*, Instituto de Contabilidad y Auditoría de Cuentas (ICAC), Madrid, June.

BOICAC No. 68 (2006), *Official Bulletin of the Spanish Institute of Accounting and Auditing (Boletín Oficial del Instituto de Contabilidad y Auditoría de Cuentas)*, Instituto de Contabilidad y Auditoría de Cuentas (ICAC), Madrid, December.

Brewster, D. and Crawford, L. (2006), 'Spanish dealers raided in stamp fraud', *Financial Times*, 10 May, p. 10.

Bruce, P. (1993), 'Roof falls in on Spanish union ambitions', *Financial Times*, 29 December, p. 2.

Business Wire (11/10/2006), 'Escala Group and its North American philatelic division report strong "Stamp Auction Week" sales', *Time*, 11 October, **15**: 37.

Calatrava, E. (2006), 'The difficult valuation of Afinsa and Fórum's stamps' ('La difícil tasación de los sellos de Afinsa y Fórum'), *Expansión*, 19 May, p. 20.

Calvo, L. (2006), 'Broken lives due to the fraud' ('Vidas rotas por la estafa'), *Tiempo*, 15 May, p. 25.

Carrera, N., Gutiérrez, I. and Carmona, S. (2005), 'Concentration in the Spanish audit market: an empirical analysis for the period 1990–2000' ('Concentración en el mercado de auditoría en España: análisis empírico del período 1990–2000'), *Revista Española de Financiación y Contabilidad*, **32**(125), 426–457.

Carrera, N., Gómez-Aguilar, N., Ruiz-Barbadillo, E. and Humphrey, C. (2007), 'Mandatory audit firm rotation in Spain: a policy that was never applied', *Accounting, Auditing and Accountability Journal*, **20**(5), 671–701.

Cinco Días (1997), 'The appointed legal experts of PSV say IGS spent the resources committed to manage the company' ('Los peritos de PSV dicen que IGS gastó lo destinado para la gestión'), 25 June.

Comisión Gescartera (2001), *Parliamentary Commission on Gescartera Case (Comisión Parlamentaria Caso Gescartera)*, Diario de Sesiones del Congreso de los Diputados, Año 2001, VII Legislatura, Núm. 9, Congreso de los Diputados, Madrid.

Congreso de los Diputados (1982), *Briefing – Treasury Commission about the situation of the entity 'Fidecaya, S.A.'*, (Sesión Informativa -Comisión de Economía y Hacienda sobre la situación de la entidad 'Fidecaya, S.A.', *Diario de Sesiones del Congreso de los Diputados*, Año 1982, I Legislatura, Núm. 39, Congreso de los Diputados: Madrid.

Congreso de los Diputados (2006), *Parliamentary Question of Catalonian Group (Convergència i Unió), about the adoption measures to protect those affected by the investigations about Fórum Filatélico and Afinsa (Interpelación del Grupo Parlamentario Catalán (Convergència i Unió), relativa a la adopción de medidas en defensa de los afectados por las investigaciones a las entidades Fórum Filatélico y Afinsa),* Cortes Generales, Diario de Sesiones del Congreso de los Diputados, Pleno y Diputación Permanente, Año 2006, VIII Legislatura, Núm. 177, Sesión plenaria núm. 166, 17 May, p. 8877.

Cortes, J.M. (2003), 'Clients and a group of shareholders of Eurobank accuse the bank's management of fraud' ('Clientes y un grupo de accionistas de Eurobank acusan de fraude a los gestores del banco'), *El País*, 25 August, p. 50.

Crawford, L. (2005a), 'Investors warned of doubtful returns', *Financial Times*, 27 September, p. 34.

Crawford, L. (2005b), 'Cheque is in the post in stamp scheme – Spanish consumer group raises concerns about an unregulated arena that has attracted Euros 5bn from thousands of small investors', *Financial Times*, 29 September, p. 34.

Crawford, L. (2006a), 'Fears held for owners' lifetime savings', *Financial Times*, 10 May, p. 10.

Crawford, L. (2006b), 'Focus on Afinsa's relations with US group', *Financial Times*, 11 May, p. 9.

Crawford, L. (2006c), 'Stamp groups "ran Spain's biggest scam"', *Financial Times*, 12 May, p. 6.

De Barrón, I. (2006), 'A risky investment plan' ('Un arriesgado sistema de inversión'), *El País*, 5 May, p. 18.

Diligencias Previas Afinsa (2007), *Order of the Central Criminal Court, No. 1,* Preliminary proceedings 134/2006 Afinsa Bienes Tangibles *(Auto del Juzgado Central de Instrucción No. 1 de la Audiencia Nacional,* diligencias previas 134/2006, Afinsa Bienes Tangibles), available at http://www.negocios.com/extras/noticias/AFINSAquerella.pdf (accessed 24 August 2007).

Diligencias Previas Fórum (2006), *Order of the Central Criminal Court No. 5,* Preliminary proceedings, simplified version 148/06J Fórum Filatélico *(Auto del Juzgado Central de Instrucción No. 5,* Diligencias previas proc. abreviado 148/06J, Fórum Filatélico), available at http://www.eleconomista.es/imag/AUTOANTONIOMERICO.doc (accessed 24 August 2007).

Dinero y Derechos (2004), *Uncontrolled Investments (Inversiones no controladas)*, No. 81, available at http://www.ocu.org/site_images/PressPdf/DD081_llenas%20de/20 riesgos.pdf (accessed 25 July 2007).

Ekaizer, E. and Romero, J.M. (2006), 'The Economy Ministry got through the 'Afinsa case' in 2002 at a request of the prosecutor without adopting any measure' ('Economía despachó el 'caso Afinsa' en 2002 a instancias del fiscal sin adoptar medidas'), *El País*, 24 May, p. 26.

*El Economista* (2006), 'The auditor of Fórum Filatélico is summoned to declare before the judge' ('Juez cita como imputado responsable auditora Fórum Filatélico'), 6 June, available at http://www.eleconomista.es/mercados-cotizaciones/noticias/25633/06/06/Juez-cita-como-imputado-responsable-auditora-Forum-Filatelico.html (accessed 28 August 2009).

*El Economista*, (2008), 'The auditor and four former directors of AVA acquitted of criminal act of bankruptcy' ('Absueltos un auditor y cuatro exdirectivos de AVA en una causa por insolvencia y delito societario'), 8 April, available at http://www.eleconomista.es/economia/noticias/465158/04/08/Economia-Absueltos-un-auditor-y-cuatro-ex-directivos-de-AVA-en-una-causa-por-insolvencia-y-delito-societario.html (accessed 28 August 2009).

*El Mundo* (1994), 'The case and sunset of Mario Conde. A provisional assessment before a pretrial (provisional) custody' ('Caso y Ocaso de Mario Conde. Una valoración provisional ante una prisión provisional'), 24 December, available at http://www.elmundo.es/papel/hemeroteca/1994/12/24/opinion/19907.html (accessed 28 August 2007).

*El Mundo* (1995), 'Members of the cooperative claim Pts. 1,500 million from PSV's auditing firm' ('Los cooperativistas reclaman 1.500 millones a la empresa que auditó PSV'), 28 January.

*El Mundo* (2006), 'Operation against a fraud in investments in stamps. Fórum and Afinsa denied the charges' ('Operación contra un fraude en inversión Filatélica. Fórum Filatélico y Afinsa niegan las acusaciones'), 9 May, available at http://www.elmundo.es/mundodinero/2006/05/09/economia/1147190777.html (accessed 4 September 2007).

*El Mundo* (2006), 'The public prosecutor's office for corruption accuses Afinsa and Fórum of fraud and says that both were bankrupt' ('Anticorrupción acusa a Afinsa y a Fórum Filatélico de estafa y dice que ambas están en "insolvencia"'), 11 May, available at http://www.elmundo.es/mundodinero/2006/05/11/economia/1147343256.html (accessed 28 August 2007).

*El Mundo* (2006), 'Executives admit that Afinsa had financial difficulties but it could face its payments' ('Los directivos admiten que Afinsa tenía un déficit pero que puede afrontar sus pagos'), 12 May, available at http://www.elmundo.es/mundodinero/2006/05/12/economia/1147399783.html (accessed 28 August 2007).

*El Mundo* (2006), 'ING opens branches for the "important moments in life"' ('ING abre oficinas para los "momentos de verdad"'), 21 June, available at http://www.elmundo.es/mundodinero/2006/06/21/economia/1150907373.html (accessed 4 September 2007).

*El Mundo* (2006), 'Fórum had a network of 14 suppliers to siphon money out of the country' ('Fórum tenía una red de 14 proveedores europeos para sacar dinero de España'), 25 May, available at http://www.elmundo.es/2006/05/25/economia/ (accessed 26 August 2009).

*El Mundo* (2006), 'The stamps fraud affects ING Direct' ('La estafa de los sellos pasa factura a ING Direct'), 26 July, available at http://www.elmundo.es/mundodinero/2006/07/26/economia/1153936974.html (accessed 4 September 2007).

*El Mundo* (2008), 'Gescartera. Trial. Sentence. Antonio Camacho sentenced to 11-year term in prison' ('Gescartera. Juicio. Sentencia. Antonio Camacho condenado a 11 años'), 30 March, p. 18.

*El País* (2007), 'Stamps valued at three million and sold at 12' ('Sellos valorados en tres millones y vendidos por 12', 6 February, p. 27.

*El País* (2007), 'Audit shows Afinsa assets fail to cover multi-million stamp fraud', English edition (W Herald Tribune), 13 April, p. 3.

*El País* (2008), 'Fraudulent stock brokerage owner given 11 years in jail', English edition (*W Herald Tribune*), 28 March, p. 1.

Europa Press (2002), 'Adicae demands regulation for investments in collectibles to avoid 'frauds' like Banco Filatélico' ('Adicae reclama regular la inversión colectiva en bienes tangibles para evitar 'fraudes' como el de el Banco Filatélico'), *Time*, 12 January, p. 9:51.

*Expansión* (2003), 'The government warns of the bargains of high profitability investing in collectiables such as works of art or stamps' ('El Gobierno alerta sobre las ofertas de alta rentabilidad con bienes de colección, como obras de arte o sellos'), 29 March, p. 77.

*Expansión* (2006), 'The great scares of the saver' ('Los grandes sustos del ahorrador'), 10 May, p. 30.

*Expansión* (2006), 'Case Afinsa-Fórum: one year of crisis' ('Caso Afinsa-Fórum. Un año de crisis'), 22 June, available at http://www.expansion.com/especiales/afinsaforum/cronologia.html, accessed 28 August 2007.

*Expansión* (2008), 'The High Court sentences Gescartera's owner to 11-year imprisonment' ('La Audiencia Nacional condena a Camacho a once años de prisión por el caso Gescartera'), 28 March, p. 37.

Fernández, M. (2006), 'Fórum and Afinsa force the government to strengthen control over the small auditing firms' ('Fórum y Afinsa fuerzan al Gobierno a estrechar el control sobre las auditoras pequeñas'), *Expansión*, 5 May, p. 23.

Fernández-Navarrete, D. (1999), 'The economy of democracy (1975–1995). Crisis and recovery' ('La economía de la democracia (1975–1995). Crisis y recuperación'), in *Historia de la España actual, 1939–1996. Autoritarismo y democracia*, Marcial Pons, Barcelona, pp. 337–376.

Form 10-K Spectrum Group International Inc, (2009), Annual Report Pursuant to Section 13 or 15(d) of the Securities Exchange Act of 1934, for the fiscal year ended June 30, 2009. Commission file number 1-11988, Spectrum Group International Inc.

Form 10-Q Escala Group, (2006), Quartely Report Under Section 13 or 15(d) of the Securities Exchange Act of 1934, for the quarterly period ended March 31, 2006. Commission file number 1 19988, Escala Group, Inc

Galindo, C. (2006), 'A chronology of fraud or the loans of Ms Baldomera' ('Cronología de la estafa o los préstamos de doña Baldomera'), *El País*, 15 May, p. 30.

García-Abadillo, C. (1999), 'A silence agreement' ('Un pacto para el silencio'), *El Mundo*, 16 February, available at http://www2.elmundolibro.com/1999/02/16/economia/16N0083.html (accessed 28 August 2009).

García-Abadillo, C. (2001), 'Gescartera invested undeclared money in Stock Selection, a firm located in the Isle of Jersey' ('Gescartera colocó el 'dinero negro' en la firma Stock Selection en la isla de Jersey'), *El Mundo*, 17 August, available at http://www.elmundo.es/elmundo/2001/08/17/economia/998018828.html (accessed 14 April 2008).

García-Benau, M.A. and Vico-Martínez, A. (2002), 'Financial scandals and auditing: loss and recovery of trust of a profession in crisis' ('Los escándalos financieros y la auditoría: pérdida y recuperación de la confianza en una profesión en crisis'), *Revista Valenciana de Economía y Hacienda*, **7**, 25–48.

García-Benau, M.A., Ruiz-Barbadillo, E., Humphrey, C. and Husaini, Walid Al (1999), 'Success in failure? Reflections on the changing Spanish audit environment', *The European Accounting Review*, **8**(4), 701–730.

Gay-Saludas, J.M. (1997), 'Legal manipulations of the accounting numbers (Alteraciones legales del resultado contable)', *Partida Doble*, **79**, 33–42.

Gómez, M. (2002), 'Gescartera case. The Ministry of Economy imposed a €540,000 fine on Deloitte in relation to the audit work of the brokerage house' ('Caso Gescartera. El Ministerio de Economía multa a la auditora Deloitte con 540.000 euros por su auditoría a la agencia de valores'), *El Mundo*, 11 February.

Gonzalo, J.A. and Garvey, A.M. (2005), 'In the aftermath of crisis: the post-Enron implications for Spanish university accounting educators', *The European Accounting Review*, **14**(2), 429–439.

Grant, R.M. and Visconti, M. (2006), 'The strategic background to corporate accounting scandals', *Long Range Planning*, **39**, 361–383.

Hill, A. (2006), 'Stamps, scandal and a timid Spanish watchdog', *Financial Times*, 11 May, p. 21.

Informe Afinsa (2007), *Proceedings of the Bankruptcy Court. Proceedings No. 8 206/2006 of 'Afinsa Bienes Tangibles S.A.'* (*Informe de la Administración Concursal de 'Afinsa Bienes Tangibles, S.A'. Concurso necesario No. 8 206/2006*), available at http://www.rdmf.files.wordpress.com/2007/04/informe-administracion-concursal-afinsa.pdf (accessed 21 July 2007).

Informe Fórum (2006), *Proceedings of the Bankruptcy Court. Ordinary proceedings 209/2006 of Fórum Filatélico, S.A.* (*Informe de la Administración Concursal. Concurso Ordinario 209/2006 de Fórum Filatélico, S.A.*), Juzgado de lo Mercantil No. 7, available at http://www.expansion.com/documentos/descarga/informeF.pdf (accessed 21 July 2007).

JUR\2000\291257 (2000), *High Court (Civil Division), Judicial Decree of 14 November 2000 (Tribunal Supremo (Sala de lo Civil). Auto de 14 de noviembre 2000.*

JUR 2000\308779 (2000), *National Court (Criminal Division, Section 4), Sentence No. 24/2000 20 September 2000 (Sentencia de la Audiencia Nacional (Sala de lo Penal, Sección 4ª), núm. 24/2000 de 20 septiembre)*.

JUR 2001\205441 (2001), *National Court (Criminal Division, Section 1), Sentence No. 33/2001 16 July 2001 (Audiencia Nacional (Sala de lo Penal, Sección 1ª), Sentencia núm. 33/2001 de 16 de julio)*.

JUR 2006\87009 (2005), *Provincial Court of Barcelona (Criminal Division, Section 2), Sentence No. 611/2005 7 June 2005 (Audiencia Provincial de Barcelona (Sala de lo Penal, Sección 2ª), Sentencia núm. 611/2005 de 7 de junio)*.

JUR 2006\200237 (2006), *National Court (Criminal Division, Section 1), Sentencia No. 27/2006 23 June 2006 (Audiencia Nacional (Sala de lo Penal, Sección 1ª), Sentencia núm. 27/2006 de 23 de junio)*.

JUR 2007\61172, (2006), *Provincial Court of Madrid (Section 5), Judicial Decree No. 4563/2006 10 November 2006 (Audiencia Provincial de Madrid (Sección 5ª), Auto núm. 4563/2006 de 10 noviembre)*.

JUR 2008\112612 (2008), *National Court (Criminal Division, Section 4), Sentence No. 18/2008 25 March 2008 (Audiencia Nacional (Sala de lo Penal, Sección 4ª), Sentencia núm. 18/2008 de 25 de marzo)*.

JUR 2010\67489 (2010), *National Court (Division for the judicial review of administrative acts, Section 3), Sentence 11 February 2010 (Audiencia Nacional (Sala de lo Contencioso-Administrativo, Sección 3ª), Sentencia de 11 de febrero)*.

JUR 2010\67490 (2010), *National Court (Division for the judicial review of administrative acts, Section 3), Sentence 11 February 2010 (Audiencia Nacional (Sala de lo Contencioso-Administrativo, Sección 3ª), Sentencia de 11 de febrero)*.

Letter (2002a), *Letter CNMV to ADICAE*, 14/03/2002, available at http://perezurena.com/docs/contestacion_carta_cnmv_adicae_2002.pdf (accessed 21 July 2007).

Letter (2002b), *Letter from the Insurance Companies Supervisory Authority to ADICAE (Letter Dirección General de Seguros to ADICAE)*, 9/04/2002, available at http://perezurena. com/docs/contestacion_carta_dgs_adicae_2002.pdf (accessed 21 July 2007).

Ley 12/2010/(2010), Law 12/2010 of June 30, modifying the Law 19/1988 of July 12 concerning Auditing, the Law 24/1988 of July 28 concerning the Stock Market, and the Public Companies Act passed by Royal Decree 1564/1989 of December 22, for its adaptation to European legislation. (Ley 12/2010, de 30 de junio, por la que se modifica la Ley 19/1988, de 12 de julio, de Auditoría de Cuentas, la Ley 24/1988, de 28 de julio, del Mercado de Valores y el texto refundido de la Ley de Sociedades Anónimas aprobado por el Real Decreto Legislativo 1564/1989, de 22 de diciembre, para su adaptación a la normativa comunitaria), Boletín Oficial del Estado (BOE), No. 159, Sec. I, Julio 1 de Julio de 2010, 57586-57625.

Ley 43/2007 (2007), Law 43/2007, December 13, on consumer protection in the procurement of goods with offer of price restitution (*Ley 43/2007, de 13 de diciembre, de protección de los consumidores en la contratación de bienes con oferta de restitución del precio*). Boletín Oficial del Estado (BOE) 299, 51327-51330. Congreso de los Diputados, Madrid.

López, P. (2006), Guijarro: 'I had more money hidden at home but you did not find it' (Guijarro: 'Tenía más dinero escondido en casa que ustedes no encontraron'), *Diario Negocio.es* December 1 2006, p. 5. Available at http://www.negocio.com/ejemplaresanteriores. php?dia=1&mes=12&ano=2006 (accessed 29 August 2009).

Marcos, P. (2001), 'Camacho sold all Gescartera's assets in the stock market in two years without a trace' ('Camacho vendió en Bolsa todos los activos de Gescartera en sólo dos años sin dejar rastro'), *El País*, 20 August, p. 47.

Martin, N.A. (2004), 'Return to sender: Greg Manning Auctions faces a sticky stamps market – and accounting questions', *Barron's*, 27 September, p. 25.

Martin, N.A. (2005), 'Sticky situation', *Barron's*, 23 May, p. 2.

Martin, N.A. (2006a), 'Review and preview follow-up – a return visit to earlier stories: stamp of disapproval', *Barron's*, 24 April, p. 17.

Martin, N.A. (2006b), 'Review and preview follow-up – a return visit to earlier stories: Spain's "Biggest Scam" ', *Barron's*, 15 May, p. 16.

Miller, G.S. (2006), 'The press as a watchdog for accounting fraud', *Journal of Accounting Research*, **44**(5), 1001–1033.

Ministerio de Economía y Hacienda, (2006), 'Press Release. The Ministry of Economy and Treasury denies the information published by the newspaper El Mundo' ('Comunicado del Ministerio de Economía y Hacienda desmiente la información publicada hoy por el diario El Mundo'), 25 May 2006. Ministerio de Economía y Hacienda, Madrid.

Morán, N. (2002), 'Is it profitable and secure to invest in stamps?' ('¿Es rentable y seguro invertir en sellos?') , *Actualidad Económica*, 11 February, p. 63.

Oliveras, E. and Amat, O. (2003), 'Ethics and creative accounting: some empirical evidence on accounting for intangibles in Spain', *University Pompeu Fabra, Economics and Business, Working Paper No. 732*, available at http://ssrn.com/abstract=563313 (accessed 21 July 2007).

Plan General Contable (1973), *Royal Decree 530/1973, of February 22, passing the Spanish GAAP (Real Decreto 530/1973, de 22 de Febrero, por el que se aprueba el Plan General de Contabilidad)*, Instituto de Contabilidad y Auditoría de Cuentas, ICAC, Madrid.

Plan General Contable (1990), *Royal Decree 1643/1990, of December 20, passing the Spanish GAAP (Real Decreto 1643/1990, de 20 de diciembre, por el que se aprueba el Plan General de Contabilidad)*, Instituto de Contabilidad y Auditoría de Cuentas, ICAC, Madrid.

Plan General Contable (2007), *Royal Decree 1514/2007, of November 16, passing the Spanish GAAP (Real Decreto 1514/2007, de 16 de noviembre, por el que se aprueba el Plan General de Contabilidad)*, Boletín Oficial del Estado (BOE), Año CCCXLVII, Martes 20 de Noviembre de 2007. Suplemento del Número 278, Madrid.

Querella Afinsa (2006), *Lawsuit of the Special Attorney General's Office for the Repression of Economic Offences related with corruption against Afinsa, sent to the Central Tribunal of the Audiencia Nacional (Querella de la Fiscalía Anticorrupción contra Afinsa remitida al Juzgado Central de Instrucción Decano de la Audiencia Nacional)*, available at http://www.expansion.com/especiales/afinsaforum/querella_afinsa.pdf (accessed 21 July 2007).

Querella Fórum (2006), *Lawsuit of the Special Attorney General's Office for the Repression of Economic Offences related with corruption against Fórum, sent to the Central Tribunal of the Audiencia Nacional, (Querella de la Fiscalía Anticorrupción contra Fórum Filatélico remitida al Juzgado Central de Instrucción Decano de la Audiencia Nacional)*, available at http://www.expansion.com/especiales/afinsaforum/querella_forum.pdf (accessed 21 July 2007).

Relaño, V. (2002), 'Very profitable collectibles. Investments in stamps reach annual yields above 10 %' ('Piezas de colección muy rentables La inversión en sellos alcanza rendimientos anuales por encima del 10 %'), *El País*, 26 May, p. 29.

Remírez de Ganuza, C. (2002), 'The Supreme Court increases from 10 to 20 years the sentence of Mario Conde in connection with "Banesto Case" ' ('El Supremo eleva de 10 a 20 años la condena impuesta a Mario Conde por el "Caso Banesto" '), *El Mundo*, 30 July, available at http://www.elmundo.es/elmundo/2002/07/29/economia/10279 37501.html (accessed 2 April 2008).

*Reuters* (1992), 'Ex-KIO manager denies wrongdoing in Grupo Torras', 26 November.

Rico, M. (2006), 'The alleged fraud of Fórum Filatélico and Afinsa. The gaps of the stamp scandal' ('La presunta estafa de Fórum Filatélico y Afinsa. Las lagunas del escándalo de los sellos'), *Tiempo*, 22 May, pp. 18–20.

RJ 1994\1121 (1994), *High Court (Criminal Division), Sentence No. 455/1994 24 February 1994 (Tribunal Supremo (Sala de lo Penal), Sentencia núm. 455/1994 de 24 de febrero)*.

RJ 2002\6357 (2002), *High Court (Criminal Division) Sentence No. 867/2002 29 July, Banesto Case (Tribunal Supremo, Sala de lo Penal, Sentencia No. 867/2002. Caso Banesto)*.

RJ 2003\7233 (2003), *High Court (Criminal Division) Sentence No. 1212/2003 9 October 2003 (Tribunal Supremo (Sala de lo Penal) Sentencia núm. 1212/2003 de 9 de octubre)*.

RJ 2004\459 (2003), *High Court (Criminal Division), Sentence No. 1036/2003 2 September 2003, (Tribunal Supremo (Sala de lo Penal), Sentencia núm. 1036/2003 de 2 de septiembre)*.

RJ\2005\1938 (2005). *High Court (Criminal Division), Sentence No. 50/2005 28 January 2005 (Tribunal Supremo (Sala de lo Penal), Sentencia núm. 50/2005 de 28 enero. RJ\2005\1938)*.

RJ 2007\5374 (2007), *High Court (Criminal Division), Sentence No. 600/2007 11 September 2007 (Tribunal Supremo (Sala de lo Penal), Sentencia núm. 600/2007 de 11 septiembre). BOE 15 febrero 2007, núm. 40 (suplement)*.

RJ 2008\1892 (2008), *High Court (Division for the judicial review of administrative acts, Section 3), Sentence 8 April 2008 (Tribunal Supremo (Sala de lo Contencioso-Administrativo, Sección 3ª), Sentencia de 8 de abril)*.

RJ 2008\1893 (2008), *High Court (Division for the judial review of administrative acts, Section 3), Sentence 8 April 2008 (Tribunal Supremo (Sala de lo Contencioso-Administrativo, Sección 3ª), Sentencia de 8 de abril 2008)*.

RJ 2008\2151 (2004), *High Court (Criminal Division, Section 1), Sentence No. 194/2004 16 February 2004 (Tribunal Supremo (Sala de lo Penal, Sección 1ª), Sentencia núm. 194/2004 de 16 febrero)*.

RJCA 2008\664 (2008), *National Court (Chamber for the judicial review of administrative acts, Section 6), Sentence 10 October 2008 (Audiencia Nacional (Sala de lo Contencioso-Administrativo, Sección 6ª) Sentencia de 10 octubre 2008)*.

Rodrigo, N. (2006), 'Auditors alerted about several irregularities in 2004 financial statements' ('Los auditores ya alertaron de diversas irregularidades en las cuentas de 2004'), *Cinco Días*, 5 May, p. 4.

Rojo, A. (2005), *Report about the nature of the activities related to stamp trading within the framework of philatelic investments schemes (Dictamen sobre la naturaleza de la actividad de comercialización de sellos en el marco de un programa de inversión filatélica dirigida)*, prepared at the request of Afinsa Bienes Tangibles, SA, 13/06/2005, available at http://www.eleconomista.es/especiales/afinsa-forum/(accessed 31 January 2007).

RTC 1987\122 (1987), *Constitutional Court (Second Chamber), Sentence No. 122/1987 14 July 1987 (Tribunal Constitutional (Sala Segunda), Sentencia núm. 122/1987 de 14 de julio). BOE 29 julio 1987, núm. 180 (suplement)*.

RTC 2006\328 (2006), *Constitutional Court (Second Chamber), Sentence No. 328/2006 20 November 2006 (Tribunal Constitucional (Sala Segunda), Sentencia núm. 328/2006 de 20 de noviembre)*.

Ruiz-Barbadillo, E. (2003), 'The role of auditors in the financial scandals' ('El papel de los auditores en los escándalos financieros'), *Partida Doble*, **146**, 48–57.

Sampedro, J. (1994), 'Sotos, ex-manager of PSV, in prison after being accused of committing fraud' ('Sotos, ex gerente de PSV, en prisión acusado de estafa'), *El País*, 30 June.

SEC vs. Escala Group, Inc. Gregory Manning, Larry Lee Crawford (2009), United States District Court. Southern District of New York, 23 March 2009. Available at http://www.sec.gov/litigation/complaints/2009/comp20965.pdf (accessed 15 July 2009).

Segovia, E. (2006), 'The huge investment in stamps in Spain is not comparable to that of any other country in the world' ('La ingente inversión en sellos en España no tiene parangón en ningún otro país del mundo'), *El Confidencial*, 11 May, available at http://www.elconfidencial.com/economia/noticia.asp?id=3494 (accessed 31 August 2007).

Sikka, P. (1997), 'Regulating the auditing profession', in *Current Issues in Auditing*, 2nd edn, eds M. Sherer and S. Turley, Paul Chapman Publishing, London, pp. 129–145.

Special Committee for the Investigation of Gescartera (2001), Session No. 21, 26 October. *Journal of Debates*, Congress, Madrid, p. 1064.

*The Economist* (2001), 'Some juicy scandals are jangling the government's nerves', 1 September, pp. 45–46.

*Tiempo* (2006), 'The audits that did not ring the bell' ('Las auditorías que no alertaron a nadie'), 15 May, p. 24.

Uriol, E. (2002), 'This year Afinsa will invest €100 million in purchases of stamps abroad' ('Afinsa invertirá este año 100 millones en adquirir sellos en el extranjero'), *Cinco Días*, 17 January.

Valero, J.C. (2003), 'Catalonian investors offer €18 million for Eurobank's licence' ('Inversores catalanes ofrecen 18 millones de euros por la ficha bancaria de Eurobank'), *ABC*, 1 December.

Vázquez, B. (1996), 'The report on the 'Banesto Case' raises by 300 million the alleged misappropriation of assets estimated by the prosecutor' ('El informe del 'Caso Banesto' eleva en 300 millones la supuesta apropiación de que les acusaba la fiscalía'), *Expansión*, 8 February.

Vico-Martínez, A. (2002), 'The Gescartera case and the future financial law: implications for the future of auditing and accounting' ('El caso Gescartera y la futura ley financiera: implicaciones para el futuro de la auditoría y la contabilidad'), *Partida Doble*, **134**, 28–35.

Villaroya, M.B. and Rodríguez, M.C. (2003), 'Accounting manipulation: the profile of companies using accounting tricks' ('La manipulación contable: el perfil de las empresas manipuladoras'), *Partida Doble*, **143**, 54–63.

Vitzthum, C. (1994), 'Spanish Union faces scandal over finances – as UGT strike draws near some members wonder where their money is', *Wall Street Journal*, 4 January, p. A7D.

# APPENDIX

| Date | Company | Accounting issues[17] |
| --- | --- | --- |
| 1981 | Caja Rural de Jaén | Allegations of manipulation of 1981 financial statements through the recording of fictitious profits and other strategies of creative accounting (RTC 1987\122, 1987; RJ 1994\1121, 1994). |

[17]Other financial scandals in the country: Fidecaya in 1981; Caja Previsora Andaluza and Caja de Crédito Andaluza in 1989; Grupo Brokers in 1992; Caja Hipotecaria de Valores in 1992; Brokerval, AV in 1994 and Sistema de Ahorro Múltiple in 1995.

| Date | Company | Accounting issues |
|------|---------|-------------------|
| 1992 | Grupo Ibercorp and Sistemas Financieros SA | Sistemas Financieros (SF) was a company belonging to Grupo Ibercorp (GI). From March to June 1990, the CEO, other top executives and other privileged shareholders sold SF's shares back to the company. The share price fell dramatically immediately afterwards when the board of directors announced a reduction of capital. There was evidence of insider trading, share price manipulation and discrimination against certain shareholders. In addition, SF's treasury stock exceeded the maximum amount permitted by Spanish law. GI failed to report significant shareholdings and the level of treasury stock, and hid the real name of the privileged shareholders (among them, GI's top executives and the then Governor of the Bank of Spain). Finally, there was evidence that funds were diverted to ends other than that of paying off the outstanding debts (Argandoña, 1999; García-Abadillo, 1999). |
| 1992 | Grupo Torras | Grupo Torras was a Spanish industrial holding company controlled by the Kuwait Investment Office (KIO). There were allegations of money transfers from Grupo Torras to offshore companies and external accounts located in offshore jurisdictions and tax havens. These payments were not recorded in Grupo Torras's accounting books. While the accounts prepared by the managers indicated a 1991 profit of Pts 4.2 billion (€25 242 million), a new audit required by KIO showed a Pts 44.44 billion loss (€267 090 million). KIO commented that the accounts were full of inconsistencies (see *Reuters*, 26/11/1992; JUR 2006\200237, 2006; RJ 2007\5374, 2007). |
| 1993 | Promotora Social de Viviendas (PSV) and Iniciativas de Gestión de Servicios (IGS) | The court's investigation focused on allegations of misappropriation of funds and fraud. There were accusations of the use of creative accounting, such as the recognition of expenses that did not exist, to justify the siphoning off of thousands of Pts (JUR 2001\205441, 2001; RJ 2003\7233, 2003). |
| 1993 | Banco Español de Crédito (Banesto) | The Spanish courts found that Conde, as the bank's chairman, manipulated the accounts using a range of questionable accounting practices. They found evidence of manipulation in the company's income statement and balance sheet positions, and non-compliance with the matching and accruals principles. The investigation also found that Banesto incurred significant losses by making excessive payments for some investments and selling assets at artificially low prices. There was also evidence of questionable transactions for the personal benefit of Conde (ARP 2000\107, 2000; RJ 2002\6357, 2002). |

| | | |
|---|---|---|
| 2001 | Gescartera | The company provided services for which it had no authorization. The company allegedly siphoned money to outside accounts. Specific details about the accounting problems were not made public (JUR 2008\112612, 2008). |
| 2006 | Afinsa and Fórum Filatélico | Both companies had accounting irregularities regarding the recording of the transactions of the stamp contracts. The accounting for the stamp contracts did not recognize the liabilities of the repurchase option held by investors; they failed to comply with the historical cost principle in relation to the repurchase of stamps; they also had problems with the recording of transactions with suppliers; and there were problems with the valuation of the stamps (Querella Afinsa, 2006; Querella Fórum, 2006; Informe Afinsa, 2007; Informe Fórum, 2006). |

# 17

# Accounting Scandals in Sweden – A Long Tradition

Gunnar Rimmel and Kristina Jonäll

## 17.1 INTRODUCTION

Sweden is not typically associated with corporate scandals involving fraud and bribes or with creative accounting. However, this impression of pristine Swedish corporate integrity and reporting transparency is not completely accurate. In the twentieth century, Sweden has experienced several major corporate scandals that have, in varying degrees, involved unethical and illegal behaviours. Other scandals, more broadly speaking, have resulted from misleading or inadequate financial disclosures of complex corporate activities.

In a description of Swedish corporate scandals, perhaps the most obvious place to begin is with the 1930s crash of Ivar Kreuger's financial empire that is still the most spectacular accounting scandal in Swedish history. (This early Swedish accounting scandal is dealt with in more detail in Chapter 7.) Starting from nothing, Ivar Kreuger created the largest corporate conglomerate in Sweden that included many renowned Swedish corporations such as Ericsson, SKF, SCA and Boliden (Wahlström, 2000). At the height of his success, Kreuger controlled about 400 companies through his acquisition of national monopolies. His International Match Company became the world's largest match manufacturer.

However, Kreuger's business empire in the USA and in Europe was a classic pyramid scheme that paid high dividends with funds obtained by the continuous issuance of financial instruments and participating debentures (Jönsson, 1991; Jönsson, 1994). During the global financial problems of the Great Depression, Kreuger & Toll, the holding company in the Kreuger empire, suffered severe liquidity problems, leading to its bankruptcy in 1932. After the Kreuger crash, it became apparent that there was almost no substance behind Kreuger's empire and its estimated value of €3.3 billion. As a result of the Kreuger crash, many legislators took action to regulate the disclosure of corporate accounting information. The US Congress enacted the Securities Act of 1933 as a direct response to Kreuger's bankruptcy (Flesher and Flesher, 1986; Jönsson, 1991), while in Sweden government regulation of external accounting information for listed companies began.

Initially, Swedish accounting practice was strongly influenced by German accounting practice that emphasised taxation rules over accounting and reporting principles. However, during the 1970s this Continental influence diminished somewhat as both the Swedish Companies Act and the Swedish Accounting Act reflected Anglo-Saxon accounting practice.

*Creative Accounting, Fraud and International Accounting Scandals*   Edited by Michael Jones
© 2011 Michael Jones. Published by John Wiley & Sons, Ltd

This shift towards Anglo-Saxon accounting practice did not break the formal link between taxation and accounting (Jönsson and Marton, 1994), but it did lead to more emphasis on corporate accounting and reporting as a separate field of interest.

In addition, during these years a new concept of *god redovisningssed* (in English, Good Accounting Practice) was introduced in Sweden that brought in the application of generally accepted accounting principles to ensure accounting was performed correctly using best practices. In large part, the major Swedish corporations have set the accounting trends that shape Good Accounting Practice in Sweden including, at a minimum, the understanding that accounting figures are trustworthy. However, the adoption of Good Accounting Practice has not ensured that there have been no accounting scandals in Sweden.

This chapter describes four financial scandals at Swedish corporations where Good Accounting Practice was not followed: Fermenta, Prosolvia, ABB and Skandia. These scandals variously involved outright fraud, misleading disclosures, fuzzy reporting and, inevitably, human greed. The aim of this chapter is to highlight how these scandals occurred in Sweden and to describe how the corporations misused accounting principles and reporting procedures. These four accounting scandals were selected because each, in its own way, had a deep impact on Swedish society. The chapter begins with the scandals at two small, publicly listed Swedish companies: Fermenta in the 1980s and Prosolvia in the 1990s. The chapter continues with the scandals at the multinational Swedish companies ABB and Skandia around the turn of the millennium. These scandals, reflecting a combination of fraud, accounting manipulation and/or top manager greed, led to the creation of Swedish commissions to regulate group accounting transactions, remuneration programmes and corporate governance codes. The chapter concludes with a discussion of the aftermath of these accounting scandals and their effect on Swedish accounting.

There have certainly been more than four such scandals in Sweden in recent decades although, as the authors' interviews with the Swedish Economic Crimes Bureau that began operations in 1998 revealed, a complete listing has not been compiled.

## 17.2 FERMENTA AND PROSOLVIA: SWEDISH STOCK MARKET DARLINGS

This section describes the financial scandals at Fermenta in the 1980s and at Prosolvia in the 1990s. At the time, the Fermenta case was considered one of the most severe misuses of accounting in Sweden in fifty years, and the Swedish media made many comparisons with the Kreuger crash. The Prosolvia case offers us a smorgasbord of accounting abuses typical of the accusations against IT companies at the end of the 1990s. In Sweden, Prosolvia was the most prominent of such cases since its collapse resulted in substantial financial problems for eight thousand small, private investors. Before their financial disasters, both Fermenta and Prosolvia were the darlings of the stock market because of their strong share prices and their many business media awards.

### 17.2.1 Fermenta – 1980s Biotech Company's Accounting Errors

Originally, Fermenta was a Swedish penicillin factory that was sold in 1981 to the entrepreneur Refaat El-Sayed by Astra, the pharmaceutical corporation. As a company, with Refaat El-Sayed as CEO as well as chairman, Fermenta's shares were floated on the

Stockholm Stock Exchange in 1984 where the company was presented as a biotech company with a dominant position in the manufacture of penicillin-based products. The Initial Public Offering (IPO) prospectus, as well as Fermenta's annual reports, described El-Sayed as a successful entrepreneur with a doctoral degree from an American university. Fermenta's share price climbed steadily, allowing the company to expand its business by the acquisitions of pharmaceutical companies in Italy, France and the US. By 1986, Fermenta's market value grew to €1.2 billion, and El-Sayed earned many awards and honours including Swedish 'Manager of the Year' in 1984 and 'Swede of the Year' in 1985 (Bränfeldt, 2006). El-Sayed was a very strong personality.[1]

In 1986, El-Sayed nearly signed a major contract with Volvo to buy their shares in Wilh Sonesson (an engineering group that controlled the pharmaceutical corporations Leo and Ferrosan and the dialysis corporation Gambro, and held shares in the biotech corporation Pharmacia). Had the purchase been completed, Fermenta would have paid Volvo with Fermenta's own shares that El-Sayed had purchased with borrowed money (Sundqvist, 1986). In February 1986, while the negotiations with Volvo were taking place, the media learned that El-Sayed had never earned a doctorate in the USA. Simultaneously, Bo Hermansson, who was Fermenta's internal auditor, blew the whistle on Fermenta to the external auditors. Hermansson stated that Fermenta's asset valuations and turnover had been inflated systematically by fictitious transactions in order to increase profit for Fermenta (Wifstrand, 1987).

After the disclosure of Fermenta's fraudulent accounting and of El-Sayed's false doctorate, Fermenta's shares fell by 50 % and trading in them was suspended for fifteen days. The Volvo deal collapsed. In December 1986, El-Sayed and the entire Fermenta board resigned. Stockholm's *Fondbörs*, the predecessor of the Stockholm Stock Exchange, began an investigation because Fermenta had violated stock exchange regulations by providing shareholders with misinformation, such as an understated price for the acquisition of the Italian bio/pharmaceutical company, Pierrel. The Fermenta Report by the investigators Walberg, Hanner and Rodhe showed that Fermenta had consistently erred in its accounting and reporting since its 1984 listing (Bränfeldt, 2006).

According to the Fermenta Report, one Fermenta strategy was to finance acquisitions by selling off divisions of acquired corporations. This acquisition strategy came to be called the 'Pierrel trick' after Fermenta's acquisition of Pierrel that was acquired with a leveraged buy-out. The deal was falsely announced to the press at €29.7 million, and according to Fermenta's interim report, two of Pierrel's three divisions were sold shortly afterwards for €27.7 million. Consequently, the shareholders wrongly believed that the Pierrel deal had paid for itself almost immediately. However, later investigations revealed that the two Pierrel's divisions were sold for only €24.4 million and that the leveraged buy-out consisted of cash payments and options that actually cost Fermenta between €47.5 and €77.8 million. This unofficial leveraged buy-out was accomplished by using parallel contracts. While there was a publicly announced contract, there were also contracts with the former Pierrel owner that were not publicly disclosed. In addition, there were different types of contracts with a number of related corporations – some owned by El-Sayed and others by

---

[1] All monetary figures in this chapter are expressed in euros. Historical amounts, in other currencies, have been restated, using exchange rates from 1995 to 2006. During these years the exchange role of the Swedish crown fluctuated from highest to lowest as follows against the €, £ and $: €8.4 to 9.2; £10.5 to 14.6; $6.7 to 10.3

his business partners. As a consequence, the financial reports and information that Fermenta provided to the stock exchange were deliberately manipulated to mislead their shareholders (Walberg, Hanner and Rodhe, 1988). In particular, insufficient information about the Pierrel deal, especially about related-party transactions, was disclosed. Fermenta had apparently overpaid for Pierrel and did not, in fact, recover the payment almost immediately as reported. Using fraudulent accounting, Fermenta disguised the transaction in its financial reports by manipulating the accounting numbers (Walberg, Hanner and Rodhe, 1988). Furthermore, as the Fermenta Report revealed, Fermenta had engaged in numerous fictitious transactions with its subsidiaries.

In addition to this accounting skulduggery, the Fermenta Report also showed that the acquisitions using leveraged buy-outs of Pierrel, SDS Biotech, Cedar and TechAmerica were all financially disastrous. In each of these acquisitions, Fermenta overpaid and losses resulted. However, to the delight of the investment community, Fermenta had reported an increase in turnover resulting from these acquisitions from €10.8 million to €330 million. Fermenta's annual reports showed growth in profit from €8.2 million in 1984 to €26.9 million in 1985, and forecasts predicted €76 million in profit for 1986 (Petersson, 1987).

Beginning with its prospectus that announced its public listing, Fermenta reported a special type of turnover, 'revenues from sales of technology,' a creative term unique to Fermenta and not used by other Swedish corporations. Over the years Fermenta's auditors had questioned this account, but their concern did not come to light until after the scandal was revealed. Because of their failure to report or strongly object to this accounting irregularity, Fermenta's auditors were criticised for not meeting their responsibilities to the stock market (Aldeholm and Olsson, 1995). Fermenta's accounting for 'revenues from sales of technology' did not follow either Swedish accounting standards or International Accounting Standards (IAS), (although Fermenta was not reporting under IAS). The Fermenta investigators even found that some 'revenues from sales of technology' numbers resulted from numerous transactions that were either fictitious or not at arm's length. One example was Fermenta's 'aspartame deal'. The sweetener aspartame had been the main profit driver of Pierrel, but after the acquisition, Fermenta tried, without success, to sell the aspartame inventories to outside parties. Therefore, El-Sayed arranged an internal sale of the inventory among Fermenta's subsidiaries using an outside sales agent to give the appearance of an external, market-based deal. The aspartame inventory worth €3.3 million was sold internally at the inflated price of €10.8 million. In total, the Fermenta Report discovered that the false 'revenues from sales of technology' were approximately €32.4 million (Walberg et al., 1988).

Another problem related to the 'revenues from sales of technology' was caused by Fermenta's lack of disclosure on its foreign subsidiaries. Although disclosure on such related parties was required by IAS 24 Related Party Disclosures, Swedish accounting standards did not require such disclosure until 1988. Therefore, Fermenta provided no related-party disclosures, and, as a result, there was no information on El-Sayed's private investments in his other corporations that dealt with Fermenta's foreign subsidiaries which appeared to act independently from Fermenta and El-Sayed. This loophole in the Swedish accounting rules allowed Fermenta to report transactions between its foreign subsidiaries and El-Sayed's other corporations without disclosing the relationships. These transactions, which inflated Fermenta's sales and profit and thus its share price, were certainly not independent, and in some cases were fictitious (Walberg, Hanner and Rodhe, 1988).

Had Fermenta followed Good Accounting Practice, Walberg, Hanner and Rodhe (1988) estimated that the company would have reported a total loss before tax of €32.4 million rather than the profits of €8.2 million and €26.9 million it reported for 1984 and 1985, respectively, and the profit of €75.7 million it forecast for 1986. Additionally, this €32.4 million loss excluded the write-off of some €23.1 million from the leveraged buy-out of the Cedar acquisition. A more 'true and fair' view of Fermenta's results would have produced a negative result of €54 million compared to the forecasted €75.7 million in profit for 1986 (Walberg, Hanner and Rodhe, 1988).

After receiving the Fermenta Report, Stockholm prosecutors charged El-Sayed with fraud, insider trading, perjury and breach of duty. Fermenta's CFO, Gaston Portefaix was charged as an accomplice on four counts of fraud. He was convicted for fraud and sentenced to a one-year jail sentence. However, he successfully appealed and his conviction was overturned. In 1989, El-Sayed was sentenced to five years in prison and was given a lifelong ban from trading in securities although he was released from prison in 1992. Venture capital companies bought Fermenta, delisting it in 1997. In the final analysis, the immediate trigger that led to the inquiry into Fermenta's accounting and reporting, and to its eventual downfall, was the media's discovery that Refaat El-Sayed had lied repeatedly about his doctorate (Bränfeldt, 2006).

### 17.2.2 Prosolvia – 1990s Experts in Simulating Virtual Reality?

Shares in Prosolvia, a Swedish virtual reality and simulation software company, were listed on the Stockholm Stock Exchange in 1997. The shares were oversubscribed at eight times the number of shares issued and the company was considered that year's darling on the Swedish Stock Exchange. In November 1997, *Dagens Industri*, the leading Swedish financial newspaper, and *Tjänstemannaförbundet*, the Salaried Employees' Union, chose Prosolvia as the 1997 Business Service Provider. Prosolvia had shown strong growth and profit in its first year as a publicly traded company, and when its 1997 annual report was issued in April 1998, the company's success was reflected in its skyrocketing share price. However, *Dagens Industri* then alleged there were accounting irregularities and intentionally inflated profits at the company (Hermele, 1998). Although Prosolvia denied the alleged irregularities, its share price soon dropped by 29 %, and seven months after the newspaper story, Prosolvia was in bankruptcy. Eight thousand Prosolvia shareholders, including many small investors, lost their money.

Manipulation of business results can occur when management deliberately takes advantage of the inevitable flexibility of interpretation allowed by accounting principles. Using such elastic interpretations, Prosolvia exploited accounting standards, and went even further by challenging the law. Using fictitious invoices, as well as invented agreements and premature income recognition, as described below, Prosolvia fabricated sales and overstated consolidated net income (Agerman, 2005). Additionally, the company lost public trust once the evidence of insider trading among the executives was revealed (Agerman, 2005).

### 17.2.3 Reconstruction of Ownership

Prosolvia had developed the concept of Virtual Reality Centres (VR-centres) to use as sales channels for the company's products and to function as education units, showrooms and product developers. All centres were owned and managed by a newly formed company called Interactive Visual Simulation International Gothenburg AB (IVS). Prosolvia owned 50.5 % of the shares of IVS, and Industrifonden (a large multi-sector, early stage investor in Swedish growth companies) owned the remaining 49.5 % of the shares. The understanding was that by the end of June 1997, Prosolvia would reduce its ownership in IVS to 49.5 % by selling shares to a non-profit association consisting of the VR-centres, their members and local partners. However, by the accounting year-end in December 1997, Prosolvia still owned the shares it had agreed to sell.

There was an agreement between Prosolvia and IVS that Prosolvia would deliver hardware and software to the VR-centres and that IVS would buy these products. Because of this agreement, a significant amount of Prosolvia's sales were to IVS, and Prosolvia's profits were therefore heavily dependent on the IVS sales.

The main accounting criticism of Prosolvia was that IVS, an unprofitable company in 1997, was not properly included in the consolidated accounts of the Prosolvia Group. According to Swedish accounting rules, IVS, which was owned 50.5 % by Prosolvia, should have been accounted for as a subsidiary company. If the inter-company sales revenues and costs of Prosolvia and IVS had been consolidated using acquisition accounting, the consolidated net income would have presented a truer and fairer result. Prosolvia's group profit would have been considerably reduced (Andersen, 1999). However, it wasn't just the 50.5 % ownership structure which suggested that Prosolvia controlled IVS; in Prosolvia's press releases, IVS was always mentioned as a company over which Prosolvia had complete control. *Prima facie*, therefore, Prosolvia had direct control over IVS and should have accounted for it as a subsidiary company. However, Prosolvia did not consider themselves to be owners. Prosolvia's critics labelled this method of increasing the consolidated net income 'reconstruction of ownership'.

### 17.2.4 Fictitious Invoices, Invented Agreements and Premature Income Recognition

At the end of 1997, a large part of Prosolvia's sales revenues for the year were uncollected as their accounts receivable balance showed. The company's practice was to invoice potential customers as soon as they merely expressed interest in Prosolvia's products. Thus, in many cases, revenue was recognised without firm agreements with the customers. Some of these sales were completed, others not. Moreover, Prosolvia recognised as sales the mere delivery of CDs with software marked product information to potential customers (Lind and Olsson, 2003). In one instance, one Prosolvia invoice was even to a non-existent Russian company.

These various bogus invoices totalled almost €4.9 million, substantially increasing Prosolvia's profits (Lind and Olsson, 2003). In addition, Prosolvia did not set up an allowance for bad debts for many of these very doubtful and even false accounts receivable that appeared on the balance sheet in their entirety without comment. Finally, the accounts receivable were overstated at the end of 1997 because sales that were not completed until

1998 were recognised prematurely, violating the principle of revenue recognition. Of course, the effect was also to increase profit for 1997 (Lind and Olsson, 2003).

### 17.2.5 Insider Trading

Besides the accounting problems at Prosolvia, there was one instance of potential insider trading that was not reported properly. Morgan Herou, a manager, failed to report his sale of 189 750 Prosolvia shares within the time period stipulated for reporting insider trades. According to Herou, he had made only an inadvertent, administrative mistake. However, an e-mail revealed that Herou had proposed to the company's financial manager that they should claim the report was made in time, despite evidence to the contrary. Herou was fined by the Swedish Financial Supervisory Authority for this mistake (Lind and Olsson, 2003; Samuelsson, 1998).

After Prosolvia entered bankruptcy, the bankruptcy trustees initiated inquiries that resulted in further analysis and many unanswered questions. A criminal investigation began and in January 2004, the chief prosecutor opened legal proceedings against Prosolvia's founders, its chief of finance and its auditors. The investigation revealed that Prosolvia had falsely reported growth and earnings. The 1997 income of €9 million was really a loss of €7 million, in the main because of Prosolvia's recognition of sales revenue without transfer of ownership before contracts were written or delivery made (Lind and Olsson, 2003). After 100 days of the legal process, the verdict was that the contracts were fictitious and sales revenues was thus overstated. While the accounting falsification was proven, all of the accused individuals, who blamed each other, were acquitted as they successfully argued that they had no knowledge of any misrepresentations in the financial statements (Agerman, 2005).

## 17.3 TWO SCANDALS IN MULTINATIONALS THAT DOMINATED THE SWEDISH MEDIA

At the beginning of the new millennium, the Enron scandal in the USA and the bursting of the worldwide dot-com bubble caused the Swedish business and financial media to shift their focus from issues of shareholder value to detailed accounting issues. Their scrutiny focused not only on the accounting practices of IT companies, like Prosolvia, but also on the wider business community. Problems at two Swedish multinationals, Asea Brown Boveri (ABB) and Skandia (two of the oldest publicly listed corporations in Sweden), attracted much media attention due to their importance on the Stockholm Stock Exchange and in Swedish society. The case of ABB is not fraud, but demonstrates the flexibility of accounting and how different sets of accounting standards will give different results.

### 17.3.1 ABB – Shaken and Stirred

ABB has a long and illustrious history of technological leadership and innovation in many industries. To its credit, the company has made many innovative breakthroughs in developing the world's first three-phase transmission system, high-speed locomotives, self-cooling transformers and synthetic diamonds. For years, ABB has fascinated business leaders, researchers, scholars, managers and management gurus around the world; it is said that ABB is the world's most popular business case study (Barham and Heimer, 1998).

ABB began as two companies that competed in a single market: the Swedish company, Asea (founded in 1883) and the Swiss company, Brown Boverie et Cie (founded in 1891). In 1988, the two companies merged to form Asea Brown Boveri (ABB), becoming one of the world's largest electrical engineering companies. The merger was politically and managerially complex and caused some turmoil in the electrical engineering industry. The acquisition strategy of the new company was to increase its competitive position in its existing, non-governmental markets as well as in new, often government-controlled, markets (Barham and Heimer, 1998). During the 1990s, the company won several business honours and was held up as a standard for management practice worldwide (Carlsson and Nachemson-Ekwall, 2003). ABB's president, Percy Barnevik, who later became ABB's chairman of the board, was repeatedly named one of the world's ten most respected business leaders.

### 17.3.1.1 Description of the Crises

For ABB, 1995 was its best year with the highest profit in its history. Nevertheless, many analysts said it was when the company's downward slide began. During 1996, the company lost several important Asian contracts and orders, and Göran Lindahl, ABB's CEO, reacted by launching a restructuring programme in which factories were closed and fourteen thousand employees in high-cost countries lost their positions. The cost of this programme was €678 million, and ABB's share price fell sharply.

However, during 1999 a programme of divestments and acquisitions in the process automation market appeared to turn the company around. In February 2000, ABB's market value was its highest ever at approximately €47 300 million. The quarterly report for the first three months of 2000 exceeded the investors' most sanguine expectations. However, the analysts failed to notice that the process automation market was struggling, and ABB's acquisitions did not make up for the revenues lost from the divestments. ABB's second-quarter results were disappointing. Additionally, because of its plans to list on a US stock exchange, ABB switched from International Accounting Standards (IAS) to US generally accepted accounting principles (US GAAP) in 2000. As a result of this change, 40 % of the reported net income for 2000 'vanished' due to different accounting treatments of non-operating revenue sources such as property and business disposals. Under IAS, ABB was legally able to inflate its operating income with the gains from the sales of these various assets. However, US GAAP did not permit this accounting practice, requiring these gains to be separately stated as items of income.

ABB's 2000 annual report also brought the company's asbestos losses to world attention. Previously, the company had quite legally effectively hidden these losses in the financial statements by offsetting them against gains from asset disposals. In January 2002, ABB's CEO announced a loss for 2001. It was the first loss in company history since 1934. In the aftermath of the public outrage, Lindahl and Barnevik had left, but repaid €157 million of their €233 million severance packages to the company. The effects of the loss and the revelation of the severance packages on ABB's reputation were shattering. ABB was no longer seen as the very successful company analysts had promoted and investors had trusted.

   Three main factors, described next, explain why ABB traded so long without investors detecting its poor performance: the use of IAS rather than US GAAP, buying back its own shares and its continual reorganisations.

## Switch to US GAAP

Listing on the New York Stock Exchange in 2001 meant that ABB had to change from IAS to US GAAP. At the time, there were various important differences between these two sets of accounting principles. Among them, broadly speaking, was the issue of how and when to account for acquisitions, disposals, restructurings and income from asset dispositions. Under US GAAP, gains and losses on such business transactions were generally accounted for in the financial years they occurred, while IAS allowed the losses to be allocated forward over time. In this issue, US GAAP therefore took a more conservative approach to income determination. According to some analysts, in the first year after a change of accounting principles to US GAAP from IAS a drop in operating profit of some 10–15 % was typically expected (Carlsson and Nachemson-Ekwall, 2003). This demonstrates the flexibility of accounting and how different sets of accounting standards will give different results.

   However, ABB had severely underestimated the difference in profit as calculated under the two sets of accounting principles. In fact, the change from IAS to US GAAP resulted in 40 % lower operating profit for ABB in the year 2000 (Carlsson and Nachemson-Ekwall, 2003). Any comparison between IAS and US GAAP for 2000 was not shown in the report. However, the 1999 operating results, restated using US GAAP, were about €1 million less than had been calculated under IAS (Carlsson and Nachemson-Ekvall, 2003). Much of this difference depended on what critics called creative accounting, whereas it was legally correct, since ABB's profit for several years had been inflated by regularly and deliberately boosting operating income with the inclusion of the extraordinary income from asset dispositions (Carlsson and Nachemson-Ekvall, 2003). Moreover, under IAS, ABB had accounted for restructuring costs as a provision that could be expensed forward; under US GAAP, these costs were written off immediately.

   The switch to US GAAP highlighted another, and probably more serious, problem for ABB. Asbestos disease-related claims had been filed against an American subsidiary of ABB that had used asbestos in its manufacturing in the 1970s. ABB estimated the asbestos liabilities at potentially at least €940 million. Although ABB was well aware of the asbestos claims, under IAS the company had not expensed them since they had not yet been settled or paid. Under US GAAP, these liabilities had to be accrued currently on the assumption they were probable and could be estimated. Thus, in ABB's 2000 financial statements, the world learned of the huge, impending financial problems facing the company. Previously, under IAS, these contingent liabilities had been described only in a note in the annual reports, in effect minimising the asbestos problem. In the 2000 financial statements, under US GAAP, the asbestos claims resulted in an additional loss provision of €355 million for 1999 and an additional amount of €76 million for 2000. Under IAS, these provisions had been treated less directly in the annual reports: sometimes as a provision in an unconsolidated company and sometimes as part of a liquidated company. In this way, ABB used other entities as a 'trash can' for different costs, including the asbestos costs. With such lack of transparency, calculating the effect of the asbestos claims on ABB's financial position was very difficult.

This meant that neither ABB board members, nor the external analysts nor the investors understood the real cost of the asbestos claims. For a number of years, the problem was ongoing as there appeared to be no limit to potential claims as the litigation dragged through the US courts (Carlsson and Nachemson-Ekwall, 2003).

*Trading in Own Shares*

For companies, there are many motives for buying back one's own shares. One possible motive may be the expectation that future dividends can be increased when there are fewer outstanding shares, leading to an increase in share price if the market weighs the increased dividend per share favourably. Of course, surplus cash is required, both for the acquisition of the company's own shares and the increased dividend payments.

Thinking it could maintain its share price at a high level, in 2001 ABB purchased 13 million of its own shares for €1.6 billion (Carlsson and Nachemson-Ekwall, 2003). Lacking surplus cash, ABB, with its good credit rating with banks, was able to finance both the purchase of the shares and the payment of the dividends to shareholders. However, the market was displeased with this strategy and the share price fell, increasing the financial pressure on the company. ABB was then forced to sell large parts of its business, including two important divisions: parts of ABB structured finance for about €2440 million (Press release ABB 2002/09/04) and the entire Swedish real estate property for about €318 million (Press release ABB/2002/06/27).

*Continual Reorganisations and Confusing Accounting*

Their many divestments and acquisitions were part of ABB's overall business and financial strategy. However effective or ineffective these various reorganisations were, they made it difficult, if not almost impossible, to draw useful comparisons of financial results between the years. Large provisions for losses, large gains on disposal and a changing mix of subsidiaries in the consolidated statements all contributed to a confusing and complex presentation of financial results. Adding to the complexity was the change of accounting principles from IAS to US GAAP. It has been said that neither the ABB board, nor the financial analysts nor the business press could interpret ABB's accounting during these years (Carlsson and Nachemson-Ekwall, 2003).

### 17.3.2 Skandia – A Shooting Star Turns into a White Dwarf

Until a few years ago, Skandia was one of Sweden's greatest success stories. The company was well known for reporting its intellectual capital (Guthrie, 2001; Guthrie and Petty, 2000; Guthrie, Petty and Johanson, 2001; Mouritsen, Thorbjørnsen, Bukh *et al.*, 2005) even though it abandoned reporting on intellectual capital in 1996 (Rimmel, 2003). However, after its most successful business year in 2000, Skandia was rocked by a number of scandals.

Skandia, incorporated in 1855, was considered the first Swedish insurance company in the modern sense to be listed on the Stockholm Stock Exchange. In 1948, an insurance law was enacted in Sweden that forced Swedish mixed insurance companies to split into separate divisions. Thereafter, the Skandia Group became two divisions. Skandia Liv (in English,

Skandia Life), acting independently on the market, sold life insurance while Skandia sold other kinds of insurance (Englund, 1982). After years of success, in 1996, following a national financial crisis in Sweden, Skandia was forced to launch a three-year restructuring programme that transformed the company from a traditional insurer into a property and casualty insurance (P&C) international financial services corporation (Skandia, 1997). At the end of 1996, Lars-Eric Petersson, a strong personality, became Skandia's CEO and initiated the creation of the Scandinavian P&C insurer named 'If' that was formed when Skandia merged its P&C division with the P&C division of the Norwegian insurer Storebrand (Skandia, 2000). Skandia's strategy, to grow aggressively, was very successful in the years 1996 to 2000. Total turnover grew from €6.96 billion in 1996 to €23.41 billion in 2000 (mainly from unit-linked products). In 1996, 50 % of Skandia's turnover was from unit-linked products, but by 2000 it was almost 80 %. The company's largest markets were the US (57 % of total sales) and the UK (28 % of total sales). Market capitalisation increased from €2.43 billion in 1996 to €19.14 billion in 2000, and Skandia's share price rose steadily from €2.37 in 1996 to €18.17 in 2000 (Skandia, 1997; Skandia, 2001).

Analysts' valuations and forecasts placed Skandia in the top league of international financial institutions with an earnings multiple of about 50. This assessment was fuelled by calculations of Skandia's future earnings expected to arise from the introduction of embedded value accounting in their contracts (explained below). Investment banks, like Morgan Stanley Dean Witter and Goldman Sachs, valued Skandia at twelve times its balance sheet equity (Rimmel, 2003).

### 17.3.2.1 *Financial Troubles and Dubious Transactions*

In 1999, despite its record earnings of €976 million, the attention by the media and the investment community on some Skandia transactions revealed a financially troubled situation. As in prior years, Skandia's total earnings were rather unusually constructed. Nachemson-Ekwall and Carlsson (2004) demonstrated, for example, that its unit-linked products never really showed a profit and in fact produced a negative cash flow of €454 million. Analysts also expressed doubts about the way the company used embedded value accounting (Nachemson-Ekwall and Carlsson, 2004). In addition, Skandia's transference of its pension fund to Skandia Liv and the sale of the Skandia asset management division raised concerns as Skandia's management, trying to ease its financial burdens, began selling off parts of its business. The background and circumstances of these three problem areas are explained next.

#### Embedded Value Accounting

Since 1997, Skandia had valued its insurance contracts using an accounting practice called embedded value, which was done quite legally. This practice had been developed in the UK in order to assess the present value of an insurance company's contract portfolio. The calculation of embedded value is strongly influenced by the underpinning assumptions used to project future earnings (e.g., surrender ratio, fees, fund growth, inflation, taxes and mortality). These assumptions can change from year to year. Moreover, the risk discount rate applied is dependent on assumptions about future earnings and future expenditures. In order to make the embedded value calculation of their contract portfolio understandable, the reporting company should disclose all its assumptions (Vanderhoof, 1998). However, even with such required disclosures, some analysts have still criticised embedded value accounting as providing opaque information on insurance contracts (Beck-Friis, 2003). In Skandia's case, embedded value accounting was used to report constantly increased turnover and increased earnings. Skandia also wrongly thought embedded value accounting would lead to increased cash flows (Nachemson-Ekwall and Carlsson, 2004).

During Skandia's 1999 and 2000 annual general meetings (AGM), some analysts claimed it was not possible to evaluate Skandia's embedded value calculation since Skandia used a methodology that was based on assumptions that other insurance companies did not use. These analysts also voiced concerns about the impact of the embedded value accounting on Skandia's balance sheet (Rimmel, 2003). Furthermore, Skandia's assumptions behind the embedded value calculation, at management's discretion, were not fully disclosed. Skandia's use of embedded value accounting, therefore, can be seen as a case of creative accounting used to manipulate the value of their insurance contract portfolio (Nachemson-Ekwall and Carlsson, 2004). The lack of transparency in the assumptions disclosure was a violation of the intent of embedded value accounting and Rydbeck and Tidström (2003) advised Skandia in their investigation report to be more transparent in their disclosure.

## The Pension Fund Transfer

Despite Skandia's reported record earnings of €976 million in 1999, mainly due to embedded value accounting, the company also reported a record negative cash flow of about €454 million caused by the losses in the unit-linked business. In order to raise cash, Skandia sold its 'If' shares to Skandia Liv even though Skandia Liv, an independent company since 1948, might not have made such an investment on its own (Rimmel, 2003). Nominally, but not really, independent Skandia Liv therefore paid cash for the shares. A good deal for Skandia, but not for Skandia Liv. Skandia Liv also transferred almost €284 million of excess capital in Skandia's pension fund to Skandia, as Skandia Liv managed pensions for Skandia. This transaction raised concerns about Skandia Liv's independence, although Skandia Liv's actions were legally correct. According to the life insurance rules, Skandia Liv should have distributed any excess capital in the pension fund to the life insurance investors. The majority of these investors were savers from the general public in Sweden and were not Skandia employees (Nachemson-Ekwall and Carlsson, 2004).

## The SAM Deal

During 2001, Skandia's sales slumped and the company reported €1.8 billion in liabilities. Skandia's management was forced to sell Skandia Asset Management (SAM) in order to raise cash. As two-thirds of SAM's €32 billion of managed assets came from Skandia Liv's 1.2 million pension investors, Skandia Liv offered to buy SAM from Skandia for €378 million and to renegotiate the asset management contract with market-based conditions for SAM. This new deal was to be valid for twelve years with the possibility of renegotiation after seven years. However, surprisingly, Skandia instead sold SAM to Den Norske Bank (DnB) at a lower price than Skandia Liv had offered.

The financial press asked why Skandia sold its asset management division to an unknown actor in the capital markets, as DnB was at the time. Skandia Liv's pension investors were angry as their savings contracts showed clearly that they could not move their pension savings to an alternative asset manager. Fifteen thousand pension savers filed a class action suit against Skandia. In their view both the 'If' sale and the SAM sale showed that Skandia had misused Skandia Liv's assets to meet Skandia's capital needs. The allegations in the suit were that in the 'If' sale, Skandia coerced Skandia Liv to buy its shares, and in the SAM sale, Skandia sold off assets belonging to Skandia Liv.

In reality, Skandia Liv's management was not really independent of Skandia's management, despite the fact that the two companies were legally independent entities. Nachemson-Ekwall and Carlsson (2004) pointed out that one of Skandia Liv's directors was on Skandia's board and could have said no to the deal. Internal controls that would have prohibited such self-dealings by Skandia were ineffective or non-existent. Although Skandia's external auditors during this period did not criticise the transactions between Skandia Liv and Skandia, the auditors were deemed not liable (Rydbeck and Tidström, 2003).

As later revealed, the sales of 'If' and SAM were creative accounting transactions undertaken to disguise Skandia's severe capital needs (Schück, 2003). The SAM deal was especially dubious as Skandia sold the management of contracts that came from Skandia Liv pension savers. The class action lawsuit by the pension savers against Skandia included compensation to the pension savers and allegations of fraudulent accounting (Bratt and Crafoord, 2003). However, on 3 October 2008 the Arbitration Board reached an out-of-court agreement between Skandia and the class action members that gave €150 million in compensation to the pension savers (Fredriksson, 2008).

### 17.3.2.2  Managers' Hands in the Cookie Jar

2002 was an even worse year for Skandia's managers. Since the SAM sale, they had constantly been in the media's focus. *Dagens Industri*, the Swedish financial newspaper, revealed that Skandia Fastigheter (Skandia's real estate company) had provided a top manager with a luxury apartment at a sub-market rate and had also renovated this apartment at Skandia's expense. In the media storm that followed these revelations, further investigations produced a long list of Skandia managers who had also been provided with such apartments that were owned by the real estate company, Diligenta, which was owned by Skandia Liv.

In the spring of 2003, following the investigative newspaper articles on Skandia's management, the Swedish Shareholders' Association demanded answers from Skandia's management about remuneration programmes, transactions between Skandia and Skandia Liv and embedded value accounting. At Skandia's 2003 AGM, Skandia Liv, which was a shareholder and had a representative on Skandia's board, initiated an official investigation headed by Otto Rydbeck, an attorney at Setterwalls Advokatbyrå AB, and Göran Tidström, an auditor at Öhlings Price Waterhouse Coopers. Skandia's auditors, Ernst & Young, unsuccessfully challenged the need for an investigation report (Sundén, 2004). The day after the 2003 AGM, Skandia's CEO Lars-Eric Petersson resigned.

The investigation led by Rydbeck and Tidström (2003) examined the remuneration programmes, the Skandia Liv transactions and the embedded value accounting as well as the many rumours circulating in the media about the company and its managers. The investigation report revealed that Skandia paid for some €2.2 million of apartment renovations for Skandia's CEO and several top managers and also rented apartments to the manager's children in the most fashionable quarters in Stockholm at unreasonably low rents.

### 17.3.2.3 Incentives Programmes: 'WealthBuilder' and 'ShareTracker'

During the investigation of Skandia's senior management, the existing incentive programmes were also scrutinised. Among the eight long-term incentive programmes at Skandia, Rydbeck and Tidström unofficially singled out two programmes 'ShareTracker' and 'WealthBuilder,' names that pretty much reflected their nature (Rydbeck and Tidström, 2003). 'ShareTracker' and 'WealthBuilder' became the focus of further legal action against Skandia's board and top management.

The Skandia board introduced ShareTracker in August 1997 as a long-term incentive programme for Skandia's executives and senior managers that was to cover the period from 1997 to 1999. ShareTracker was an options programme that granted managers cash equivalent to the increased value of Skandia's share price if the current long-term benchmark interest rate of 8 % was exceeded. Each ShareTracker participant was granted a number of options that fixed these additional salaried cash payments from Skandia. At the beginning of 2000, participants were to be offered a replacement stock option programme. However, because of institutional shareholder resistance, the Skandia board decided to extend ShareTracker until 15 May 2000 (Rydbeck and Tidström, 2003; Nachemson-Ekwall and Carlsson, 2004). Eventually, the total cost of ShareTracker rose to €129 million as Skandia's share price had increased by more than 500 %. More than half of these payments resulted from the board's decision to extend ShareTracker until mid-May 2000. The highest award in this programme was €21 million and the lowest €71 000 (Rydbeck and Tidström, 2003; Nachemson-Ekwall and Carlsson, 2004).

The second focus of the investigation was the global incentive programme 'WealthBuilder' that the Skandia board created in April 1998 in Skandia's Assurance & Financial Services (AFS) business. WealthBuilder participants were granted shares whose value depended on the increased value of certain AFS companies, especially American Skandia, Skandia Life UK and Swedish Skandia Link. Initially, the AFS business was valued at €179 million, and the WealthBuilder calculations were based on the increase in the embedded value and the value of new business. The WealthBuilder programme was originally planned for 1998 and 1999, and the value of the share options was restricted to a maximum of €34 million. Thirty-eight employees qualified for these share options. In 1998 and 1999, the original timeframe of WealthBuilder, Skandia's AFS business more than doubled (Rydbeck and Tidström, 2003; Nachemson-Ekwall and Carlsson, 2004). Like ShareTracker, a replacement stock option programme was proposed for WealthBuilder participants for the year 2000. Again, some institutional shareholders requested that this decision be taken at the April 2000 AGM, but the Skandia board extended the original programme until 15 May 2000. However, the cap of €34 million was not applied. The total value of the share options under WealthBuilder was €114 million (Rydbeck and Tidström, 2003).

#### 17.3.2.4   Lawsuits Against Management and the End of Skandia

During the Rydbeck and Tidström investigation, the new Skandia management hired additional lawyers in order to take legal action against the former top managers. In October 2004, State Attorney Christian van der Kwast filed charges against former Skandia CEO Lars-Eric Petersson, former Skandia CFO Ulf Spång and former Skandia Liv CEO Ola Ramstedt for misusing corporate assets.

In May 2006, Petersson was sentenced to two years in prison by the Stockholm District Court for abusing a bonus scheme and for removing the ceiling on the management incentive programme WealthBuilder without authorisation. However, the court found Petersson not guilty of inflating his pension by approximately €4 million more than the Skandia board had approved. Consequently, Petersson did not have to repay the €18.7 million in claims Skandia had sued for (Carlberg, 2006). On 10 December 2007, Petersson successfully appealed the two years sentence for abusing the bonus scheme and his conviction was overturned by the Svea court of appeal (Westerlund and Lindqvist, 2007).

After replacing Petersson and the other top managers involved in the scandal, Skandia undertook a massive marketing campaign to rebuild its battered reputation. However, at almost the same time, in 2006, Skandia lost a hostile takeover bid by Old Mutual, a South African insurance firm, which Skandia management opposed but shareholders supported. In three years, a few managers ended Skandia's more than a century and a half tradition as an independent corporation.

# 17.4 CONCLUSIONS

When corporate financial scandals have occurred in Sweden, involving dubious accounting creativity at best and accounting fraud at worst in addition to the immediate legal ramifications, there is typically a renewed public debate concerning the aim and scope of accounting, its regulation and the role of auditors. Traditionally, such a debate has resulted in revisions to Swedish accounting standards and Swedish laws with the purpose of closing any loopholes that may have contributed to the errors of commission or omission that led to the scandals.

The Kreuger crash in the 1930s probably had the most significant impact on Swedish accounting regulation since it led to the enactment of securities laws in Sweden and in the US and to increased regulation of corporate financial information disclosures by listed companies (Flesher and Flesher, 1986). In Sweden, the existing Companies Act was revised to make accounting irregularities a prosecutable crime. The role of auditors in Sweden also changed radically after the 1930s. The new regulations made it mandatory for all corporations listed on the Stockholm Stock Exchange to have a statutory audit by an authorised or approved public accountant (Jönsson, 1991).

The Fermenta Report by Walberg, Hanner and Rodhe made a number of recommendations to the Stockholm Stock Exchange aimed at strengthening control of companies. One recommendation was to amend the Swedish Companies Act vis-à-vis related-party disclosures to forbid the domination of entrepreneurial companies by one person responsible for a combination of different functions (e.g. one person as both chairman of the board and

CEO). Another recommendation was to tighten the laws on insider trading. The Stockholm Stock Exchange itself recommended increasing the contact between auditors, management and shareholders, reserving to itself the option of appointing auditors in cases where it suspected irregularities (Walberg *et al.*, 1988). However, none of these recommendations was enacted.

The cases (like Prosolvia) involving economic crime have resulted in several proactive steps by the Swedish government. In 1998, the Swedish National Economic Crimes Bureau was established with its primary purpose being to detect and impede economic crime. The Bureau's main task is to investigate tax evasion and illegal insider dealing, but it also deals with financial fraud, embezzlement and economic swindles (Bureau, 1997, p. 898). The Swedish scandals, particularly the Skandia case, have also led to legislation requiring different regulations for independent auditors (i.e. stricter on whistleblowing and auditor independence) for life insurance companies than for other corporations. Moreover, since 1999, Swedish external auditors have a duty to report economic crimes they suspect are being committed by managers or board directors to the public prosecutor. This last law was also a recommendation in the Fermenta Report.

It is of interest that in the cases described in this chapter, top management was heavily involved in the events that led to the loss of investor confidence, investigations and/or prosecutions. In three cases, the companies were led by very powerful, charismatic and trusted leaders – El-Sayed at Fermenta, Barnevik at ABB and Petersson at Skandia – who seemingly were outside the reach of normal accounting controls. If internal control over management had been better, the problems at all four companies described in this chapter might have become known sooner, possibly in time to avoid the catastrophic financial events that followed. Nor was there any evidence of whistle-blowing by the external auditors. It was only in the Fermenta case that an auditor blew the whistle, and he was an internal auditor. In all four cases, the external auditors, as well as management, seemed in some sense to fail in their fiduciary responsibility to protect the companies' resources and reputations and to provide the investment community with reliable financial reporting.

These corporate scandals, whether from fraud or creative accounting, especially at ABB and Skandia, caused a tremendous loss of confidence in major parts of Swedish business. In September 2002, the Swedish government appointed a Commission on Business Confidence to establish a dialogue with key members of the business sector for the purpose of improving confidence in the business sector and considering changes in regulations and norms. The Commission set up a special working group to look into these issues.[2] Concluding that poor corporate governance was a key factor in the loss of confidence in business, this group developed a voluntary, self-regulated Swedish Code of Corporate Governance, introduced in 2004 and intended for Swedish companies listed on the Stockholm Stock Exchange. Under the Code, companies can either choose to comply with the regulations or explain, in their annual reports or elsewhere, why they do not.

---

[2] This group was comprised of FAR (Institute of Swedish Accountancy Profession), the Swedish Industry and Commerce Stock Exchange Committee, the Stockholm Stock Exchange, the Swedish Bankers' Association, the Swedish Securities Dealers' Association, the Confederation of Swedish Enterprise, the Swedish Shareholders' Association and the Swedish Insurance Federation (SOU, 2004, p. 46).

The Swedish Code of Corporate Governance aims to create transparency in company reporting that will benefit shareholders, the capital markets and society. In particular, the Code pays attention to creating transparency of disclosure in remuneration programmes for senior management. Companies that apply the Swedish Code of Governance should report such remuneration programmes, their estimated costs as well as the dilution that such incentive programmes may have on a company's share price. The Swedish financial media, however, remains rather sensitive, if not suspicious, toward new remuneration programmes. In early 2006, there was outrage in the Swedish media when SEB, the Swedish bank, disclosed that its 2006 remuneration scheme for 800 managers in 2006 cost €62 million (Cervenka, 2006).

In Sweden, the new regulations and increased press scrutiny have not, however, halted the practice of creative accounting entirely. In 2006, ABB caught the media's attention again as new cases of creative accounting came to light. Additionally, Swedish banks revealed large bonus schemes for top management, and the Scandinavian airline SAS had to confirm, before the publication of its 2006 annual report, that their Spanish subsidiary had reported costs as revenues. In these cases, however, the external auditors and the corporations were careful to be very transparent about the problems before they developed into scandals.

# REFERENCES

For convenience, the references have also been translated into English.

Agerman, P. (2005), 'Lessons from the Prosolvia case', (Lärdomar av Prosolviadomen). *Affärsvärlden.*

Aldeholm, P.-A. and Olsson, H. (1995), 'Auditor's legal responsibilities – referring to the background of Fermenta and Gusum', (Revisorns juridiska ansvar – mot bakgrund av Fermenta och Gusum), *Balans,* **1**(11), 8–14.

Andersen, A. (1999), *Investigation on Behalf of Ackordcentralen* (Utredning på uppdrag av ackordcentralen).

Barham, K. and Heimer, C. (1998), *ABB the Dancing Giant: Creating the Globally Connected Corporation,* Financial Times/Pitman, Prentice Hall. London.

Beck-Friis, U. (2003), 'There's more to investigate' (Det fins mer att utreda). *Svenska Dagbladet.*

Bränfeldt, L.-E. (2006), 'Fermenta – the scandal everyone would like to forget' (Fermenta: Skandalen som alla vill glömma). *Affärsvärlden.*

Bratt, P. and Crafoord, C. (2003), 'Court appeal for class action suit against Skandia' (Ansökan Om Stämning Grupptalan mot Skandia). Advokatbyrån Bratt & Feinsilber AB.

Bureau, S. N. E. C. (1997: 898), *Ordinance Containing Instruction for the Swedish National Economic Crimes Bureau.*

Carlberg, P. (2006), 'He won against Skandia: Lars-Eric Petersson slips 173 million kronors claim' (Han vann mot Skandia : Lars-Eric Petersson slipper skadestånd på 173 miljoner kronor). *Svenska Dagbladet (SvD).*

Carlsson, B. and Nachemson-Ekwall, S. (2003), *Dangerous management: the history of the ABB crash* (Livsfarlig ledning: historien om kraschen i ABB), Ekerlid, Stockholm.

Cervenka, A. (2006), 'SEB top managers share 2 billion SEK' (SEB-toppar delar på 2 miljarder), *Affärsvärlden.*

Englund, K. (1982), *Insurance Companies on the Move – from Skandia to Skandia Group – 1855–1980*. Skandia Insurance Co. Ltd. Stockholm, Sweden.

Flesher, D.L. and Flesher, T.K. (1986), 'Ivar Kreugar's Contribution to U.S. Financial Reporting', *The Accounting Review*, **61**(3), 421.

Fredriksson, T. (2008), 'Savers in Skandia Liv gets money back' (Sparare i Skandia Liv får pengar tillbaka), *Sveriges Radio*.

Guthrie, J. (2001), 'The management, measurement and the reporting of intellectual capital'. *Journal of Intellectual Capital*, **2**(1), 27–41.

Guthrie, J. and Petty, R. (2000), 'Intellectual capital: Australian annual reporting practices'. *Journal of Intellectual Capital*, **1**(3), 241–251.

Guthrie, J., Petty, R. and Johanson, U. (2001), 'Sunrise in the knowledge economy: Managing, measuring and reporting intellectual capital', *Accounting, Auditing & Accountability Journal*, **14**(4), 365–384.

Hermele, B. (1998), 'Mistakes and problems in Prosolvia's annual report' (Fel och oklarheter i Prosolvias bokslut). *Dagens Industri*. Stockholm.

Jönsson, S. (1991), 'Role making for accounting while the state is watching', *Accounting, Organizations and Society*, **16**(5–6), 521–546.

Jönsson, S. (1994), 'Changing Accounting Regulatory Structures in the Context of a Strong State', *Critical Perspectives on Accounting*, **5**(4), 341–360.

Jönsson, S. and Marton, J. (1994), 'Sweden'. In J. Flower and J.O. Elling (eds), *The Regulation of Financial Reporting in the Nordic Countries*, Fritze, Stockholm.

Larsson, B. (2005), 'Auditor regulation and economic crime policy in Sweden, 1965–2000'. *Accounting, Organizations and Society*, **30**(2), 127–144.

Lind, P. and Olsson, A. (eds) (2003), *Court appeal for TR lawsuit B1799-00* (Ansökan om stämning, TR mål B1799-00).

Mouritsen, J., Thorbjørnsen, S., Bukh, P.N. and Johansen, M.R. (2005), 'Intellectual capital and the discourses of love and entrepreneurship in new public management'. *Financial Accountability and Management*, **21**(3), 279–290.

Nachemson-Ekwall, S. and Carlsson, B. (2004), *Golden rain – Skandia's saga* (Guldregn – sagan om Skandia), Bonnier Fakta.

Petersson, C. (1987), *Refaat och spelet kring Fermenta*, Stockholm, Gedin.

Rimmel, G. (2003), *Human Resource Disclosures – A Comparative Study of Annual Reporting Practice About Information, Providers and Users in Two Corporations*, BAS Publishing House, Göteborg.

Rydbeck, O. and Tidström, G. (2003), *Investigation Report* (Granskningsrapport). Försäkringsbolaget Skandia (PUBL).

Samuelsson, M. (1998), 'Prosolvia: 'Orderliness of the financial statements' (Ordring och reda i redovisuingen). *Tidningarnas Telegrambyrå*.

Schück, J. (2003), 'Skandia's inflated earnings' (Skandias sätt att räkna blåste upp vinsterna). *Dagens Nyheter*.

Skandia (1997), *Skandia Annual Report 1996*, Stockholm, Sweden, Skandia Insurance Company Ltd.

Skandia (2000), *Skandia Annual Report 1999*, Stockholm, Sweden, Skandia Insurance Company Ltd.

Skandia (2001), *Annual Report 2000*, Stockholm, Sweden, Skandia Insurance Company Ltd.

SOU (2004), Swedish Code of Corporate Governance. In Report, S.G.O. (ed.) Ministry of Finance, p. 46.

Sundén, M. (2004), 'Full auditors' war in Skandia scandal' (Fullt reviorskrig i Skandiahärvan). *Svenska Dagbladet.*

Sundqvist, S.-I. (1986), 'Volvo buy themselves free from arrangements: El-Sayed may loan half a billion' (Volvo 'köper sig fri' från uppgörelse: El-Sayed får låna halv miljard). *Dagens Nyheter (DN)*

Vanderhoof, I.T. (1998), 'Introduction'. In I.T. Vanderhoof and E.I. Altman (eds), *The Fair Value of Insurance Liabilities,* Kluwer Academic Publishers, Boston, MA.

Wahlström, G. (2000), *New Prerequisites to Regulate Financial Accounting – a Study on Accounting Practice Regarding Financial Instruments* (Nya förutsättningar för reglering av extern redovisning – en praxisundersökning mot bakgrund av finansiella instrument). Parajett AB.

Walberg, S., Hanner, P.V.A. and Rodhe, K. (1988), *Fermenta fakta och erfarenheter – en rapport till Stockholms Fondbörs (Fermenta facts and experiences – a report for the Stockholm Exchange),* Stockholm.

Westerlund, K. and Lindqvist, R. (2007), 'Svea Court of Appeal freed Lars-Eric Petersson' (Svea hovrätt friar Lars-Eric Petersson). *Dagens Nyheter (DN)*

Wifstrand, J. (1987), 'Auditor's critique against Fermenta: Here is the secret protocol' (Revisorernas kritik mot Fermenta: Här är det hemliga protokollet). *Dagens Nyheter (DN).*

# Creative Accounting – The UK Experience

David Gwilliam and Richard H.G. Jackson

## 18.1 INTRODUCTION

In early May 1993 Asil Nadir, a prominent UK businessman of Turkish Cypriot origin, left his London house and was driven to a small, picturesque airfield in Dorset where he boarded a light plane which flew him to Beauvais in Northern France. There he transferred to a private jet which flew, via Vienna (where refreshments of caviar and champagne were taken on board) and Istanbul, to northern Cyprus[1]. Nadir, who at that time was on trial for the alleged theft of £34 million, and thought to be subject to bail conditions, did not return to the UK but continued to reside, in same luxury, in northern Cyprus, which does not have an extradition treaty with the UK.[2] However, in August 2010, following a high court ruling that Nadir would be allowed bail if he voluntarily returned to the UK, and accompanied by a high level of publicity and media attention, Nadir flew into Luton airport ahead of a case management hearing at the Old Bailey in early September.[3] Nadir's earlier departure, which caused no little embarrassment to the authorities, was just one more dramatic incident in the extraordinary saga of Polly Peck – the business which Nadir had, within a decade, virtually single-handedly, transformed from an obscure garment manufacturer with turnover of just £1 million into a fruit packing and electrical conglomerate which was one of the UK's largest, and apparently most successful, companies. More than two and a half years before Nadir's flight from justice, Polly Peck had collapsed almost overnight, with reported balance sheet net assets of almost £1 billion being transformed in the subsequent administrators' report to a deficiency of over £550 million.

In this chapter, we delve into the manner in which financial reporting, and the underlying accounting policy choice, played a role in creating and sustaining the fiction of Polly Peck. We do this against a contextual background which briefly traces salient episodes in the

---

[1] The northern part of Cyprus was invaded by Turkey in 1974, and is styled by Turkey as the 'Turkish Republic of Northern Cyprus' (TRNC). It is not, however, recognised by the UN as an independent state and is essentially an adjunct of Turkey. In this chapter we use the term 'northern Cyprus' to refer to the Territory.

[2] The conviction for perverting the course of justice of Peter Dimond, the pilot who assisted Nadir to leave the UK, was subsequently quashed when the Court of Appeal held that technically Nadir was not on bail at the time of his departure.

[3] We note that Nadir has consistently claimed to be innocent in relation to all the allegations made against him and has long held the position that he would return to the UK provided agreement as to bail conditions could be reached. According to *The Observer*, 1 May 2005: 'The former tycoon has always loudly protested his innocence, and tried to broker a jail-free return to London last year, but was firmly rebuffed by British prosecutors.' However, he has now returned to face trial as the Serious Fraud Office has agreed not to oppose bail (Adams, 2010).

*Creative Accounting, Fraud and International Accounting Scandals*   Edited by Michael Jones
© 2011 Michael Jones. Published by John Wiley & Sons, Ltd

narrative of accounting manipulation in the UK – which includes the 1991 collapses of the Bank of Credit and Commerce International and the Mirror Group.[4] These, which occurred slightly later than the Polly Peck debacle, are not covered in the depth we afford Polly Peck (there is already a wealth of literature upon them) – but they are important both because of their sheer scale and public impact and also because of the impetus they provided to regulatory and governance reform. We then consider the detail of the Polly Peck case and its implications for changes in accounting standard setting and in the mechanisms of governance of corporations. This is followed by a short reprise of developments in the UK subsequent to the demise of Polly Peck, and the chapter concludes with some observations and reflections as to the wider lessons to be learnt.

Although this chapter considers several of the notorious commercial episodes of the early 1990s, it does not aim to provide a treatment of all the major corporate insolvencies (some associated and some unassociated with accounting issues) of that era: such would constitute a book in itself.

## 18.2 HISTORICAL BACKGROUND

Financial accounting and financial reporting in the UK have a long and, for the greater part, distinguished history (see, for example, Edwards, 1989). There is little doubt that the accounting discipline has directly and indirectly contributed to the growth and success of modern commercial entities. Financial reporting through income statements, balance sheets, cash flow statements and associated disclosures has made a significant contribution to the development of capital markets in the UK and beyond. That is not to say, however, that there have not been a number of episodes of controversy which have caused crises of confidence – many of which have been associated with what might be generically termed 'creative accounting'.

Paradoxically, whereas in most areas of human activity creativity is considered to have positive connotations, in financial reporting creativity is not seen as a virtue at all. As discussed in the introduction to this book, however, the term is applied very broadly and may cover a variety of activity – from that where the purpose is purely to present a more informative picture of the entity's activities to that where the intent is to cover up fraud. Within this domain lie an almost infinite variety of different scenarios and, as we shall see in the specific case considered in more detail below, these may well overlap and indeed intertwine.[5]

Consequent to the industrial revolution, it was in the UK in the nineteenth century that periodic financial statements first came to acquire an importance in commercial life, given impetus by the accounting and audit requirements of the 1844 Joint Stock Act. This was accompanied by increasing interest in accounting issues, initially primarily those relating to asset valuation and to the legality of dividend distributions (Edwards, 1989; French, 1977). Periodically, these issues would come to further prominence when apparently prosperous businesses came to nought as confidence and credit deserted them.

---

[4] Strictly speaking, the Mirror Group was one part of the Maxwell empire which did not, in fact, collapse, surviving until it later merged to form Trinity Mirror. We continue with the common, if slightly inaccurate, usage and refer to Mirror Group throughout this chapter.

[5] There would, however, not appear to have ever been creative accounting in the UK of a similar nature to that perpetrated on a small US hosiery manufacturing company whose accountant created on paper, for no apparent motive other than his own amusement, a highly successful enterprise (see McCarten, 1939).

At the end of the nineteenth century one of the most notable of such cases was the collapse of the Liberator Building Society (McKie, 2004), then the largest UK building society, which saw the downfall of the business empire of Jabez Balfour – once described as 'striding like a colossus' across the London business world. Following a decline in property valuations and a run on the London and General Bank (another company within the Balfour empire), a mass of intercompany transactions imploded. The businesses collapsed and Balfour fled to Patagonia where, with a degree of local assistance, he managed to resist extradition for three years. He was ultimately returned to the UK, convicted of fraud and sentenced to a long term of imprisonment. Here the accounting issues related primarily to valuations. One website describes Balfour's *modus operandi* as follows:

> However as was soon to become all too clear his entire business empire was built on deceit; the declared profits were an illusion and nothing more than mere accounting entries. The nature of the fraud perpetrated by Jabez was fairly straightforward; it simply involved moving assets between his various companies at inflated prices, allowing the selling companies to declare paper profits and thus permitting the payment of large bonuses to Jabez and his cronies and handsome dividends to the shareholders.[6]

These accounting practices and the quality of the audit procedures led to civil and criminal litigation. This included the landmark London and General Bank case (1895) which, together with Kingston Cotton Mill (1896), set the basis for the determination of UK auditors' duties. But although these, and other Victorian and Edwardian cases (e.g. Irish Woollen Co., 1900; London Oil Storage, 1904), are well known, there was little sophistication in the accounting manipulations.

The inter-war period brought forth a spectacular *cause célèbre*: the Royal Mail Steam Packet Company (RMSP) case (dealt with in more depth in Chapter 7) saw the prosecution of both the chairman and the auditor, a senior Price Waterhouse partner. The parent company had, in the 1920s, consistently reported profits during a period of depressed trading conditions. This apparent profitability was provided by a combination of the release of provisions against income tax and duty, and the receipt of dividends from subsidiaries – which, in part, are likely to have been from profits of earlier years (RMSP, like many other companies at the time, did not prepare group accounts: see Bircher, 1988).[7] There was almost no disclosure in the financial statements of RMSP of the breakdown of the reported change in the profit and loss reserves, other than that in 1926 and 1927 where the phrase 'Including adjustment of Taxation Reserves' was inserted at the behest of the audit partner. In the trial, the jury found the audit partner and the chairman not guilty of charges relating to the financial statements themselves; but the chairman was found guilty on an associated prospectus charge. The impact of the Royal Mail case was fundamental. Although the successful defence claimed that 'secret reserve accounting' was an accepted practice,[8] the attention drawn to it indubitably contributed to its general demise (Arnold

---

[6] http://everything2.com/index.pl?node_id=1829575.

[7] The group structure was a complicated one, with complex cross holdings between companies and high gearing. See Davies and Bourn (1972) for analysis of the structure and Arnold (1991) for a detailed analysis of the make-up of the reported profitability of the company.

[8] Lord Plender, a former President of ICAEW, said in evidence that it was 'quite usual for large commercial and industrial companies to set aside out of an unusually prosperous year sums to secret reserves'. A review of corporate disclosure practice of the time (Arnold, 1997) suggests that the use of secret reserve accounting increased markedly in the first quarter of the twentieth century, with more than a quarter of his sample using such practices extensively.

and Collier, 2007). Furthermore, the case provided an impetus both for the introduction of more comprehensive profit and loss disclosures and compulsory requirements for group accounting – although these did not enter UK company law until 1947 (see Bircher, 1988).

The remainder of the 1930s, the 1940s and the 1950s was a relatively fallow period as measured by the number of accounting scandals. A number of reasons may account for this, including the recovery of the economy and corporate profitability in the later 1930s, and the very different commercial conditions in war time as compared to those in the immediate post-war period (including the absorption into public ownership of very significant parts of British industry). In the absence of *ex post* investigation, it is difficult to establish the extent or nature of creative accounting over this period – which was still one characterized by an almost complete absence of formal UK standards[9] and limited disclosure requirements. Some would conjecture that at this time the accounting and auditing profession exercised their duties with a greater degree of rigour than subsequently; others would suggest that the lack of standards enabled forms of creative accounting to continue.

In the 1960s the continuing growth in the economy, increasing importance of capital markets and emergence of a market for corporate control saw accounting issues thrust again into the limelight – most notably by the bitterly contested struggle for control of electrical manufacturing company AEI by GEC (see Chapter 7 for more details). During the battle AEI issued a 1967 profit forecast of £10 million; after its acquisition of AEI, in July 1968 GEC released figures which indicated that the 1967 result for AEI was a loss of £4.5 million. Much of this gap was ostensibly caused by differences of judgement with respect to long-term contracts. Whether or not those judgements were appropriate at the time is difficult to determine (see Macve, 1997 and Rutherford, 1996 for further details). Shortly after this the collapse in 1971 of one of the UK's most prestigious manufacturers, Rolls Royce, and the realization that its profitability and balance sheet had been sustained for many years by capitalizing aero engine development costs, also occasioned much adverse comment with respect to the relative freedom of existing accounting policy choices (DTI, 1973; Edwards and Shaoul, 1999).

The publicity, controversy and subsequent recriminations generated by the GEC/AEI affair had significant implications for the development of UK financial reporting as, following an ICAEW initiative, it prompted the professional accounting bodies to come together in 1969 to form the Accounting Standards Steering Committee, the forerunner of the Accounting Standards Committee (ASC), and its successor the Accounting Standards Board (ASB) (see Rutherford, 2007).[10]

## 18.3 SOME RECENT ACCOUNTING SCANDALS

Although the 1970s and early 1980s saw the first tranche of formalized UK accounting standards, it is the 1980s which are usually characterized as the golden era of creative

---

[9] The Institute of Chartered Accountants in England and Wales (ICAEW), then the largest and most important body of professional accountants in the UK, issued 29 influential but non-mandatory *Recommendations on Accounting Principles* between 1942 and 1969.

[10] From 1971 until 1990 the ASC was responsible for setting Statements of Standard Accounting Practice (SSAPs) in the UK. The ASB, an independent body operating as a sub-board of the newly created Financial Reporting Council (FRC), replaced the ASC in 1990. It took over the existing SSAPs and commenced the issue of a series of Financial Reporting Standards (FRSs).

accounting in the UK. Indeed, it was at this time that the term 'creative accounting' first entered the public domain, popularized by Griffiths (1986). Why this should be is difficult to explain, but a combination of the following factors probably contributed: the ever-growing importance of financial and capital markets; more complex commercial practice; innovations in executive compensation mechanisms; a possible decline in auditing professional values and ethics as considerations of revenue growth and the sale of non-audit services began to dominate within the large firms; and a growing willingness of companies to utilize legal opinions as to the appropriateness of particular accounting policy choices.

Notwithstanding both the enhanced appreciation of the notion of creative accounting and the increased disclosure requirements, the opacity of the financial statements of certain companies continued to defeat the most financially knowledgeable analysts. It is in the investigations and legal actions following spectacular frauds and collapses that we have the most detailed, although by no means complete, information on accounting issues. Three such cases where we do have access to such *ex post* investigation are those relating to the Bank of Credit and Commerce International (BCCI), the Mirror Group and Polly Peck. Although the main focus of this chapter is on Polly Peck, first we jump ahead very slightly in chronological terms to sketch out the circumstances surrounding the collapse in July 1991 of BCCI and that in November 1991 of the group of companies known as the Mirror Group.

### 18.3.1 Bank of Credit and Commerce International (BCCI)

In July 1991, following the receipt of a report commissioned from Price Waterhouse,[11] the Bank of England coordinated the actions of regulatory authorities across the world to close down the operations of BCCI – a bank with a parent company registered in Luxembourg but which operated in more than 70 countries around the world (Wearing, 2005) and which had claimed assets of $25 billion. Following its closure, substantial shortfalls were identified, with estimates of the amount in default ranging up to $13 billion. Unsurprisingly, there was extensive subsequent investigation into the activities of the bank and the circumstances surrounding its closure.[12] The main focus of this investigation in the UK was on regulatory issues and, in particular, on whether the Bank of England should have been more proactive in terms of oversight and regulation (Bingham, 1992). As noted above, an extensive literature exists regarding the collapse of the bank and its aftermath, which saw a number of its officers and employees sentenced to long terms of imprisonment (see, for example, Adams and Frantz, 1993; Arnold and Sikka, 2001; Beaty and Gwynne, 1993; Mitchell *et al.*, 2001). But it is not that straightforward to obtain from publicly available documentation a clear account of the overall level and mechanisms of financial manipulation – perhaps because the whole entity was a mass of deception and fraud. The US Senate inquiry (Kerry and Brown, 1992) characterized the bank's *modus operandi* in the following terms:

---

[11] The Sandstorm report (Sandstorm was a code word for BCCI). This report was not, and has not been, made publicly available in the UK but a restricted version was provided to, and published by, the US Senate Committee investigation (Kerry and Brown, 1992).

[12] Together with litigation activity by the liquidators as they sought to recover money from various parties. This resulted in significant settlements with Price Waterhouse, Ernst & Whinney and the government of Abu Dhabi. A long-running court battle to recover money from the Bank of England failed completely.

BCCI's criminality included fraud by BCCI and BCCI customers involving billions of dollars; money laundering in Europe, Africa, Asia, and the Americas; BCCI's bribery of officials in most of those locations; support of terrorism, arms trafficking, and the sale of nuclear technologies; management of prostitution; the commission and facilitation of income tax evasion, smuggling, and illegal immigration; illicit purchases of banks and real estate; and a panoply of financial crimes limited only by the imagination of its officers and customers.

The inquiry report continued:

Among BCCI's principal mechanisms for committing crimes were its use of shell corporations and bank confidentiality and secrecy havens; layering of its corporate structure; its use of front-men and nominees, guarantees and buy-back arrangements; back-to-back financial documentation among BCCI controlled entities, kick-backs and bribes, the intimidation of witnesses, and the retention of well-placed insiders to discourage governmental action.

This is a formidable indictment. Abstracting from the wider charges of corruption and criminality, it is clear that BCCI's balance sheet contained many loans which were irrecoverable, or wholly fictitious, and that this deceit was covered up by two mechanisms. First, by accounting manoeuvres – when BCCI lost money due to poor lending practices, rather than accept provisions for the losses it simply disguised them with what Price Waterhouse described as 'a very complicated series of manipulations of loan and deposit accounts, treasury activities and purchases of its own shares'; and second, by direct collusion with the (alleged) counterparties who were prepared to provide documentation to support the existence of non-existent loans and deposits. The JDS Tribunal Report[13] relating to the role of Price Waterhouse in this debacle noted that 'the extent of the massive BCCI fraud was, as is now known, unparalleled and unusual and was such that auditors were actively deceived not only by BCCI management but, in addition, by customers and shareholders acting in collusion with management'. There was also evidence that such manipulation had been taking place for many years, the Senate committee noting that:

Price Waterhouse found significant accounting manipulation at BCCI beginning as early as 1976. It now appears that over the period from 1977 to 1985, the treasury operations of Sandstorm [i.e., BCCI] made significant losses. These losses were concealed and at the same time significant profits were manufactured. The precise amount of loans/fictitious profits cannot now be established, but may well have been of the order of \$600–\$700 million before funding costs, or approaching \$1 billion if funding costs are added. (Kerry and Brown, 1992)

In 1989, a senior employee of BCCI alerted Price Waterhouse to the possibility of fraud and the likelihood that senior management had systematically misled the auditors. This led to discussions between Price Waterhouse and the Bank of England as to the appropriate course of action and also further investigation and enquiry by Price Waterhouse into BCCI's affairs, an investigation carried out initially with the sanction of BCCI senior management. This uncovered both a significant financial shortfall and evidence of the falsification of accounts by senior management. The possibility of restructuring supported by Abu Dhabi

---

[13] JDS 2006 report available at http://www.castigator.org.uk/index.html?bcci_tr.html. Here, and subsequently in this chapter, 'JDS' refers to The Accountants' Joint Disciplinary Scheme which was set up in 1986 by the professional accounting bodies for the purpose of conducting independent investigations into the work and conduct of chartered accountants in cases of public concern. Its functions have now been taken over by the Accountancy and Actuarial Discipline Board (AADB), itself a subsidiary board of the FRC.

interests acting at the behest of Abu Dhabi's ruler was mooted but when, in June 1991, Price Waterhouse passed on the findings of their investigation to the Bank of England, the Bank decided to close down BCCI immediately.

### 18.3.2  The Mirror Group

In 1968 Pergamon Press, a UK publishing house then subject to a bid from Leasco (a US conglomerate), published financial statements, bearing a clean audit report, which showed a profit of more than £1.5 million. The bid was later withdrawn amid allegations of dishonesty and a subsequent reappraisal of Pergamon's financial statements by another audit firm disclosed a loss of £60 000 – approximately half the difference being attributable to inflated stock prices resulting from write-backs of previous provisions for obsolescence, and the other half to inappropriate accounting for transactions between Pergamon and private companies controlled by Robert Maxwell, the chairman and driving force behind Pergamon. In the subsequent Department of Trade and Industry report (DTI, 1971) into the circumstances surrounding the Leasco bid for Pergamon, the range of issues documented that contributed to the overstatement of profit also included classification of overseas stock at cost (rather than the lower net realizable value), failure to provide adequately for sales returns, inappropriate early income recognition and inadequate provisions for bad debts. Maxwell, who had built up his publishing empire on the basis of copyrights associated with scientific journals in the years following World War II and who was, at the time of the Leasco bid, a member of parliament was heavily criticized in the DTI inquiry. The Inspectors concluded that 'he is not in our opinion a person who can be relied upon to exercise proper stewardship of a publicly quoted company' (DTI, 1971, para. 343). Brushing aside this damning, oft-quoted reference to his commercial propriety, Maxwell rebuilt his business empire via a series of acquisitions commencing with the reacquisition of Pergamon in 1974, British Printing Corporation in 1981 (later Maxwell Communications Corporation (MCC)), Mirror Group Newspapers (MGN) (publishers of the *Daily Mirror* and *Sunday Mirror*) in 1984, and in 1988 both the US arm of Macmillan and the Official Airline Guide. Whilst Maxwell had been successful in returning the Mirror Group to profitability, the 1988 acquisitions were at too high a price – $3.4 billion – financed by $3 billion of short-term unsecured debt. The resulting liquidity problems were a major factor in the collapse of Maxwell's business interests shortly after his death in 1991.

Although the earlier DTI inquiry had identified many examples of creative accounting in respect of the Pergamon accounts, the more high-profile concerns in the Mirror Group collapse related to the misuse of pension fund assets and the question of whether or not the flotation of MGN in 1990 should have been allowed to proceed by the regulatory authorities and the relevant advisers. After the collapse these issues were analysed and documented in detail in a DTI report (DTI, 2001). This report concluded that from 1985 onwards the assets of the MGN pension fund had been utilized to lend money to Maxwell's private companies (more than £100 million was borrowed by the end of 1990), to engage in related-party dealings (primarily for the benefit of the private companies), to engage in transactions solely designed for the benefit of the private companies, to invest in shares and debt instruments of related companies, primarily MCC, and to provide collateral for borrowings by the private companies (more than £200 million of collateral was outstanding at end 1990). Many of these transactions had been carried out without the knowledge of the majority of the pension scheme trustees. Apart from the transactions relating to the pension fund, within the group Maxwell had sold assets which had previously been pledged as collateral elsewhere, diverted shares and cash from within the Mirror Group to companies controlled by Maxwell, and engaged in a variety of transactions designed to support the share price of MCC and MGN (Wearing, 2005). More specific accounting issues associated with the flotation of MGN related to the manner in which 'brand valuations' of approximately £625 million (significantly more than the flotation value) were created for the Mirror Group mastheads – valuations obtained by reference to a process of negotiation between the auditors of Mirror Group and Robert Maxwell.[14]

Perhaps unsurprisingly, the failure of Coopers & Lybrand, the auditors of the Maxwell group companies, to detect or in any way prevent these abuses occasioned subsequent comment and criticism. In 1999, the JDS levied a significant fine on Coopers & Lybrand citing as grounds for this sanction:

(i) Inadequate respect for, and incompetent performance in compliance with, obligations to the Investment Management Regulatory Organization (IMRO).
(ii) Deficient work in establishing primary audit facts.
(iii) Undue acceptance of representations [from MCC to the auditors], sometimes accompanied by inappropriate use or content of letters of representation, which in turn reflected a lack of independent judgement of the character, propriety and purposes of transactions which merited objective consideration.
(iv) Deficient consideration of the interest of third parties and persons with fiduciary duties.
(v) A lack of robust implementation of a basically sound system of audit.
(vi) Deficient partner review and overview.

## 18.4 POLLY PECK[15]

Polly Peck was, ahead of the acquisition of a majority shareholding by Nadir, a very small company with interests in the East End garment trade. A private company controlled by Nadir acquired 58 % of Polly Peck's share capital for cash of £270 000 (Wearing, 2005). Capitalized at under £300 000 before Nadir's initial investment in 1980, Polly Peck grew rapidly consequent to a rights issue and investment in, and acquisition of, businesses in Turkey and northern Cyprus. Beyond this it diversified more widely, its acquisition strategy aided by its soaring share price, culminating in its 1989 purchase of the Del Monte fresh food business for £557 million. The market value of shares in the group, which started trading on the London market at 5p, rose to peak just a few years later at more than £35.

---

[14] Appendix 14, DTI (2001) (appendices available at http://www.insolvency.gov.uk/cib/inspectorreports/appencomplete. pdf) provides a wealth of detail as to the valuation practices employed. Appendix 13 considers the suitability of the accounting for certain share interests on an equity basis.

[15] The parent company at the time of the collapse of the group was Polly Peck (International). This chapter uses the nomenclature 'Polly Peck' to cover the group as a whole except where it is necessary to identify individual companies for the purposes of clarity.

Underlying the growth in the share price was a commensurately spectacular pattern of success in terms of financial reporting – in particular:

- Turnover rose from £21 million in 1982 to £1.16 billion in 1989.
- Pre-tax profits rose from £9 million in 1982 to £161 million in 1989.
- Net assets increased from under £12 million in 1982 to £845 million in 1989.

The last full set of financial statements for the group were those for the year ended 31 December 1989, but interim figures for the six months to 30 June 1990, released in September of that year, showed both record profits for the first six months of the year and also that net assets had increased further to £933 million, including cash and bank balances of £405 million (of which £303 million was said to be held by subsidiaries). Notwithstanding this apparently healthy position, in the same month Polly Peck was unable to meet its payments to its creditors and, with sentiment adversely affected by a Serious Fraud Office raid on the headquarters of Nadir's management company, administrators were appointed in October 1990. A report to creditors issued by the administrators in May 1991 showed there to be an overall deficit of £551 million, the principal explanation for which was an anticipated £927 million shortfall in the realization of inter-company debtor balances.

The aftermath was protracted and, as we have seen, involved the criminal prosecution in the UK of Nadir who, although since 1982 no longer a majority shareholder, continued to dominate the entity and effectively control the board and the company. At the 1989 year end Nadir had an interest in approximately 25 % of Polly Peck's ordinary share capital. The JDS Tribunal referred to his position in the following terms: 'The unfettered power of this single individual over the group's most significant area of activities was a key contributory factor in the difficulties that ensued' (S8).[16] Further, one of Nadir's aides, who worked for Nadir's management company, was initially convicted of dishonestly handling stolen goods and imprisoned, but this conviction was overturned on appeal. In addition, there was a raft of litigation relating to the administration process including an action, settled out of court, against the group auditors, Stoy Hayward and also quasi-judicial investigation under the aegis of the JDS of both Stoy Hayward and members of Erdal & Co., a local firm of auditors in northern Cyprus who were the primary auditors of three of the key subsidiaries. The JDS investigations resulted in separate reports published in 2001 and 2002 and it is these reports which, together with information from the published statements of Polly Peck for the relevant period, form the basis for the account detailed below. (There was an earlier report, *Polly Peck International and its Subsidiaries (Mr John Turner)*, published in 1998, which focused specifically on the role of the former group accountant of Polly Peck. In coming to its decision to exclude him from membership of ICAEW, the Tribunal concluded that: 'his ignorance of the reality of the situation, the consequence of his taking no steps to

---

[16] Paragraph number references in this chapter to the 2001 JDS report (Polly Peck/Stoy Hayward) are prefaced by S and those to the 2002 JDS report (Polly Peck/Erdal & Co.) are prefaced by E. Both reports are available on the Joint Disciplinary Scheme website (at http://www.castigator.org.uk/index.html?ppistoys_tr.html and http://www.castigator.org.uk/index.html?erdal_tr.html, respectively). For ease of exposition the two reports, which overlap in their coverage of the relevant material, are referred to here as 'the Tribunal Report'.

verify what he was told, amounted to the equivalent of "clapping the glass to his sightless eye"').

The allegations against Nadir related to the extraction of cash from Polly Peck for his own purposes. Payments would be made on a regular basis from the holding company, Polly Peck International (PPI), to an account of a subsidiary company (usually, but not always, Unipac) and then transferred on by Nadir for his own use. In the year ending 31 December 1989, PPI made 64 payments totalling £141 million to the Turkish subsidiaries. In the previous year, 24 such payments totalling £57 million had been made (S10). In total, the Serious Fraud Office identified transfers totalling £383 million between August 1987 and October 1990 (E85). These transfers were made possible by 'the lack of any meaningful high-level control environment or system of detailed control procedures within PPI's Head Office in London. This fundamental weakness included the absence of even the most basic control, namely the requirement for dual signatures on all substantial bank disbursements' (S8). The payments appear in the books of the holding company as an amount owed by the subsidiary and would be eliminated on consolidation as an inter-company balance. As the Tribunal Report noted, however, '[these] loans in turn could only be justified by inflation of assets and profitability shown in the subsidiaries' accounts' (E45).

The three key subsidiaries central to the manipulations were as follows (descriptions abbreviated from E39(1)–(3); these three subsidiaries are hereinafter collectively referred to as 'the Turkish subsidiaries'):

**Meyna**, which purported to be a substantial and highly profitable company whose food purchase, production and processing business was located in Turkey with a head office in Istanbul. In the 1989 accounts it contributed approximately 33 % of the group's bank balances and cash, that is about £82 million.

**Vestel**, another Turkish company, described by Wearing (2005) as a joint venture with Thorn-EMI. It manufactured electrical goods under licence from Thorn-EMI but Thorn-EMI do not appear to have had an equity interest. It contributed 33 % of group profit before interest and tax in 1989 and £212 million (or 25 %) of group net assets.

**Unipac**, a company based in northern Cyprus which manufactured corrugated cardboard boxes for food packaging. It only had about 150 employees (compared with more than 17 000 Polly Peck group employees worldwide by the end of 1989), but its contribution to the group's reported financial performance was very significant. In the 1989 accounts it contributed £82 million (or 51 %) to profit before interest and tax, £307 million (or 36 %) to net assets and £93 million (or 37 %) to bank balances and cash.

The reality would appear to have been that Polly Peck largely invented the 'assets' in its subsidiaries which would offset the substantial balances which these subsidiaries purportedly owed to the parent company, and similarly constructed almost entirely fictitious numbers for turnover and income. Evidence as to the scale of this creation is found in the tables contained within the Tribunal Report, which contrast, for both Meyna and Vestel, the financial statements provided to the Turkish authorities (primarily for taxation purposes) and the group consolidation returns. The statements provided to the Turkish authorities might be considered as the equivalent of the subsidiary statutory accounts in the UK; and, although 'not prepared to take the local accounts as gospel' (E62), the Tribunal does appear to have accepted them as a reasonable approximation to the actual financial situation

**Table 18.1**   Balance sheet extracts from Meyna (abstracted from E61)

|  | 31 December 1988 | | | 31 December 1989 | | |
|---|---|---|---|---|---|---|
|  | Local £m | Reported £m | Difference £m | Local £m | Reported £m | Difference £m |
| Fixed assets | 14.4 | 72.9 | 58.5 | 19.4 | 192.3 | 172.9 |
| Debtors | 3.6 | 50.3 | 46.7 | 7.7 | 116.2 | 108.5 |
| Cash and bank | 1.2 | 16.2 | 15.0 | 3.2 | 82.5 | 79.3 |
| Group co. balances | (6.2) | (172.6) | (166.4) | (15.0) | (345.2) | (330.2) |
| Net assets | 9.0 | (35.3) | (44.3) | 15.0 | 64.2 | 49.2 |

pertaining to the subsidiaries. These tables are reproduced here with 'Local' referring to the domestic financial statements and 'Reported' to the consolidation returns.

### 18.4.1  Meyna

Cursory inspection of Tables 18.1 and 18.2 reveals the enormous scale of the differences. By the end of 1989 Meyna's reported fixed assets were all but 10 times those in the local returns. Taken together, reported fixed assets, debtors and cash exceeded the local figures by £361 million, an amount very largely offset by reported inter-company balances which totalled £330 million more than those in the local returns. Whereas the local returns for 1988 show Meyna to be a barely profitable enterprise with turnover of just £16 million, the consolidation returns for the 16-month accounting period report turnover of £215 million (which grew to £264 million in 1989) and profit of more than £56 million (£52 million in 1989), representing a very significant proportion of the overall claimed profitability of the group.

**Table 18.2**   Income statement extracts from Meyna (abstracted from E61)

|  | Period ended 31 December 1988 | | | Year ended 31 December 1989 | | |
|---|---|---|---|---|---|---|
|  | Local £m | Reported £m | Difference £m | Local £m | Reported £m | Difference £m |
| Turnover | 16.1 | 214.9 | 198.8 | 39.8 | 264.2 | 224.4 |
| Profit before tax | 0.2 | 56.5 | 56.3 | 1.3 | 52.5 | 51.2 |

Even allowing for the impact of accounting policy differences and possible errors in the local accounts, the Tribunal was of the opinion that the local accounts, which were consistent both with the underlying books and records and the circumstances discovered by the administrators, were sufficiently reliable 'to provide a yardstick against which to gauge the measure by which Meyna's position was inflated' (E62).

### 18.4.2  Vestel

Although in total the differences for Vestel are not quite so large as those for Meyna, Tables 18.3 and 18.4 show that they are still striking, in particular in relation to the balance sheet numbers for fixed assets, stocks and work in progress and, of course, intercompany balances; and in the income statement the comparison between the £0.3 million of other income reported locally and the £32.5 million in the consolidated returns for 1989 is highly significant. The Tribunal was prepared to accept that submissions, by the local firm of auditors, as to the explanations for these differences (in particular in relation to the accounting treatment of goods in transit) had some merit but, nevertheless, they could not, even if accepted in their entirety, provide more than 'a partial explanation of the significant discrepancies' (E74).

**Table 18.3**   Balance sheet extracts from Vestel (abstracted from E73)

|                     | 31 December 1988 | | | 31 December 1989 | | |
|---------------------|------------|-------------|----------------|------------|-------------|----------------|
|                     | Local £m   | Reported £m | Difference £m  | Local £m   | Reported £m | Difference £m  |
| Fixed assets        | 7.3        | 45.0        | 37.7           | 8.6        | 110.8       | 102.2          |
| Stocks and WIP      | 7.1        | 25.7        | 18.6           | 9.8        | 41.3        | 31.5           |
| Debtors             | 25.8       | 31.2        | 5.4            | 46.6       | 57.8        | 11.2           |
| Cash and bank       | 0.9        | 8.0         | 7.1            | 9.8        | 17.4        | 7.6            |
| Group co. balances  | (15.1)     | (142.9)     | (127.8)        | (30.8)     | (205.4)     | (174.6)        |
| Net assets          | 16.7       | (49.7)      | (66.4)         | 29.3       | 6.7         | (22.6)         |

### 18.4.3  Unipac

For Unipac, incorporated in northern Cyprus, full local financial statements were not made available to the Tribunal. A combination of analytical review and more specific evidence, however, persuaded the Tribunal that the Unipac consolidation returns were implausible, indeed incredible. Turnover for both 1988 and 1989 represented at least 20 % of the GDP of northern Cyprus. For cash balances – 'Some £87.2 million was said to be "blocked". In

**Table 18.4**   Income statement extracts from Vestel (abstracted from E73)

|                   | Period ended 31 December 1988 | | | Year ended 31 December 1989 | | |
|-------------------|------------|-------------|----------------|------------|-------------|----------------|
|                   | Local £m   | Reported £m | Difference £m  | Local £m   | Reported £m | Difference £m  |
| Turnover          | 71.1       | 75.0        | 3.9            | 87.9       | 89.9        | 2.0            |
| Other income      | 1.2        | 22.0        | 20.8           | 0.3        | 32.5        | 32.2           |
| Profit before tax | 5.4        | 21.7        | 16.3           | 8.8        | 19.0        | 10.2           |

reality, the funds were not there and we are satisfied that they had never been there' (E91). For other assets – 'The Expenditure on Projects Schedule produced in December 1990 which purported to show payments by Unipac totalling £163.9m by way of deposits concerning leisure projects and £63.2 million as "deposits to building contractors" was bogus' (E91).

The overall conclusion of the Tribunal was that 'we are sure that in both 1988 and 1989 there were neither bank balances, nor purchased properties, nor contractual rights which could begin to justify the consolidated returns' (E92).

### 18.4.4  Accounting Policies at Polly Peck

At one level Polly Peck would appear to be a straightforward case of deceit, conducted without any particular degree of subtlety, which continued for as long as it did only because of the internal governance failings, the inadequacies of the local firm of auditors,[17] the startling naivety and all but incredible gullibility of a long established firm of UK auditors, and the failure of city analysts and others to maintain objectivity and indeed a necessary degree of scepticism as to both the source and the sustainability of Polly Peck's spectacular growth. Even when criminal proceedings were initiated against Nadir soon after Polly Peck's collapse, commentators appeared reluctant to believe that fraud on the scale alleged could have taken place. For example, the second edition of *Accounting for Growth* published five years after the collapse stated: 'Even now it is difficult to judge whether Polly Peck failed because of malpractice or from more fundamental flaws in currency mismatching, working capital controls or even just the absolute level of debt' (Smith, 1996, p. 212). Beyond this, however, there are wider issues – particularly in respect of the nature and role of accounting standards and whether or not these played a part, wittingly or unwittingly, in facilitating the extraordinary, almost unparalleled, growth of Polly Peck ahead of its denouement. Here the question arises as to whether the perceived success of Polly Peck was in part the result of accounting which might be considered to be creative but was within the parameters of accepted accounting practice – indeed perhaps arguably required by formalized standards. Although this aspect was touched upon by commentators immediately after the demise of Polly Peck (see e.g. Gwilliam and Russell, 1991; Smith, 1992), the academic and professional literature contains relatively little in the way of a systematic analysis of the financial statements of Polly Peck over the 10 years for which Nadir had control, or of how these policies may have contributed to the relentless growth in profitability documented in the financial statements over this period. Table 18.5 contains extracts from Polly Peck's audited financial statements for the 10 years from Nadir's takeover until the collapse, which document the spectacular growth of turnover, profitability and net assets of the company over the period but also shed light on the construction of that profitability, in particular: the significant growth in interest receivable from 1985 through to 1989; the relatively low level of the taxation charge (in no single year did the taxation charge exceed 20 % of reported profit and the overall average for the period was less than 16 %); and crucially the very

---

[17] The Tribunal did not find that the local firm of auditors were actually aware of the nature of the misrepresentations, stating: 'Although there is evidence from which it would be possible to infer that they were complaisant in what was undoubtedly a fraudulent disguise carried out at the behest of Mr Nadir, on the evidence we consider that it would be wrong so to conclude and we acquit them of any such implied accusation' (E111).

**Table 18.5** Polly Peck financial statement extracts (compiled from Polly Peck International Annual Reports: 1980–1984, Polly Peck (Holdings); 1985–1989, Polly Peck International, all available from Companies House; all figures in £million)

| | 1980 | 1981 | 1982 | 1983 | 1984 | 1985 | 1986 | 1987 | 1988*** | 1989 |
|---|---|---|---|---|---|---|---|---|---|---|
| Turnover | 1.0 | 6.5 | 21.1 | 62.2 | 137.2 | 205.5 | 273.7 | 380.9 | 967.1 | 1162.3 |
| Interest receivable | | 0.1 | 0.4 | 0.6 | 1.7 | 0.2 | 7.6 | 11.8* | 27.8* | 68.1* |
| Interest payable | | | | | | 5.5 | 14.1 | 21.4* | 40.6* | 55.6* |
| Profit before tax | (0.1) | 2.1 | 9.0 | 24.7 | 50.6 | 61.1 | 70.4 | 86.2 | 144.1 | 161.4 |
| Taxation | (0.1) | 0.7 | 0.2 | 4.0 | 6.4 | 10.7 | 9.1 | 16.6 | 24.5 | 22.8 |
| Profit after taxation, minority interest and extraordinary items | (0.1) | 1.4 | 9.2 | 20.7 | 43.8 | 50.5 | 61.2 | 69.4 | 118.8 | 137.7 |
| Net assets | 0.4 | 3.1 | 11.6 | 24.4 | 87.2 | 108.7 | 163.9 | 197.2 | 386.2 | 843.7 |
| Credit to revaluation surplus | | | | | 8.3 | nil | 44.8 | 45.4** | 122.8 | 113.5 |
| Foreign exchange movements | | | | | | | | | | |
| Movements on exchange, being: | nil | n.a. | (2.4) | (5.2) | (13.4) | (40.2) | (43.4) | (84.3) | (182.4) | (46.4) |
| • Translation of opening balances | | | (0.9) | (2.2) | (7.3) | (28.1) | (36.3) | (70.0) | (170.3) | (44.7) |
| • Difference between average and closing rate | | | (1.5) | (3.0) | (6.1) | (12.1) | (7.1) | (14.3) | (12.1) | (1.7) |

*Notes:*

n.a. not available.

The 1981 and 1982 figures are based on the historical cost figures produced as a supplement to the current cost financial statements. The 1982 figures are as reported, i.e. they do not reflect the subsequent prior year adjustment. The 1988 prior year adjustment, discussed further below, did not affect any of the above figures.

*Interest receivable was netted off against interest payable in the main profit and loss statement for 1987 and 1988 but disclosed separately in the notes; in 1989 interest receivable was included in other income.

**There was an offsetting £8.5 million exchange variance.

***16-month period to 31 December 1988 (the 1981 accounts were drawn up for a 17-month period to 31 August 1981).

large sums being taken to reserves relating to movements on exchange, broken down in terms of the retranslation of the opening balances and the difference between average and closing rate translation of income and expense items.

The discussion below focuses on the foreign currency and valuation issues, but it is worth noting that Polly Peck was a child of its time in its approach to other accounting policy choices, and employed a *pot pourri* of group accounting techniques (see e.g. Holmes and Sugden, 1990; McBarnet and Whelan, 1999). In 1984 it used merger accounting to reflect what was described in the relevant accounting policy note as the 'acquisition' of a textile manufacturer, Wearwell. In respect to a number of subsequent acquisitions it utilized the merger relief provisions, contained initially in the 1981 Companies Act, to write purchased goodwill off against a merger reserve effectively created from the premium on the shares issued for the purpose of the acquisition (in 1985, 1988 and 1989, £14 million, £32 million and £14 million, respectively of purchased goodwill were written off against a merger reserve). In 1989 it treated all but the entirety of the difference between the price it paid for Del Monte's fresh fruit business (£557 million) and the fair value of the assets acquired (£271 million) as a brand valued at £281 million rather than purchased goodwill, thereby avoiding the need either to amortize this amount or to write it off against reserves. It is, however, difficult to say that these techniques, frequently associated with creative accounting, were chosen for creative accounting purposes. The use of merger accounting for the Wearwell 'acquisition' was justifiable on the grounds that Polly Peck and Wearwell shared extensive common management ahead of the merger; the write-offs to merger reserve would not be permissible today but were commonplace at the time; and the recording of a substantial brand value, subject to future impairment tests, in respect to the Del Monte acquisition is effectively the accounting treatment required under current international accounting standards (whether the 'asset' is described as 'brand' or 'purchased goodwill'). Beyond this, Holmes and Sugden (1994) highlight the fact that the 1989 Polly Peck funds flow statement, prepared in accordance with SSAP 10, showed funds generated from operations of £172 million (a figure close to the reported profit of £161 million), whereas a cash flow statement prepared under the format subsequently required under FRS 1 would have shown an outflow from operations of £129 million. Polly Peck, however, was doing no more than following the then applicable standard and again it is difficult in this respect to convict it of creative accounting per se.

### 18.4.4.1  *Foreign Currency Translation*

In 1981 and 1982, when Polly Peck began its meteoric rise, the primary financial statements were current cost accounts in accordance with SSAP 16 *Current Cost Accounting* (issued in 1980, application suspended in 1985) although conventional historical cost accounts were also prepared. An accounting policy note refers to the treatment of foreign currencies in the following terms: 'All items arising in overseas currencies are translated into sterling at the rates ruling at the balance sheet date, other than fixed assets and opening balance on reserves which are translated at historical rates. Any translation differences, together with those on conversion of foreign currencies, are treated as normal trading transactions.' There is no information in the 1982 financial statements as to the magnitude or composition of these translation differences (although the nature of the restatement following the change in accounting policy in 1983 discussed further below provides indicative evidence that losses on translation of the opening balances were quite small).

In April 1983, the ASC published SSAP 20 *Foreign Currency Translation*, mandatory for accounting periods commencing after April 1983 with early adoption encouraged. This effectively established a default policy for the treatment of subsidiaries operating in foreign currencies as the closing rate method with translation gains or losses on the opening net investment being taken through reserves. The underlying thinking behind this policy was, and is, that it removes from the income statement the significant volatility which may arise as a result of fluctuations in currency values largely irrelevant to the operations of the business (SSAP 20, para. 19). The suitability of such a policy is in itself, however, dependent upon the nature of the business and its income-generating activities, the composition of its asset and liability mix, and the presence or otherwise of a significant long-term trend in the relationship between relevant currencies. In the extreme example of an entity for which the only line of business of the parent company is that of providing hard currency for an overseas subsidiary to lend or deposit in a soft currency then, if the interest rates reflect perceptions of a continuing deterioration in the position of the soft currency, the all but inevitable outcome is that each year there will be significant interest income in the income statement being offset by sizeable translation losses taken through the reserves.

In its 1983 accounts, Polly Peck changed its accounting policy so as to bring it into line with the requirements of SSAP 20. SSAP 20 allowed the choice of either average or closing rate for translation of profit and loss items and Polly Peck opted to use the average rate (FRS 23 and IAS 21 now require the use of the average rate). The restatement of the 1982 figures in line with the implementation of SSAP 20 in 1983 led to an increase in turnover of £2.7 million and in net income of nearly £1.5 million for that year.

Polly Peck continued to use the closing rate/net investment method with average rate translation of profit and loss items for the remainder of its existence and, as the figures extracted from the published accounts set out above show, implementation of this policy had a very significant impact on the financial numbers reported by Polly Peck. From 1983 through to 1989, Polly Peck reported total profits before tax of approximately £599 million, whilst over the same period it debited £415 million to profit and loss reserves as a result of movements on exchange. These movements represented a combination of translation of the opening net investment (£359 million) and the difference between the use of an average and closing rate for conversion of profit and loss items (£56 million). In each and every year movements on exchange were adverse, and they grew in size consistently from 1982 to reach a maximum of £182 million in 1988 before falling sharply to only £46 million in 1989. Interest receivable, however, grew rapidly from just £0.2 million in 1985 to £68.1 million in 1989 (in which year it amounted to £12.5 million more than interest payable, notwithstanding the fact that at year end 1989 Polly Peck had £735 million outstanding in long-term debt).

### 18.4.4.2  *Asset Revaluation*

Cushioning the impact on the balance sheet of the adverse exchange movements were asset revaluations which, over the same period, 1983–89, generated credits of £335 million to revaluation reserve. The 1983 Polly Peck accounts were compiled on a strictly historical cost basis, but in 1984 Polly Peck revalued its freehold property giving rise to a revaluation reserve of more than £8 million. There was no revaluation in 1985, but further revaluations based on a mix of independent and directors' valuations took place in all subsequent years. In 1988, Polly Peck adopted a policy of bringing the current value of fixed assets into the local financial statements ahead of their translation into sterling, the relevant additional paragraph in the foreign currency accounting policy note reading:

> With effect from 30th August, 1987, in countries affected by exceptional inflation, the financial statements of subsidiary companies are adjusted to reflect the current value of tangible fixed assets before translation into sterling. In previous years, these companies' financial statements were translated directly into sterling. The effects of this change have been treated as a prior year adjustment and comparative balance sheet figures have been accordingly restated ... Comparative profit and loss account figures have not been restated as any effect on the previous year's results is not considered material.

The immediate balance sheet effect of this change was to increase (by means of a prior year adjustment) 1988 opening fixed asset balances and reserves by £21.5 million, almost entirely as a result of revaluation of short leasehold and plant and equipment assets. The increase in opening net assets was reflected as a £75.3 million credit to opening retained profit and an offsetting £53.8 million debit to opening revaluation reserves. Unfortunately, the extent of disclosure and explanation with respect to these changes in opening reserves is quite limited and this makes it difficult for any user of these financial statements, then and now, to establish the justification for what at first sight may appear to be an accounting sleight of hand. Without this increase in opening retained profits, retained profits would, on the face of it, have been negative at the end of 1988, which may have had implications for the legality of the 1988 dividend payment of £26.1 million. Going forward, application of this policy of revaluation saw a credit to the revaluation reserve in 1988 of £123 million and in 1989 of £113 million.

The alternative accounting rules of the 1985 Companies Act allowed the revaluation of tangible fixed assets and the Tribunal Report takes the view that in itself the accounting policy change was not inappropriate. Referring to: 'The change in accounting policy, whereby the value of tangible fixed assets in areas of exceptional inflation (chiefly Turkey and the TRNC) were indexed upwards before translation to Sterling in order to reduce the impact on retained profits of the losses on exchange on translation of the year end balance sheets' the Report continues: 'This change in accounting policy was acceptable, but it should have reminded Stoy Hayward of the very serious impact which the devaluation of the Turkish Lira was having on the group's affairs' (S50(c)).

### 18.4.4.3   Interpretation

As we have seen and documented, the majority of the creativity in the Polly Peck accounts would appear to have been in the form of pure invention – but this is with the benefit of hindsight, itself based on subsequent detailed investigation, by the disciplinary tribunals.[18]

---

[18] Even now we do not have full information as to the role which accounting per se played in the development and continuation of the fiction of Polly Peck. Neither the administrators' reports nor the expert witness report to the Joint Disciplinary Tribunal are publicly available. From the Tribunal Report we know that Unipac accounted in sterling, whereas

Contemporary users, investors, analysts and even the auditors of the Polly Peck financial statements were faced with a number of possible scenarios which might have explained, at least in part, the disclosed financial statement numbers.

One interpretation was linked to the perception of Polly Peck as a highly successful packager and distributor of agricultural products. If Polly Peck was advancing funds to fruit growers in a soft currency ahead of their delivery, then the interest on these advances would be reflected in the profit and loss account whilst the losses on the capital value of the loans would go to reserves. There is no evidence, however, that this was in fact the case; and the sheer scale and growth of interest income and adverse exchange movements in the late 1980s would suggest other explanations. Two further possibilities were that Polly Peck was placing money in high interest-yielding local bank accounts or that it was effectively conducting an unregulated private banking operation. To an extent Polly Peck encouraged both perceptions, in particular the idea that it could in some way benefit from the very high local currency interest rates whilst avoiding, wholly or in part, the concomitant losses caused by the decline in the value of that currency. Here the Tribunal report noted that:

> [i]n the course of Stoy Hayward's work on the [1989] rights issue, they were told by PPI that UNIPAC (which prepared its accounts in Sterling) had a special arrangement with its banks whereby it received 5 % per month interest on accounts denominated in Turkish Lira. It was said that the banks effectively treated the capital amount of the balance as being in Sterling terms and there was therefore no Sterling exchange risk (S55).

Unsurprisingly, the Tribunal was sceptical of the existence of such an arrangement:

> It was not easy to understand why any bank or banks would have offered UNIPAC an extended interest rate of 60 % with no foreign exchange risk on deposits of such magnitude ... over the entire duration of the forecast period ... and in the context of the weakening Turkish Lira ... (S59).

Despite this, there is no doubt that some credence was given to this possibility in the investing community. Gwilliam and Russell (1991) illustrate this with a quotation from a contemporary analyst's report noting that approximately 20 % of the 1990 interim profit came from 'borrowing some £200m in hard currencies at around 10 % and lending it to a Turkish bank at around 30 %, below the current market rate but including a currency translation guarantee' and explained that 'most companies with active treasury departments are taking advantage of similar interest rate differentials. These are unlikely to account for such a large proportion of profits, but then they probably don't have the right connections.'

In the outcome there was no evidence of any such guarantees and, as far as one can tell, they were not taken into account in the construction of the financial statements.

A related possibility was that Polly Peck was taking advantage of its ability to circumvent exchange control restrictions to run a private banking operation for individuals and organizations in Turkey and northern Cyprus. The Tribunal was prepared to accept that some limited private banking activities may have taken place but did not consider that these facilities were being provided on a substantial scale. In one sense, however, this explanation is perhaps closest to the truth in that the reality would appear to be that Polly Peck was effectively providing a private banking service to Nadir. If the assets which were claimed

---

Meyna and Vestel accounted in Turkish lira – but the Tribunal was uncertain as to, *inter alia*, how differences on intercompany balances were treated.

to exist in the Turkish subsidiaries represented anything at all, they represented unsecured amounts owed by Nadir to these companies – rather than the types of assets which they purported to be. Such borrowings would almost certainly have been illegal under UK company law, but more importantly the perception of the group in the financial markets would have been radically different if investors and others had appreciated the true situation.

Each of these interpretations may have contributed to a surprising absence of scepticism and a lack of critical awareness by those responsible for analysis of the Polly Peck financial statements (see Gwilliam and Russell, 1991). However, in the absence of more detailed information as to the construction of the Polly Peck accounting numbers, it is difficult to come to any conclusion as to whether the application of SSAP 20 in tandem with asset revaluation accidentally led to apparent profitability and balance sheet growth. Nor is it clear what the interaction was, if any, between accounting policy choice and more straightforward accounting invention designed to cover up the abstraction of assets to which Polly Peck (which might here be considered to be a personification of Nadir) resorted.

### 18.4.4.4 Governance and Audit

The Polly Peck saga illustrated weaknesses of internal governance and control mechanisms which facilitated the removal from the group of very large sums of money belonging to shareholders and, indirectly, to creditors and other stakeholders beyond. The ability of Nadir to transfer cash, purportedly to the Turkish subsidiaries, on a large scale and over a considerable period without serious questioning by employees, directors or the auditors does, with the benefit of hindsight, seem quite extraordinary. It was only possible because of the extent and manner in which Nadir, acting as both chairman and chief executive, exercised largely unfettered power within Polly Peck and the inability or, indeed, possibly lack of desire of the other directors and the external auditors to put or seek out answers to pertinent questions.

The failings of the group accountant to question the purpose and nature of the transfers were, as mentioned above, documented in JDS report *Polly Peck International and its Subsidiaries (Mr John Turner)*. The failure of the other board members (both executive and non-executive) to act in any meaningful way as a check on Nadir is also striking. At the time of the Nadir takeover of Polly Peck in 1980 there were four other directors, all of whom resigned in March 1981. New directors were appointed and in 1984 two of these were described as non-executive directors (one of whom resigned after less than two years with the company). By 1985 three non-executive directors were in place, all of whom were still in office at the time of the company's collapse, and in 1988 an additional non-executive director was appointed who was also still *in situ* at the time of the collapse. Although, on the basis of the brief biographies contained within the annual reports, these directors appeared to have reasonable business experience and qualifications (two were chartered accountants), it is far from clear what, if any, contribution they made to the appropriate governance of Polly Peck. An indication of the autocratic manner in which Nadir ran Polly Peck may be obtained from the fact that in August 1990, just ahead of the final implosion, Nadir summoned, at two days' notice, the directors of Polly Peck to a meeting at which he announced his intention to take the group private. This plan was dropped five days later, but a statement issued by the London Stock Exchange almost immediately afterwards noted that the very short notice of the emergency board meeting contributed both to the fact that only seven of the 13 directors were able to attend, and also that it restricted their ability to access adequate professional advice with respect to Nadir's proposals (Wearing, 2005).

The role of the auditors, both Erdal & Co. (auditors of the Turkish subsidiaries which were key to the underlying manipulations) and Stoy Hayward, the group auditors since 1981, came under direct scrutiny in the Tribunal Report referred to above. In the outcome the Erdal partners were excluded from membership of the Institute of Chartered Accountants in England and Wales and each fined £1000. The Tribunal Report did absolve the local auditors from direct complicity in the accounting manipulations, but the sheer scale of the differences between the accounts filed locally and those returned for consolidation purposes does suggest audits carried out in a manner very far removed from the standards that those who place reliance upon audited financial statements would normally expect. Stoy Hayward was also subject to significant stricture from the Tribunal in respect of the 1988 and 1989 audits (and their association with the 1989 rights issue). Criticisms levelled at Stoy Hayward by the Tribunal related to:

- The manner in which they assessed the suitability of Erdal to conduct the audit of the Turkish subsidiaries which comprised such an important part of the group.
- Failure at the planning stage to identify audit risks or to modify and enhance their group audit procedures notwithstanding the rapid growth of the group.
- The limited extent of the review of Erdal's working papers (in both 1988 and 1989 two audit partners and an audit supervisor visited northern Cyprus for three days to review Erdal's work) and, in particular, the failure to pursue the manner in which inter-company balances were agreed and reconciled.
- Failure to enquire as to the reasons for the rapid growth of the subsidiaries; acceptance of uncorroborated assurances from Nadir as to the ownership of group assets which they knew were not legally held by PPI or its subsidiaries (assets amounting to £47.7 million in the 1989 accounts).
- Failure, in circumstances when they were aware that the PPI bank accounts were controlled by sole signatory authorities, to consider the reasons for the entirely one-way cash flow from PPI to subsidiaries which were reportedly profitable and maintained significant cash reserves.
- Failure to conduct an appropriate closing review of the accounts of either the group or the parent company. This review should have identified issues relating to the overall significance of the Turkish and northern Cyprus subsidiaries, to the larger and rapidly growing level of interest income, to the change in accounting policy regarding asset revaluation in the context of overall retained profits, the very large sums owed by the subsidiaries and the likely recoverability of these sums (S18–S115 provide more detail as to the failings in the Stoy Hayward audits).

## 18.5 THE IMMEDIATE AFTERMATH

### 18.5.1 Accounting Regulatory Change

The collapse of Polly Peck, followed shortly after by the demise of BCCI and the Mirror Group, no doubt contributed to strengthening the hand of the newly formed ASB as, under the leadership of David (now Sir David) Tweedie, it set out on its mission to cleanse what it perceived to be the Augean stables of creative accounting. Among the early targets of the ASB were cash flow statements (addressed in FRS 1), group accounts (initially addressed in FRS 2 and FRS 6), financial statement presentation (addressed in FRS 3) and off-balance sheet financing (addressed in FRS 5). As noted above, the presentation of Polly Peck's funds flow statement under the rules contained in SSAP 10 gave a very different picture from that which would have resulted from use of FRS 1, but the extent to which the Polly Peck story contributed to the new standard (which was issued a year after the collapse of Polly Peck) is not clear.

Perhaps the most immediate, direct effect of the Polly Peck saga was a firming up of the requirements for accounting for foreign exchange transactions in circumstances where business was transacted in a depreciating local currency. SSAP 20, in its original version, did note that where a foreign enterprise operates in a country with a very high level of inflation then it may not be possible to 'present fairly in historical accounts the financial position of a foreign enterprise simply by a translation exercise' and that in such circumstances 'the local currency financial statements should be adjusted where possible to reflect current price levels before the translation process is undertaken'. There is no evidence that Polly Peck undertook such a translation for Meyna and Vestel (Unipac used sterling as its functional currency) although, as we have seen, fixed assets were revalued to current value from 1988 onwards – which may be seen as being in the spirit of the SSAP 20 requirements.

In June 1993, an UITF Abstract[19] was issued which noted the uncertainty as to the operationalization of some provisions of SSAP 20, in particular, the possibility of profits, for example interest income, reported through the group income statement being offset by movements on reserves. The abstract required adjustments to be made where the cumulative inflation rate over three years was approaching, or over, 100 % and where the overseas operations were material. Adjustment could be made either by adjusting the local currency financial statements to current price levels (as suggested in SSAP 20) and taking any gain or loss on the net monetary position through the income statement or, alternatively, by the use of a stable currency as the functional currency for the overseas operation.[20]

The BCCI, Maxwell and Polly Peck scandals also slightly post-dated the formation in 1990 of the Financial Reporting Review Panel (FRRP), another offspring of the FRC. The aim of the FRRP was, and is, to ensure that the provision of financial information by public and large private companies complies with relevant accounting requirements. FRRP press notices, which document circumstances in which companies agree to revise their accounts or take other corrective action, reveal a wide range of issues (see Beattie, Fearnley and Hines, 1997 and McBarnet and Whelan, 1999 for reviews of the work of the panel in its early years). Although neither the Polly Peck collapse nor those of BCCI and the Mirror Group were directly instrumental in the setting up of the FRRP, there is little

---

[19] UITF Abstract 9 *Accounting for operations in hyper-inflationary economies*, ASB 1993. UITF (Urgent Issues Task Force) Abstracts are issued with the approval of the ASB to deal with matters which either do not warrant a full standard or where the relevant standard-setting process would be too time-consuming. (International Financial Reporting Interpretations are the closest equivalent to UITF Abstracts in the international accounting setting.)

[20] UITF 9 was withdrawn following the issue of FRS 24 *Financial Reporting in Hyperinflationary Economies* in 2004. FRS 24 effectively implemented the provisions of IAS 29 *Financial Reporting in Hyperinflationary Economies*. IAS 29 only allows restatement in terms of the measuring unit current at the balance sheet date, restatement being achieved by the use of a general price index.

doubt that this concatenation of spectacular accounting and business scandals in the early 1990s contributed significantly to the manner in which the FRRP approached its role, then and subsequently.

### 18.5.2 Governance and Enforcement

Beyond the enforcement activities of the FRRP, there were also far-reaching changes in terms of the approach to, and the importance accorded to, wider aspects of corporate governance following the report of the Cadbury Committee in 1992 (the Cadbury Report; Cadbury, 1992). This committee, commissioned to report on 'the financial aspects of corporate governance', was set up in May 1991 because of 'the perceived low level of confidence both in financial reporting and in the ability of auditors to provide the safeguards which users of company reports sought and expected' (Cadbury, 1992, para. 2.1, 2.2). These concerns had been 'heightened by some unexpected failures of major companies and by criticisms of the lack of effective board accountability for such matters as directors' pay'. There is little doubt that the collapse of Polly Peck was one of those 'unexpected failures', which prompted the setting up of this committee; and although the setting up of the Cadbury Committee predated the BCCI and Mirror Group failures, these two cases significantly influenced the committee in its deliberations and in the drafting of its final report. Indeed, following the Mirror Group collapse the terms of reference of the Cadbury Committee were amended so as to encompass corporate governance in its entirety as compared with just that relating to financial reporting.

The principal recommendation of the Cadbury Report was the institution of a non-statutory Code of Best Practice on financial governance for all listed companies: the 'Combined Code'. The Code emphasized the governance responsibilities of non-executive directors and effectively required the setting up of an audit committee with overall responsibility to review the financial statements and the accounting policies employed. It also required separation of the positions of chairman and chief executive and emphasized the responsibilities of directors for the institution of adequate systems of internal control. The Code was, and is, non-statutory but compliance for listed companies has been effectively ensured by Stock Exchange (and now Financial Services Authority) requirements for disclosure of aspects of non-compliance.

## 18.6 SUBSEQUENT DEVELOPMENTS

It is now more than 15 years since the collapse of Polly Peck and the near-contemporary failures of BCCI and the Mirror Group. Since that time UK accounting standards have continued to be developed and refined, initially by the ASB and now under the effective aegis of the International Accounting Standards Board. There has also been revision and strengthening of the original Combined Code (incorporating the later Hampel 1998 report and, post-Enron, the Higgs 2003 and Smith 2003 reports). In this time there have, inevitably, been many occasions on which corporate failure and corporate irregularity have come to public attention, perhaps most notably in respect of the terminal losses sustained by Barings Bank as a result of unauthorized trading by just one employee. In Barings, however, the creativity in the accounting consisted almost entirely of the trader not reporting loss-making trades by hiding them in the now infamous Error Account 88888; and the fundamental issue was the lack of controls within the entity which allowed these losses to build up until, when revealed, they overwhelmed the company. The extensive unauthorized trading was sustained by the provisions of large amounts of cash by the bank's head office, purportedly for margin purposes[21] – with only a very belated realization that either the extent of trading taking place far exceeded authorized levels or that the cash was being used to settle losing trades (in fact both appear to have been the case).[22]

The losses sustained by some policy holders of the mutual insurer Equitable Life in consequence of the need for the company to meet its obligations in terms of guaranteed annuities to other policy holders were also given much publicity and have been intensively investigated and litigated. Here the question was essentially whether the company could adjust final bonuses so as to reduce payouts to those policy holders who were entitled to guaranteed annuities. During periods of high inflation and high nominal returns, Equitable had routinely provided policy holders with an option to convert their policy to an annuity on termination – but without any expectation that such conversion would take place. The sharp fall in inflation from the early 1990s onwards meant that these annuities became very attractive to policy holders. The accounting issues revolved around the question of how and when Equitable should have recognized the potential losses attaching to these annuities, itself a question irrevocably tied up with the legality of Equitable's attempt to reduce the terminal bonuses for one subset of its policy holders for the purpose, as they saw it, of achieving equity between groups of policy holders.[23]

Other more recent cases of perceived accounting misstatement which have been investigated by the JDS have included: Wickes (immediate recognition of material supplier rebates which were conditional upon the attainment of future purchase levels); Wiggins (recognition of profit on development contracts ahead of the grant of planning permission) and Versailles (massive and fraudulent overstatement of turnover in relation to a credit lending business – in the 1999 accounts claimed turnover of £232 million was subsequently restated as just £37 million and debtors of £80 million to just £5 million).[24] Space does not permit detailed discussion of these cases other than to say that they illustrate the range and variety in which accounting and financial reporting can be utilized to achieve outcomes varying from those which might be seen as being on or a little over the borderline of what is acceptable practice, to scenarios such as that at Versailles where the accounting was an integral part of a fraud involving a complex and detailed artifice of false accounting records with circulating payments between group companies being treated as genuine third-party business.

---

[21] In this context, margin is the collateral that the holder of a position in financial instruments has to deposit to cover the credit risk of its counterparty.

[22] See the JDS 1998 and 2002 reports (available at http://www.castigator.org.uk/index.html?coopers_tr.html) for further discussion of Barings with specific reference to the role of the auditors.

[23] See the Penrose report available at http://www.hm-treasury.gov.uk/independent_reviews/penrose_report/indrev_pen_index.cfm for further details of the relevant accounting and regulatory issues.

[24] See the Serious Fraud Office press release at http://www.sfo.gov.uk/news/prout/pr_264.asp?id=264 for further details of the background to the case and the outcome of the criminal proceedings.

## 18.7 CONCLUSIONS

The nature and practice of creative accounting runs from earnings management through to fraudulent misrepresentation. The focus in this chapter has been on a case study approach which, perhaps inevitably, has concentrated on the more extreme and spectacular cases. To conclude, we bring out some aspects linking the three main cases (BCCI, Mirror Group, Polly Peck) which we have discussed – highlighting in particular common themes relating to issues of internal control and governance. In each case, a single dominant personality exercised largely unfettered control within the company. There is no doubt that these individuals had abilities which marked them out from the average corporate executive and in each case it was widely perceived that the commercial entity was their own creation. Kerry and Brown (1992) note that '[b]y all accounts – ranging from statements made by Bert Lance [a former member of the US administration] to Jimmy Carter [a former US president] to the Pakistani bankers who went to work for him at BCCI – Agha Hasan Abedi [the founder and driving force behind BCCI] was a man of extraordinary personal charisma. That charisma was the glue which held BCCI together.' They characterize the entity's organizational structure in the following terms: 'There was Mr Abedi at the very top, there was Mr Naqvi who was like a chief operating officer, who converted . . . Mr Abedi's ideas and things into practical shapes. And then there was a big gap between these two and the other executives who were all called general managers.' Kerry and Brown (1992) note that: 'BCCI's conception, growth, collapse, and criminality are inextricably linked with the personality of its founder, Agha Hasan Abedi, who in turn was a product of the unique conditions of Muslim India in the final period of British rule prior to partition, and the first years after partition.'

The DTI report following the collapse of the Mirror Group stated that it was clear to many people who dealt with Robert Maxwell that 'he was a bully and a domineering personality, but could be charming on occasions' (DTI, 2001, p. 19, quoted by Wearing, 2005). But many people admired the way that he had rebuilt his business empire, and to an extent his reputation, following the Pergamon/Leasco affair. Maxwell too treated the Mirror Group as very much his personal fiefdom, 'acting, as always, as if he owned everything and he had the absolute right to do as he wished with any of the companies, public or private, of which he held the stewardship' (Davies, 1993, p. 332, quoted by Wearing, 2005).

Asil Nadir too possessed great charisma and force of personality in his business dealings – but, as we have seen, appears on occasion to have demonstrated (as, to perhaps an even more marked extent, did Maxwell) a degree of disdain for the opinions of his fellow board members. Maxwell and Nadir were both perceived to be outsiders seeking acceptance in part from the conventional financial and commercial world; and both were known to have private business interests. Abedi also appears to have considered himself as an interloper. Abedi was quoted as attributing BCCI's problems in obtaining a full UK banking licence to opposition from both the Bank of England and 'the Club' (Kerry and Brown, 1992). To an extent there was an air of mystery about each of the three entities' businesses and as to how they generated their profitability. This was particularly true of BCCI: 'BCCI's amazing rate of growth continued in good years and bad, without regard to macro-economic conditions' (Kerry and Brown, 1992).

Maxwell's business interests were a little more straightforward than Asil Nadir's, although there was always a perception of significant wealth resources tied up in 'the private side', resources which, if they had existed at any time, were wholly inadequate to support the losses in the public companies. The almost unprecedented growth and profitability of Polly Peck, based as it apparently was on the activities of a rather mundane fruit packaging business, also gave rise to a perception, usually expressed very indirectly, that questions as to the legitimacy of its business operations were unhelpful and inappropriate lest they 'killed the goose that laid the golden egg'.

In each case these factors combined to produce a 'control culture' and governance environment very far removed from that which might be considered ideal. Polly Peck had non-executives (there is no reference to an audit committee in the annual reports) but there is little evidence that these were effective in any way. The Mirror Group companies had non-executive directors but again the contribution, if any, to governance is difficult to determine. The DTI report (DTI, 2001) claimed that Robert Maxwell's attitude was that non-executives might be appointed to seek to obtain political influence, to add lustre in terms of lending their name to the company or even as a means of helping friends who had lost office – but 'beyond that, non-executive directors had no function in Robert Maxwell's world' (DTI, 2001, pp. 185–186). If BCCI had formalized institutions and procedures of governance it is fair to say on the basis of the *ex post* inquiry that their influence was completely non-existent.[25] The governance failures went hand in hand with control weaknesses which, in each case, enabled the more directly fraudulent transactions to take place.

The control weaknesses at BCCI were referred to by the Bank of England when it took its decision to shut BCCI down: 'It appears from the Price Waterhouse Report [of June 1991] that the accounting records [of BCCI] have completely failed and continue to fail to meet the standard required of institutions authorised under the Banking Act. It further appears that there is not [a] proper or adequate system of controls for managing the business of BCCI.' In the Mirror Group, the lack of any sort of high-level control to prevent inappropriate and illegal transfers of cash and pension fund assets is extensively documented in the DTI report – and as we have seen, a similar failure of controls enabled very large sums of cash to leave Polly Peck.

A final aspect relates to the failure in all three cases of external audit to perform the role ascribed to it by society and by regulators. Criticism of Price Waterhouse's role with respect to BCCI was relatively muted in both the Bingham report and the subsequent JDS investigation and report, which noted the complexities of the audit and the concerted attempt to mislead and deceive the auditors. But the US Senate Report was critical, stating: 'Regardless of BCCI's attempts to hide its frauds from its outside auditors, there were numerous warning bells visible to the auditors from the early years of the bank's activities, and BCCI's auditors could have and should have done more to respond to them.' As we have seen, the auditors of both the Mirror Group and Polly Peck were heavily criticized by the relevant professional disciplinary tribunals.

---

[25] There is a brief reference in the Senate Committee report to the existence of an audit committee at BCCI and the submission of a report to it by Price Waterhouse in 1988 – but there is no discussion of the composition or effectiveness of the audit committee.

Significant changes in governance, control and audit have taken place since the three major *causes célèbres* which we document. Accounting standards and related regulations are now far more wide-ranging in their scope and coverage, and enforcement mechanisms are more structured and systematic than they previously were. There is little doubt that the introduction of the Combined Code has significantly influenced both formal governance structures and also modes of thinking about the nature and practice of governance (although some have questioned the effectiveness of the changes introduced in terms of generating 'better' corporate governance – see, for example, Gwilliam and Marnet, 2007; Spira, 2003). Of course, these new governance structures have not wholly eliminated either creative accounting or the use of financial statements to mask major fraud and defalcation (as, for example, in the Versailles case). Nevertheless regulators, the representatives of the accounting profession and of the major auditing firms, believe that these changes have moved the goal posts, in the UK at least, so that blatant accounting manipulation and actual or alleged fraud of the nature that took place at BCCI, the Mirror Group and Polly Peck could not take place today.

At the time of writing, economies around the globe are suffering as a result of a crisis in the financial services sector – itself allegedly following from, *inter alia*, imprudence in risk management and consequent imbalance in funding and asset portfolios. Governmental and regulatory efforts at present are focused on stabilization of financial markets and restoration of confidence. It seems likely, however, that wide-reaching, formal investigations will follow. In the UK, there is as yet no suggestion of any associated problems or impropriety in financial accounting and reporting, albeit issues around the use of mark-to-market accounting have been raised. We might predict that governance will again be in the spotlight, and this, together with financial accounting and reporting issues of financial asset valuation and risk assessment, and their associated disclosure and transparency, may well figure large in the deliberations of investigators and regulators in the months and years to come.

## 18.8 ACKNOWLEDGEMENTS

We would like to thank Professors Rachel Baskerville, Mike Jones, Richard Macve and Christopher Napier for their insights and very helpful comments on earlier drafts of this chapter.

## REFERENCES

Adams, J. and Frantz, D. (1993), *A Full Service Bank: How BCCI Stole Billions Around the World*, Simon & Schuster, New York.

Adams, S. (2010), 'Fugitive Polly Peck tycoon granted bail for fraud trial' *Daily Telegraph*, 31 July, p. 16.

Arnold, A. (1991), 'Secret reserves or special credits? A reappraisal of the reserve and provision accounting policies of the Royal Mail Steam Packet Company, 1915–1927', *Accounting and Business Research*, **21**(83), 203–214.

Arnold, A. (1997), 'Publishing your private affairs to the world: corporate financial disclosures in the UK 1900–1924', *Accounting, Business & Financial History*, **7**(2), 143–173.

Arnold, A. and Collier, P. (2007), *The Evolution of Reserve and Provision Accounting in the UK, 1938–50*, ICAS, London.

Arnold, P. and Sikka, P. (2001), ' "Globalisation" and the state–profession relationship: the case of the Bank of Credit and Commerce International', *Accounting, Organizations and Society*, **26**(6), 475–499.

Beattie, V., Fearnley, S. and Hines, A. (1997), 'The Financial Reporting Review Panel: an analysis of its activities', in *Financial Reporting Today, Current and Emerging Issues*, Accountancy Books, Milton Keynes.

Beaty, J. and Gwynne, S. (1993), *The Outlaw Bank: A Wild Ride into the Secret Heart of BCCI*, Random House, New York.

Bingham, Lord Justice (1992), *Inquiry into the Supervision of the Bank of Credit and Commerce International*, HMSO, London.

Bircher, P. (1988), 'The adoption of consolidated accounting in Great Britain', *Accounting and Business Research*, **19**(73), 3–13.

Cadbury (1992), *Report of the Committee on the Financial Aspects of Corporate Governance*, Professional Publishing Ltd, London.

Davies, N. (1993), *The Unknown Maxwell*, Pan, London.

Davies, P. and Bourn, A. (1972), 'Lord Kylsant and the Royal Mail', *Business History*, June, 103–123.

DTI (1971), *Report on the affairs of International Learning Systems Corporation Limited and interim report on the affairs of Pergamon Press Limited – investigation under Section 165(b) of the Companies Act 1948*; by Rondle Owen Charles Stable QC and Sir Ronald George Leach CBE FCA, HMSO, London.

DTI (1973), *Rolls-Royce Limited: investigation under Section 165[a][i] of the Companies Act 1948*; report by R.A. MacCrindle and P. Godfrey, HMSO, London.

DTI (2001), *Mirror Group Newspapers plc – investigations under Sections 432(2) and 442 of the Companies Act 1985*; report by the Honourable Sir Roger John Laugharne Thomas and Raymond Thomas Turner FCA, HMSO, London.

Edwards, J. (1989), *A History of Financial Accounting*, Routledge, London.

Edwards, P. and Shaoul, J. (1999), 'Reporting accounting?', *Accounting Forum*, **23**(1), 59–92.

French, E. (1977), 'The evolution of the Dividend Law of England', in *Studies in Accounting*, eds W. Baxter and S. Davidson, ICAEW, London, pp. 306–331.

Griffiths, I. (1986), *Creative Accounting*, Firethorn Press, London.

Gwilliam, D. and Marnet, O. (2007), 'Audit in the Corporate Governance Paradigm: a Cornerstone Built on Shifting Sand', Working Paper, University of Exeter.

Gwilliam, D. and Russell, T. (1991), 'Polly Peck: Where were the Analysts?,' *Accountancy*, January, 25–26.

Holmes, G. and Sugden, A. (1990), *Interpreting Company Reports and Accounts*, 4th edn, Woodhead Faulkner, London.

Holmes, G. and Sugden, A. (1994), *Interpreting Company Reports and Accounts*, 5th edn, Prentice Hall/Woodhead Faulkner, London.

Kerry, J. and Brown, H. (1992), *The BCCI Affair. A Report to the Committee on Foreign Relations United States Senate*, December 102d Congress 2d Session Senate Print 102–140, http://www.fas.org/irp/congress/1992_rpt/bcci/.

Macve, R. (1997), *A Conceptual Framework for Financial Accounting and Reporting: Vision Tool or Threat?* Garland, New York.

McBarnet, D. and Whelan, C. (1999), *Creative Accounting and the Cross-Eyed Javelin Thrower*, John Wiley & Sons Ltd, London.

McCarten, J. (1939), 'The greatest accountant in the world', *The New Yorker*, December, reproduced in W. Baxter and S. Davidson (eds) (1977), *Studies in Accounting*, ICAEW.

McKie, D. (2004), *Jabez: The Rise and Fall of a Victorian Rogue*, Atlantic Books, London.

Mitchell, A., Sikka, P., Arnold, P., Cooper, C. and Willmott, H. (2001), *The BCCI Cover-Up*, Association for Accountancy and Business Affairs (available at http://visar.csustan.edu/aaba/BCCICOVERUP.pdf).

Rutherford, B. (1996), 'The AEI GEC gap revisited', *Accounting, Business & Financial History*, **6**(2), 141–161.

Rutherford, B. (2007), *Financial Reporting in the UK: A History of the Accounting Standards Committee, 1969–1990*, Routledge, London.

Smith, T. (1992), *Accounting for Growth*, Century, London.

Smith, T. (1996), *Accounting for Growth*, 2nd edn, Century, London.

Spira, L. (2003), Audit committees: begging the question, *Corporate Governance*, **12**(4), 489–499.

Wearing, R. (2005), *Cases in Corporate Governance*, Sage Publications, London.

# 19

# Creative Accounting and Accounting Scandals in the USA

Charles W. Mulford and Eugene E. Comiskey

## 19.1 INTRODUCTION

The list of US firms involved in accounting scandals in recent years is frighteningly long. The names of many roll off one's tongue as readily as a list of professional athletes, musical artists or even movie stars. In contrast to athletes, musical artists and movie stars, however, these firms are famous for the wrong reasons. Consider names like Cendant Corp., Tyco International, Ltd or W.R. Grace & Co. These are names of firms that readers may not have heard had they not been involved in some form of accounting scandal. Others include HealthSouth Corp. and, of course, Enron Corp. and WorldCom, Inc. All of these companies and, unfortunately, many others are firms that became engulfed in the accounting maelstrom that developed in the USA in the 1990s and extended into the early part of this century.

A reasonable question that any informed reader should ask is: why were there so many accounting scandals in the USA during the 1990s and early 2000s? Many would say that reduced diligence and a decline in independence on the part of outside auditors were the primary contributing factors. Others would point to a set of accounting standards that was very rule-oriented with bright-line guides or strict dictums that were just begging to be thwarted by smart accountants. Consider too the history-making bull market for equities that developed in the late 1990s. It would be argued by some that high stock prices became the end that was justified by the means – even the means of creative accounting practices. As stock prices rose, in many cases for no apparent reason, the onus fell on management to provide justification in the form of higher earnings, whether those earnings were truly earned or not. But these managers found solace in the dubious observation that higher prices benefited all stakeholders and thus accounting acts to support them were not harmful. As the bull market continued and stock prices moved ever higher, many of these same managers gained a sense of entitlement that never seemed to be sated, even as option grants to them increased to what would appear to be preposterous levels.

Like any major event, whether social, political, economic or even natural, there was no single identifiable cause for the significant number of accounting scandals that developed in the USA. Many factors, including those identified and probably many others played

*Creative Accounting, Fraud and International Accounting Scandals*   Edited by Michael Jones
© 2011 Michael Jones. Published by John Wiley & Sons, Ltd

contributing roles. A natural follow-up to the question of why there were so many accounting scandals in the USA is the question: where was the Securities and Exchange Commission, the US regulatory watchdog? Is it not the job of the SEC to review corporate financial statement filings? While counter arguments can be made that focus on limits to the SEC's staff and the Commission's reliance on external auditors who were arguably compromised at times, the fact of the matter is that the SEC made public its collective concern about a building accounting-scandal storm. In 1998, in a speech known as the 'numbers game' speech, Arthur Levitt, the former chairman of the SEC, called attention to what he termed, '. . . a widespread, but too little-challenged custom: earnings management . . . [that] can best be characterized as a game . . . that, if not addressed soon, will have adverse consequences . . .,' (Levitt, 1998).

At the time of the speech the wave of accounting scandals in the USA had already begun. By then the world had already witnessed the widely known scandals of Cendant Corp., W.R. Grace & Co. and Sunbeam Corp. Yet, in their review of filings, the SEC's staff were witnessing an alarming increase in creative accounting practices that extended well beyond this limited set of companies. What they were seeing suggested to them that many managers had learned and embraced the concept of creative accounting and were using such practices to the likely detriment of investors. The SEC saw the problem as it was developing, announced it to others and took action in the form of a nine-point plan. The plan was designed to return reliability and transparency to financial reporting in the USA. In the end, however, the SEC's actions were probably too little, too late.

At the time of writing, the USA is in the midst of a mortgage-related credit crisis that has resulted in the failure of many venerable financial institutions, including Fannie Mae, Freddie Mac, American International Group, Inc., The Bear Stearns Companies, Inc., IndyMac Federal Bank, and Washington Mutual, Inc. While the causes of the crisis are not due to accounting scandals, per se, accounting policy has played a role in the multi-faceted developments that continue to play out. In particular, securitization accounting permitted lenders to account for loans as sales and remove loan balances from their balance sheets. Such accounting was permitted even in cases where sellers retained a continuing obligation to the loans that were sold. Such a lack of accountability encouraged reckless lending. As a result, loans were originated that should not have been made. Recently, the Financial Accounting Standards Board addressed the accounting for financial asset securitizations and soon will begin requiring that such loans must be true sales before they are accounted for as such. Fair value accounting also played a role as financial institutions were required to mark their financial asset portfolios to market. While the point is arguable, we would maintain that fair value accounting served investors well by highlighting earlier the problems that were developing.

The scandals that occurred in the USA could happen anywhere and new regulations notwithstanding, will probably happen in the USA yet again. While not a comforting thought, by studying past scandals, readers will be better equipped to avoid being misled by future ones.

In this chapter we look at some of the more noteworthy accounting scandals occurring in the USA in recent years. However, given the large number of scandals, we felt it necessary to organize them according to the manner in which each of the scandals was effected. We use the following four general categories to classify the scandals:

1) Premature or fictitious revenue recognition
2) Capitalized costs and/or extended amortization periods
3) Overstated assets and/or understated liabilities
4) Other creative accounting practices.

In the fourth category, the other creative accounting practices, we include such topics as the abuse of restructuring charges, creative financial statement classifications, derivatives-related schemes and the very recent scandal involving backdated stock options. Certainly more groups could be added, but this is a good working set. Also, while some scandals can be included in more than one category, we group them according to what we view as the primary creative accounting steps taken.

Our focus is on accounting practices that extend beyond the boundaries of generally accepted accounting principles (GAAP). Without repercussions from regulators, firms may use accounting practices that are aggressive but within the boundaries of GAAP. Examples include the capitalization of costs that are permitted under GAAP but that are expensed by most of a firm's key competitors or the selection of optimistic useful lives for property, plant and equipment. However, aggressive practices that are within the boundaries of GAAP would hardly be considered to entail an accounting scandal.

Accounting practices that extend beyond the boundaries of GAAP may not necessarily be considered to constitute fraud. In the USA, the decision as to whether an action is fraudulent is up to the SEC to demonstrate (in the case of civil fraud and violation of the anti-fraud provisions of the US securities laws) or subject to prosecution by the Department of Justice (in the case of criminal fraud) or some other court of proper jurisdiction. Fraudulent financial reporting is considered to involve material misstatements with a preconceived intent to mislead. Thus, in this chapter, we write about accounting scandals in the USA that entail evidence of material misstatements involving actions that extend beyond the boundaries of GAAP. However, the actions taken may or may not entail alleged civil or criminal fraud.

In identifying our examples of US accounting scandals, we relied primarily upon publicly announced enforcement actions of the SEC. The Commission's Division of Enforcement investigates potential violations of the securities laws and makes recommendations as to when enforcement actions should be pursued against alleged violations. A settlement may be negotiated, or, depending on the seriousness of the alleged wrongdoing, a hearing may be held before an administrative law judge, or through a civil action filed with a US District Court. When settled, the details of a case, together with the SEC's findings and the resulting penalty, are reported in what is termed an SEC *Accounting and Auditing Enforcement Release*. These enforcement releases contain a treasure trove of information regarding US accounting scandals. Beyond these enforcement actions, we also looked to financial publications for more background information on the accounting scandals discussed here.

There are two frauds that occurred in the USA that deserve special note. Because of their size and impact on accounting practice and the securities laws in the USA, Enron Corp. and WorldCom, Inc. are two frauds that stand apart from all others. Both frauds, which included criminal prosecutions of key officers in both companies, are discussed near the end of the chapter, outside the chapter's classification scheme. The chapter concludes with a look at the aftermath of the accounting scandals and the changes that have occurred in response to them.

## 19.2 SCANDALS SINCE THE 1990s

### 19.2.1 Premature or Fictitious Revenue Recognition

Accounting standards generally call for revenue to be recognized when it is earned and realizable. Earned revenue entails completion of the earnings process, including a valid order and delivery of the goods or services in question. Realizability requires that the selling company have a valid claim from a creditworthy customer.

The difference between premature revenue and fictitious revenue is one of degree. Premature revenue typically results from revenue recognition pursuant to a valid order but prior to delivery. Fictitious revenue results from the recognition of non-existent revenue. A valid customer order does not exist. Whether revenue is recognized as premature or fictitious, it is done outside the boundaries of GAAP. However, depending on the circumstances, fraud is typically not alleged for premature revenue whereas it is for fictitious revenue.

While not considered an accounting scandal, the case of Bausch & Lomb, Inc. is one that can be characterized as premature revenue recognition. In the third quarter of 1993, the company used an especially aggressive promotion and marketing campaign, including deep discounts for contact lenses, to effectively push more product onto distributors than they would normally purchase. In some cases, distributors bought enough product to last them two years at normal resale levels. In effect, Bausch & Lomb borrowed sales from future quarters in order to boost the current quarter.

Such channel-stuffing, as the practice is known, is not illegal. Many would view it as a smart business practice and certainly one that has been practiced in many industries for years. However, Bausch & Lomb's transgression was that it did not properly disclose its practices and made it appear that reported sales increases were both real and sustainable.

In 2000, Lucent Technologies, Inc. restated its financial statements for revenue that had been recognized prematurely. Most of the restatement was due to higher than normal returns from distributors that had not sold product that had been shipped to them. The company had really overshipped to its distributors in an effort to meet short-term sales goals that were overly ambitious. As quoted in the *Wall Street Journal*, the company's CEO noted, 'We mortgaged future sales and revenue in a way we're paying for now ...,' (Schacht, 2000, B2).

Xerox Corp. may also be characterized as a premature revenue story. The company used sales-type lease accounting, which called for recognizing revenue up-front on its office equipment leases. In a sales-type lease, revenue is recognized for the present value of future rent amounts. The interest rate used in calculating present value should properly incorporate the credit risk level of the lessee. The riskier the lessee, the higher the discount rate; the lower the present value of the rental stream and accordingly, the lower the amount of revenue recognized. Many of Xerox's lessees were in South America, where interest rates were much higher than in the USA. However, Xerox did not properly incorporate those higher interest rates into its present value calculations, resulting in overstated revenue. The company was forced into a major restatement of its financial statements for the late 1990s. In its restatement, the company abandoned sales-type lease accounting for many of its leases, moving instead to recognizing revenue over the lease terms.

While there were many accounting problems at Sunbeam Corp., fictitious revenue recognition was primary among them. One of the actions taken by the company was the abuse of a permitted practice known as 'bill and hold' accounting. When properly applied, accounting for a bill and hold transaction entails recognition of revenue for the sale of merchandise that is segregated and held for a customer awaiting a future delivery date. Such an action is done to accommodate the customer who may not be able to take immediate delivery of its purchased product. In essence, there is a valid order from a creditworthy customer. However, rather than delivering the purchased merchandise, it is temporarily segregated in the seller's warehouse. Title is transferred to the customer and the seller would not include the purchased goods in a count of its own inventory.

Sunbeam stretched bill and hold accounting to include delivery delays that were designed to achieve its own revenue goals. For example, Sunbeam might approach a customer with a special price if the customer were to place a large order. Sunbeam would offer to hold all merchandise purchased pursuant to the order until the customer was ready to take delivery – even if delivery occurred months later. Sunbeam would improperly recognize revenue upfront on such a sale, even without delivery. These practices were done to boost revenue in 1997, effectively borrowing sales from the early quarters of 1998.

There is one example in particular that captures the essence of fictitious revenue recognition, California Micro Devices Corp. In a criminal trial of the company's chairman, testimony noted that revenue recognition practices involved one particularly bold move, '... booking bogus sales to fake companies for products that didn't exist' (MacDonald, 2000, A1). As was learned during discovery leading up to the criminal trial, one-third of the company's reported revenue of $45 million in financial year 1994 was non-existent. As revenue goals in the company became ever more aggressive, managers began relaxing their definition of what constitutes a sale. For example, the company began recognizing revenue for product shipped to real companies, even in the absence of orders. Moreover, those sales were not reversed when the product was returned. As the fraud developed, sales were even recognized for fake shipments. In fact, as the fraud grew, the company's staff became involved in an ongoing joke, where staff persons would say to each other, '... like in a Bugs Bunny cartoon, "What's wevenue?"' (Macdonald, 2000, A1).

No discussion of premature or fictitious revenue would be complete without reference to the use of what are referred to by the SEC as side letters. Side letters, or really 'secret' side letters, are side agreements or contract addendums. While there is nothing wrong with contract addendums, problems surface when such addendums are kept secret and are not properly accounted for. Such side letters may actually neutralize a sales transaction between a company and its customer, rendering it either non-existent, or making it subject to future efforts on the part of the selling company. An improper side letter might include liberal rights of return; rights to cancel orders at any time; contingencies, such as the need to raise funds on the part of the customer that if not met make the sale null and void; being excused from payment if goods purchased are not resold; or, even worse, a total absolution of payment. With such side-agreement provisions, which are outside normal accounting channels, there is really no sale agreement between the selling company and its customer.

Certainly, no revenue should be recognized. Any shipment of merchandise in such cases should be treated as a consignment sale, in effect, a transfer of inventory that is still held by the selling company.

Informix Corp. was a particularly egregious user of side agreements. During the 1990s, company personnel used a variety of both written and oral side agreements to encourage customers to place orders that effectively rendered their sales agreements unenforceable.

While not precisely an example of premature or fictitious revenue recognition, the case of US FoodService, Inc. (a subsidiary of a Dutch Company, Royal Ahold, NV) is one of improper *income* recognition. That is, rather than recognizing revenue in a premature or fictitious way, the company recognized vendor rebates, a reduction in cost of goods sold, which should not have been recognized. US FoodService, Inc. is covered briefly here and in more detail in Chapter 15.

Like many resellers, US FoodService was offered rebates from its vendors for volume purchases. As a hypothetical example, the company may be offered a 10 % discount if purchases from one vendor reached $10 million. The rebate might be increased, say to 15 % and applied to all purchases, if purchase levels reached $12 million. At issue, should rebates be accrued as purchases are made? If they should be accrued, what percentage rebate should be used? That is, should the company begin accruing rebates at the 15 % level, even when purchases have not yet justified that level, on the premise that the higher purchase level will be reached and the higher rebate will be earned? Also, how should the accrued rebate be accounted for? Should it be recorded as a reduction of inventory or of cost of goods sold?

US FoodService accrued the rebates at the higher anticipated percentage level and credited them to cost of goods sold, boosting income. Generally accepted accounting principles permit the practice, provided the rebates were probable and could be estimated. Credits to cost of goods sold were permitted as long as the purchased goods were resold. On the surface it would appear that US FoodService was not breaking any rules. However, later it was learned that during 2001 and 2002 the company's program of obtaining and accruing rebates really became more of its own line of business. A so-called 'initiative' at the firm gave employees an opportunity to earn bonus money based on purchases made. As the company made purchases of unusual quantities of products like frozen pies and bottled water, higher and higher rebates were earned and recorded, boosting income. However, the company did not resell all of the products purchased and, in fact, had to rent additional space and hire cold-storage trucks to hold it all. As such, the credits should have been to inventory cost and not cost of goods sold.

Soon after the company's 2002 earnings were announced, in the face of investigations by the US Attorney's office in Manhattan and the SEC, Royal Ahold, the US FoodService parent company, acknowledged that it had improperly accounted for vendor rebates. According to the company, earnings for 2001 and 2002 would be restated downward by amounts totalling more than $500 million.

### 19.2.2 Capitalized Costs and/or Extended Amortization Periods

When an incurred expenditure benefits future reporting periods, generally accepted accounting principles call for its capitalization and amortization to expense against those future periods. In effect, the expenditure is for the purchase of an asset and is not an expense that benefits only the current period. Consider costs incurred for an oil change and servicing of a company car versus the replacement of that car's engine. The oil change should be expensed currently as it does not benefit future periods, while the expenditure for the engine replacement does benefit future periods and should be capitalized and amortized over the periods that benefit.

Of course, professional judgement plays a prominent role in deciding whether an expenditure will benefit future reporting periods. As a result, different companies will make varying decisions on whether expenditures should be capitalized. Often they are plying the flexibility in GAAP to reach desired earnings results – all within the boundaries of GAAP.

Consider, for example, software development costs. While GAAP specify that such costs should be capitalized once software development reaches 'technological feasibility' (basically, that the software will be able to function as it is designed to do), a majority of companies actually expense all software development costs incurred. Flexibility in GAAP permits it. It is not that their software does not reach technology feasibility, but rather that only immaterial amounts of software costs are incurred after technological feasibility is reached. Flexibility in GAAP permits it.

Consider too the accounting for advertising costs. In the USA, advertising costs are expensed as incurred. While it can be argued that advertising does in fact result in future benefits in the form of higher sales, it is difficult if not impossible to link most advertising with actual sales. Thus, advertising costs incurred are accounted for as though they provide no future benefit. In contrast to traditional advertising expenditures, however, accounting practices differ for so-called direct-response advertising. Here, capitalization is permitted, opening the way for differing accounting practices across firms.

Direct-response advertising entails costs incurred to elicit sales from customers who can be shown to have responded to specific offers. The idea is that the company can demonstrate that historically, the incurrence of a certain expenditure will generate sufficient revenue to cover that expenditure and provide a return. There is a definite future benefit and historical evidence is available to demonstrate it. Examples of direct-response advertising costs include the mailing of coupons and catalogues. With sufficient historical evidence as to realizability, costs incurred in printing and distributing coupons and catalogues can be capitalized. However, some firms choose to expense the costs as incurred.

While GAAP does provide for flexibility in cost capitalization, a problematic case arises when a company stretches its capitalization policies beyond any reasonable level. For example, a firm might capitalize costs that clearly provide no future benefit. Capitalization in such a case moves beyond the boundaries of GAAP and, depending on the materiality of the amounts involved, an accounting scandal may ensue.

During 1995 and 1996, America Online, Inc. capitalized certain direct-response advertising costs, in particular, the cost of recording and mailing new disks with membership applications, that the Securities and Exchange Commission felt should be expensed as incurred. While AOL argued that the company had the necessary historical evidence to support capitalization, the SEC disagreed. The SEC argued that the company's industry was new and dynamic and that prior evidence of realizability was not sufficiently representative of future results to warrant capitalization. Ultimately, AOL was required by the SEC to expense the capitalized costs. The company's capitalization policy had, according to the

SEC, moved beyond the boundaries of GAAP. While not a 'scandal' per se, the example does demonstrate the role of judgement in capitalization decisions and the grey line that can often exist in such decisions.

It is not difficult to identify companies that used capitalization policies to improperly boost income. In fact, some of the biggest USA frauds involve improper cost capitalization.

To most, the story of Tyco International Ltd is one of corporate greed and looting. The company's CEO, Dennis Kozlowski, was found guilty of essentially stealing shareholders' money – lots of it. It was money he spent on purchasing and decorating his own residences, on travel, lavish parties and, of course, expensive art. However, while prosecutors were successful in pressing their looting case and did not prosecute the CEO on accounting misdeeds, there were major accounting problems at Tyco. One of them entailed improper cost capitalization.

One of the company's business lines was the sale of security systems. The company ran this business through a network of independently owned dealers. The dealers would sell the systems, complete with equipment and a monitoring contract. Tyco would acquire the customers from the dealers. The dealers incurred marketing and administrative costs to attract and sign up new customers. These are costs that Tyco would have incurred and expensed. However, because Tyco purchased these customers from the dealers, the full costs incurred, including a *de facto* reimbursement to the dealers for their marketing and administrative expenses, could be accounted for as assets.

One could argue whether the costs incurred by Tyco to acquire its customers entailed some form of reimbursement for marketing and administrative costs that should have been expensed. It is a grey area. However, the company also used its customer acquisition program to boost earnings further. That is, while Tyco might pay say $800 to purchase a customer from a dealer, the company would account for the acquisition as though it paid $1000, with $200 of the purchase price being accounted for as a 'connection fee' – a reimbursement to Tyco for administrative costs incurred in setting up the new customer. It worked well as it gave Tyco immediate income at the time of a purchase of a new customer (see Maremont, 2004). Ultimately, Tyco restated its results for 1998 through 2003. The company admitted to past accounting mistakes totalling more than $2 billion.

In 1998, Cendant Corp. came into being with the acquisition of CUC International, Inc. by HFS, Inc. Within weeks after the deal closed, significant irregularities were found on the books of CUC International. The bad news chopped about $14 billion off the market value of Cendant. Somewhat embarrassing for the company is that even with its due diligence, the problems at CUC International, which included improper cost capitalization, were not found before the acquisition. What is particularly interesting, however, is that CUC had taken a special charge for improper cost capitalization some 10 years earlier. Thus, there was fair warning of improper tendencies at CUC.

CUC International was a membership shopping club. Members would pay fees to shop in company-sponsored stores, which the company recorded as deferred income and recognized over a one-year membership period. Costs incurred by the company to market its memberships and sign up new members, so-called membership acquisition costs, were capitalized and amortized over a three-year period. The company argued that the costs were a form of direct-response advertising. However, the significance of the amounts capitalized, which net of amortization amounted to 59 % of pre-tax income in 1988, raised some eyebrows. Moreover, the company capitalized many other costs, including promotion costs for which no new members had been obtained, and costs for what appeared to be severance pay for some terminated sales personnel. Ultimately, the vast majority of the costs that were capitalized under questionable circumstances were written off.

HealthSouth Corp. is an Alabama-based medical services firm. The SEC found evidence of fraud at the firm dating back to its founding in the 1980s. In fact, as part of the Justice Department's and SEC's investigation of the firm, many of its officers, including virtually all of its chief financial officers, pleaded guilty to financial statement fraud. The company's founder, Richard Scrushy, was found not guilty of financial fraud. However, in separate proceedings, he was found guilty of other criminal charges.

The HealthSouth fraud is one that entailed significant amounts of improperly capitalized costs. The company recorded approximately $1 billion in improper assets on its books. Items, including routine expenses such as advertising costs, or even sponsorship of a junior-league hockey team in Pennsylvania, were capitalized and reported as components of property, plant and equipment. Managers at the company knew that its auditors typically would not carefully audit expenditures for less than $5000 each on the premise that such amounts were not material. Thus, the company would capitalize small amounts, a few thousand dollars here, a few thousand dollars there, and the totals really added up. It is remarkable to think about the amount of effort that was needed to effect such a large fraud.

In the late 1980s, an elaborate fraud involving fictitious property, plant and equipment was carried out at the electronics manufacturer Comptronix Corp. The fraud included misstated inventory. In a regular fashion, typically monthly, management journalized an increase to inventory and a reduction to cost of goods sold. By reducing cost of goods sold, net income was increased. Aware that an unexplained increase in inventory would be a warning sign to some analysts, periodically some of the bogus inventory was transferred to property, plant and equipment. Fake invoices for equipment purchases were prepared to make it appear as though equipment additions were actually made. The thinking here was that bogus amounts could be carried longer in property, plant and equipment than in inventory. Management was right. The fraud was not detected until it was disclosed by company personnel.

A final, but extremely significant example of capitalization is at WorldCom. The fraud at WorldCom, Inc. was very much a cost-capitalization story. Given its significance, the details of the fraud at WorldCom are provided in a separate section later in this chapter.

When expenditures are capitalized, they must subsequently be amortized. Amortization requires selection of an appropriate amortization period. For financial reporting purposes, there are no hard and fast rules dictating what amortization period should be used. Judgement is necessary. Application of that judgement, however, can have a significant effect on reported results. For example, as reported in Mulford and Comiskey (2002, p. 222), Vitesse Semiconductor Corp., a company not implicated in the major scandals of the period, depreciates its property and equipment over a period of three to five years. If, instead, the company were to use six years – a very small change – its depreciation charge for 2000 would be reduced in an amount sufficient to increase pre-tax income by 14 %.

The selection of an unreasonably long amortization period results in a build-up of amortizable assets on the balance sheet. As such, future charges may be needed to write down those assets if they become value-impaired. Waste Management, Inc. is a case in point. While not considered a scandal, in 1997, the company took an impairment loss and restated its financial statements for 1994, 1995 and 1996. The culprits were unrealistically long amortization periods and residual values that were set too high.

### 19.2.3  Overstated Assets and/or Understated Liabilities

In this section, we consider assets that are not subject to amortization, such as inventory and investments. Also included are scandals that entailed the understatement of liabilities.

Some of the more outlandish accounting scandals entail the overstatement of inventory. Consider Bre-X Minerals, Ltd, for example. The gold mining company reported a significant gold find in the jungles of Indonesia. Following the discovery, there was a flurry of public announcements, including press releases and television appearances that touted ever-increasing amounts of discovered gold at the site. Investors got uneasy, however, when the company's geologist committed suicide by 'jumping' from a company helicopter. Eventually it was determined that Bre-X personnel had 'salted,' or added gold to, core test samples. The company actually owned little, if any, gold (see Heinzl, 1998).

Earnings can be overstated by the overstatement of other assets, including investments. Consider the case of Presidential Life Corp. The company had an investment portfolio of junk bonds that included holdings in such low-quality issues as Circle K Corp., Eastern Airlines, Inc. and Southland Corp. The fair values of these securities had declined significantly below cost. Recovery was unlikely. Yet, the company continued to carry its investments at cost under the premise that their values might yet recover. While not a scandal, the SEC did force the company to face reality and record a write-down.

When accrued liabilities are understated, earnings are conversely overstated, as the offset to an accrued liability account is expense. Consider, for example, Miniscribe, Inc. The company overstated income by understating its accruals for warranty obligations. This misstatement was, however, only a small part of the financial fraud committed at the company. The computer disk-drive manufacturer also packaged scrap items as good inventory and counted those packages as part of its finished goods.

In an effort to impart the impression to financial statement readers that a company has a reduced debt burden, steps may be taken to understate actual borrowed amounts. That was the case at Enron Corp., where debt reduction also resulted in an increase in shareholders' equity. Given its significance, details of the Enron Corp. fraud are discussed in a separate section later in this chapter.

The case of Adelphia Communications Corp. also involved off-balance sheet debt. However, this was more an example of undisclosed loan guarantees. At Adelphia, the founding family used the public company's credit quality to back what were effectively private loans with little associated disclosure. Judith Fischer, managing director of Executive Compensation Advisory Services, called it 'an abuse of the system' (see Sandberg and Lublin, 2002).

### 19.2.4  Other Creative Accounting Practices

#### 19.2.4.1  Abuse of Restructuring Charges

In an effort to become more competitive, companies may reorganize and restructure their operations. Markets often respond in a positive way to announcements of such events, even as companies indicate that significant charges will be taken in order to effect the restructurings. The charges are the companies' best estimates of the total future costs to be incurred in completing the necessary actions. They include such costs as severance pay and benefits, plant closing costs, lease termination fees and losses related to the impairment of inventory, property, plant and equipment and other assets. With restructurings, unscrupulous managers are afforded an opportunity to record charges that are larger than even high-end estimates of the costs needed to complete the process. The goal is to provide reserves that can be reversed, providing a boost to earnings in future periods.

Consider the example of W.R. Grace & Co. The SEC found that the company used its restructuring reserves to mislead investors between 1991 and 1995. Pursuant to the SEC's actions, the company was forced to restate its financial statements. What the SEC found was that the company used its restructuring reserves, accounts such as accruals for future payments of severance and benefits and plant closing costs, to boost future earnings. When managers determined that earnings were not going to meet previously set targets, the shortfall was offset by reversing a portion of the restructuring reserves.

### 19.2.4.2  Creative Financial Statement Classification

More than reported net income, analysts and investors are influenced by the amount of recurring income reported by a company. Such sustainable earnings receive higher stock price multiples than earnings generated by non-recurring sources such as gains on asset sales or litigation settlements. To this end, the more a company can impart the impression that its earnings are generated from sustainable sources, the more the markets will pay for those earnings.

Consider International Business Machines Corp., for example. In 1999, IBM netted against selling, general and administrative expenses (or SG&A) $2.7 billion in gains from the sale of its Global Network business. On the one hand, the inclusion of the gain as an offset to SG&A does not alter net income. On the other hand, to a casual reviewer of the income statement, the treatment suggests that earnings are derived from a more recurring source, expense control, than from a non-recurring one, a gain on sale. In late 2001, the company recorded another gain on the sale of an asset in the amount of $300 million, which it once again netted against SG&A. Worse, as part of a discussion of the company's results for the fourth quarter of that year, chairman Louis Gerstner said, 'We also once again demonstrated exceptional management of our cost and expense structure' (see Maremont and Bulkeley, 2002). However, without the sale, SG&A expenses would have been higher. While not considered an accounting scandal, in 2002, under SEC review, the company did revise the presentation of its income statement for 2001, moving the gain out of SG&A and into a special line of other income.

The creative classification of cash flows, taking steps to report higher operating cash inflows offset by outflows in the investing or financing sections, is another way that managers might create a heightened impression of sustainable financial performance. In fact, creative cash flow reporting was an important part of the accounting scandal at Enron discussed later in this chapter.

### 19.2.4.3  Derivatives-related Schemes

US GAAP requires firms to carry derivative instruments on the balance sheet at their fair value (Financial Accounting Standards Board, 1998). When first proposed, there was considerable resistance to this requirement from members of the business community who were concerned about increased earnings volatility. The increase in earnings volatility would be most severe in cases where derivatives were used to hedge exposure in situations where there was no contemporaneous offsetting gain or loss to record in the income statement. However, relief from this potential earnings volatility is available for certain hedging applications of derivatives.

If a number of conditions are satisfied and ongoing monitoring is conducted, a firm is permitted to initially record gains and losses from the revaluation of derivatives into shareholders' equity. Subsequently, these gains and losses are reclassified into the income statement when the offsetting gains or losses from the hedged items are also included in income. This *hedge accounting* eliminates the earnings volatility that would otherwise result from the revaluation of the derivative.

The top management of the Federal National Mortgage Association (usually referred to as Fannie Mae), a giant US financial firm, found hedge accounting to be very appealing. The use of hedge accounting could result in a smoother, more predictable stream of earnings and, as a result, help them to meet their earnings targets. Hitting defined earnings targets was critical to Fannie Mae management because exceeding defined earnings thresholds could result in millions of dollars of employee incentive compensation.

However, in its application of hedge accounting, Fannie Mae failed to follow the requirements necessary to qualify for this income-smoothing accounting method. Moreover, in applying hedge accounting, a *shortcut* method was elected by Fannie Mae that permits the hedger to assume that the gains and losses of the derivative and the hedged position are perfectly offsetting. The failure of Fannie Mae to follow the relevant GAAP requirements meant that their use of the shortcut method was improper. As a result, *hedge ineffectiveness*, the amount by which the gains and losses of the derivative and the hedged position do not offset, should have been included in the income statement, increasing volatility and making the achievement of earnings targets much more difficult.

By failing to meet all of the requirements for the use of hedge accounting, Fannie Mae recorded gains and losses from changes in the value of its derivatives in shareholders' equity, whereas they should have been recorded in the income statement. The improper accounting treatment for its derivatives, among other items, resulted in the overstatement of the earnings and capital of Fannie Mae.

The consequences of Fannie Mae's efforts to manage earnings by the misapplication of GAAP are proving to be very costly. The restatement of its financial statements and the updating of its accounting systems are expected to cost a billion dollars. Moreover, in May of 2006, Fannie Mae agreed to pay the Securities and Exchange Commission a fine of $400 million. An effort is also underway to recover the incentive compensation received by top Fannie Mae officers that was the result of their overstatement of earnings. A news release associated with the filing of charges by the Office of Federal Housing Enterprise Oversight (the regulatory body that oversees Fannie Mae) against former Fannie Mae officers declares (Office of Federal Housing Enterprise Oversight, 2006):

> The Notice of Charges details the harm to Fannie Mae resulting from the conduct of these individuals from 1998 to 2004, said Director Lockhart. The 101 charges reveal how the individuals improperly manipulated earnings to maximize their bonuses, while knowingly neglecting accounting systems and internal controls, misapplying over twenty accounting principles and misleading the regulator and the public.

### 19.2.4.4 Backdated Share Options

Share options give company officers and employees the right to purchase shares at a pre-established exercise price. The exercise price for options is typically set at the market price of the underlying share on the date of grant. The idea here is that the option recipient will earn incentive compensation in the form of gains as the company's share price increases above the exercise price. Under Accounting Principles Board Opinion No. 25, *Accounting for Stock Issued to Employees* (Accounting Principles Board, 1972), the relevant accounting standard at the time, a company would only need to record compensation expense related to its options grants for an amount equal to the difference between the exercise price and the market price on the date of grant. Thus, for option grants where the exercise price is set equal to the market price on the date of grant, no compensation expense would need to be recorded.

At the time of an option grant in a so-called backdated option grant arrangement, management would look back across previous periods to pick an earlier date on which the company's share price was lower than at present. In many backdated option grants, the lowest price of the year might be chosen. That earlier date would then be selected as the grant date and the exercise price would be set at the closing price on that day. Since the present price of the company's share would be higher than that earlier amount, the recipient would have an immediate gain related to the options received. However, because the exercise price and market price were equal on the specified date of grant, no compensation expense would need to be recorded.

Many US companies were found to have used option backdating to varying degrees in the late 1990s and early 2000s. In many cases, honest errors caused by a lack of controls over the option-granting process led to errors in grant-date selections. In some instances, however, there was a concerted effort on the part of management to boost compensation and minimize expense – all outside the boundaries of GAAP. Consider the case of UnitedHealth Group, Inc. While not an accounting scandal, internal investigations at the company show many cases of backdated options.

Option backdating in the USA is less of a problem today than it was even five years ago. New and stronger internal controls and more diligent boards of directors and outside auditors have helped to reduce the risk of backdating. Also, under new accounting guidelines, Statement of Financial Accounting Standards No. 123R, *Share Based Payment* (Financial Accounting Standards Board, 2006), option expense is now recorded for the fair value of options granted. As such, companies may no longer avoid compensation expense by simply setting the exercise price equal to the market price.

## 19.3 ENRON AND WORLDCOM

### 19.3.1 Enron Corp.

From humble beginnings as a slow-growth, energy production and distribution company, Enron Corp. morphed into a trading company that was, for a while, known as an exemplar of how a 'new economy' company should be run. It became one of America's most respected companies, frequently admired as one of the country's 'best places to work'. In 2000, the company ranked seventh on the Fortune 500 list and generated $100 billion in reported revenue. A year later in 2001, the company was a bankrupt shell, facing liquidation.

Today, the words Enron and accounting fraud are inextricably linked. The company's fraud was truly of mega proportions, involving off-balance sheet liabilities, fictitious income and misreported cash flow.

Management at Enron Corp. used separate, single-purpose entities, known as special purpose entities, to off-load its burgeoning debt and to generate phantom income. A special purpose entity, or SPE, is a company organized to perform a specific activity. Usually, SPEs are established to hold assets that are being refinanced. For example, an SPE might take ownership and hold a building that is subject to a sale and leaseback transaction. In the case of Enron, however, SPEs were the perfect vehicle for conducting a complicated and growing financial fraud.

Enron sponsored the creation of an SPE and guaranteed a sizable bank loan to the entity, typically constituting 97 % of its total financing. That left 3 % of its total financing to be comprised of equity. Enron's objective was to avoid consolidation of the SPE. Accounting rules at the time specified that if no less than 3 % of an SPE's total financing was in the form of equity owned by an independent third party, and if that equity were a controlling equity interest in the entity, then the sponsoring company, Enron in this case, need not consolidate the entity. Notice the arrangement. Out of 100 % of an entity's total financing, 97 % was debt, guaranteed by Enron. Someone else held the entity's equity, but that equity constituted only 3 % of its total financing. Still the arrangement was consistent with the rules, at least on paper, and Enron would not have to consolidate the entity.

There was, however, another twist. An independent third party did not truly own the equity piece in the Enron SPEs. Rather, through guarantee arrangements designed to protect the equity holders, Enron was effectively the equity holder of last resort. Accordingly, Enron should have consolidated the SPEs.

This was the perfect arrangement for Enron. Here was a company that Enron effectively controlled that did not have to be consolidated. On several occasions, Enron negotiated sizable bank loans providing debt proceeds to its SPEs. Enron then issued shares to the entities, which were purchased with the borrowed funds. Enron accounted for the transactions as an equity issue, even though the funds received were borrowed and Enron guaranteed the debt.

Enron could also use its SPEs to boost income by selling them Enron assets at a gain. Asset sales might include 'dark' fibre optic cable or even poorly performing power plants. Such transactions help to explain Enron's ability to report higher income even as many of its businesses suffered.

Beyond allowing Enron to hide debt and generate phantom income, the company's SPEs also allowed it to report operating cash flow. We think that this component of the fraud, especially during 2000 and into 2001 when the real business of the company was truly struggling, was what helped to keep the concerns of analysts and investors assuaged.

In more than one transaction, and often for hundreds of millions of dollars, Enron's SPEs used borrowed funds to buy oil from Enron that was paid for in advance. Enron received the funds and accounted for them as a prepayment, a customer deposit. In particular, the company would increase its cash account (debit cash) and increase the customer deposits account, a current liability (credit customer deposits). Enron then contracted with the bank that had loaned the SPE its funds to also purchase oil in advance, effectively settling the prepay agreement for oil. The same funds were then transferred to the bank, but in the next financial year. Accounting for the transfer of cash, including ultimate settlement of the prepayment agreement, entailed a reduction in cash (credit cash) and a reduction in customer deposits (debit customer deposits). That bank transferred the funds back to the SPE, settling its open position. The SPE used the funds received to repay its bank loan. Only cash moved between the companies involved, no oil was ever transferred between them.

At the end of 2000, Enron was holding the funds, which, as noted, it accounted for as a customer deposit. The increase in that deposit, which occurred during 2000, was reported on Enron's statement of cash flows as an operating source of cash. The cash flow was really the result of a bank loan and should have been reported as a financing source of cash. However, by reporting the proceeds as an operating cash source, Enron was able to impart an impression of heightened financial well-being.

The borrowed funds that were reported by Enron as operating cash flow in 2000 were transferred to the bank in early 2001 as Enron's side of the prepayment agreement was settled. That disbursement presented a new problem for the company that year – how to report operating cash flow in 2001? However, the inflow in 2000 still enabled the company to report significant operating cash flow that year. The likely plan was to repeat the transaction(s) in 2001, but that year, the business ended before new similar transactions were completed.

In the end, Enron's guarantees were much to blame for what killed the company. The guarantees were often backed by Enron's own shares. As long as those shares increased in price, or at least, held their own, the arrangements worked. However, when the shares began to decline in price, and more and more shares were needed to make good on the many and growing guarantees, the charade began to unravel.

Unable to meets its obligations, Enron Corp. was declared bankrupt in late 2001. The company's Chief Financial Officer, Andrew Fastow, pleaded guilty to criminal fraud and received a six-year sentence. The company's chairman, Kenneth Lay, and its former CEO, Jeffrey Skilling, were tried and also found guilty of fraud. Mr Lay died before he could be sentenced. Mr Skilling received a 24-year prison term.

Today in the USA, SPEs are referred to as Variable Interest Entities, or VIEs. They work much the same as SPEs. However, for a sponsoring entity to avoid consolidation now, the entity's equity must be sufficient to allow it to absorb any expected losses. That is, the entity's equity must be sufficiently large to virtually eliminate the risk that the sponsoring company will need to provide additional financing to the entity. Generally, equity equal to at least 10 % of the entity's total financing is viewed as the required minimum.

Much of the blame for Enron's rise and ultimate decline has been placed on its CEO, Jeffrey Skilling. Mr Skilling's brilliance and early successes attracted dedicated followers. A lack of internal controls at the company, in particular, absent checks and balances that permitted managers to effect desired accounting misdeeds, permitted the company to veer off course. Finally, Arthur Andersen, the company's auditor, was an ineffective stop gap. Criminal indictments of the audit firm led to its ultimate demise.

### 19.3.2 WorldCom, Inc.

In the summer of 2002, only months after the fraud at Enron Corp. became news, the fraud at WorldCom, Inc. was thrust upon the nation's consciousness. It was a somewhat surreal development. US markets were just beginning to recover from the hangover left after the fraud-induced bankruptcy at Enron, and then another multi-billion fraud became news. How could it be? Were no earnings or balance sheets to be trusted? Fortunately, WorldCom was the last *big* USA fraud at the time. There would be other frauds, but not of that size.

A major piece of the WorldCom fraud entailed accounting practices that were much less complex than the steps taken at Enron. While amounts involved were truly spectacular, on the order of billions of dollars, the basic fraud itself was really quite simple. It was a capitalization story. Operating expenses incurred for leasing other telecommunications companies' phone lines – primarily for last-mile access to homes and businesses – were capitalized. That is, rather than being charged to expenses with an accompanying reduction in earnings, the expenses were reported as capital expenditures and added to the balance sheet as property, plant and equipment. Those assets were then depreciated over extended periods.

One wonders how nearly $4 billion could be added improperly to property, plant and equipment and not get noticed. The fact of the matter is that at the time, normal capital expenditures at the company were reduced. When the improperly capitalized line costs were combined with them, capital expenditures at the firm appeared to be about right.

The WorldCom scandal, however, went beyond cost capitalization and included the manner in which the company accounted for its acquisitions. From humble beginnings as a regional telephone carrier in the southeastern USA, WorldCom, Inc. grew quite rapidly to become a national player. The company grew through acquisitions, using its stock as currency to gobble up other telephone firms. Quickly, the company grew in reach and stature, putting itself on the national stage with its more recent acquisition of MCI Communications, Inc. However, its method of accounting for its many acquisitions also permitted the firm to boost earnings artificially.

Investigators began to take a much closer look at WorldCom's accounting once the cost capitalization fraud was uncovered. It did not take long before they noticed the firm's aggressive practices related to acquisition accounting. When another firm is acquired, a reserve or liability is often established to absorb anticipated costs related to effecting the combination. These costs may entail costs expected to be paid for facilities consolidation, lease terminations and personnel reductions. When payments are made in future periods to cover these costs, the payments are charged against the previously established reserves. In addition to such business combination reserves, WorldCom also established reserves for such items as uncollectible receivables and the estimated future cost of litigation. The plan was to charge these reserves when uncollectible receivables were written off or litigation-related payments were made.

While in theory WorldCom's reserves were used properly, in practice they provided a means to increase earnings. The company typically overstated its reserves, which it could then reverse, as needed, providing a boost to earnings.

Another item related to acquisitions at WorldCom that was used to boost assets, equity and earnings was the overvaluation of goodwill. Under GAAP in the USA, goodwill, the difference between the acquisition price and the fair value of identifiable assets, is reported as an asset on the balance sheet. At the time, US GAAP called for the amortization of goodwill over periods ranging up to 40 years. However, a charge was also needed when evidence indicated that goodwill was value-impaired. The investigations that followed the discovery of the WorldCom improprieties found that the company failed to write down goodwill that was clearly worth less than the amount reported on the balance sheet.

Ultimately, as WorldCom emerged from bankruptcy, the company's fraud-inspired restatement totalled tens of billions of dollars. Shareholders in the firm had lost all of their money and Bernard Ebbers, the company's long-time CEO, was sentenced to prison for 25 years.

Bernard Ebbers, the product of a small southern town, was apparently swept up in the many successes that surrounded the telecom industry of the 1990s. His drive to grow his company, primarily through acquisitions, may have taken his attention away from the need to consolidate his winnings. The resulting behemoth that he created did not have the controls, or the checks and balances, needed to ensure that untoward accounting practices would be uncovered and corrected. In the end, it was a careful internal auditor, doing her job, who found evidence of the mess that had been created.

## 19.4 AFTERMATH OF THE SCANDALS

With the many USA accounting scandals that followed in short succession, there was an outcry from the public for Congress to 'do something'. The calls for action became particularly acute when the fraud at WorldCom, Inc. gained attention so soon after the fraud at Enron Corp. was discovered. Both frauds resulted in dramatic bankruptcies that rendered worthless billions of dollars in shareholder investments. Congress responded and passed the Sarbanes-Oxley Act of 2002 (US Congress, 2002). The financial reporting landscape in the USA was changed dramatically as new requirements were put in place for managers, their firms and auditors.

The Sarbanes-Oxley Act contains many provisions, all of which are focused on the financial reporting system in the USA. Among the more prominent changes brought by the Act are the creation of the Public Company Accounting Oversight Board, increased auditor independence, changes to corporate governance and responsibility, and evaluations of internal controls.

The Public Company Accounting Oversight Board, or PCAOB, is a government-sponsored entity given authority to set standards for auditing, quality control and ethics, to inspect the work of registered accounting firms, to conduct investigations and take disciplinary actions. As a check on its power, PCAOB is subject to SEC review and oversight. While the concept for regular review of audit firm work is not new, the public disclosure of the results of those reviews and sanctions for substandard work is new.

Because of concern that audit firms may not be sufficiently independent of the companies they audit, Sarbanes-Oxley introduced provisions for stricter independence. Auditors would now be limited in the scope of non-audit services they can provide their clients. Examples of services that may no longer be provided to clients include work on the design for a financial reporting system and the conducting of internal audits.

In terms of corporate governance and responsibility, the independence and financial expertise of audit committees was increased. The Act emphasized that the primary responsibility of a company's auditors was to its board of directors and the investing public and not to its managers. Also, the Act requires CEOs and CFOs to certify that the company's financial statements are free of material error. There is also a threat of criminal prosecution, including sentences of 20 years in prison, when an officer knowingly misstates a company's financial results and position.

Regarding internal controls, provisions of the Act require management to assess the effectiveness of the company's internal controls and make a statement of responsibility in annual filings. The auditors must review management's assessment of internal controls and identify any material weaknesses uncovered.

Whether Sarbanes-Oxley will be effective in reducing financial reporting fraud remains to be seen. While it cannot, and will not, eliminate accounting scandals and fraud, it will reduce the opportunity and increase the penalties for doing so. We are optimistic that it will be successful in at least reducing the number and size of financial reporting frauds in the USA.

# REFERENCES

Accounting Principles Board (1972), 'Accounting Principles Board Opinion No. 25', *Accounting for Stock Issued to Employees*, American Institute of CPAs, New York.

Financial Accounting Standards Board (1998), 'Statement of Financial Accounting Standards No. 133', *Accounting for Derivative Instruments and Hedging Activities (amended)*, Financial Accounting Standards Board, Norwalk, CT.

Financial Accounting Standards Board (2006), 'Statement of Financial Accounting Standards No. 123R', *Share Based Payment*, Financial Accounting Standards Board, Norwalk, CT.

Heinzl, M. (1998), 'Bre-X hid rock-sampling technique, touted non-existent gold, probe finds', *Wall Street Journal*, 19 February, A8.

Levitt, A. (1998), 'The "numbers game"', *Remarks to New York University Center for Law and Business*, 28 September, para. 4.

MacDonald, E. (2000), 'Regulators seek to penalize auditors who missed fraud', *Wall Street Journal*, 6 January, A1.

Maremont, M. (2004), 'Tyco probe focuses on ADT unit; current, ex-workers subpoenaed', *Wall Street Journal*, 17 May, http://www.wsj.com.

Maremont, M. and Bulkeley, W. (2002), 'IBM is resolute on accounting cited by SEC', *Wall Street Journal*, 28 February, C1.

Mulford, C. and Comiskey, E. (2002), *The Financial Numbers Game: Detecting Creative Accounting Practices*, John Wiley & Sons, Inc., New York.

Office of Federal Housing Enterprise Oversight (2006), *OFHEO Files Notice of Charges against Former Fannie Mae Executives Franklin Raines, Timothy Howard and Leanne Spencer, Charges Seek Restitution, Civil Money Penalties*, OFHEO, Washington, DC, p. 1.

Sandberg, J. and Lublin, J. (2002), 'Adelphia draws market criticism over debt, loans to Rigas family', *Wall Street Journal*, 29 March, http://www.wsj.com.

Schacht, H. (2000), 'Lucent slashes first quarter outlook, erases revenue from latest quarter', *Wall Street Journal*, 22 December, B2.

US Congress (2002), *The Sarbanes-Oxley Act*, July, Washington, DC.

# 20

# Bank Failures and Accounting During the Financial Crisis of 2008–2009

Simon D. Norton

## 20.1 INTRODUCTION

Jensen and Meckling (1976, p. 9) observed that '[t]he firm is not an individual. It is a legal fiction which serves as a focus for a complex process in which the conflicting objectives of individuals ... are brought into equilibrium within a framework of contractual relations.' Agency theory suggests that management will be self-serving and where information is asymmetrical, this will be exploited to the detriment of the uninformed owner (Schipper, 1989). Creative accounting may be viewed as a technique or form of behaviour whereby management attempts to exploit information or limit its disclosure to maintain its superiority of bargaining power vis-à-vis the owner. Definitions of creative accounting, as we saw in Chapter 1, tend to focus upon the manipulation of levels of earnings in a way which affects reported income but which, in most scenarios, makes no genuine contribution to the economic well-being of the organisation (Merchant and Rockness, 1994).

In the context of the financial markets, creative accounting may occur for complex reasons which significantly exceed the relatively simplistic objective of earnings manipulation derived from traditional agency theory (Kothari, 2001). Owners (shareholders) or investors (for example, bondholders) or lenders in the interbank markets invariably have access to risk evaluation models as well as the ability to exit when management is perceived to be attempting to deceive or withhold vital information. In other words, in sophisticated, highly liquid markets the traditional elements required for the management-owner conflict as deemed necessary by traditional agency theory are absent (Breton and Taffler, 1995). Owners have access to resources and models which deprive management of its ability to manipulate information over the medium term. Informational inequality can be further undermined by ratings agencies which can downgrade credit scores of bonds of shares issued by banks regarded as evasive or involved in creative accounting (Gode and Sunder, 1993). The purpose of creative accounting in such a restrictive context is to describe or value assets or trading activity in a favourable (lawful) manner, entirely within the rules as established by international bodies such as the Basel Committee on Banking Supervision, even if such description or valuation may sometimes be at variance with underlying reality. In the absence of asymmetrical information, presentation becomes paramount.

*Creative Accounting, Fraud and International Accounting Scandals*   Edited by Michael Jones
© 2011 Michael Jones. Published by John Wiley & Sons, Ltd

Financial institutions may embark upon creative accounting, despite the sophistication of shareholders and bondholders and their ability to react adversely to such behaviour, for several reasons including the following:

• To conceal the true state of the organisation's earnings (McNichols and Wilson, 1988). This encompasses the traditional definitions of creative accounting and includes, for example, an attempt by management to hide substantial losses or the existence of fraud. One of the most extreme examples is the Bank of Credit and Commerce International (Sikka and Willmott, 1997) (this is discussed in more detail in Chapter 18).

• To suggest that assets available in the balance sheet for collateral for future lenders to the bank are of greater value or greater liquidity than is the case. Creative accounting in this context would enable a bank to over-leverage its balance sheet, borrowing heavily from lenders on the assurance that it has sufficient asset strength that should the lenders later need to call in their loans, liquidation of collateral will more than suffice to meet their claims.

• To suggest that the level of risk associated with a bank's balance sheet is lower than it actually is. A bank adjudged by the ratings agencies to be overly committed to a particularly volatile market or to a narrow class of borrowers will usually see this reflected in a downgrading of its credit score and a 'knock-on' effect of an increase in its borrowing costs (Morgan, 2002). To circumvent such a downgrading banks have occasionally embarked upon 'off-balance sheet' activities as a means of relocating risky assets from the balance sheet to special purpose vehicles (SPVs) which, through bond issues, pass on this risk to investors who are willing to assume it in return for an attractive premium (Henderson, 2000). Banks holding highly illiquid bonds have been known to 'recycle' these assets, particularly if some are trading in the secondary market at substantial discounts to face value, via securitisation. In simple terms, such assets have been 'bundled up' and sold to an SPV set up especially for this purpose. A 'new' homogenised bond is then issued to investors, the coupon (or interest payments) being met from the cash flows accruing to the 'old' illiquid bonds. In this way an illiquid portfolio is 'freed up' and the balance sheet relieved of the weight of otherwise 'toxic' material (Niu, 2007).

• To justify excessively generous remuneration schemes. In exuberant, booming, highly volatile markets in which banks need to attract and retain 'star traders' or deal makers, the generosity of remuneration structures becomes paramount. However, if a bank's fundamentals, as revealed in its balance sheet, are insufficient to sustain such structures, perhaps because of unrealised losses accruing to a particular class of assets such as complex derivatives, creative accounting may provide a short-term solution (Pourciau, 1993). For example, if assets which would otherwise generate substantial unrealised losses when 'marked to market' are reclassified into an asset category in respect to which no market price reference can be made, unrealised losses decline, increasing the level of profits from which high levels of remuneration can continue to be funded. In the longer term if such assets recover in value, a re-transference can be made and a more favourable mark-to-market undertaken.

During recent years banks have become preoccupied with the accurate measurement of portfolio risk, using highly sophisticated models to 'stress test' assets and their vulnerability to normal fluctuations in equity markets or mild disturbances in secondary bond markets.

The exercise is not an academic one. The degree of risk pertaining to particular assets must be taken into account when deciding upon the level of capital provision made in accordance with the Basel capital adequacy rules. Recently three principal activities have affected this risk-assessment process. First, the use of so-called value at risk or VaR models. Second, the involvement of banks in off-balance sheet activities such as securitisation. Third, the accumulation by banks of highly complex, highly illiquid assets in the balance sheet, such as derivatives and repackaged debt. All three of these, it may be argued, ignored the 'black swan' phenomenon, consciously or by accident. A black swan phenomenon is the occurrence of a highly unusual, 'once in a trader's lifetime' set of circumstances or even a single event which, in happening, undermines all previous assumptions. The recent 'credit crunch' may be described as such a 'black swan' event: the meltdown in the markets, the drying up of interbank lending, coupled with a stagnation affecting many markets in such a way that it became impossible to 'mark to market' assets held because there was no such market in existence against which prices could be estimated. VaR, it has been suggested, failed to prepare banks for the recent turmoil since it substantially underestimated the possibility of extreme and unexpected events and the potential impact that these might have in precipitating liquidity crises.

In recent years, VaR gained an aura of infallibility, leading many banks to rely upon it to the exclusion of consideration of any other forms of internal stress testing. When the credit crisis began, many banks were unprepared since the event had not been factored into their calculations using internal VaR models.

VaR models are used to hypothesise the probability or likelihood of losses on a particular portfolio over a particular time horizon based upon a statistical analysis of prior trends and price fluctuations (Duffie and Pan, 1997). As such VaR is a useful tool for evaluating the necessity or otherwise of hedging specific types of risk accruing to a portfolio, bearing in mind that such a strategy itself is a cost which, all things being equal, will reduce potential gains on that portfolio should the need to take advantage of the hedge not arise. For example, if a series of options are taken against shares held in a portfolio which enables the financial institution to sell at certain prices notwithstanding a general fall in market prices this will be a successful hedging strategy. The losses which would otherwise have arisen in respect of those shares will have been avoided. However, if instead the price of those shares has risen and the hedge is not implemented and the options are allowed to expire then the cost, the premium paid for that quasi-insurance, will be written off against the gain on the shares. In this latter scenario a 'naked' or unhedged position would have resulted in profit undiminished by the cost of the hedge. But the benefit of hindsight is by definition never available when the decision whether or not to hedge has to be made. A further criticism of VaR models is that they inevitably fail to provide for or anticipate 'black swan' events (Beder, 1995).

The purpose of this chapter is not to consider in detail the causes of failure of each of the many banks, including Icelandic bank Kaupthing, Royal Bank of Scotland and Northern Rock in the United Kingdom, Hypo Real Estate Bank in Germany, to name but a few. Instead the chapter will focus upon the demise of three financial institutions, Lehman Brothers, Bernard Madoff Securities, and Bear Stearns, since each demonstrates the consequences of creative accounting in the context of balance sheets which did not accurately represent the value of collateral or the magnitude of the risk presented, and thus reported, to the wider investment community. Brief mention of the causes of failure of Hypo Bank, Fortis Bank, Kaupthing and Northern Rock will however assist in introducing themes to be explored in greater detail in the remainder of the chapter. The next section therefore considers the causes of failure of these banks.

## 20.2

Creative accounting and failures in the banking sector are, of course, nothing new. As we saw in Chapter 7, the City Bank of Glasgow failed spectacularly in the 1890s. More recently, Billings and Capie (2009) have shown that creative accounting was alive and kicking in the UK banking system in the 1950s. This demonstrates Jones and Oldroyd's (2009) thesis that there is nothing new under the sun. However, perhaps the extent of the recent bank failures and its impact upon the whole economic life marks out the present banking crisis as something substantially different from that which has occurred in the past.

### 20.2.1 Kaupthing Bank

There were several causes underlying Kaupthing Bank's collapse in 2008, not all of which are agreed upon by the principal parties associated with its downfall. The bank, based in Iceland, but included in the United Kingdom's top 20 largest banks, had been experiencing a draining away of confidence in its ability to survive for several months preceding its demise. The cost of insuring its debt via credit default swaps had increased significantly in early October 2008 as investors holding its bonds became increasingly concerned that it would be unable to meet its future interest payment obligations. In the same month the ratings agency Fitch downgraded the bank's rating to 'sub investment' or junk status, coinciding with a near-halting of deposits into the bank. As the Icelandic banking sector had for several years relied upon funds raised in the international markets rather than domestic savings to finance its expansion both at home and abroad, a loss of international confidence was to prove fatal for Kaupthing. In October 2008 the bank was taken over by the Icelandic government after the United Kingdom government seized the bank's UK operation. At the same time the bank was refused permission to participate in the £500 billion rescue package for UK lenders (*The Daily Telegraph*, 9 October 2008). However, it was also true that British savers had been withdrawing funds from the bank's UK-regulated subsidiary, Kaupthing Edge, for several weeks preceding the nationalisation, panicked by the collapse of a similar but weaker Icelandic internet-based bank, Landsbanki Icesave.

The bank's chairman Sigurdur Einarsson, contended that the bank's collapse had been precipitated in large part by the UK government's seizure of its UK arm, undermining the bank's entire network. Of even greater damage to the bank and the Icelandic government, the United Kingdom Chancellor, Alistair Darling, had used anti-terrorist legislation to authorise the seizure, contending that the action was necessary to protect the stability of the UK financial system and the interests of depositors. In essence this was a bank which had expanded too quickly, was too dependent upon international rather than domestic sources of funding, and which ultimately fell victim to the United Kingdom government's pre-emptive measures to settle and reassure its own domestic depositors and bank shareholders.

## 20.2.2 Northern Rock

In the United Kingdom Northern Rock plc floundered in September 2007 as its business model came apart as a consequence of the nascent credit crunch. In that month the bank received a liquidity support facility from the Bank of England, but by February 2008 its position had worsened to such an extent that full nationalisation became necessary. In essence, the bank's demise had been brought about by over-reliance upon the international credit markets to finance its domestic lending; approximately 25 % of its loan capital came from domestic savers, the remaining 75 % from borrowing in the interbank market. As the US sub-prime crisis escalated in late 2007 so it became increasingly difficult for Northern Rock to access liquidity to fund its day-to-day activities. Its business model, premised upon an assumption of indefinite availability of cheap credit, could not adapt quickly enough to the new world of seized-up credit markets. The bank had become one of the early victims of the draining-away of trust and confidence in the interbank loan markets.

There were of course several other large banks which fell victim to the credit crunch as it swept across global financial markets. In Germany in the first few days of October 2008 Hypo Real Estate (HRE), one of the country's largest providers of property finance and the country's fourth largest bank, collapsed after an attempted €35 billion rescue by private banks and the European Central Bank came to nothing. HRE had become overwhelmed by a mountain of debt incurred by a German-Irish subsidiary, Depfa, bought in October of the previous year and a matter of months before collapse of the US sub-prime market triggered the credit crunch. The final nail in HRE's coffin was hammered home when a consortium of German banks refused to provide the bank with liquidity lines to enable it to refinance existing debt. Without such commitment, and despite initial determination by German Chancellor Angela Merkel to support the rescue plan, the bank's fate had been sealed by the liquidity crisis over which not even the national government appeared to have any influence.

Similar liquidity difficulties were to lead to the disintegration of another European bank, the Dutch-Belgian-owned Fortis Bank. The bank had previously bought ABN-AMRO bank through debt borrowing, leaving it exceptionally vulnerable to upward spikes in LIBOR rates and the general downturn in interbank lending which followed so close on the heels of the US sub-prime crisis. The bank was also exposed to the US sub-prime market. After a staggering 95 % fall in Fortis's share price over the year to 21 November 2008, the three governments of Luxembourg, the Netherlands and Belgium mounted a rescue in which €1 billion was injected into the bank, each government taking a 50 % stake in respective local presences of the bank (www.bloomberg.com, 26 September 2008). Despite the bail-out by the Benelux countries, disintegration of the bank and the selling off of acquisitions made in previous years was to follow. This was a case of a bank brought low by a strategy of expansion by acquisition funded by high-cost debt. This strategy was to be fatally undermined by a liquidity crisis brought about by the US sub-prime debacle, as well as the bank's over-ambitious expansion into that market.

Northern Rock, Kaupthing, Hypo Bank and Fortis were of course not the only banks, financial institutions or ordinary companies to get into trouble in the next couple of years. Companies as diverse as Anglo-Irish Bank, Fannie Mae and Freddie Mac, AIG, Stanford, Royal Bank of Scotland and HBOS all experienced difficulties. In the context of these and other world-renowned financial institutions that have experienced fundamental problems during the credit crunch, it is too early to say whether or not these have been brought about by either creative accounting or poor management or a combination of both.

Having considered the background to the current credit crisis, the next sections will consider the specific origins of the current bank instability, and the extent to which creative accounting has contributed to or facilitated the volatile trading environment in financial services. The remainder of the chapter will show how, although perfectly lawful, creative accounting techniques utilised by several banks which have either failed or experienced severe trading or liquidity difficulties have served to cloud or obscure the true level of risk across the global banking system rather than promoting a culture of transparency and accuracy in financial reporting. The true level of toxicity of assets held in portfolios, principally in the form of assets-backed securities, has been underestimated by the financial institutions themselves, investors, and the global bond rating agencies. As one of the consequences of perfectly lawful creative accounting, collateral underpinning complex financial instruments has in several cases been overestimated by participants in the financial markets. This has contributed to and exacerbated the effects of the global downturn and the drying up of lending in the interbank markets. In this chapter, overvalued portfolios and underestimated risk will be shown to have caused severe undercapitalisation by leading banks, brought down in part by the very creative accounting techniques which they quite legally utilised. In the case of Bernard Madoff such complexity and deliberate obfuscation of financial truth, principally through a Ponzi scheme, enabled the perpetration of a fraud of near-unparalleled dimensions. The next section considers several bank practices which led to the credit crunch.

## 20.3 ORIGINS OF THE 'CREDIT CRUNCH'

There are several causes for the recent credit crunch but the most important are arguably the role of sub-prime lending, off-balance sheet activities by banks and inadequate risk evaluation of assets which ultimately turned out to be highly volatile and highly illiquid. Creative accounting played a major part in facilitating or making possible these practices. Each of these activities will be considered in turn.

### 20.3.1 Sub-prime Lending

In the aftermath of the terrorist attacks on the Twin Towers of the World Trade Center on 11 September 2001 one of the principal concerns of the US government, apart from preventing further attacks, was to contain the potential for a 'knock-on' adverse effect upon the wider economy. Specifically, there was a fear that economic confidence could become undermined as Americans grew fearful for the country's security, leading in a short time to a general decline in confidence in the stock market. To head off this potential crisis in confidence the Federal Reserve initiated a series of substantial interest rate cuts, facilitating President Bush's exhortation to Americans to keep spending to stave off economic malaise. By December 2001, the Federal Reserve Board (the 'Fed') had cut overnight interest rates to 1.75 per cent, the lowest level for more than four decades and a culmination of no less than eleven cuts in that one single year. By December 2002, the costs of 30-year fixed rate loans in the US had fallen to their lowest level for 30 years (*New York Times*, 15 December 2002), but still borrowers continued to take up adjustable rate loans which, while lower in cost than the exceptionally low fixed rate alternatives, had the potential to spike upwards in the medium term.

The availability of cheap money led to what could be characterised as a borrowing frenzy, the Federal Reserve's strategy of cuts persisting for a further two years through to mid-2003. Consumer demand for home equity loans, car finance, and variable rate mortgages was near-insatiable. The political consideration underpinning the policy was that such an expression of governmental confidence in the future would postpone into the distant future any possibility of an economic slowdown or, even worse, a recession. After all, spending by American consumers represented two-thirds of the US economy and 20 % of global economic activity at that time; it was accordingly crucial that such confidence be sustained (*New York Times*, 6 November 2001).

As a consequence of the prolonged period of low interest rates it became increasingly possible for banks to raise capital at low cost on the interbank market and then lend it out again at significantly higher rates. In addition, property prices had been rising steeply; mortgage lenders were now significantly discounting or ignoring entirely the possibility of future price declines. In this environment, lenders were less concerned with the payment histories of those to whom they lent but instead focused upon the assumption that, even if it became necessary to enforce or seize and sell the underlying security, this would not matter because property values would inevitably have increased during the term of the loan. This practice of lending to the asset and not to the borrower was termed 'sub-prime' because the quality of the payer was a secondary consideration to the value of the property against which the loan was being made and which provided security in respect of the loan. Sub-prime lending entailed making available credit or loans or mortgages to borrowers whose income was poor, credit rating weak or non-existent (perhaps as a consequence of previous loan defaults), and future earning capacity highly volatile or subject to sustained interruption (for example, long-term unemployment). Two main types of mortgage were made available to sub-prime borrowers. First, interest only mortgages which at the beginning imposed a very low interest rate but which rose sharply after a few years. Second, mortgages where the borrower was required only to make payments of capital, interest accumulating towards a future date. Under the terms of this latter repayment mortgage, each payment made by the borrower gradually reduced the outstanding capital by an agreed amount, resulting in interest payments being reduced over time. However, the accumulated interest still needed to be paid. Both forms were a response by the mortgage industry to house price inflation which gave lenders the false impression that loans would always be secure as a corollary of the general increases in house prices. Negative equity, the phenomenon in which the underlying asset falls below the value of the loan used to purchase it, was viewed as a remote possibility. Sub-prime lending was particularly strong in poorer areas, particularly in the US, where salespeople, compensated not through salaries but instead through commissions on sales of loans and target-driven bonuses, were actively encouraged to offer mortgages to borrowers with dubious credit histories.

### 20.3.2  Types of Mortgage

Prudent practices followed in the mortgage industry in previous years were ignored. Specifically it had been the case, and remained so in most countries of the European Union, that in order to borrow for a house purchase, a deposit of at least 25 % was required. By contrast in the UK and US, in the few years leading up to the sub-prime crisis borrowers were able to raise up to 125 % of the purchase price and in many cases were not required to provide a deposit. This risky strategy was exacerbated by 'self certification': borrowers were not required to provide independent proof of income but instead merely to make unsupported declarations of earnings. Borrowers with severely impaired credit ratings or with highly volatile or unpredictable earnings were provided with mortgages when previously their applications would have been rejected.

### 20.3.3  Economic Downturn and Rising Unemployment

When the recession arrived in 2008 the levels of mortgage defaults increased as unemployment escalated. House repossessions soared, particularly in the US, driving down property values. The value of collateralised assets came to be adversely affected by two factors. First, prices of the underlying security were declining. Second, the cash flows accruing to those assets, the mortgage payments, were now increasingly in default as borrowers failed to meet their payment obligations. Banks which had invested in the collateralised assets were faced with the prospect of either significant write-downs to reflect their declining value, or alternatively finding a way to reclassify these non-performing assets. In such circumstances banks looked to creative accounting in order to maintain the appearance of a healthy balance sheet, sustainable profits and cash flow. The next section considers some of the financial products created by the banks which both contributed to and, in turn, exacerbated the extent of the credit crunch.

## 20.4  FINANCIAL INSTRUMENTS ASSOCIATED WITH THE CREDIT CRUNCH

In practical terms it is possible to make a distinction between financial instruments and creative accounting. With regard to the former, these usually comprise, in the main, bonds and derivatives traded on recognised exchanges. In contrast, the latter comprises the methods by which the former are recorded in banks' balance sheets the principal intention being, through legal means, the presentation of information in an optimal or most beneficial way, taking into account the holder's own financial circumstances and those prevailing in the wider economy. For example, during the recent credit crunch it was not deemed beneficial for a bank to be seen to be holding illiquid financial instruments (products which could not be easily sold at an acceptable price) which had declined significantly since the date of purchase. A significant holding of risky financial instruments invariably resulted in time in a downgrading of the holder by the international credit ratings agencies. In these circumstances creative accounting was used to present the best picture, notwithstanding the underlying reality.

In recent years the financial markets have evolved new mechanisms for risk reallocation from financial institutions to investors and vice versa. New products designed by financial engineers or so-called 'rocket scientists' repackaged balance sheet risk into tradable bonds and other derivatives. The underlying assumption was that sophisticated investors, with assistance from the ratings agencies, would be equipped to evaluate underlying risk and reflect this in the rate of interest to be demanded of the issuer or originator of the product. In turn, further instruments were created to 'hedge' or reduce the degree of risk implicit in some of these products, these devices becoming tradable instruments in their own right. Several of these instruments deserve mention and explanation here.

### 20.4.1 Collateralised Debt Obligations (CDOs)

CDOs are asset-backed securities the coupon (interest) payments on which are derived from a portfolio of underlying fixed income assets. These securities are invariably tranched when offered to investors, senior tranche holders having priority over junior debtholders in the event of the issuer becoming bankrupt. In recognition of the higher risk to junior tranche holders, the rate of interest payable usually exceeded that payable to investors in the higher tranches. The advantage of this technique to banks was that it enabled debt to be shifted off-balance sheet to be pooled with comparable debt of other institutions, and then brought back into the balance sheet in the form of synthetic CDOs. These later instruments obscured the extent of the original risk in the issuer's balance sheet (Duffie and Garleanu, 2001). A further reality was that the ratings agencies found evaluation of the underlying risk in these products extremely problematic, often resulting in a higher credit rating being assigned than was justified given the riskiness of the underlying assets.

### 20.4.2 Credit Default Swaps (CDS)

Under a CDS the buyer of the instrument makes payments to the seller, invariably a financial institution with significant capital reserves, in exchange for a commitment by the seller to make a payment to the buyer in the event of default on specified bond (Longstaff *et al.*, 2005). These CDSs are tradable instruments in their own right and thus can be bought and sold. Unlike insurers who maintain reserves to meet potential claims, sellers of CDSs are not required to maintain any reserves to meet buyers' claims, and do not necessarily have to be entities overseen (or policed) by financial regulators. In practice the arrangement has the characteristics of insurance: the buyer is insuring against the possibility of some class of assets within its portfolio going into default. However, the analogy is not entirely accurate since in many instances the buyer will not even own the bond to which the CDS is referenced but will instead be buying the CDS for entirely speculative rather than risk hedging purposes. In this sense it is different from a normal insurance contract where the buyer of the policy must have some underlying interest (an 'insurable interest') in the subject-matter to which it relates, otherwise the policy is void and unenforceable against the seller. Both sides of the transaction assume counterparty risk. The buyer takes the risk that the seller may default in paying out should there be default on the underlying security: the owner of the bond (and the buyer of the CDS) will take a loss on its sale without a commensurate compensation payment from the seller as per the terms of the CDS. The seller takes the risk that the buyer will default in making further payments on the CDS. Buyer default is particularly worrying to the seller when the CDSs have been bundled up and sold on, as the seller still retains a contingent default risk. Usually the seller will offset all or part of its own risk by buying protection from a third party (Houweling and Vorst, 2005).

In September 2008 the US Federal Reserve provided 'life saving' financial assistance to one of the largest sellers of CDSs in the world, American International Group (AIG). In essence AIG had been selling CDSs against the debt of a large number of financial institutions including Lehman's and Bear Stearns but, believing the risk of default to be negligible, had not taken steps to offset this risk, leaving it with a potentially fatal payout exposure exceeding one hundred billion dollars. During the credit crunch, AIG's payment obligations for CDSs of financial institutions previously regarded as too big to fail were triggered; if it failed to meet these payments the dire consequences for the global banking system were considered too extensive for the Federal Reserve to permit to happen, hence the rescue finance package. The CDS market had graphically illustrated the degree of interconnectivity within the global financial system; total credit risk had not been reduced or hedged but merely reallocated and then underestimated elsewhere within that system.

### 20.4.3 Collateralised Mortgage Obligations (CMOs)

A CMO is a financial instrument in which mortgages provide the underlying collateral or security to investors. Groups of mortgages are 'bundled' together and different classes of bonds created with varying degrees of risk attached to each. In essence the higher tranches pay a lower rate of interest than that paid to holders of lower tranches since the right or claim to prepayment upon default or bankruptcy of the issuer is higher. During the recent credit crunch it became apparent that ratings agencies had been unable to accurately evaluate the precise degree of risk attaching to many CMO issues, principally because 'good' or prime mortgages had been mixed with 'bad' or sub-prime mortgages where the risk of default was significant. In this way 'financial engineers' in the banks had managed to create higher quality bonds from lower quality material, these being mortgages provided to borrowers who were unlikely to be able to meet their payment obligations over the medium term. Base metal had been converted into gold, but as the US economy entered a downturn the true risk attaching to these instruments quickly became apparent. As mortgage default rates soared and properties were repossessed it became increasingly difficult for portfolio managers to unload these CMOs; simply put, there were no buyers for what soon became known as 'toxic assets'.

### 20.4.4 Securitisation and Off-balance Sheet Financing

As banks increased their involvement in the mortgage markets, the new income streams made financial innovation possible. Specifically, banks were now able to create fungible assets (bonds which could be bought and sold in the secondary markets) through the technique of securitisation. Mortgage books were 'bundled up' and repackaged as 'asset-backed

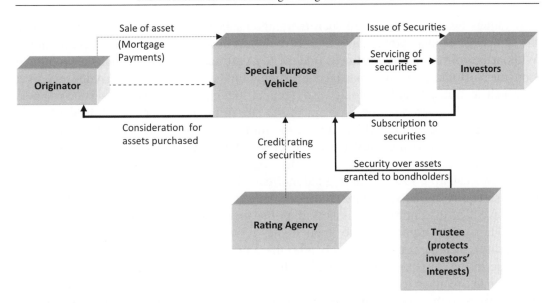

**Figure 20.1**  Securitisation structure

securities', offered to investors through special purpose entities ('SPEs') set up specifically for the purpose of making bond offerings. These repackaged mortgages comprised both high quality cash flows from reliable payers but also low quality-high default risk streams from sub-prime borrowers. Investors and credit rating agencies were increasingly unable to evaluate accurately the quality of the underlying loan portfolio which had been securitised, or the quality of the mortgage payees servicing payments on the assets (the ability of borrowers to continue servicing their debts). Since the original lenders were now mere collection agents under the terms of the securitisation ('conduits') the risk was effectively moved 'off-balance sheet', now becoming the responsibility of the SPE. A typical securitisation structure can be seen in Figure 20.1. Bonds which were issued, secured by these cash flows, were often 'tranched' or offered in different classes. For example, some of the bonds were secured, to be paid off first in the event of bankruptcy of the SPE. The interest payment made on these bonds was lower as a consequence. Unsecured bonds which attracted lower credit ratings would pay higher rates of interest. Paradoxically, the high risk assessment ascribed to the mortgages when on the lender's balance sheet (reflecting the potential for default by individual borrowers) was now transformed into lower risk by reason of the optimistic rating ascribed to the securitised bonds by the ratings agencies (which did not look as closely at the quality of the assets collateralising the bonds – the mortgage payments themselves – as perhaps they should have done). With the removal of these loans from their balance sheets, banks were now free to repeat the process, making fresh mortgages available to a new group of sub-prime borrowers. Risk had not been reduced, but instead moved elsewhere within the financial system. Although securitisation of mortgages was commonplace by 2007–8, the flaw inherent in these bundled up products was that they included low grade mortgages where the risk of payment default was high and the vulnerability to price falls in the underlying collateral significant.

If ratings agencies scrutinised such mortgage-backed products the risk would be that the sub-prime element would have a negative impact upon the bond's overall credit rating. Without the gold standard investment grade of AAA rating, the products would be prohibited from the portfolios of leading managed investment funds. In turn and with a reduced market in which to trade, liquidity would also decline, making the assets of even less appeal to investors. To overcome the problem of the sub-prime components within the bonds, the investment community which created the initial 'raw' products sliced the bonds into tranches, these now being known as collateralised debt obligations (CDOs), the intention being to offer to the investment community higher risk assets and safer but lower yield alternatives (Sharpe, 1992). The original mortgage backed securities were now sliced into high-risk equity, middle-risk mezzanine and investment grade low-risk low-yield bonds. In the event of the entire bond issue failing the first class of investors to lose would be the holders of the equity tranche (their higher return was in return for this higher risk possibility), then mezzanine, and only after these two classes were exhausted could resort be made to the investment grade bonds. Theoretically this last group of investors could receive back their entire investment, leading the ratings agencies to allocate investment grade ratings to the tranche and thereby facilitating its marketing to managed investment funds to which previously sales had been prohibited.

### 20.4.5 Repurchase agreements or 'repos'

A repurchase agreement or 'repo' is used by borrowers to raise short-term capital secured by the transfer of assets to a lender. In terms of accounting treatment such transactions are recorded as 'sales' and not as short-term loans, with the asset being removed from the borrower's balance sheet. This was the principal consequence of the accounting standard SFAS 140 introduced in the United States in 2001. The repo transaction comprises a parallel undertaking by the borrower to buy back the same security from the lender at a later date at a fixed price. In essence the arrangement is a cash transaction combined with a forward contract. The borrower raises funds in return for the transfer to the lender of a security which can be easily disposed of in the event of default. The contract commits the borrower to take back the asset within a very short timeframe. The difference between the two figures – the value of the assets exchanged for a loan of a lesser value – enables the transaction to be treated as a true sale since the seller retains no legal rights in the assets transferred. The lender takes unqualified legal title to the security and holds it pending repurchase by the borrower. Following repayment of the loan the borrower repurchases the asset which is then restored to the balance sheet.

In the United States, Repo 105 enables cash raised from the lender to be used to pay down debt during the short period preceding the preparation of accounts, reducing liabilities and leverage. After the accounts have been issued, the borrower can proceed to borrow cash to buy back the assets previously transferred to the lender in accordance with the obligation under the repo. On the closing out of the repo the borrower's leverage and holdings of risky assets are restored to the position ex ante, but in the meantime a healthier than perhaps warranted balance sheet has entered the public domain.

# 20.5 CREATIVE ACCOUNTING IN THE BANKING SECTOR

### 20.5.1 Loan-loss Allowances

There is a variety of creative accounting techniques deployed by banks, all entirely legal and in accordance with GAAP. For example, in April 2009 Bloomberg.com discussed in an article titled 'Wells Fargo's Profit Looks Too Good to Be True' some of the factors enabling the bank to report one of its most profitable quarters ever in the midst of the global credit crisis. In the previous year, Wells had purchased Wachovia Corporation for US$12.5 billion, and carried over a US$7.5 billion loan-loss allowance from Wachovia's balance sheet onto its own books. This practice was lawful at the time but has since been prohibited. Bloomberg defined loan-loss allowances as the reserves lenders set up on their balance sheets in anticipation of future credit losses. The expenses lenders record to boost their loan-loss reserves are called provisions, and as loans are written off lenders record charge-offs, reducing their allowance (as a loan is deemed irrecoverable, so the loss becomes crystallised or actual as opposed to provided for; the allowance is accordingly reduced). After taking control of Wachovia, Wells was able to effectively transfer new credit losses, including on loans made by Wells itself, to this fund, and in this way present a more favourable impression regarding its own performance (since its exposure or allowance appeared to have been reduced). When the US$7.5 billion allowance from the Wachovia acquisition had been exhausted, the scale of the bank's own losses would become apparent. However, by that time, assuming an economic recovery and the ending of the credit crunch, these would be either minimal or non-existent (since the loan default rate would have reduced). In this way Wells was able to manage the disclosure of losses on loans made in a perfectly legal manner. This resulted in the declaration of loan losses which were smaller than might otherwise have been the case if the Wachovia allowance had not been available.

This specific practice has now been prohibited under new rules issued by FASB. However, banks still remain able to make use of 'reserves,' or the fund set aside to protect against bad loans as part of lawful creative accounting. Subject to GAAP considerations a bank is entitled to determine the size of this reserve by looking at the quality of its loans, history of previous non-performance and default rates, and other factors. If the bank wishes to inflate its profits through a one-off adjustment, it can reduce the value of the reserve on the pretext that loans have somehow become less risky, and book the reduction as profit. Although this strategy can result in the bank under-reserving in respect of a realistic evaluation of future losses, the short-term boost to profits can make it an attractive option.

### 20.5.2 Adjustment of Reporting Dates

In April 2009, Goldman Sachs reported impressive first quarter earnings, enabling the bank to announce that it would soon be in a position to repay money made available to it by the US Treasury under the Troubled Assets Relief Program ('TARP') which had effectively 'stripped out' or bought toxic assets from the balance sheets of banks requesting assistance. However, in December 2008 Goldman's had booked a pre-tax loss of US$1.3 billion. By switching to reporting results from a financial year to a calendar year, this meant that its financial year ended in November 2008 while its first quarter began in January 2009, leaving December, according to the *Irish Times* of 25 August 2009, an 'orphan month'. Creative accounting had been used, entirely legally, to adjust the months in which information was reported. The *Irish Times* observed: 'A Goldman spokesman pointed out that "we didn't make the rules". Still, by burying the December figures in a table on page 10 of a news release, it certainly didn't seek to draw attention to the losses.'

### 20.5.3 Enhancing Profits through Disposals of Assets

Other lawful methods of creative accounting used by banks include enhancing declared profits by taking one-off gains on the sales of stakes taken in other banks during the earlier heady days of banking exuberance. A bank's performance may not have improved at all. However, by declaring profits generated by the disposal of such assets, the share price of the disposer invariably increased. Similarly, it is quite permissible for one bank which has acquired another to increase the value of the assets transferred under the takeover using revised prices which significantly exceed those previously used by the original holder. This is done by the acquirer stating that assets had been recorded in the acquired bank's accounts at historic rather than marked-to-market value reflecting the price as pertaining at the time of the takeover. For example, the assets may have been purchased some time earlier at a lower price but had not been revalued to reflect price increases over time. In this way an instant 'paper' gain can be produced without any change in the acquirer's underlying business performance. If the price used by the acquirer is unrealistic or inflated, this will be revealed in time when assets have to be written down to their fair value, but if in the meantime the value has improved with general market conditions, then the overly optimistic revaluation simply will not matter.

### 20.5.4 Lawful Adjustments to Composition of 'Level 3' Assets in Banks' Balance Sheets

According to Federal Accounting Standards Board (FASB) Statement 157, balance sheet assets were to be classified within one of three possible categories. Level 1 comprises assets which are very liquid, in which there is a market in which they can be easily and readily traded, and are as a consequence relatively easy to price. Level 2 assets are assets which can be priced by reference to similar or comparable assets or market-based prices. For example, if a complex bond trading in a secondary or mature market is priced in US dollars and has a certain variable coupon structure, it would be legitimate to price a bond of similar characteristics held in a bank's portfolio by reference to such a bond. Level 3 assets are those assets whose fair value cannot be estimated with any degree of accuracy by reference to existing market prices, or models (Nelson, 1996). With regard to existing market prices, such a market reference point does not exist. With regard to the models, these are essentially historical and not capable of providing a price in highly volatile and unpredictable trading conditions.

To some extent this latter scenario is associated with the so-called 'black swan' scenario: the proposition that some market conditions are as rare as black swans and therefore beyond the predictive or interpretive capabilities of models more suited to historical events. Level

3 valuations are principally an outcome of management assumptions or expectations; they can neither be supported nor challenged with any degree of accuracy by outside observers (Venkatachalam, 1996). One of the principal advantages of allocating assets to the Level 3 classification is that holders often do not feel obliged to write them down during a crisis such as the recent credit crunch since, they argue, the fair value cannot be accurately determined.

In such circumstances, unlike assets held in Levels 1 and 2, a significant write-down does not take place notwithstanding the reality that those assets held in Level 3 have also probably plunged in value (Whittington, 2008). This last class can result in reported profits being significantly greater than would otherwise be the case if an unrealised loss had to be provided for. Furthermore, if a bank is of the view that a Level 2 asset has become illiquid, it is legally entitled to reallocate it to Level 3, manipulating reported unrealised losses in the process.

It was noted by a 'Moneymorning.com' Contributing Editor, Martin Hutchinson, on 28 April 2008, that prior to the sub-prime crisis mortgage-backed securities, although complex, were priced according to Markit's ABX Index, which used the average weight of four series in the index to track the price of housing derivatives. However, when the ABX Index collapsed a reference point for pricing of such derivatives was no longer available. Instead of marking down Level 2 assets with the negative publicity which would inevitably follow, some firms instead elected to reclassify those assets as Level 3 assets. The logic of such a reclassification is that if there is no market into which an asset can be sold, it cannot technically be written down since there is no price (collapsed or otherwise) to which reference can be made to make such a write-down possible. Marking to market is impossible since there is no market in existence. Accordingly, the price allocated to Level 3 assets can theoretically be anything. The prospect of huge losses on assets held in Level 2 does not materialise since they have effectively been moved elsewhere within the balance sheet. A second advantage of inflating the holdings of Level 3 assets is that, if they are revalued upwards through the use of internal pricing models, it remains possible to continue paying high levels of bonuses and salaries even though the true value of the holdings is, in the extreme, zero. A further advantage of allocating assets to Level 3 is that, when market conditions eventually begin to improve and liquidity returns to those asset-backed securities, it then becomes possible to reallocate these again to Level 2. This is a further example of legally permissible creative accounting; when the value of the ABS collapses and there is no market into which it can be sold, setting a figure for an unrealised loss becomes impossible since there is no price to which reference can be made. At that point it becomes possible to allocate the asset to Level 3. However, if the market for the ABS subsequently improves, then at that point a price at which it can be sold becomes apparent. It then becomes possible to set a price for the ABS and restore it to Level 2, making an unrealised gain in the process.

### 20.5.5 Decline in Value of Outstanding Debt

A final creative accounting technique utilised by banks consists of taking advantage of declines in the value of their own debts (issued bonds). If the market value of this debt has fallen a 'credit value adjustment' may be made since the issuer, the bank, would be able, if so inclined, to buy back the debt for less cash than it originally received when the bonds were issued. In this way a profit can be taken on the adjustment equal to the difference between the issue price and the current discounted value. Having considered the various techniques of creative accounting used by banks, the next section will discuss these in the context of recent financial crises and scandals.

## 20.6 LEHMAN'S, MADOFF AND BEAR STEARNS; FAILURES AND CONSEQUENCES

### 20.6.1 Lehman Brothers

#### 20.6.1.1 The Fall

In the straggly final days of September 2008 one of the most prestigious, respected banks on Wall Street staggered on the point of collapse, desperately seeking a 'white knight' to save it, like a boxer staggering around the ring waiting for the final knock-out blow. During the previous year shares in the bank had fallen by a record 94 %, and yet by the end of the first week in September the shares had fallen by another 45 %. Blow followed upon blow. On 9 September one prospective knight, the Development Bank of Korea, decided against a purchase of a 50 % stakeholding in the 158-year-old bank. Its formal withdrawal was confirmed on 10 September and coincided with the announcement by Lehman's of a third-quarter loss of US$3.9 billion. 14 September witnessed a further withdrawal, this time by Barclays Bank and Bank of America from rescue talks. Lehman's share price collapsed a further 42 %.

On 12 September the US government, still floundering to identify policy options and instruments to deal with what appeared a financial services Armageddon, announced via the Federal Reserve and the Treasury that taxpayers' funds would not be used to bail out the bank or to 'broker a marriage' between it and a white knight keen to purchase the bank for perhaps a dollar. This was perhaps driven by the fear on the part of the Federal Reserve that bailing out Lehman's would convey a message to the markets that the State would ride to the rescue of all crisis-ridden financial institutions, relieving other stakeholders of their obligation of oversight. Moreover, the US government refused to give UK bank Barclays a guarantee for Lehman's trading commitments as a prerequisite to the purchase of the bank. It was unwilling to put taxpayers' money at risk when the true extent of the losses at Lehman, or the residual strength of its asset base, were not yet known with any degree of certainty.

By 15 September the game was up. Lehman's finally filed for Chapter 11 bankruptcy which in the US provides protection while the applicant negotiates either a rescue package with creditors or a strategy by which they can be repaid. The bank cited bank debt of US$613 billion, US$155 billion in bond debts, and assets valued at US$639 billion. Of these assets, a large component was constituted by Level 3 assets (assets such as mortgage-backed securities, collateralised debt obligations and other complex derivatives which are notoriously difficult to value). In a filing with the Securities and Exchange Commission in November 2008 the bank had indicated that Level 3 assets had risen relative to overall assets from 6.1 % in November 2007 to 6.5 % as of May 2008. Although this figure was to decline in the months leading up to the bank's collapse, it still remained a significant element in the bank's balance sheet. Approximately half Lehman's balance sheet was in the form of asset-backed securities, principally mortgages, which were to steeply decline in value as underlying assumptions regarding the future direction in property values and default rate increasingly proved to have been erroneous. On 16 September one of the earlier potential rescuers, Barclays, finally came forward, but this time to buy up those parts of Lehman's activities which offered the best prospects of future survival and profitability, rejecting those lines of business, clogged with debt, which were now well beyond the point of redemption.

### 20.6.1.2   *Aftermath of the Fall: The Investigation Begins*

After the collapse of Lehman's the investigations into the causes of its demise were commenced with alacrity. In oral testimony before the Committee on Oversight and Government Reform of the United States House of Representatives, Luigi Zingales, Professor of Entrepreneurship and Finance at University of Chicago Graduate School of Business, spoke on the 'Causes and Effects of the Lehman Brothers Bankruptcy'. According to Zingales, the bank's collapse had in essence been brought about by a 'very aggressive leverage policy in the context of a major financial crisis'. 'CNN Money' noted on 11 September 2008 that between 2004 and 2007 Lehman increased its balance sheet by nearly US$300 billion through the purchase of securities collateralised by commercial and domestic property loans, but during the same period the firm's equity base increased by a paltry US$6 billion. As a consequence assets increased from an already difficult to sustain 24 times capital to 31 times.

Between 2007 and 2008 the bank increased the balance sheet by US$120 billion of additional debt, driven in part by a need to leverage or increase by debt rather than retained profits the bonus pool and sustain compensation schemes for higher paid employees. The bank itself had also become one of the principal underwriters of mortgage-backed securities on Wall Street, one of the core assumptions underlying this commitment to the market being that property prices would continue to boom over the medium term, and mortgage payment default rates would persist at sustainable, relatively insignificant levels into the future. Both assumptions proved to be incorrect. The short-term collapse in overpriced property values was proving spectacular, whilst defaults on mortgages were rapidly escalating as workers across the country became victims of the economic slowdown, no longer able to maintain payments on properties which had overstretched meagre resources even during the good times. As the 'sub-prime crisis' took hold ratings agencies quickly downgraded bonds previously rated as having limited default risk. Investors reacted to the downgrading by holding back from the market and unloading mortgage-backed securities from their portfolios, significantly depressing the market and leaving Lehman's with large holdings which were plummeting in value, precipitating substantial write-downs and a further tumbling in the bank's share price.

There are several possible explanations for the increase in the holdings of Level 3 assets in Lehman's and other US banks' balance sheets during the sub-prime crisis. First, banks may have reclassified existing holdings across from Level 2 to Level 3. Second, firms may have sought to inflate the values of existing commitments in Level 3. Since these assets are notoriously difficult to price, during a financial crisis where there is a complete failure of the market in which these can be traded, the figure or estimate for the Level 3 component can be massaged through the use of internal models which, in truth, can simply pluck a figure from the air in such circumstances, offsetting a massive 'hit' taking place elsewhere within Levels 1 and 2.

In his testimony, Zingales identified how a prolonged and perhaps artificial period of real estate price increases combined with unrestrained boom in a parallel and corollary activity, securitisation, had led to a relaxation of lending standards within Lehman's. Traditional rules of conservative, prudent banking had given way to an exuberance which resulted in a substantial and soon-to-be disastrous failure by the capital markets properly to assess the quality of the mortgages underpinning the securitised asset-backed market.

However, according to Zingales there were several reasons why effective risk monitoring had fallen into such a state of disrepair and inaccuracy (McAnally, 1996). First, mortgages were priced based upon historical records which did not factor in the probability of a significant drop in real estate prices at the national level, nor did they take into account the potential effect of changes in lending standards on the probability of default (for example, payments rising sharply at the end of an interest rate 'holiday' provided as a 'sweetener' or inducement to borrowers at the commencement of the loan).

It seems that there may have been another factor in this weak approach to risk evaluation. During the several years leading up to the collapse in the securitised mortgages industry, there were players in the financial markets which had a vested interest in seeing risk assessment criteria substantially weakened or ignored altogether. Mortgage brokers, often earning commissions from selling mortgages, had an interest in encouraging a booming property market. Urban myth holds that, on the freeway leading away from a state penitentiary in Maryland, there was a poster reading, 'Just leaving prison? Not got a job? Not got any savings? No problem! Give us a call and we'll arrange a mortgage so you too can become a home owner!'

The second reason identified by Zingales for the weak credit check environment was the massive amount of collateralised assets issued by a limited number of players, including Lehman's. This had altered the fundamental relationship between credit rating agencies and the investment banks issuing these asset-backed securities. Instead of submitting an issue to a ratings agency, at arm's length, and awaiting its evaluation, investment banks 'shopped around' for the best ratings and even, according to Zingales, received handbooks explaining how to produce the riskiest security whilst at the same time qualifying for the top AAA rating.

Demand for asset-backed securities in general, and mortgage-backed securities in particular, was being driven from two major sources. First, The Federal National Mortgage Association ('Fannie Mae') and the Federal Home Loan Mortgage Corporation ('Freddie Mac') were allowed and encouraged to invest their funds into these securities. Second, money market funds, required by law to hold only highly-rated securities, craved these securities which simultaneously satisfied regulatory requirements whilst at the same time boosted their yields. According to Zingales managers hoped that if there was a crisis (and they were aware of the risk of their over-commitment to this market) it would adversely affect their competitors to the same extent. This would neutralise any reputational damage which they might otherwise suffer if they were the only ones to suffer losses in this way. There was also a prevailing view that, just as the government had protected the market on 19 September by insuring all money market funds it would step in again if a new crisis were to begin. The earlier quasi-bail-out decision for AIG had created a moral hazard in which money market managers were disincentivised from evaluating in any truly meaningful sense the true nature of the risk they were taking when investing in AAA-rated mortgage backed securities. Indeed, in many quarters these were known to be overvalued.

There was a further reason why AAA-rated mortgage backed securities, known to many to be of a higher risk than the ratings agencies were implying, were of such appeal. Under recommendations made by the Basel Committee on Banking Supervision banks are required to maintain a relationship between levels of risk in investments and the allocated level of capital in the balance sheet. The greater the level of risk being taken on by a bank, the greater the capital it has to hold in relatively risk-free assets such as UK Gilts or US Treasuries to provide security for stakeholders such as depositors or investors in the event of it experiencing difficulties. These collateralised assets were producing higher yields than comparable corporate paper but at the same time had the same rating. The capital allocation burden was the same (because risk was adjudged under the Basel criteria to be the same), but the returns greater, creating a simple regulatory arbitrage opportunity. Mortgage-backed securities were generally receiving the same AAA rating as risk-free Gilts and Treasuries; the favourable regulatory capital allocation implication was obvious.

### 20.6.1.3   The Role of Securitised Sub-prime Mortgages in Lehman's Demise

The pooling of mortgages, the assets backing the securities, also proved to be major cause of the crisis to affect Lehman's. High-quality mortgages with improbable default rates became 'mixed' with very low-quality mortgages in which the default risk was highly probable. The securities issued thus represented a homogenisation of these very different types of risk with the result that it became impossible to 'tease out' the good from the bad or achieve any level of transparency as to who owned what in the underlying security. The good became recycled or repackaged with the bad. An additional and comparatively new problem was that many of the issuers repurchased those asset-backed bonds which they had issued in the first place. In the absence of any achievable transparency regarding the degree of risk implicit in these securities the market became suspicious of banks and the extent of what had now become known as the 'toxicity' in their balance sheets, (i.e. the presence of mortgage-backed securities where the default risk was now much more significant than when they had been issued and evaluated by the ratings agencies).

It thus became increasingly difficult for banks to tap the interbank market. Even when this was still possible it was at a much higher rate of interest than had previously prevailed. In Lehman's case, Zingales asserted in his testimony before the House of Representatives Committee that the problem was exacerbated by two factors. First, Lehman's had an extremely high level of leverage or asset to equity ratio. While US commercial banks cannot leverage their equity more than 15 to 1, Lehman had a leverage of more than 30 to 1. A mere 3.3 % drop in the value of assets would thus wipe out the entire value of Lehman's equity and make the company insolvent. The bank was already highly vulnerable to bond market volatility, but the fall in asset-backed securities, which now comprised a significant component of its own portfolio as a consequence in part of its underwriting activity, was to prove disastrous in driving its leverage to a level unsustainable even in the short term. It was also now impossible to sell off its existing portfolio of mortgage-backed securities into a collapsing market. Aware of Lehman's involvement and commitment to the mortgage-backed securities market both as an underwriter and as an investor, the markets were quick to withdraw from meaningful engagement with the bank and failed to assist it in dealing with its short-term funding difficulties.

The second factor which undermined Lehman's position was its over-reliance on the use of short term debt. In the context of a highly volatile and panicking market, such reliance can be catastrophic as lines of credit are quickly withdrawn as interbank lenders recoil from those institutions merely rumoured to be experiencing solvency difficulties. Zingales observed:

> The Lehman CEO will likely tell you that his company was solvent and that it was brought down by a run. This is a distinct possibility. The problem is that nobody knows for sure. When Lehman went down, it had 26 billion in book equity, but the doubts about the value of its assets combined with its high degree of leverage created a huge uncertainty about the true value of this equity: it could have been worth 40 billion or negative 20. It is important to note that Lehman did not find itself in that situation by accident; it was the unlucky draw of a consciously-made gamble.

### 20.6.1.4  *Remuneration Structures at Lehman's; a Contributory Factor in the Fall*

One of the main drivers of Lehman's accumulation of debt was its remuneration schemes for senior staff. At the head of the bank was Richard S. Fuld Jr who earned US$34.4 million in 2007. During that same year and after reporting a record profit, Lehman's compensation rose 9.5 % to US$9.5 billion, including bonuses estimated at US$5.7 billion. The top five executives also received US$81 million during that year (US House of Representatives Oversight and Government Reform Committee, 7 October 2008). The bank's in-house legal adviser, Thomas Russo, received US$12 million in 2007 (Bloomberg.com, 19 September 2008). Both Fuld and Russo contended that these payments were not disproportionate, being commensurate with the bank's increased profitability as a result of Fuld's stewardship and the extent of Russo's duties and responsibilities. The administration of the bank was kept highly secretive. Strategy and all other decision-making concerning the bank was run from the '31st floor' at the bank's headquarters to which only a very few employees of the most senior rank were granted access (BBC World News America, 2009).

In 2008–9 approximately 30 % of the shares in Lehman's were owned by employees, either directly or through share options and restricted shares. Two consequences followed from this generous remuneration structure. First, when the stock began to fall at an astonishing rate preceding the collapse, employees who had been paid in shares and other stock options incurred enormous unrealised losses. In normal circumstances employees would hold such shares and wait for the upturn, but in the context of Lehman's the market collapse was so spontaneous and unexpected that it became almost immediately impossible to exit or sell without incurring vast actual losses. Stock options, which depended upon the share price reaching a certain (higher) level than prevailed when they were allocated, effectively became worthless overnight. However, many of the more shrewd senior management had diversified away from Lehman shares, preferring instead to invest their huge salaries, bonuses and proceeds of liquidations of shareholdings into property purchases, yachts, other shares and similar trappings of the lifestyles of the rich. The second consequence of such a significant proportion of the equity being in the hands of employees was that the degree of activism which would usually be associated with a high proportion of external investors such as pension funds and private investors was absent.

### 20.6.1.5  Repurchase Agreements; Creative Accounting and Balance Sheet Impression Management

In March 2010 Anton Valukas, the examiner appointed by New York's Southern District Bankruptcy Court to investigate the collapse of Lehman Brothers, issued his report, 'Lehman Brothers Holdings Inc. Chapter 11 Proceedings'. In the report Valukas noted that through the use of repos Lehman's had been able to remove risky assets from its books for between seven and ten days, artificially but lawfully improving the ostensible health of its balance sheet. According to the report, Lehman's use of Repo 105 transactions doubled from about US\$24 billion (£15.8 billion) in the fourth quarter of 2006 to US\$49.1 billion and US\$50.4 billion in the first and second quarters of 2008. Risky assets and other liabilities were temporarily removed from Lehman's balance sheet in this way, and entirely within the law. This use of creative, but entirely legal, accounting meant that markets, investors, regulators and other stakeholders were unable to gain an accurate and consistent view of the true scale of Lehman's holdings of risky assets, or of its leverage.

Overall, therefore, Lehman's is an example of a company which adopted a business strategy based on an unsustainable economic base. This was compounded by the use of financial instruments and creative accounting, especially reliance on CMOs and Level 3 valuations. The role of repo agreements was also significant, as reported by Anton Valukas in his report to New York's Southern District Bankruptcy Court. The principal effect of these agreements was to present a balance sheet to the world which, entirely lawfully, underrepresented the true extent of the company's leverage and its holding of risky assets.

## 20.6.2  Bernard Madoff

### 20.6.2.1  Origins of the Fraud

On 29 June 2009 Bernard 'Bernie' Madoff was sentenced to 150 years in prison for perpetrating a US\$65 billion swindle and one of the biggest financial frauds in history. At his trial Madoff pleaded guilty to 11 offences including securities fraud, money laundering, perjury, and making false filings with the SEC. In sentencing him the Judge Denny Chin referred to his fraud as being one of 'extraordinary evil,' which was both 'staggering and unprecedented' in its magnitude. Madoff's business had been a gigantic 'Ponzi' scheme of accounting trickery originating, according to the prosecutors, in the 1980s, although the culture of criminality, evasion, and deliberate obfuscation had formed within the Madoff organisation in earlier decades. Madoff himself stated in his court plea that the Ponzi scheme had been initiated in 1991.

Bernie Madoff had started his career on Wall Street in 1960 with the founding of the firm 'Bernard L. Madoff Investment Securities LLC'. In the early days the firm's principal line of business had been market-making: matching buyers and sellers of securities on Wall Street and taking a small 'turn' or marginal percentage on each transaction. Madoff's principal goal had been to achieve a high volume of orders or so-called 'pass through business,' and to achieve this he agreed to pay a commission to those firms which passed business to him. Leading firms to pass business to him in this way included established names such as Fidelity Capital and Charles Schwabb. However, Madoff also ran a 'sideline' business, providing investment advisory services to private clients. It was this latter, secretive activity which first generated the potential for fundamental conflicts of interest. Madoff was capable in these early years of 'front running,' or executing deals in shares on behalf of himself and his advisees before his market-making firm put in greater transactions on behalf of buyers or sellers which, by the nature of their size, would move the price of the shares (Danthine and Moresi, 1998). Madoff depended on 'feeder' firms to pass business through to him. In order to incentivise and encourage this flow, feeders were provided with promissory notes which generated fixed interest payments to their own clients of around 18 %, this being at a 2 % discount from the 20 % Madoff would pay to the feeder. The feeders thus gained 2 % for very little work and behaviourally would not have wished to upset Madoff. Although SEC rules require that if a firm has anything more than 15 clients it must be registered as an investment advisor, Madoff, in time managing the investments of 3200 clients, never registered. As far as clients of the feeders were concerned, they had no knowledge of Madoff's involvement with their investments, instead believing that it was the feeder firms which were generating such high returns on their portfolios. This was one of the very few rules on which Madoff insisted when accepting funds from feeders: total secrecy should be maintained and he should not be named as the investor advisor. In this way he also evaded the registration rule required by the SEC of investment firms with more than 15 clients.

### 20.6.2.2  Bernie's Little Secret: the Ponzi Scheme

On 11 December 2008 Agent Theodore Cacioppi of the FBI arrived at Madoff's apartment to ask if there was an innocent explanation for recent activities at his securities firm. Madoff told Cacioppi and another agent, 'There is no innocent explanation,' admitting that 'he paid investors with money that wasn't there,' and expected to go to jail.

Madoff had admitted that his investment fund was a giant Ponzi scheme. Such a scheme is named after an American fraudster, Charles Ponzi, who, in the 1920s promised investors a 40 % return on their investments over a 90-day period, compared with a comparable 5 % which was being paid on standard deposit accounts at that time. Ponzi anticipated making significant short-term profits on exchange rate fluctuations between the dollar and other currencies through buying and selling foreign-currency denominated international mail coupons. When these increased in value, he realised the profits before the date fixed for meeting the payment obligation to investors arrived. But in time the exchange rate fluctuations were not of a magnitude Ponzi had anticipated and, in an increasingly desperate attempt to maintain cash flow, he diverted the money of fresh investors into the scheme to meet payments to earlier investors as well as enriching himself (Kedia and Philippon, 2007).

Madoff was active in the hedge fund sector but specialised in a specialist highly opaque division within this sector, this being 'funds of funds'. These have been defined by the *Washington Post* of 17 December 2008 as hedge funds that raise money from pension funds, university endowments and trusts, and high net worth individuals and, for a fee of

1.5 % a year, invest in other hedge funds which then pay even higher fees. In return for paying double fees, these middlemen market themselves as being capable of seeking out the best and most profitable hedge funds, and also conducting the required level of due diligence regarding those funds with which they invest. Many of these 'funds of funds' invested billions of dollars of clients' money with Madoff without taking any cognisance of the series of red flags which should have put them on enquiry. For example, the auditing of the fund's books by a three-person audit firm rather than an international firm of auditors which would normally have been expected to be appointed to such a business. The ability of Madoff to generate consistent returns when the rest of the market was suffering significant downturns in performance failed to generate serious concern or suspicion amongst the majority of affected parties, although competitors and a minority of investors had started to raise questions. There was also a suspicion that confirmation tickets for trades were routinely sent through the post rather than electronically to give Madoff the potential of an additional five days' trading before the client was in possession of legal documentation relating to trades. Businesses which had 'funds of funds' and which incurred substantial losses with Madoff included Man Group of the United Kingdom, Spain's Banco Santander and Switzerland's Union Bancaire Privee.

### 20.6.2.3  *Aftermath and Investigation*

In testimony before the Senate Banking Committee Enquiry into the Madoff affair on 27 January 2009, John Coffee, Professor of Law at Columbia Law School, identified the difference between mutual funds which as a business had no prior association with Ponzi Schemes, and hedge funds of the sort administered, fraudulently, by Madoff. A mutual fund has an independent custodian who is a trustee and holds the investor's funds in a separate bank or broker-dealer account and does not let the money manager (the investment adviser) have access to that fund. Instead the custodian buys or sells securities at the instruction of the investment adviser but crucially, does not remit the funds to the care of the adviser, instead passing the money directly back and forth to the investors (Liang, 2000). Coffee noted in his testimony that where there have been failures in the hedge fund industry this has usually been in the context of a small minority of hedge funds which do not use an independent external custodian. Madoff had been until 2006 a broker-dealer who gave investment advice. After 2006 he registered himself as an investment adviser and was at that point, according to the Investment Advisers Act, required to use a 'qualified custodian'. As permitted under the law, Madoff creatively appointed himself as the 'qualified custodian,' and in this capacity was his own watchdog, his own overseer. Commenting on this flaw in the law Coffee observed:

> It still allows the investment adviser – where it has a broker-affiliate – to use its own broker-dealer to be its own custodian and I think that permits incest. The small closely held broker-dealer firm wants to keep everything in-house, and thus there is no accountability, no watchdog.

Stability is fundamental to the success of a Ponzi scheme; if it is dependent upon predictable exchange rate or interest rate movements and these prove unexpectedly volatile, 'cash flow in' can become insufficient to meet 'cash flow out,' resulting in panic by existing investors, an inability to meet their claims for return of their capital, and an inevitable collapse of the scheme itself. In 2007, a crash in the housing market unsettled the markets. Hedge funds began to shut down or refused clients who now wanted to withdraw money. Despite the rush of cash out of the system, Madoff appeared to be 'bucking the trend,' making money on behalf of clients despite the general downturn. But eventually money began to flow out from Madoff's funds as clients required liquidity to meet their own personal financial crises. At first Madoff's response was to launch new funds, the BBH Emerald Fund and the Greenwich Emerald Fund, but when this failed to attract sufficient investors it became impossible to continue meeting the demands of existing clients desperate to be repaid. The collapse of Madoff's empire became inevitable at this point. In this case Madoff had managed to bend, and also break, the regulations existing at the time. He was able then to use accounting trickery through a Ponzi scheme to defraud depositors.

### 20.6.3 Bear Stearns

#### 20.6.3.1 Origins of the Liquidity Crisis

Prior to its collapse, Bear Stearns (Bear hereafter) had an aura of confidence and durability borne of survival through wars and catastrophes since first opening its doors to business in 1923, becoming by 2008 the fifth largest investment bank on Wall Street. Bear used creative accounting in a perfectly legal manner to convey signals to the market regarding the strength of the collateral provided in respect of its complex series of financial transactions with other banks and investors. However, over-leveraging of the balance sheet, insufficient stress testing of the underlying collateral and a culture of aggressive pursuit of management fees was to eventually bring about the bank's demise in 2008. Fung and Hsieh (1997) have shown how hedge funds follow strategies that are dramatically different and significantly more risk-inclined than mutual funds, such strategies being significantly more dynamic. Most mutual fund managers have investment mandates similar to traditional asset managers with relative modest return targets, whereas, according to Fung and Hsieh (1997), hedge fund managers tend to have mandates to make an absolute return target, regardless of the wider market environment. They state (1997 at p. 276):

> To achieve the absolute return target, managers are given the flexibility to choose among many asset classes and to employ dynamic trading strategies that frequently involve short sales, leverage, and derivatives.

The roots of Bear's crisis were to be found in the mortgage-backed securities market, as was the case for so many other investment banks which were to fail during the credit crunch. It appeared that the bank had 'magicked away' the weakness of mortgage-backed securities in their initial form, replacing them with CDOs of high grade and low default risk. This was not the case but enabled the bank to leverage its balance sheet, at least in the early months after the reformulation, to an extent which would simply not have been possible if mortgage-backed securities alone were the sole or principal component of the bank's balance sheet. Coval et al. (2009) explain how the ability to repackage risks and create apparently safe assets from otherwise risky collateral led to a dramatic expansion in the issuance of tranched securities, many of the components of which came to be regarded as almost risk-free and certified as such by the ratings agencies. The principal factors in the later catastrophic fall in the structured finance market for these collateralised assets were, according to Coval *et al.*, the extreme fragility of the ratings to 'modest imprecision in evaluating underlying risks', and the exposure of such assets to systematic risks, including economic downturns in which unemployment rises and the ability to continue mortgage payments declines.

### 20.6.3.2  Two Hedge Funds: Courting a Funding Crisis?

Bear established two hedge funds, the Bear Stearns High Grade Structured Credit Fund and the Bear Stearns High Grade Structured Credit Enhanced Leveraged Fund. These Funds bought some of the CDO tranches from Bear. In effect, in a clear piece of financial engineering, the bank was buying assets from itself. Since the CDOs were generating a return over and above the cost paid by the Funds on borrowings to make these purchases, the attraction to investors of these booming vehicles was obvious. With the general increase in property prices, the security underlying the Funds, there was a consequent decline in default risk (Cohan, 2009). As a result, the value of the equity CDO also increased, providing further collateral against which higher borrowing from other banks could be secured. This was the process which originated the overleveraging undertaken by Bear (Miller, 1991). The risk inherent in this strategy is that the underlying security, the CDOs, was relatively illiquid from conception since the size of the potential market into which they could be sold was small. Many investors, private and institutional, lacked the sophisticated risk evaluation tools necessary to understand these instruments and consequently held back from purchasing them. But in the early days of the process the third-party financiers looked only to the value of the collateral itself, marked up by Bear, which had sliced up the mortgage-backed securities and created the CDOs in the first place. To partially protect against adverse movements in the underlying CDOs Bear purchased credit default swaps, discussed earlier in this chapter in section 20.4.2. These involved payments akin to insurance premia to a third party (Hull *et al.*, 2004). With every additional unit of leverage the performance of the Funds increased. Banks increased their lending to the Funds on the assumption that the underlying collateral, the CDOs, had increased in value and would continue to do so. In turn the Funds bought more CDOs from Bear which continued creating these from mortgage-backed securities which it bought in the market place, slicing them into CDOs as it had done from the beginning.

The crisis began, at first as a trickle, when the mortgage market started experiencing increasing levels of default. Banks which had previously lent to the Funds now insisted that if the Funds were not able to provide cash as security (the 'pool' to which lenders would have recourse should the Funds fail), then part of the collateral, the CDOs, had to be liquidated to realise additional cash (Krishnamurthy, 2003). Unable to find the required cash the Funds commenced sales. Although credit insurance was in place against the underlying security in the Bear Funds to protect Bear's position under the arrangement, it was not so extensive as to protect the Funds in this new scenario. The Funds, having significantly leveraged their positions, began to suffer substantial losses. Eventually, after having sold all the underlying security and causing the market for CDOs to crash in the process, the Funds could not survive without cash infusions from Bear. In June 2007 the Bear Stearns High Grade Structured Credit Fund received a US$1.6 billion bail-out from Bear, enabling it to fund its positions while it liquidated out of its CDOs. A letter dated 17 July 2007 sent to investors by Bear chief executive officer Jim Cayne explained:

> As you know, in early June, the funds were faced with investor redemption requests and margin calls that they were unable to meet. The funds sold assets in an attempt to raise liquidity but were unable to generate sufficient cash to meet the outstanding margin calls.... As a result, counterparties moved to seize collateral or otherwise terminate financing arrangements they had with the funds.

### 20.6.3.3  *Bankruptcy and Investor Flight*

In late July 2007 both Funds filed for bankruptcy, but the cash call upon Bear to bail out the Funds had been nothing short of catastrophic. The bank's perceived exposure to both the mortgage-backed securities market in general, and hedge funds investing in them in particular, triggered wider concerns amongst investors as to the bank's short-term solvency. Bear's difficulties were exacerbated by other banks which, knowing that the Funds needed to make immediate sales of assets to meet the cash demands of their investors, aggressively drove down the prices of those assets in the secondary markets by selling their own holdings. By March 2008 lines of credit upon which Bear depended to fund its business were being closed down. Lenders feared that the bank would be unable to pay back its borrowings. Existing clients were now extremely reluctant to trade with the bank, and hedge funds which had also previously been a source of cash now switched their assets away from Bear's prime brokerage, substantially eroding its already precarious commission flows. The bank was rapidly running out of cash, meeting the cash calls being made on the Funds which by this time had become completely exhausted of capital. The irony of Bear's debacle is that it was its own accounting 'magick alchemy' of converting base assets or sub-prime mortgages into investment grade material which was eventually to contribute in large part to its demise.

# 20.7  CONCLUSION

Recent events have shown how complex financial instruments and funding arrangements can be used to manipulate the apparent strength of balance sheets when ratings agencies, investors and even management itself fail adequately to evaluate risk or 'stress test' trading or portfolio investment strategies. Leverage or borrowing against a healthy balance sheet is a sustainable and often wise business practice, but when this becomes over-leveraging or raising capital against overvalued or potentially highly volatile assets, the foundation stones of a funding crisis are put in place. Regulators who permit banks to weigh the risks accruing to their balance sheets through the use of their own internal risk measurement or value at risk models should not be surprised when it eventually transpires that the true levels of exposure to particular markets are either underplayed or underreported.

Banks too have a vested interest in perpetuating such creative accounting. Overvalued collateral can be used as a basis for securing levels of borrowing from lenders which would not be possible, or only possible at a much higher rate of interest, if the true value of the underlying security was known. However, when banks become 'too clever' in creating or deploying financial instruments with implicit risk which even the devisors do not understand, they also create the possibility of their own future demise. Such was the case with Bear Stearns. The artificiality of the balance sheet value attached to the 'diced and sliced' mortgage-backed securities purchased by the bank as part of its strategy to create investment grade bonds from 'toxic waste' eventually led to the disastrous cash crisis which ruined the bank when forced to meet the funding demands of its two Funds. Non-etheless, the role of market psychology should not be overlooked in the context of creative accounting; the reality is that in booming markets investors and ratings agencies have a tendency to dilute their level of scrutiny of new business strategies. And when a firm is maintaining healthy returns even during a market downturn, those taking the shilling of its success are often too willing to overlook the thicket of 'red flags' which would suggest to the objective bystander that groundless exuberance or even worse, criminality, may be lurking in the undergrowth. Such was the case with Bernard Madoff.

# REFERENCES

BBC World News America (11 September 2009), 'Washington diary: a year of crisis'.

Beder, T.S. (1995), 'VAR: Seductive but Dangerous', *Financial Analysts Journal* **51**(5), 12–24.

Billings, M. and Capie, F. (2009), 'Transparency and financial reporting in mid-20th century British banking', *Accounting Forum*, **33**(1), 38–53.

Bloomberg.com, 26 September 2008, 'Fortis names Dierckx Chief Executive Officer after shares fall'.

Bloomberg.com, April 2009, 'Wells Fargo's profit looks too good to be true'.

Breton, G. and Taffler, R.J. (1995), 'Creative accounting and investment analyst response', *Accounting and Business Research*, **25**(98), 81–92.

Cohan, W.D. (2009), *House of Cards*, Allen Lane.

Coval, J., Jurek, J., and Stafford, E. 'The economics of structured finance', *Journal of Economic Perspectives*, **23**(1), 3–25.

Danthine, J. P., and Moresi, S. (1998), 'Front-Running by Mutual Fund Managers: a Mixed Bag', *European Finance Review*, **2**(1), 29–56.

Duffie, D. and Pan, J. (1997), 'An overview of value at risk', *Journal of Derivatives*, **4**(3), 7–49.

Duffie, D. and Garleanu, N. (2001), 'Risk and valuation of collateralized debt obligations', *Financial Analysts Journal*, **57**(1), 41–59.

Fung, W. and Hsieh, D.A. (1997), 'Empirical characteristics of dynamic trading strategies: the case of hedge funds', *Review of Financial Studies*, **10**(2), 275–302.

Gode, D.K. and Sunder, S. (1993), 'Allocative efficiency of markets with zero-intelligence traders: market as a partial substance for individual rationality', *Journal of Political Economy*, **101**, 119–137.

Henderson, J. (2000), 'Off-balance sheet financing and trusts: a competitive advantage', *Business Journal*, **64**(4), 12–16.

Houweling, P. and Vorst, T. (2005), 'Pricing default swaps: empirical evidence', *Journal of International Money and Finance*, **24**(8), 1200–1225.

Hull, J., Predescu, M., and White, A. (2004), 'The relationship between credit default swap spreads, bond yields, and credit rating announcements', *Journal of Banking and Finance*, **28**(11), 2789–2811.

Hutchinson, M. 'Rising Tide of Level 3 Assets a "Disaster Waiting to Happen"', http://www.moneymorning.com/rising-tide-of-level-3-assets-a-disaster-waiting-to-happen/.

Jensen, M.C. and Meckling, W.H. (1976), 'Theory of the firm: managerial behaviour, agency costs and ownership structure', *Journal of Financial Economics*, **3**, 306–360.

Jones, M.J. and Oldroyd, D. (2009), 'Financial accounting: past, present and future', *Accounting Forum*, **33**(1), 1–10.

Kedia, S. and Philippon, T. (2009) 'The economics of fraudulent accounting', *Review of Financial Studies*, **22**(6), 2169–2199.

Kothari, S. P. (2001), 'Capital markets research in accounting', *Journal of Accounting and Economics*, **31**(1–3), 105–231.

Krishnamurthy, A. (2003), 'Collateral constraints and the amplification mechanism', *Journal of Economic Theory*, **111**(2), 277–292.

Liang, B. (2000), 'Hedge Funds: the Living and the Dead', *Journal of Financial and Quantitative Analysis*, **35**(3), 309–326.

Longstaff, F.A., Mithal, S. and Neis, E. (2005), 'Corporate yield spreads: default risk or liquidity? New evidence from the credit default swap market', *Journal of Finance*, **60**(5), 2213–2253.

McAnally, M.L. (1996), 'Banks, risk, and FAS 105 disclosures', *Accounting, Auditing and Finance*, **11**(3), 453–491.

McNichols, M. and Wilson, G.P. (1988), 'Evidence of creative accounting from the provision for bad debts', *Journal of Accounting Research* **26**, Supplement, 1–33.

Merchant, K.A. and Rockness, J. (1994), 'The ethics of managing earnings: an empirical investigation', *Journal of Accounting and Public Policy*, **13**, 79–94.

Miller, M.H. (1991), 'Leverage', *Journal of Finance*, **46**(2), 479–488.

Morgan, D.P. (2002), 'Rating banks: risk and uncertainty in an opaque industry', *American Economic Review*, **92**(4), 874–888.

Nelson, K.K. (1996), 'Fair value accounting for commercial banks: An empirical analysis of SFAS No. 107', *Accounting Review*, **71**(2), 161–182.

Niu, F. (2007), 'Accounting for transferring financial assets', *Review of Accounting and Finance*, **6**(2), 195–213.

Pourciau, S. 'Earnings management and non-routine executive changes', *Journal of Accounting and Economics*, **16**(1–3), 317–336.

Schipper, K. (1989), 'Commentary on creative accounting', *Accounting Horizons*, December, 91–102.

Sharpe, W.F. (1992), 'Asset allocation: management style and performance measurement', *Journal of Portfolio Management*, **18**, 7–19.

Sikka, P. and Willmott, H. (1997), 'Practising critical accounting', *Critical Perspectives on Accounting*, **8**(1–2), 149–165.

Valukas, A.R. (2010), 'Lehman Brothers Holdings Inc. Chapter 11 Proceedings Examiner's Report'.

Venkatachalam, M. (1996), 'Value-relevance of banks' derivatives disclosures', *Journal of Accounting and Economics*, **22**(1–3), 327–355.

Whittington, G. (2008), 'Fair value and the IASB/FASB conceptual framework project: an alternative view', *Abacus*, **44**(2), 139–168.

# Part C

# 21

# Identifying Some Themes

Michael Jones

## 21.1 INTRODUCTION

In the first part of this book I looked at the background to creative accounting and fraud. This involved looking at the motives for companies indulging in creative accounting and fraud, and into the methods which they used. This was followed by an examination of the academic literature and a look at 20 celebrated accounting scandals and scams that had occurred throughout history up to about 1980. These scandals proved very varied, both geographically and historically.

Then in the second part of the book, we looked at scandals that had occurred across 12 different countries worldwide since 1980. These chapters were all written by nationals and experts of the countries involved. The chapters were diverse, ranging from developed countries such as the UK and USA to developing countries such as China and India.

In addition, a separate chapter looked at accounting scandals and the role of accounting in the global credit crunch. Despite their differences, in every country there was no shortage of accounting scandals from which to choose. The scandals covered are the most important ones to occur in each country, but they are by no means exhaustive.

In this chapter I seek to provide an overview of the different themes which I have synthesized and interpreted from the 13 chapters in Part B. Readers are referred to the individual chapters for the sources and details of the cases discussed. I start by outlining the major scandals that have been covered. I then look at the most commonly used methods, whether the scandals were mainly about creative accounting or fraud, the major methods used, the motives of management, the role of overstrong personalities in the scandals, the failures of internal controls and of internal auditing. I have relied upon individual authors for the factual accuracy of information in each chapter to provide this synthesis. Given the individual nature of each country chapter, it has not always been possible to ascertain a full set of information for each scandal. The frequencies, therefore, reported in this chapter should thus be seen as more for illustration and guidance rather than as being prescriptive. Then, in Chapter 22, I look at the consequences of the scandals.

## 21.2 SOME THEMES

### 21.2.1 Background

In Table 21.1 below I outline major examples of creative accounting and major accounting scandals (Table 21.2). This is based on the scale, impact and prominence of the

*Creative Accounting, Fraud and International Accounting Scandals*   Edited by Michael Jones
© 2011 Michael Jones. Published by John Wiley & Sons, Ltd

**Table 21.1**    Major instances of accounting issues covered in the book

| Country | Company (bold indicates most significant coverage) | Main accounting issues |
| --- | --- | --- |
| Australia | Adelaide Steamship | Consolidation and asset revaluations |
|  | Bond Corporation | Overstating acquisition assets, gains and losses on sale of business, convertible bonds |
|  | Harris Scarfe | Inventories overstated, understated liabilities |
|  | **HIH Insurance** | Provisions, financial reinsurance and goodwill overstated |
|  | One.Tel | Overstating debtors and other assets |
| China | Daqing Lianyi | Forgery, misappropriated assets, bribery |
|  | Great Wall Fund Raising | Financial statement misrepresentation |
|  | Hongguang | Inflated profits, misrepresentation in prospectus |
|  | Kangsai Group | Related-party sales, bribery, misrepresented statements |
|  | Lantian Gufen | Fabricated listing applications, forged bank statements and inflated profits |
|  | Shenzen Yuanye | Inflated profits, forged assets and management embezzlement |
|  | **Zhengzhou Baiwen** | Fraudulent sales, capitalised and deferred expenses, inflated assets, related party transactions, bad debts |
| Germany | Arques | Missing disclosures on acquisitions and mergers |
|  | Balsam | Falsified documents, false factoring of debtors |
|  | Bremer Vulkan Verbund | Provision accounting |
|  | Co op | Unconsolidated equity, related party transactions, pension funds |
|  | **ComRoad** | Inflated and non-existent sales, fictitious supplier/customers |
|  | **Flowtex** | Fictitious manufacture and leasing of drilling equipment |
|  | Philipp Holzmann | Optimistic management forecasts, overvaluation contracts |
| Greece | **Bank of Crete** | Large-scale embezzlement |
|  | Dynamic Life | Understated expenses and overstated income, hiding loss |
|  | ETBA Finance | Fictitious expenses and embezzlement |
| India | Apollo Tyres | Transfers from reserves |
|  | Asian Electronics | Impairments through reserves and not P&L |
|  | Bombay Dyeing and Manufacturing | Provision accounting |
|  | Hindustan Zinc | Reclassifying investments as intangible assets |
|  | Larsen & Toubro | Income recognition through transfer of loan liabilities |
|  | Oil and Natural Gas Commission | Capitalised interest |
|  | **Satyam** | Cooking the books, creative accounting, fictitious assets and insider trading |

**Table 21.1** (*Continued*)

| Country | Company (bold indicates most significant coverage) | Main accounting issues |
|---|---|---|
| | Tata Motors | Direct write-off to reserves |
| | WIPRO | Transfer of fixed assets to stock |
| Italy | **Parmalat** | Redeemable preference shares, false sales, related party, duplicate invoices, debt as equity, overstated assets |
| | Pirelli | Choice of consolidation technique |
| | Top football clubs, e.g. Internazionale Milan F.C. and A.C. Milan | Sale of registration rights |
| Japan | Fuji Sash | Inflates sales via affiliated companies, overstates obsolete inventories |
| | **Kanebo** | Boosts earnings through sale and buyback of goods, deferring expenditure and temporary sale of shares |
| | **Livedoor** | Fictitious revenues, off-balance sheet financing |
| | Morimoto-gumi | Understating cost of goods sold by deferring expenses to the next period |
| | **Nikko Cordial** | Booking false valuation gain on a share-exchangeable bond of special purpose company |
| | Riccar | Fictitious sales |
| | Sanyo Special Steel | Inflates sales via subsidiaries |
| | Sawako | Inflates sales under the percentage-of-completion method on construction contract |
| | Yamaichi Securities | 'Tobashi' securities deals to keep valuation losses off-balance sheet |
| | Yaohan Japan | Books gains on property sales to a dummy company, then repurchases after financial year |
| Netherlands | Fokker | Capitalization of development costs. |
| | Rijn-Schelde-Verolme (RSV) | Impression management in annual report, deferred tax accounting, restructuring costs, government grants |
| | **Royal Ahold** | Consolidation abuses (US GAAP), vendor allowance balances |
| Spain | **Afinsa Bienes Tangibles (Afinsa) and Fórum Filatélico (Fórum)** | Financial as trading activities, overvalued assets, pyramid selling, unrecognized liabilities |
| | Banesto | Expenses as assets, questionable transactions for personal benefit |
| | Banfisa | Asset valuations |
| | Caja rural de Jaen | Fictitious profits |

(*Continued*)

**Table 21.1**   (*Continued*)

| Country | Company (bold indicates most significant coverage) | Main accounting issues |
|---|---|---|
| | Gescartera | Unauthorised financial services, money siphoned off |
| | Promotora Social De Viviendas (PSV) and Iniciativas de Gestión de Servicios (IGS) | Non-compliance matching, double recording |
| Sweden | **ABB** | Sales boosted through extraordinary items, hidden liabilities, trading own shares |
| | Fermenta | Misreported acquisitions, invented sales terminology, related-party disclosures |
| | Prosolvia | Consolidation, fictitious and premature income recognition |
| | **Skandia** | Embedded value, executive remuneration |
| UK | Bank of Credit and Commerce International (BCCI) | Fraud, money laundering and bribery |
| | Mirror Group | Misuse pensions |
| | **Polly Peck** | Inflated fixed assets, debtors, cash; foreign currency, asset revaluations |
| USA | Adelphia Communications Corp. | Off-balance sheet debt |
| | America Online | Capitalised costs |
| | Bausch & Lomb | Premature revenue recognition |
| | **Bear Stearns** | Overleveraged, underestimation of risk |
| | Bre-X Minerals | Stock overstatement, fictitious stock |
| | California Micro Devices Corp. | Fictitious sales |
| | Cendant Corp. | Cost capitalisation at subsidiary |
| | **Enron Corp.** | Off-balance sheet entities, fictitious income, misreported cash flow |
| | **Fannie Mae** | Improper treatment of derivative instruments |
| | HealthSouth Corp. | Capitalized costs |
| | IBM | Offsets non-operating gain against operating expenses |
| | Informix | Premature revenue recognition |
| | **Lehman Bros** | Overleveraged, underestimation of risk and collateralised assets |
| | Lucent Technologies | Premature revenue recognition |
| | **Madoff Securities International Ltd.** | Ponzi scheme, extensive fraudulent behavior |
| | Miniscribe Ltd | Understated warranty accruals |
| | Presidential Life Corp. | Overstated investments |
| | Sunbeam Corp. | Premature revenue recognition |

**Table 21.1**    (*Continued*)

| Country | Company (bold indicates most significant coverage) | Main accounting issues |
|---|---|---|
| | Tyco International Ltd | Capitalised costs, misreported cash flow |
| | United Health Group | Backdated share options |
| | US Foodservice, Inc. (subsidiary of Royal Ahold, Netherlands) | Improper income recognition |
| | **WorldCom, Inc.** | Capitalisation of expenses, aggressive acquisitions, overvalued goodwill |
| | W.R. Grace & Co. | Restructuring reserves |
| | Xerox | Premature revenue recognition |

accounting irregularities. In Chapters 8–19, the major accounting scandals were detailed across 12 countries. Then in Chapter 20 recent cases involving banking failures during the credit crunch were investigated. These are outlined in Table 21.1, with the major scandals in each country outlined in bold. In Appendix 2, summary abstracts of these cases, prepared by individual authors, are presented.

These accounting scandals and issues of creative accounting and fraud (see Table 21.1) were to be found across the developed countries (e.g. BCCI, Mirror Group and Polly Peck in the UK) and in the developing countries (e.g. Shenzhen Yuanye and Zhengzhou Baiwen in China and Satyam in India). They were thus to be found in Asia (China, India and Japan), Australasia (Australia), Europe (Germany, Greece, Italy, Netherlands, Spain, Sweden and the UK) and in North America (USA). It should, however, be stressed that this is the number of scandals and the issues of creative accounting covered by individual authors and not necessarily the exhaustive and complete set of major scandals within particular countries. Generally, there is a concentration upon individual decided cases rather than those that are sub judice. In Appendix 1, using the data supplied by the individual authors, a more comprehensive table is compiled of major instances of problematic accounting issues that have occurred across time. Appendix 2 then provides a summary of the most important scandals in the book compiled from data provided by the individual authors.

### 21.2.2  Creative Accounting or Fraud

As can be seen from Table 21.1, there are many examples of both creative accounting and fraud. It is generally the high-profile and well-known cases where fraud has been alleged, such as Enron, Madoff Securities International Ltd, Parmalat and Polly Peck. In many of the Chinese scandals there is also apparent fraud. Thus, Shenzhen Yuanye, Great Wall Fund Raising, Hongguang, Daqing Lianyi, Kangsai, Lantian Gufen and Zhengzhou Baiwen provide examples of apparently falsified statements. In some Chinese cases, there are also examples of inflated profits, management embezzlement, and bribery and corruption. In Germany, there is ComRoad which is the rather extreme case of a fictitious supplier/customer and Flowtex which supplied fictitious drilling equipment. In other cases, the scandals involved creative accounting rather than fraud. These instances used the maximum flexibility permitted by prevailing regulations. For example, in Australia, Adelaide Steamship used loopholes on consolidation and asset revaluations, in the prevailing Australian regulations, creatively to boost net assets. Finally, in Sweden, ABB used extraordinary income to boost operating income (Carlsson and Nachemson-Ekwall, 2003).

There are also frequent examples in Table 21.1 of companies using creative accounting practices that probably fall short of an accounting scandal. Taking, for example, one country, India, there were a variety of companies which creatively used accounting policies, for example, to capitalise income or to indulge in window-dressing.

In Italy and the USA, there appear to have been some creative accounting practices that became endemic. In both Italy and the USA, creativity in stock options was a common occurrence. In addition, in Italy at football clubs there was the swapping of players' registration rights and the sale of brands. In the USA, there appear to be innumerable examples of premature or fictitious revenue recognition, capitalised costs, overstated assets and understated liabilities, and the abuse of restructuring charges and other creative accounting practices.

In some other cases, there appears to have been both creative accounting and potential fraud and the boundary between them is not always clear. In HIH, in Australia, the insurance company appears to have used provisions for expected future claims quite creatively. However, there were also side letters for financial reinsurance which negated the transfer of risk and which the investigating judge called audacious. In China, there appears to have been an admixture of creative accounting and fraud in Zhengzhou Baiwen. In this case, there appears to have been fraudulent sales and the misuse of raised capital. It would also seem that a series of creative accounting practices have been used, such as capitalised expenses, deferred recognition of expenses and misreporting of debtors.

In many of these cases, creative accounting and fraud co-exist and there is little evidence as to whether management first indulged in creative accounting and gradually then crossed the border into fraud. In Italy, however, in the case of Parmalat it seems that at first the company used redeemable preference shares creatively. Then, later, it seems to have indulged in fraud. In this case the creative accounting clearly came first.

## 21.3 THE MAJOR METHODS USED

Across all the cases there were a huge variety of different methods of creative accounting and fraud. These embraced all parts of the balance sheet and income statement. All of the methods that we looked at in Chapter 4 occurred. I discuss them below under the four broad headings that were used in Chapter 4: increasing income, decreasing expenses, increasing assets and decreasing liabilities. I separate out the main methods of fraudulent reporting and deal with them at the end. However, the boundary between creative accounting and fraud is very fluid.

I highlight, in particular, those methods that are used by at least two companies as a significant method. These were the methods that were identified by the individual authors as being important for the individual cases. Given the variety in approaches taken by the authors and the focus on major methods, the frequency of methods should not be taken as

**Table 21.2**   Some major methods of increasing income

| Method | Frequency |
| --- | --- |
| Boost sales/earnings through related parties | 12 |
| Premature sales recognition | 11 |
| Include non-operating profits | 6 |
| Treat loans as sales | 2 |
| Transfers to reserves | 2 |
| Long-term contracts | 2 |
| Swaps | 1 |
| Pyramid sales | 1 |
| Gains and losses on sales | 1 |
| Sales terminology | 1 |
| Other | 7 |

comprehensive or exhaustive, rather as illustrative. Many other companies may well have also indulged in these methods, but they are not listed as they are not the major methods of companies.

### 21.3.1  Strategy 1: Increasing Income

There was a great variety of types of creative accounting which primarily involves increasing income. Some of these are listed in Table 21.2.

The three most commonly occurring techniques are increasing sales and/or income through related-party transactions, premature sales recognition and including non-operating profits. By far the most common technique was the use of associates, nominee or other related companies to boost sales and earnings. Four good examples of how this can be achieved are provided from Japan, the Netherlands and the USA. The Japanese case is worth citing even though it predates 1980, which is the main focus of the book. Sanyo Special Steel, which was one of the largest ever Japanese bankruptcies, used subsidiaries to boost sales and inflate earnings by 13 billion yen. Sanyo Special Steel was the biggest ever bankruptcy in Japan at that time, with 50 billion yen debt. The Dutch example is also interesting due to the managerial motivations which underpinned it. Royal Ahold was, in 1989, a large retail company mainly active in the Netherlands. It, however, wanted to grow bigger and be in the same category as Walmart and Carrefour. One way that it sought to do this was to increase its sales by consolidating four companies that were joint ventures. So that it could include these companies' sales in its results, it used side letters. It disclosed letters to the auditors indicating that Royal Ahold had the decisive say. However, the side letters not shown to the auditors from the joint venture partners said that they did not agree with this. Royal Ahold, therefore, should not have consolidated these joint ventures according to US GAAP. In this use of side letters the Royal Ahold case parallels that of Australian insurance company HIH, which used side letters to attempt to mislead auditors over reinsurance contracts. Finally, at Enron, special purpose entities were used to boost

Enron's income, by the simple device of selling them assets ranging from optic cables to poorly performing power plants at a profit.

Two examples of premature revenue recognition come from Australia and Sweden, although, as detailed by Mulford and Comiskey, it is a very common technique in the USA. In Australia, One.Tel, a company dealing in mobile telephone services, adopted an extremely aggressive marketing policy. The result was that it booked sales to many customers without adequate credit checks. It consequently built up substantial uncollected and uncollectible debtors. Meanwhile in Sweden, Prosolvia, a Swedish virtual reality and simulation software company, adopted similar aggressive selling techniques, billing customers as soon as they expressed an interest in the product. In addition, sales delivered in 1998 were treated as income for 1997.

The methods of including non-operating profits were varied. Three examples of potential creative accounting are given here: from India, Sweden and the USA. In the Indian example, Apollo Tyres transferred funds into the profit and loss account from the general reserve to counterbalance additional excise duty it had to pay the Indian government. The result was that the profit was 320.85 million rupees higher than it would otherwise have been. In the Swedish example ABB, a global electrical engineering company, was able continually to inflate its sales by extraordinary income from the sale of fixed assets. In the USA, the well-known company IBM boosted its operating income by netting off $2.7 billion in gains from the sale of its Global Network business. This gave the impression that its operating income was more than it actually was.

There are a variety of other techniques which were used. Here I single out just two interesting, and illustrative, cases from Sweden and Spain. In the Swedish case, Fermenta was a penicillin manufacturer. In an extremely creative use of accounting language, it invented a special term 'revenues from sales of technology'. This term proved not only to be unique to Fermenta, but also much of the alleged revenue was, in fact, made up. The Spanish case is interesting as it was, in effect, an old technique used in a modern setting. Afinsa and Fórum were companies that sold stamps with associated investment plans to Spanish investors. In essence, it was not just philatelists, but also ordinary savers who thought that buying and holding stamps was a good investment strategy. These companies' growth, however, was predicated on the fact that the new funds from new investors were being used to pay interest to the old investors. This technique was also used by Madoff Securities International where funds invested by new investors were used to pay returns to existing investors.

### 21.3.2 Strategy 2: Decreasing Expenses

There were a variety of methods used by companies to decrease expenses. These are shown in Table 21.3.

All of the methods outlined in Chapter 4 are to be found. The two most common methods are old favourites that have been around for a long time: capitalising expenses and using provision accounting. In the USA, capitalising costs was a common method of creative accounting, for example, with advertising and software development costs. Perhaps the most famous US and, indeed, global case is that of WorldCom. In the WorldCom case nearly $4 billion was added to the balance sheet as property, plant and equipment. However,

**Table 21.3**  Some major methods of decreasing expenses

| Method | Frequency |
|---|---|
| Capitalise expenses | 12 |
| Provision accounting | 10 |
| Defer expenses | 6 |
| Expenses to reserves | 4 |
| Increase depreciation/amortization periods | 3 |
| Stock options | 2 |
| Generous with bad debts | 2 |
| Reduce taxation charge | 1 |
| Big Bath | 1 |
| Increase closing inventory | 1 |
| Use goodwill account | 1 |

capitalising interest is not only a technique of the developed world. In China, Zhengzhou Baiwen, a company dealing with household appliances and department stores, capitalised RMB 16.17 million in 1995. In 1997, such capitalization represented 125 % of its net profit. Meanwhile, in India, the Oil and Natural Gas Commission capitalized interest on loans.

The use of provision accounting was also found not only in the developed countries, but also in the developing world. Two examples are illustrative, from Australia and from India. The Australian example is provided by HIH, which was an insurance company and became the largest ever collapse of an Australian company in 2001. HIH adopted an aggressive approach to the provisioning of future insurance claims. In other words, instead of adopting a prudential approach and setting aside a greater than average amount to meet expected claim liabilities, HIH used a central estimate so that it had an equal chance of being right or wrong. Not only is this basic approach incautious, but this was compounded by the fact that HIH seemed to arrive at a targeted profit and then adjust its provisions to meet the profit. Therefore, profit drove the provisions rather than the more logical scenario where provisions drive profit.

The Indian case of creative provisioning is a much more classical example. It concerned Bombay Dyeing and Manufacturing Company. In 2003–4, this company made a provision for an expected loss that would be incurred when raw material it had in stock was converted into product. At that time the net realisable value of the stock was less than the cost. A speculative, rather creative, notional loss was therefore established. However, this provision was reversed in 2004–5 and the reversal formed nearly 25 % of profit. The company had thus quite legally, but creatively, moved profits from one year to another.

Two other common techniques of decreasing expenses and, therefore, increasing income were to defer expenses (six cases) and to take expenses to reserves rather than to the income statement (four cases). Deferring expenditure is in effect treating the expenses as prepaid assets. In many ways, it is analogous to capitalisation, but usually involves a shorter time horizon. To take an Australian example: One.Tel evidently capitalised certain advertising and staff costs as expenses. Meanwhile, in Japan, Kanebo also deferred its advertising and sales promotion expenses to the next year. The four cases of writing off expenditures to reserves all came from India (Tata Motors, Bombay Dyeing, Mahindra and Himachal Futuristic). In all four cases, large amounts of miscellaneous expenditure and other forms of direct expenditure were written off to the securities premium account quite legally with the approval of the High Court. This avoided write-offs (and thus reduced profit) in the profit and loss account.

Five companies were identified as either being overgenerous in their treatment of bad debts or having extended amortisation periods. In the UK, for example, Mirror Group, among other creative accounting practices, arguably had inadequate provisions for bad debts, while in Italy, football clubs were allowed to lengthen the period over which their transfer costs could be amortised. In the USA, Waste Management, Inc. used unrealistically long amortisation periods.

There are a variety of other examples of companies reducing expenses. Two instances will be discussed here from Italy. The Italian experience as illustrated concerns a running sore for standard-setters: stock options. Stock options relate to potential future costs if employees exercise these options for buying shares. They are a sort of deferred remuneration. Companies globally strive not to recognise these options as costs in the income statement. This was the case in Italy, before 2005, until the adoption of International Financial Reporting Standards made it mandatory for Italian companies to account for them. Before this, the general practice was quite legally to exclude them. In the case of companies, such as Fullsix and Safilo, the cost of these options represented 124 % and 27 % of their reported income, respectively.

HIH provides a good example of goodwill enhancement. Goodwill is supposed to be the residual of the purchase price of a subsidiary less the fair value of its identifiable net assets. However, the goodwill account was treated with much more flexibility by HIH. The goodwill account became a dustbin account for all sorts of unwanted losses which should have gone through the income statement. Goodwill was charged rather than the income statement.

### 21.3.3 Strategy 3: Increasing Assets

As can be seen from Table 21.4, many examples of methods of increasing assets were found. These methods should be taken in conjunction with those used in Table 21.3 as often the impact of increasing assets is, at the same time, to reduce expenses.

**Table 21.4**   Major methods of increasing assets

| Method | Frequency |
| --- | --- |
| Inventory | 8 |
| Revalue fixed assets | 4 |
| Inflate debtors | 4 |
| Acquisition-related | 3 |
| Current assets | 2 |
| Enhance brands | 1 |
| Prepaid assets | 1 |
| Investments | 1 |
| Other | 1 |
| Intangibles | 1 |

One of the most popular methods of increasing assets while also increasing profit by reducing expenses is by increasing inventory. At least eight instances of this occurred. Three examples will suffice. In the USA, Bre-X Minerals claimed it had large stocks of gold; however, these proved illusory. Meanwhile, in Japan, Fuji Sash had overstated obsolete inventories and thus understated cost of sales and overstated profits. Finally, an Australian case concerns Harris Scarfe, a discount department store. In this company, inventories were evidently stated at artificially high levels. As a result, its net income for the year was accordingly inflated.

There were three instances where companies used acquisition-related techniques as a major method of enhancing assets or distorting their results. These individual cases are very varied and two examples are given here from Sweden and the USA. In Sweden, Fermenta used acquisitions to mislead the shareholders. In a series of acquisitions, the same technique was used. This was exemplified by the purchase of Pierrel. The reported price of the acquisition was understated and then the monies received for selling off acquired businesses were overstated. It looked as if the company had benefited more than the reality. Its net assets were hence apparently increased. In the case of WorldCom, it was found that the company had made numerous acquisitions and incurred large amounts of goodwill. It should have expensed these when evidence indicated that the goodwill was value-impaired. This would have reduced earnings. However, WorldCom failed to do so.

Assets can be revalued to increase their worth. This is what happened in the case of Adelaide Steamship, in Australia; there was a selective, over-optimistic revaluation of assets. For Skandia in Sweden, the problem was not inappropriate revaluation, but rather the systematic adoption of an over-optimistic method of valuing the insurance portfolio. The result was an inflated asset portfolio as well as enhanced earnings. Finally, for Zhengzhou Baiwen the problem was not the manipulation of asset values but rather the booking of losses as assets.

A relatively easy method of inflating assets is to have unreasonably high levels of debtors. The most common technique here is not to record, or to inadequately record, bad or doubtful debts. This is in effect what happened at One.Tel in Australia, Zhengzhou Baiwen in China and Parmalat in Italy. In the case of Parmalat, for example, bad debts were removed from the books by transferring them to nominee accounts. They therefore failed to appear on the consolidated balance sheet.

Another method of increasing assets is demonstrated by Italian football clubs. It shows how creative accounting practices can be adopted by whole industries. In Italy it was common practice for football clubs to sell each other registration rights of players at inflated prices. This happened, for example, between local rivals Internazionale Milan F.C. and A.C. Milan. These players' registration rights were then capitalised and inflated the balance sheet.

### 21.3.4 Strategy 4: Decreasing Liabilities

The need to reduce one's apparent liabilities is often pressing, especially for companies in trouble. This accounts for the popularity of accounting manipulations in this area (Table 21.5). Indeed, there are more examples of off-balance sheet financing than any of the other techniques used. In almost every large accounting scandal the use of subsidiary,

**Table 21.5**   Major methods of decreasing liabilities

| Method | Frequency |
| --- | --- |
| Off-balance sheet financing | 10 |
| Understating liabilities | 10 |
| Reclassifying debt as equity | 2 |
| Other | 4 |

related-party, associate company, nominee or special purpose entity is present to some degree.

The two most common methods of decreasing liabilities were the use of one form or other of off-balance sheet financing and generally understating liabilities. Off-balance sheet financing was a very common method of manipulating accounts. It was particularly prevalent in developed countries such as Australia, Japan and the USA. The most famous example is probably US energy giant Enron. It used special purpose entities to hide huge amounts of debts. Meanwhile, in Australia, Adelaide Steamship used prevailing accounting rules to avoid consolidating the results of entities it effectively controlled. Then, in Japan, Livedoor also used off-balance sheet vehicles to hide debts. Pirelli is an interesting example of a company choosing not to consolidate a subsidiary with an unusual motive. The management of Pirelli did not wish to breach Italian law, which stated that Italian banks could not loan more than 25 % of their capital. By quite legally not consolidating Pirelli, this threshold was not breached. In Japan, Sanyo Electric failed to account correctly for the impairment of a subsidiary's loss in its parent companies' accounts.

The methods of understating liabilities were diverse. Four examples will suffice to give a flavour of some different methods. One example of a calculated attempt to understate liabilities is provided in Australia. Insurance company, HIH, set up reinsurance contracts which transferred the risk for liabilities. At least this is how it appeared. However, HIH committed itself to using side letters, the backdating of documents and other techniques to negate the original contract. In reality, it thus retained the risk. Meanwhile, in Spain, Afinsa and Fórum Filatéco, the stamp companies, failed to recognise in their balance sheets the stamps that they had promised to repurchase at the start of the contract with customers. They did not, therefore, recognize the liability associated with the repurchase agreement. Finally, from Australia, the Bond Corporation effectively offset a non-current asset (future income tax benefit) against a current liability (provision for income tax).

### 21.3.5  Other Methods of Creative Accounting

In order to try to conceal debt, companies may also try to disguise debt as equity. Both Bond Corporation, an Australian company, and Parmalat, from Italy, did this. Bond Corporation treated convertible loans as equity rather than as liabilities. Meanwhile, Parmalat used quite sophisticated schemes, such as special purpose financing vehicles, to try to disguise debt as equity.

In at least three cases, there was evidence of attempts to improve the companies' cash flow position. This was the case in the USA, for Tyco and Enron. In Tyco's case, Tyco used improper acquisition accounting to boost earnings and cash flow. At Enron, the company indulged in circular transactions with banks and SPEs apparently with the purpose of enabling borrowed funds to be reported as cash flows. Interestingly, Enron used borrowed funds to boost its sales and cash flows. Enron's SPEs used these funds to buy oil from Enron in advance. By using timing differences between years it looked like Enron was making sales; however, in effect there were no sales and no movement of oil. Only cash moved and it appeared wrongly that Enron had a positive cash flow. Finally, in Sweden ABB sold off property which improved its cash flows after it had bought back its own shares.

There were two examples of accounting techniques which do not fit easily within the above classification scheme. In Spain, at Gescartera, a brokerage house, the company indulged in intraday selling and purchasing activities to give the impression of activity where there was really none. Finally, also in Spain the two stamp companies Afinsa and Fórum Filatélico strove to have their activities classified as financial rather than trading activities so that they could continue their rather dubious financial activities.

### 21.3.5.1  Impression Management

The main focus of this book has been on accounting scandals, creative accounting and fraud. In these high-profile cases, most attention is usually quite naturally focused on earnings management and less on impression management. However, two examples which are arguably impression management stand out: RSV from the Netherlands and Philipp Holzmann from Germany.

In the RSV case, the company was going through difficult times in the late 1970s and early 1980s. However, in its annual report the company was optimistic about the financial future. This contrasted with its actual accounting policy on government grants which were credited to income. This accounting policy was only permissible if the company was in a permanent loss-making situation. There was thus a mismatch between the message in the company's narratives in its annual report and its actual policies. Both were, in effect, self-serving but self-contradictory: a positive message to shareholders accompanied by the creative crediting of a government grant to boost income.

With Philipp Holzmann, the company was in financial difficulties in 1998–9. However, Dr Heinrich Binder, the chairman in the 1998 management report, provided a positive financial forecast for 1999 and of profitable growth for the future. This appears, in hindsight, to have been over-optimistic, as four-and-a-half months after the AGM in which the chairman had made such a positive speech, the company informed the shareholders of a spectacular loss of about 2.4 billion marks which almost completely wiped out the equity of the company.

## 21.4 METHODS OF FRAUD

The boundary between creative accounting and fraud is not always clear. Fraud is normally decided by the courts or the regulatory authorities. This section is thus best taken in conjunction with the previous ones. In this section, I focus on those cases which appear

**Table 21.6**  Methods of fraud

| | |
|---|---|
| *Misappropriation of assets* | 22 |
| (i) Embezzlement | 17 |
| (ii) Other | 5 |
| *Fictitious transactions* | 30 |
| (i) Sales | 19 |
| (ii) Financial documentation | 7 |
| (iii) Subsidiaries | 3 |
| (iv) Loans | 1 |

*prima facie* to involve either fraud or alleged fraud. In Table 21.6, I use the same broad classification that I did in Chapter 4. In particular, I distinguish between the misappropriation of assets and fictitious transactions. Evidence of all types of fraud was found, with the exception of theft of inventory. Given the focus of this book on management-led fraud and financial statement fraud, this is not too surprising. The theft of inventory is normally associated with individual employees rather than with management.

As can be seen from Table 21.6, there were at least 22 cases of identifiable misappropriation of assets and 30 identifiable cases of fictitious transactions. Management embezzlement was common, especially in China (e.g. Shenzhen Yuanye, Great Wall Fund Raising). However, the most spectacular documented embezzlements were arguably carried out in Greece and the UK. In the Bank of Crete scandal, George Koskotas managed to get himself an important managerial role as Deputy Head of the Accounting Section of the Bank of Crete. From this position he was able to misappropriate huge sums of money. He, for example, transferred US $1 507 515 from the Bank of Crete foreign currency accounts of customers to Westminster Bank Ltd in London in August 1980 to accounts he, in effect, controlled. In total one observer maintains that he stole the equivalent of 31 million US dollars. In the Madoff case, Bernard Madoff perpetrated a $65 billion swindle, probably the biggest financial fraud in history. He used new investors' money to pay the returns for existing investors in a typical Ponzi scheme. Meanwhile, in the UK, Asil Nadir, head of Polly Peck, a company which specialized in fresh food, was alleged by the Serious Fraud Office to have abstracted large amounts of cash from the company and used them for his own purposes. However, this case has still, after 20 years, not come to trial. Asil Nadir remained until very recently, in the occupied part of Cyprus from where he consistently protested his innocence, but could not be extradited.[1]

Three other kinds of misappropriation of assets concerned the misuse by the company of share capital, the misuse of pension funds and the misuse of deposit interest earned. Zhengzhou Baiwen, in China, was accused of misusing share capital. Baiwen fraudulently inflated its assets by RMB 149 million (about £11 million) through the misapplication of a rights issue (Ding, Zhang and Zhu, 2005). It used funds raised from shareholders to repay bank loans. This had not been specified in the prospectus.

---

[1] The north of Cyprus was invaded by Turkey in 1974. It is not recognised by the UN as an independent nation. As this book goes to press, however, Asil Nadir, after years of protesting his innocence has now voluntarily returned to face trial as the Serious Fraud Office has now agreed not to oppose bail (Adams, 2010).

Co op in Germany and Mirror Group in the UK both stand guilty of misusing the company pension funds in order to benefit the company itself. In the Co op case, the financial press suspected that the pension fund wrongly acquired Co op shares (Peemöller and Hofmann, 2005), In Mirror Group, there appears to have been an even more systematic abuse of the independent status of pension funds. The company raided the pension funds. The DTI report (DTI, 2001) concluded that from 1985 onwards the Mirror Group Newspapers pension funds had been used to lend more than £100 million to companies that were owned privately by Robert Maxwell. They were also used to trade with Maxwell companies and to buy shares in Maxwell companies. Many of these transactions were without either the approval or knowledge of the majority of the pension fund trustees. Finally, in Greece, ETBA Finance used invested sums of money to speculate on the stock market instead of being deposited to earn interest. The scam was for those involved to share in the profits from the stock market speculation after returning the interest.

There were, at least, 30 examples of major fictitious transactions, although in reality there were probably many more. The most common method was the creation of fictitious sales (19 instances). This was followed by the more general production of false financial documentation (seven cases). Generally, this involved more extensive forgeries than just sales. Even more extensive was the forgery of almost complete subsidiaries (three instances). Finally, there was one case of fictitious loans. Often these cases involve multiple and extensive fraud across more than one category. However, for convenience we focus here on the major methods of fabrication.

In most cases, the aim of fabricating sales was to increase profit. In China, falsifying sales was particularly popular (e.g. Kangsai Group, Hongguang and Shenzen Yuanye). For example, Hongguang inflated its profits by RMB 150 million by, *inter alia*, forging sales. In Sweden, both Prosolvia and Fermenta inflated sales. For instance, for Prosolvia, a Swedish virtual reality and simulation software company, at least one of the invoiced companies was an entirely fictitious company in Russia. It is worthwhile looking in detail at four examples: one from the USA, two from Greece and one from Germany, which may be seen as fairly typical, if extreme, examples of sales fabrication. First, California Micro Devices Corp. booked bogus sales to fake companies for non-existent products. The fraud was so extensive that staff joked with each other about the fictitious sales. In Greece, Dynamic Life sales were falsified by a non-existent transaction of €3 million with a wholly owned subsidiary abroad. The Greek company ETBA Finance had fees for 'fictitious services', in one case 3.9 million drachmas for liquidation expenses for which apparently no voucher or proof existed. Finally, in Germany, Balsam had a whole edifice of fictitious receivables sold to a factor. In the end, there was a staggering 1.8 billion German marks of fictitious receivables.

In seven cases, there was extensive forgery of non-sales documentation (although often this included sales). In at least four cases, these were Chinese companies (Great Wall Fund Raising, Daqing Lianyi, Hongguang and Lantian Gufen); in two cases, Spanish companies and one Italian company, Parmalat. If we take the case of the Great Wall Fund Raising, there is clear evidence of extensive forgeries. For example, there was a fixed asset of RMB 187 million that was based on a fake invoice. In the two Spanish cases, for Gescartera, an investment house, there was evidence of the falsification of documents, for example, from other banks. In the case of Afinsa and Fórum Filatélico, there was concern that some of the underlying assets of the companies, stamps, were faked. Many other stamps were considered by independent experts to be overvalued.

In the case of Parmalat, there were also extensive forgeries. For example, assets were either improperly measured or simply created. The most impressive example of this was the use of a forged depository account. In the consolidated financial statements, there was a cash equivalent asset of €3.95 billion deposited in a Bank of America account in the name of Bonlat. A forged letter had been produced to the auditors from the Bank of America stating that the amount was actually in existence. As well as this spectacular fraud, Parmalat had substantial sales of assets such as powdered milk that never existed. In addition, Parmalat double-billed (i.e. sent duplicate invoices to distributors) and also reported inflated and fictitious income from trademarks. There was an impressive array of other fictitious and fabricated transactions.

There were also three cases of companies creating almost totally fictitious subsidiaries (or customer/supplier) or using the subsidiaries as a framework to create virtual accounts. The three most notable examples of this stem from Germany and the UK. In the German cases, two companies were particularly active in the creation of almost totally fictitious trade. The first of these companies was Flowtex. Flowtex was a German company that distributed an innovative drilling system. Basically, banks bought non-existent drilling systems from a subsidiary company. These systems were supposedly then leased to customers who paid leasing payments back to the bank. However, in effect, later payments from the banks were used to pay the leasing charges. There were thus circular transactions. In the end, there were supposed to be 3400 drilling systems worldwide. However, in fact there were only 250. Creditors lost about DM 2 billion in this fraud. In another German case there was an even more extensive network of fabricated accounts. ComRoad supplied so-called satellite navigation systems for cars. A journalistic investigation revealed that the CEO and his wife prepared falsified accounts relating to the manufacture of equipment from a non-existing supplier, VT Electronics in Hong Kong. The fictitious units made by VT Electronics were then delivered to fictitious customers. The scale of these fictitious transactions was immense. In 1998, for example, sales were DM 20 million, of which DM 17 million came from VT Electronics. Unfortunately, in a special audit done by auditors Rodl & Partner, no evidence of actual business transactions or customers was found. Basically, Mr and Mrs Schnabel had constructed a whole network of fraudulent transactions.

In the UK, investigators found that the results of Meyna and Vestel, two subsidiaries of Polly Peck, were vastly inflated. If we take the results of Meyna, the 'true' results based on local accounts were much lower than the reported results. For instance, fixed assets and cash were reported under local accounts in December 1988 to be £14.4m and £1.2m, respectively. However, the reported figures were vastly inflated at £72.9m and £16.2m, respectively. These balance sheet figures were mirrored and accentuated by the figures for Meyna from the income statement. For sales at December 1988, the local figures were £16.1m, while the reported figures were 13 times higher at £214.9m. For the figure of profit before tax the discrepancy was even greater. There was only a bare profit using local figures at £0.2m, while the reported profit came in at £56.3m. The reality appears to have been that Polly Peck largely invented assets and that these were then set off against the substantial debts owed by the subsidiaries to the parent company. In addition, the income statement appears to have been almost entirely made up of fictional figures.

The final case of fraud also involved a British company, BCCI. This company got into difficulties at the start of the 1990s, which was at a similar time to Polly Peck. However, in this case the company appears to have had many loans on its balance sheet that were essentially irrecoverable or, indeed, wholly fictitious. This deception was covered up by collusion between the bank and the third parties to whom the loans had been made.

## 21.5 INCENTIVES FOR CREATIVE ACCOUNTING AND FRAUD

In Chapter 3, I looked at a range of possible incentives for creative accounting and fraud. These ranged from general incentives to market incentives to special circumstances. Many of these incentives had been established as the result of academic research. The cases from the individual chapters were examined to see if it was possible to ascertain the motives across the countries. This was usually possible in a general way. However, it was not usually possible to be very specific. For instance, it was often possible to identify that the management were seeking personal advantage, but not necessarily so straightforward to link managerial actions to, for instance, bonus-related pay. Often one can only try to draw tentative conclusions from individuals' apparent actions.

In Table 21.7, I have divided the incentives into four broad areas: (i) cover up bad performance (30 cases), including two of meeting managerial or analysts' expectations; (ii) personal benefit (35 cases), including 12 cases where it was possible to identify improving share price as the main general incentive; (iii) five cases of meeting listing requirements and (iv) finally, six other cases. I discuss some of the more interesting cases below. Many of the incentives are not easy to pigeonhole, for example increasing share price.[2]

**Table 21.7**   Incentives for creative accounting and fraud

| General incentives | Frequency |
| --- | --- |
| *a, cover up bad performance* | 30 |
| (i) Meet expectations | 2 |
| *b, personal benefit* | 35 |
| (i) Improve share price | 12 |
| *c, meet listing requirements* | 5 |
| *d, other* | 6 |

There were numerous examples of companies apparently attempting to use creative accounting and fraud to cover up poor financial performance across practically all countries. Under this broad heading, I include a more specific motive which is to meet analysts' expectations. If we look at three examples from Italy, the Netherlands and Sweden. In Italy, Parmalat, although appearing profitable was, in fact, technically insolvent since 1990. A key rationale for the Parmalat fraud was, therefore, using many dubious accounting irregularities to keep the company afloat. Parmalat Finanziara reported profits in every period from 1990

---

[2] Although I include improving share price, for convenience, under personal benefit, companies may also be trying to improve share price to meet analysts' expectations, and this could also be classified under covering up bad performance.

to 2003, when usually it should have reported losses. Cumulatively reported earnings were €1513 million while there was an actual cumulative loss reported of €3694 million.

In the Netherlands, management at US Foodservice, a subsidiary of Royal Ahold, apparently sought to cover up bad financial performance by misclassifying vendor allowances that were given to them, often as up-front cash, by suppliers. The result of this misstatement was that in the group accounts net income was overstated by €103 million in 2000 and €215 million in 2001. In Sweden, Skandia, an important insurance company, ran into financial difficulties in the late 1990s. By using a special type of accounting, embedded value accounting, Skandia managed to show profits. However, its underlying financial position was far from healthy. For example, in 1999, while Skandia showed a record revenue of €976 million it also had a negative cash flow of about €454 million from its unit-linked business. In effect, embedded value accounting appears *prima facie* to have been used to cover up Skandia's poor financial position.

There were two specific cases identified of covering up worse than expected performance so as to meet performance expectations. These were Harris Scarfe in Australia and Com-Road in Germany. Harris Scarfe was an Australian discount store chain. Inventories appear to have been overstated while liabilities appear to have been understated. The reason seems to have been for senior management to meet the profit expectations of directors. In Com-Road, however, the situation was far more extreme. A husband and wife partnership was forced to indulge in fraudulent accounting apparently to meet aggressive earnings forecasts.

There were 35 examples of personal incentives driving individuals to indulge in creative accounting and fraud. Many of the cases for personal benefit involve the extraction of cash by individuals from the company. However, individuals also gain more indirectly by, for example, an increase in share price. Three examples of personal benefit are discussed next (Flowtex, Bank of Crete and Polly Peck). Then two more specific cases which involve share price manipulation are examined. In the German case, Manfred Schmider was a charismatic, dominating and well-connected individual. He set up a complicated scheme using fictitious drilling machines. As a result of his fraud he is believed to have tunnelled approximately €350 million of creditors' money to secret accounts in tax havens. In Greece, George Koskotas also misappropriated huge amounts of money. In this case it was customers' money and it has been estimated that he managed to steal the equivalent of $31 million by transferring the money from accounts in the name of the Bank of Crete to his own account. In the UK, Asil Nadir, head of Polly Peck, was also allegedly active in misappropriating the money of Polly Peck International. He has, however, consistently protested his innocence. Just as this book is going to press, in August 2010 he has voluntarily agreed to return from exile to face trial. In essence, Asil Nadir is accused of treating some of the assets of Polly Peck as his own personal assets. Payments were allegedly made on a regular basis from the parent company to a Turkish subsidiary and then on to Asil Nadir's personal account. In 1989, 64 payments totalling £141 million were identified by the UK's Serious Fraud Office, while in 1988 transfers of £57 million had been made. In total, the Serious Fraud Office identified transfers totalling £383 million from August 1987 to October 1990. Finally, in the US, Madoff who perpetrated a large financial fraud appears to have been driven by personal benefit.

In total, 11 specific cases were identified which appeared to involve creative accounting or fraud so as to support the price of a company's shares. Two of these are examined in more detail here: Sawako from Japan and WorldCom from the USA. Sawako was a medium-sized general contractor. It appears to have boosted sales by using an incorrect percentage-of-completion method on long-term construction contracts. In addition, it issued convertible bonds. It did this in an apparent attempt to stimulate convertible bondholders to exercise their rights. In the USA, one motive for the WorldCom fraud can be seen as an effort to maintain the company's share price. This was done by boosting income by capitalising inappropriate expenses. Bernard Ebbers, the CEO, was a significant shareholder in WorldCom. In addition, the company was very acquisitive and a high share price helped finance the company's acquisitions.

There were five cases where the creative accounting or fraud seemed to be linked to meeting a company's listing requirements. Interestingly, all of these involved companies in China (Shenzhen Yuanye, Daqing Lianyi, Kangsai, Lantian Gufen and Zhengzhou Baiwen). I will take a closer look at Zhengzhou Baiwen. In China, Zhengzhou Baiwen was a company dealing with household appliances and department stores. It was listed on the Shanghai Stock Exchange in 1996. However, to obtain that listing it had falsified its financial statements. It had fabricated sales and excluded 22 subsidiaries because of their bad performance.

I found six other identifiable motives for the adoption by companies of creative accounting or fraud. In Italy there are two cases. First, Pirelli adopted creative accounting quite legally so that it did not have to consolidate two of its subsidiaries, Olimpia and TI. As a result of non-consolidation, it was able to keep inside Italian banking regulations. These allowed a bank only to lend a maximum of 25 % to one group of companies. Second, Italian football clubs' licences to participate in the national football league depend upon their not breaching certain financial covenants. These are often endangered by the high costs of players' salaries. Consequently, Italian clubs have indulged in a variety of creative accounting practices to stop breaching the covenants. These include selling registration rights to each other at inflated prices, creatively writing down the intangible asset (i.e. players' contracts) and the inter-company sale of brands.

Next, in two cases the motives for the creative accounting appear to have been to meet unrealistic managerial targets for growth. Thus, ABB in Sweden seems to have wished to become a more powerful player in the electrical engineering business while Royal Ahold in the Netherlands wanted to become one of the largest retailers in the world. Finally, in Japan, there were two cases. First, Sanyo Electric manipulated its accounts with the apparent intention of continuing to pay a dividend. Then, lastly, the case of Morimoto-gumi provides an interesting example of the variety of reasons for adopting creative accounting. Morimoto-gumi was a long-established midsize construction company. In Japan, companies are ranked by size and the public construction contracts they are awarded are determined by that ranking. Morimoto-gumi manipulated its earnings in order to be able to bid for public construction contracts from 1999 to 2003.

## 21.6 OVERSTRONG PERSONALITIES

In many cases of accounting scandals individuals play a key role. These individuals are generally charismatic, and persuade and convince the investing community that everything is fine and generally by the strength of their personality carry all before them. In total, across the 12 countries, 24 overstrong individuals were identified from 10 countries. In this section, we will briefly look at the role that such individuals played in accounting scandals. Australia: Alan Bond, John Spalvins, Ray Williams and Jodee Rich; China: Zhaoyu Qu and Taifu Shen; Sweden: Lars-Eric Petersson, Refaat El-Sayed and Percy Barnevik; Germany: Manfred Schmider; Greece: Natasha Bougatioti and George Koskotas; Japan: Hagino, Hiraki, Horie, Ohira and Morimoto; Spain: Mario Conde and Antonio Camacho; UK: Agha Hasan Abedi, Asil Nadir and Robert Maxwell; USA: Jeff Skilling and Bernard Ebbers.

I will explore the role of individuals by specifically looking at China, Japan, the UK, the USA, Spain and Sweden. In China, Zhaoyu Qu at Lantian was a powerful individual who had a wide network of personal relationships. He was particularly active in bribing officials, such as Heling Sun and Yanhua Wan at the Ministry of Agriculture and Faxiong Wang at the Organisational Department of the Central Committee, the Communist Party of China (CPC). In Japan, five individuals (Hiraki of Riccar; Horie of Livedoor; Hagino of Sanyo Special Steel; Ohira of Sawako; and Morimoto of Morimoto-gumi) had very strong personalities. Focusing on two, Hiraki and Horie: Hiraki was so strong that it was reported chiefs of the finance division did not dare to stand up to him, while Horie enjoyed widespread popularity amongst young people and tried to acquire a baseball team and a major television network. In the UK, three individuals had extremely strong personalities that carried all before them. In the case of the Mirror Group, there was a previous history of dubious practice such that it was widely known that Robert Maxwell was a potential business risk. However, he was still allowed to build up a powerful business empire. In Asil Nadir's case, Polly Peck was controlled almost as a personal fiefdom. He was the mastermind behind the company's aggressive accounting. Agha Hasan Abedi, the founder and driving force of BCCI, was a man of extraordinary personal charisma. In the USA, at Enron, Jeff Skilling had a larger than life personality. Meanwhile, at WorldCom, Bernard Ebbers, the CEO, was instrumental in setting unrealistic growth targets and in encouraging dubious accounting policies. In Spain, at Banesto Mario Conde won many plaudits. He was an emblematic figure who symbolized the Spanish economic boom of the 1980s. Finally, in Sweden there are two examples of men who were festooned with awards. Refaat El-Sayed, head of Fermenta, became Manager of the Year in 1984 and 'Swede of the Year' in 1985. It was, however, discovered later that the doctorate he claimed was false. Meanwhile, Percy Barnevik, President of ABB, when it won many business honours, was repeatedly considered one of the world's 10 most respected business leaders.

## 21.7 FAILURE OF INTERNAL CONTROLS

It is interesting to reflect on why the scandals occurred and, in particular, whether a failure of internal controls played any part. These internal controls can vary from country to country. They may include, *inter alia*, an effective board of directors, the presence of independent non-executive directors, supervisory boards, state shareholders or internal audit controls. In some cases, we have clear evidence of such failures. In China, at Zhengzhou Baiwen, for example, there was a failure of the supervisory board, a failure of independent directors and of the state-controlled shareholder. In Germany, at both Bremer Vulkan Verbund and

ComRoad, the supervisory board failed to exercise due diligence. At Parmalat, in Italy, there seems to have been a multiple failure of internal controls. There were no independent directors, the role of the audit committee appeared compromised, the roles of CEO and Chair were held by the same man and there was a failure by some institutional investors to appreciate what was happening. In Spain, at Afinsa and at Fórum Filatélico, there was a lack of a paper trail for suppliers and inventory. In the UK too, there was an evident failure in internal controls. For example, at Polly Peck, there was a surprising lack of control over cash. In this case, as with El Sayed at Fermenta, Nadir was both CEO and chairman. In Greece, there was evidence of a lack of basic internal controls at both ETBA Finance, where there was a dearth of written, individual employees' roles and duties, and at the Bank of Crete, where there were inadequate internal controls and, in particular, a lack of segregation of duties. Finally, in the USA, there was a failure at both Enron and WorldCom of top-level reporting controls and at WorldCom this was compounded by a lack of control over the classification of expenses.

## 21.8 FAILURE OF EXTERNAL AUDITORS

In many cases, across the accounting scandals, there was evidence of a failure of external auditing. The severity of this failing varied. It ranged from the auditor being deceived by management, to failure to exercise due oversight, to conniving with management, to active involvement. Generally, however, in most of the major accounting scandals, the failure of external audit is notable. In many cases, even the most straightforward checks appeared not to have been done. In Germany from 2005–7, in only three out of 24 cases of misstatements detected by the German Financial Reporting Enforcement Panel had those misstatements resulted in qualified auditors' reports.

As a result of failures in external auditing, there have been many incidences where the external auditors were fined or cautioned. In possibly the most extreme cases, Enron and Kanebo, the apparent lack of due professional diligence of the auditors Arthur Andersen and ChuoAoyama PricewaterhouseCoopers led to the collapse of the audit firm as a viable business. Similarly, in China, the Shenzhen Special Economic Zone Accounting Firm and the Zhongcheng audit firm were shut down after the Shenzhen Yuanye and Great Wall Fund Raising cases.

In the Chinese cases, there is a clear failure of the external auditors in most cases. Generally, in all seven cases in China (Shenzen Yuanye, Great Wall Fund Raising, Hongguang, Daqing Lianyi, Kangsai, Lantian Gufen and Zhengzhou Baiwen) the auditors failed to display the due professional diligence that might have been expected. Indeed, in extreme cases the auditors appeared to be complicit in the accounting scandal. In Great Wall Fund Raising, for example, there were multiple auditing failures. Three CPAs provided unfounded certificates confirming RMB 300 million capital and no audited number in the client's financial statement was verified through any due auditing process. As a result the Chinese government took a number of actions against individual auditing firms such as fining them or disqualifying individual CPAs. In Germany, with ComRoad there seems to have been a failure of the external auditor to spot the fact that there was a fictitious customer. In fact, the failure was such that it was apparently an independent journalist not the auditors that detected the massive fraud. The journalist had revealed her findings in 2001 and the existing auditors, KPMG stepped down in 2002. In Italy, too, the auditors failed to impress. At Parmalat, as we saw in Chapter 13, 'there was little evidence of complex accounting techniques or sophisticated earnings management'. However, despite systematic creative accounting and fraud the auditors were not as vigilant as might have been hoped. In particular, Italian prosecutors reported that the auditors apparently allowed the company to post off a letter requesting confirmation of a balance of €3.95 billion in cash and investments in the Bank of America. The result was that a letter was returned agreeing a fictitious balance. The auditors then relied upon this fraudulent letter, and the fact that there was no such money held by the company went undetected. By contrast, in the Netherlands at Royal Ahold, there were no apparent failures of audit procedures. In fact, on the contrary, it was the external auditor, Deloitte, that discovered the vendor allowances fraud by a standard auditing procedure – the confirmation of vendor allowances.

However, it seems that the Spanish auditors were less vigilant than their Dutch counterparts. In the Spanish cases, there is generally evidence of a failure of external audit. In Banesto, two months before its collapse Price Waterhouse had raised no doubts when Banesto had completed two parts of the largest ever share issue in Spanish banking history. They subsequently were fined Pts 127 million. At Gescartera, Deloitte & Touche had given the company a clean audit report for the 2000 annual reports and then six months before the company ran into trouble it again received a favourable report. The auditors later claimed that the sophistication of the irregularities meant that they were impossible to detect. The Spanish authorities apparently disagreed, fining them €1 318 319. In the case of Promotora Social de Viviendas and Afinsa, the auditors were also found liable and fined. In the Promotora Social de Viviendas case the auditors were fined €426 720 and faced a civil suit by cooperative members who alleged the firm had failed to detect accounting irregularities. In the Afinsa case, Gestynsa Auditores Externos was fined. Although the audit firm did spot certain irregularities, it failed to question the accounting treatment of sales and repurchase agreements. In the final Spanish case, Fórum, Carrera Auditores SA did qualify the accounts on the grounds of the debts of several companies in the group. However, the auditors failed to question the nature of the sales and repurchase agreements. Carrera Auditores was fined €150 000 for its audit of Forum's financial statements of 2002. The fine for the partner in charge of the audit work amounted to €3050. This case is, however, ongoing.

In the UK, the auditors of BCCI, Mirror Group and Polly Peck were all criticised. Although criticism within the UK was relatively muted, the US Senate report was highly critical of BCCI. Meanwhile, the auditors of the Mirror Group and Polly Peck were heavily criticised by the relevant professional disciplinary tribunals. Finally, in the USA, there were severe auditing failures. In the Enron case, there was a clear failure of the auditors, Arthur Andersen, to perform the independent review role which is traditionally expected of auditors. It has been argued that they were compromised by the large amount of consultancy work that they were doing for the company. They agreed to, and arguably were even complicit in, dubious accounting practices (but not the fraud itself). Similarly at WorldCom, there was another failure in auditing. The auditors failed to notice that the capitalized assets were vastly overstated and also failed to question the company's treatment of its consolidation procedures.

## 21.9 CONCLUSION

This chapter provides an overview of the major accounting scandals covered in this book. There were 58 scandals across 12 countries. In addition, there were frequent instances of creative accounting. These companies used a great variety of different methods to indulge in creative accounting and fraud. In some cases, such as Parmalat, Enron or Madoff, fraud appears paramount. Creative accounting was shown to be endemic in certain countries, such as Italy and the USA. In addition, in many individual cases, such as Adelaide Steamship, and ABB, creative accounting appears to have been used.

There is great variety in the methods used. Some, such as in WorldCom, were very simple – for example, the capitalisation of expenses. In other cases, the techniques were more complicated, such as Skandia's use of embedded accounting. Some of the most popular methods were boosting sales/earnings through related parties, premature sales recognition, capitalisation of expenses, provision accounting, increasing inventory, off-balance sheet financing and understating liabilities. There were also numerous examples of the misappropriation of assets, – especially embezzlement – and fictitious transactions – especially sales.

There were a variety of motives that appeared to drive managerial actions. The main broad motives were to cover up bad performance and for personal benefit. More specifically, cases of meeting managerial or analysts' expectations, improving share price and meeting listing requirements were identified.

Also the role of overstrong individuals seems to play a part in a significant minority of cases. To single out just a few, in the UK, Robert Maxwell at Mirror Group and Asil Nadir at Polly Peck appear to have exercised undue control over their companies. The same appears to have been true, perhaps to a lesser extent, of Jeff Skilling at Enron, Bernard Ebbers at WorldCom and Mario Conde at Banesto.

A major contributory factor in the accounting scandals was the failure of internal controls. In most countries, in most of the accounting scandals there was a failure in one or more of the following internal controls: an effective board of directors, the presence of non-executive directors, audit committees, state shareholders or internal audit controls.

In addition to a failure of the internal controls, the external auditor was usually notable by its absence. In most cases, there was a signal failure to provide qualified accounts or, indeed, any warning at all of a company's troubles. In some cases, especially in China, the auditors were actually found to be apparently complicit in the accounting irregularities. In many cases, the auditors were fined and in the extreme cases of Arthur Andersen, ChuoAoyama PricewaterhouseCoopers, Shenzhen Special Economic Zone Accounting Firm, Zhongcheng, the collapse of the companies being audited (i.e. Enron, Kanebo, Shenzhen Yuanye and Great Wall Fund Raising) also led to the collapse of the auditing firms themselves.

Overall, therefore, this chapter has shown that in 12 important countries worldwide there have been a series of successive accounting scandals. Managements have been motivated to indulge in creative accounting/fraud for a variety of reasons. Often key, very charismatic individuals in the company have been implicated in the accounting scandals. These scandals have usually not been detected, until too late, either by internal controls – which have often failed lamentably – or by external auditors.

# REFERENCES

Note: Most of the material upon which this chapter is based is drawn from individual country chapters. I am, therefore, dependent on the individual authors for the factual accuracy of the material cited. It is at the end of these chapters that relevant references will be found.

Adams, S. (2010), 'Fugitive Polly Peck tycoon granted bail for fraud trial', *Daily Telegraph*, 31 July, p. 16.

Ding, Y., Zhang, H. and Zhu, H. (2005), 'Accounting failures in Chinese listed firms: origins and typology', *International Journal of Disclosure and Governance*, **4**(2), 395–412.

DTI (2001), *Mirror Group Newspapers plc – investigations under Sections 432(2) and 442 of the Companies Act 1985*; report by the Honourable Sir Roger John Laugharne Thomas and Raymond Thomas Turner FCA, HMSO, London.

Nachemson-Ekwall, S. and Carlsson, B. (2004) *Golden rain – Skandia's saga* (Guldregn – sagan om Skandia), Bonnier Fakta.

Peemöller, V.H. and Hofmann, St. (2005), *Accounting Scandals* (Bilanzskandale), Erich Schmidt Verlag, Berlin.

# 22

# The Impact of Accounting Scandals and Creative Accounting

Michael Jones

## 22.1 INTRODUCTION

This chapter looks at the aftermath of accounting scandals. I relied upon the factual accuracy of the material from individual chapters for the international background, while Chapter 7 provides a more longitudinal perspective.[1] This is important as the effects of accounting scandals are often cumulative, stretching over long time periods.

One of the major impacts of accounting scandals is that consequences often stretch far beyond the immediate confines of the firm. The impact of accounting scandals and, more pervasively, creative accounting can thus be divided into the short-term, immediate effects on those involved and longer, more diffuse effects. The immediate consequences are that the company itself often either collapses, is taken over or at the very minimum its share price slumps and investors lose money. When a scandal occurs there are usually casualties: both innocent and guilty. There is usually an immediate outcry and calls for something to be done. Often the guilty are punished, more rarely the innocent are compensated in some way for their financial loss. Those culpable in the accounting scams are often punished. This can mean individuals like Jeffrey Skilling, Bernard Ebbers and Bernard Madoff in the USA, who are often fined or sent to prison. However, it can also mean sanctions against the auditors. Mostly they are, as with the Spanish cases, fined. However, in more extreme cases such as Arthur Andersen post-Enron in the USA or in Japan with ChuoAoyama PricewaterhouseCoopers post-Kanebo, the audit firm itself may collapse. There are then the longer-term effects. These may be increased regulation and more subtly, a creative accounting arms race may develop.

## 22.2 SHORT-TERM IMMEDIATE EFFECTS

Creative accounting usually goes unnoticed until it either develops into a fraud or there is a corporate collapse or some other form of accounting scandal. When this happens, there are usually casualties. These can be divided into 'insiders' and 'outsiders'. Insiders can broadly be classified as the internal management of the companies involved. Often there is an inner circle of perpetrators of the fraud, such as directors, who are guilty. Many other

---

[1] Interested readers are thus referred to the individual chapters for full details of the cases mentioned here.

*Creative Accounting, Fraud and International Accounting Scandals*   Edited by Michael Jones
© 2011 Michael Jones. Published by John Wiley & Sons, Ltd

insiders, however, such as lower management and other employees may be blameless. By contrast, the outsiders are much more diffuse. They may comprise auditors, shareholders or creditors. In the sections that follow, I have analysed the cases from the individual chapters and attempted to provide a synthesis from the factual information provided by the individual authors. The tables should be treated as illustrative, as the information from the chapters is neither exhaustive nor complete for all cases.

### 22.2.1 Insiders

It is very easy to identify the effects on directors who are accused or found guilty of accounting malpractice. In the case of suspected fraud, the directors are usually tried. I have analysed the cases in the individual chapters from the information available and they are synthesized in Table 22.1. As Table 22.1 shows, the most common penalty facing directors across all countries is imprisonment. However, there were a variety of other options, such as being fined, having personal wealth seized and even execution.

**Table 22.1**   Penalties facing directors

| Penalty | Frequency |
| --- | --- |
| Jail | 32 |
| Fined | 14 |
| Step down | 4 |
| Seize personal wealth | 2 |
| Death | 1 |
| Settlement out of court | 1 |

By far the most frequent penalty was thus a jail sentence. As can be seen in Table 22.2, in those cases where a jail sentence was applied it was generally reasonably short.

The majority of jail sentences were thus up to 10 years. In fact, 17 jail sentences were less than six years. There were only four jail sentences of 20 years or more. Interestingly, two of these four were from the USA. At Enron, Jeffrey Skilling, the former CEO, was sentenced to a 25-year term and Bernard Ebbers, the CEO of WorldCom, was also sentenced to 25 years. In Greece, Koskotas was sentenced to 25 years, but only served 12 years. In Spain, Mario Conde was sentenced to 20 years after the Banesto bank scandal. Indeed,

**Table 22.2**   Length of jail sentence

| Length | Frequency |
| --- | --- |
| 1 to 2 years | 9 |
| 3 to 5 years | 8 |
| 6 to 10 years | 7 |
| 6 to 12 years | 1 |
| 16 years | 3 |
| 20, 24 or 25 years | 4 |

the sentence tariffs themselves have often been shortened or, as was common in Japan, suspended. The directors were imprisoned: first as a punishment and then to discourage others. Overall, given the misery and financial loss that a lot of these directors caused, *prima facie*, the prison sentences meted out were often quite light.

The next most common penalty that some directors and/or managers faced was being fined. This occurred for instance in respect to HIH in Australia, involving pecuniary penalties imposed on certain directors who also served jail terms and in Sweden concerning Prosolvia. At Royal Ahold there was an out-of-court settlement in which two of the directors settled the case without admitting wrongdoing in the US.

Three unusual cases were in Germany, China and Japan. In Germany, the court of Bavaria using a special state law seized the personal wealth of Bodo Schnabel, the CEO of ComRoad. In China, as a consequence of the Great Wall Fund Raising scandal, the President of the Great Wall Fund Raising company was sentenced to death. Finally, in Japan, Nikko Cordial, as a company, claimed 3.4 billion yen damages against three former top officials. They eventually settled for 300 million yen.

Where a company goes into liquidation, the consequences for the employees are often severe. They lose their jobs and often, being stigmatised by association, will find it difficult to find new ones. However, generally these consequences cannot be quantified.

### 22.2.2 Outsiders

By outsiders, I mean those not privy to the accounting scandal, and not directly implicated in the scandal. This may mean, for example, auditors, employees and investors. Auditors may have a close involvement in the scandal; however, they will generally not be directly implicated. They are, however, often blamed when things go wrong. For employees, if the company runs into difficulties or even goes into receivership or bankruptcy, they may lose their jobs. Investors will also lose their money if there is a corporate collapse or if there is a sharp fall in the share price.

We look first at the impact on auditors. Auditors are supposed to be independent of the companies they audit, and to exercise professional care and scepticism. It is, therefore, inevitable that after major cases of financial irregularities or financial collapse, auditors are often censured. Indeed, auditors are often the only ones associated with corporate collapse that have any money left. They are frequently seen as repositories of potential compensation by investors, creditors and the government. However, in many cases, unfortunately, auditors appear to be notable by their absence. In Germany, for example, only three of the 25 cases the German Financial Reporting Enforcement Panel investigated from July 2005 to November 2007 were qualified by the auditor in respect of the misstatement mentioned by the Panel. In Table 22.3 I identify, from the prior individual country cases, where possible, the actions taken against auditors.

As can be seen, the four most extreme cases are where the collapse led to the demise of the audit firm. In Japan, after the Kanebo scandal, ChuoAoyama Pricewaterhouse-Coopers, one of the Big 4 auditing firms, was broken down into two smaller firms: Misuzu and Arata. Then, subsequently Misuzu was forcibly dissolved having been involved in another accounting scandal at Nikko Cordial. In China, two audit firms were disbanded after accounting scandals. First, after the delisting of Shenzhen Yuanye, the Shenzhen

**Table 22.3**   Actions against auditors

| Action | Frequency |
| --- | --- |
| Audit firm disbanded | 4 |
| Fined or settled out of court | 15 |
| Auditors jailed (suspended) | 2(1) |
| Individuals sanctioned | 5 |
| Audit firm warned | 3 |
| Auditors acquitted | 3 |
| Auditors criticized but no action taken | 8 |

Special Economic Zone Accounting Firm was shut down. Then, after the Great Wall Fund Raising scandal, five CPAs were disqualified and Zhongcheng, the auditing firm, was dismantled. Meanwhile, in the USA Andersen's perceived involvement in the demise of Enron, particularly the alleged shredding of documents, led to the spectacular collapse of Arthur Andersen, one of the world's leading accounting partnerships, in the USA and then worldwide. Such accounting firm failures contribute to changing stereotypes of accountants which may constitute 'negative signals of movement' for accounting as a profession.

In many cases (I identified at least 15) the auditing firm was fined or settled out of court. Let us take just three examples. First, in Spain, the auditing firm Deloitte & Touche (D&T) had given a clean audit report on Gescartera, an investment services firm, for the 2000 financial statements, just six months before the Spanish Stock Exchange seized control of the company. The auditors were subsequently fined €1 318 319. In Germany, KPMG were the auditors of Flowtex and gave a set of fictitious accounts an unqualified report. Having failed to spot such a widespread fraud, the auditor paid the banks an out-of-court settlement of DM 100 million although without admitting any wrongdoing. Finally, in China, the auditors of Lantian Gufen, a company involved in pharmacy, agricultural and aquatic products, were sued by investors together with the listed firm, and had to compensate them with RMB 5.4 million.

In other cases, action of various types was taken not necessarily against the firm, but against individual auditors. Some examples are given below. There were very few cases where the auditors themselves were jailed. However, in Greece, the chartered accountant who had audited the Bank of Crete was jailed for 12 years and six months. Also in Greece, the chartered accountant of ETBA Finance was initially sentenced to jail for 11 years, but appealed against the severity of the sentence. Then at the appeal trial charges were dropped because of the statute of limitation. In Japan, three of the auditors who had audited Kanebo were sentenced to jail, but the sentences were suspended. However, an auditor from Koyo Audit Corporation that had audited Livedoor was not so lucky, and received a 10-month sentence without suspension. Also, in Japan, in the Fuji Sash case, the licences of two auditors were revoked, while in the Sawako case, the auditor was punished by the Japanese Institute of Certified Public Accountants with one month's cessation of business. In China, after the Daqing Lianyi case, as well as warning the audit firm, two auditors were disqualified and one was fined. In the UK, the Accountants Joint Disciplinary Scheme (JDS) investigated the role of members of Erdal & Co., who were the local northern Cyprus auditors of Polly Peck's subsidiaries. They excluded the Erdal partners from being members of the ICAEW and fined them each £1000.

Finally, there was a range of other lesser action against auditors. In several cases in China various actions were taken against the auditors of Daqing Lianyi (warned) and Kangsai (penalized). In Germany, the auditors were acquitted or no action was taken against them in the cases of Bremer and ComRoad. In most cases, such as HIH in Australia, if nothing else the auditors were criticized, but were not implicated in any criminal action. In this case, it has been reported that they entered into a confidential settlement with the liquidator.

Employees are usually the victims rather than the villains in these accounting scandals. However, this is not always so. For example, a manager of Promotora Social de Viviendas (PSV), a Spanish real estate and housing cooperative, was sent to prison for fraud and misappropriation of funds. Meanwhile, in the case of the Chinese company, Daqing Lianyi, 39 officials of the Communist government or the company were given administrative disciplinary punishments.

More normally, the employees just lose their jobs. This is often the case in spectacular bankruptcies such as Enron. The loss by employees of their jobs has always been a consequence of corporate collapse. For example, in the nineteenth-century City of Glasgow Bank accounting scandal 750 employees lost their jobs (Lee, 2004).

There are also knock-on effects on other areas of the economy. Investors and creditors are often the main losers. For example, in the German cases of Co op and Balsam, shareholders and creditors lost millions. The same was true at WorldCom and Enron in the USA. Typically, even if the company does not go bankrupt the share price, as in the case of Zhengzhou Baiwen, plummets and investors consequently lose. For example, at Afinsa in Spain, thousands of investors lost money while in the Great Wall Fund Raising scandal it is estimated that 225 000 investors lost money. However, today investors are usually arguably better off than they were at some periods in the past. Thus, to take the City of Glasgow Bank in 1878 as an example, the investors were hit particularly badly. In this case, there was unlimited liability. Therefore, the investors lost not only the money that they had originally invested, but also any other assets needed to pay for the shortfall. As a result, eight out of the 10 investors in the bank were forced into bankruptcy (Lee, 2004). Only 250 out of 1819 shareholders remained solvent (French, 1984).

Sometimes injured investors attempt to recover money by taking out court actions against the company. Thus, in China, Hongguang paid compensation of RMB 225 000 to 11 investors; two officials from Daqing Lianyi were successfully sued by 679 investors for RMB 12 million; and at Lantian Gufen, 83 investors successfully sued the accounting firm and eight officials for RMB 5.4 million.

There are sometimes wider short-term economic and political consequences. For example, an accounting scandal may adversely affect the stock market. An impressive example of this occurred in Japan. The accounting scandal at Livedoor prompted not only the widespread sale of Livedoor's shares, but also the panic spread to the Tokyo Stock Exchange. On 18 January 2006 the whole Tokyo Stock Exchange was shut down when the sell-off of shares threatened to crash the Exchange's computer system. This became known as the 'Livedoor Shock'.

Political consequences also arise from some scandals. In China, for example, many government officials were implicated in the Daqing Lianyi case. In Spain, as a result of the collapse of Gescartera, an investment services firm, a junior minister in the government was forced to resign and the President of the Spanish Stock Exchange stepped down two months later. Probably, the most important recent case with political implications was the Bank of Crete. Koskotas had close connections with the Greek Socialist Party through his media interests. When the fraud was uncovered, several government ministers were forced to resign. The Greek Socialist government fell in 1989 and the Bank of Crete scandal was one of the contributing factors. Papandreou, the leader of the Greek Socialist Party, was himself charged with several offences. However, he was acquitted.

## 22.3 LONG-TERM EFFECTS

The wider consequences are much more general. They may be a loss of economic confidence in a country or the introduction of new regulatory measures to stop the abuses. In this case, there is thus a continuing evolution. The regulations are changed when a new scandal occurs. As a result, there is a new need for regulatory change. I look at some of these wider consequences below.

The more long-lasting effects of the accounting scandals are those relating to the wider society such as social, economic and political consequences and then those more specifically relating to the country's regulatory framework. The effects of the South Sea Bubble on the UK were, for example, profound both economically and politically. In the case of the City of Glasgow Bank, the economic consequences were dramatic. Over a thousand firms ran into difficulties. Interest rates fell and the other Scottish banks became ultra-cautious (French, 1984).

The long-term effects may be a knee-jerk regulatory, one-off response. However, there is also a cumulative effect over time of continual accounting scandals and creative accounting. In this section, I look first at the one-off regulatory responses which over time become impressive. I then look at four examples of specific cases that have caused significant regulatory change.

### 22.3.1 One-off Regulatory Responses

Once an accounting scandal has occurred, the aftermath of the scandal typically follows a similar pattern. There is extensive media interest, and some sort of investigation follows (either by the government, accounting professional bodies or the fraud office). There is then criticism of the accounting regulations and often a trial. Then, often new legislation or accounting regulations are introduced.

As can be seen in Table 22.4, in most countries there has been a legislative or regulatory response to the accounting scandals. Perhaps the most famous was the introduction of the Sarbanes-Oxley Act in the USA. This has subsequently also formed the basis for changes in Japan. Perhaps the most common response has been the introduction of a new code of corporate governance. Indeed, the growth of interest in corporate governance and in corporate governance codes has been quite dramatic. This started in the UK with the Cadbury Committee, which was set up in response to UK financial reporting deficiencies heightened by unexpected failures of UK companies, particularly Polly Peck. However, since 1992 when the Cadbury Committee set out a corporate governance framework for the

**Table 22.4**  Regulatory consequences of accounting scandals

| Country | Consequences |
|---|---|
| Australia | (i) AAS 24 Consolidated Financial Statements (1990)<br>(ii) Corporate Law Economic Reform Programme (2004)<br>(iii) Major review of auditor independence<br>(iv) ASX Principles of Good Corporate Governance and Best Practice Recommendations |
| China | (i) Rules on Information Disclosure to the Public by Chinese Securities Regulatory Commission<br>(ii) Corporate Governance Guidelines<br>(iii) New legal provisions |
| Germany | (i) Auditor Oversight Commission<br>(ii) 1998 Act on Corporate Control and Transparency<br>(iii) Financial Reporting Enforcement Act |
| Greece | (i) Changes in internal controls at banks<br>(ii) Corporate Governance Code introduced<br>(iii) Accounting Standardization Committee<br>(iv) Measures to limit creative accounting |
| India | (i) Changes in Companies Acts<br>(ii) Measures by SEBI to protect investors<br>(iii) Prudential norms established for banks |
| Italy | (i) Savings Law<br>(ii) Changes in auditors' engagement<br>(iii) Changes in 8th Directive |
| Japan | (i) New accounting standards on consolidated financial statements (1975, 1997, 2006, 2007, 2008)<br>(ii) Corporation Law and Financial Instruments and Exchange Law modified (Japanese SOX Law, 2006)<br>(iii) Standards for Management Assessment and Audit concerning Internal Control Over Financial Reporting (Council Opinions) |
| Netherlands | (i) Corporate Governance Code 2004<br>(ii) New oversight role of the Netherlands Authority Financial Markets<br>(iii) Changes to Civil Code and Criminal Law |
| Spain | (i) Financial Law includes amendments<br>(ii) Audit law reformed<br>(iii) New regulation for protection of customers of collectibles |
| Sweden | (i) Code of Corporate Governance<br>(ii) Swedish Economic Crimes Bureau established<br>(iii) Amendments to audit requirements and Companies Act |
| UK | (i) Accounting Standards Steering Committee<br>(ii) Accounting Standards Board and specific standards, e.g. FRS 1, 2, 3, 5, 6<br>(iii) Cadbury Report on Corporate Governance |
| USA | (i) Sarbanes-Oxley<br>(ii) Public Companies Accounting Oversight Board<br>(iii) Power of audit committees increased |

UK, there have been numerous other corporate governance codes set up, for example, in Australia, China, Greece, the Netherlands and Sweden.

In addition, there have been attempts to strengthen the role of external audit. Thus, in Australia, Italy and Spain, attempts have been made to boost the independence of auditors. Indeed, the Italian experience on the importance of auditor regulation has led to revisions to the 8th Directive in 2006 with recommendations that EU members adopt mandatory audit partner rotation as well as strict rules on auditor independence and responsibility.

### 22.3.1.1 Specific Instances of Regulatory Change

We take four examples to serve as illustrations: Kreuger & Toll in the USA in the 1930s; the Associated Electrical Industries takeover by the General Electric Company in the UK in 1967; Polly Peck in 1990; and Enron in 2001 in the USA.

#### Kreuger & Toll

In this case, the accounting scandal was discovered after the death of the company's founder, Ivar Kreuger. The company went bankrupt in 1932 and was the largest bankruptcy in US history at that time. The fraud was detected by the auditors Price Waterhouse, who conducted an enquiry after Kreuger's death. Once the scandal broke, there was intense press interest. Flesher and Flesher (1986) state that over 300 articles about the fraud appeared in 1932 and 1933, as well as five books.

The US Congress became involved and then there were hearings in the US Senate. The Senate concluded that simpler corporate structures and more straightforward accounting and auditing were required. The Senate took testimony from many leading accountants and financiers. As a result of the Kreuger scandal, there was renewed interest in a federal securities law. Perhaps as a result of the scandal, in April 1932, the New York Stock Exchange required new listees to agree to audits in subsequent years. In January 1933, the New York Stock Exchange required audits prior to new listings and, most importantly, in May 1933, the US Securities Act of 1933 was signed into law (Flesher and Flesher, 1986).

#### AEI takeover by GEC

This takeover caused great controversy when it was discovered afterwards that the profit which AEI made for GEC in the year after it was taken over was much less than had been forecast. There was intense press interest. Academics and practitioners became involved in a heated debate about the inadequacy of UK accounting principles. As Rutherford put it (1996, p. 143): 'The cumulative effect of much commentary on the AEI–GEC gap, including that cited here, is to lead the reader, directly or by implication, to the conclusion not only that a substantial proportion of the gap was attributable to what would now be called flexibility in accounting policy choice, but further that it was generally accepted at the time that, as a consequence, the gap demonstrated the need for standards to reduce such flexibility.'

As a result of all the publicity surrounding the AEI takeover, the Institute of Chartered Accountants in England and Wales threw its weight behind mandatory standards in the UK. As a result, in 1970, the Accounting Standards Steering Committee was set up. This led to the formation of the Accounting Standards Committee. This body was charged with developing and publishing mandatory UK standards. For the first time in the UK, there was an officially recognised standard-setting body.

### Polly Peck

Polly Peck was an important accounting scandal in both the UK and globally. It was apparently an extremely successful company run by a well-known businessman, Asil Nadir. Its sudden, unexpected collapse had a profound effect on the financial reporting environment in the UK. It helped, following the replacement of the Accounting Standards Committee (ASC), to shape the thinking of the new Accounting Standards Board. There was a recognition in the UK that standard-setting ought to be tightened. In addition, the collapse of Polly Peck, with its evident failure of corporate governance (for example, there was a clear failure of controls over cash, segregation of duties and a combination of the twin roles of chief executive and chairman in one man), led to an appreciation of the importance of corporate governance. This contributed to the setting up in the UK of the Cadbury Committee. This produced the world's first Code of Corporate Governance. It was soon followed by Corporate Governance Codes elsewhere.

### Enron

Enron, the seventh largest US company at the time, collapsed in 2001. It was the subject of intense media speculation, innumerable articles in the press and in academia. There were also discussions in the US Congress and Senate. As the accounting scandal also involved the demise of auditors Arthur Andersen, there was intense speculation about the role and function of auditing in the USA. The directors of Enron and various other individuals were brought to trial on fraud charges and found guilty.

As a result of all this analysis and discussion, the US federal government introduced new legislation. The Sarbanes-Oxley Act brought in new accounting and auditing regulations. In particular, there were strengthened corporate governance requirements. Ironically, given the fact that auditors appear to have been complicit in the collapse, the new legislation introduced substantive new compliance work. As a result, there was substantially more work for the US auditing profession.

## 22.4 CUMULATIVE EFFECTS

As a result of countless examples of creative accounting and many accounting scandals, there has been a gradual trend towards increasing regulation in accounting. This began with government legislation in most countries and the introduction of accounting standards. The situation in the UK is typical.

There was a gradual introduction of accounting legislation in Companies Acts in the nineteenth century. The general trend was that successive Companies Acts introduced progressively more stern accounting rules and regulations. Then, in 1970, the Accounting Standards Committee was introduced. The GEC–AEI accounting scandal proved instrumental in its introduction. This was followed, in 1990, by the Accounting Standards Board.

Once again UK accounting scandals helped to shape its early thinking. In addition, in the UK, especially following Polly Peck, a new voluntary code of corporate governance was set up. Then, finally, in 2005, International Accounting Standards were introduced for UK (and all European) listed companies. Over time there has thus been a gradual strengthening of the accounting regulatory framework. Much of this is down to the cumulative effect of accounting scandals and creative accounting.

The increasingly detailed rules and regulations do not, however, mean that the motives for individuals to indulge in creative accounting disappear. As a result, financial manipulations still occur but they become more sophisticated. In effect, a creative accounting arms race occurs. In essence, it works something like this. Initially, creative accountants use a simple scheme of creative accounting to boost profits or increase assets. The regulators then introduce legislation which outlaws these simple schemes. The creative accountant, often with the help of a merchant bank, devises a new scheme which effectively bypasses the regulations. The regulators respond by legislating against this even more complicated scheme. Thus, both creative accounting and the regulatory framework develop in tandem. Tweedie and Whittington (1990, p. 87) comment on this: '[S]ome recent innovations [in financial reporting] can be regarded as problematic for two reasons. First, they introduce new types of contract or transaction with which existing standards fail to cope, or second, by "repackaging" transactions they allow them to be treated in a different manner from that prescribed by standards.' The problem is actually compounded by detailed rules and regulations. Granof and Zeff (2002) examine the US situation where, at that time, there were 101 statements running to 2300 pages. 'What results is a detailed rule for almost every conceivable transaction. It takes the FASB [US Standard Setting Body] two or more years to issue such a detailed standard. It then takes a clever investment banker or accountant about two hours to figure out how to circumvent it.'

There are several examples of a creative accounting arms race. Two examples from the UK are given here. First, the case of off-balance sheet financing. In the early 1980s, two accounting standards, SSAP 17 (*Accounting for Post Balance Sheet Events*) and SSAP 21 (*Accounting for Leases and Hire Purchase Contracts*), addressed the topic. As a result, the off-balance sheet schemes became more complicated. In 1986, the ICAEW, therefore, issued Technical Release TR 603 arguing that the economic substance of a transaction rather than its legal form should predominate. Then, in 1994, there was more regulatory activity with the publication of Financial Reporting Standard 5, *Reporting the Substance of Transactions*, which took a similar line to the ICAEW's Technical Release. Overall, this increased regulation reflected the increasing sophistication of the creative accounting schemes which had been devised, often by merchant banks.

The second example is given by Shah in a series of articles (1996, 1997, 1998). He looked at the case of complex convertible securities issued by UK listed companies from 1987 to 1990. These convertible securities combine a convertible bond or loan with an option to convert the bond into equity shares of the underlying company. Shah (1996) noted an active pattern of creative compliance with a shift from avoidance to rules and then back to avoidance. There were four different regulatory pronouncements in four years, either made by the accounting profession or the standard-setters. Shah found that the auditors were reactive and complicit rather than being active and policing. He found a dialectic of creativity from avoidance to rules to avoidance. Overall,

Shah (1996, p. 36) concluded: 'regulators were slow to respond, and when they did make pronouncements, companies once again circumvented the rules with the help of various professionals'.

The evolution of these convertible securities is documented over time (Shah, 1997). They were a quite legal development in that they respected the letter of the law. In effect, they were an innovation in 1987. Prior to 1987, there were only convertible bonds and convertible preference shares. The market was small, with issues not exceeding £30 million. These financial instruments were relatively unsophisticated and only allowed companies to convert bonds into the underlying shares at a pre-specified time and a pre-specified place. However, from January 1987 there was a steady evolution in the sophistication of these financial instruments. First, a premium-put convertible bond was invented. Second, in January 1988, it was followed by an offshore convertible preference share.

Burton's quite legally first issued the premium-put convertible bond. It had a lower interest coupon rate (3–4 % lower), but a higher conversion premium (25–30 % share price) to compensate. In accounting terms, companies' income statements benefited as the interest coupon rate was the rate charged rather than the effective rate of 9.98 %. Burton's issued £110 million of premium-put convertibles and saved £5.75 million per annum on interest. Fourteen companies then used premium-put convertibles and raised $1390 million. All of them charged the coupon interest rate and thus exploited a gap in the accounting rules. Shah (1997, p. 89) quotes an investment banker as stating: 'There is an awful lot of pressure on UK companies to perform, and the performance evaluation is purely based on reported profits. On the balance sheet side, *providing gearing was reasonable*, the analysts were not bothered.'

However, a major disadvantage of the convertible bond, from an accounting perspective, is that until the bonds were converted they were treated as debt. This increased gearing. In April 1988, a financial instrument was developed which circumvented this: the offshore convertible preference share (OCPS). It was first issued quite legally by United Biscuits. It was invented by S.G. Warburg, a UK merchant bank. It retained the advantages of the premium-put convertible bond. These instruments were issued through a special purpose financial subsidiary in a tax haven, the Netherlands Antilles. As they were classed as preference shares, they were counted as equity not debt. As they were offshore, and not taxable, they got around the tax disadvantage of preference dividends vis-à-vis coupon interest. 'This instrument was an ingenious invention in that it combined tax and accounting benefits in one instrument' (Shah, 1997, p. 89).

United Biscuits used the OCPS to make a major acquisition for £335m. As the fair value of the net assets was £145m, goodwill of £190m was recorded. United Biscuits chose to write this goodwill off to reserves. However, to do this it needed adequate reserves. Creative accounting again proved useful. The OCPS had a nominal value of £1, but an issue price of £5000. This created substantial reserves against which the goodwill could be written off, according to Standard Statement of Accounting Practice 22. This instrument was specifically tailored for this issue. The investment banker who developed the instrument, when interviewed, stated: 'We therefore developed the Netherlands Antilles preference share which could be sold in good terms, and have the accounting benefits of creating a reserve for goodwill write off. From a tax perspective, as it was an offshore issue, the loan from the Netherlands Antilles subsidiary would qualify for deduction. Thus accounting and tax benefits were combined in one issue. *It was a wonderful instrument designed to meet a particular need* (emphasis added)' (*Banker*, January 1992).[2]

The goodwill accounting standard itself that permitted the write-off of goodwill to reserves was also felt by many to be a source of creativity. Shah (1997, p. 90) quotes an interview with a senior audit partner in a large UK firm:

> I think the goodwill standard was a precursor to many of the evils of current financial reporting – convertibles, brands, and asset revaluation. I often give lectures showing how different treatments have been used by companies to write off large chunks of goodwill, with or without court approval (to use the share premium account). Personally, the way the court gives permission to use the share premium account for goodwill write off is a joke. Firms have used many creative schemes in order *not* to amortise goodwill against profits but to write it off in one stroke against reserves.

## 22.5 CONCLUSION

Overall, therefore, there are short-term and long-term consequences of creative accounting and accounting scandals. The consequences of these accounting scandals often extended far beyond the actual participants. In the short term in accounting scandals there are generally investigations and trials. As a result, directors may be imprisoned or fined. There may also be sanctions taken against the auditors. However, there are wider economic and societal consequences. In most cases, there was a loss of confidence created by the accounting scandal. In the longer term, in order to address this, governments and/or the accounting profession brought in new laws and regulations. These have taken the form of mandatory regulation, such as Companies Acts in the UK or Federal Laws in the USA. Or there may be Voluntary Codes of Corporate Governance. These regulations are often knee-jerk official reactions to the scandals. Over the longer time period, the legislation becomes cumulative. In this longer time frame, regulations will become more complex as will creative accounting schemes. The overall result will be that firms will have to follow ever-increasing accounting regulations, and there is likely to be a creative accounting arms race. Both legislation and the creative accounting schemes used to combat them become more sophisticated.

## REFERENCES

*Note:* Most of the factual material upon which this chapter is based is drawn from individual country chapters. It is at the end of these chapters that relevant references will be found.

Flesher, D.L. and Flesher, T.K. (1986), 'Ivar Kreuger's contribution to US financial reporting', *The Accounting Review*, **LXI**(3), 421–434.
French, E.A. (1984), *Introduction to City of Glasgow Bank. Report and Trial of the Directors and Managers of the City of Glasgow Bank*, Yale, USA.
Granof, M.H. and Zeff, S.A. (2002), 'Open the Andersen archives to find a way out of today's mess', *Houston Chronicle*, 7 April.
Lee, T.A. (2004), 'The dominant manager in the history of auditing', *Accounting Business and Financial History Conference*, Cardiff, September.

---

[2] As quoted in Shah (1997, p. 90).

Rutherford, B.A. (1996), 'The AEI–GEC gap revisited', *Accounting, Business and Financial History*, **6**(2), 141–161.

Shah, A.K. (1996), 'Creative compliance in financial reporting', *Accounting Organizations and Society*, **21**(1), 23–29.

Shah, A.K. (1997), 'Regulatory arbitrage through financial innovation', *Accounting, Auditing and Accountability Journal*, **10**(1), 85–104.

Shah, A.K. (1998), 'Exploring the influences and constraints on creative accounting in the United Kingdom', *The European Accounting Review*, **7**(1), 83–104.

Tweedie, D. and Whittington, G. (1990), 'Financial reporting: current problems and their implications for systematic reform', *Accounting and Business Research*, **21**(81), 87–102.

# 23

# Conclusion – Looking Backwards and Forwards

Michael Jones

This book has provided an overview of international accounting scandals. It shows that accounting scandals have always been with us, from Mesopotamia in the third millennium BC, to the South Sea Bubble in 1720, to Enron and Parmalat today. Accounting manipulations generally form a crucial part of such scandals. Management may use creative accounting which, in effect, bends the spirit of existing Generally Accepted Accounting Principles. Alternatively, management may doctor the results – performing illegal activities or stepping outside the regulatory framework. This chapter will first provide a brief overview of the contents of the book, focusing on creative accounting and fraud in the past and present. Then it will look at some lessons that can be learnt. Finally, it will provide a prognosis for the future.

## 23.1 OVERVIEW

In the first part of the book, the themes underpinning creative accounting and fraud are explored with reference to the prior literature and to past accounting scandals. The differing self-interest of the main actors in creative accounting (managers, investment analysts, auditors and regulators, shareholders, merchant banks and other users) was examined in order to see those who would benefit and those who would be harmed by creative accounting. In addition, the incentives for creative accounting and fraud were explored. Personal incentives for managers ranged from increasing their salaries and bonuses to enhancing their shares and share options. City expectations meant that managers would try to meet analysts' forecasts.

Prior research was reviewed in order to consider the main strategies that could be adopted for creative accounting and also for fraud. Four main strategies were reviewed. First, companies can maximise revenues by, for example, the premature recognition of sales. In extreme cases, and many were identified in the book, fictitious sales are created. Second, expenses can be decreased, for example, by capitalisation, reclassifying bad debts or extending amortization or depreciation periods. Alternatively, provisions can be created to reduce immediate expenses and then fed back into the income statement in the future to smooth profits. Third, assets can be increased, often in conjunction with decreasing expenses (e.g. capitalizing interest also boosts fixed assets). Other methods are also identified, such as enhancing goodwill, brands and other intangible assets. Fourth, liabilities can be decreased. Two popular methods identified are off-balance sheet financing and reclassifying debt as equity.

A review of the prior literature identified both descriptive and statistical studies. In the descriptive studies, a number of influential books and reports presented an impressive set of evidence about creative accounting in Australia, the UK and the USA. The academic literature is also reviewed and synthesised. Broad conclusions are drawn, such as that managers manipulated earnings so that they could receive higher bonuses. In addition, the literature on the use of accounting numbers, graphs and photographs to manage impressions was reviewed. This provided a broad framework in which to frame creative accounting and fraud.

Accounting scams and scandals are a perennial problem. This was identified by a study from ancient to modern times. Examples ranged from the doctoring of a cruciform monument in the third millennium BC in Mesopotamia to creative accounting in New Zealand in the 1980s. Eighteen examples were provided from all these time periods and from geographically diverse countries such as Australia, Italy, Mesopotamia, New Zealand, the UK and the USA. These scandals show that essentially human nature does not change and that there are always individuals who will try to gain personal advantage by manipulating accounting numbers in their own favour.

In Chapters 8–19, individual authors provide an overview of accounting in 12 countries from about the 1980s. These cover Australia, China, Germany, Greece, India, Italy, Japan, the Netherlands, Spain, Sweden, the UK and the USA. The writers of these chapters, all natives of the country concerned, explore in depth the context of individual countries and the major accounting scandals that have occurred, generally since about 1980, with their consequences.[1] In Chapter 20, there is a consideration of the credit crunch and banking failures from 2008–9. Some of these accounting scandals are already well known internationally, such as Enron, Madoff and WorldCom from the USA, Parmalat from Italy and Polly Peck from the UK. In these cases, there were spectacular examples of accounting manipulation. Enron was the seventh biggest company in the USA before its demise and is well known for its misuse of special purpose entities. WorldCom is famous for its scandalous abuse of capitalisation, treating what were, in accounting terms, really expenses as fixed assets. Madoff is a good example of a Ponzi scheme where an audacious individual managed to pay existing investors from the receipts of new investors. Parmalat was an example of a company that may never actually have been solvent, but was kept afloat by the massive falsification of earnings, assets and liabilities with poor internal control and lax external auditing. Finally, Polly Peck is an example of a company which was involved in spectacular growth where one man, Asil Nadir, combining the offices of chairman and chief executive, has been accused by the UK's Serious Fraud Office of transferring huge sums of money out of the UK to Turkey. Asil Nadir has, however, consistently protested his innocence and may now return to face trial in the UK. In addition, there were many examples of dubious accounting practices.

In other countries too, both developed and developing, examples were presented of important accounting scandals. From Europe, there was ComRoad, Flowtex and Balsam

---

[1] I synthesise some of the main points in this section relying upon the factual material provided by the individual authors. However, readers are referred to the individual chapters for the details and references of individual cases.

from Germany; the Bank of Crete from Greece; Royal Ahold from the Netherlands; Afinsa and Fórum Filatélico from Spain and ABB and Skandia from Sweden. The German cases are spectacular examples of accounting fraud. In ComRoad, there was, in essence, a fictitious subsidiary, VT Electronics, with which ComRoad supposedly traded actively. The fraud was detected by a journalist rather than by the auditors. Flowtex was another widespread fraud in which banks and leasing companies bought non-existent drilling machines and these systems were then rented to other (fictitious) companies. There were supposed to be 3400 drilling machines in existence. In actual fact, there were only 250. With Balsam, a whole edifice of fictitious receivables and revenues was built up through fraudulent factoring. Fictitious sales were five times actual sales. In Greece, the main case identified was the Bank of Crete. George Koskotas, a clever fraudster, achieved rapid promotion within the bank. Taking advantage of his position, lax internal controls and banking secrecy, he misappropriated 32 billion drachmas from customers.

In the Netherlands, at Royal Ahold, there was an accounting fraud at head office. Management used control letters and side letters (hidden from the auditors) to justify fully consolidating four joint ventures that were not really subsidiaries. In addition, in a US subsidiary vendor allowances were manipulated which resulted in lower cost of sales and higher profits.

The major Spanish accounting scandal is interesting as it shows how companies can exploit people's passions, in this case stamps. Afinsa and Fórum Filatélico were two stamp companies. They offered investment contracts backed by stamps. However, the stamps were overvalued and the companies failed correctly to recognize liabilities. Finally, in Sweden, ABB and Skandia had very different accounting problems. When ABB changed from IAS to US GAAP, hidden asbestos liabilities came to light as well as problems with ABB trading in its own shares. For Skandia, an insurance company, it was found that Skandia used embedded value, an unusual accounting methodology. There were also dubious financial deals and suspicions about the questionable use of incentives programmes.

The four Asian and Australasian countries showed a variety of different accounting scandals. For Japan, the three main accounting scandals were probably Livedoor, Nikko Cordial and Kanebo, while for Australia the major case was HIH, an insurance company. The two developing countries, India and China, also had a number of major accounting scandals, most notably Zhengzhou Baiwen for China and Satyam in India.

In Japan, 10 accounting scandals were identified. However, the three most important scandals were all very different. In Livedoor's case, a fourfold increase in consolidated income was reported when in reality there would have been a consolidated operating loss without manipulation. The accounting scandal caused the Tokyo Stock Exchange to shut down temporarily. With Kanebo, there was massive earnings manipulation from 2000–4. As a result of this, the auditing firm ChuoAoyama PricewaterhouseCoopers was broken up into Misuzu and Arata. Then, in Nikko Cordial's case, there was manipulation of performance-related compensation so that management could benefit. Misuzu was implicated in this case and then broken up. In Australia, frequent cases of creative accounting were identified. However, the most important prominent failure was HIH Insurance. This was Australia's largest corporate collapse. HIH had under-reserved, effectively understating the group's liabilities and overstating the group's profits. The HIH Insurance case caused a major shake-up in corporate governance in Australia.

China and India provide interesting examples of creative accounting and accounting scandals. Seven Chinese examples were covered in some depth and outline frequent cases of accounting fraud, particularly attempts by companies to manipulate their results ahead of a stock market listing. Zhengzhou Baiwen is covered in depth. Zhengzhou Baiwen was one of the biggest accounting scandals in China. The company was charged with manipulating publicly reported financial results, inflating profits and lying to the Chinese Securities Regulatory Commission. In the Indian chapter, there is an extensive list of companies which have indulged in creative accounting, ranging from reclassification of assets to the creation of provisions and the capitalization of interest. In the Satyam case, the promoter/chairman of the company, Mr Raju, admitted he had been cooking the books of the company in what is suspected to be India's biggest ever fraud.

## 23.2 THEMATIC ANALYSIS

Overall, 58 major accounting scandals were detailed across 12 countries. However, there were many other examples of creative accounting, especially from Italy, India and the USA. In Italy, for example, creative accounting for stock options and by football clubs was common. Meanwhile, in India, a raft of creative accounting techniques (such as the capitalization of interest) was identified. In Germany, too, many examples of potential creative accounting were identified. Across the major accounting scandals, it was possible to synthesise certain patterns in terms of the methods of creative accounting and fraud used, the incentives that could be identified for creative accounting and fraud, overstrong personalities, failure of internal controls and failure of external auditors.

The first important point about the methods of creative accounting and fraud used was the sheer diversity of different methods. Although there were some common identifiable methods, each firm used a unique set of methods. Generally, companies used multiple methods of creative accounting to arrive at their desired accounting outcomes rather than just one. There were different methods relating to increasing income, decreasing expenses (often in conjunction with increasing assets), increasing assets and decreasing liabilities. The two most popular ways of increasing sales were boosting sales and earnings by conducting transactions with related parties and by premature sales recognition. Another popular method was by including non-operating profits. For decreasing expenses, the two most popular methods were capitalising expenses and provision accounting. Two other frequently used methods were deferring expenses to future periods (other than capitalisation) and putting expenses through to reserves rather than to the income statement. Generally, there were fewer cases identified of increasing assets. The most frequent were increasing inventory, increasing debtors, revaluing fixed assets and acquisition-related methods. Finally, the two major methods of decreasing liabilities were off-balance sheet financing and generally understating liabilities.

It was often difficult to distinguish methods of fraud from methods of creative accounting, so the two sets of methods should be taken in conjunction with each other. Generally, frauds will have been proved at court or by the regulatory authorities. The underpinning motive for the fraud appeared to be embezzlement. The most common method was fictitious sales transactions, although there were many identifiable cases of false financial statement documentation. Particularly interesting and impressive were three cases of totally fictitious subsidiaries. Two German cases involved the creation of non-existent drilling systems (Flowtex) and the invention of what seems to have been a totally fictitious subsidiary (ComRoad). In the third case, from the UK, the results of two overseas subsidiaries of Polly Peck were vastly inflated.

The incentives for creative accounting and fraud were most often to cover up bad performance, often to maintain the company's share price and meet market expectations, and also for personal benefit. Two notable examples of the latter were the Bank of Crete and Polly Peck, where George Koskotas and Asil Nadir, respectively, appear to have extracted huge amounts of cash from their respective businesses. In the UK, Asil Nadir has been accused of transferring millions of pounds out of the country by the UK's Serious Fraud Office (although Nadir has never returned to the UK to face trial and has consistently protested his innocence). As this book goes to press, however, in August 2010 Asil Nadir has returned to face trial as the Serious Fraud Office has now agreed not to oppose bail (Adams, 2010). Another important motive, particularly in the developing countries of China and India, appeared to be to meet listing requirements. However, it is often difficult to get precise motivations. One unusual case from Japan, Morimoto-gumi, involved the fabrication of results to allow the company to bid for larger public construction contracts than would otherwise have been warranted.

A particular feature of accounting scandals was the role that overstrong individuals played in them. Across most countries, examples of charismatic individuals who managed to persuade the business community that all was well when actually it was not can be found. For example, in the three UK scandals Agha Hasan Abedi of BCCI, Asil Nadir of Polly Peck and Robert Maxwell of Mirror Group were all able to control their companies through the strength of their personalities, often combining the role of CEO and chairman.

For any accounting scandal to occur, there must be some failure of either internal control or external auditor. These failures are often difficult to identify though, through the secrecy of companies and the defensiveness of auditors. However, across the cases studied, there were numerous examples of failures of independent directors, audit committees, supervisory boards and basic internal controls such as paper trails or division of responsibilities. In addition, the external auditors rarely escaped without censure – although in some cases, such as Royal Ahold in the Netherlands, it was the external auditors who discovered the financial irregularities. More often, the auditors spotted nothing and, as with Arthur Andersen and Enron and in many of the Chinese scandals, appear to have been complicit in the dubious accounting practices adopted (although not necessarily in the underlying fraud). In extreme cases, the external audit failure led to the break-up of the external audit firms in China, Japan and the USA.

The impact of accounting scandals and creative accounting can be broadly divided into short-term immediate effects and longer-term effects. The short-term impact on management and directors can be profound. In many cases (at least 30), the directors were jailed, in others they were fined. However, these jail sentences were generally not substantive and often, especially in Japan, were suspended. Over half of the prison sentences (17 out of 32) were less than five years. Indeed, in only seven cases were they more than 16 years. Even when the maximum sentence of 25 years was awarded, it could be commuted. For example, in Greece, George Koskotas served only 12 years out of a 25-year sentence for a major case of embezzlement. Overall, it seems that white collar crime carries very low tariffs. In other cases, the directors were fined. However, there was usually very little sequestration of assets – except for Germany, where the personal wealth of Bodo Schnabel, CEO of ComRoad, was seized. Capital punishment too was rare, occurring only once in China where the President of the Great Wall Fund Raising Company was sentenced to death.

If the penalties on directors were relatively light, then this was also true for auditors. Generally, auditors escaped with censure, or with fines (on individuals or the firms themselves). More rarely, actions were taken directly against named individuals. In only four notable cases were the audit firms dismantled. First, in Japan, where ChuoAoyama PricewaterhouseCoopers was broken down after the Kanebo scandal into Misuzu and Arata; Misuzu, then finding itself on the wrong side of another accounting scandal, Nikko Cordial, was itself dissolved. Second, in the infamous Enron case, when Arthur Andersen was broken up after the spectacular collapse of Enron. Third, in the Chinese Great Wall Fund Raising scandal, where the auditing firm was dissolved. And, finally, also in China, where the Shenzhen Special Economic Zone Accounting Firm was shut down after the collapse of Shenzhen Yuanye. Indeed, the most common action against auditors was that they were fined or criticized, but no action was taken. Occasionally, action was taken against individual auditors, but only rarely. In two cases, in Japan, the auditors were jailed or received suspended sentences. And in Greece, the auditor of the Bank of Crete was sentenced to jail for 12.5 years.

Frequently, the main losers appear to be employees, who often lost their jobs (and often their pensions), and investors and creditors, who often lost their money. Indeed, there is generally little recompense for any of these three groups, although, thankfully, the days when, because of unlimited liability, the investors could lose all their money, as in the nineteenth century City of Glasgow Bank accounting scandal, appear to be long gone. In some cases, there have been impressive short-term economic and political consequences, with the Livedoor scandal in Japan causing a short-term shutdown in the Tokyo Stock Exchange and in China, Greece and Spain government officials being forced to resign.

The longer-term consequences of the accounting scandals tend to be one-off regulatory responses which, over time, led to a cumulative increase in legislation. Across all 12 countries studied, there was evidence of this – often implicitly, but sometimes explicitly. Across these countries over time, there has been a steady increase in general accounting and auditing legislation, specific accounting and auditing measures, and corporate governance codes and principles of best practice. To take some illustrations, in India and Spain, there were some general changes to the companies/financial law caused by the accounting scandals. In Australia and Japan, there were specific developments in accounting standards on consolidated financial statements. In Italy, there were changes in auditors' engagement rules and, throughout the EU, a change to the European 8th Directive caused directly by the Parmalat case. In many countries, starting in the UK, and including Australia, China, Greece, the Netherlands and Sweden, corporate governance codes have been introduced, largely it would seem to combat perceived failings in corporate governance in *causes célèbres* in the respective countries.

Over time, the effect of these regulations has become cumulatively impressive. In the UK, for example, accounting legislation has often followed accounting scandals starting with the South Sea Bubble Act after the South Sea Bubble in 1720. More recently, the takeover by the General Electric Company of Associated Electrical Industries, which caused much controversy, led to the formation of the Accounting Standards Committee. This formed the UK's standard-setting regime for 20 years until the formation of the Accounting Standards Board in 1990. The Accounting Standards Board's early thinking was influenced by accounting scandals such as Polly Peck. Polly Peck was one of the contributory causes of the formation in the UK of the Cadbury Committee which, in turn, produced the first Code of Corporate Governance in 1992. This Code was then emulated in other countries.

In the USA there was a similar pattern, with accounting scandals causing regulatory change. Thus, in 1932, Kreuger & Toll went bankrupt, the largest bankruptcy in US history at the time. As a result, the USA embarked on a path of regulation. In 1933, the US Securities Act was signed to regulate US listed companies. Another significant change occurred in the USA, after the Enron scandal, when the Sarbanes-Oxley Act introduced new accounting and auditing regulations.

In essence, therefore, an accounting evolutionary war of the fittest developed, with accounting scandals causing regulatory change. These changed the mechanism of creative accounting and fraud, but not its basic nature. New regulations just mean that new methods of accounting manipulation need to be found. This is not too hard for motivated, intelligent and resourceful creative accountants.

## 23.3 LESSONS FOR THE FUTURE

The first, and most important, lesson learnt from this examination of cases is probably that creative accounting, fraud and accounting scandals are perennial problems stemming from basic human nature. They are thus unlikely to go away. Over the four years it has taken to put this book together, new potential accounting scandals have emerged. There have been, for example, a raft of companies that have run into problems through the credit crunch, for example, Bear Stearns and Lehman Brothers. Therefore, our best hope is to understand and perhaps mitigate the problem.

Figure 23.1 is an attempt to do this using a theoretical model to reduce creative accounting and fraud. It represents a fairly simplistic diagram in which conceptually I look at the potential for creative accounting and fraud. I will use this schema as a basis for investigating the lessons and what can be done.

### 23.3.1 Factors Increasing the Possibilities of Creative Accounting and Fraud

Several factors enhance the possibility of accounting manipulations and, in turn, accounting scandals. These can be broken down into motives and environmental opportunities.

#### 23.3.1.1 Motives

The presence of strong motives enhances the possibility of accounting shenanigans. These motives may be generated internally from individual needs or externally via city pressures. An individual's circumstances may pressure him or her (more usually him!) to indulge in creative accounting or fraud. For example, if an individual has huge debts or is facing bankruptcy this may enhance the pressures to be creative.

Similarly, if a company is under strong pressure to perform on the stock market this will increase the motivations to indulge in creative accounting. For example, the company may

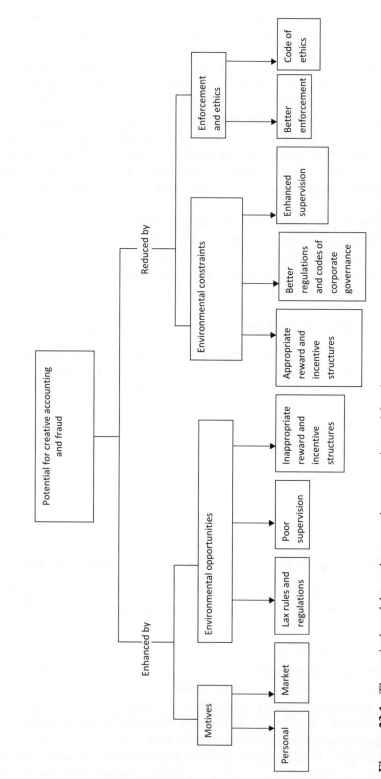

**Figure 23.1** Theoretical model to reduce creative accounting and fraud

be struggling to meet analysts' forecasts, to cover up bad performance or even to avoid bankruptcy. This might have serious consequences for managerial remuneration in terms, for example, of share options.

### 23.3.1.2  Environmental Opportunities

These can also enhance the potential to indulge in creative accounting and fraud. They can be divided, for example, into three broad areas: lax rules and regulations, poor supervision, and inappropriate reward and incentive structures.

#### Lax rules and Regulations

The rules and regulations in a country may need revision. This may require Companies Acts, specific standards or indeed effective codes of governance. Generally, nowadays every country has a fairly impressive regulatory structure. However, often there are still loopholes that would benefit from being plugged.

#### Poor Supervision

Supervisory structures can exist within a company and also from outside. Therefore, the potential for creative accounting and fraud can be enhanced by poor internal controls and lax external auditing. Poor internal controls can be at board level or at company level. At board level, it may be lack of independent directors, ineffective or non-existent audit committees, or supervisory boards, or combined roles of CEO and chairman. The involvement of senior executives in fraud highlights the importance of effective monitoring by boards and audit committees, especially of the managerial incentives for financial statement fraud (Beasley, Carcello and Hermanson, 1999). At company level, it might involve lack of division of responsibilities or lack of controls over cash. Lax external auditing may be caused by a variety of failures such as poor provision for auditor independence. In many accounting scandals, there were both poor internal and external supervision.

#### Inappropriate Reward and Incentive Structures

Individuals respond to incentives. Donoher, Reed and Storrud-Barnes (2007), for example, show that managerial equity ownership and stock options are related to the issue of misleading financial disclosures. If, therefore, managerial remuneration is excessively geared to share prices or share options, then there are enhanced incentives for individuals to use creative accounting and, in extremes, fraud to shore up share prices. If they do not, then their remuneration may suffer severely.

### 23.3.2  Factors Reducing the Potential for Creative Accounting and Fraud

Just as there are several factors which enhance the potential for creative accounting and fraud, several can reduce them (see Figure 23.1). I divide these into two areas: environmental constraints, and enforcement and ethics. In some cases, the proposed factors would represent a fairly big change to the *modus operandi* of companies in particular countries. These factors are set out to encourage debate rather than as prescriptive solutions.

### 23.3.2.1  Environmental Constraints

I have broadly divided the constraints into three: reward and incentive structures, better regulations and enhanced supervision.

#### Appropriate Reward and Incentive Structures

The current reward and incentive structures in some countries encourage individuals to try to maximise profits, if necessary through creative accounting. This not only maximises any performance-related pay, but also helps to support the share price. In many countries, shares and share options are often an important element in management's compensation. A return to a more balanced remuneration structure, where individuals are more dependent on a basic salary, might help to remove incentives to enhance profits. However, such a move would obviously have to be balanced against the advantages of performance-related pay, such as the alignment of shareholder and managerial interests.

#### Better Regulations and Codes of Corporate Governance

In most countries, there is a comprehensive set of rules and regulations for accounting and auditing. A strong regulatory framework has been proved necessary because of lapses in human ethical standards. Indeed, some commentators, such as Clarke and Dean (2007), argue that there is already sufficient regulation. However, there are still areas which arguably could be improved – for example, in many countries the rules on consolidating subsidiaries would benefit from close inspection. Similarly, in most countries the codes of corporate governance remain voluntary. If certain basic rules were implemented in every country, such as the separation of the roles of CEO and chairman, this might considerably enhance the potency of internal controls. In *Financial Reporting at a Crossroads*, Sutton (2002, p. 326) spells this out clearly: we need to 'rewrite our corporate governance policies and guidelines to clearly break the bonds between management and the independent auditor, and to unmistakably spell out the responsibilities of boards of directors and audit committees to shareholders and the investing public'. Certainly, some research shows a relationship between fraud and poor corporate governance (e.g. Beasley, 1996; Bell and Carcello, 2000; Crutchley, Jensen and Marshall, 2007; Farber, 2005; Persons, 2005). Most commonly, the failings in corporate governance relate to ineffective audit committees and boards which lack independence. However, even when there are strong audit committees and independent boards, this will never prove a complete guarantee against the determined creative accountant or fraudster.

When setting rules and regulations, a balance needs to be set. Too many rules may well lead to regulatory overload and box ticking. It may be that a more principles-based approach may be better where the 'spirit' rather than the 'letter' of the law becomes more important. For example, at Enron, Benston and Hartgraves (2002) argue that the US rules-based approach allowed Andersen's to accept procedures that complied with the letter of the law even though they violated the basic objectives of GAAP. They prefer a 'true or fair' type of approach. Clarke and Dean (2007, p. 217) concur, suggesting for example that the 'true and fair' criteria should not be subservient to compliance with detailed accounting standards. Baker and Hayes (2004) meanwhile emphasise substance over form. At Enron, Baker and Hayes argue this would have provided a more realistic view of the company's financial statements. This view was echoed by Martens and McEnroe (1992), who felt that by following rules rather than substance over form the profession will lose legitimacy.[2]

Some commentators actually call for a major revamping of present rules. Clarke, Dean and Oliver (2003), in an Australian context, severely criticise current rules and procedures on group accounting. They call for a rethink. Later, Clarke and Dean (2007, p. 2005) call for a totally different approach where the holding company's share in a subsidiary is shown as an investment in the holding company's balance sheets. Under their proposed model, this would represent the proportionate current money's worth of the underlying net assets valued at their current cash equivalents.[3] They also call for a comprehensive mark-to-market accounting system. Radical approaches like this are certainly worth considering. However, fair value has been much-criticised for its role in the credit crunch.

*Enhanced Supervision*

There are certain things which can be done to enhance both internal controls and also external auditing. For internal controls, for example, the setting up of supervisory boards, increasing the percentage of independent, non-executive directors for boards and audit committees would help internal control in many companies. In addition, it might well enhance the independence and effectiveness of external auditing if fixed auditing periods were introduced. On independence, too, Reinstein and McMillan (2004) note the particular problems which consultancy causes for independence. In addition, there are certain areas of the financial statements that deserve increased attention by both internal and external auditors, such as premature revenue recognition, transactions with related parties, capitalisation, provisions, asset valuation and off-balance sheet financing (see also Beasley, Carcello and Hermanson, 1999, p. 45).

There is also a need for external auditors to take a holistic view of a company and its environment. This should incorporate: the company's control environment, the company's economic, social and political environment, as well as the motivations of management. A healthy professional scepticism should be adopted (Beasley, Carcello and Hermanson, 1999, p. 46).

### 23.3.2.2  *Enforcement and Ethics*

*Better Enforcement*

Enforcement can be divided into enforcement of accounting rules and enforcement on individuals. Broadly, the introduction of investigatory panels, such as the Financial Reporting

---

[2] In Reinstein and McMillan (2004).

[3] Currently a group balance sheet is prepared where the assets and liabilities are combined, but with goodwill and minority interest separately calculated.

Review in the UK or the Financial Reporting Enforcement Panel in Germany, helps to scrutinise the financial reporting within countries. Such panels, particularly if vested with proactive investigatory powers, could prove a powerful weapon in detecting and deterring aberrant accounting practices.

For individuals, the sanctions imposed in the courts appear very light. As pointed out earlier, in only seven instances were prison sentences of more than 16 years meted out to individuals. Even post-Enron, the penalties seem quite light. In the USA in 2005, the penalty for making false statements was a fine of up to $5 million, or imprisonment for up to 20 years, or both (Dnes, 2005). Given that some of the accounting scandals caused hardship to many employees, investors and creditors, these sentences seem surprisingly lenient.[4] It would seem advisable for countries to look at their current sentencing policies for both directors and auditors. Longer sentences would not only signal that countries took accounting fraud seriously, but could also act as a deterrent. As in the USA, directors could be personally liable. In addition, it would be advisable to look at the definitions of false accounting and fraud. Higson (1999), for example, believes that the reason there has been so much reticence in reporting fraud in the UK is the impreciseness of its definition. Also, in the Enron trial, it is reported anecdotally that the prosecution often focused on general issues given the difficulties of proving the specifics of financial statement fraud.

### Code of Ethics

In a sense, the solutions to creative accounting and fraud proposed so far are all controlling and punitive. They involve tightening up current reward and incentive standards, improving current regulatory and supervisory structures, better regulatory enforcement and harsher penalties on individuals. Another alternative solution is to improve the ethical awareness of individuals (see, for example, Satava, Caldwell and Richards, 2006). Ethics requires obeying both the spirit and letter of the codes. Ethical behaviour needs to be set at the top and be part of the organisational culture (Guynn, 2005). Many of the accounting scandals *prima facie* were associated with a lack of ethical awareness. For example, Duska (2005) identified a compliance mentality rather than a sense of ethical responsibility in Arthur Andersen, auditors of Enron. Enhancing ethical awareness may be done nationally, through companies, or professionally. National codes of ethics, company codes or professional ethical codes could all be developed, and where they exist already, strengthened. Such written codes of ethics will set forth what the government, company or profession expects from its citizens, employees or professionals (Association of Certified Fraud Examiners, 1996).

Most professional institutes already have such written codes, such as the American Institute of Certified Accountants (The Code of Professional Conduct of the American Institute of Certified Public Accountants 1973, revised 1988) and the US Management Accounting Code (Standards of Ethical Conduct for Practitioners of Management Accounting and Financial Management, 1997). There are also codes for accountants in other countries, such as Canada, Germany and the UK and also internationally (IFAC, 2003a). Generally,

---

[4] Certainly compared to medieval times, when the ultimate penalties for fraud were death and disfigurement (Jones, 2008).

these codes cover areas such as responsibilities, public interest, integrity, objectivity and independence, due care, and the scope and nature of services. These codes provide a useful reference point. However, flagrant abuses of ethics, such as the case of Arthur Andersen in the USA, show that they are not universally followed. These codes need to be revised and, in particular, they need to be more specific and enforced more rigorously (Duska and Duska, 2003). This call for more effective codes of ethics for the profession is mirrored by the need for more effective corporate ethics codes and more active monitoring (IFAC, 2003b). Indeed, Schaub *et al.* (2005) see the solution as not only articulating ethical values to employees, but also rewarding employees who uphold those values.

Fortunately, there are some signs of enhanced ethical awareness. For example, one of the world's leading accounting professional institutes, the UK's Association of Chartered Certified Accountants (ACCA), has recently introduced a 'Professional Accountant', final level paper, to increase candidates' awareness of ethical issues when taking their final exams. Such developments may also help to strengthen the independent mental attitude which should underpin auditor independence (Clarke and Dean, 2007). Finally, there need to be codes of conduct for other bodies involved in the broader accounting environment, such as corporate lawyers and merchant banks. In addition, it would be useful if users were made aware, through education, that accounting is not objective, but subjective (Dellaportas *et al.*, 2005) and, therefore, subject to potential abuse. This book will hopefully play its part by increasing awareness, and thus wariness, among readers of the potential for creative accounting.

## 23.4 PROGNOSIS

However, when reviewing the possible solutions to creative accounting and fraud, it is necessary to take the long view and be realistic. By instituting enhanced controls and enforcement as well as increasing ethical awareness, it may indeed be possible to curb the worse excesses of financial manipulation. However, given the perennial nature of the problem, it is unlikely that creative accounting and fraud will ever be eliminated. Indeed, history is likely to repeat itself. As more and more legislation is enacted, there will be more advanced methods of circumventing the new rules.

At the time of completing the writing of this book (July 2010), it seems that we have entered into a new period of economic insecurity. Starting with the sub-prime collapse in the USA, economic problems have spread across the world. In the UK, this resulted in the collapse of the Northern Rock Building Society – although this appears to have had more to do with poor management than with creative accounting. In the US, numerous companies, such as Bear Stearns and Lehman Brothers, have collapsed. The banking system itself has since come under close scrutiny. Creative accounting techniques have been shown to play their part in the banking crisis. In addition, spectacular fraud such as that at Madoff Securities International has been uncovered. We have entered a severe economic downturn, and it is likely that more companies will feel under pressure to turn in better financial performances. Past history informs us that they are *in extremis* likely to indulge in creative accounting and fraud. If this happens and there are new accounting scandals, then there will be more calls for action by governments. As a result, there is likely to be more legislative action and the creative accounting cycle will continue.

## 23.5 CONCLUSION

This book has provided a comprehensive, global investigation of creative accounting, fraud and international accounting standards. After reviewing many past cases of accounting malpractice, it looked at the accounting environment in which accounting scandals occur, the motivation for individuals to indulge in creative accounting and fraud, and the main methods of creative accounting, fraud and impression management. There was a comprehensive examination of the extant descriptive and statistical literature on creative accounting, fraud and impression management. Moreover, there was a detailed examination of 18 accounting scandals that had occurred from the third millennium BC in Mesopotamia to New Zealand in the 1980s.

In addition, individual country studies written by individual country specialists looked at accounting scandals globally in both developed and developing countries. Twelve countries from North America (USA), Europe (Germany, Greece, Italy, the Netherlands, Spain, Sweden, the UK), Australasia (Australia) and Asia (China, India and Japan) were covered. The accounting scandals in each country were set in the context of that country's accounting environment. The motives, methods, internal controls and external accounting failings were covered, as well as the regulatory consequences. There was, in addition, a chapter which looked at the accounting aspects of bank failures during the recent global credit crunch.

The main findings were that there was an incredible diversity in methods of creative accounting and fraud. Some of the most popular methods were boosting sales and earnings through related-party transactions and premature sales recognition, reducing expenses by the capitalisation of expenses and provision accounting, increasing assets by increasing stock and debtors, and decreasing liabilities through off-balance sheet financing and generally understating liabilities. The main incentives for creative accounting fraud were to maintain the company's share price and for personal benefit. Poor internal controls and lax external auditing generally contributed to the accounting scandals. In addition, strong and charismatic individuals often played a major role.

The short- and long-term impacts upon directors, employees, auditors and other interested parties were examined. Very few directors were found guilty and jailed for long periods. Similarly there were, perhaps surprisingly, very few dire consequences for the auditors. Generally, they were either criticised or fined.

The potential for creative accounting and fraud appeared to be enhanced by managerial motivation (such as personal rewards and big incentives) as well as by environmental opportunities (such as inappropriate reward and incentive structures, tax rules and regulations, and poor supervision). It was suggested that the potential for creative accounting and fraud might be reduced by environmental constraints and more enforcement and ethics. Environmental constraints might involve a decreased focus on performance-related managerial compensation, better regulations and enhanced supervisory structures (such as supervisory boards, increased numbers of non-executive directors and audit committees). Better enforcement might involve harsher penalties for individual directors and enhanced enforcement regimes such as Financial Reporting Review Panels to regulate financial reporting in annual reports. Improved ethical codes might be introduced by countries, companies or professional institutes (e.g. in their examination structures).

Overall, therefore, creative accounting and fraud is endemic (across time and space). No era or country appears to be without its fair share of accounting scandals. Enron, WorldCom and Parmalat are just the tip of the iceberg. At the back of the book, I have compiled two appendices from the factual information provided by the individual authors. In Appendix 1, for example, there is a chronological list of 58 accounting scandals across 12 countries, while summaries of 144 cases are provided in Appendix 2. It is true that countries can attempt to reduce the number of accounting frauds and mitigate the amount of creative accounting and fraud through better environmental constraints and improved enforcement and ethics. However, given the perennial pressures upon human beings and companies to perform, it is almost inevitable that creative accounting, fraud and international accounting scandals will continue in one form or another. Where there is accounting, there will, it seems, always be accounting malpractice.

# REFERENCES

*Note:* Most of the material upon which this chapter is based is drawn from the factual information from the individual country chapters provided by the authors. It is at the end of these chapters that relevant references will be found.

Adams, S. (2010), 'Fugitive Polly Peck tycoon granted bail for fraud trial', *Daily Telegraph*, 31 July, p. 16.

Association of Certified Fraud Examiners (1996), *Report to the Nation on Occupational Fraud and Abuse (Wells Report)*, Association of Certified Fraud Examiners, USA.

Baker, C.R. and Hayes, R. (2004), 'Reflecting form over substance: the case of Enron Corp.', *Critical Perspectives on Accounting*, **15**, 767–785.

Beasley, M.S. (1996), 'An empirical analysis of the relation between the board of director composition and financial statement fraud', *The Accounting Review*, **71**(41), 443–465.

Beasley, M.S., Carcello, J.V. and Hermanson, D.R. (1999), *Fraudulent Financial Reporting 1987–1997: An Analysis of U.S. Public Companies*, research commissioned by the Committee of Sponsoring Organizations of the Treadway Commission, COSO, USA.

Bell, T.B. and Carcello, J.V. (2000), 'A decision aid for assessing the likelihood of fraudulent financial reporting', *Auditing: A Journal of Practice and Theory*, **19**(11), 169–184.

Benston, G.J. and Hartgraves, A.L. (2002), 'Enron: what happened and what we can learn from it', *Journal of Accounting and Public Policy*, **21**, 105–127.

Clarke, F.L. and Dean, G.W. (2007), *Indecent Disclosure: Gilding the Corporate Lily*, Cambridge University Press, Melbourne.

Clarke, F.L., Dean, G.W. and Oliver, K.G. (2003), *Corporate Collapse: Accounting, Regulatory and Ethical Failure*, Cambridge University Press, Cambridge.

Crutchley, C.E., Jensen, M.R.H. and Marshall, B.B. (2007), 'Climate for scandal: corporate environments that contribute to accounting fraud', *The Financial Review*, **42**, 53–73.

Dellaportas, S., Gibson, K., Alagiah, R., Hutchinson, M., Leung, P. and Homrigh, D.V. (2005), *Ethics, Governance and Accountability*, John Wiley & Sons Australia Ltd, Milton, QLD.

Dnes, A.W. (2005), 'Enron, corporate governance and deterrence', *Managerial and Decision Economics*, **26**, 421–429.

Donoher, W.J., Reed, R. and Storrud-Barnes, S.F. (2007), 'Incentive alignment, control and the issue of misleading financial disclosures', *Journal of Management*, **33**, 547–569.

Duska, R. (2005), 'The good auditor – skeptic or wealth accumulator? Ethical lessons learned from the Arthur Andersen debacle', *Journal of Business Ethics*, **57**, 17–29.

Duska, R.F. and Duska, B.S. (2003), *Accounting Ethics*, Blackwell, MA, USA.

Farber, D.B. (2005), 'Restoring trust after fraud: does corporate governance matter?' *The Accounting Review*, **80**(2), 539–561.

Guynn, J. (2005), 'Ethical challenges in a market economy', *Vital Speeches of the Day*, **LXXI**(13), 386–390.

Higson, A. (1999), *Why is Management Reluctant to Report Fraud? An Exploratory Study*, The Fraud Advisory Panel, London.

IFAC (2003a), *Proposed Revised Code of Ethics for Professional Accountants*, International Federation of Accountants, New York.

IFAC (2003b), *Rebuilding Public Confidence in Financial Reporting: An International Perspective*, International Federation of Accountants, New York.

Jones, M.J. (2008), 'Internal control, accountability and corporate governance: medieval and modern Britain compared', *Accounting, Auditing and Accountability Journal*, **21**(7) 1052–1075.

Martens, S.C. and McEnroe, J.E. (1992), 'Substance over form in auditing and the auditor's position of public trust', *Critical Perspectives on Accounting*, **3**, 389–401.

Persons, O.S. (2005), 'The relationship between the new corporate governance rules and the likelihood of financial statement fraud', *Review of Accounting and Finance*, **4**(2), 125–145.

Reinstein, A. and McMillan, J.J. (2004), 'The Enron debacle: more than a perfect storm', *Critical Perspectives on Accounting*, **15**, 955–970.

Satava, D., Caldwell, C. and Richards, L. (2006), 'Ethics and the auditing culture: rethinking the foundation of accounting and auditing', *Journal of Business Ethics*, **64**, 271–284.

Schaub, M.K., Collins, F., Holzmann, O. and Lowensohn, S.H. (2005), 'Self-interest vs. concern for others', *Strategic Finance*, **86**(9), 41–45.

Sutton, M.H. (2002), 'Financial reporting at a crossroads', *Accounting Horizons*, **16**(4), 319–328.

# Appendix 1

# Chronological List of Major Instances of Accounting Issues Across 12 Countries and Beyond

The details in the table below have been provided by individual authors. It is not necessarily complete or exhaustive, but hopefully gives some indication of the nature and extent of the problems.

| Year | Company | Country | Nature of Accounting Issues |
|------|---------|---------|------------------------------|
| 1879 | Afrikaanse Handelsvereeniging (Pincoffs Affair) | Netherlands | Falsifying profits |
| 1895 | Liberator Building Society/London General Bank | UK | Valuation of assets; intra-group sales |
| 1896 | Kingston Cotton Mill | UK | Existence and valuation of stock |
| 1900 | Irish Woollen | UK | Non-detection of frauds |
| 1904 | London Oil Storage | UK | Existence of cash |
| 1930 | Royal Mail Steam Packet Company | UK | Release of provisions; payment of subsidiary dividends; prospectus irregularities |
| 1932 | Kreuger | Sweden | Financial instruments |
| 1965 | Sanyo Special Steel | Japan | Fictitious sales on its parent-only financial statements through subsidiary sales |
| 1967 | AEI (acquisition by GEC) | UK | Valuation of long-term contracts |
| 1968 | Pergamon Press (acquisition by Leasco) | UK | Provisions (and write-backs); valuation of stock; timing of income recognition; transactions with Maxwell private companies |
| 1970–79 | OGEM | Netherlands | Non-consolidation of subsidiaries |
| 1971 | Rolls Royce | UK | Capitalisation of development costs |
| 1973 | Nihon Netsugaku Industries | Japan | Boosting sales to related companies just before year end with covering contract to buy goods back |

*(Continued)*

*Creative Accounting, Fraud and International Accounting Scandals*   Edited by Michael Jones
© 2011 Michael Jones. Published by John Wiley & Sons, Ltd

| Year | Company | Country | Nature of Accounting Issues |
| --- | --- | --- | --- |
| 1973–76 | Fuji Sash | Japan | Boosting sales by forcing an associated company to purchase the products at an improper high price and understating cost of goods by overstating obsolete inventories |
| 1974 | Sofico | Spain | Falsification of documents of property sold multiple times (sale of apartments that turned out to be fictitious) |
| 1975–82 | RSV | Netherlands | Deferred tax asset; restructuring costs direct in equity; government grant not recorded as liability |
| 1976–84 | Riccar | Japan | Issuing fictitious sales invoices and hiding merchandise in a warehouse as an off-balance sheet asset |
| 1980–88 | Bank of Crete | Greece | Embezzlement of about $200 million by Koskotas by the manipulation of bank accounts |
| 1981 | Caja Rural de Jaén | Spain | Fictitious profits and other creative accounting strategies |
| 1981 | Fidecaya | Spain | Unauthorized services and other irregularities |
| 1982 | Neue Heimat | Germany | Undisclosed related-party transactions |
| 1984 | Cafisa | Spain | Overvaluation of inventory (stamps); irregularities in sale of fixed assets; irregularities in foreign subsidiaries' transactions |
| 1986 | Miniscribe, Inc. | USA | Revenue recognition and understated accruals |
| 1987 | Saunders et al. ('Guinness affair') | UK | False accounting; market manipulation |
| 1988 | Barlow Clowes | UK | Investment fraud; extent of oversight and regulation |
| 1988 | Co op | Germany | Undisclosed related-party transactions; undisclosed ownership of treasury shares |
| 1988, 1990–95 | Fokker | Netherlands | Capitalization of aircraft development costs |
| 1989 | Fermenta | Sweden | Inflated sales and fraudulent revenue recognition in Initial Public Offering prospectus |
| 1990 | Polly Peck | UK | Debt structure and collateral; alleged false accounting; internal controls |
| 1990 | British and Commonwealth/Atlantic Computers | UK | Risk in leasing businesses; valuation of asset residuals |

| Year | Company | Country | Nature of Accounting Issues |
|------|---------|---------|------------------------------|
| 1991 | Comptronix | USA | Revenue recognition and cost capitalisation |
| 1991 | Adelaide Steamship | Australia | Consolidation using majority ownership rather than control, overstating certain assets |
| 1991 | Bond Corporation | Australia | Window-dressing (e.g. overstating acquisition assets; gains and losses on the sale of businesses as operating income; treating hybrid instruments as equity not debt) |
| 1991 | Bank of Credit and Commerce International | UK | Recoverability (and existence) of loans; extent of oversight and regulation |
| 1991 | Mirror Group | UK | Improper use of pension fund monies |
| 1992 | Shenzhen Yuanye | China | Falsifying capital contributions; inflating profits and assets appreciation; fraudulent applications for listing; management embezzlement |
| 1992 | Grupo Ibercorp and Sistemas Financieros | Spain | Insider trading, share price manipulation and discrimination; excessive repurchase of shares |
| 1992 | Grupo Torras | Spain | Dubious money transfers |
| 1993 | Bausch & Lomb | USA | Revenue recognition: channel stuffing |
| 1993 | Presidential Life | USA | Overstated investments |
| 1993 | Great Wall Fund Raising | China | Financial statement misrepresentation; management embezzlement of raised funds |
| 1993 | Metallgesellschaft | Germany | Sales of subsidiaries treated as operating results; hidden reserves via related-party transactions; undisclosed guarantees; valuation of forward oil contracts |
| 1993 | Südmilch AG | Germany | Property sales shown as ordinary sales; fictitious transactions |
| 1993 | Promotora Social de Viviendas (PSV) and Iniciativas de Gestión de Servicios (IGS) | Spain | Misappropriation of funds and fraud; recognition of nonexistent expenses |
| 1993 | Banco Español de Crédito (Banesto) | Spain | Manipulated financial statements; non compliance with matching; excessive payments for some investments; selling assets at artificially low prices; questionable transactions by CEO |

*(Continued)*

| Year | Company | Country | Nature of Accounting Issues |
|------|---------|---------|-----------------------------|
| 1993–2000 | ETBA Finance | Greece | €32 million embezzled by misappropriating client companies' interest income and investing into shares or charging clients with expenses without vouchers |
| 1994 | California Micro Devices | USA | Revenue recognition; nonexistent revenue |
| 1994 | Jürgen Schneider | Germany | Fictitious transactions (e.g. sham rental agreements) |
| 1994 | Balsam | Germany | Sale of fictitious receivables to a factoring firm |
| 1995 | W.R. Grace | USA | Restructuring charges |
| 1995 | Barings Bank | UK | Risk on futures contracts; record keeping and internal controls |
| 1995 | Wickes | UK | Timing of recognition of conditional supplier rebates |
| 1995 | Schneider Rundfunkwerke | Germany | Related-party transactions (selling self-developed patents to a joint venture) |
| 1995 | Strabag | Germany | Doubtful reversal of a written-down receivable; sale-and-lease-back |
| 1995–97 | Yamaichi Securities | Japan | 'Tobashi' securities deals, in which shares were shuffled through a complex web of the customers with a pledge that the unrealised losses would be covered, to keep valuation losses off balance sheet |
| 1996 | America Online | USA | Capitalised direct-response marketing costs |
| 1996 | Waste Management | USA | Extended depreciation periods |
| 1996 | Bayerische Hypotheken- und Wechsel-Bank (Hypo-Bank) | Germany | Overvaluation of assets; refraining from write-downs |
| 1996 | Bremer Vulkan | Germany | Related-party transactions; loss compensation by provisions accounting |
| 1996 | Yaohan Japan | Japan | Sales of real estate to a dummy company before the year end; repurchased next year |
| 1997 | Informix | USA | Revenue recognition; side letters |
| 1997 | Houwang Gufen | China | Related-party transactions; lending loans to parent company; large shareholder tunnelling |
| 1997 | Hongguang | China | Fraudulent applications for listing by inflating profits and misrepresentations in the prospectus |

| Year | Company | Country | Nature of Accounting Issues |
|------|---------|---------|------------------------------|
| 1997 | Daqing Lianyi | China | Bribery and corruption; fraudulent applications for listing; forging documents and statements |
| 1997 | Baan Company | Netherlands | Related-party transactions to increase revenue |
| 1998 | Bre-X Minerals | USA | Fictitious inventory |
| 1998 | Cendant (CUC International) | USA | Revenue recognition; cost capitalisation; reserves manipulation |
| 1998 | Kangsai Group | China | Bribery; financial statement misrepresentations; inflating profits by related-party transactions |
| 1998 | ST Tongda | China | Reported fake restructuring plans to exchange assets with Shenzhen City Yuehai Qiye Group |
| 1998 | Qiong Minyuan | China | Share price manipulation; invented contracts with related parties |
| 1998 | Jiabao Shiye | China | Inflated 1998 profits; opened over 300 fake individual accounts between 1996–98 to inflate profits for listing |
| 1998 | Babcock Borsig | Germany | Goodwill previously deducted from reserves capitalised |
| 1998 | EWS Euro Waste (Sero Lösch) | Germany | Fictitious journal entries of receivables |
| 1998 | AVA Agencia de Valores/Socimer | Spain | Inadequate disclosure and transparency; inadequate internal controls |
| 1998 | Long-Term Credit Bank of Japan | Japan | Failing to write off 313 billion yen in irrecoverable loans using lax assessment standards. However, the Supreme Court delivered a judgment of acquittal because a rational estimation of irrecoverable loans is very difficult. |
| 1998–99 | Sawako | Japan | False invoice by project co-worker under the percentage-of-completion method on long-term construction contract to rig sales |
| 1999 | Sunbeam | USA | Revenue recognition; bill and hold transactions |
| 1999 | UnitedHealth Group | USA | Backdated options |
| 1999 | Xerox | USA | Revenue recognition; sales-type leases |
| 1999 | Equitable Life | UK | Liabilities for policy bonuses |
| 1999 | Lantian Gufen | China | Falsifying assets and manipulating profits; fraudulent applications for listing |

*(Continued)*

| Year | Company | Country | Nature of Accounting Issues |
|---|---|---|---|
| 1999 | Dongfang Guolu | China | Inflated profits for listing; reported false financial statements |
| 1999 | Liming Gufen | China | Inflated assets, sales revenues and profits; fabricated accounts and invoices; CPAs provided auditing reports with misrepresentations |
| 1999 | Hypo-Vereinsbank | Germany | Overvaluation caused large write-downs after merger |
| 1999–2001 | Landis | Netherlands | Incorrect merger and acquisition accounting |
| 1999–2001 | LCI Computer | Netherlands | Capitalisation of development costs; ghost invoices and accounts receivable |
| 1999–2002 | Royal Ahold (US Foodservice) | Netherlands/ USA | Consolidation of joint ventures; accelerated recognition of vendor rebates (US subsidiary) |
| 1999–2003 | Morimoto-gumi | Japan | Understating cost of goods sold by deferring expenses to the next period to get a good ranking to put in a bid for larger public construction contracts |
| 2000 | Lavreotiki | Greece | Insider trading and share manipulation |
| 2000 | Wiggins | UK | Recognition of profit |
| 2000 | Versailles | UK | Fraud; overstatement of turnover |
| 2000 | Zhengzhou Baiwen | China | Inflated profits for listing; management embezzlement; related-party transactions; fraudulent applications for listing |
| 2000 | Flowtex | Germany | Sham deals (e.g. sale and leasing of non-existent drilling machines) |
| 2000 | EM.TV | Germany | Misstatements in interim reports; insider trading; false ad-hoc reports |
| 2000 | Infomatec | Germany | Intentional false information, e.g. contract volumes; overly optimistic press releases |
| 2000 | Freedomland | Italy | Fraudulent accounting; falsification of revenues |
| 2000 | Lucent Technologies | USA | Revenue recognition; channel stuffing |
| 2000–4 | Kanebo | Japan | Selling merchandise just before end of year and then buying back next year, understating cost of goods by overstating obsolete inventories |
| 2001 | Enron | USA | Off-balance sheet financing; loans as operating cash flow |
| 2001 | International Business Machines | USA | Income statement classification; gains netted against operating expenses |

| Year | Company | Country | Nature of Accounting Issues |
|---|---|---|---|
| 2001 | Harris Scarfe | Australia | Overstating inventories; understating creditors |
| 2001 | HIH Insurance | Australia | Understating liabilities, especially provisions for expected future claims; earnings management using reinsurance contracts; overstating goodwill |
| 2001 | One.Tel | Australia | Overstating debtors and other assets (e.g. licenses; capitalising certain expenses) |
| 2001 | Shandong Bohai | China | Faked accounts |
| 2001 | Zhang Jia Jie Tourism Development | China | Reported false financial statements 1996 to 1998 |
| 2001 | Jinzhou Port | China | Overstating revenues and assets; understating financial expenses and depreciation; management embezzlement; accounts falsification; earnings management by inflating sales and reducing bad debt provisions |
| 2001 | mg technologies | Germany | Undisclosed results from discontinuing operations; false recognition of restructuring provisions, etc. |
| 2001 | Gescartera | Spain | Unauthorized services; siphoning off money |
| 2001–6 | Sanyo Electric | Japan | Impairment loss of subsidiaries' shares on its parent-only financial statements not recorded properly; paid illegal dividends |
| 2002 | Adelphia Communications Corp. | USA | Undisclosed loan guarantees |
| 2002 | HealthSouth | USA | Excessive cost capitalisation; reserves manipulation |
| 2002 | WorldCom | USA | Acquisition reserves; excessive cost capitalisation |
| 2002 | Sichuan Electrical Apparatus | China | False financial statements |
| 2002 | Philipp Holzmann | Germany | Overvaluation of unfinished building projects; discretionary reversal of provisions; missing provisions for contracts |
| 2002 | ComRoad | Germany | False financial statements; fictitious transactions |
| 2002 | Phenomedia | Germany | False financial statements 1999–2001; fictitious transactions (e.g. sales to non-existent customers) |

(*Continued*)

| Year | Company | Country | Nature of Accounting Issues |
|------|---------|---------|----------------------------|
| 2002 | Hugo Boss | Germany | Channel stuffing (e.g. sales with a return option) |
| 2002 | MLP | Germany | Mismatched commission fees; lack of provisions; doubtful accounting of reinsurance transactions |
| 2002 | Bankgesellschaft Berlin | Germany | Contingent liabilities not disclosed; provisions for guarantees not recognised; fees for guarantees not recognised in the correct period |
| 2002 | Banfisa | Spain | Problems of asset valuation of stamps; non-recognition of repurchase liabilities |
| 2002 | ABB | Sweden | Creative accounting until introduction of US GAAP |
| 2002 | Prosolvia | Sweden | Premature invoices booked as revenues |
| 2003 | Tyco International | USA | Acquisitions; capitalised costs; overstated operating cash flow; undocumented officer loans |
| 2003 | Giacomelli | Italy | Fraudulent accounting; falsification of revenues and overstatement of inventories |
| 2003 | Parmalat | Italy | Fraudulent accounting; falsification of earnings, assets and debts |
| 2004 | Sex Form AE | Greece | €5 million misappropriation that led to the closure of the company |
| 2004 | Kelon | China | Management embezzlement; accounts falsification and earnings management by inflating sales and reducing bad debt provisions |
| 2004 | Livedoor | Japan | Using special purpose entities to hide losses and illegally book capital transaction as income in its accounts |
| 2004 | Finmatica | Italy | Fraudulent accounting; falsification of revenues and overstatement of intangibles |
| 2004 | Federal National Mortgage Association | USA | Derivatives used to manage earnings swings |
| 2004–5 | Ipirotiki Software | Greece | A manipulation scheme that artificially influenced the price and marketability of the company's shares |
| 2004–7 | Dynamic Life | Greece | Falsified financial statements; hiding a loss of €6 million |

| Year | Company | Country | Nature of Accounting Issues |
|---|---|---|---|
| 2004/5–2008/9 | Satyam Computer Services Ltd | India | Cooking the books, insider trading and misgovernance |
| 2005 | Zapf Creation | Germany | Reclassification of expense items; unrecognised provisions (e.g. for bonus payments, returns); failure to allocate marketing and sales expenses to proper period; restatements resulting from barter transactions |
| 2005–6 | Nikko Cordial | Japan | Booking false valuation gain on a share-exchangeable bond of special purpose company |
| 2006 | Nici | Germany | Fictitious transactions; sale of non-existent receivables to factoring firms and banks ('Ponzi scheme') |
| 2006 | Afinsa and Fórum Filatélico | Spain | Non-recognition of repurchase liabilities; non-compliance with historical cash on repurchase; non-recording of transactions and valuation of stamps |
| 2006 | Skandia | Sweden | Questionable apartment renovations and remuneration programme; embedded value insurance accounting |
| 2006–7 | IHI | Japan | Recognised improper revenue on a long-term construction contract based on the percentage-of-completion method |
| 2008 | Bear Stearns | USA | Overleveraging; underestimate of risk associated with sub-prime assets; valuation of CDOs |
| 2008 | Madoff Securities International Ltd | USA | Ponzi Scheme; extensive fraudulent behaviour |
| 2008 | Lehman Brothers | USA | Overleveraging; underestimate of risk associated with holdings of collateralised assets |

# Appendix 2

## Alphabetical List of Most Important Accounting Scandals Across 12 Countries and Beyond since about 1980

This summary of the most important accounting scandals covered in this book has been provided by the individual authors. Generally, with a couple of rare, interesting cases, such as Fuji Sash and Riccar from Japan and RSV from the Netherlands, these date from 1980 onwards.

### ABB (SWEDEN)

ABB is a company with a long and illustrious history of technological leadership and innovation in many industries. In order to list on the New York Stock Exchange in 2001, the company was required to change accounting principles from IAS to US GAAP. Reporting under the new set of accounting principles resulted in greatly reduced profits, and also brought to light the asbestos liability claims that had previously been hidden using what critics called creative accounting. In addition, the large repurchase of its own shares and the numerous acquisitions and dispositions made the financial statements very complex and difficult to compare between years and within the industry.

### ADELAIDE STEAMSHIP (AUSTRALIA)

Adsteam was hailed as an entrepreneurial and well-managed corporation for most of the 1980s and yet built a group structure which involved a complex web of cross-shareholdings where companies' accounts were consolidated on the basis of majority ownership rather than on the basis of effective control of other entities under the 'substance over form' notion of presenting a 'true and fair view'. A number of the associated entities that were not consolidated into the group accounts carried high levels of debt. Concerns were also raised about Adsteam's approach to asset revaluations, which tended to be over-optimistic, and the valuation basis for certain assets.

### ADELPHIA COMMUNICATIONS (USA)

From humble beginnings, Adelphia Communications Corp. grew to become the sixth largest cable TV operator in the USA. Allegations against members of the Company's founding family relate to employing company assets for personal use and also steps taken to hide developing financial problems. The transgressions include using company assets to secure loans to private, family-run partnerships that were not disclosed, using company funds to cover margin calls on the family's personal ownership of company stock and overstating cable TV subscription numbers. For their role in the fraud, key members of the founding family were found guilty of financial fraud.

## AFINSA BIENES TANGIBLES (AFINSA) AND FÓRUM FILATÉLICO (FÓRUM) (SPAIN)

Afinsa and Fórum offered investment contracts backed by stamps. The contracts promised investors a fixed return at the maturity of the contract. The companies promised to buy back the stamps at maturity. Both companies failed to recognise the liabilities of the repurchase option of the investors. They also failed to comply with the historical cost principle in relation to the repurchase of stamps (the stamps were recorded at the purchase price, leading to the overvaluation of their stamp inventory). Problems were also found with the recording of the transactions with suppliers (over-invoicing and a lack of documentation) and valuation of the stamps.

## BALSAM (GERMANY)

Balsam AG was initially a successful manufacturer and distributor of synthetic floors for sports stadiums. An excessive focus on growth and market share led to serious financial troubles and liquidity problems. The CEO and CFO over a long period used the sale of more and more fictitious receivables to a factor to cover huge operation losses. The fraud was connected with the booking of some of the fictitious receivables and revenues in the financial statements. Control failure of the supervisory board and the auditor facilitated this financial statement fraud.

## BANESTO (SPAIN)

The Bank of Spain seized control of Banesto, one of the most important Spanish banks, in 1993 with an accounting deficit near €4 million. The Spanish courts found that Conde, the bank's chairman, manipulated the company's income statement and balance sheet positions using questionable accounting practices, including non-compliance with the matching and accruals principles. There was evidence of recording current expenses as assets in the balance sheet, significant losses resulting from paying excessively for some investments and selling assets at artificially low prices, and transactions not related to Banesto's operations done for the personal benefit of Conde.

## BANK OF CREDIT AND COMMERCE INTERNATIONAL (BCCI) (UK)

The operations of BCCI were closed down by regulatory authorities across the world in July 1991 following production of the Sandstorm report. From a position of claimed assets of $25 billion, post-closure estimates of the amount in default ranged up to $13 billion. Extensive investigations and legal process across a range of jurisdictions later resulted in: scathing criticism of the business practices and interests of BCCI; a catalogue of the mechanisms and deceits by which BCCI was able to undertake large-scale criminal activity and financial manipulation; a number of its officers and employees being sentenced to long terms of imprisonment; and a focus on the role of regulators and auditors.

## BANK OF CRETE (GREECE)

George Koskotas was hired in the bank's financial administration department in 1979. He advanced very quickly and soon began making transfers of payments in Greece or overseas as the bank's authorised legal representative. He took advantage of his position and managed to misappropriate a total amount of 32 billion drachmas, mainly stolen from customers' cheques. Soon he managed to own 95% of the bank's shares and became President of its Board of Directors, a position which helped him cover up his misappropriations for some time. Koskotas had exploited the then existing inefficiency in the accounting banking information systems in Greece, whereby accounting events that affected two or more branches could not be processed simultaneously. A delay in the reconciliation of inter-branch accounts allowed Koskotas to transfer money outside his bank. For his crimes, Koskotas served a 12-year prison term in Greece and the USA.

## BEAR STEARNS (USA)

The collapse of Bear Stearns did not involve fraudulent behaviour but instead originated in an over-leveraged portfolio which ultimately precipitated a liquidity crisis for the bank. One of the components of Bear's funding strategy was the setting up of two investment funds offering income streams derived from collateralised securities bought on the open market and then repackaged by Bear for subsequent sale to its investors. Creative accounting was used by Bear, entirely lawfully, to convert high risk assets into lower risk repackaged products which could be sold at lower yields than would otherwise have been the case if they had remained in their original disaggregated state.

## BOND CORPORATION (AUSTRALIA)

Bond Corporation adopted a growth by acquisition strategy, characterised by leveraged purchases, followed by promptly executed asset revaluations of the assets acquired. This tactic was combined with the window-dressing of accounts, involving the use of accounting policies and practices which tended to disguise rather than reliably portrayed the underlying financial impacts of its aggressiveness, especially when rapidly increasing interest rates began to stifle the ultimately debt-ridden group. Bond Corporation's auditors, Andersen, later settled out of court, allegedly for approximately $100 million, over the firm's handling of the 1988 audit.

# BREMER VULKAN VERBUND (GERMANY)

Bremer Vulkan Verbund AG (BVV) was a shipyard with a long-lasting tradition. An unsound diversification strategy, in conjunction with competitive pressure, led to chronic strained liquidity. Because BVV was a huge employer, the City of Bremen supported BVV via guarantees and other state subsidies. Close personal ties between the City and the management and supervisory board played an important role and inhibited an active monitoring of the management. The financial statements showed an overly optimistic picture of the financial situation, and state subsidies for specific purposes were misused to cover operating losses.

# BRE-X MINERALS (USA)

While included among the accounting scandals of the USA, Bre-X Minerals Ltd was actually a Canadian gold mining company. In 1997, an independent mining consultant concluded that the company had 'salted' or added to its gold samples, overstating the size of the Busang gold deposit in Indonesia by tens of millions of ounces. Investors had grown uneasy when the company's geologist committed suicide by 'jumping' from a company helicopter. Shares in the company that were once valued at more than $6 billion became worthless. The company's founder and CEO, who died of natural causes soon after the fraud became public, was never charged in the matter.

# CAJA RURAL DE JAEN (SPAIN)

In 1982, the Bank of Spain seized control of Caja Rural de Jaen, a savings bank. The inspection service of the Bank of Spain detected several accounting irregularities in the company's financial statements. According to the news published at the time, Caja Rural de Jaen recorded fictitious profits and attempted to reduce an 'accounting hole' of around Pts 3500 million (€21 million). The main reason behind the accounting manipulation was to hide the high level of indebtedness from the financial authorities. In 1984, the directors of the savings bank were accused of accounting manipulation in the 1981 financial statements. Although the managers were sentenced to three years in jail, the penalties were repealed three years later. The case continued in the courts and in 1992 the Court of Jaen sentenced the managers for fraud and forgery. The appeal lodged by the managers against the decision was rejected by the Supreme Court in 1994.

# CALIFORNIA MICRO DEVICES (USA)

The case of California Micro Devices Corp. is one of particularly egregious revenue recognition. Like many small technology firms, the company was under constant pressure to keep revenues and profits growing in order to justify a high and rising share price. In 1994, more than one-third of the company's revenue was fictitious. In the fraud, many different revenue recognition tricks were employed. For example, revenue was recorded for orders that were shipped in subsequent quarters and returned shipments were never reversed. In some cases, customers were asked whether early shipments could be made. If permission was not received, phony packing documents were prepared and the goods were shipped to a company-controlled location and stored there until the customer requested shipment. Fake invoices were also prepared and revenue recorded for non-existent shipments. Receivables ballooned and were written off in stealth, offset with fictitious returns and revenue from a later, unrelated sale. The company's CEO and its most senior financial officer were found guilty of financial fraud.

## COMROAD (GERMANY)

ComRoad, a supplier of so-called telematik traffic systems, was listed in November 1999 on the exchange for the first time. Tough inquiries by a journalist revealed later that over 90 % of its revenues stemmed from fictitious transactions with a non-existent customer in Hong Kong. In this case, a journalist acted like an auditor and applied a risk-oriented audit strategy. Because of close personal ties between members of the supervisory board and the CEO, no active and independent oversight role by the supervisory board could be expected.

## CO OP (GERMANY)

The management of Co op AG, a retail chain, tried to gain near total control of the firm via the wrongful acquisition of treasury shares. The Co op case showed that pressure to be creative in the financial statements was caused by the ongoing bad financial condition of Co op and the need to disguise management enrichment. Some dominating members of the top management appear to have used their power to try to enrich themselves via high salaries and other monetary benefits (e.g. Co op shares). Opportunities were given because of a lax supervisory board and lenient auditors who arguably did not adequately discharge their monitoring function.

## DAQING LIANYI (CHINA)

Daqing Lianyi Petrochemical Shareholding Co. Ltd (Daqing Lianyi) was established by Daqing Lianyi Petrochemical Plant (a state-owned enterprise established in 1985) in 1996 and acquired a listing on the Shanghai Stock Exchange in 1997. In 1999, the company was discovered forging documents to meet its listing requirements, misusing assets and funds raised, and bribing government officials. Its main officers, auditors and securities underwriters were implicated and 39 Party and government officials were punished. It was also the first Chinese securities lawsuit in which the victimised investors successfully sued the company and were compensated.

## DYNAMIC LIFE (GREECE)

Towards the end of 2004, the Capital Market Commission revealed that Dynamic Life, a health club chain, was involved in improper accounting practices and imposed a fine of €1.5 million on Natasha Bougatioti, the owner and the company's main executive. By falsifying financial statements she augmented results by €3 million through a transaction concerning future receipts with a wholly owned subsidiary abroad. Later on losses of €6 million were not explicitly shown in the financial statements. Natasha Bougatioti, upon these revelations and the investigation of the Hellenic Capital Market Committee, left the country.

## ENRON (USA)

Growing rapidly from a small energy firm into one of America's most respected companies, Enron Corp.'s reversal of fortune was truly of epic proportions. The company generated $100 billion in reported revenue in 2000 only to face bankruptcy and liquidation in 2001. The company's fraud was big and complicated, entailing off-balance sheet liabilities, fictitious income and misreported cash flow. The company used separate, single-purpose entities, known as special purpose entities, to effect its fraud. While controlled by Enron, these SPEs were not consolidated for reporting purposes. The convenient arrangement permitted the company to transact with the entities as though they were separate, independent companies, borrowing money but reporting income, increases in shareholders' equity and operating cash flow in the process. Key officers of the company were ultimately found guilty of financial fraud.

## ETBA FINANCE (GREECE)

In 1998 it was revealed that company executives of ETBA Finance, a subsidiary of ETBA Bank, had embezzled 11 billion drachmas (about €32 million). The lack of defined responsibilities allowed company employees to handle their own transactions in all phases, from execution to supervision. Among other things, to achieve better returns, they combined all available cash of ETBA Finance and of client companies under liquidation and invested them into one large fixed deposit account or a repurchase agreement. This resulted in 'extra' interest due to the size of the deposit, which was then transferred into their personal accounts.

## FERMENTA (SWEDEN)

Fermenta was a Swedish pharmaceutical company headed by the entrepreneur, Refaat El-Sayed. The company grew rapidly through leveraged buy-outs and its share price soared. These acquisitions were publicised as highly profitable, although in reality they were financially disastrous. When it was revealed that El-Sayed had falsely claimed he had a doctoral degree and when Fermenta's internal auditor blew the whistle on the accounting irregularities, a criminal investigation began that revealed that turnover and asset valuations had been inflated systematically. Accounting had been used very creatively as well as fraudulently in order to disguise the company's financial crisis. In 1989, Refaat El-Sayed was sentenced to five years in prison for fraud and received a life-long ban from securities trading.

## FLOWTEX (GERMANY)

Flowtex was a mid-sized, non-listed, owner-dominated company. Flowtex developed and distributed a new horizontal drilling system. The charismatic founder and CEO sold non-existent drilling systems to banks or leasing firms. The proceeds from the sales were used to pay the leasing charges ('Ponzi scheme'). Obviously this system needed more and more cash. In the end, Flowtex claimed that 3400 drilling systems were operating all over the world, but only 250 drilling systems really existed. In this large-scale fraud no independent control, except for the auditor, existed. The auditor paid €51 million to the banks in an extrajudicial settlement, the largest sum so far paid by a German audit firm.

## FOKKER (NETHERLANDS)

Fokker is a case of creative accounting, with capitalisation of aircraft development costs and capitalising programme losses of specific types of aircraft (F 50 and F 100). The management of Fokker was very optimistic in capitalising these costs, while the payback period of these series of aircraft was quite long (in total approximately 20 years). There was harsh competition in the aircraft industry with low prices per aircraft, priced in US$ which was depreciating. Moreover, Fokker had overruns with respect to development costs of new types of aircraft. As a consequence, Fokker had programme losses which were also capitalised. These amounts should have been, but were not, impaired.

## FUJI SASH (JAPAN)

The metal products manufacturer's shares were listed on the Tokyo Stock Exchange. It illegally boosted earnings from 1973 to 1976 by 42.5 billion yen, which was the largest ever earnings manipulation at that time. The company forced its associated company to buy its products at a high price and understated cost of goods by overstating obsolete inventories. After this case, the equity method for consolidated financial statements to increase (decrease) periodically the investment's carrying amount by the investor's proportionate share of the earnings (losses) of the investee was required in Japan.

## GESCARTERA (SPAIN)

The Comisión Nacional del Mercado de Valores (CNMV) seized control of Gescartera, a brokerage house, in 2001. According to the CNMV, Gescartera did not have the required accounting entries and had weak internal controls. Investigations showed that Gescartera did not invest its clients' money; rather, money was 'siphoned off' to 'unknown' places. There was evidence of the falsification of documents and lack of information to investors. There were also concerns about the excessive number of intraday transactions. These transactions were allegedly to show the authorities and the auditors that the company carried out a certain level of investment activity. The court estimated the fraud at €57 million.

## GREAT WALL FUND RAISING (CHINA)

Great Wall Electrical Engineering Science and Technology Co. (Great Wall) was set up in Beijing in 1984, engaging in electronic engineering. Between 1992 and 1993, the company illegally issued very high coupon securities to over two million private investors in 17 large cities of China and raised one billion RMB. The money raised was partly embezzled. The company president was given a death penalty and a vice government minister was sentenced to imprisonment for 17 years for accepting bribes. The accounting firm and individuals implicated were all also severely punished.

## HARRIS SCARFE (AUSTRALIA)

Despite a track record in excess of 150 continuous years in the retail industry, Harris Scarfe was identified in March 2001 as having employed misleading accounting practices in order to remain profitable in accordance with the group profit expectations of the corporation's directors. For a period of at least six years, the consolidated financial statements had overstated the group's net assets, as management overstated inventories and understated creditors in order to engineer the financial results to meet the prevailing profit expectations. The board of directors subsequently announced that it had acted in good faith on the financial information made available by senior management.

## HEALTHSOUTH (USA)

At HealthSouth Corp. the SEC found evidence of fraud that dated back many years, possibly as early as the company's founding in the 1980s. The fraud entailed the capitalization of significant amounts of expenditure that should have been expensed. Such routine expenses as advertising costs and other operating expenses were in fact reported as components of property, plant and equipment. Virtually all of the company's chief financial officers since its founding pleaded guilty to participating in the fraud. However, the company's founder was not found guilty of financial fraud. He was, however, convicted of other unrelated charges.

## HIH INSURANCE (AUSTRALIA)

On its collapse, HIH Insurance was Australia's largest corporate collapse and was the second largest insurance company in Australia. Its collapse had wide-reaching implications for the Australian insurance industry and for the general public, and resulted in a Royal Commission into the demise of the insurer. It was found that HIH Insurance had engaged in the practice of under-reserving and had effectively understated the group's claims liabilities and thereby overstated group profits. It had also entered into poorly conceived and badly executed acquisitions, such as of FAI Insurances, which evidently contributed to the adoption of inappropriate accounting practices for goodwill.

## HONGGUANG (CHINA)

Transformed from a state-owned electronic tube factory in Sichuan Province in 1993, Chengdu Hongguang Industrial Shareholding Co. Ltd (Hongguang) made its initial public offering (IPO) in May 1997. It was the first listed firm in China to report a loss in the first year of listing. It was discovered later that the company had inflated its profit by RMB 150 million for its IPO. The related parties and employees were penalised and the company was sued by private shareholder(s) in 1998 and 1999. This was the first securities lawsuit in China.

## KANEBO (JAPAN)

Kanebo, whose shares were listed on the Tokyo Stock Exchange, was once a leading textile and cosmetics company established more than a hundred years ago. The accounting fraud at Kanebo from 2000 to 2004 is referred to as a Japanese-style Enron accounting scandal because Kanebo's case was the largest ever amount of earnings manipulation and the audit firm was forcibly broken up just like Arthur Andersen in Enron's accounting scandal. The ways in which earnings were boosted were varied. For example, the company sold unsaleable merchandise just before the end of the financial year with a covering contract and bought them back at the beginning of the next financial year.

## KANGSAI GROUP (CHINA)

Kangsai Group Shareholding Co., Ltd (Kangsai Group) was a company manufacturing clothes in Hubei Province. In 1996, the company obtained a listing on the Shanghai Stock Exchange. The company later reported a loss of RMB 62.03 million in 1999 and was publicly reprimanded by the Shanghai Stock Exchange in 2000 due to its commitment to a series of wrongdoings, such as bribery and corruption, fraudulent financial statements and unfair related-party transactions.

## LANTIAN GUFEN (CHINA)

Shenyang Lantian Shareholding Co. Ltd (Lantian Gufen) was originally established by a merger of three firms in Shenyang, Liaoning Province in 1992, covering pharmacy and agricultural and aquatic products. It was listed on the Shanghai Stock Exchange in June 1996 and became one of the 'star' companies reporting continued rapid growth until the CSRC discovered that the directors had committed a series of financial frauds including fabrication of listing application materials and falsification of the bank account balance and intangible assets. It was then acquired by a Hubei company and changed its name to Hubei Ecological Agriculture Shareholding Co. Ltd in 2001.

## LEHMAN BROTHERS (USA)

Lehman Brothers was one of the more well-known casualties of the credit crunch. Its demise was precipitated by over-dependence upon debt financing, the need to maintain its remuneration structure, and creative accounting which clouded the true scale of the risk associated with derivatives in its investment portfolio. Between 2004 and 2007 the bank significantly increased its leverage, aggressively purchasing collateralised securities. At no point before or after the bank's collapse was any allegation of wrongful or fraudulent behaviour made. The bank used the flexibility permitted under US GAAP to classify a proportion of its portfolio as 'Level 3 Assets' (assets which, due to their level of illiquidity, could not be accorded a risk weighting with any degree of accuracy). It was then able, quite legally, to avoid writing these down even though not doing so would seem in retrospect to have been optimistic. As the 'sub-prime crisis' took hold in the collateralised debt markets investors withdrew, leaving Lehman's with considerable holdings which eventually precipitated a fatal short-term funding crisis.

## LIVEDOOR (JAPAN)

The internet conglomerate company whose shares were traded on the Tokyo Stock Exchange reported a fourfold increase in consolidated operating income from 2003 to 2004. However, it was revealed that the company had reported fictitious revenue of 5.2 billion yen and that the company would have reported a consolidated operating loss without manipulation. The company used special purpose entities as off-balance sheet vehicles to hide losses and illegally book capital transactions as income in its accounts. As soon as the news of the accounting scandal spread, a sell-off of Livedoor's shares was sparked and the benchmark Nikkei 225 declined by 5.4 %. The Tokyo Stock Exchange shut down its entire trading operations after the news prompted a sell-off threatening to crash its computer system. The event became known as the 'Livedoor Shock'.

## MADOFF SECURITIES INTERNATIONAL LTD (USA)

Bernard Madoff used creative accounting to perpetrate one of the largest frauds in history involving a series of financial crimes for which he was sentenced to 150 years' imprisonment in a US state penitentiary. At the heart of his strategy was the setting up of a 'Ponzi' scheme in which investors were paid returns far in excess of market performance funded from capital provided by new entrants to the scheme. Such a scheme can continue to operate only for so long as fresh capital is forthcoming from new duped investors; if existing investors demand the return of their funds and this coincides with an inability to attract in new capital, a Ponzi scheme will invariably collapse. Rumours of fraud led to a refusal by investors to subscribe to Madoff's new investment trusts, set up in a desperate attempt to raise fresh capital. The funding crisis precipitated the collapse of Madoff's Ponzi scheme and revealed the extent to which investors had been defrauded.

## MIRROR GROUP (UK)

Having been heavily criticized in the Leasco/Pergamon scandal of the late 1960s, Robert Maxwell rebuilt his business empire into the Mirror Group. Its collapse in 1991, just after Maxwell's death, was precipitated, in large part, by over-priced acquisitions in the late 1980s and associated debt funding. The key issues highlighted in subsequent investigations were the misuse of pension fund assets (by wide and varied means) and the degree of perspicacity of regulatory authorities and professional advisors in allowing the 1990 flotation of a Maxwell company. Heavily criticised for a range of shortcomings, leading to failure in detection or prevention of the abuses in the Mirror Group, were the group's auditors, Coopers & Lybrand.

## MORIMOTO-GUMI (JAPAN)

This long-established, medium-sized construction company illegally manipulated earnings amounting to 98 billion yen from 1999 to 2003. The objective of the manipulation was to get a better construction rating and join in a public bid for larger public constructions. The company understated cost of goods sold by deferring expenses to the next financial year in order to boost the ratio of operating income to construction revenue and paid illegal dividends as the company would have had a deficit without earnings manipulation.

## NIKKO CORDIAL (JAPAN)

This company, one of the three big securities houses in Japan, manipulated its consolidated net income in 2005 and 2006 by booking false valuation gain on the share-exchangeable bond which was issued by a special purpose company. The performance-related compensation of the management was one of the most important motivations for the earnings manipulation. The company set up a management compensation scheme which was linked to an annual consolidated net income just before the accounting scandals. The reported compensation of the executives was actually much higher than the average amount of other companies, and the proportion of performance-based compensation total was very high.

## ONE.TEL (AUSTRALIA)

Operating in the mobile telephone services sector, One.Tel adopted an aggressive approach to business development on its establishment in 1995 by developing a customer base by internal growth which involved entering into contracts with customers of all types who were not necessarily able to meet their financial obligations under such contracts. Combining this aggressiveness to business development with the adoption and use of inadequate accounting systems, the practice of capitalising certain expenses and the acquisition of licences at amounts that were later identified as excessive contributed to the group's financial woes and to its demise only six years after formation.

## PARMALAT (ITALY)

Parmalat represents the most spectacular and important case of accounting fraud which has occurred in Italy. Accounting issues at Parmalat included creative accounting practices (e.g. the creative practice of 'redeemable' preference shares recorded as equity) but, mostly, accounting practices that were well beyond the boundaries of existing GAAPs. Fraudulent accounting at Parmalat was significant, and included the falsification of reported earnings, assets and liabilities, via a great variety of techniques. The Parmalat case occurred due to the failure of the corporate governance structures that allowed and/or did not hamper the fraud.

## PHILIPP HOLZMANN (GERMANY)

Philipp Holzmann AG was one of Europe's largest construction and engineering companies. Despite a difficult restructuring and turnaround situation, the management report contained a positive forecast for the following year and the CEO confirmed this at the annual general meeting. Only four months later, huge losses were disclosed and the company opened bankruptcy proceedings. The Holzmann case can be seen as an example of creative accounting because of the probable overvaluation of unfinished building contracts, the missing or underestimated provisions for onerous contracts and the insufficient reporting about risk factors in the management reports. Poor internal control facilitated the preparation and disclosure of misleading financial statements.

## POLLY PECK (UK)

Polly Peck collapsed in 1990 with a shortfall of £551 million, after a decade of extraordinary growth under the leadership of the charismatic yet autocratic Asil Nadir. The crux of the case was the apparent extraction of cash from the group by Nadir for his personal use; and central was the use of the subsidiaries Meyna, Vestel and Unipac. The key issues subsequently investigated include: the existence, valuation and revaluation of assets; the existence of income; the accounting policy choice and application of accounting standards; and modes of governance. The auditors of both the group and the Cyprus subsidiaries were subject to significant criticism for a range of failures. Nadir fled the UK in 1993 and has always protested his innocence. In August 2010 he returned to the UK to face trial.

## PROMOTORA SOCIAL DE VIVIENDAS (PSV) AND INICIATIVAS DE GESTIÓN DE SERVICIOS (IGS) (SPAIN)

PSV was a housing cooperative. IGS was the holding company that managed the cooperative. In 1993, PSV announced that the company would need around €601 012 million to meet its financial obligations. Two years later, PSV was declared bankrupt because its liabilities exceeded its assets by €85 million. The accounting irregularities in PSV and IGS included non-compliance with the matching principle. In 1993, PSV recorded as expenses amounts relating to future services to be provided by IGS. Recording these expenses led to the overestimation of expenses by €50 million. There was also evidence of the double recording of expenses and a lack of documentation supporting many transactions.

## PROSOLVIA (SWEDEN)

Prosolvia was a young company that developed a software programme for the so-called virtual reality technology and was briefly a darling of the stock market according to journalists and analysts. One year after its public listing, however, accounting irregularities with the intention of inflating profits were alleged. The share value plummeted immediately and within seven months, Prosolvia declared bankruptcy. Using multiple methods of manipulating its business results, including reconstruction of ownership, fictitious invoices, invented agreements and premature income recognition, Prosolvia reported false levels of turnover and earnings. In addition, misleading information about insider trading by a Prosolvia executive contributed to investors' loss of confidence in the company.

## RICCAR (JAPAN)

This leading Japanese sewing machine manufacturer, whose shares were listed on the Tokyo Stock Exchange, had been suffering excessive debts and applied for court protection from creditors under the Corporate Rehabilitation Law in August 1984. The accounting fraud by the company was discovered after its application for the Corporate Rehabilitation Law. The company reported fictitious revenue of 53.6 billion yen in total and boosted earnings by 32.9 billion yen during the period from 1976 to 1984, which was the second largest ever value of fictitious earnings in Japan at that time. The company issued fictitious sales invoices and hid corresponding merchandise in a warehouse, treating it as an off-balance sheet asset.

## ROYAL AHOLD (NETHERLANDS)

At Royal Ahold, there was an accounting fraud at head office. Some members of the former management signed one or more almost similar control letters (and side letters, which were hidden from the external auditors) to justify the full consolidation of four joint ventures. In this way the consolidated turnover was much higher. Further, there was a huge accounting fraud with vendor allowances at US Foodservice (a subsidiary of Royal Ahold). The investigations at US Foodservice identified fraud relating to fictitious and overstated vendor allowance receivables and an understatement of cost of goods sold. This accounting fraud relating to vendor allowances was covered by US Foodservice employees, who prepared incorrect balance statements within the scope of the confirmation of balance procedure (auditing procedure). The irregularities were revealed by the confirmation of balance procedure conducted by the external auditor of US Foodservice, Deloitte USA.

## RSV (NETHERLANDS)

This is mainly a case of management being over-optimistic by debiting deferred tax liabilities on the basis of carry forward in combination with, at the same time, a pessimistic view related to the ability to pay back received government grants. This is a *prima facie* irreconcilable position. In 1977 a government grant was recorded not as a liability, but directly in the profit and loss account, so the management of RSV thought that RSV would be in a permanent financial loss situation. In these circumstances they did not have to repay the government grant. This contrasts with debiting a deferred liability, as a carry forward needs an optimistic view with respect to the future of the company. This resulted in much too low losses from 1976 to 1979 and much too high profits in 1975.

## SANYO SPECIAL STEEL (JAPAN)

This special steel manufacturer, whose shares were listed on the Tokyo Stock Exchange, became bankrupt owing 50 billion yen which was the biggest ever value for a failed company at that time. After the bankruptcy, it was revealed that the company had reported fictitious sales and illegally inflated earnings by 13 billion yen from 1952 to 1965. The company forced its subsidiaries to buy its products at a high price and recorded fictitious sales on the parent-only financial statements. After this case, auditing standards were revised and the new accounting standards for consolidated financial statements were introduced.

## SATYAM (INDIA)

The Satyam Computer Services Ltd scandal came into the limelight in January 2009 with a confessional statement made by its promoter (i.e. person in overall charge of the company)-chairman, Mr B. Ramalinga Raju, involving a Rs.78 000 million fraud. Starting in 1987 in the private sector, the company soon became a global organisation and the fourth-ranking IT company in India in 2008. The scandal involved cooking the books of accounts, insider trading and corporate misgovernance over a number of financial years. The managing director and the chief finance manager are now in jail. The chairman has recently been granted bail by the Supreme Court of India. Criminal cases are going on in several forums in respect of all three individuals. The Institute of Chartered Accountants of India (ICAI) has also instituted proceedings against the auditors, PricewaterhouseCoopers. The Government of India replaced the board of directors and appointed a new board to steer the disgraced company out of danger. Now Tech Mahindra, an M&M-promoted company, runs 'Mahindra Satyam Ltd' as an independent company with a new six-member board of directors .

## SAWAKO (JAPAN)

This medium-sized general contractor, whose shares were traded over-the-counter in Japan and on the NASDAQ in the USA, issued convertible bonds of 3 billion yen and bonds with share purchase warrants of 500 million yen and boosted earnings to maintain higher share prices in order to encourage bond-holders to exercise their conversion rights. The company recognised sales on a long-term construction contract based on the percentage-of-completion method and rigged the period's costs incurred by forcing a co-worker in the construction project to make out a false invoice. It falsified the periods' sales by 6 billion yen in 1998 and 1999.

## SHENZHEN YUANYE (CHINA)

Shenzhen Yuanye Industrial Corporation Limited was established in 1987, as a state-owned enterprise (SOE) manufacturing textiles. It became the first listed Sino-foreign joint venture in China in 1990 after transforming into a Sino-foreign joint-venture shareholding company in 1989. It was delisted in 1992 because it had committed fraudulent accounting and financial practices such as forging sales and illegal profit transfers. It was the first publicly exposed case of financial fraud in China. The company's audit firm was shut down because it provided false capital contribution certificates and unqualified audit reports for the client. This was also the first case of this nature in Chinese accounting history.

## SKANDIA (SWEDEN)

In the 1990s, following a restructuring programme, Skandia, the oldest listed insurance company on the Stockholm Stock Exchange, was a renowned Swedish success story among international financial institutions. When various parts of Skandia were sold off, in transactions of dubious legitimacy, 15 000 pension savers brought a class action suit against the company. The use of the questionable methodology of embedded value accounting to value their insurance contracts portfolio also led to accusations that Skandia had deliberately inflated its balance sheet. Following a criminal investigation, the former CEO Lars-Eric Petersson was sentenced to two years in prison for removing the payout ceiling on the executive incentive programme called WealthBuilder without board authorisation. In 2006, in a hostile takeover, a South African insurance company acquired Skandia. However, in December 2007, Petersson successfully appealed against the two-year sentence and his conviction was overturned by the Svea Court of Appeal.

## TYCO INTERNATIONAL (USA)

To most, the story of Tyco International, Ltd was one of corporate greed and looting. The company's CEO was found guilty of misappropriating shareholders' funds. It was money he spent on purchasing and decorating his own residences, on travel, lavish parties and, of course, expensive art. However, while prosecutors were successful in pressing their looting case and did not prosecute the CEO on accounting misdeeds, there were major accounting problems at Tyco. A key element of the misdeeds entailed improper cost capitalisation. The company capitalised costs that should have been expensed, boosting assets and income in the process. There must have been a viable business model behind the company's fraudulent exterior as it did not file for bankruptcy and is today a prosperous concern.

## WORLDCOM (USA)

At its heart, the fraud at WorldCom, Inc. was relatively simple. It was a capitalisation story, though one that entailed billions of dollars in fictitious assets. In particular, operating expenses incurred for leasing other telecommunications companies' phone lines – primarily for last-mile access to homes and businesses – were not expensed but reported as additions to property, plant and equipment. Those assets were then depreciated over extended periods. Beyond cost capitalisation, the fraud at WorldCom also included the manner in which the company accounted for its acquisitions. The company overstated business combination reserves, which were used to boost income in future periods. Acquisition-related assets, such as goodwill, were also overstated. Ultimately, the firm filed for bankruptcy and the company's CEO was found guilty of financial fraud.

## YAMAICHI SECURITIES (JAPAN)

Japan's fourth-largest securities house shut down in November 1997 after 100 years in business with debts of about three trillion yen, which was the largest financial failure since the Second World War. After that, accounting frauds hiding losses of more than 200 billion yen and the payment of illegal dividends were detected. The massive losses had been incurred through years of dubious 'tobashi' securities deals, in which shares with market value sinking below book value were valued at historical cost based on accounting standards at that time and shuffled through a complex web of Yamaichi's customers with a pledge that the unrealised losses would be covered. Finally, pressured by funding difficulties amid the revelations of the off-the-book losses, Yamaichi announced it was closing trading.

## YAOHAN JAPAN (JAPAN)

This supermarket chain, consisting of more than 400 stores in 15 countries around the world, was listed on the Tokyo Stock Exchange. It collapsed in September 1997 leaving more than 185.5 billion yen in debts, the biggest failure in the Japanese retail industry. The company had issued convertible bonds from 1990 to 1994 amounting to about 47 billion yen. The company then made desperate efforts to maintain a high share price in order to encourage bond-holders to convert their convertible bonds into common shares. The company rigged earnings by booking gains on sales of real estate to a dummy company and then repurchasing the real estate after the end of the financial year.

## ZHENGZHOU BAIWEN (CHINA)

Baiwen was a typical, inefficient and diversified state-owned enterprise (SOE). It was established in September 1989 as a retail and wholesale company, and listed on the Shanghai Stock Exchange in April 1996. Three years later, it was discovered to have been systemically faking its accounts. In 2000, Baiwen filed for bankruptcy as it was unable to pay off its debts, worth RMB 2.5 billion (around £16 million). Baiwen was charged with securities frauds (i.e. manipulating publicly reported financial results, inflating profits and lying to the China Securities Regulatory Commission (CSRC). The Baiwen scandal, as one of the biggest accounting scandals in China, was the first case where the CSRC had fined board directors as well as independent directors and where the CSRC itself was sued by an independent director. The Baiwen scandal stirred huge turbulence in the Chinese financial markets at that time and ushered in an urgent need for significant reform to accounting and corporate governance in China.

# Index

*Indexed by TERRY HALLIDAY*
*(HallidayTerence@aol.com)*